ANALYSIS AND DESIGN OF PARALLEL ALGORITHMS
Arithmetic and Matrix Problems

McGraw-Hill Series in Supercomputing and Parallel Processing

Consulting Editor
Kai Hwang, *University of Southern California*

Hwang and Briggs: *Computer Architecture and Parallel Processing*
Hwang and DeGroot: *Parallel Processing for Supercomputers and Artificial Intelligence*
Lakshmivarahan and Dhall: *Analysis and Design of Parallel Algorithms: Arithmetic and Matrix Problems*
Quinn: *Designing Efficient Algorithms for Parallel Computers*

ANALYSIS AND DESIGN OF PARALLEL ALGORITHMS
Arithmetic and Matrix Problems

S. Lakshmivarahan

Sudarshan K. Dhall

School of Electrical Engineering and Computer Science
University of Oklahoma

McGraw-Hill Publishing Company

New York   St. Louis   San Francisco   Auckland   Bogotá   Caracas
Hamburg   Lisbon   London   Madrid   Mexico   Milan   Montreal
New Delhi   Oklahoma City   Paris   San Juan   São Paulo
Singapore   Sydney   Tokyo   Toronto

Analysis and Design of Parallel Algorithms:
Arithmetic and Matrix Problems

3 4 5 6 7 8 9 0 DOC DOC 9 4 3 2 1 0

ISBN 0-07-036139-8

The editor was David M. Shapiro;
the production supervisor was Denise L. Puryear.
R. R. Donnelley & Sons Company was printer and binder.

Library of Congress Cataloging-in-Publication Data
Lakshmivarahan, S.
   Analysis and design of parallel algorithms.

   (McGraw-Hill series in supercomputing and parallel processing)
   Includes bibliographical references.
   1. Parallel programming (Computer science)
2. Algorithms   3. Supercomputers — Programming.
I. Dhall, Sudarshan Kumar, (date).   II. Title.
III. Series.
QA76.642.L35   1990   004'.35   89-13329
ISBN 0-07-036139-8

For information about our audio products, write us at:
Newbridge Book Clubs, 3000 Cindel Drive, Delran, NJ 08370

Dedicated to

Shantha, Subha and Bharathram

S. Lakshmivarahan

My father and the sweet memory of my mother

Sudarshan K. Dhall

CONTENTS

CONTENTS

PREFACE

The past decade has witnessed a tremendous explosion of research on various aspects of parallel processing covering parallel architectures, parallel models and complexity classes, parallel algorithms, programming languages (with parallel constructs), compilers, and operating systems for parallel computers. Since the whole field of parallel processing is in a state of flux, any book in this area has a risk of being quickly outdated. However, many of the the basic principles that are germane to the analysis and design of parallel algorithms have become well understood. Many of these results have been until now confined to journal articles, conference proceedings, survey and tutorial papers, and a few anthologies. While there are a number of good textbooks covering the basic principles of algorithm design for serial machines, there has not been a corresponding development for parallel algorithms. This book is meant to fill this gap.

This book arose out of a set of lecture notes used for a course on parallel algorithms at the School of Electrical Engineering and Computer Science, University of Oklahoma. In developing these notes, we have assumed that readers will already have a good understanding of the basic principles of the analysis and design of serial algorithm. This book can be used as text for a first year graduate or senior level course on parallel algorithms. In order to make it accessible to a larger audience including mainstream computer scientists, engineers, and scientists, at the risk of a slight redundancy we have made the chapters reasonably independent. This gives great flexibility to the instructor, who can weave a sequence of coverage depending on the type and interest of the audience. Outlines for different course developments are given at the end of this preface.

The book is divided into seven chapters. Each chapter ends with a set of exercises which constitute an integral part of the overall development of the main text. Preceding the exercises is a section with comments and citations of relevant sources. Three small appendixes at the end of the book supplement the main development, and the volume concludes with a list of all cited references.

The seven chapters are grouped into three parts. Part 1, consisting of Chapters 1 and 2, provides the necessary background for the analysis and design of parallel algorithms. Chapter 1 begins with a review of various parallel models, namely the CRCW, CREW, EREW, circuit models and their interrelations. After discussing many of the standard performance measures such as the speed-up ratio, processor efficiency, redundancy factor, utilization factor, and degree of parallelism, the role and importance of the now well-known parallel complexity class called the *NC*-class is described. This chapter concludes with a derivation of a number of interesting lower bounds on the parallel time complexity.

Most of the commercially available parallel machines may, at a gross level, be divided into two classes: *shared memory* multiprocessors and *non-shared memory* multicomputers. In Chapter 2, our treatment of the non-shared memory architecture is centered on the ubiquitous hypercube interconnection scheme. We present the generic organizational aspects of this class of architectures using a new hierarchy of hypercube interconnection scheme called the *N*-node, base-*b* hypercube of dimension *k*. Embedding of a number of standard interconnection schemes, including the ring, two-dimensional mesh, and binary tree, onto the standard binary hypercube is discussed. Many of these embedding schemes very cleverly exploit the properties of base-*b* reflected Gray codes. Using these embedding schemes, one can readily transport algorithms developed for those architectures onto the hypercube.

Dynamic multistage interconnection networks constitute the back-bone of the shared memory computers such as the GF-11 and the butterfly System. Section 2.3 is devoted to the analysis, design, and control of two basic categories of networks, namely, the blocking networks and non-blocking networks.

Chapters 3 and 4 comprise Part 2 of the book, which is devoted to arithmetic problems. Bit-level parallelism, in the form of circuit-based algorithms for basic arithmetic operations, is described in Chapter 3. Since fast algorithms for multiplication and division critically depend on the results from elementary number theory and on fast Fourier transforms, we have included results from these areas at appropriate places. In fact, the fast Fourier transform is also used in Chapter 7 for finding the approximate solution of certain class of Toeplitz systems.

Chapter 4 contains a comprehensive survey of techniques for restructuring arithmetic expressions. The fundamental properties such as associativity, commutativity, and distributivity play a key role in achieving speed-up in the parallel evaluation of arithmetic expressions. These methods are useful in the design of compilers for parallel computers.

Part 3 contains Chapters 5 through 7 and is devoted to matrix problems. In particular, Chapter 5 develops parallel direct methods for the solution of bidiagonal and tridiagonal systems. Bidiagonal systems correspond to linear first-order recurrence systems. The treatment of tridiagonal systems is divided into two parts: the scalar tridiagonal matrix in Section 5.3 and the block tridiagonal matrix in Section 5.4. The effect of diagonal dominance on speed-up, numerical stability, and mapping algorithms into hypercube architectures are presented.

Chapter 6 generalizes the algorithms for solving bidiagonal systems to banded and lower triangular systems. This is followed by a discussion of the classical **LU** decomposition algorithm and its implementations.

The concluding Chapter 7 contains an assortment of matrix problems -- computation of inverse, product, powers, determinant, and characteristic polynomial of a matrix, eigenvalues of a real symmetric matrix, and approximate solution of a certain class of Toeplitz systems. This chapter also contains a discussion of the trade-off between speed and numerical stability.

The coverage has a mix of both practically useful algorithms and theoretically interesting ones. The book is adaptable for a variety of classes depending on interest and background. For example, Chapters 1 to 4 and selected portions of Chapters 5 and 7 could constitute a one-semester course for computer science / computer engineering students. A course on large-scale scientific computing can be built around Chapters 1 and 2 and 5 through 7. This course is of interest to engineers, scientists, and computer scientists involved in the efficient use of commercially available parallel computers. The book can also be used for a seminar on parallel computing.

S. Lakshmivarahan
Sudarshan K. Dhall

ACKNOWLEDGMENTS

We are indebted to a number of individuals for helping us in this project either directly or indirectly. First, our thanks are due to a number of graduate students who suffered through many stages of the development of the manuscript. In particular, we wish to record our thanks to A. Y. Al-Hallaq, Linda Barasch, Deepak Bharadwaj, Joe Bradley, Javed Butt, Fa-Chung Chen, Melvin DeVilbiss, Ken Dowers, Miltos Grammatikakis, Clifford Green, Fernand Galiana, Chi H. Hwang, Jung-Sing Jwo, Abul L. Haque, Chin Hsieh, Jay Liang, Yong Liang, Chandi Mohanty, Tommy McGehee, M. Malik, Seshu Madabhushi, Gyo Moon, Srinath Narayan, Il-Kyung Oh, Bob Palmer, Mark Packard, Simin Pakzad, Hassan Peyravi, M. Purswani, C. Rhee, C. Song, C. J. Shim, U. Shroff, Fred Sutarjo, S. Surendran, Jong Siang, Hugo Terashima, Bih-Ding Tung, Chi-Ming Yang, S. B. Yang, Adrian Yeung, Jim Womack, Steve Watkins, S. K. Wang and Man-Hung Wu for various suggestions. Ken Dowers, Jung-Sing Jwo, and Yong Liang deserve special mention for their help in laser printing and in drafting the figures.

Our thanks are due to Jerry Wagener, Rex Page, Amoco Production Company, Tulsa, Oklahoma, and Gordon Lyon, National Institute of Standards and Technology (formerly National Bureau of Standards) for supporting our research in parallel processing for many years. A. S. Krishnakumar of A.T. & T. Laboratory helped us in writing Section 7.7.2. We will remain grateful to the following reviewers whose incisive comments and observations helped us improve the presentation and coverage -- Narsingh Deo, University of Central Florida; Marilyn Livingston, University of Michigan; V.K. Prasanna Kumar, University of Southern California; Lionel Ni, Michigan State University; and Harold S. Stone, The Interfactor Inc.

Kai Hwang made a number of critical comments that set the tone for the final manuscript. His commitment to this project went far beyond the call of duty as the

Consulting Editor and to him we remain grateful. It has been a pleasure to work with David Shapiro, Computer Science Editor at McGraw-Hill. Our thanks are due to him and his staff, in particular Ingrid Reslmaier.

    We are thankful to Ted Batchman, J. C. Diaz, Martin Jischke, Seun K. Kahng, and Daniel Meade for their constant encouragement.

    Finally, we express our deep sense of gratitude to members of our family for helping us in ways too numerous to list here. Without their understanding this arduous task would have never made it to the finish line.

ANALYSIS AND DESIGN OF PARALLEL ALGORITHMS
Arithmetic and Matrix Problems

PART
1

PARALLEL
MODELS
AND
ARCHITECTURES

CHAPTER 1

PARALLEL MODELS: BASIC CONCEPTS

1.1 INTRODUCTION

Chapters 1 and 2 constitute Part 1 of this book and together lay the groundwork for the analysis and design of parallel algorithms. This chapter provides an introduction to three types of parallel models -- shared memory and non-shared memory models and circuit models. In Chapter 2, we describe the salient architectural features of shared and non-shared memory computers. Thus these chapters complement each other, with Chapter 1 dealing with the theoretical possibilities in algorithm design and Chapter 2 describing the practical realities of contemporary architectures.

The models provide a very useful framework for the development of parallel algorithms. The literature on the formal analysis of the individual merits and the relative power of shared memory and circuit models is extensive and could be the subject of a monograph. Admittedly, our treatment of models merely scratches the surface. Nevertheless, a number of salient features of these models are brought out in sufficient detail that even a beginner can comfortably build from this treatment.

Shared memory models are conceptually simple and yet are versatile enough to capture all the nuances of a parallel model. Circuit models, on the other hand, are quite natural and directly capture the spirit of the underlying parallel hardware. These models have virtually dominated the developments in parallel complexity theory. After a brief discussion of these models and their interrelationship, in Chapter 1, we discuss a number of commonly used measures, such as speed-up, processor efficiency, and redundancy, for characterizing the performance of parallel algorithms. One of the major achievements of the parallel complexity theory is the isolation of a class called the *NC-class* of problems, so named in honor of Nick Pippenger (also for notoriously concurrent). The distinguishing feature of this class is that problems in it admit ultrafast algorithms (using unbounded parallelism) compared to the best known serial algorithms.

Chapter 1 concludes with a discussion of some rather surprising upper bounds and a number of elementary yet useful lower bounds.

1.2 PARALLEL COMPUTERS AND MODELS

1.2.1 Parallel Computers

With the advances in VLSI technology, it has become feasible to build computing machines with hundreds or even thousands of processors cooperating in solving a given problem. Computing machines with various types and degrees of parallelism built into their architectures are already available in the market, and many more are in various stages of development. Examples include CRAY Research machines (Cray X-MP, Cray Y-MP, Cray-2, etc.), Cyber-205, the Cyberplus system, ETA-10, Fujitsu VP-200, Hitachi S-810/20, array processors, data flow machines, the Intel hypercube, NCUBE, PYRAMID, FLEX-32, Butterfly, Convex C-family, Ultracomputer, ICL DAP, Massively Parallel Processor (MPP), C.mmp and Cm^* developed at the Carnegie-Mellon University, Denelcor's HEP, Encore Multimax, Balance 8000 of Sequent, Alliant machines, Elxsi machines, experimental machines including Cedar Project at the University of Illinois, GF-11, RP-3 Project at IBM, systolic arrays, and the Connection Machine.[1]

However, in practice the tremendous increase in the *raw computational power* available through these machines does not directly translate into a comparable

---

[1]This list of machines is by no means complete and is only meant to indicate the range of possibilities. In fact, before the publication of this book many more newer architectures will come into existence.

increase in *performance*. There are a number of reasons for this disparity between the *available* computing power and *achievable* performance. In order to attain the maximum performance, one must keep as many processors *active* as possible. But this is critically dependent on the algorithm used. It could be that the problem itself is such that it does not admit an "efficient" parallel algorithm. Or the type of parallelism that the chosen algorithm exhibits may not readily fit into the architecture of the underlying machine. That is to say, not every parallel algorithm is "efficiently" mapped onto a realistic parallel machine, or the processors are all active all the time but perform a large amount of *redundant* computations. Further, when two or more processors cooperate in solving a problem, there will definitely be a need for communication and coordination between them. Understanding the nature and extent to which each of these factors affects the performance of parallel algorithms and architectures constitutes one of the fundamental goals of the theory of parallel computation.

1.2.2 Parallel Models

To perform such an analysis one needs to create a framework which is independent of the idiosyncrasies of the design and implementation of any specific architecture. Such a framework is provided by *parallel models*. From the viewpoint of modeling, most of the existing machines may be broadly grouped into two classes: (1) machines with *shared* memory architecture (examples include Cray Y-MP, Cray-2, Butterfly, HEP, Multimax, Balance 8000, etc.), and (2) machines with *non-shared* memory architecture (hypercube). Refer to Fig. 1.2.2.1 for an illustration of the general scheme and specific examples of interconnections. Analysis of the properties of these and other specific interconnections are given in Chapter 2. In shared memory architecture, processors communicate by *reading* from and *writing* into the shared memory. But in non-shared memory architectures, processor communication is essentially through *message passing*. While the shared memory models need global synchronization, in non-shared memory machines, synchronization is essentially data driven. One of the advantages of non-shared memory machines based on specific or fixed interconnection networks is that one can readily exploit their topology to efficiently solve a specific class of problems. But the main advantages of shared memory models are that it makes the data access more transparent to the algorithm designer and it can simulate any of the communication patterns of non-shared memory models based on any fixed interconnection scheme. In the following, we describe various refinements of the shared memory model.

A very general model for the study of parallel computation is often called a *paracomputer*. It consists of a set of identical general purpose processors, P_i, $1 \leq i \leq p$, each with its own local memory. The local memory holds the programs and each processor uses it as a scratch pad for its own computations. It is assumed that each processor knows its own *index*. The processors may run *synchronously* or *asynchronously*. In a synchronous model all the processors run

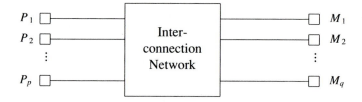

(a) A scheme for shared memory machines with p processors and a system of q-way interleaved shared memory

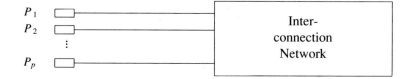

(b) A scheme for non-shared memory machines

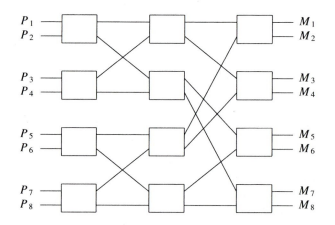

(c) An example of a network called the baseline network used in the design of shared memory machines to interconnect eight processors to a system of eight-way interleaved memory. The boxes are 2×2 complete cross-bar switches.

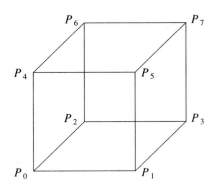

(d) An example of a network called binary hypercube used
in the design of non-shared memory machines.

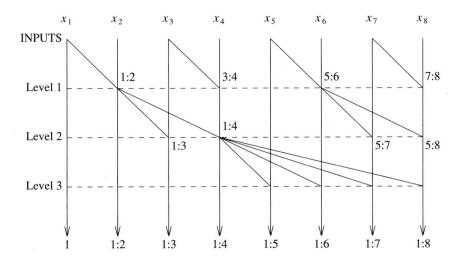

(e) An example of a Boolean circuit. Operation nodes at each
level compute the Boolean OR of the two inputs. The
label $i:j$, with $j \geq i$, denotes the OR of $x_i, x_{i+1}, \ldots, x_j$.

FIGURE 1.2.2.1
An illustration of various computing models.

identical programs but may operate on different segments of data depending on their own index. In an asynchronous setup, each processor may run on different sets of programs. In the following, unless specified otherwise, it is assumed that processors work synchronously. The processors *communicate* with each other by writing into and reading from the *shared memory* with an *unlimited* number of memory cells. It may be assumed that the input is contained in the first N cells $M_1, M_2, \cdots, M_N$ of the shared memory and all the other cells are suitably initialized (zero, for example). The number p of processors may be a function of the size of the problem $(p = N, N \log N, 2^N$, etc.), that is, depending on the need, the number of processors is assumed to be a suitable function of N. In a given step, each processor may either perform some computation or read from or write into the shared memory. By limiting the ways in which various processors write into and read from the shared memory, we obtain a variety of successively weaker models.

(a) *Models with Concurrent Read and Concurrent Write (CRCW) Capability:* In this case simultaneous reading from and writing into the same memory location by different processors is allowed. We can further subdivide this model depending on the way in which write conflict is resolved. When multiple writes occur, one way to resolve the conflict is to let the processor with the least index, for example, write. This is called the *priority write CRCW* model. However, in the design of parallel algorithms for this model, the proof of correctness becomes much less involved if we require that all processors write the *same* quantity when simultaneous write takes place. This latter requirement is often called the *common write* rule, and the model with this requirement is often called the *common write CRCW* model. Throughout this book, unless specified otherwise, we will use the CRCW model with the common write rule restriction.

(b) *Models with Concurrent Read but Exclusive Write (CREW) Capability:* These models, while permitting simultaneous reading from a given memory cell by more than one processor, do *not* permit writing into a given cell by more than one processor. Thus, like the CRCW model, this model also allows fetch conflicts. This model is also known as P-RAM (for parallel random access memory) model.

(c) *Models with Exclusive Read and Exclusive Write (EREW) Capability:* In this model, neither simultaneous writing into nor reading from a given memory cell is allowed. This model is also known as P-RAC (for parallel random access computer) and is more realistic, since this does not permit fetch conflicts while restricting the writing to only one processor.

The EREW model can be restricted to have a fixed (as opposed to unlimited) number of memory cells. One can further restrict the read/write *access* to individual memory cells. In fact, if there is a unique processor that has the read access and a unique processor that has the write access to each of the memory cells, then each of the memory locations acts as a *unidirectional* link that connects two processors. In this way, the EREW model can readily simulate non-shared memory models with fixed interconnection schemes, such as a hypercube. One of the important consequences of this latter observation is that at the highest level of conceptual design of parallel algorithms, the designer can, without loss of generality, use the framework of the shared memory models and later suitably modify the algorithm for implementation on actual machines.

Since the shared memory model is a natural extension of the conventional RAM model (Aho, Hopcroft, and Ullman [1974]), virtually all the conclusions and results of the contemporary complexity theory based on the classical Turing machine model carry over to parallel models. For example, since parallel models can be readily simulated by a serial RAM model, *unsolvable* problems remain so even under parallelism. A discussion of a very useful parallel complexity class is contained in Section 1.4.

Another class of models that has received considerable attention is called the *combinational* or *Boolean circuit models*. A Boolean circuit C is a finite, directed acyclic graph with nodes classified into two groups: *input* and *operation* nodes. Refer to Fig. 1.2.2.1(e) for an example. The input nodes have *indegree* zero and carry the input $x_1, x_2, \cdots, x_r$ and perhaps the constants 0 and 1 when needed. The operation nodes labeled NOT have indegree 1 and perform the NOT operation. The operation nodes labeled AND or OR have indegree 2 and perform the logical *conjunction* or *disjunction* of their inputs, respectively. There is no restriction, however, on the fan-out or the *outdegree* of any node. Some of the input and/or the operation nodes may be designated as the *output* nodes. If there are r input nodes and q output nodes, the circuit C is said to compute the function

$$f:\{0, 1\}^r \to \{0, 1\}^q.$$

From every input node there is *at least one* path to some operation node. The *depth* d_v of an operation node v is defined to be the length of the longest path from some input node to v. The *depth d of circuit C* is defined to be the *maximum* of the depths of all its output nodes. The total number s of operation nodes in C is called the *size* of the circuit C. The number w_i of operation nodes at depth i is called the *width of the circuit at depth i*. (It is assumed that the inputs are at depth zero.) The *maximum* of the width at all levels is called the *width, w, of the circuit C*. Clearly $s \le dw$.

Let $f = <f_N>$ be a family of functions with

$$f_N : \{0, 1\}^{g(N)} \to \{0, 1\}^{h(N)},$$

where $g(N)$ is a monotonically increasing function of N. Let $C = <C_N>$ be a family of Boolean circuits, where C_N computes f_N, that is, C_N has $g(N)$ inputs and $h(N)$ outputs.

For example, let $f_N(x, y) = x + y$ denote the addition of two N-bit integers. Then, clearly $g(N) = 2N$ and $h(N) = N + 1$. If, on the other hand, f_N computes the transitive closure of a graph, then $f_N(x) = y$, where x is a bit string of length N^2 corresponding to the adjacency matrix and y is the bit string of length N^2 corresponding to the transitive closure. In this case $g(N) = N^2 = h(N)$.

Often, it may be possible to design *optimal* circuits (in the sense of minimum size or depth, etc.) for specific instances of a problem. For example, we can design an optimal depth circuit to compute eight-bit carry in depth 5 (Kallman [1983]). The "tricks" used in these *ad hoc* optimizations may not often carry over to other instances of the problem. From the point of view of parallel complexity theory, there is virtue in focusing on the design of a family of circuits where different members of the family solve different instances of a problem. This discussion leads to the following definition. A family $C = <C_N>$ of circuits is said to be *uniform* if for a given N there is an *algorithm* to generate the Nth member C_N of the family C. Algorithms for designing uniform circuits for many of the basic arithmetic operations are described in Chapter 3.

Uniform circuit families (introduced by Borodin [1977]) have played a key role in the definition of various parallel complexity classes as well as in establishing relations between various parallel complexity classes and the well-known complexity classes based on *time* and *space* using the Turing machine model. We now quote without proof a number of interesting relations between the size and depth of circuits and space and time in Turing machine models. Pippenger and Fischer [1979] proved that for every deterministic Turing machine that computes the solution to a problem in time $T(N) (\geq N)$, there corresponds a circuit computing the solution to the same problem with *size* bounded above by $d\, T(N) \log T(N)$ for some constant $d > 0$. Borodin [1977] proved the correspondence between the (extra) space needed to compute a function using a non-deterministic Turing machine to the depth of the circuit computing the same function. More specifically, if a problem is solvable by a non-deterministic Turing machine using $S(N) (\geq \log N)$ extra space, then there exists a circuit for solving the same problem with the *depth* bounded above by $dS^2(N)$ for some constant $d > 0$. Since the depth of the circuits is related to the parallel time, this result relating the sequential space to parallel time is quite fundamental. There exists much deeper correspondence simultaneously relating the size and depth of uniform family Boolean circuits to the space and time of alternating Turing machines. For an account of this and other relationships, refer to Pippenger [1979] and Ruzzo [1981].

These facts relating the resources of a parallel model, such as parallel time and hardware, to those of serial models, such as space, time, and reversals, have come to be known as the *parallel computation thesis*. For a discussion of this latter thesis, refer to Parberry [1987] and Blum [1983].

1.2.3 Relations Between Parallel Models

We now examine the relation between various parallel models. The following theorem proves that the uniform Boolean circuits can be readily simulated by CREW models.

Theorem 1.2.3.1. Let $C = <C_N>$ be a uniform family of Boolean circuits computing $f = <f_N>$. Let s_N and d_N be the size and depth of C_N. Then, there exists a CREW algorithm for computing f_N in $O(d_N)$ steps using

$$p = \left\lceil \frac{s_N}{d_N} \right\rceil$$

processors.[2]

Proof

The proof consists in simulating the circuit by a CREW model with p processors. (In fact, most of the proofs in complexity theory relating to the equivalence of various models rely on simulation.) Assume that the N inputs are stored in the first N cells in the shared memory.

Let N_i be the number of gates (nodes) in C_N at depth i, where

$$\sum_{i=1}^{d_N} N_i = s_N.$$

Simulating a gate with two inputs consists in *reading* the relevant pair of data from the shared memory (in at most two steps), performing the gate operation (in one step), and writing the result into a distinct cell in the shared memory (in one step). To understand the need for the concurrent read, let $u_1, u_2, \cdots, u_k$ be a set of nodes at depth $i + 1$ one of whose inputs is the output of a node v at depth i. Then, in simulating the nodes at depth $i + 1$, processors corresponding to the nodes $u_1, u_2, \cdots, u_k$ simultaneously read the memory cell containing the result of node v. Thus, using p processors the gates at depth i can be simulated in at most $k \left\lceil N_i/p \right\rceil$ steps, where $k \leq 4$. If T is the total time for the entire simulation, then

$$T \leq \sum_{i=1}^{d_N} k \left\lceil \frac{N_i}{p} \right\rceil.$$

Since $\lceil x \rceil < x + 1$ and $p = \left\lceil s_N/d_N \right\rceil$, we obtain $T = O(d_N)$, and the proof is complete.

The reader is encouraged to apply this simulation to the circuit in Fig. 1.2.2.1(e). (See also Exercise 1.3.)

The properties of the Boolean circuits are not quite symmetric with respect to the fan-in and fan-out of gates. From the practical point of view both the fan-in and fan-out must be a small constant. Hoover, Klawe, and Pippenger [1984] showed that, from the complexity theory point of view, restricting the fan-out to be a small constant has an inconsequential effect of increasing the size and depth by only a constant factor. The story with fan-in is quite different, however. It has been shown by Furst, Saxe, and Sipser [1981] that Boolean circuits with *unbounded* fan-in

---

[2] The big-O notation is explained in Appendix A at the end of the book.

constitute the *correct* circuit analog of CRCW models. In developing this correspondence between CRCW models and circuits with unbounded fan-in, the *number of edges* (as opposed to the number of nodes) is defined to be the size of the circuit. The following theorem is immediate.

Theorem 1.2.3.2. Let s_N and d_N be the size (number of edges) and the depth of an unbounded fan-in circuit computing a Boolean function f_N of N Boolean variables. Then there exists a CRCW algorithm that computes f_N in d_N steps using s_N processors.

Proof

First associate one processor with each edge and one memory cell for each gate in the circuit. These latter memory cells are distinct from the ones that carry the N inputs. All the cells corresponding to the AND gates are initialized to 1, and those corresponding to OR gates are initialized to 0. As in Theorem 1.2.3.1, the proof is by simulation through the levels.

Let a node u at level i be connected to v_{j_k}, a node at level j_k by an edge e_k, where $j_k < i$ for $k = 1, 2, , \cdots, m$, that is, the m inputs of node u are the outputs of the m nodes v_{j_k}, $k = 1, 2, \cdots, m$. If u is an AND (respectively OR) gate, then the processor corresponding to the edge e_k writes 0 (respectively 1) into the cell corresponding to u if and only if it reads a 0 (respectively 1) at the cell v_{j_k}, $k = 1, 2, \cdots, m$ (recall that simultaneous write with common write is permitted in the CRCW model). Clearly, the entire simulation takes d_N steps and the theorem is complete.

The proof of the converse of Theorem 1.2.3.2 is conceptually simple but tedious, and we refer the reader to the paper by Stockmeyer and Vishkin [1984]. For a characterization of the parallel complexity classes based on unbounded fan-in circuits, refer to the papers by Furst, Saxe, and Sipser [1981], Chandra, Stockmeyer, and Vishkin [1984], and Wegener [1987].

It may be tempting to discount the usefulness of CREW and CRCW models and circuits with unbounded fan-in as being impractical. Admittedly, they are impractical, but their real usefulness stems from the fact that they provide a framework for deriving a number of interesting lower bounds on parallel time. It must be realized that lower bounds based on these *euphoric* models still continue to hold for more realistic models. For example, using the circuit model with unbounded fan-in, one can prove that the parity function (given N bits $x_1, x_2, \cdots, x_N$, checking if the sum $\sum_{i=1}^{N} x_i$ is divisible by 2) *cannot* be computed by circuits with polynomial size and constant depth (Furst, Saxe, and Sipser [1981]). Second, there are two components to every parallel algorithm: the computational part and the communication part. By assuming that the processors are powerful enough to compute any function in *one* step, we could often isolate the communication overhead involved in a parallel algorithm. We illustrate this possibility in Section 1.5.

Another interesting variation of the circuit model is the *arithmetic* circuits, which is defined quite like the Boolean circuits with inputs containing the real or complex variables $x_1, x_2, \cdots, x_N$ and a set of real or complex constants, say, $c_1, c_2, \cdots, c_k$. The operation nodes perform one of the four standard operations $\{+, -, \times, \text{and} /\}$. All the other concepts relating to the size, width, depth, fan-in, and fan-out readily carry over to these circuits. While it follows that the basic Boolean operations x AND y, x OR y, and NOT x can be simulated by $x \times y$, $x + y - x \times y$, and $1 - x$, respectively, there are no direct analogs between arithmetic and Boolean circuit models (Borodin [1977]).

We conclude this section by describing an $O(\log N)$ time and $O(N)$ space algorithm that simulates one simultaneous read step of the CRCW model with N processors on an N-processor EREW model. A similar result holds for the simultaneous write. Consequently, any algorithm that takes $T(N)$ steps in the CRCW model can be simulated on an EREW model in *at most* $O(T(N) \log N)$ steps with $O(N)$ additional memory cells.

The algorithm in Fig. 1.2.3.1 proceeds by assuming that the processors occupy the leaves of a $\lceil \log N \rceil$ level complete binary tree associated with each of the locations to be read. At each level, between each pair of processors, the lower-indexed one is allowed to move up until the least-indexed processor reaches the root node. This processor reads the information which is then propagated to other processors using the same binary tree.

The following example illustrates the various stages of the algorithm of Fig. 1.2.3.1.

Example 1.2.3.1. Assume a total of eight processors. Processors 1, 2, and 4 request to read location $l1$, processor 6 requests to read location $l2$, and processors 3, 5, 7, and 8 request to read location $l3$. Arrays W and P are initialized as shown in Figs. 1.2.3.2 and 1.2.3.3, respectively.

At the end of the first, second, and third iterations through the first j loop, array P changes successively as shown in Figs. 1.2.3.4 through 1.2.3.6.

The positions of the various processors on the tree associated with locations $l1, l2$ and $l3$ during the various stages of the algorithm are illustrated in Figs. 1.2.3.7 through 1.2.3.9, respectively.

At this time, processors 1, 6, and 3, read from locations $l1, l2$ and $l3$ respectively, and write in array T. Going through the three iterations of the last j loop, the snapshots of the successive changes of array T are given in Figs. 1.2.3.10 through 1.2.3.13.

In the case of simultaneous *writes,* all that needs to be done is to allow only one processor to write and ignore the write requests from the other processors. The first part of the above algorithm chooses in $O(\log n)$ steps one processor from each set of n processors that need simultaneous access to the same location. The chosen processor is then allowed to write, while the requests of the other processors are ignored.

/* Given N processors and an array $W[1:N]$. Element $W[i]$ indicates the element of $C[1:m]$ that processor i intends to read. Array $P[1:N, 1:\lceil \log N \rceil + 1]$ indicates the active processor. $T[1:m, 1:N]$ and $TEMP[1:N]$ are working arrays. */

```
    FOR i ∈ {1, 2, ··· , N} DO IN PARALLEL
        P [i, 1] = i;
        FOR j = 2 TO 1 + ⌈ log N ⌉ DO
            P [i, j] = 0;
        END
        FOR j = 1 TO ⌈ log N ⌉ DO
/* Each processor indicates what data it wants to read. */
            IF P [i, j] ≠ 0
                THEN BEGIN
                    T [W [i ], P [i, j ]] = P [i, j ];
/* Each processor tells its neighbor that it wants to proceed further. */
                    IF P [i, j ] IS ODD
                        THEN T [W [i ], P [i, j ] + 1] = P [i, j ]
                        ELSE T [W [i ], P [i, j ] – 1] = P [i, j ];
/* The lower-indexed processor proceeds forward. */
                    IF P [i, j ] ≤ T [W [i ],P [i, j ]]
                        THEN P [i, j + 1] = ⌈ P [i, j ]/2 ⌉ ;
                END
        END
/* Processors reaching the root first read the data. */
        IF P [i, 1 + ⌈ log N ⌉ ] ≠ 0
            THEN T [W [i ], 1] = C [W [i ]];
/* Now each processor, recursively, passes on information to its children. */
        FOR j = 1 + ⌈ log N ⌉ DOWNTO 2 DO
            IF P [i, j ] ≠ 0
                THEN BEGIN
                    TEMP [i ] = T [W [i ], P [i, j ]];
                    T [W [i ], 2×P [i, j ] – 1] = TEMP [i ];
                    T [W [i ], 2×P [i, j ]] = TEMP [i ];
                END
        END
    END
```

/* Processor i can now read information from $T[W[i], i]$ without any conflict. */

FIGURE 1.2.3.1
Algorithm to simulate concurrent read.

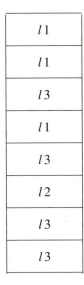

l1
l1
l3
l1
l3
l2
l3
l3

FIGURE 1.2.3.2
Array *W* initialized.

1	0	0	0
2	0	0	0
3	0	0	0
4	0	0	0
5	0	0	0
6	0	0	0
7	0	0	0
8	0	0	0

FIGURE 1.2.3.3
Array *P* initialized.

1	1	0	0
2	0	0	0
3	2	0	0
4	2	0	0
5	3	0	0
6	3	0	0
7	4	0	0
8	0	0	0

FIGURE 1.2.3.4
Array *P*. End of first iteration.

1	1	1	0
2	0	0	0
3	2	1	0
4	2	0	0
5	3	2	0
6	3	2	0
7	4	0	0
8	0	0	0

FIGURE 1.2.3.5
Array *P*. End of second iteration.

1	1	1	1
2	0	0	0
3	2	1	1
4	2	0	0
5	3	2	0
6	3	2	1
7	4	0	0
8	0	0	0

FIGURE 1.2.3.6
Array *P*. End of third iteration.

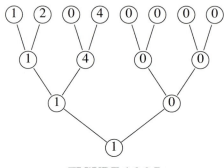

FIGURE 1.2.3.7

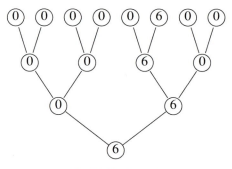

FIGURE 1.2.3.8

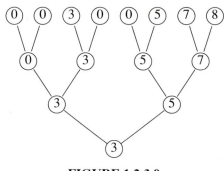

FIGURE 1.2.3.9

				T				
row	col 1	col 2	col 3	col 4	col 5	col 6	col 7	col 8
$l1$	$C[l1]$							
$l2$	$C[l2]$							
$l3$	$C[l3]$							

FIGURE 1.2.3.10
Array T at the beginning of last j loop.

				T				
row	col 1	col 2	col 3	col 4	col 5	col 6	col 7	col 8
$l1$	$C[l1]$	$C[l1]$						
$l2$	$C[l2]$	$C[l2]$						
$l3$	$C[l3]$	$C[l3]$						

FIGURE 1.2.3.11
Array T at the end the first iteration.

				T				
row	col 1	col 2	col 3	col 4	col 5	col 6	col 7	col 8
$l1$	$C[l1]$	$C[l1]$						
$l2$	$C[l2]$	$C[l2]$	$C[l2]$	$C[l2]$				
$l3$	$C[l3]$	$C[l3]$	$C[l3]$	$C[l3]$				

FIGURE 1.2.3.12
Array T at the end of the second iteration.

				T				
row	col 1	col 2	col 3	col 4	col 5	col 6	col 7	col 8
$l1$	$C[l1]$	$C[l1]$	$C[l1]$	$C[l1]$				
$l2$	$C[l2]$	$C[l2]$	$C[l2]$	$C[l2]$	$C[l2]$	$C[l2]$		
$l3$	$C[l3]$	$C[l3]$	$C[l3]$	$C[l3]$	$C[l3]$	$C[l3]$	$C[l3]$	$C[l3]$

FIGURE 1.2.3.13
Array T at the end of the third iteration.

1.3 PERFORMANCE MEASURES

There are a number of different ways to characterize the performance of both parallel computers and parallel algorithms. Usually, the peak performance of a machine is expressed in units of millions of instructions executed per second (MIPS) or millions of floating point operations executed per second (MFLOPS). However, in practice, the *realizable* performance may be far lower than the peak performance. The actual realizable performance is clearly a function of the *match* between the algorithms and the architecture. An understanding of this match is often gained by *benchmarking* (Dongarra [1986] and Lubeck, Moore, and Mendez [1986]). In this section we are, however, concerned with different ways to characterize the performance of parallel algorithms within the framework of the models described in Section 1.2. In this pursuit, the *time* (measured in terms of the number of basic operations) and *space* (number of storage locations) required to solve the given problem on a serial machine is often taken as the standard for comparison.

1.3.1 Speed-up, Efficiency, and Redundancy

Perhaps the best known measure of the effectiveness of parallel algorithms is the *speed-up ratio* (S_p) with respect to the best serial algorithm, which is defined as the ratio of the time required to solve a given problem using the *best known serial* method to the time required to solve the same problem by a parallel algorithm using p processors. Thus, if $T(N)$ denotes the time required by the best known serial algorithm to solve a problem of size N, and $T_p(N)$ denotes the time taken by a parallel algorithm using p processors in solving a problem of the same size, then

$$S_p = \frac{T(N)}{T_p(N)}.$$

Clearly, S_p is a function of N, the size of the problem, and p, the number of processors. For notational simplicity, we often do not explicitly denote this dependence. Another related measure is known as the processor efficiency, E_p , which is the ratio of the speed-up to the number of processors. Thus

$$E_p = \frac{S_p}{p} = \text{Speed-up per processor.}$$

Not all serial algorithms admit speed-up through the use of parallel implementation. But all the parallel algorithms can be serially implemented in a straightforward way. Thus, since a parallel algorithm using p (> 1) processors must perform at least as fast as a serial algorithm, it is desired that

$$S_p \geq 1.$$

In the above definition of speed-up, the parallel algorithm may be quite different from the serial algorithm. It is conceivable that in many cases one might be interested in comparing the performance of the same algorithm on the serial machine and on a given parallel processor. In such cases, the speed-up with respect to a given algorithm is simply defined as

$$S_p^* = \frac{T_1(N)}{T_p(N)}.$$

Recall that $T_i(N)$ is the time needed to execute the algorithm on i processors. Likewise, the processor efficiency in this case is

$$E_p^* = \frac{S_p^*}{p}.$$

Clearly,

$$S_p^* \geq 1.$$

Further, one step of a parallel algorithm using p processors takes at most p steps when implemented serially. Thus

$$T_1(N) \leq pT_p(N).$$

This in turn implies that

$$1 \leq S_p^* \leq p \qquad \text{and} \qquad 0 \leq E_p^* \leq 1.$$

Since $T(N) \leq T_1(N)$ (why ?), it readily follows that

$$S_p \leq S_p^*.$$

In the following, to simplify the notation, in either case, we denote the speed-up by S_p. (See Exercises 1.1 and 1.2.)

Any parallel algorithm which asymptotically attains linear speed-up, that is,

$$S_p(N) = \Omega(p)$$

is said to have the *optimal* speed-up. It is conceivable that an algorithm with optimal speed-up may have very low processor efficiency, and likewise, an algorithm with good processor efficiency may not have large speed-up. (A good serial algorithm may be a bad parallel algorithm, and a throwaway serial algorithm may end up being a reasonable parallel algorithm.)

Another factor that would reflect the performance of a parallel algorithm is the total number of scalar operations required by an algorithm. In the case of serial algorithms, the serial time complexity function itself denotes the number of scalar operations. But it is a common practice to design parallel algorithms by introducing extra or *redundant* scalar computations to achieve speed-up. The redundancy factor, R_p, of a p-processor algorithm is defined as the ratio of the total scalar operations performed by a parallel algorithm to the total scalar operations of a serial algorithm. Clearly,

$$R_p \geq 1.$$

The following examples illustrate these ideas.

Example 1.3.1.1. Suppose we want to add N numbers $x_1, x_2, \cdots, x_N$ stored in the first N memory cells $M_1, M_2, \cdots, M_N$. A parallel algorithm for computing the sum of the N numbers using $\dfrac{N}{2}$ processors is given in Fig. 1.3.1.1. The contents of the memory cells during various phases of the algorithm are given in Fig. 1.3.1.2(a). Functionally, the computation in the algorithm in Fig. 1.3.1.1 may be represented in a binary tree as in Fig. 1.3.1.2(b).

This algorithm, called the *associative fan-in algorithm* (Heller [1978]), basically exploits the *associative* property of the addition operation, which naturally suggests the following *divide-and-conquer* type of strategy. Clearly,

$$\sum_{i=1}^{N} x_i = \sum_{i=1}^{N/2} x_i + \sum_{i=1}^{N/2} x_{N/2+i},$$

and each of the terms on the right-hand side may likewise be expressed as the sum of $\dfrac{N}{4}$ of the input quantities. Continuing this way, eventually we end up adding $\dfrac{N}{2}$ pairs of numbers using $\dfrac{N}{2}$ processors. A number of observations are in order. This

---

/* Let $N = 2^n$ for some $n \geq 1$. Let $x_1, x_2, \cdots, x_N$ be stored in $M_1, M_2, \cdots, M_N$. In the end, the sum of the x_i's is stored in M_1. We assume there are N processors but only $\dfrac{N}{2}$ of them will be used. */

> $inc = 1;$
> FOR $j = 1$ TO log N DO
> FOR $i \in \{ 1 + 2 \times k \times inc \mid k = 0, 1, \cdots, (\dfrac{N}{2^j} - 1) \}$ DO IN PARALLEL

/* Processor P_i does the following */

> > READ M_i and M_{i+inc};
> > ADD contents of M_i and M_{i+inc};
> > WRITE the sum in M_i;
> > $inc = 2 \times inc;$
> END
END

FIGURE 1.3.1.1
A parallel algorithm for adding a set of N numbers using $N/2$ processors on a CREW shared memory model.

---

j	M_1	M_2	M_3	M_4	M_5	M_6	M_7	M_8
0	1	2	3	4	5	6	7	8
1	3		7		11		15	
2	10				26			
3	36							

(a) Contents of the memory cells during various stages of the algorithm in Fig. 1.3.1.1.

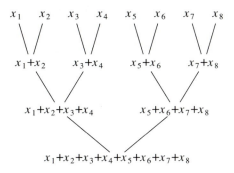

(b) Another way of representing the computations of the algorithm in Fig. 1.3.1.1.

FIGURE 1.3.1.2
An illustration of the algorithm of Fig. 1.3.1.1.

---

algorithm, quite like the serial counterpart, requires $N - 1$ operations. The number of operations and hence the number of active processors decreases by a factor of 2 through each stage of the algorithm. Because of this the speed-up and the processor efficiency are unacceptably low for large N. For

$$S_{N/2} = \frac{N-1}{\log N} \approx \frac{N}{\log N}$$

and

$$E_{N/2} \approx \frac{2}{\log N} \to 0 \text{ as } N \to \infty.$$

The key to increasing the speed-up and processor efficiency is to require that the problem size be much larger than the processor size as the next example illustrates. After all, the desire to solve larger problems grows with the size and power of computers. (See Exercise 1.5.)

The associative fan-in algorithm is quite fundamental and is used repeatedly in the solution of a number of problems -- computing the inner product of vectors, finding the maximum and minimum of numbers, computing the disjunction/conjunction of Boolean variables, computing prefixes (Chapter 3), and solving linear recurrence using the cyclic reduction method (Chapter 5), to mention a few.

From the preceding example, it is clear that given any tree-based parallel strategy, we can readily convert it into a parallel program on a suitable shared memory model. In view of this, in the following we shall be content with specifying any tree-based algorithm by its logical structure.

Example 1.3.1.2. Consider the problem of adding N numbers $x_1, x_2, \cdots, x_N$ using p processors, where $1 < p < N$. First, divide the set of N numbers into p groups, each of which contains no more than $\left\lceil \dfrac{N}{p} \right\rceil$ numbers. Assign a group to each of the p processors. Let each processor compute serially and deliver the sum of numbers in each group in at most $\left\lceil \dfrac{N}{p} \right\rceil - 1$ steps. The p partial sums so obtained can be added using one of many strategies. Typically, the p partial sums can be combined in the form of a binary tree in not more than $\lceil \log p \rceil$ steps. Refer to Fig. 1.3.1.3 for an example. Thus, the total elapsed time $T_p(N)$ is given by

$$T_p(N) = \left\lceil \frac{N}{p} \right\rceil - 1 + \lceil \log p \rceil .$$

$$S_p = \frac{N - 1}{\lceil N/p \rceil + \lceil \log p \rceil - 1}.$$

group 1 group 2 group 3 group 4

$$S_1 + S_2 \qquad S_3 + S_4$$

$$S_1 + S_2 + S_3 + S_4$$

FIGURE 1.3.1.3
S_i is the sum of elements in group i.

Thus, if $N = L\,p\,\log p$, then each processor will have $L \log p$ items to process. Clearly,

$$S_p \approx \frac{L\,p\,\log p}{(L+1)\,\log p} = \frac{Lp}{L+1}.$$

L is often denoted as the *load factor*. Thus, for large L, S_p is linear in p, since the constant of proportionality tends to 1 as $L \to \infty$.

Clearly,

$$E_p \approx \frac{L}{L+1}.$$

Example 1.3.1.3. Let $X = (x_1, x_2, \cdots, x_N)$ and $Y = (y_1, y_2, \cdots, y_N)$ be two vectors. Let us analyze a class of strategies for computing $\sum_{i=1}^{N} x_i y_i$, the scalar product of X and Y. Let p divide N, and the kth processor compute

$$\sum_{(N/p)(k-1)+1}^{(N/p)k} x_i y_i, \quad \text{for} \quad k = 1, \cdots, p.$$

Clearly, each processor takes $\dfrac{N}{p}$ time units for multiplication and $(\dfrac{N}{p} - 1)$ time units for addition. Then the resulting sums can be added in a binary tree fashion in $\lceil \log p \rceil$ units of time. Thus

$$T_p(N) = (2\frac{N}{p} - 1) + \lceil \log p \rceil.$$

If $p = N$, then

$$T_N(N) = \lceil \log N \rceil + 1.$$

If, on the other hand, $p = \dfrac{N}{2}$, then

$$T_{N/2}(N) = \left\lceil \log \frac{N}{2} \right\rceil + 3.$$

Clearly,

$$S_p = \frac{2N - 1}{(2\dfrac{N}{p} - 1) + \lceil \log p \rceil}.$$

Let $p = 2^k$, and $N = L\,p\,\log p$. Then,

$$S_p \approx \frac{2\,L\,p\,\log p}{2\,L\,\log p + \log p} = \frac{2L}{2L+1}p.$$

A problem is said to be *asymptotically completely parallelizable* if there exists an algorithm with *optimal speed-up*. The summation problem and the inner product computation are completely parallelizable since, for any p and large L, by choosing $N = L \, p \, \log p$ for some $L \geq 1$, we readily see that $S_p(N)$ is linear in p. Clearly such optimal speed-up is obtained by choosing the problem size to be a function of the processor size p. (See Exercises 1.4 to 1.6 and 1.9.)

1.4 A PARALLEL COMPLEXITY CLASS

The contemporary computational complexity theory is basically built around two (distinct ?) classes of problems known as the *P*-class and the *NP*-class, in particular the *NP*-complete (*NPC*) class of problems. The problems in the *P*-class are characterized by the fact that they admit *polynomial* (in the size of the input) time algorithms on a serial machine. The problems in the *NPC*-class, on the other hand, are such that in the worst case they require an *exponential* (in the size of the input) time on a serial machine. Examples of the problems in the *P*-class include *sorting, matrix product, shortest path, transitive closure, two-dimensional matching, FFT computations,* and *linear programming,* to mention a few. The *NPC*-class includes such important problems as the *satisfiability problem,* the *bin-packing problem,* and the *knapsack problem.* Since polynomial functions do not grow as fast as the exponential functions, the *P*-class is often identified with the class of problems that are "feasibly" solved, as opposed to the *NPC*-class for which the solution process is "infeasible."

1.4.1 The *NC*-Class

A relevant and important problem in this context is to characterize the impact of parallelism on problem solving. From the definition of the *NPC*-class, it follows that in order for a problem in the *NPC*-class to be solvable in polynomial time, it is required to ensure the availability of an *exponential* number of processors. But requiring an exponential amount of resources -- be it space, time, or processors -- is quite impractical in present-day technology. What at best is possible in the foreseeable future is only a polynomial (in the size of the problem) bound on the number of processors. While this type of limitation on the number of available processors has little effect on the *NPC*-class, using this restriction of a polynomial bound on the number of processors, complexity theorists have identified an important class called the *NC*-class.

Following Cook [1985], we define the *NC*-class as follows:

$$NC = \bigcup_{r \geq 1} NC^{(r)}$$

where $NC^{(r)}$ is the set of all problems solvable by uniform Boolean circuit family $C = <C_N>$, where the size s_N and depth d_N of the Nth circuit C_N are such that for some $t \geq 1$

$$s_N = O(N^t)$$

and

$$d_N = O((\log N)^r),$$

that is, the size of C_N is bounded by a polynomial in N and the depth of C_N is bounded by a polynomial in the logarithm of N, where N is the size of the problem. (Notice that the fan-in in this class of circuits is bounded by 2.)

The above definition of *NC* critically depends on the notion of uniform family of Boolean circuits and is known as U_{E^*} uniformity (Cook [1985], Ruzzo [1981]). There are at least two other notions of uniformity called *P-uniformity* and *log space uniformity*. A detailed treatment of these definitions and their interrelation is of intrinsic interest in complexity theory but is beyond our scope. We refer the reader to an excellent expository paper by Cook [1985] for details.

Using Theorem 1.2.3.1, we can roughly translate this definition for the shared memory models as follows: The *NC*-class consists of all problems that are solvable in time that is polynomial in the logarithm of the size of the problem (poly-log time in short) using only a polynomial number of processors. Clearly, the problems in *NC* are in *P* since any problem in *NC*, when solved serially, would take at most polynomial time. One might suspect at first sight that all the problems in *P*, using a polynomial number of processors, could be solved in poly-log time. This is not the case, however. For example, the best known parallel algorithm for the well-known maximum flow problem takes $O(N^2 \log N)$ steps using $O(N)$ processors (Shiloach and Vishkin [1982]); that is, the maximum flow problem is not yet known to be in *NC*. However, for planar graphs, fast parallel algorithms for the max-flow problem are known (Johnson and Venkatesan [1982]). While the membership in *NC* has the stringent requirement of poly-log time using only a polynomial number of processors, as a first step, in analyzing the class *P* with respect to parallelism, the requirement of a polynomial number of processors is often relaxed.

One of the reasons for concentrating on poly-log time algorithms in parallel computation stems from the intrinsic relation between sequential space and parallel time. According to the parallel computation thesis, "sequential space is polynomially related to parallel time" (Parberry [1987]). More specifically, if a class of problems can be solved on a deterministic Turing machine using an extra space bounded by a polynomial in the logarithm of the input (called *poly-log space* class), then it can be solved in poly-log time in parallel.

To understand and isolate the difficulties in solving problems in *P* using only poly-log space, the notion of a complete problem for *P* (*P*-complete for short) is very useful. A problem π is said to be *P*-complete if and only if

    (a) $\pi \in P$, and
    (b) Any problem π' can be "algorithmically" reduced to π, denoted by $\pi' \leq \pi$.

For this reduction to be useful, we need to constrain the resources needed by this reduction process, and such constraints are essentially derived from the properties of the target class, namely the class of problems solvable in poly-log space. One such reduction is called the log space reduction (Jones and Lasser [1977]) and is denoted by $\leq_{\log}$. Informally, this reduction is an algorithm which, when implemented on a deterministic Turing machine, requires an extra space bounded by the logarithm of the input size. A fundamental property of this reduction is that it is *transitive*, that is, if $\pi_1 \leq_{\log} \pi_2$ and $\pi_2 \leq_{\log} \pi_3$, then $\pi_1 \leq_{\log} \pi_3$. Consequently, if we can prove that any *P*-complete problem π is solvable in poly-log space, then every problem in *P* is also solvable in poly-log space.

    However, the existence of *P*-complete problems suggests that *P*-complete problems may not be solvable in poly-log time. An important implication of this development is that if we suspect that a problem in the *P*-class is not in *NC*, then it may be worthwhile to prove that it is *P*-complete.

    There is an impressive list of *P*-complete problems which includes the maximum network flow problem (with capacities in binary notation), linear programming, circuit value problem, the emptiness and the infiniteness of the language $L(G)$ generated by a context-free grammar G, the membership problem for context-free languages, etc. Refer to Jones and Lasser [1977] and Cook [1985] for other problems.

    In much the same way as the *P*-class helped to identify the set of feasible computations, the *NC* and poly-log space classes provide a yardstick for measuring parallelizability of the solution process for various problems. However, one of the basic difficulties of *NC* is that most algorithms in this class are *reasonable* only if the number of processors is very large. Besides, $(\log N)^k$ grows very rapidly even for small N. Refer to Table 1.4.1.1 for relative values of N, $\sqrt{N}$, and $(\log N)^k$, $k = 1, 2, 3$, and 4. From this table, it follows that a parallel algorithm with complexity $(\log N)^4$ is not as good as a serial algorithm with complexity N, unless $N \geq 65{,}536$. Likewise, $(\log N)^2$ is better than $\sqrt{N}$ only if $N \geq 65{,}536$, and $(\log N)^3$ is better than $\sqrt{N}$ only if $N \geq 621{,}350{,}000 > 2^{29}$, which is astronomically large. Thus, the role of *NC* and poly-log space classes in parallelism is quite akin to that of *P*-class in feasible computations. Showing that a problem is *not* in *NC*, however, implies that it is intrinsically serial and does not readily lend itself to parallelization.

    For problems not in *NC*, lower-order speed-up may still be achievable, witness the general max-flow problem with serial time $O(N^3)$ and parallel time $O(N^2 \log N)$. To capture this and other possibilities Vitter and Simons [1986] introduced two new classes. A problem in *P* is said to be in *PC* if its serial time can be speeded up by more than a constant factor by a parallel algorithm on the CRCW model. Likewise, PC^* consists of all those problems in *PC* whose speed-up on the CRCW model is proportional to the number of processors.

TABLE 1.4.1.1

Values of Various Functions of N ($N = 2^t$).

t	$\sqrt{N}$	t^2	t^3	t^4
2	2	4	8	16
4	4	16	64	256
6	8	36	216	1,296
8	16	64	512	4,096
10	32	100	1,000	10,000
12	64	144	1,728	20,736
14	128	196	2,744	38,416
16	256	256	4,096	65,536
18	512	324	5,832	104,976
20	1,024	400	8,000	160,000
22	2,048	484	10,648	234,256
24	4,096	576	13,824	331,776
26	8,192	676	17,576	456,976
28	16,384	784	21,952	614,656
30	32,768	900	27,000	810,000
32	65,536	1,024	32,768	1,048,576
34	131,072	1,156	39,304	1,336,336

There are a number of other interesting parallel complexity classes. One of them is called AC, where

$$AC = \bigcup_{r \geq 1} AC^{(r)},$$

and $AC^{(r)}$ consists of all problems solvable by the uniform circuit family with *unbounded fan-in,* poly-log depth, and polynomial size.

To understand the relation between $AC^{(r)}$ and $NC^{(r)}$, consider an operation node performing the AND operation, with fan-in $p(N)$, where $p(.)$ is a polynomial. From Exercise 1.7, it can be seen that the above node with $p(N)$ inputs can be replaced by a binary tree with $p(N)$ leaves and $O(\log N)$ depth, using the AND gates with a fan-in of two. From this argument, it readily follows that $AC^{(r)} \subseteq NC^{(1+r)}$. Further, from the definition, it follows that $NC^{(r)} \subseteq AC^{(r)}$. Combining these, we obtain $NC = AC$.

Another parallel complexity class is called *random NC* (*RNC*, for short) which permits the use of randomization in parallel algorithm. For a discussion of this *RNC* class, refer to Cook [1985] and Karp and Ramachandran [1988].

1.5 BASIC LOWER AND UPPER BOUNDS

One of the challenges in computational complexity theory is to characterize the intrinsic complexity of solving problems. A standard approach to such characterization is to derive a (non-trivial) lower bound on the resources needed to solve the problem. In this section, we derive lower bounds for a number of simple problems, thereby illustrating the power of these models. We also derive a rather surprising upper bound on the parallel time for computing the disjunction of N Boolean variables using the CREW model.

1.5.1 Simple Lower Bounds

We begin by presenting another useful way of characterizing the computations in a parallel model, called *p-computation*. Let p denote the size, namely, the number of processors in the model. It is assumed that each processor is capable of performing the standard arithmetic (addition, subtraction, multiplication, and division) operations.

Let I_0 be a finite set of real numbers (often corresponds to the set of input). A p-computation from I_0 is a sequence of sets $I_1, I_2, \cdots$, such that for each i

$$I_{i+1} = I_i \bigcup \{ y_{i_1}, y_{i_2}, \cdots, y_{i_p} \},$$

where

$$y_{i_j} \in \{ z_1 \, \text{o} \, z_2 \mid z_1, z_2 \in I_i \text{ and o } \textit{is a binary arithmetic operation} \}.$$

Thus, I_{i+1} contains all of I_i and all those results of binary operation on the pairs of elements chosen from I_i. Clearly I_i is a non-decreasing sequence of sets.

A set I is said to be p-computable from I_0 in t time steps if there is a p-computation from I_0 such that $I \subset I_t$. Notice that the above definition of a p-computation formalizes the notion of a sequence of results that can be successively generated by a set of p identical processors, without regard to any overhead involved in memory accesses, conflict resolutions, etc. In other words, p-computation is an abstraction of the type of computations that are possible using a parallel model with p processors.

Any algorithm when expressed as a p-computation does not increase the number of operations. Hence any lower bound on the p-computation is also a lower bound on the corresponding algorithm.

Lemma 1.5.1.1.
(a) x^{2^N} is 1-computable in N units of time.

(b) x^N is 2-computable from x in $\lceil \log N \rceil$ time.

(c) $[x, x^2, x^3, \cdots, x^N]$ is $\dfrac{N}{2}$-computable in $\lceil \log N \rceil$ time using only $N - 1$ multiplications.

Proof

(a) The only way to accomplish this is to compute serially $x^2, x^4, x^8, \cdots, x^{2^N}$, in N steps. No amount of parallelism can speed this up.

(b) Let $b_r b_{r-1} \cdots b_2 b_1$ be the representation of N in binary. If one of the two processors continue computing $x^2, x^4, x^8, \cdots, x^{2^r}$, the other processor can accumulate the product of the appropriate powers of x corresponding to each 1 in the binary expansion of N.

(c) The scheme in Fig. 1.5.1.1 provides an algorithm. At time i, let 2^{i-1} processors compute $x^{2^{i-1}+1}$ through x^{2^i}. Thus if $2^{k-1} < N \le 2^k$, clearly in k units of time using at most 2^{k-1} processors all the first N powers of x can be computed. The number of operations is bounded by $\sum_{j=0}^{k-1} 2^j = 2^k - 1 = N - 1$.

Notice that the claims of this lemma are true on both the CREW and the CRCW models. The following theorem due to Munro and Patterson [1973] is quite fundamental.

Theorem 1.5.1.2. Let the serial computation of a single quantity, say, Q, take $N \ge 1$ binary arithmetic operations. If $t = T_p(N)$ is the time taken by the shortest p-computation of Q, then

$$t \ge \left\lceil \frac{N + 1 - 2^{\lceil \log p \rceil}}{p} \right\rceil + \lceil \log p \rceil, \quad \text{if } N \ge 2^{\lceil \log p \rceil},$$

and

$$t \ge \lceil \log (N + 1) \rceil, \qquad\qquad \text{otherwise.}$$

Time	Processor			
	1	2	3	4
1	x^2			
2	x^3	x^4		
3	x^5	x^6	x^7	x^8

FIGURE 1.5.1.1
Schedule of computation of powers of x for Lemma 1.5.1.1.

Proof

In the sequence of computations leading to the result Q, at time t, at most one processor is usefully employed. Since each operation involved in the computation of Q is a binary operation, at time $t - 1$, at most two processors are useful. Continuing like this, it is seen that for any $j \geq 0$, at time $t - j$, at most $\min(p, 2^j)$ processors can actively take part in computing Q.

Thus, using p processors, the total number of operations that can be performed in $\lceil \log p \rceil$ time is given by

$$\sum_{i=1}^{\lceil \log p \rceil} 2^{i-1} = 2^{\lceil \log p \rceil} - 1.$$

Two cases arise:

Case 1. If $N > 2^{\lceil \log p \rceil} - 1$, then, clearly, $t > \lceil \log p \rceil$. Thus, during the first $\lceil \log p \rceil$ units of time, the total number of operations performed is given by

$$1 + 2 + 2^2 + \cdots + 2^{\lceil \log p \rceil - 1} = 2^{\lceil \log p \rceil} - 1.$$

In the rest of $t - \lceil \log p \rceil$ units, since the maximum number of operations performed in a given time is limited by p, a total of $p(t - \lceil \log p \rceil)$ operations are performed. Thus,

$$N \leq p(t - \lceil \log p \rceil) + 2^{\lceil \log p \rceil} - 1,$$

from which it follows that

$$t \geq \left\lceil \frac{N + 1 - 2^{\lceil \log p \rceil}}{p} \right\rceil + \lceil \log p \rceil.$$

Case 2. $t \leq \lceil \log p \rceil$ or $N \leq 2^{\lceil \log p \rceil} - 1$. Since the maximum number of useful operations that can be performed in t units of time is $\sum_{i=0}^{t-1} 2^i = 2^t - 1$, it follows that

$$N \leq 2^t - 1,$$

or

$$t \geq \lceil \log (N + 1) \rceil.$$

Thus Theorem 1.5.1.2 suggests a class of optimal algorithms for computing

$$x_1 \; o \; x_2 \; o \; \cdots \; o \; x_N,$$

where o is an associative binary arithmetic operation. Compare this with the *associative fan-in* algorithms in Section 1.3. Stated in other words, Theorem 1.5.1.2 implies that any p-computation involving only addition, subtraction, multiplication, or division and producing a single result by performing $\Omega(N)$ operations on a serial machine requires $\Omega\left(\dfrac{N}{p} + \log p\right)$ steps using p processors. In the above discussion, restriction to the binary arithmetic operations is essential since Valiant [1975] derived a p-computation (using the CREW model) involving only comparison operations to find the maximum of N numbers in Θ (log log p) steps.

In the following we present a lower bound similar to Theorem 1.5.1.2 again using the concept of p-computation in a non-shared memory model. Define a parallel processor of *size p* and *degree k* as one with p processors where each processor *can communicate with at most k neighbors*. Thus, a degree-k parallel processor of size p can be represented by a graph with p nodes representing processors, and each node is connected to at most k distinct neighbors. A degree-k, p-computation is a p-computation on a degree-k (and size p) parallel processor. It is assumed that the degree-k, p-computation consists of a sequence of time steps during which each processor can do one of the following:

(1)   Perform a binary operation (any associative binary operation) on two local data items and generate a new result.

(2)   Perform a binary test (such as comparison) on two local data items and generate a test result.

(3)   Receive a data item from one of the k neighbors, and

(4)   Receive some test result from one of the k neighbors.

Notice that the unary operations and tests are special cases of (1) and (2). It is assumed that each processor, at the end of every step, on the basis of the test results it has established or received from one of its neighbors, decides instantaneously which operation to perform next. It should be interesting to note that the above assumptions, while permitting arbitrary binary operations, restrict the interconnection pattern. This is to be contrasted with the assumptions of Theorem 1.5.1.2, where the binary operations were restricted to the form of basic arithmetic types and the p processors were assumed, in a sense, to be "completely" connected. Thus, the results given below also apply to the problem of finding the maximum.

Let $Q = [P_0, P_1, \cdots, P_{p-1}]$ be the p processors in a degree-k parallel processor of size p. Let $d(P_i, P_j)$ be the distance between P_i and P_j which is measured in terms of the minimum number of edges in a path joining the node P_i to the node P_j. The following lemma is immediate.

Lemma 1.5.1.3. Let S be a subset (of Q) of processors within distance d. Then

$$|S| \leq 1 + \sum_{i=0}^{d-1} k(k-1)^i.$$

In particular,

$$|S| \leq 2d + 1, \quad \text{if } k = 2,$$

and

$$| S | \le \frac{k(k-1)^d - 2}{k - 2}, \quad \text{if } k > 2.$$

Proof

For any processor P_i there are at most k neighbors at a unit distance. For each of these neighbors there are at most $k - 1$ neighbors (not counting P_i) at unit distance. Thus, there are at most $k(k-1)$ processors within a distance of 2 from P_i. Continuing likewise, the number of processors within a distance of d from P_i is given by

$$k + k(k-1) + k(k-1)^2 + \cdots + k(k-1)^{d-1}.$$

Since P_i is at distance 0 from P_i, the total number of processors within a distance of d is given by

$$| S | \le 1 + \sum_{i=0}^{d-1} k(k-1)^i = \frac{k(k-1)^d - 2}{k - 2}.$$

Clearly, when $k = 2$,

$$| S | \le 2d + 1.$$

Corollary 1.5.1.4. For each P_i in a degree $k > 1$ parallel processor, the number of processors within distance d of P_i is less than $k^{d+1} - 1$.

Proof

Clearly, for $k > 1$,

$$| S | \le 1 + k + k^2 + \cdots + k^d = \frac{k^{d+1} - 1}{k - 1} < k^{d+1} - 1.$$

Lemma 1.5.1.5. Let $P_i \in Q$ and $S \subset Q$. Then, for $k > 1$,

$$\max_{P_j \in S} d(P_i, P_j) \ge \log_k (|S| + 1) - 1.$$

Proof

Let $d = \max_{P_j \in S} d(P_i, P_j)$. Thus, the members of S are within a distance d from P_i. From Corollary 1.5.1.4, it follows that

$$k^{d+1} - 1 > | S |,$$

from which the lemma follows.

For related properties, see Exercises 1.16 and 1.17.

We now state a fundamental property of a degree-k p-computation, where $1 < k < p$.

Theorem 1.5.1.6. A degree-k p-computation of a single quantity y depending on N given data requires $\Omega(\frac{N}{p} + \log_k N)$ steps, where $1 < k < p$.

Proof
The first term follows from the fact that N operations cannot be completed by p processors in less than $\frac{N}{p}$ units of time. If any processor examines $\Omega(\log N)$ data items and test results, the theorem holds trivially. Thus, we may assume that each processor examines $O(\log_k N)$ data items and test results. Thus, $\Omega(\frac{N}{\log_k N})$ processors must communicate either directly or indirectly with the processor that will eventually compute y. Since $\log(\frac{N}{\log_k N}) = \Omega(\log N)$, by Lemma 1.5.1.3, the proof of Theorem 1.5.1.6 is now complete.

Corollary 1.5.1.7. A bounded degree p-computation of a single item y depending on n items requires (with $N \geq p$) $\Omega(\frac{N}{p} + \log p)$ time units.

1.5.2 New Upper and Lower Bounds

We conclude this section by deriving upper and lower bounds for elementary problems which illustrate the relative power of the shared memory models. Define

$$f_{OR}(x_1, \cdots, x_N) = x_1 \vee x_2 \vee \cdots \vee x_N$$

and

$$f_{AND}(x_1, \cdots, x_N) = x_1 \wedge x_2 \wedge \cdots \wedge x_N,$$

where $\vee$ and $\wedge$ are the logical OR and AND operations, respectively. Let x_i be stored in memory cell M_i, $i = 1$ to N, and all the other memory cells be suitably initialized.

In a CRCW model, we can compute $f_{OR}(x_1, \cdots, x_N)$ in constant time as follows. Processor p_i first *reads* memory cell M_i, for $i = 1$ to N, in parallel. Then, for $i = 1$ to N, each processor p_i *writes* a 1 in a designated cell, say, M_{N+1} (which is assumed to be initialized to zero) if and only if $x_i = 1$. Since all the processors involved in writing write the common value, the entire algorithm takes at most three steps (read, compare, and conditionally write). By a similar argument, we can show that $f_{AND}(x_1, \cdots, x_N)$ can be computed in *constant* time.

On CREW and EREW models, by using the algorithm similar to the one given in Example 1.3.1.1, we can compute $f_{OR}(x_1, \cdots, x_N)$ and $f_{AND}(x_1, \cdots, x_N)$ in $\log N + O(1)$ steps. (A similar conclusion follows if we simulate the concurrent write step by exclusive write using the algorithm given at the end of Section 1.2.)

Further, since AND and OR are binary operations, using the fan-in argument of Theorem 1.5.1.2, we would normally conclude a lower bound of $\log N$ on the time required to compute $f_{OR}(x_1, \cdots, x_N)$ and $f_{AND}(x_1, \cdots, x_N)$. (See Exercise 1.14.) However, Cook, Dwork, and Reischuk [1986], using a very clever and subtle argument, derived an algorithm that on a CREW model computes $f_{OR}(x_1, \cdots, x_N)$ in less than $\log_2 N + O(1)$ steps. If $T(f_{OR})$ is the time to compute $f_{OR}(x_1, \cdots, x_N)$ in a CREW model, they proved that

$$\log_\beta N \le T(f_{OR}) \le \log_\alpha N + O(1), \tag{1.5.2.1}$$

where $\alpha = 2.618$ and $\beta \approx 4.79$. (Also refer to Cook and Dwork [1982].)

The upper bound depends on a crucial observation that a processor can *communicate certain information by not writing*. Let p be a processor and let R be one of its local memory cells containing a Boolean variable r. Let A and B be two memory cells resident in the shared memory, containing Boolean variables a and b, respectively. Processor p first *reads* the contents of A and computes $a \vee r$. Then p *writes* 1 into the cell B if and only if $a \vee r = 1$. From

$$a \vee r \vee b = \begin{cases} 1, & \text{if } a \vee r = 1 \\ b, & \text{otherwise,} \end{cases}$$

it is clear that in the end memory cell B contains $a \vee r \vee b$. Since p writes only in the case that $a \vee r = 1$, in the other case it "transmits" the information by *not* actually writing anything.

An algorithm for computing f_{OR} exploiting this idea is given in Fig. 1.5.2.1, where F_k denotes the kth Fibonacci number. In analyzing this algorithm, first recall the definition of F_k, namely, $F_0 = 0$, $F_1 = 1$, and

$$F_{k+2} = F_{k+1} + F_k.$$

It follows that (Reingold, Nievergelt, and Deo [1977])

$$F_k = \frac{1}{\sqrt{5}} [(\frac{1+\sqrt{5}}{2})^k - (\frac{1-\sqrt{5}}{2})^k].$$

Thus,

$$F_{2k} \ge \frac{1}{\sqrt{5}} (\frac{1+\sqrt{5}}{2})^{2k} = \Omega((2.618)^k). \tag{1.5.2.2}$$

Let $N = F_{2T+1}$ for some $T \ge 1$. The variable x_i is stored in cell M_i, for $i = 1$ to N, and in M_j for $j > N$ are initialized to 0. Each processor p_i has the local variable Y_i initialized to zero for $i = 1$ to N. The processors work synchronously. An illustration of the algorithm is given in Table 1.5.2.1.

During the kth step, processor p_i first writes the disjunction of the *old values* of Y_i and $M_{i+F_{2(k-1)}}$ into the location Y_i for $1 \le i \le N - F_{2(k-1)}$. Then, processor p_i writes 1 in cell $M_{i-F_{2k-1}}$ if and only if the value of Y_i computed during the kth step is 1. From the above consideration, it is clear that for $i > F_{2k-1}$, cell $M_{i-F_{2k-1}}$ after the kth step contains the disjunction of its value from the $(k-1)^{th}$ step and Y_i computed during the kth step.

/* The Boolean variable x_i is stored in memory cell M_i, $i = 1$ to N. M_j, for $j > N$, are initialized to 0. Y_i is a local memory cell for the processor p_i, which is initialized to 0 for $i = 1$ to N. M_1 contains the result. T is such that $F_{2T+1} = N$. */

```
FOR k = 1 TO T
      FOR i ∈ {1, 2, ⋯ , N} DO IN PARALLEL
            IF (i + F_2(k-1) ≤ N) THEN
                  Y_i = Y_i ∨ M_{i + F_2(k-1)}
            IF (i > F_{2k-1} AND Y_i = 1) THEN
                  M_{i - F_{2k-1}} = 1
      END
END
```

FIGURE 1.5.2.1
Cook-Dwork-Reischuk algorithm for computing the disjunction of N Boolean variables in a CREW model.

TABLE 1.5.2.1
An Illustration of the Algorithm in Figure 1.5.2.1
$(x_i : x_j = x_i ∨ x_{i+1} ∨ \cdots ∨ x_j, \text{ for } j > i)$

i	After Step $k = 1$		After Step $k = 2$		After Step $k = 3$	
	M_i	Y_i	M_i	Y_i	M_i	Y_i
1	$x_1 : x_2$	x_1	$x_1 : x_5$	$x_1 : x_3$	$x_1 : x_{13}$	$x_1 : x_8$
2	$x_2 : x_3$	x_2	$x_2 : x_6$	$x_2 : x_4$	$x_2 : x_{13}$	$x_2 : x_9$
3	$x_3 : x_4$	x_3	$x_3 : x_7$	$x_3 : x_5$	$x_3 : x_{13}$	$x_3 : x_{10}$
4	$x_4 : x_5$	x_4	$x_4 : x_8$	$x_4 : x_6$	$x_4 : x_{13}$	$x_4 : x_{11}$
5	$x_5 : x_6$	x_5	$x_5 : x_9$	$x_5 : x_7$	$x_5 : x_{13}$	$x_5 : x_{12}$
6	$x_6 : x_7$	x_6	$x_6 : x_{10}$	$x_6 : x_8$	$x_6 : x_{13}$	$x_6 : x_{13}$
7	$x_7 : x_8$	x_7	$x_7 : x_{11}$	$x_7 : x_9$	$x_7 : x_{13}$	$x_7 : x_{13}$
8	$x_8 : x_9$	x_8	$x_8 : x_{12}$	$x_8 : x_{10}$	$x_8 : x_{13}$	$x_8 : x_{13}$
9	$x_9 : x_{10}$	x_9	$x_9 : x_{13}$	$x_9 : x_{11}$	$x_9 : x_{13}$	$x_9 : x_{13}$
10	$x_{10} : x_{11}$	x_{10}	$x_{10} : x_{13}$	$x_{10} : x_{12}$	$x_{10} : x_{13}$	$x_{10} : x_{13}$
11	$x_{11} : x_{12}$	x_{11}	$x_{11} : x_{13}$	$x_{11} : x_{13}$	$x_{11} : x_{13}$	$x_{11} : x_{13}$
12	$x_{12} : x_{13}$	x_{12}	$x_{12} : x_{13}$	$x_{12} : x_{13}$	$x_{12} : x_{13}$	$x_{12} : x_{13}$
13	x_{13}	x_{13}	x_{13}	x_{13}	x_{13}	x_{13}

We now prove by induction that for $0 < k < T$ and $1 \leq i \leq N = F_{2T+1}$,

$$Y_i = x_i \vee x_{i+1} \vee \cdots \vee x_{i-1+F_{2k}}$$

and

$$M_i = x_i \vee x_{i+1} \vee \cdots \vee x_{i-1+F_{2k+1}}.$$

Initially, that is, at $k = 0$, $Y_i = 0$ (since disjunction over an empty set is 0) and $M_i = x_i$. After the first step, $k = 1$, $Y_i = M_i$, and $M_i = x_i \vee x_{i+1}$. (Recall that $M_j = 0$ for $j > N$ and hence interpret $x_j = 0$ for $j > N$.) Let Y_i^k and M_i^k be the contents of Y_i and M_i after k steps. From the algorithm, and using the hypothesis,

$$Y_i^{k+1} = Y_i^k \vee M_{i+F_{2k}}$$

$$= (x_i \vee \cdots \vee x_{i-1+F_{2k}}) \vee (x_{i+F_{2k}} \vee \cdots \vee x_{i+F_{2k}+F_{2k+1}-1})$$

$$= (x_i \vee \cdots \vee x_{i-1+F_{2(k+1)}}).$$

Similarly,

$$M_i^{k+1} = M_i^k \vee Y_{i+F_{2k+1}}$$

$$= x_i \vee x_{i+1} \cdots \vee x_{i-1+F_{2k+1}+F_{2(k+1)}}$$

$$= x_i \vee \cdots \vee x_{i-1+F_{2(k+1)+1}}.$$

Thus, after T steps M_1 contains $x_1 \vee x_2 \vee \cdots \vee x_N$, where $N = F_{2T+1}$. The following theorem summarizes the above discussion.

Theorem 1.5.2.1. There exists an algorithm to compute $f_{OR}(x_1, x_2 \cdots x_N)$ in a CREW model in at most $0.72 \log_2 N + O(1)$ steps.

Proof
From (1.5.2.1), since

$$N = F_{2T+1} \geq \frac{1}{\sqrt{5}} \left(\frac{1+\sqrt{5}}{2}\right)^{2T+1}$$

$$= c(2.618)^T \quad \text{for some } c > 0,$$

we obtain

$$T \leq \log_{2.618} N + O(1) = 0.72 \log_2 N + O(1).$$

We now turn to deriving a *lower* bound on computing $f_{OR}(x_1, x_2, \cdots, x_N)$ on a CREW model. Let $\{p_1, p_2, \cdots\}$ be a set of processors, $\{M_1, M_2, \cdots\}$ be a set of memory cells, Σ be an alphabet set, and Q_i be the set of all states of processor p_i for $i = 1, 2, \cdots$. Let $<N>$ and $<N^+>$ denote the set of non-negative and positive integers. Associated with each processor is a set of functions to do a number of routine tasks such as reading, writing, and state transitions, which are defined as follows:

$$R_i : Q_i \;\rightarrow\; <N^+>,$$

$$W_i : Q_i \;\rightarrow\; <N>,$$

$$\sigma_i : Q_i \;\rightarrow\; \Sigma,$$

and

$$\delta_i : Q_i \times \Sigma \;\rightarrow\; Q_i, \text{ the state transition function.}$$

For any state $q \in Q_i$, and symbol $a \in \Sigma$, $R_i[q]$ denotes the index of the next cell that is *read* by p_i; $W_i[q]$, the index of the next cell *written* onto by p_i, with $W_i[q] = 0$ denoting that no writing takes place; $\sigma_i[q]$ denotes the symbol that is currently written, and finally $\delta_i[q_i, a]$ denotes the next state of processor p_i.

Let $q_i(t)$ and $m_j(t)$ be the state of processor p_i at time t and the contents of memory cell M_j at time t, respectively, where $t = 0, 1, 2, \cdots$. Initially, at $t = 0$, cell M_i contains x_i for $i = 1$ to N and all the other cells $M_j, j > N$, contain the distinguished symbol $\# \in \Sigma$, denoting the blank. Let $q_i(0)$ be the state of the processor at $t = 0$. For later consistency, we define, for all $i = 1, 2, \cdots$,

$$W_i[\, q_i(0)] = 0. \tag{1.5.2.3}$$

Given this initial setup, it is convenient to describe the sequence of events using the semiclosed interval $(t, t + 1]$, for $t = 0, 1, 2, \cdots$. During the interval $(t, t + 1]$, while in state $q_i(t)$, processor p_i first *reads* the contents $m_j(t)$ of cell M_j, where $j = R_i[q_i(t)]$. It then computes the next state,

$$q_i(t + 1) = \delta_i[q_i(t), m_j(t)]. \tag{1.5.2.4}$$

From the new state, p_i then writes $\sigma_i[q_i(t + 1)]$ into cell $W_i[q_i(t + 1)]$. This cycle of reading, changing state, and writing continues for $t = 0, 1, 2, \cdots, T - 1$, for some $T \geq 1$.

The contents of a cell M_k change only if some processor writes into it. Thus

$$m_k(t + 1) = m_k(t)$$

if, for all j,

$$W_j[q_j(t + 1)] \neq k,$$

that is, no processor p_j writes into memory cell M_k. On the other hand, if for some j

$$W_j[q_j(t+1)] = k,$$

then

$$m_k(t+1) = \sigma_j[q_j(t+1)],$$

that is, M_k contains the symbol written by processor p_j from state $q_j(t+1)$.

Since the CREW model does not permit simultaneous write into any memory cell, for the correctness of the algorithm it is required that for all $i \neq j$, either

$$W_i[q_i(t+1)] \neq W_j[q_j(t+1)]$$

or

$$W_i[q_i(t+1)] = 0 = W_j[q_j(t+1)].$$

Some more preparatory definitions are in order. Let $g:\{0, 1\}^N \rightarrow \{0, 1\}$ and let

$$I = (x_1, x_2, \cdots, x_N) \in \{0, 1\}^N$$

be an input to g. Define $I(k) = (x_1, x_2, \cdots, \overline{x}_k, \cdots, x_N)$, where $\overline{0} = 1$ and $\overline{1} = 0$, that is, $I(k)$ differs from I at the kth position, $1 \leq k \leq N$. An input I is said to be *critical* for g if and only if

$$g(I) \neq g(I(k)),$$

for all $k = 1$ to N. As an example, $I = (0, 0, \cdots, 0)$ is critical for $f_{OR}(x_1, \cdots, x_N)$. Assume that an algorithm for computing g on the CREW model takes T steps and that the value of g is stored in a designated cell, say, M_1. As will be seen later, the concept of the critical input plays a fundamental role in the derivation of the lower bound on T.

Let $(q_i(t) \mid I)$ and $(m_j(t) \mid I)$ denote the state of processor p_i, and the contents of cell M_j, respectively, at time t starting with input I. An input *index* k is said to *affect* or *influence* processor p_i and influence memory cell m_j if and only if

$$(q_i(t) \mid I) \neq (q_i(t) \mid I(k))$$

and

$$(m_j(t) \mid I) \neq (m_j(t) \mid I(k)),$$

respectively.

Let $A(p, t, I)$ and $B(M, t, I)$ denote the set of input indices that affect or influence processor p and memory cell M, respectively, at time t on input I.

We now pause to understand the need for this framework. Recall that if a function g has a critical input, then the value of g for this critical input will be dependent on each and every component of the input. In other words, the *information* contained in each of the input bits sooner or later has to influence the value of g. Thus, our aim is to understand the *dynamics* of the flow of information from each input bit position to the memory cell M_1 that contains the final value of g. Clearly, any characterization of this dynamics must involve the *interaction* between the processors and the contents of the memory cells in terms of reading, change of state, and writing and $B(M_1, t, I)$, the set of input indices that has influenced the contents of the cell M_1 at time t.

We now proceed to analyze the properties of the sets $A(p, t, I)$ and $B(M, t, I)$. To this end, we introduce a system of recurrences defined as follows:

$$a_0 = 0, \quad b_0 = 1,$$

and

$$\left.\begin{array}{l} a_{t+1} = a_t + b_t \\ b_{t+1} = 3a_t + 4b_t. \end{array}\right\} \tag{1.5.2.5}$$

Rewrite (1.5.2.5) as

$$\mathbf{Z}_{t+1} = \mathbf{A}\,\mathbf{Z}_t, \tag{1.5.2.6}$$

where

$$\mathbf{Z}_t = \begin{pmatrix} a_t \\ b_t \end{pmatrix}, \quad \mathbf{Z}_0 = \begin{pmatrix} 0 \\ 1 \end{pmatrix}, \quad \text{and} \quad \mathbf{A} = \begin{bmatrix} 1 & 1 \\ 3 & 4 \end{bmatrix}.$$

Since the eigenvalues of the matrix $\mathbf{A}$ are

$$\lambda_1 = \frac{5 + \sqrt{21}}{2} = 4.7913,$$

$$\lambda_2 = \frac{5 - \sqrt{21}}{2} = 0.2087,$$

using the standard methods, it can be seen that (Exercise 1.20),

$$\left.\begin{array}{l} a_t = \dfrac{1}{\sqrt{21}}\,(\lambda_1^t - \lambda_2^t) \le c_1 (4.7913)^t, \\[4mm] b_t = \dfrac{1}{2\sqrt{21}}\,[(\sqrt{21}+3)\,\lambda_1^t + (\sqrt{21}-3)\,\lambda_2^t\,] \le c_2 (4.7913)^t, \end{array}\right\} \tag{1.5.2.7}$$

for some positive constants c_1 and c_2.

The following lemma provides the key to the lower bound.

Lemma 1.5.2.2. For all p, M, t, and I,

$$\left.\begin{array}{l} |\,A(p, t, I)\,| \le a_t \\ \text{and} \\ |\,B(M, t, I)\,| \le b_t. \end{array}\right\} \tag{1.5.2.8}$$

Proof

The proof is by induction. Since the initial state of a processor is independent of the input data, $A(p, 0, I)$ is empty. Likewise, $B(M_i, 0, I) = \{i\}$, since x_i is initially written into M_i, $1 \le i \le N$. (Notice that $B(M_j, 0, I)$ is a null set for $j > N$.) Combining this with (1.5.2.5) and (1.5.2.8), the basis is established. Assume that (1.5.2.8) holds up to the instant t. From

$$q_i(t + 1) = \delta_i[q_i(t), m_j(t)],$$

it follows that there are only two ways in which an input index k can affect (the state of) the processor p_i at time $t + 1$. The index k either affected the processor p_i at time t or it affected the memory cell that is read by the processor p_i at time t. Thus,

$$A(p, t + 1, I) \subset A(p, t, I) \cup B(M, t, I).$$

Now from the induction hypothesis, we obtain

$$| A(p, t + 1, I) | \le | A(p, t, I) | + | B(M, t, I) |$$

$$\le a_t + b_t = a_{t+1}.$$

The proof of the second inequality in (1.5.2.8) is more involved. We consider two cases.

Case 1. Some processor p writes into a cell M at time $t + 1$, starting with input I. Then, all that was contained in M is replaced, and M is totally influenced by those indices that influence p. Thus

$$B(M, t + 1, I) \subset A(p, t + 1, I);$$

that is,

$$| B(M, t + 1, I) | \le a_{t+1} = a_t + b_t$$

$$\le 3a_t + 4b_t = b_{t+1}.$$

Case 2. Let no processor p write into a cell M at time $t + 1$ starting with input I. One possibility is that M continues to be affected by those indices that affected it at time t starting with I.

To describe an alternative possibility, we introduce the following definition: Let $C(M, t + 1, I)$ denote the set of all input indices k that *cause* some processor p to write into M at time $t + 1$ starting with $I(k)$ but not with I.

Since a cell can be affected at time $t + 1$ by affecting it earlier or changing a single bit of the input, we obtain

$$B(M, t + 1, I) \subset B(M, t, I) \cup C(M, t + 1, I). \qquad (1.5.2.9)$$

This is possible because we are interested in computing a function with critical inputs, and the bounds (1.5.2.9) are uniform in p, M, t, and I.

We now estimate the size of the set $C(M, t + 1, I)$. Let

$$C(M, t+1, I) = \{u_1, u_2, \cdots, u_r\}. \tag{1.5.2.10}$$

For definiteness, suppose that the index u_i *causes* processor p_{u_i} to write into M at time $t+1$ starting with $I(u_i)$. Let $\alpha, \beta \in C(M, t+1, I)$ be such that $p_\alpha \neq p_\beta$.

By definition, p_α writes into M at time $t+1$ starting with $I(\alpha)$. Now, changing the bit at position β of $I(\alpha)$ causes p_α *not* to write into M at time $t+1$, that is, β affects p_α at time $t+1$ starting with $I(\alpha)$. Interchanging α and β, it follows that α affects p_β at time $t+1$ starting with $I(\beta)$.

To compute the bound on r, define a bipartite graph $G = (V, E)$, where

$$V = \{u_1, u_2, \cdots, u_r\} \cup \{v_1, v_2, \cdots, v_r\},$$

with u_i's defined in (1.5.2.10), v_i's a distinct set of symbols, and $(u_i, v_j) \in E$ if and only if u_i affects p_{u_j} at time $t+1$ starting with $I(u_j)$, that is, $u_i \in A(p_{u_j}, t+1, I(u_j))$. Thus, the degree of the node v_j in G is bounded by $|A(p_{u_j}, t+1, I(u_j))| \le a_{t+1}$. Consequently,

$$|E| \le r a_{t+1}. \tag{1.5.2.11}$$

We now estimate $|E|$ in another way by deriving a lower bound on the number of pairs u_i, u_j in $C(M, t+1, I)$ such that $p_{u_i} \neq p_{u_j}$. From the above analysis we obtain that there are at most two edges (u_i, v_j) and (u_j, v_i) in G for each such pair u_i, u_j. Clearly, there are r choices for u_i. Now, given u_i, there are at most $|A(p_{u_i}, t+1, I)| \le a_{t+1}$ indices that can cause p_{u_i} to write into M at time $t+1$ starting with I. Hence, there are at most $r - a_{t+1}$ choices for u_j. Combining these, we have

$$\tfrac{1}{2} r(r - a_{t+1}) \le |E|. \tag{1.5.2.12}$$

From (1.5.2.11) and (1.5.2.12), since

$$\tfrac{1}{2} r(r - a_{t+1}) \le r\, a_{t+1},$$

we obtain (using (1.5.2.5))

$$r \le 3 a_{t+1} = 3 a_t + 3 b_t. \tag{1.5.2.13}$$

From (1.5.2.9), (1.5.2.10), (1.5.2.13), and the induction hypothesis, it follows that

$$|B(M, t+1, I)| \le 3 a_t + 4 b_t = b_{t+1},$$

and the proof is complete.

The following is one of the principal results of this section.

Theorem 1.5.2.3. If $g : \{0, 1\}^n \to \{0, 1\}$ has a critical input, then every algorithm that computes g on a CREW model requires at least $\log_b N$ steps, where $b \approx 4.7913$.

Proof

Let T be the number of steps needed to compute g on the critical input. Then, at the final step T, every one of the N input indices must affect cell M_1, which contains the value of g. That is,

$$| B(M_1, T, I) | = N.$$

Combining this with Lemma 1.5.2.2 and relation (1.5.2.7), we have

$$| B(M_1, T, I) | = N \leq b_T \leq c_2 \lambda_1^T,$$

from which the theorem follows, by taking logarithms on both sides.

Since $f_{OR}(x_1, x_2, \cdots, x_N)$ is a function with critical input, the lower bound in (1.5.2.1) follows from Theorem 1.5.2.3.

1.6 NOTES AND REFERENCES

Section 1.2. There are a number of excellent textbooks and monographs on serial algorithms -- Aho, Hopcroft and Ullman [1974], Baase [1978], Brassard and Bratley [1988], Bellman, Cooke, and Lockett [1977], Borodin and Munro [1975], Deo [1974], Even [1980], Horowitz and Sahni [1978], Hu [1982], Knuth [1968, 1969, 1973], Kronsjo [1987], Kuck [1978], Lorin [1975], Mehlhorn [1984a, 1984b, 1984c], Papadimitriou and Steiglitz [1982], Purdom and Brown [1985], Reingold, Nievergelt, and Deo [1977], Sedgewick [1983], Swamy and Thulasiraman [1983], Syslo, Deo, and Kowalik [1983], Traub, Wasilkowski, and Wozniakowski [1983], and Traub and Wozniakowski [1980]. Weide [1977], Reingold [1972], and Cohen [1979] present an interesting survey of techniques that are widely used in the analysis and design of algorithms.

A historical perspective on the development of parallel architectures is given in Kuck [1978], Hockney and Jesshope [1981], and Hwang and Briggs [1984]. A standard classification of parallel architectures as single instruction stream and multiple data stream (SIMD) and multiple instruction stream and multiple data stream (MIMD) is due to Flynn [1972]. or other taxonomies refer to Kuck [1978], Hockney and Jesshope [1981], and Bell [1985]. A clear exposition of a number of pipelined and parallel architectures can be obtained from Hockney and Jesshope [1981], Hwang [1984, 1987], Hwang and Briggs [1984], Kuhn and Padua [1981], and Ramamoorthy and Li [1977].

Illiac-IV, the forerunner of all the parallel processors, is described in Barnes et al [1968]. The related ICL-DAP is described in Hockney and Jesshope [1981], and MPP in Batcher [1980].

Cray Research machines and Cyber-205 systems are described in Hwang and Briggs [1984] and Hockney and Jesshope [1981]. The Cyber-Plus system is described in Cyberplus [1984].

A description of the Encore family of multiprocessors is contained in Bell

[1985], and that of the Balance-8000 family of multiprocessors is contained in Sequent Computer Systems [1985].

The Cosmic Cube, the forerunner of Intel's hypercube, called iPSC, is described by Seitz [1985]. The design and development of the ultracomputer is contained in Gottlieb et al [1983]. A closely related research project leading to the architecture called RP-3 is described in Pfister et al [1985]. For information on the HEP, refer to Jordan [1984], for Butterfly to Crowther et al [1985], for GF-11 to Beetem, Denneau, and Weingarten [1985], for the Pyramid family to Maples [1985], for Flex/32 multicomputer systems to Matelan [1985], for Alliant machines to Alliant [1985], for The Connection machines to Hillis [1985], for BSP to Kuck and Stokes [1982], and for configurable parallel machines to Snyder [1982]. The goals of the CEDAR project are described in Kuck et al [1983].

For a tutorial exposition of data flow architectures, refer to Dennis [1980], Agerwala and Arvind [1982], and Chambers et al [1984]. The special issue of *IEEE Computer*, edited by Theis [1981] is devoted to all aspects of array processors. Cellular automata machines (Toffoli and Morgolus [1987]) have long been known for their versatility in simulation of distributed systems. Wulf and Bell [1972] and Swan, Fuller, and Siewiorek [1977] describe the now classic project that led to the early MIMD machines, called C.mmp and Cm^*. Also refer to Satyanarayanan [1980] for more information on C.mmp and the related project called Cm^*.

There are equally as many expositions such as expository surveys, tutorials, anthologies, and monographs on various aspects of parallel computation. Akl [1989], Almasi and Gottlieb [1989], Andre, Herman, and Verjus [1985], Baba [1987], Babb [1988], Baer [1974], Bertsekas and Tsitsiklis [1989], Borodin and Munro [1975], Gentzsch [1983], Harel [1987], Heller [1978], Hockney and Jesshope [1981], Karp and Ramachandran [1988], Lipovski and Malek [1987], Lorin [1972], McKeown [1980], Miranker [1971], Moitra and Sitharama Iyengar [1987], Ortega [1988], Parberry [1987], Quinn [1987], Reed and Fujimoto [1988], Sameh [1977], Schendel [1984], Siegel [1985], and Wegener [1987] constitute definitive work on parallelism.

Kuck [1976, 1978] succinctly summarizes the problems and challenges confronting the translation of ordinary serial programs into parallel programs, and parallel algorithms for the evaluation of recurrences, arithmetic expressions, etc.

The book by Hockney and Jesshope [1981] well summarizes the various desirable attributes of a parallel programming language.

A general taxonomy of parallel algorithms is presented in Kung [1980] and Cook [1985]. Chambers, Duce, and Jones [1984], Evans [1980], Haynes, Lau, Siewiorek, and Mizzell [1982], Hwang [1984], Kuhn and Padua [1981], Lorin [1972], Riganati and Schneck [1984], Stone [1971], Uhr [1984], and Zakharov [1984] are general references on parallel processing.

Kowalik [1985] and Lakshmivarahan [1985] contain papers on parallel algorithms specially designed for the very promising but short-lived parallel machine called HEP.

Hirschberg [1982], Karp and Ramachandran [1988], Reghbati and Corneil [1978], and Quinn and Deo [1984] present parallel algorithms for graph problems.

Akl [1985] and Lakshmivarahan, Dhall, and Miller [1984] present a survey of parallel sorting algorithms. Batcher [1968] broke new ground in the design of parallel sorting networks. Ajtai, Komlos, and Szemeredi [1984] gave an optimal design for parallel sorting networks.

Csanky [1976] describes a conceptual framework for parallel algorithms for a number of matrix-related problems, such as inversion, and evaluation of determinants.

A study of parallelism in a rule-based production system, which is of intrinsic interest in artificial intelligence, is contained in Gupta [1987].

The role and importance of communication in parallel computation is discussed in Lint and Agerwala [1981], Gannon and Rosendale [1984], and Gentleman [1978].

The concept of a *paracomputer* was first introduced in a very influential paper by Schwartz [1980]. Parallel models are discussed in a number of papers including Borodin [1977], Borodin and Hopcroft [1982], Cook and Dwork [1982], Cook, Dwork, and Reischuk [1986], Fortune and Wyllie [1978], Galil [1985], Galil and Paul [1983], Goldschlager [1978, 1982], Gottlieb and Kruskal [1984], Lev, Pippenger, and Valiant [1981], Schwartz [1980], Shiloach and Vishkin [1981], and Snir [1985]. Parallel computation tree models are discussed in Borodin and Hopcroft [1982] and Valiant [1975]. Kozen [1976] examines parallelism in the framework of Turing machines. Chandra, Fortune, and Lipton [1983], Fagin, Klawe, Pippenger, and Stockmeyer [1983], Furst, Saxe, and Sipser [1981], and Pippenger and Fischer [1979] deal with various aspects of combinational circuit models and their relation to other models.

The $O(\log N)$ algorithm for simulating one read/write step of a CRCW model on an EREW model is due to Eckstein [1979].

Section 1.3. Hockney and Jesshope [1981] present an extensive discussion on modeling the performance of parallel computers, in particular the asymptotic vector performance. Dongarra [1986] and Lubeck, Moore, and Mendez [1986] contain a number of interesting benchmarks. The concept of problems admitting asymptotically completely parallelizable algorithms is discussed in Schwartz [1980] and Gottlieb and Kruskal [1984].

Section 1.4. Garey and Johnson [1979] is a standard reference on complexity theory, especially dealing with *NP*-complete problems. The *NC*-class is due to Nick Pippenger [1979]. For a thorough discussion of the *PC*- and PC^*-classes, refer to Vitter and Simons [1986]. Log-space complete problems for *P* are discussed in Jones and Lasser [1977]. The survey papers by Cook [1985] and Karp and Ramachandran [1988] provide a wealth of information on various parallel complexity classes. Another useful class of models called *vector machines* is described in Pratt and Stockmeyer [1976]. Hofri [1987] is a good source on probabilistic algorithms.

Section 1.5. Theorem 1.5.1.2 is from Munro and Patterson [1973]. Lemma 1.5.1.3 through Theorem 1.5.1.6 are from Gottlieb and Kruskal [1984]. The rest of Section

1.5 closely follows Cook, Dwork, and Reischuk [1986]. For further discussion of lower and upper bounds, refer to Beame [1986], Beame, Cook, and Hoover [1986], Wegener [1987], Parberry [1987], and Savage [1987].

1.7 EXERCISES

1.1 Let a binary operation take k cycles to complete when done serially. If this operation is pipelined using a k-segment pipe, show that the resulting speed-up in computing N operations is

$$S_k = \frac{Nk}{N + k - 1}.$$

1.2 (Calahan and Ames [1979]). The time to add two vectors of length l on a pipelined unit may be modeled as

$$t_v = t_s + l \times t_e,$$

where t_s is known as the vector start-up time and t_e is the time taken by a segment of the pipe (it is assumed that all the segments of the pipe are of the same duration). Show that the number of floating point operations delivered in a second (by the pipe) is give by

$$\text{FLOPS} = \frac{l}{t_s + l \times t_e}.$$

Under ideal conditions ($t_s = 0$), the pipe can deliver results at the rate $r_e = t_e^{-1}$. Thus, define *vector efficiency* VE as the ratio of FLOPS to r_e. Show that

$$\text{VE} = \frac{1}{1 + x^{-1}}, \qquad \text{where } x = \frac{l}{r_e \times t_s}.$$

Analyze the behavior of VE as a function of x. Find the length of the vector necessary to deliver 75%, 50%, 25% vector efficiency.

Note: For further analysis of this measure and its role in characterizing the performance of various architectures and algorithms, refer to the book by Hockney and Jesshope [1981].

1.3 (Brent [1974], Heller [1978]). Assume that an algorithm requires N operations. Let T_p and T_q be the times required to complete the algorithm using p and q processors, respectively. If $q < p$, then show that

$$\frac{N}{q} \leq T_q \leq T_p + \frac{N - T_p}{q}.$$

Hint: Let N_i be the number of operations performed at stage i using p processors. Then $\sum_i^{T_p} N_i = N$ and $T_q \leq \sum_{i=1}^{T_p} \left\lceil \frac{N_i}{q} \right\rceil$. Recall $\left\lceil \frac{x}{y} \right\rceil \leq \frac{x - 1}{y} + 1$.

1.4   Consider a computer which essentially operates in two modes: the high-speed and the low-speed mode. (The high speed may correspond to an attached parallel processor and the low speed to the main serial processor.) Let t_h and t_l ($t_l > t_h$) be the times taken to complete a generic operation at the high and low speed, respectively. Then, $B_h = t_h^{-1}$ and $B_l = t_l^{-1}$ are known as the bandwidths of the high-speed and the low-speed modes. Given an algorithm, let f_h (≥ 0) and f_l (≥ 0) ($f_h + f_l = 1$) be fractions of the computations done at the high-speed and low-speed mode, respectively. The average bandwidth B is given by

$$B = \frac{1}{f_h \times t_h + f_l \times t_l} = \frac{B_h}{r + f_h \times (1 - r)},$$

where $r = \dfrac{B_h}{B_l}$.

Analyze the behavior of B as a function of f_h for various values of r.

Note: This is called the Amdahl's law (Amdahl [1967]) which states that the overall processor bandwidth realizable by an algorithm is limited by the fraction of computations performed at the low-speed mode. Notice that the problem size is assumed to be *fixed*.

1.5   (a) Given an algorithm, let f_i ($f_i \geq 0$) be the fraction of computations that can be executed using i processors where $f_1 + f_2 + \cdots + f_p = 1$. Then,

$$\text{Speed--up,} \quad S_p = \frac{T_1}{\displaystyle\sum_{i=1}^{p} f_i \times \frac{T_1}{i}} = \frac{1}{\displaystyle\sum_{i=1}^{p} \frac{f_i}{i}}.$$

(1) Analyze the behavior of s_p as a function of p (for large p) when $f_i = p^{-1}$.

(2) Consider the special case when

$$f_2 = f_3 = \cdots = f_{p-1} = 0,$$

and let $f_1 = f_l$ and $f_p = f_h$. Then

$$S_p = \frac{p}{pf_l + f_h}. \tag{$*$}$$

Analyze the behavior of S_p as a function of f_l.

Note: This is an extension of Amdahl's law due J. Wharlton. Also refer to U. Banerjee's Ph.D. dissertation (Banerjee [1979]) and Exercise 1.6.

(b) Amdahl's law as stated above analyzes the effect of changing f_i on the speed-up achievable under the assumption that the problem size is *fixed*. However, with increasing processor size, it is natural to correspondingly increase the problem size as well. To analyze the speed-up under the assumption of *increasing problem size*, let f_l and f_h be the fractions of the serial and parallel parts, respectively, of a problem, where $f_l + f_h = 1$. Let T be the time taken to complete this computation on a parallel processor with p processors. These computations, when executed in a serial processor, would take

$$Tf_l + Tf_h p$$

steps. Thus, the speed-up S'_p is given by

$$S'_p = \frac{Tf_l + Tf_h p}{Tf_l + Tf_h} = p + (1 - p)f_l. \qquad (**)$$

Analyze the behavior of S'_p with f_l and compare it with that of S_p in (*) in part (a).

Note: This new form of Amdahl's law is due to Gustafson [1988]. For a comparative discussion of these two forms -- fixed vs. variable problem size of Amdahl's law -- refer to Gustafson, Montry and Benner [1988], Heath and Worley [1989] and Gustafson [1989].

1.6 Let f_i be defined as in Exercise 1.5. Let

$$F_i = \sum_{j=1}^{i} f_j \quad \text{and} \quad H_p = \sum_{j=1}^{p} \frac{1}{j}.$$

Show that

(a) If $F_i \geq \dfrac{i}{p}$, then $s_p \leq \dfrac{p}{H_p}$.

(b) If there exists an integer k such that $0 \leq k \leq p$, $f_1, f_2, f_3, \cdots, f_k \geq (\leq) \dfrac{1}{p}$ and $f_{k+1}, f_{k+2}, \cdots, f_p < (>) \dfrac{1}{p}$, then

$$s_p \leq (\geq) \frac{p}{H_p}.$$

(c) If $f_1 \geq f_2 \geq \cdots \geq f_p$, then $S_p \leq \dfrac{p}{H_p}$.

(d) If $f_1 \leq f_2 \leq \cdots \leq f_p$, then $S_p \geq \dfrac{p}{H_p}$.

(e) If for each $i = 1$ to p, $F_i \leq \dfrac{i}{p} \times H_p$, then $s_p \geq \dfrac{p}{H_p^2}$.

Note: Since $H_p > \log_e p$ and $(H_p - \log_e p) = $ constant (nearly 0.577, called Euler's constant), notice that $\dfrac{p}{\log p}$ and $\dfrac{p}{(\log p)^2}$ are some of the typical values that S_p can take in the interval 1 to p.

1.7   (a) Show that an N-way fan-in can be realized by a circuit using at most $\dfrac{N-1}{k-1}+1$ components, with only k-way fan-in ($2 \le k < N$), where the longest path in the circuit does not contain more than $\lceil \log_k N \rceil$ components.

(b) When $k = 2$, show that the minimum number of components needed is $N - 1$ and the length of the longest path contains a minimum of $\lceil \log N \rceil$ components.

(c) Illustrate these bounds for $N = 8$ and $k = 2$ and 3.

1.8   Let $E(N)$ be an arithmetic expression with N atoms (where by definition, an atom is a constant or a variable taking numeric values). If $T(E(N))$ is the time required to evaluate $E(N)$ using processors with two-way fan-in, then show that

$$\lceil \log_2 N \rceil \le T(E(N)) \le N - 1.$$

1.9   Another attribute of a parallel algorithm relates to the *degree of parallelism,* which is defined as the maximum of the number of operations it performs in various stages. If the algorithm is such that the number of operations is not a constant across the stages, then a related measure is called the *average* degree of parallelism, which is defined as the ratio of the total number of operations to the total number of stages.

Compute the degree and the average degree of parallelism for the algorithms in Examples 1.3.1.1, 1.3.1.2, and 1.3.1.3.

1.10 The *utilization factor, U_p,* of a parallel algorithm is defined as

$$U_p = \frac{\text{total scalar operations required by a parallel algorithm}}{pT_p(N)},$$

where $T_p(N)$ is the time needed to complete the algorithm using p processors.

(a) Show that $U_p \le 1$.

(b) Compute R_p, U_p, and E_p, for the problems in Examples 1.3.1.1, 1.3.1.2, and 1.3.1.3.

(c) Show that $U_p = E_p R_p$ and discuss the implications of (i) $U_p = 1$, and $E_p < 1$, (ii) $E_p = U_p$ and (iii) $U_p < E_p$.

1.11 Compute the product $p \times T_p(N)$ for $p = 1, 2, 4, \log N, \dfrac{N}{\log N}, \dfrac{N}{\log \log N}$, and $\dfrac{N}{2}$ in Example 1.3.1.2.

1.12   (Galil [1985]).

(a) Show that a parallel algorithm that takes t units of time using p processors can be transformed into a serial algorithm of time tp.

(b) Show that a parallel algorithm that takes t_0 units of time using p_0 processors can be transformed into a family of parallel algorithms using p processors requiring t units of time where $tp \leq t_0 p_0$ and $p \leq p_0$. (Compare this with Example 1.3.1.2.)

Hint: Follows from direct simulation.

1.13   (Galil [1985]). Using the notation of Exercise 1.12, a family of algorithms for a problem are said to be *optimal parallel algorithms* if $tp = O(N)$ for $1 \leq p \leq p_0 \leq N$, where N is the size of the problem and p_0 is close to N such as $\dfrac{N}{\log N}$, $\dfrac{N}{\log^2 N}$, etc. Clearly, optimal parallel algorithms in this sense are contained in linear time serial algorithms.

(a) Show that any $f(x_1 \cdots x_N) = x_1 \text{ o } x_2 \text{ o } x_3 \text{ o } \cdots \text{ o } x_N$, where o is an associative binary operation, can be computed on a CREW model in $tp = O(N)$, where the number of processors $p \leq \dfrac{N}{\log N}$.

Note: It has been shown by Cook, Dwork, and Reischuk [1986] (see Section 1.5) that the N-variable AND (or OR) function needs $\Omega(\log N)$ time in a CREW model, even if an unlimited number of processors are available. Thus $tp = O(N)$ is not attainable if p is considerably larger than $\dfrac{N}{\log N}$. This is the reason that when $p = N/2$, t is still $\log N$, but $tp = O(N \log N)$. Compare with Exercise 1.12.

(b) (Valiant [1975]) Show that the maximum of N variables can be computed on a CRCW model in $tp = O(N)$, where $p \leq \dfrac{N}{\log \log N}$.

1.14   Derive parallel algorithms on CRCW, CREW, and EREW models for the following problems:

(a) Finding whether a Boolean N-vector contains a 1.

(b) Finding the maximum/minimum of a set of N numbers.

(c) Finding the number of 1's in a Boolean N-vector.

1.15 (Heller [1978]). Define a set $BT(p)$ of labeled binary trees as follows:

(1) A tree with one node with label 0 is in $BT(p)$. This corresponds to the tree with only one node, namely, the root. The depth of the tree is defined to be the label of the root node (0 in this case).

(2) Given a depth k tree in $BT(p)$, by increasing all the labels by 1 and replacing at most p leaves with a tree of the type given in Fig. E1.1, a new tree in $BT(p)$ of depth $k + 1$ is obtained.

(3) No tree is in $BT(p)$ unless it arises due to steps 1 and 2.

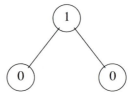

FIGURE E1.1

Clearly a depth t binary tree in $BT(p)$ corresponds to t steps of parallel computation using p processors. Let $L(p, t)$ be the maximum number of leaves on a depth-t tree in $BT(p)$ and $M(p, N)$ the minimum depth of a tree in $BT(p)$ with N leaves.

(a) Show that

$$L(p, 0) = 1,$$

$$L(p, t + 1) = L(p,t) + \min(p, L(p, t)),$$

and

$$M(p, N) = t, \quad \text{if } L(p, t - 1) < N \leq L(p, t).$$

(b) If $k = \lceil \log p \rceil$, then

$$L(p, t) = 2^{\min(k,t)} + p \max(0, t - k),$$

and

$$M(p, N) = \min(k, \lceil \log N \rceil) + \max\left(0, \left\lceil \frac{N - 2^k}{p} \right\rceil\right).$$

(c) Draw the minimum depth tree for $N = 8$ and $p = 3$, and relate this with Theorem 1.5.1.2.

1.16 Show that in a degree-k parallel processor of size p, the maximum diameter is at least $\log_k (p + 1) - 1$.

1.17 In a degree-k parallel processor of size p, if $P_i \in Q$ and $S \subset Q$, then show that

$$\max_{P_j \in Q} d(P_i, P_j) = \Omega(\log_k |S|).$$

1.18 A computation of m output quantities $(y_1, y_2, \cdots, y_m)$ depends on N input quantities $(x_1, x_2, \cdots, x_N)$ if each x_i is required for the computation of at least one y_j, that is, there exists a function $f(.)$ such that $(y_1, y_2, \cdots, y_m) = f(x_1, x_2, \cdots, x_N)$ and for each $i = 1, 2, \cdots, N$, there exist distinct values a and b such that

$$f_{x_i=a}(x_1, \cdots, x_N) \neq f_{x_i=b}(x_1, \cdots, x_N).$$

Give examples of such computations with $m = N$.

1.19 Let $T(N)$ and $T_p(N)$, respectively, be the serial and parallel time (using p processors) taken to solve a problem. Define $G_p(N)$ as the gain in time resulting from the introduction of parallelism as

$$G_p(N) = T(N) - T_p(N),$$

and the relative gain $RG_p(N)$ as

$$RG_p(N) = \frac{G_p(N)}{p}.$$

Analyze the behavior of $RG_p(N)$ for various algorithms and compare it with speed-up ratio and processor efficiency.

1.20 Show that the solution of system (1.5.2.5) is given by (1.5.2.7).

1.21 (Cook, Dwork, and Reischuk [1986]). Let $W = w_1 w_2 \cdots w_n$ be a binary string of length n. Given W, define a function $f_W : \{0, 1\}^n \rightarrow \{0, 1\}$ such that its value is 1 if and only if $w_i = x_i$ for all $i = 1$ to n. Prove the correctness of the following algorithm for computing the function f_W.

(a) Given $(x_1, x_2, \cdots, x_n)$, first complement x_i if $w_i = 1$ for $1 \leq i \leq n$ and let $Y = (Y_1, Y_2, \cdots, Y_n)$ be the resulting vector, where $Y_i = \bar{x}_i$ if $x_i = 1$, otherwise $Y_i = x_i$.

(b) Compute $Z = Y_1 \vee Y_2 \vee \cdots \vee Y_n$ using the algorithm given in Section 1.5.

(c) Show that $f_W(x_1, x_2, \cdots, x_n) = \bar{Z}$, where $\bar{0} = 1$ and $\bar{1} = 0$.

1.22 (Cook, Dwork, and Reischuk [1986]). The following is an algorithm for computing the logical OR of N variables $x_1, x_2, \cdots, x_N$ in a CRCW model. It is assumed that *at most k of the input variables can have value 1 (that is, at least $N - k$ of them are 0's)*, and that x_i is stored in M_i, $1 \leq i \leq N$.

(1) For each subset $r_k = \{i_1, i_2, \cdots, i_k\}$ of $\{1, 2, \cdots, N\}$ with $i_1 < i_2 < \cdots < i_k$, a processor p_{r_k} in k steps reads $M_{i_1}, M_{i_2}, \cdots, M_{i_k}$ and writes 1 into M_1 in step k if and only if $M_{i_1} = M_{i_2} = \cdots = M_{i_k} = 1$.

(2) At step $k + 1$, for each $r_{k-1} = \{i_1, i_2, \cdots, i_{k-1}\}$, there is a processor $p_{r_{k-1}}$ (which has already read input cells $M_{i_1}, M_{i_2}, \cdots, M_{i_{k-1}}$) which now reads M_1 and writes 1 in M_1 if and only if $\{M_1 = 0 \text{ and } M_{i_1} = M_{i_2} = \cdots = M_{i_{k-1}} = 1\}$.

(3) This process is repeated in steps $k + 2, k + 3, \cdots, 2k - 1$. That is, at step $k + t$, some processor writes a 1 in M_1 if and only if no 1 has been written before and there are exactly $k - t$ 1's in the input.

(a) Prove the correctness of the algorithm by showing that M_1 contains the correct output after $2k - 1$ steps. Compute the number of processors needed to achieve this bound.

(b) Prove that there is no write conflict if the input has at most k 1's in it.

(c) Analyze the special cases when $k = 1, 2$, and N.

(d) Since there is no write conflict for inputs with at most k 1's in it, show that using the algorithm for computing f_{OR} on a CREW model given in Section 1.5, the above upper bound can be reduced to $k + O(\log k)$.

(e) Compare this bound with the lower bound $0.442 \log_2 N$ given in Theorem 1.5.2.3.

CHAPTER
2

MULTIPROCESSORS AND MULTICOMPUTERS

2.1 INTRODUCTION

The parallel models described in Chapter 1 provide the framework for the development of parallel algorithms. The equivalence between the various models further enables the designer to pick the model that is better suited for a given problem. Ultimately, however, an algorithm is measured by its performance, such as speed-up and efficiency in solving problems on actual machines. At the model level, one can assume that multiple read and/or write or unbounded fan-out are allowed. But in practice, even if we disallow multiple read and write, the actual read/write time in a parallel computer is critically dependent on the data storage scheme as well as on the properties of the network that interconnects processors or processors and memory. Thus, to predict the performance of algorithms on actual machines, a good understanding of the interconnection schemes is necessary. In this chapter, we describe the salient features of two types of parallel computers, called *multiprocessors* and *multicomputers*. Our aim is to provide a backdrop that will help focus on the key issues germane to algorithm design, such as the effect of data organization on parallel access, communication cost, mapping, and/or portability of algorithms across architectures. The literature on these topics is quite extensive, and we have avoided the temptation to describe the specific features of many of the commercially available machines.

Parallel computers in general may be *loosely* classified into two groups -- (1) *multiprocessors with shared* memory organization and (2) *multicomputers with non-shared* or *distributed* memory organization. In a shared memory organization an array of processors and an array of common bank of memory units are connected through a fast bus or one of many types of *multistage dynamic* interconnection networks. In this organization, the processors communicate by writing onto and reading from the common or shared memory. The GF-11 supercomputer, the Butterfly multiprocessor, the Ultracomputer, and C.mmp are some examples of this type of organization. Other examples are the Alliant machines and Cray X-MP. In a non-shared memory organization, on the other hand, an assemblage of processors each with its own local memory are connected in a *static* or *fixed* interconnection scheme. Examples of this type of organization include the Cosmic Cube, Intel's hypercube, NCUBE machine, the Connection Machine.

Our treatment of the multicomputer organization in Section 2.2 is centered around the ubiquitous hypercube interconnection scheme. The approach is quite generic in nature and can be adopted to analyze any other static interconnection scheme. We first introduce the recursive structure of a class of hypercube interconnection schemes, called the N-node, base-b hypercubes that includes the binary ($b = 2$) hypercube at one end and the complete graph ($b = N$) at the other. The topological properties of this class of networks, such as degree, number of edges, diameter, edge and/or node disjoint parallel paths between pairs of nodes are then derived. These properties are crucial for the efficient design of routing tables that constitute a major component of the network operating system.

Another fundamental issue of both theoretical and practical importance is related to the *portability* of algorithms across various parallel architectures. Analysis of portability naturally leads to the simulation or embedding of one set of graphs by another. The two key parameters that characterize the quality of an embedding are called *expansion* and *dilation*. Expansion relates to the hardware overhead in terms of the number of processors needed, and dilation to the communication overhead involved in simulating one graph by the other. We present a comprehensive discussion of the embedding of many topologies including linear arrays, rings, two-dimensional meshes, and complete binary trees into the hypercube. A proven strategy for deriving many of these embeddings into a binary hypercube is to use the binary reflected Gray codes. In extending these embeddings to base-b cubes, we also introduce a class of generalized Gray codes called *base-b reflected Gray codes*.

Two types of multistage dynamic networks that constitute the backbone of the multiprocessors with shared memory organization are described in Section 2.3. One class, called the *blocking* networks, includes the well-known omega network, a variation of which is used in the Butterfly multiprocessor. The other class, called the *rearrangeable* networks, is used in the GF-11 supercomputer. The *combinatorial power (CP)* of an $N \times N$ dynamic network is defined as the ratio of the number of permutations realized by the network to the total number of permutations over N objects. Under synchronous operations, CP relates to the variety of data access patterns realizable by the network. The discussion includes the derivation of combinatorial power, the generic routing algorithm, and the effect of data organization on parallel access.

2.2 THE HYPERCUBE MULTICOMPUTER

2.2.1 The Recursive Structure of the N-Node Base-b Hypercube

Let N and b be two integers where $N \geq b \geq 2$. Let k be an integer such that $b^{k-1} < N \leq b^k$. In the rest of this section, a hypercube will be represented by its underlying graph. Let $< m > = \{ 0, 1, 2, \cdots , m-1 \}$.

An N-node base-b hypercube denoted by (N, b, k) hypercube is a graph $G = (V, E)$, where

$$V = \{ x \mid x \text{ is a } k\text{-digit base-}b \text{ integer, i.e. } x = x_k x_{k-1} \cdots x_1, \text{ and } x_i \in < b > \},$$

and

$$E = \{ (x, y) \mid x, y \in V, \text{ and } there \text{ } exists \text{ } 1 \leq j \leq k$$

$$\text{such that } x_j \neq y_j \text{ and } x_i = y_i \text{ for } all \text{ } i \neq j \}$$

Thus, two nodes in G are connected if and only if their labels differ in exactly *one* base-b digit. Since this is a generalization of the definition of the base-2 cube, this graph is called an (N, b, k) hypercube. If $N = b^k$, then the graph G is called a *complete* (N, b, k) hypercube of *dimension* k or simply an (N, b, k) cube. Otherwise, G is called an *incomplete* (N, b, k) cube.

Figure 2.2.1.1 gives an example of the complete $(5, 5, 1)$ cube. The five nodes are labeled 0 through 4, and it is a complete graph on five nodes. Figure 2.2.1.2 is an example of an incomplete $(6, 3, 2)$ cube, and Fig. 2.2.1.3 is an example of a $(9, 3, 2)$ cube. The conventional eight-node hypercube in Fig. 2.2.1.4 is a complete $(8, 2, 3)$ cube.

The (N, b, k) cube admits a simple *recursive* characterization. If A is a set of strings over $< b >$, then define

$$B = xA = \{ x\alpha \mid \alpha \in A \text{ and } x \in < b > \}, \tag{2.2.1.1}$$

where $x\alpha$ is a string obtained by concatenating x and α. Define a sequence of sets $V^{(i)}$, $i = 0, 1, \cdots , k - 1$, where

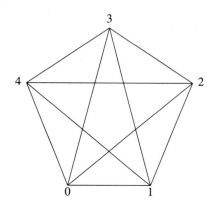

FIGURE 2.2.1.1
Example of a complete (5, 5, 1) cube.

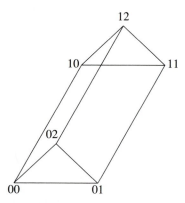

FIGURE 2.2.1.2
Example of an incomplete (6, 3, 2) cube.

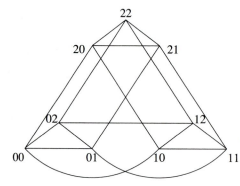

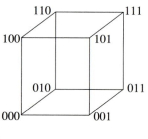

FIGURE 2.2.1.3
Example of a complete (9, 3, 2) cube.

FIGURE 2.2.1.4
Example of a complete (8, 2, 3) cube.

$$V^{(i)} = \bigcup_{x \in <b>} V_x^{(i)}, \qquad (2.2.1.2)$$

and $V_x^{(i)}$ is defined recursively as follows:

$$V_x^{(0)} = \{ x \} \quad \text{for all } x \in <b>, \qquad (2.2.1.3)$$

and (using 2.2.1.1)

$$V_x^{(i)} = xV^{(i-1)} \quad \text{for all } x \in <b>. \qquad (2.2.1.4)$$

It follows that $V_x^{(i)}$ consists of strings over $<b>$ of length $i + 1$, whose leading (leftmost) symbol is x. Further,

$$|V_x^{(0)}| = 1 \quad \text{for all } x \in <b> \quad \text{and} \quad |V^{(0)}| = b, \quad (2.2.1.5)$$

and, for $i \geq 1$,

$$|V_x^{(i)}| = b^i \quad \text{for all } x \in <b> \quad \text{and} \quad |V^{(i)}| = b^{i+1}. \quad (2.2.1.6)$$

The following example illustrates the structure of these sets for $b = 4$.

$V_0^{(0)}$	$=$	$\{0\}$	$V_1^{(0)}$	$=$	$\{1\}$
$V_2^{(0)}$	$=$	$\{2\}$	$V_3^{(0)}$	$=$	$\{3\}$
$V^{(0)}$	$=$	$\{0, 1, 2, 3\}$			
$V_0^{(1)}$	$=$	$\{00, 01, 02, 03\}$	$V_1^{(1)}$	$=$	$\{10, 11, 12, 13\}$
$V_2^{(1)}$	$=$	$\{20, 21, 22, 23\}$	$V_3^{(1)}$	$=$	$\{30, 31, 32, 33\}$

$V^{(1)} = \{00, 01, 02, 03, 10, 11, 12, 13, 20, 21, 22, 23, 30, 31, 32, 33\}.$

$V_3^{(2)} = \{300, 301, 302, 303, 310, 311, 312, 313, 320, 321, 322,$
$323, 330, 331, 332, 333\}.$

In the following, depending on the context, a member of $V_x^{(i)}$ will be considered either as a string of length $i + 1$ with the leftmost symbol x or as an $i + 1$-digit base-b integer with x as the leading digit. When considered as an integer, the usual ordering on the integers will be imposed on $V_x^{(i)}$. Thus, in $V_3^{(2)}$, it is readily seen that $300 < 301 < 302 < \cdots < 332 < 333$. Clearly, the ordering on $V_x^{(i)}$ induces the natural ordering on $V^{(i)}$.

The basic building block of the (N, b, k) cube is the graph $G^{(0)}$ defined as

$$G^{(0)} = (V^{(0)}, E^{(0)}), \quad (2.2.1.7)$$

where $V^{(0)}$ is defined in (2.2.1.2) and (2.2.1.3) and

$$E^{(0)} = \{(s,t) \mid s, t \in V^{(0)}, s < t\}. \quad (2.2.1.8)$$

Clearly, $G^{(0)}$ is a complete graph on $V^{(0)}$ and

$$|E^{(0)}| = \frac{b(b-1)}{2}. \quad (2.2.1.9)$$

Figure 2.2.1.5 is an example of $G^{(0)}$ with $b = 4$.

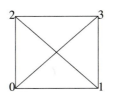

FIGURE 2.2.1.5
Example of a $(4, 4, 1)$ cube $G^{(0)}$.

Now define

$$G_x^{(1)} = (V_x^{(1)}, E_x^{(1)}),$$ (2.2.1.10)

where $V_x^{(1)}$ is defined in (2.2.1.2) through (2.2.1.4), and

$$E_x^{(1)} = \{(x\alpha, x\beta) \mid (\alpha, \beta) \in E^{(0)}\}.$$ (2.2.1.11)

Thus, $G_x^{(1)}$ is obtained by simply adding a prefix x to each node of $G^{(0)}$; that is, $G_x^{(1)}$ is isomorphic to $G^{(0)}$ for all $x \in <b>$.

Let

$$G^{(1)} = (V^{(1)}, E^{(1)}),$$ (2.2.1.12)

where $V^{(1)}$ is given in (2.2.1.2) through (2.2.1.4), and

$$E^{(1)} = \bigcup_{x \in <b>} E_x^{(1)} \cup \{(s\alpha, t\alpha) \mid \alpha \in V^{(0)} ; s, t \in V^{(0)} \text{ and } s < t\}.$$ (2.2.1.13)

Obviously,

$$|E^{(1)}| = b^2(b-1).$$ (2.2.1.14)

Stated in words, first take b copies of $G^{(0)}$ and rename them as $G_x^{(1)}$ for $x \in <b>$. Now considering each of these $G_x^{(1)}$ as a *supernode*, $G^{(1)}$ is obtained by building a base-b cube on them. A supernode $G_x^{(1)}$ is connected to a supernode $G_y^{(1)}$ if and only if a node $x\alpha$ in $G_x^{(1)}$ is connected by an edge to its *corresponding* node $y\alpha$ in $G_y^{(1)}$ for each α in $V^{(0)}$. (Notice that the labels of corresponding nodes in $G^{(1)}$ have the same suffix α of length 1.)

An example of $G^{(1)}$ is given in Fig. 2.2.1.6. For simplicity in representation, the same (16, 4, 2) cube in Fig. 2.2.1.6 will be represented as in Fig. 2.2.1.7, where the connections between the supernodes are shown by the thick dark connections.

Now, in general, $G^{(i)}$ is defined by

$$G^{(i)} = (V^{(i)}, E^{(i)}),$$ (2.2.1.15)

where $V^{(i)}$ corresponds to (2.2.1.2) through (2.2.1.4), and

$$E^{(i)} = \bigcup_{x \in <b>} E_x^{(i)} \cup \{(s\alpha, t\alpha) \mid \alpha \in V^{(i-1)}; s, t \in V^{(0)} \text{ and } s < t.\}.$$ (2.2.1.16)

From (2.2.1.16), using the previous development, it follows that

$$|E^{(i)}| = b \; |E^{(i-1)}| + \frac{b^{i+1}(b-1)}{2},$$ (2.2.1.17)

the solution of which is

$$|E^{(i)}| = \frac{i+1}{2} b^{i+1}(b-1).$$ (2.2.1.18)

Clearly $G^{(k-1)}$ corresponds to the $(N = b^k, b, k)$ cube. For an example of $G^{(3)}$ refer to Fig. 2.2.1.8.

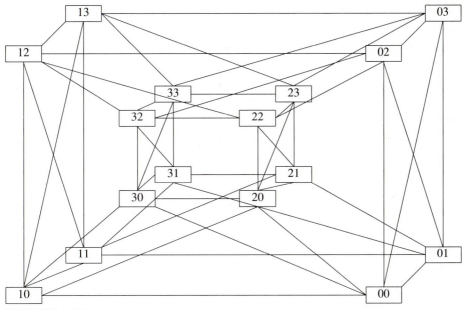

FIGURE 2.2.1.6
Example of a complete (16, 4, 2) cube $G^{(1)}$.

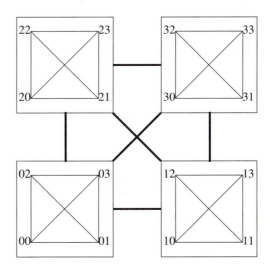

FIGURE 2.2.1.7
Recursive structure of a complete (16, 4, 2) cube.

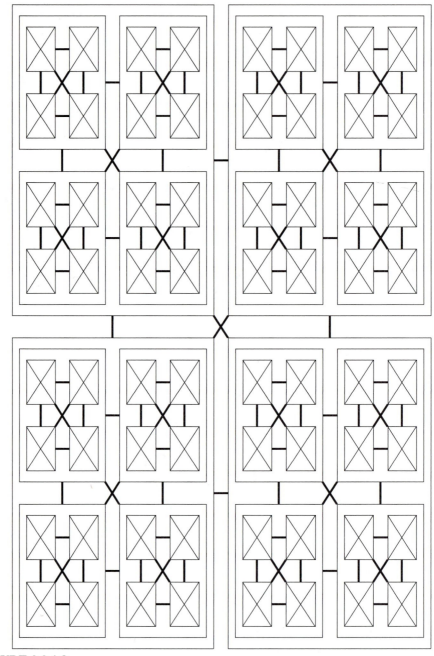

FIGURE 2.2.1.8
Recursive structure of a (256, 4, 4) cube -- $G^{(3)}$.

The following theorem is a direct consequence.

Theorem 2.2.1.1. For $j \geq 1$, the graph $G^{(j-1)}$, recursively defined above, is a (b^j, b, j) cube.

Proof

The proof is by induction. That $G^{(0)}$ is a $(b, b, 1)$ cube readily follows from the definition (2.2.1.7) and (2.2.1.8). Assume it is true for $j = i - 1$. To show that it is true for $j = i$, consider

$$G^{(i)} = (V^{(i)}, E^{(i)}).$$

Referring to (2.2.1.16), it is clear that the edges in $E^{(i)}$ are divided into two groups: (a) those in $G_x^{(i)}$, and (b) those interconnecting various $G_x^{(i)}$. Since $G_x^{(i)}$ are isomorphic to $G^{(i-1)}$, all the edges in $E_x^{(i)}$ by inductive hypothesis satisfy the definition of the hypercube. Now the edges in the second group by their very definition (refer to (2.2.1.16)) again satisfy the conditions of definition of the hypercube given at the beginning of this section. Hence the theorem.

One way to construct an incomplete (N, b, k) cube is to first build a (b^k, b, k) cube. Then the subgraph defined on the nodes with labels 0 through $N - 1$ in $G^{(k-1)}$ corresponds to the required incomplete (N, b, k) cube. This subgraph is obtained by removing all the nodes with labels ranging from N through $b^k - 1$ and all the edges incident on them. In practice, an incomplete cube arises principally due to faulty nodes in a complete cube. Since faults occur randomly, there are many possibilities for considering an incomplete (N, b, k) cube, when $b^{k-1} < N < b^k$.

The following corollary establishes the existence of a hierarchy of hypercubes.

Corollary 2.2.1.2. Let d, k, and m be positive integers. Then a (d^{mk}, d^m, k) cube contains a $(d^{mk}, d^{m/p}, kp)$ cube for every positive integer p dividing m.

Proof

Consider two nodes x and y. When considered as nodes in the (N, d^s, t) cube, with $s < m$, let $x = x_t x_{t-1} \cdots x_2 x_1$ and $y = y_t y_{t-1} \cdots y_2 y_1$, where x_i and y_i belong to $< d^s >$. For the same pair of nodes, when considered as nodes in the complete (N, d^m, k) cube, let $x = \bar{x}_k \bar{x}_{k-1} \cdots \bar{x}_1$ and $y = \bar{y}_k \bar{y}_{k-1} \cdots \bar{y}_1$, where $\bar{x}_i$ and $\bar{y}_i$ belong to $< d^m >$. Since $s < m$ and $m = ps$, it follows that $< d^s >$ is a subset of $< d^m >$ and that $\bar{x}_1 = x_p x_{p-1} \cdots x_1$, that is, $\bar{x}_1$ in base-d^m is equal to $x_p x_{p-1} \cdots x_1$, in base-d^s. Similarly, $\bar{x}_2 = x_{2p} x_{2p-1} \cdots x_{p+1}$, and more generally, for $1 \leq i \leq k$,

$$\bar{x}_i = x_{ip} x_{ip-1} \cdots x_{(i-1)p+1} .$$

A similar relation holds for $\bar{y}_i$ and the y_j's.

There will be an edge connecting x and y in the (N, d^s, t) cube if and only if there exists $1 \le q \le t$ such that $x_q \ne y_q$ and $x_i = y_i$ for $i \ne q$, that is, if and only if x and y are adjacent in this cube. But this latter condition implies that

$$\bar{x}_{\lceil q/p \rceil} \ne \bar{y}_{\lceil q/p \rceil} \quad \text{and} \quad \bar{x}_j = \bar{y}_j \quad \text{for all } j \ne \left\lceil \frac{q}{p} \right\rceil ,$$

that is, x and y are adjacent nodes in the (N, d^m, k) cube. Since x and y are arbitrary, the corollary follows.

Thus every $(N, 4, k)$ cube contains an $(N, 2, 2k)$ cube. Clearly, the $(16, 4, 2)$ cube in Fig. 2.2.1.6 contains a $(16, 2, 4)$ cube.

Given the (N, b, k) cube, by virtually reversing the recursive procedure given above, different subgraphs with prespecified properties can be obtained by properly *tearing* the given cube. The process of tearing is equivalent to systematic removal of certain edges in the given graph to obtain the required subgraphs. Thus, tearing relates to the possibility of *reconfiguring* the given interconnection network into a number of desirable subnetworks. Obviously, the number of different ways of tearing depends critically on the properties of the subgraphs to be obtained. In the following, different ways of reconfiguring the given (N, b, k) cube are characterized. To fix the ideas, the concept of a *basic projection* is introduced.

An (N, b, k) cube admits k different basic projections, one along each of the k base-b digits (or dimensions). In each dimension, there are b such projections, one for each value of the base. Each of these projections is an $(N/b, b, k - 1)$ cube.

As an example, consider the $(16, 4, 2)$ cube in Fig. 2.2.1.6. The two different basic projections of this cube are given in Figs. 2.2.1.9 and 2.2.1.10. Using these basic projections, the set of all possible reconfigurations of an (N, b, k) cube may be enumerated, which is the content of the following theorem.

Theorem 2.2.1.3. An (N, b, k) cube may be reconfigured by tearing it into an incomplete $(rN/b, b, k)$ cube and an incomplete $((b-r)N/b, b, k)$ cube in $k \begin{pmatrix} b \\ r \end{pmatrix}$ different ways.

Proof

Consider the jth basic projection containing b copies of $(N/b, b, k - 1)$ cubes. These b copies may be partitioned into two groups -- one containing r copies and the other with $b - r$ copies of the $(N/b, b, k - 1)$ cube. The r copies may be combined using the recursive procedure to form an incomplete $(rN/b, b, k)$ cube. Likewise, the rest of the $b - r$ copies may be combined to obtain an incomplete $((b-r)N/b, b, k)$ cube. The r copies may be picked in $\begin{pmatrix} b \\ r \end{pmatrix}$

different ways. Since $\begin{pmatrix} b \\ r \end{pmatrix} = \begin{pmatrix} b \\ b-r \end{pmatrix}$ by repeating this for each possible projection, the theorem follows.

When $r = 2$, the three different reconfigurations obtained by combining the basic projections in Fig. 2.2.1.9 are given in Fig. 2.2.1.11. Likewise, the three different reconfigurations obtained by combining the basic projections in Fig. 2.2.1.10 are given in Fig. 2.2.1.12. When $r = 1$, the four different reconfigurations obtained by combining the basic projections in Fig. 2.2.1.9 are given in Fig. 2.2.1.13 and those for Fig. 2.2.1.10 in Fig. 2.2.1.14.

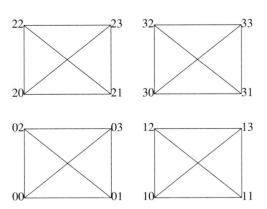

FIGURE 2.2.1.9
Basic projections of the cube in Fig. 2.2.1.6 along the second dimension.

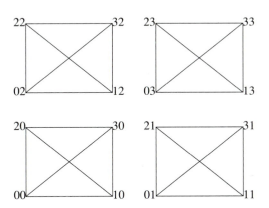

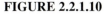

FIGURE 2.2.1.10
Basic projections of the cube in Fig. 2.2.1.6 along the first dimension.

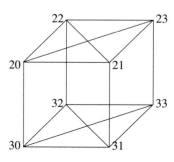
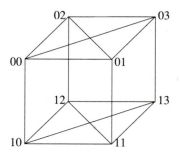

(a)

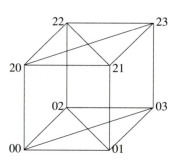
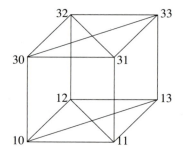

(b)

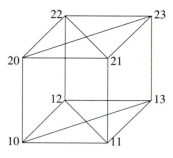
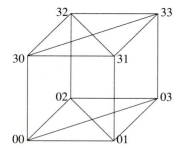

(c)

FIGURE 2.2.1.11

Three ($r = 2$) reconfigurations of a complete (16, 4, 2) cube obtained from the basic projections in Fig. 2.2.1.9.

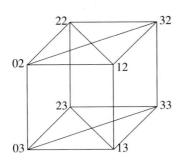

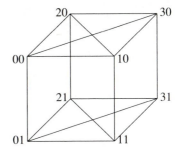

(a)

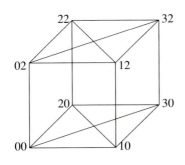

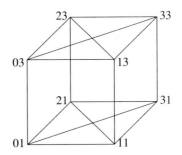

(b)

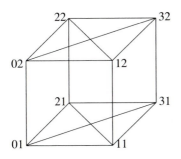

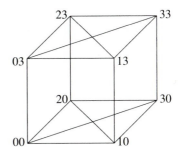

(c)

FIGURE 2.2.1.12

Three ($r = 2$) reconfigurations of a complete (16, 4, 2) cube obtained from the basic projections in Fig. 2.2.1.10.

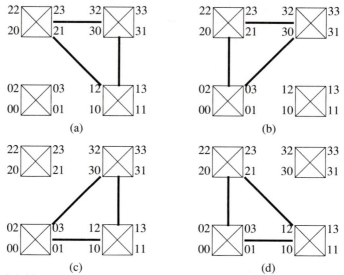

FIGURE 2.2.1.13

Four ($r = 1$) reconfigurations of a complete (16, 4, 2) cube obtained from the basic projections in Fig. 2.2.1.9.

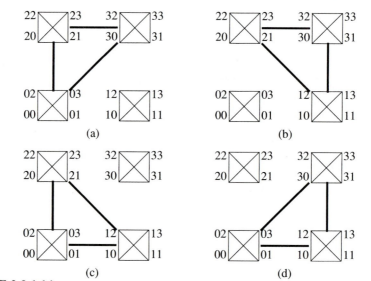

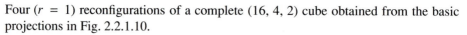

FIGURE 2.2.1.14

Four ($r = 1$) reconfigurations of a complete (16, 4, 2) cube obtained from the basic projections in Fig. 2.2.1.10.

2.2.2. Topological Properties of an (N, b, k) Cube

In this section we derive a number of interesting topological properties relating to sparsity, diameter, existence of node disjoint parallel paths, and existence of odd and even cycles in an (N, b, k) cube.

Theorem 2.2.2.1. If $b = N$, then the $(N, N, 1)$ cube is a complete graph on N nodes.

Proof
The proof readily follows from the definition in Section 2.2.1.

Theorem 2.2.2.2. In a complete (N, b, k) cube,

(a) The degree of each node is $(b - 1) \log_b N$, and

(b) There are a total of $\dfrac{1}{2}(b - 1)N \log_b N$ edges.

Proof
(a) The nodes in $G^{(k-1)}$ are labeled with k-digit base-b integers. By construction, a node is connected by an edge to each of those nodes which differ from it in exactly one digit position. Since there are $b - 1$ nodes that differ in a given digit and a total of $k = \log_b N$ digits, the degree of each node is $(b - 1) \log_b N$.

(b) There are a total of N nodes. Using (a), we readily obtain that the total number of edges is $\dfrac{1}{2}(b - 1)N \log_b N$ (since each edge is counted twice).

An alternative and perhaps a more direct way to prove claim (b) is to use the solution (2.2.1.18) of the recurrence (2.2.1.17). Thus, in $G^{(k-1)}$ there are $(\dfrac{k}{2})b^k(b - 1)$ edges. Hence the theorem.

Theorem 2.2.2.3. The *diameter* of an (N, b, k) cube is $\log_b N$.

Proof
The diameter is the maximum of the shortest distance between a pair of nodes in $G^{(k-1)}$. Clearly, this maximum occurs when the labels of a pair of nodes differ in each of the k digit positions. Since there are k digit positions, the theorem follows.

Since the diameter relates to the maximum communication delay, algorithms implemented on base-b cubes (with $b > 2$) will have shorter communication delay than on base-2 cubes.

The next theorem is fundamental and provides an easy algorithm for building an interconnection scheme for N processors with prespecified diameter.

Theorem 2.2.2.4. Given N and d, there exists a k and b such that the diameter of the (N, b, k) cube is less than or equal to d.

Proof

Define $b = \left\lceil N^{1/d} \right\rceil$ and recursively build the (b^d, b, d) cube. By removing nodes from $(N + 1)$ to b^d and the corresponding edges, the resulting graph will have the required property.

Characterizing the cost of the network by the number of edges (assuming unit cost per edge), an important cost *vs.* delay trade-off can be derived. Table 2.2.2.1 gives the cost and delay for various values of b.

The recursive procedure for building the (N, b, k) cube along with Theorem 2.2.2.4 gives an upper bound on the number of edges needed to construct a *cube* with pre-specified diameter. In a sense, this bound is tight since, when $d = 1$, the number of edges given in Theorem 2.2.2.1 coincides with the known value $\frac{N(N - 1)}{2}$. Further, for any fixed $b < N$, the graph $G^{(k-1)}$ is a sparse graph, since the number of edges is asymptotically $O(N \log_b N)$.

TABLE 2.2.2.1
Cost -- Delay Trade-off

b	Delay (Diameter)	Cost (Number of Edges)
N	1	$\frac{1}{2}(N^2 - N)$
$N^{1/2}$	2	$N^{3/2} - N$
16	$(1/4) \log_2 N$	$(15/8)N \log_2 N$
8	$(1/3) \log_2 N$	$(7/6)N \log_2 N$
4	$(1/2) \log_2 N$	$(3/4)N \log_2 N$
2	$\log_2 N$	$(1/2)N \log_2 N$

We now turn to characterizing the paths in an (N, b, k) cube. Let x and y be any two nodes, where

$$x = x_k x_{k-1} \cdots x_1 \quad \text{and} \quad y = y_k y_{k-1} \cdots y_1.$$

Let $h_b(x,y)$ be the Hamming distance between x and y, which is defined as the number of base-b digits in which x and y differ. Thus, $h_2(010, 101) = 3$ and $h_4(00, 31) = 2$.

Define $x \mid y_j$ to be the node whose label is obtained by replacing the x_j in x by y_j. Likewise, define $x \mid x_i \leftarrow j$ to be a node whose label is obtained by replacing the ith digit x_i by $j \in \; < b >$. The following theorem is immediate.

Theorem 2.2.2.5. Let $h_b(x, y) = t$. Then,
(a) The minimum distance between x and y is t.
(b) There are a total of $(b - 1)k$ node disjoint base-b paths between x and y of which

    (i) t paths are of length t,
    (ii) $t(b - 2)$ paths are of length $t + 1$, and
    (iii) $(k - t)(b - 1)$ paths are of length $t + 2$,

where $b^k = N$.

Proof

Let $i_1 < i_2 < \cdots < i_t$ be the t digit positions in which x and y differ. Thus the shortest path between x and y is obtained by successively correcting x in the t bit positions in which it differs from y. A typical base-b path from x to y is

$$x \rightarrow x \mid y_{i_1} \rightarrow (x \mid y_{i_1}) \mid y_{i_2} \rightarrow \cdots \rightarrow (\cdots ((x \mid y_{i_1}) \mid y_{i_2}) \cdots) \mid y_{i_t} = y.$$

Now, instead of starting the correction at the $i_1{}^{th}$ digit, we could have started at the $i_j{}^{th}$ digit first and corrected through the $i_t{}^{th}$ digit. Then, carrying the corrections from i_1 through the $i_{j-1}{}^{th}$ digits, we obtain all the t different paths between x and y of length t.

To prove their node disjointness, consider two paths

$$x \rightarrow x \mid y_{i_1} \rightarrow (x \mid y_{i_1}) \mid y_{i_2} \rightarrow ((x \mid y_{i_1}) \mid y_{i_2}) \mid y_{i_3} \rightarrow \cdots \rightarrow y$$

and

$$x \rightarrow x \mid y_{i_2} \rightarrow (x \mid y_{i_2}) \mid y_{i_3} \rightarrow ((x \mid y_{i_2}) \mid y_{i_3}) \mid y_{i_4} \rightarrow \cdots \rightarrow y.$$

Comparing these paths, it is readily seen that the corresponding intermediate nodes are distinct and hence they are disjoint. The same arguments carry over to every pair of paths of the type described above from which claims (a) and (b)(i) follow.

To prove (b)(ii), consider the following path:

$$x \rightarrow (x \mid x_{i_j} \leftarrow s) \rightarrow \cdots \rightarrow (y \mid y_{i_j} \leftarrow s) \rightarrow y,$$

where $x_{i_j} \neq s$ and $y_{i_j} \neq s$, and $s \in <b>$.

Since

$$h_b(x \mid x_{i_j} \leftarrow s, \, y \mid y_{i_j} \leftarrow s) = t - 1,$$

by claim (a), the above path is of length $t + 1$. There are $t - 1$ node disjoint paths between $(x \mid x_{i_j} \leftarrow s)$ and $(y \mid y_{i_j} \leftarrow s)$, and we pick one path from this set. Since there are $b - 2$ values for s (why?), by varying j from 1 through t we obtain all the $t(b - 2)$ base-b paths of length $t + 1$, each of which is node disjoint with the paths described in (b)(i).

To prove (b)(iii), let

$$m_1 < m_2 < \cdots < m_{k-t}$$

be such that

$$x_{m_j} = y_{m_j} \quad \text{for } j = 1, \cdots, k - t.$$

Consider a path

$$x \rightarrow (x \mid x_{m_j} \leftarrow s) \rightarrow \cdots \rightarrow (y \mid y_{m_j} \leftarrow s) \rightarrow y,$$

where $x_{m_j} = y_{m_j} \neq s$ and $s \in <b>$.

Clearly,

$$h_b(x \mid x_{m_j} \leftarrow s, \, y \mid y_{m_j} \leftarrow s) = t$$

and the above path is of length $t + 2$. Since there are $b - 1$ values for s, by changing j from 1 through $k - t$, we obtain all the $(k - t)(b - 1)$ base-b node disjoint paths of length $t + 2$, each of which is node disjoint with the paths described in (b)(i) and (b)(ii). Hence the theorem.

Notice that if $b = 2$, there are no paths of length $t + 1$. Further, in any base-2 cube, if $t < \log_2 N$, then there are t paths of length t and $\log_2 N - t$ paths of length $t + 2$. If $b = d^k$, then in an (N, b, k) cube there are base-d^s paths for all $1 \leq s \leq k$. However, the set of base-d^s paths and the set of base-d^t paths for $s \neq t$ are not mutually edge disjoint, as the following example illustrates.

Consider the $(16, 4, 2)$ cube in Fig. 2.2.1.6, and consider $x = 00$ and $y = 13$ (in base 4). The set of all base-4 paths between x and y is:

Path 1: $00 \rightarrow 03 \rightarrow 13$
Path 2: $00 \rightarrow 10 \rightarrow 13$
Path 3: $00 \rightarrow 01 \rightarrow 11 \rightarrow 13$
Path 4: $00 \rightarrow 02 \rightarrow 12 \rightarrow 13$
Path 5: $00 \rightarrow 30 \rightarrow 33 \rightarrow 13$
Path 6: $00 \rightarrow 20 \rightarrow 23 \rightarrow 13$

The set of all base-2 paths between the same $x = 0000$ and $y = 0111$ (in base 2) is:

Path 1:   0000→0001→0101→0111
Path 2:   0000→0010→0011→0111
Path 3:   0000→0100→0110→0111
Path 4:   0000→1000→1010→1011→1111→0111

Notice that the base-4 path 2 and base-2 path 3 are not edge disjoint. The next theorem is a direct consequence of Theorem 2.2.2.5.

Theorem 2.2.2.6. Let x and y be two nodes in an (N, b, k) cube, where $h_b(x, y) = t$. Then, there are

(a) $\begin{bmatrix} t \\ 2 \end{bmatrix}$ base-b even cycles of length $2t$.

(b) $\begin{bmatrix} t(b-2) \\ 2 \end{bmatrix} + t(k - t)(b - 1)$ base-b even cycles of length $2(t + 1)$.

(c) $\begin{bmatrix} (k - t)(b - 1) \\ 2 \end{bmatrix}$ base-b even cycles of length $2(t + 2)$.

(d) $t^2(b - 2)$ base-b odd cycles of length $2t + 1$.

(e) $t(k - t)(b - 1)(b - 2)$ base-b odd cycles of length $2t + 3$.

Proof
Two distinct paths of length t can be combined to obtain an even cycle, and claim (a) follows. Any path of length t between x and y can be combined with a path of length $t + 1$ to obtain an odd cycle of length $2t + 1$. Since there are t paths of the first kind and $t(b - 2)$ paths of the second kind, claim (d) follows. Claims (b), (c), and (e) follow from similar arguments.

Corollary 2.2.2.7. In a base-2 cube there are no odd cycles.

Proof
The proof follows from claims (d) and (e) of Theorem 2.2.2.6.

2.2.3 Embedding of Simple Topologies

The need for the embedding arises from at least two different directions. First, with the widespread availability of distributed memory architectures based on the hypercube interconnection scheme, there is an ever-growing interest in the portability of algorithms developed for architectures based on other topologies, such as linear arrays, rings, two-dimensional meshes, and complete binary trees, into the hypercube. Clearly, this question of portability reduces to one of embedding the above interconnection schemes into the hypercube. Second, the problem of mapping parallel algorithms into parallel architectures naturally gives rise to graph embedding problems. It has been known for a long time that the general graph embedding problem is *NP*-complete. Recently, it was shown that the embedding of general graphs into the binary hypercube is also *NP*-complete. Further strengthening of this result indicates that the problem of embedding arbitrary trees in a binary hypercube is *NP*-complete as well. All of these results point to the fact that for easy embedability, one must look for highly structured graphs, such as arrays, rings, and complete binary trees.

Let $G_g = (V_g, E_g)$ be the (guest) graph to be embedded in the (host) graph $G_h = (V_h, E_h)$, where the host is taken to be the (N, b, k) cube. It is assumed that $|V_g| \leq |V_h|$. Let $d(x, y)$ denote the shortest path, measured in terms of the number of edges, between nodes x and y in G_g. Let $f : V_g \rightarrow V_h$ be an embedding function such that $f(x) \neq f(y)$ if $x \neq y$, that is, f is injective. The *dilation factor* $D_f(x, y)$ for $x \neq y$ is defined by

$$D_f(x, y) = \frac{h_b(f(x), f(y))}{d(x, y)}.$$

Let

$$D_f = \max_{x \neq y} \{D_f(x, y)\}. \tag{2.2.3.1}$$

Clearly $D_f = 1$ implies that the edges in G_g are mapped to edges in G_h and that the embedding function preserves the neighborhood property of the graph being embedded. The ratio

$$E_f = \frac{|V_h|}{|V_g|} \geq 1 \tag{2.2.3.2}$$

is called the *expansion factor*.

A number of observations are in order. In the case of embedding of architectures, the nodes in the guest and host graphs correspond to processors, and the edges to the physical communication links. But in mapping a parallel algorithm into an architecture, the nodes in the guest graph denote the chunks of computation and the edges define the communication needs of the algorithm. In either case, D_f relates to the cost of simulating one communication step and E_f to the hardware needs in terms of the number of processors. Further, the requirement that the embedding function be injective helps to *preserve* the inherent parallelism of the guest architecture or the algorithm to be mapped. Thus, one of the challenges in embedding is to derive an embedding function f that simultaneously minimizes D_f and E_f.

As for the tools, binary reflected Gray codes have been extensively used in embedding arrays, rings and meshes into the binary hypercube. In extending these embeddings to an (N, b, k) cube, we need a new class of generalized codes, called base-b Gray codes.

A. Base-b Reflected Gray Codes. Fundamental to many of these embeddings is the definition of a class of codes called Gray codes. We begin by defining a version of these codes called base-b *reflected Gray* codes. To make the presentation simple, it is assumed that $b = 2^m$, $m \geq 1$, $N = 2^{km}$, and $n = km$. The generalization to *even* and *odd* b is treated in Exercises 2.13, 2.14 and 2.15. Let $G^{(b)}(n)$ denote the set of all n-digit code words of the base-b reflected Gray code. When $m = 1$ (that is, $b = 2$), it is called a *binary* reflected Gray code. While there is considerable literature on this latter class of codes, we introduce the new class of base-b reflected Gray codes as a natural extension of the well-known base-2 codes. The following definition of $G^{(2)}(n)$ is standard.

Define

$$G^{(2)}(1) = \{0, 1\}.$$

Let

$$G^{(2)}(n) = \{G_0^{(2)}(n), G_1^{(2)}(n), \cdots G_{2^n-1}^{(2)}(n)\},$$

where $G_i^{(2)}(n)$ is called the encoding of integer i for $i = 0$ to $2^n - 1$.

Now define $G^{(2)}(n+1)$ recursively as follows:

$$G^{(2)}(n+1) = \{0G_0^{(2)}(n), 0G_1^{(2)}(n), \cdots, 0G_{2^n-1}^{(2)}(n),$$

$$1G_{2^n-1}^{(2)}(n), 1G_{2^n-2}^{(2)}(n), \cdots, 1G_1^{(2)}(n), 1G_0^{(2)}(n)\}.$$

Clearly,

$$|G^{(2)}(n)| = 2^n.$$

Refer to Table 2.2.3.1 for examples of $G^{(2)}(4)$.

To understand the encoding and decoding process involved in the definition of $G^{(2)}(n)$, let $i \in <N>$, where

$$i = i_n i_{n-1} i_{n-2} \cdots i_2 i_1 i_0,$$

in binary. Since $0 \leq i < 2^n$, it follows that $i_n = 0$.

Let

$$G_i^{(2)}(n) = g_n g_{n-1} \cdots g_2 g_1.$$

Let $E^{(2)}$ and $D^{(2)}$ be the corresponding encoding and decoding functions, that is,

$$E^{(2)} : <N> \rightarrow G^{(2)}(n)$$

and

$$D^{(2)} : G^{(2)}(n) \rightarrow <N>.$$

If $\oplus$ denotes the exclusive-OR addition of binary bits, then it can be shown that

$$E^{(2)}(i) = G_i^{(2)}(n),$$

where

$$g_j = i_j \oplus i_{j-1}, \quad \text{for all } j = 1, 2, \cdots, n,$$

and

$$D^{(2)}(G_i^{(2)}(n)) = i,$$

where $i_j = g_{j+1} \oplus g_{j+2} \oplus \cdots \oplus g_n$ for all $j = 0$ to $n - 1$.

Examples of $G^{(2)}(4)$ and $G^{(2)}$ (6) are given in Tables 2.2.3.1 and 2.2.3.2, respectively.

TABLE 2.2.3.1
$N = 16, n = 4, k = 2, m = 2$

i	$(i)_2$	$(i)_4$	$G^{(2)}(4)$	$G^{(4)}(2)$	Another Base-4 Gray Code
0	0000	00	0000	00	00
1	0001	01	0001	01	01
2	0010	02	0011	03	02
3	0011	03	0010	02	03
4	0100	10	0110	12	13
5	0101	11	0111	13	12
6	0110	12	0101	11	11
7	0111	13	0100	10	10
8	1000	20	1100	30	20
9	1001	21	1101	31	21
10	1010	22	1111	33	22
11	1011	23	1110	32	23
12	1100	30	1010	22	33
13	1101	31	1011	23	32
14	1110	32	1001	21	31
15	1111	33	1000	20	30

An intrinsic property of these codes is that two successive code words differ in exactly one bit and hence the Hamming distance between successive code words is unity. The following lemma is an extension of the above property.

Lemma 2.2.3.1. Let $i, j \in\ <N>$. If $j = (i + 2^d) \bmod N$, for some $0 < d < n$, then

$$h_2(G_i^{(2)}(n), G_j^{(2)}(n)) = 2,$$

where $h_2(x, y)$ is the Hamming distance between binary strings x and y.

Proof

Let $s \geq d$ be the bit position in which the carry (in adding 2^d to i) stops propagating. It follows that if

$$i = i_n i_{n-1} \cdots i_{s+1} i_s \cdots i_{d+1} i_d i_{d-1} \cdots i_1 i_0,$$

$$j = j_n j_{n-1} \cdots j_{s+1} j_s \cdots j_{d+1} j_d j_{d-1} \cdots j_1 j_0,$$

then

$$i_r \neq j_r, \quad \text{for } r = d, d+1, \cdots s,$$

and all the other corresponding bits in i and j are the same. If

$$E^{(2)}(i) = a_n a_{n-1} \cdots a_2 a_1 \tag{2.2.3.3}$$

and

$$E^{(2)}(j) = b_n b_{n-1} \cdots b_2 b_1 \tag{2.2.3.4}$$

then from the definition of $E^{(2)}$ and those of i and j, we readily obtain

$$a_d \neq b_d \quad \text{and} \quad a_{s+1} \neq b_{s+1}, \tag{2.2.3.5}$$

and the rest of the corresponding bits are the same, from which the lemma follows.

We now extend the above definition to obtain a base-b reflected Gray code for $b = 2^m$ and $m > 1$. To this end, introduce a one-to-one and onto function

$$f: \{0, 1\}^{km} \to \{0, 1, \cdots b - 1\}^k.$$

If

$$x = x_{km} x_{km-1} \cdots x_{(k-1)m+1} x_{(k-1)m} \cdots x_{(k-2)m+1} \cdots x_m \cdots x_2 x_1,$$

and

TABLE 2.2.3.2
$N = 64, n = 6, k = 3, m = 2.$

i	$(i)_2$	$(i)_4$	$G^{(2)}(6)$	$G^{(4)}(3)$	Another Base-4 Gray Code
0	000000	000	000000	000	000
1	000001	001	000001	001	001
2	000010	002	000011	003	002
3	000011	003	000010	002	003
4	000100	010	000110	012	013
5	000101	011	000111	013	012
6	000110	012	000101	011	011
7	000111	013	000100	010	010
8	001000	020	001100	030	020
9	001001	021	001101	031	021
10	001010	022	001111	033	022
11	001011	023	001110	032	023
12	001100	030	001010	022	033
13	001101	031	001011	023	032
14	001110	032	001001	021	031
15	001111	033	001000	020	030
16	010000	100	011000	120	130
17	010001	101	011001	121	131
18	010010	102	011011	123	132
19	010011	103	011010	122	133
20	010100	110	011110	132	123
21	010101	111	011111	133	122
22	010110	112	011101	131	121
23	010111	113	011100	130	120
24	011000	120	010100	110	110
25	011001	121	010101	111	111
26	011010	122	010111	113	112
27	011011	123	010110	112	113
28	011100	130	010010	102	103
29	011101	131	010011	103	102
30	011110	132	010001	101	101
31	011111	133	010000	100	100

TABLE 2.2.3.2
(Continued)

i	$(i)_2$	$(i)_4$	$G^{(2)}(6)$	$G^{(4)}(3)$	Another Base-4 Gray Code
32	100000	200	110000	300	200
33	100001	201	110001	301	201
34	100010	202	110011	303	202
35	100011	203	110010	302	203
36	100100	210	110110	312	213
37	100101	211	110111	313	212
38	100110	212	110101	311	211
39	100111	213	110100	310	210
40	101000	220	111100	330	220
41	101001	221	111101	331	221
42	101010	222	111111	333	222
43	101011	223	111110	332	223
44	101100	230	111010	322	233
45	101101	231	111011	323	232
46	101110	232	111010	321	231
47	101111	233	111000	320	230
48	110000	300	101000	220	330
49	110001	301	101001	221	331
50	110010	302	101011	223	332
51	110011	303	101010	222	333
52	110100	310	101110	232	320
53	110101	311	101111	233	321
54	110110	312	101101	231	322
55	110111	313	101100	230	323
56	111000	320	100100	210	310
57	111001	321	100101	211	311
58	111010	322	100111	213	312
59	111011	323	100110	212	313
60	111100	330	100010	202	303
61	111101	331	100011	203	302
62	111110	332	100001	201	301
63	111111	333	100000	200	300

$$Z = Z_k Z_{k-1} \cdots Z_2 Z_1,$$

then $f(x) = Z$ if and only if, for all $r = 1$ to k,

$$(Z_r)_b = (x_{rm} x_{rm-1} \cdots x_{(r-1)m+2} x_{(r-1)m+1})_2,$$

that is, the right-hand side of this equation is a binary encoding of the base-b digit Z_r. As an example, if $k = 3$, $m = 2$, then

$$f(011111) = 133$$

and

$$f(001101) = 031.$$

Now this function f and $E^{(2)}$ can be combined in a natural way to obtain the new base-b encoding function

$$E^{(b)}: <N> \rightarrow G^{(b)}(k)$$

and

$$E^{(b)} = f^{-1} E^{(2)} f.$$

This latter definition is illustrated by the commutative diagram in Fig. 2.2.3.1, where the composition operation is to be interpreted as

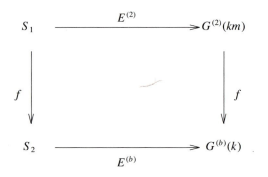

FIGURE 2.2.3.1
Commutative diagram. $S_1 = \{0, 1\}^{km}$, and $S_2 = \{0, 1, \cdots, b-1\}^k$.

$$E^{(b)}(i) = f^{-1} E^{(2)} f(i) = f(E^{(2)}(f^{-1}(i))).$$

Clearly, the base-b decoding function $D^{(b)}$ is given by

$$D^{(b)} = f^{-1} D^{(2)} f.$$

Examples of $G^{(4)}(2)$ and $G^{(4)}(3)$ are given in Tables 2.2.3.1 and 2.2.3.2. It is clear that two successive code words differ in exactly one base-b digit position, and hence the base-b Hamming distance between them is unity.

There are other ways of defining $G^{(b)}(k)$, and an example of another base-4 reflected Gray code is given in the last column of Tables 2.2.3.1 and 2.2.3.2.

The following lemma is a direct analog of Lemma 2.2.3.1 and is used repeatedly in the applications covered in the later chapters.

Lemma 2.2.3.2. Let i and j belong to $< N >$ be such that $j = (i + 2^d) \bmod N$, for $0 < d < n$. Then

$$h_b(G_i^{(b)}(k), G_j^{(b)}(k)) =$$

$$\begin{cases} 2 & \text{for } \textit{all } s \geq d & \text{if } 0 \equiv d \ (\bmod m) \\ 1 & \text{for } \textit{all } d \leq s \leq (d+m-1-t) & \text{if } 0 \neq t \equiv d \ (\bmod m) \\ 2 & \text{for } \textit{all } s > (d+m-1-t) & \text{if } 0 \neq t \equiv d \ (\bmod m), \end{cases}$$

where s is defined in the proof of Lemma 2.2.3.1, and $1 \leq t \leq m-1$.

Proof
Let

$$f(E^{(2)}(i)) = A_k A_{k-1} \ \cdots \ A_2 A_1$$

and

$$f(E^{(2)}(j)) = B_k B_{k-1} \ \cdots \ B_2 B_1,$$

where, using (2.2.3.3) and (2.2.3.4), it follows that

$$A_r = a_{rm} a_{rm-1} \ \cdots \ a_{(r-1)m+1},$$

$$B_t = b_{tm} b_{tm-1} \ \cdots \ b_{(t-1)m+1}.$$

Since $d > 0$, $0 \equiv d \ (\bmod m)$ implies that $d = rm$ for some $1 \leq r \leq k$. From this and Lemma 2.2.3.1 it follows that $A_r \neq B_r$. Further, since $s + 1 > d$ and $a_{s+1} \neq b_{s+1}$, it follows that there exists a $p > r$ such that $A_p \neq B_p$. This proves the lemma for the case when $0 \equiv d \ (\bmod m)$. The proof of each of the other two cases is quite similar and is left as an exercise.

From Corollary 2.2.1.2, since every N-node base-2^m cube contains an N-node base-2 cube, using Lemma 2.2.3.1 it readily follows that

$$h_b(G_i^{(b)}(k), G_j^{(b)}(k)) \leq 2,$$

if $j = (i + 2^d) \bmod N$. While this conclusion is enough for many applications, our Lemma 2.2.3.2 further characterizes the values i and j for which the distance between $E^{(b)}(i)$ and $E^{(b)}(j)$ is exactly 1 and 2, respectively.

B. Embedding of Linear Arrays, Rings, and Two-Dimensional Meshes. From Theorems 2.2.2.5 and 2.2.2.6, it follows that given any two nodes x and y on an (N, b, k) cube, there exist a variety of simple paths between x and y and simple cycles containing x and y. This observation suggests the possibility of embedding linear arrays and rings on a base-b cube, where b is a power of 2. In the following, we further explore these embeddings.

Let a *linear array* with p processors $P_0, P_1, \cdots, P_{p-1}$, $p \leq N$, be given. The key to embedding this array is to preserve the adjacency or the proximity structure of this array according to which a processor P_i is directly connected to P_{i-1} and P_{i+1} except for $i = 0$ and $p - 1$. P_0 is connected to P_1, and P_{N-1} is connected to P_{N-2}. Since the code words in $G^{(b)}(k)$ naturally possess this adjacency property, a simple embedding is to map the processor P_i onto the node with label $G^{(b)}_i(k)$ for $i = 0, 1, 2, \cdots, p - 1$. Clearly, this mapping achieves unit dilation.

The adjacency structure of a *ring* of N processors $P_0, P_1, \cdots, P_{N-1}$ can be readily embedded on an (N, b, k) cube, b even, by mapping processor P_i onto a node with label $G^{(b)}_i(k)$ for $i = 0, 1, 2, \cdots, N - 1$. Clearly, such a mapping corresponds to the *Hamiltonian* cycle [1] on the graph $G^{(k-1)}$. Thus, by referring to Table 2.2.3.1, we can obtain a Hamiltonian cycle on the graph of Fig. 2.2.1.6 by using $G^{(4)}(2)$. It is readily seen that this Hamiltonian cycle uses only the edges in a base-2 cube. This unit-dilation embedding, however, is *not* unique as a second embedding can be obtained by using the other base-4 reflected Gray code given in the last column of Table 2.2.3.1. This second Hamiltonian cycle uses the base-4 connections such as the edges $(01, 02)$, $(10, 20)$, $\cdots$, and $(30, 00)$.

Let r be even, $r < N$, and $m = \dfrac{r - 2}{2}$. Then an r-node ring can be embedded in an (N, b, k) cube as follows. Map the r processors onto the r nodes of the cube whose labels are in the following ordered subset of $G^{(b)}(k)$,

$$\{ \ G^{(b)}_{0:m}(k), \ G^{(b)}_{N-m-1:N-1}(k) \ \},$$

where $G^{(b)}_{i:j}(k)$ refers to the set $\{ \ G^{(b)}_i(k), G^{(b)}_{i+1}(k), \ldots, G^{(b)}_j(k) \ \}$. The following example illustrates this embedding on a $(16, 4, 2)$ cube.

$r = 8 : \{ \ 00, 01, 02, 03, 33, 32, 31, 30 \ \}$

$r = 6 : \{ \ 00, 01, 02, 32, 31, 30 \ \}$

$r = 4 : \{ \ 00, 01, 31, 30 \ \}$

$r = 12 : \{ \ 00, 01, 02, 03, 13, 12, 22, 23, 33, 32, 31, 30 \ \}$

Likewise, on an $(8, 2, 3)$ cube, we have for

$r = 6 : \{ \ 000, 001, 011, 111, 101, 100 \ \}$

---

[1] A cycle in a graph is said to be a *simple* cycle if no vertex other than the start-end vertex appears more than once. A *Hamiltonian cycle* is a simple cycle involving every vertex of a graph.

Further, by suitably combining Theorem 2.2.2.6 and the definition of Gray codes, we can obtain embedding of a variety of rings of odd and even lengths on an (N, b, k) cube. This discussion is summarized in the following theorem.

Theorem 2.2.3.3. An (N, b, k) cube $(b \geq 2)$ admits an embedding of linear arrays of length $p \leq N$ and embeddings of a variety of rings of odd (when $b > 2$) and even (when $b \geq 2$) lengths. In all these embeddings the proximity structure is preserved (that is, $D_f = 1$) by associating the ith node of the linear array and the ring with the node of the cube whose label corresponds to the ith code word in $G^{(b)}(k)$.

The following example illustrates the embedding of a *two-dimensional mesh* onto a base-b cube, with obvious generalizations.

Consider a two-dimensional mesh formed by the 16×4 grid points as shown in Fig. 2.2.3.2. There are 16 points in the x-direction numbered 0 through 15 and four points in the y-direction, numbered 0 through 3. Assign a two-digit base-4 reflected Gray code word $G_i^{(4)}(2)$ to the ith point in the x-direction. Likewise, assign the jth code word $G_j^{(4)}(1)$ to the jth point in the y-direction. Thus, if

$$G_i^{(4)}(2) = a_{i_2} a_{i_1},$$

and

$$G_j^{(4)}(1) = b_j,$$

then, the grid point (i, j) is assigned a label $a_{i_2} a_{i_1} b_j$. This assignment of labels defines an embedding of the 16×4 two-dimensional array onto the complete $(64, 4, 3)$ cube, which clearly preserves the proximity structure with or without the wraparound connections. Thus, referring to Fig. 2.2.3.2, the grid point $(2, 1)$ is assigned the code word 031. Its four neighbors are assigned 011, 021, 030, and 033. This embedding achieves unit dilation.

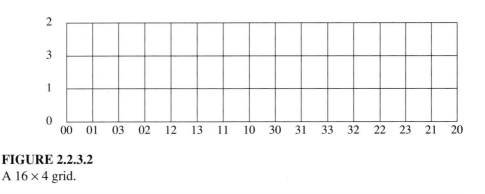

FIGURE 2.2.3.2
A 16×4 grid.

The following theorem is immediate.

Theorem 2.2.3.4. A $b^l \times b^m$ grid can be embedded onto a (b^d, b, d) cube where $d = l + m$, where the proximity is preserved (that is, $D_f = 1$) by assigning the label $G_i^{(b)}(l)G_j^{(b)}(m)$ to the grid point (i, j).

This embedding can be extended to meshes in higher dimensions in an obvious way, provided the number of grid points in each dimension is a power of b. The optimal embedding of meshes when the number of grid points is not a power of b is more complex and is pursued in the exercises.

C. Embedding of Binary Trees. Since the graph $G^{(n-1)}$ of an (N, b, n) cube is a *connected* graph (why?), there is a spanning tree. We first describe an algorithm for defining a spanning tree with minimum depth on a $(N, 2, n)$ cube.

Spanning Tree Algorithm for Base-2 Cubes

Step 1. Let $j = 1$. Starting at node 0^n, the tree contains the edge connecting 0^n to $0^{n-1}1$ (where 0^x refers to the concatenation of 0's x times).

Step 2. For $j = 2$ to n, place the edges connecting the node $0^{n-j+1}x_j$ to $0^{n-j}1x_j$ in the tree, where x_j is a $(j-1)$-bit binary string.

An example of a spanning tree on a $(16, 2, 4)$ cube is given in Fig. 2.2.3.3(a). This type of spanning tree can be readily used in broadcasting data from a single processor to all the other nodes. (Refer to Exercise 2.17.) Instead of the node 0^n, if we want to build a tree from any other node Z, we can obtain the latter from the previous tree by replacing each node label by the exclusive-OR of the node label with the label of the node Z. Figure 2.2.3.3(b) provides an example of this process. This operation is called *translation*. However, since many of the tree-based parallel algorithms, such as, associative fan-in algorithms use binary trees, we turn our attention to embedding complete binary trees.

A $(2^n, 2, n)$ cube contains 2^n nodes. A natural question is whether it is possible to embed a complete binary tree with $2^n - 1$ nodes in this cube. The following theorem answers this question in the negative for the case when $n > 2$. Note that a tree with three nodes can be embedded in the $(4, 2, 2)$ cube.

Theorem 2.2.3.5. It is not possible to embed a complete binary tree with $2^n - 1$ nodes (n levels) in a $(2^n, 2, n)$ cube, for $n \geq 3$.

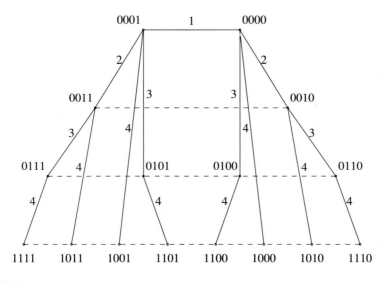

FIGURE 2.2.3.3(a)
A spanning tree of depth 4 embedded in a (16, 2, 4) cube, starting at 0000.

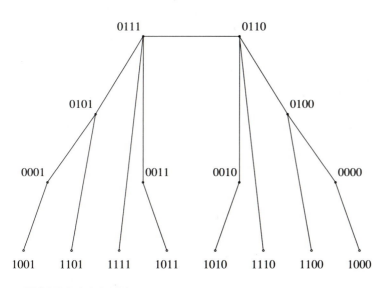

FIGURE 2.2.3.3(b)
A spanning tree of depth 4 embedded in a (16, 2, 4) cube, starting at 0110.

Proof

It is enough to show that starting from a complete binary tree with $2^n - 1$ nodes and adding the additional node and all relevant edges, it is not possible to obtain the $(2^n, 2, n)$ cube. Showing this hinges on the fact that there are no odd cycles in a binary n-cube. The absence of an odd cycle in the binary n-cube precludes the presence of two neighboring nodes of the cube at the leaf level. Thus from a node on the leaf level there can be no edge to another node on the leaf level. Similarly, from a node on the leaf level, there cannot be any edge to a node whose level differs from the leaf level by an even number. (Recall that the root is at level 1.)

Each node at the leaf level already has one edge to its parent. Therefore, for each leaf node, $n - 1$ other neighbors need to be found. The totality of remaining edges leaving the leaf nodes is $(n - 1)2^{n-1}$. We can now count the number of edges which can be absorbed by the remaining nodes. Two cases need to be considered.

Case 1. n is odd. In this case, the number of nodes which can receive edges from the leaf nodes is given by

$$\sum_{i=1}^{(n-1)/2} 2^{2i-1}.$$

Each of these nodes already has three edges. The extra node, which is not part of the tree, can absorb n edges. Thus the total edges which can be absorbed is given by

$$(n-3)\left(\sum_{i=1}^{(n-1)/2} 2^{2i-1}\right) + n = \frac{n-3}{3}(2^n - 2) + n.$$

Since for $n \geq 3$,

$$\frac{n-3}{3}(2^n - 2) + n < (n-1)\,2^{n-1},$$

there are not enough vertices, including the extra vertex, which can absorb the edges emanating from the leaf nodes. Hence, in this case the complete binary tree cannot be embedded in the $(2^n, 2, n)$ cube.

Case 2. n is even. In this case, the number of nodes which can receive edges from the leaf nodes is given by

$$\sum_{i=0}^{(n-2)/2} 2^{2i}.$$

Each of these nodes already has three edges, except the root node which has degree 2. Since the extra node, which is not part of the tree, can absorb n edges, the total number of edges which can be absorbed is given by

$$(n-3) \sum_{i=0}^{(n-2)/2} 2^{2i} + n + 1 = (n-3)(\frac{2^n - 1}{3}) + n + 1.$$

Again, for $n \geq 3$, since

$$(n-3)(\frac{2^n - 1}{3}) + n + 1 < (n-1) \, 2^{n-1},$$

all the edges emanating from the leaf nodes cannot be absorbed. Hence, in this case also no embedding is possible.

If a complete binary tree of size $2^n - 1$ cannot be embedded in a $(2^n, 2, n)$ cube, what, then, is the maximum size of such a tree that can be embedded in this cube? The following theorem shows that a complete binary tree which uses only about half the nodes of the cube can always be embedded in it.

Theorem 2.2.3.6. A complete binary tree with $2^{n-1} - 1$ nodes can be embedded in an $(N, 2, n)$ cube, with $D_f = 1$.

Proof

The theorem is proved by showing that the following graph $G_n = (V_n, E_n)$ can be embedded in an $(N, 2, n)$ cube, where

$$V_n = V_n' \cup V_n''$$

and

$$E_n = E_n' \cup E_n''.$$

(V_n', E_n') is a complete binary tree with $2^{n-1} - 1$ nodes.

$$V_n'' = \{l_1, l_2, \cdots, l_{n+1}\}$$

and

$$E_n'' = \{(l_i, l_{i+1}) \mid i = 1, 2, \cdots, n\} \cup \{(r, l_1), (l_{n+1}, l)\},$$

where r is the root and l is the rightmost leaf of the binary tree (V_n', E_n'). An example of this graph for the case $n = 2$ is given in Fig. 2.2.3.4.

The proof of this embedding is by induction on n. Clearly, when $n = 2$, the $(4, 2, 2)$ cube is a cycle containing four nodes. Any one of these nodes can be taken as the binary tree with $2^{n-1} - 1 = 1$ node, and this node plays the roles of r and l, referred to above. The remaining nodes form the set V_2''. Figure 2.2.3.5 provides another illustration for $n = 4$.

Assume that the above embedding is possible for all $n < m$, where $m \geq 3$. Now consider the case when $n = m$. Recall that the $(N, 2, n)$ cube can be reconfigured into two $(\frac{N}{2}, 2, (n-1))$ subcubes, which are merely the projections along any dimension -- say, without loss of generality, along the leading bit. Referring to Fig. 2.2.3.6, first fix an embedding of $G_{(n-1)}^{(0)}$ in one of the two subcubes. Since these embeddings are independent of the choice of labeling of the nodes in the cube, we pick an embedding for $G_{n-1}^{(1)}$ in the other subcube, where the nodes $r^{(1)}$ and $l_1^{(1)}$ are neighbors of $l_1^{(0)}$ and $l_2^{(0)}$ in $G_{n-1}^{(0)}$, respectively. The required embedding of G_n is then obtained by letting $l_1^{(0)}$ of $G_{n-1}^{(0)}$ be the root node, introducing the edges $(l_1^{(0)}, r^{(1)})$ and $(l_2^{(0)}, l_1^{(1)})$, and deleting the nodes $(l_3^{(0)}, l_4^{(0)}, \cdots, l_n^{(0)})$ and the corresponding edges, as in Fig. 2.2.3.7. Clearly, G_n contains the required binary tree. Hence the theorem.

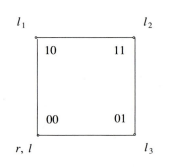

FIGURE 2.2.3.4
Graph G_2 embedded in a (4,2,2) cube.

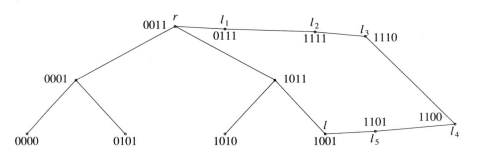

FIGURE 2.2.3.5
Graph G_4 embedded in a (16, 2, 4) cube.

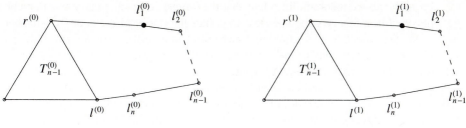

$G_{n-1}^{(0)}$

$G_{n-1}^{(1)}$

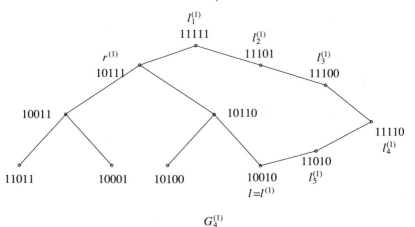

$G_4^{(0)}$

$G_4^{(1)}$

FIGURE 2.2.3.6

Two copies of G_{n-1} embedded in the two $(\dfrac{N}{2}, 2, n-1)$ subcubes of a $(N, 2, n)$ cube, one in each subcube. Illustration for $n = 5$.

From the above theorem, it is clear that the largest complete binary tree that can be embedded in a binary cube uses less than half the nodes of the cube. To further investigate the embedding of complete binary trees in base-2 cubes, we now define a variation of a complete binary tree, called the *double-rooted complete binary tree,* as follows. A double-rooted complete binary tree of level 1 has two nodes connected by an edge. A double-rooted complete binary tree of level n consists of two nodes at level 1 as above, and each of these two nodes in turn is connected to a node which is the root of a complete binary tree of $n-1$ levels. Figure 2.2.3.8 provides examples of double-rooted complete binary trees.

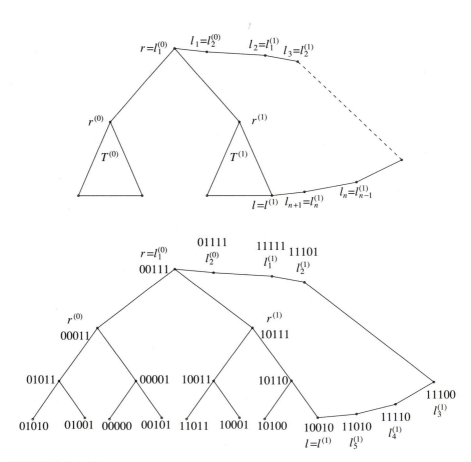

FIGURE 2.2.3.7
Graph G_n obtained by combining the subgraphs G_{n-1} in Fig. 2.2.3.6, along with an illustration for $n = 5$.

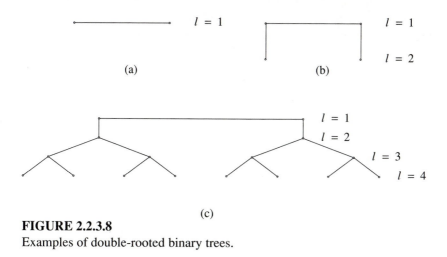

FIGURE 2.2.3.8
Examples of double-rooted binary trees.

There are 2^{l-1} nodes at level l (> 1) of a double-rooted complete binary tree. Since level 1 also contains two nodes, an n-level double-rooted complete binary tree obviously contains 2^n nodes. As such, an interesting question is whether there exists an embedding of an n-level double-rooted complete binary tree in an $(N, 2, n)$ cube. This question is answered in the affirmative by the following theorem.

Theorem 2.2.3.7. A double-rooted complete binary tree with 2^n nodes can be embedded in a $(2^n, 2, n)$ with $D_f = 1$.

Proof
The proof is by induction on level n of the tree.
When $n = 1$ or 2, the double-rooted complete binary tree is easily seen to be embedded in the corresponding binary cube, as shown in Fig. 2.2.3.9.

FIGURE 2.2.3.9
Embedding double-rooted binary trees in (2, 2, 1) and (4, 2, 2) cubes.

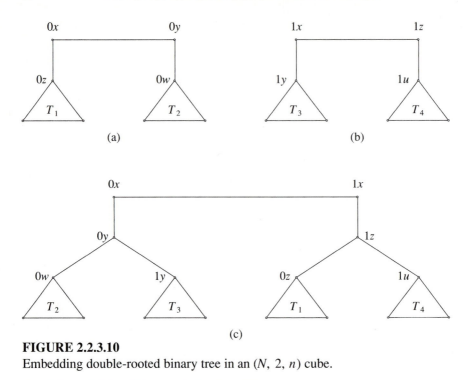

FIGURE 2.2.3.10
Embedding double-rooted binary tree in an $(N, 2, n)$ cube.

Assume that the theorem holds for all $n < m$, for some $m > 2$. Consider the case when $n = m$. This cube can be reconfigured into two subcubes of dimension $n - 1$, with the nodes in one of the subcubes having labels containing a 0 in the most significant bit position, while the nodes in the other contain a 1 in the most significant bit position. For the sake of simplicity, let us call these two subcubes the zero-subcube and the one-subcube, respectively. By the induction hypothesis, there is a double-rooted complete binary tree with 2^{n-1} nodes in each of these subcubes. Let the double-rooted complete binary tree embedded in the zero-subcube be as shown in Fig. 2.2.3.10(a). Since the cube is completely symmetric, there exists a double-rooted complete binary tree embedded in the one-subcube as shown in Fig. 2.2.3.10(b). These two trees can now be combined into a double-rooted complete binary tree with 2^n nodes by inserting edges $(0x, 1x)$, $(0y, 1y)$, and $(0z, 1z)$ and deleting edges $(0x, 0z)$ and $(1x, 1y)$, as shown in Fig. 2.2.3.10(c), which is the desired embedding. Hence the theorem.

Refer to Fig. 2.2.3.11 for an example. Stated in other words, the double-rooted tree is a spanning tree for the $(2^n, 2, n)$ cube. The following result is an immediate consequence.

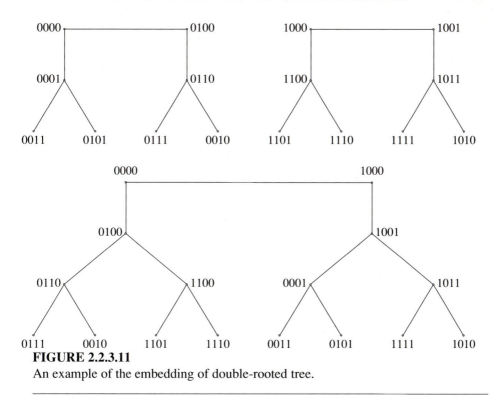

FIGURE 2.2.3.11
An example of the embedding of double-rooted tree.

Theorem 2.2.3.8. There exists an embedding of a complete binary tree with $2^n - 1$ nodes in a $(2^n, 2, n)$ cube, with $D_f = 2$.

Proof
The double-rooted complete binary tree shown in Fig. 2.2.3.10(c) can be easily transformed into the desired tree by joining one of the nodes, say $0x$, at level 1 to $1z$ at level 2. Refer to Fig. 2.2.3.12. Since the new edge $(0x, 1z)$ connects nodes which have a common neighbor at distance 1 from each of them, the distance between these two nodes is exactly 2, and the proof is complete.

We now turn to embedding complete binary trees in base-4 cubes. Figures 2.2.3.13 and 2.2.3.14 indicate an embedding of two- and three-level complete binary trees in a $(4, 4, 1)$ cube and an incomplete $(8, 4, 2)$ cube, respectively. Likewise, Figs. 2.2.3.15 through 2.2.3.17 describe embeddings of complete binary trees on base-4 cubes.

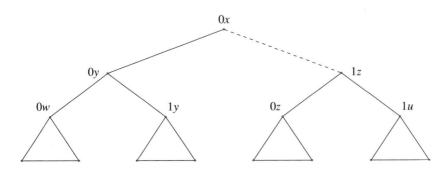

FIGURE 2.2.3.12(a)
An example of complete binary tree with $2^n - 1$ nodes in an $(N, 2, n)$ cube with $D_f = 2$. The dotted line connecting $0x$ and $1z$ is the only edge with dilation 2.

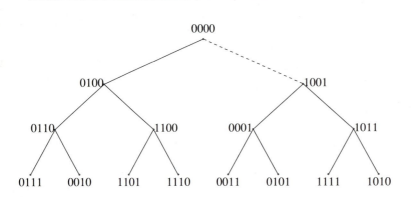

FIGURE 2.2.3.12(b)
An example illustrating the above embedding with $D_f = 2$.

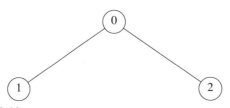

FIGURE 2.2.3.13
A three-node complete binary tree in a four-node, base-4 cube.

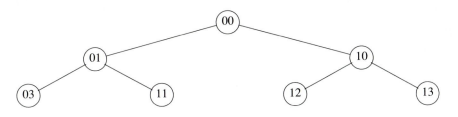

FIGURE 2.2.3.14
A seven-node complete binary tree in an eight-node, base-4 cube.

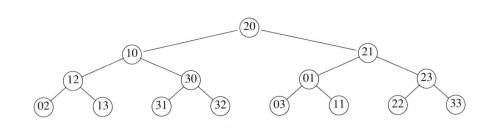

FIGURE 2.2.3.15
A 15-node complete binary tree in a 16-node, base-4 cube.

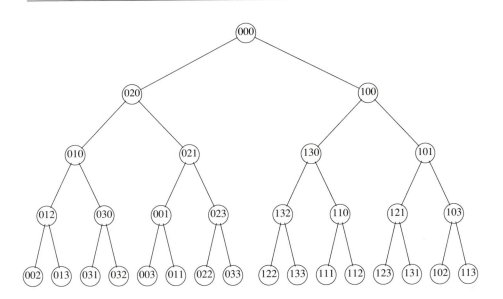

FIGURE 2.2.3.16
A 31-node complete binary tree in a 32-node, base-4 cube.

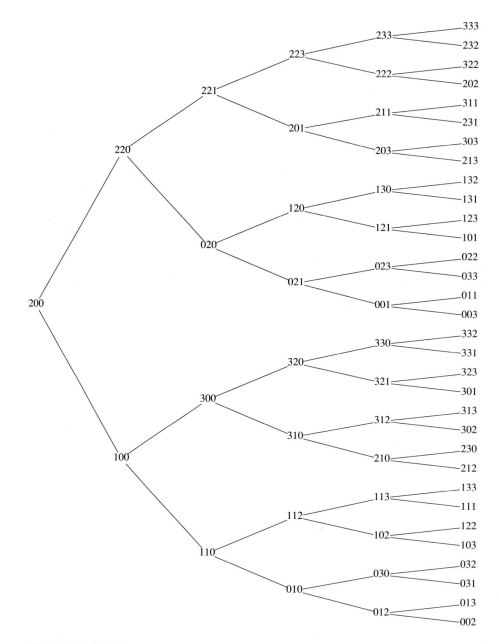

FIGURE 2.2.3.17
A 63-node complete binary tree on a 64-node base-4 cube.

The following theorem generalizes these examples.

Theorem 2.2.3.9. There exists an embedding of a $2n$-level complete binary tree with $2^{2n} - 1$ nodes onto a complete $(4^n, 4, n)$ cube, with $D_f = 1$.

Proof
For $n = 1$, the embedding is trivial. A $(4^n, 4, n)$ cube can be divided into two halves. One of these halves contains nodes whose most significant digit is either a 0 or a 1 (same as 00 and 01 in base 2). Let us denote this half as a 0-1 half. The other, denoted as the 2-3 half contains all nodes whose most significant digit is either a 2 or a 3 (same as 10 and 11 in base 2). Each of these halves is a $(2^n, 2, n)$ cube. By Theorem 2.2.3.4, a double-rooted tree with 2^n nodes can be embedded in each of these two halves. Let these trees be as shown in Fig. 2.2.3.18. By inserting the edges $(1x, 2x)$, $(0y, 2y)$, and $(1x, 3x)$ and deleting the node $0x$ and the corresponding edges $(0x, 1x)$ and $(0x, 0y)$, the two double-rooted trees can be combined into a binary tree with $2^{2n} - 1$ nodes, as shown in Fig. 2.2.3.19. This proves the theorem.

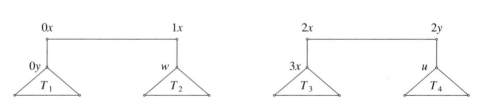

FIGURE 2.2.3.18
Double-rooted binary trees used in the proof of Theorem 2.2.3.6. All labels are in base 4.

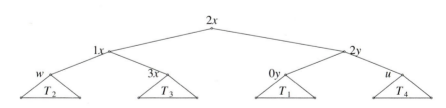

FIGURE 2.2.3.19
A complete binary tree embedded in a $(4^n, 4, n)$ cube. All labels are in base 4.

Thus, all but one node of a base-4 cube can take part in forming a complete binary tree (with $D_f = 1$), and this complete binary tree can be used for broadcasting in a base-4 cube.

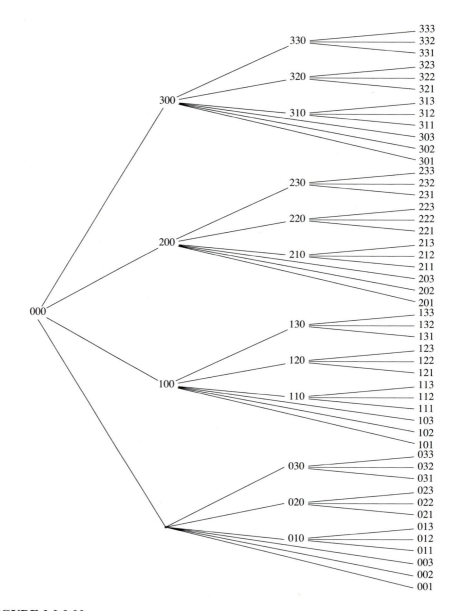

FIGURE 2.2.3.20
An example of a spanning tree in a (64, 4, 3) cube.

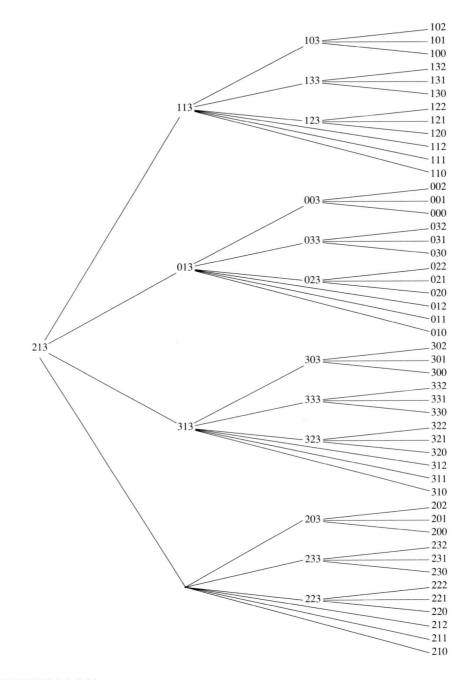

FIGURE 2.2.3.21
A spanning tree obtained from the one in Fig. 2.2.3.20 by translation.

Broadcasting in a base-b cube can be done using another kind of tree, namely, the spanning tree in an (N, b, k) cube. In developing this tree, it is assumed that each processor is capable of simultaneously communicating with $b - 1$ of its neighbors. The following algorithm, which is an extension of the one given at the beginning of this section for base 2, defines this spanning tree.

Spanning Tree Algorithm for Base-b Cube

Step 1. Starting at 0^k, the tree contains the edge to each node $x0^{k-1}$ for $x = 1, 2, \cdots, b - 1$.

Step 2. For $j = 2$ to k, place an edge connecting $x0^{k-j+1}$ to $xy0^{k-j}$ for all $y = 1, 2, \cdots, b - 1$, and x is a $(j - 1)$-digit base-b integer.
　　　Examples of this spanning tree for $b = 4$ and $k = 3$ are given in Figs. 2.2.3.20 and 2.2.3.21.

2.3 SHARED MEMORY MULTIPROCESSORS

2.3.1 Basic Concepts

The characteristic feature of shared memory multiprocessors is that a common bank of interleaved memory modules are connected to a collection of processors through a network, where each processor is a stand-alone machine with its own local memory and may use parallelism at the arithmetic level in the form of pipelined arithmetic units with vector registers. Refer to Fig. 2.3.1.1 for an illustration.

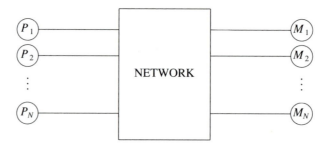

FIGURE 2.3.1.1
A shared memory architecture.

A major factor that often degrades the overall performance of this type of parallel computer organization relates to the *access conflicts.* If k ($1 < k \le N$) of the N processors generate addresses that are resident in a single memory module, then it would take k cycles to deliver the data and the performance of the algorithm could, in principle, be *degraded* by a factor of k. Thus, for overall efficiency, it is necessary that

(a) the processors generate addresses such that *no* two processors request data from the same module, that is, the access pattern is a *permutation,*

(b) the data must be spread across the memory modules to permit *parallel access,* and

(c) the network connecting the processors and memory must be powerful enough to *align* and deliver the requested data to the respective processors.

In this section, we concentrate on analyzing the alignment properties of interconnection networks with special reference to realizing permutations. An example of a data organization that permits parallel access of various cross sections of matrices such as rows, columns, and diagonals is pursued in Exercises 2.49 and 2.50.

The simplest of the connecting networks is the high-speed bus, which is described in Fig. 2.3.1.2. In this network, while the processors *cannot* simultaneously access the memory, by fixing the number of processors and memory modules in advance, we can compute the bandwidth of the bus necessary to serve all the access (fetch/store) requests within the prespecified delay. A number of successful designs have appeared in the commercial arena, and the Encore Multimax with 20 processors is an example of this organization. This scheme, however, is not suitable for a very large number of processors, because of the bus saturation problem, etc.

At the other end of the spectrum is the $N \times N$ cross-bar switch, which is a connecting network with N inputs and N outputs. It is assumed that the processors are connected to the input side and the memory modules to the output side of the network. Refer to Fig. 2.3.1.3 for examples of cross-bar networks. At the intersection of the ith input line and j^{th} output line is a *two-state* (on/off) switch. Setting this switch *on* provides a connecting link between the processor P_i and memory M_j. Thus, in all, there are N^2 switches in an $N \times N$ cross-bar.

Let $\pi : \; < N > \; \rightarrow \; < N >$ be a permutation. A network is said to *realize* the permutation π if there exists a setting of the switches in the network such that the ith input is connected to the $\pi(i)^{th}$ output for $0 \le i < N$. It is easily verified that an $N \times N$ cross-bar network can realize all the $N!$ permutations. Thus, the *combinatorial power (CP)* (which is defined as the ratio of the number of permutations realized to the total number of permutations) of an $N \times N$ cross-bar network is unity. The C.mmp, an early experimental multiprocessor at Carnegie-Mellon University, was built using the 16×16 cross-bar.

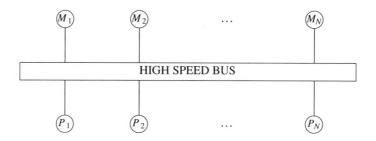

FIGURE 2.3.1.2
A high-speed bus based interconnection.

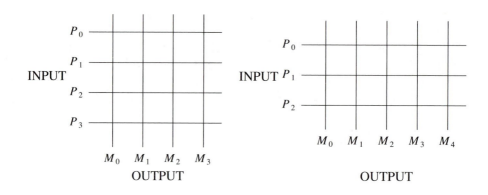

FIGURE 2.3.1.3
Examples of 4×4 and 3×5 cross-bar networks.

The process of computing the states (on/off) of the individual switches to realize a permutation is called *routing*. The cross-bar network admits a very simple routing strategy which can be implemented in *parallel*. One of the major disadvantages of the cross-bar, however, is its *cost* (measured in terms of the number of on/off switches), which is the product of the number of inputs and outputs. In addition, there are a number of engineering considerations, such as *pin limitations, fault tolerance,* and *maintainability,* that do *not* favor building large cross-bars. From the technological point of view, it is often economical to mass produce highly reliable, small cross-bar switches, such as 2×2 or 4×4. Thus, one of the principal problems of interconnection is to design networks, using small, say, 2×2, (cross-bar) switches that are functionally equivalent ($CP = 1$) to the $N \times N$ cross-bar.

In the following, we will use the 2×2 switches as the basic building block. Referring to Fig. 2.3.1.4, the 2×2 cross-bar has four on/off switches, $s_{ij}, 0 \leq i, j \leq 1$, at the intersection of the input line i and the output line j. A useful representation of the 2×2 switch is given in Fig. 2.3.1.4(b). By setting s_{00} and s_{11} *on* and the other two *off*, we can realize the identity permutation

$$\pi = \begin{pmatrix} 0 & 1 \\ 0 & 1 \end{pmatrix}.$$

This is called the *on* or *through* state of the switch. Likewise, setting s_{01} and s_{10} *on* and the other two *off*, we can realize the permutation

$$\pi = \begin{pmatrix} 0 & 1 \\ 1 & 0 \end{pmatrix}.$$

This is called the *off* or *cross* state of the switch. Representations of the through and cross states of the 2×2 switch are given in Figs. 2.3.1.4(c) and (d). While there are other modes of operation of the 2×2 switch (see Exercise 2.30), in this discussion we confine our attention to the realization of permutation between inputs and outputs. Thus, the states of the switch can be controlled by one bit -- the *0* value of the *control* bit corresponds to the *through state* and the *1* value to the *cross state*. The *state of a network* made of 2×2 switches corresponds to the settings of the individual switches. Clearly, a network with L 2×2 switches has a total of 2^L distinct states.

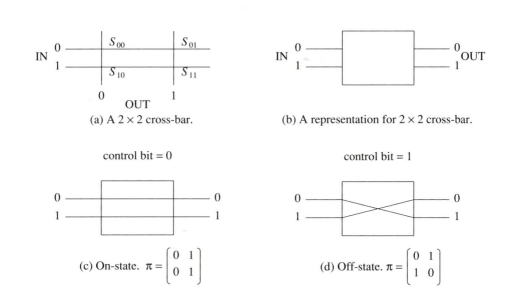

(a) A 2×2 cross-bar.

(b) A representation for 2×2 cross-bar.

control bit = 0

control bit = 1

(c) On-state. $\pi = \begin{pmatrix} 0 & 1 \\ 0 & 1 \end{pmatrix}$

(d) Off-state. $\pi = \begin{pmatrix} 0 & 1 \\ 1 & 0 \end{pmatrix}$

FIGURE 2.3.1.4
The 2×2 cross-bar switch.

Using this model of the 2×2 switch, we now describe a number of examples. A 4×4 network must have a minimum of one *stage* with two 2×2 switches. Refer to Fig. 2.3.1.5(a). Examples of two- and three-stage networks are given in Figs. 2.3.1.5(b) through (d). Tables 2.3.1.1 and 2.3.1.2 enumerate the set of all permutations realized by the networks in Figs. 2.3.1.5(a) and (c), respectively. It is readily seen that the network in Fig. 2.3.1.5(b) realizes the same set of permutations as that in Fig. 2.3.1.5(a). Computing the number of permutations realized by the network in Fig. 2.3.1.5(d) is left as Exercise 2.31.

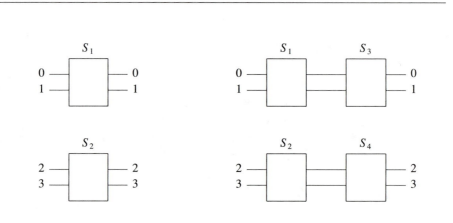

(a) A single stage 4×4 network.　　　　(b) A two-stage 4×4 network.

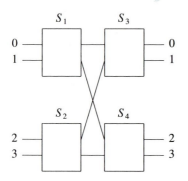
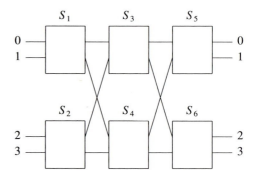

(c) Another two-stage 4×4 network.　　　　(d) A three-stage 4×4 network.

FIGURE 2.3.1.5
Examples of 4×4 networks using 2×2 switches.

TABLE 2.3.1.1

Permutations Realized by Network in Fig. 2.3.1.5(a) (0, through state; 1, cross state)

State of the Network		Permutation Realized			
S_1	S_2	$\pi(0)$	$\pi(1)$	$\pi(2)$	$\pi(3)$
0	0	0	1	2	3
0	1	0	1	3	2
1	0	1	0	2	3
1	1	1	0	3	2

TABLE 2.3.1.2

Permutations Realized by Network in Fig. 2.3.1.5(c)

State of the Network				Permutation Realized			
S_1	S_2	S_3	S_4	$\pi(0)$	$\pi(1)$	$\pi(2)$	$\pi(3)$
0	0	0	0	0	2	1	3
0	0	0	1	0	3	1	2
0	0	1	0	1	2	0	3
0	0	1	1	1	3	0	2
0	1	0	0	0	2	3	1
0	1	0	1	0	3	2	1
0	1	1	0	1	2	3	0
0	1	1	1	1	3	2	0
1	0	0	0	2	0	1	3
1	0	0	1	3	0	1	2
1	0	1	0	2	1	0	3
1	0	1	1	3	1	0	2
1	1	0	0	2	0	3	1
1	1	0	1	3	0	2	1
1	1	1	0	2	1	3	0
1	1	1	1	3	1	2	0

A network in which there exists *at least one* path from each of the input terminals to every output terminal is called a *full access* network. If there exists a unique path between every input/output pair of terminals, then the network is called a *unique path* network or Banyan network (Goke and Lipovski [1973]). A network is called a *blocking* network if there exists at least one permutation not realized by the network (that is, $CP < 1$), otherwise (that is, $CP = 1$) it is called a *non-blocking* network. (See Exercise 2.45.) Refer to Fig. 2.3.1.6 for a classification of network topologies.

The networks in Figs. 2.3.1.5(c) and (d) are full access networks, but those in Figs. 2.3.1.5(a) and (b) are *not* full access networks. In the networks in Figs. 2.3.1.5(a) and (b), there is no path connecting input 0 to outputs 2 and 3. Figure 2.3.1.5(c) is an example of a unique path network. There are exactly two paths between each input/output pair of terminals of the network in Fig. 2.3.1.5(d). The network in Fig. 2.3.1.5(c) is also a blocking network, since it does not realize the identity permutation. Fig. 2.3.1.5(d) is an example of a network which is non-blocking (see Exercise 2.31).

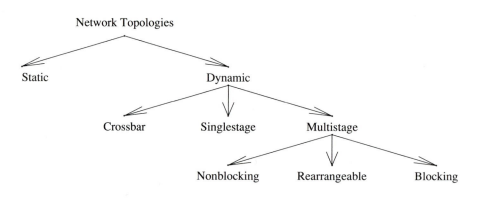

FIGURE 2.3.1.6
Taxonomy of network topologies.

Thus, the number of paths and the combinatorial power of a network depend critically on the number of stages and the interstage interconnection scheme. A number of useful properties are pursued in Exercises 2.32 to 2.34.

The following observations immediately follow from the above examples. Let $N = 2^n$ and consider a k-stage network, built out of 2×2 switches.

(N1) In a k-stage network, there are at most $\dfrac{kN}{2}$ 2×2 switches.

(N2) In a k-stage network, $k \leq n$, there exists *at most one* path between every input/output pair of terminals [see Figs. 2.3.1.5(a), (b), and (c)].

(N3) n stages are *necessary* for this network to possess the full access property. The sufficiency, however, depends on the interstage interconnections. [See the difference between Figs. 2.3.1.5(b) and (c).]

(N4) The number of permutations realized by a k-stage network is at most $2^{kN/2}$ for $1 \leq k \leq n$ [see Figs. 2.3.1.5(a) and (c)].

(N5) In a unique path network, the number of permutations realized by it is equal to the number of distinct states of the network. (See Fig. 2.3.1.5(c).)

(N6) If π is a permutation realized by a full access network, then, in general, more than one state of the network realize the same permutation π. (See Fig. 2.3.1.5(d).)

Two classes of networks have been singled out for further analysis: (1) the class of full access, unique path blocking networks (generalization of the example in Fig. 2.3.1.5(c)), and (2) the class of full access, multipath networks which are non-blocking (generalization of the example in Fig. 2.3.1.5(d)). These networks are discussed in Sections 2.3.2 and 2.3.3, respectively.

In closing this section, we derive a lower bound on the number of 2×2 switches necessary to realize the set of all permutations. Let $N = 2^n$ and let an $N \times N$ network be made of L 2×2 switches. Then, there are 2^L distinct states of the network. For full combinatorial power, since the number of states of the networks must be at least as large as the number of permutations, we obtain that

$$2^L \geq N!,$$

that is,

$$L \geq \log N!.$$

Using Stirling's approximation, namely,

$$N! \approx (2\pi)^{-1/2} N^N \ e^{-(N + 1/2)},$$

we have (for some constants c_1 and c_2)

$$L \geq N \log N - c_1 N + c_2.$$

Summarizing, we obtain the following theorem.

Theorem 2.3.1.1. The minimum number of 2×2 switches necessary to realize $N!$ permutations, is $N \log N$, that is $L = \Omega(N \log N)$.

Comparing this lower bound with the cost of the $N \times N$ cross-bar, it follows that the cross-bar is far from optimal. Optimal non-blocking networks are described in Section 2.3.3.

2.3.2 Analysis of Blocking Networks

In this section, we describe the class of unique path, full access blocking networks. We begin by describing a class of networks called the baseline networks, BL_N, with N inputs and outputs. This network admits a recursive characterization. Let $N = 2^n$. BL_2 is the single-stage network consisting of a 2×2 cross-bar switch. For $N \geq 4$, assuming that copies of $BL_{N/2}$ are available, the construction of BL_N is illustrated in Fig. 2.3.2.1. The *first stage* consists of a *column* of $\frac{N}{2}$ 2×2 switches numbered 0 through $\frac{N}{2} - 1$. This is followed by *two* copies of $BL_{N/2}$, called the top and bottom subnetworks. Let the input terminals in each sub-network be numbered 0 through $\frac{N}{2} - 1$. The interconnection between the first stage and the two subnetworks is such that the two outputs of a 2×2 switch are distributed equally between the two subnetworks. More specifically, the top (bottom) output of the ith switch is connected to the ith input of the top (bottom) subnetwork. The output terminals of the top subnetwork are numbered 0 through $\frac{N}{2} - 1$, and those of the bottom subnetwork from $\frac{N}{2}$ through $N - 1$.

From this definition, it follows that this network has $\log N$ *stages* with $\frac{N}{2}$ 2×2 switches in each of them. Thus, BL_N has a total of $\frac{N}{2} \log N$ 2×2 switches. In view of the lower bound in Theorem 2.3.1.1, it may be tempting to ask if BL_N can realize the set of all $N!$ permutations. The answer is no, since there are only

$$2^{(N/2) \log N} = \sqrt{N^N}$$

distinct states in BL_N, which is clearly less than $N!$. More directly, we can verify that BL_N does not realize the identity permutation. Thus, we obtain the following lemma.

Lemma 2.3.2.1. BL_N is a blocking network.

By exploiting the recursive structure, the following result can be proved by induction (see Exercise 2.23).

Lemma 2.3.2.2. BL_N is a unique-path, full-access network.

An immediate consequence of the unique path, full access property is the following.

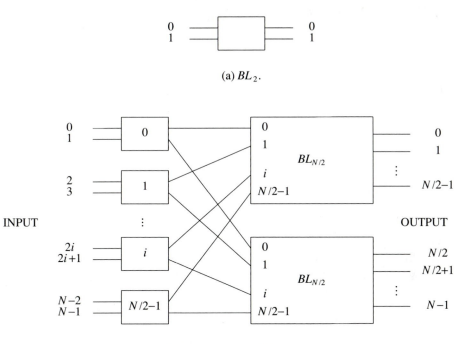

(a) BL_2.

(b) The structure of BL_N.

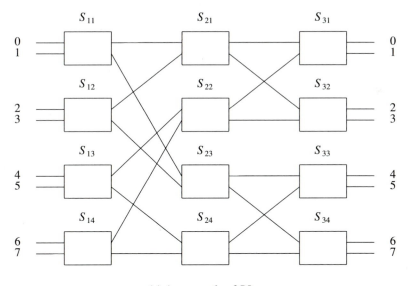

(c) An example of BL_8.

FIGURE 2.3.2.1
The structure and examples of BL_N.

Lemma 2.3.2.3. The number of permutations realized by BL_N is $\sqrt{N^N}$ and $CP \to 0$ as $N \to \infty$.

Proof

From the unique path and full access property of BL_N, it follows that distinct states of the network correspond to distinct permutations realized by the network. Hence BL_N realizes $\sqrt{N^N}$ permutations. Since

$$CP = \frac{\sqrt{N^N}}{N!},$$

using Stirling's approximation, the second claim follows.

The BL_N is only one of many $(\log N)$-stage blocking networks made of 2×2 switches that have the unique path, full access property. We now describe some of the other networks that are closely related to BL_N. To this end, we define some useful permutations.

Let $x \in\ <N>$, where $N = 2^n$, and

$$x = x_n x_{n-1} \cdots x_2 x_1$$

in binary. The *perfect shuffle* σ is a permutation $\sigma: <N> \to <N>$ such that

$$\sigma(x) = x_{n-1} x_{n-2} \cdots x_2 x_1 x_n,$$

that is, $\sigma(x)$ is a *left circular shift* of the bits in the binary representation of x. Expressed in decimal notation,

$$\sigma(x) = (\ 2x + \lfloor 2x/N \rfloor\ ) \bmod N.$$

For $1 \le k \le n$, define k^{th} *subshuffle* $\sigma_{(k)}(x)$ by

$$\sigma_{(k)}(x) = x_n x_{n-1} \cdots x_{k+1} x_{k-1} x_{k-2} \cdots x_2 x_1 x_k,$$

which is a perfect shuffle (left circular shift) on the k *trailing* or least significant bits of x. Similarly, define $\sigma^{(k)}(x)$ as the kth *supershuffle*:

$$\sigma^{(k)}(x) = x_{n-1} x_{n-2} \cdots x_{n-k+1} x_n x_{n-k} \cdots x_2 x_1,$$

that is, the kth supershuffle is a perfect shuffle on the k *leading* or most significant bits of x. The *inverse*, σ^{-1}, of the perfect shuffle is called the *unshuffle*. If σ^k denotes the k-fold composition (or product) of σ, that is, $\sigma^k = \sigma \cdot \sigma \cdot \sigma \cdots \sigma$ (k times), then it follows that

$$\sigma^{-1} = \sigma^{n-1}.$$

The *bit reversal* permutation is $\rho: <N> \to <N>$, where

$$\rho(x) = x_1 x_2 \cdots x_{n-1} x_n.$$

The *butterfly* permutation is $\beta: <N> \to <N>$ such that

$$\beta(x) = x_1 x_{n-1} x_{n-2} \cdots x_3 x_2 x_n.$$

For $1 \leq k \leq n$, $\rho_{(k)}(x)$ and $\rho^{(k)}(x)$, the kth sub and super bit reversals are defined as the bit reversal operations on the trailing and leading k bits of x. A similar definition leads to $\beta_{(k)}(x)$ and $\beta^{(k)}(x)$.

An *exchange* permutation $e_i : \; <N> \; \rightarrow \; <N> \;$ is such that

$$e_i(x) = x_n x_{n-1} \cdots x_{i+1} \bar{x}_i x_{i-1} \cdots x_2 x_1,$$

where $\bar{y}$ is the complement of y (see Exercise 2.24).

Let E denote the set of $2^{N/2}$ permutations realized by a column of $\dfrac{N}{2}$ 2×2 cross-bar switches. With this background, we now define several other networks.

An $N \times N$ *omega* network Ω_N has $\log N$ stages of 2×2 switches where the interstage interconnection is a perfect shuffle. In addition, the input terminals and the input to the first stage are also connected by a perfect shuffle. An example of Ω_8 is given in Fig. 2.3.2.2. Thus, Ω_N can be succinctly denoted by

$$\Omega_N = (\sigma E)^n.$$

The *indirect binary n-cube* network C_N is defined by

$$C_N = E \, \beta_{(2)} \, E \, \beta_{(3)} \, E \, \cdots \, E \, \beta_{(n)} \, E \, \sigma^{-1}.$$

An example of C_8 is given in Fig. 2.3.2.3.

This network is called an indirect binary n-cube because it holds a special relation to the binary hypercube described in Section 2.2. In examining this relation, pretend that both the input node i and the output node i are connected to the two ports of the processor p_i, $0 \leq i \leq N - 1$. That is, the network is *wrapped* around as a processor interconnection network. Now in Fig. 2.3.2.3, by setting the 2×2 switches in stage 1 to the *cross* state and all the other switches to the *through* state, network C_8 realizes the connections between the processors along the first dimension of the eight-node (direct) binary cube shown in Fig. 2.3.2.4. That is, processor pairs (000, 001), (010, 011), (100, 101), and (110, 111) are connected in C_8.

More generally, by setting the switches in the ith stage to the cross state and all the others to the through state, it is readily seen that C_N simulates the connections of the N-node (direct) binary cube along the ith dimension. Hence, the name indirect binary-n cube, where $N = 2^n$. (See Exercise 2.25.)

Given a multistage interconnection network, by interchanging its inputs and outputs, we obtain a new network called the *inverse* of the network. The inverse of BL_N is given in Fig. 2.3.2.5. Two networks are said to be *topologically equivalent* if one network can be obtained from the other by relabeling the switches and/or the input/output terminals. Two networks are said to be *functionally equivalent* if they realize the same set of permutations.

By examining the labels in Figs. 2.3.2.2, 2.3.2.3, and 2.3.2.5, the reader can verify that the omega network Ω_8, the indirect binary n-cube network C_8, and the inverse of the baseline network BL_8 are topologically equivalent to BL_8. By

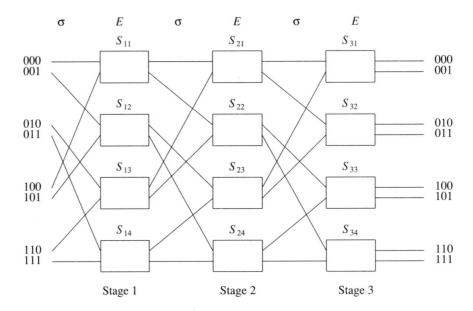

FIGURE 2.3.2.2

An example of omega network $\Omega_8 = (\sigma E)^3$.

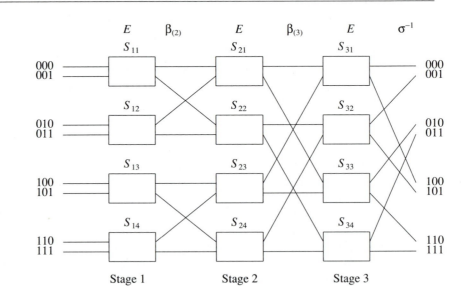

FIGURE 2.3.2.3

An example of an indirect binary three-cube network $C_N = E\beta_{(2)}E\beta_{(3)}E\sigma^{-1}$.

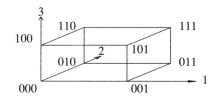

FIGURE 2.3.2.4
An eight-node (direct) binary cube.

---

suitably relabeling the input/output terminals, it follows that these networks are in fact identical. Clearly, topological equivalence naturally leads to functional equivalence. The above examples can be generalized to networks with N inputs and outputs. (See Exercise 2.26.) The importance of the topological equivalence of networks is that parallel computers using these networks can easily simulate one another.

The analysis of the blocking network would be incomplete without a discussion of the routing algorithm. We illustrate this process for the omega network. Invoking the topological equivalence, we can derive analogous algorithms for other equivalent networks.

Let $N = 2^n$ and let the input and the output terminals of each stage of the omega network made of 2×2 switches be numbered 0 through $N - 1$ in binary. Assume that we want to connect the processor at the input node s (called the *source tag*) to the memory at the output node d (called the *destination tag*), where

$$s = s_n \, s_{n-1} \, \cdots \, s_2 \, s_1$$

and

$$d = d_n \, d_{n-1} \, \cdots \, d_2 \, d_1.$$

Let $path(s, d)$ denote the path through the network connecting s to d. A consequence of the unique path and full access property is that we can *embed* a *complete binary tree* with n levels with each input node as the root and all the N output nodes as the leaves. An example of a tree with $s = 110$ as the root is given in Fig. 2.3.2.6. At each node of this tree, label the upper edge 0 and the lower edge 1. By concatenating the labels of the edges along each path from the root to the leaf, we obtain the labels of the output terminals corresponding to the leaf. This labeling scheme immediately suggests a routing algorithm.

Let $u_1, u_2, \cdots, u_n$ be the switches along $path(s, d)$. Refer to Fig. 2.3.2.7 for an example. This path is incident on switch u_k in stage k. Set switch u_k in such a way (cross or through state) that $path(s, d)$ passes through the *top* output of u_k if $d_{n-k+1} = 0$ and the *bottom* output of u_k if $d_{n-k+1} = 1$. Since the state of switch u_k depends on d_{n-k+1}, it is often called the *control* bit, and this routing algorithm is called a *destination tag* based control algorithm. Figure 2.3.2.7 illustrates such a path connecting 110 and 010.

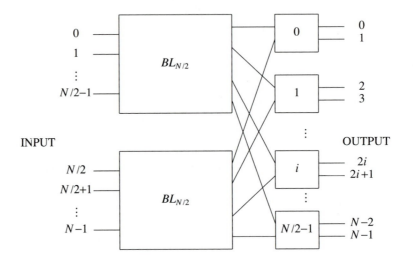

(a) The structure of the inverse BL_N.

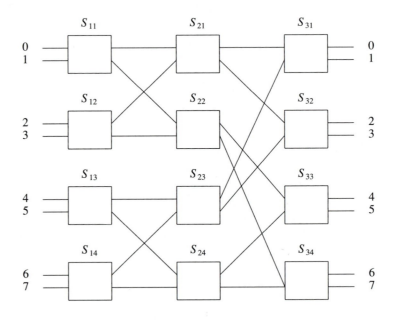

(b) An example of an 8×8 inverse baseline network.

FIGURE 2.3.2.5
The inverse of the baseline network.

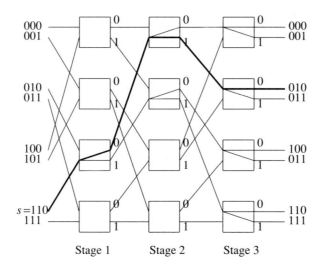

FIGURE 2.3.2.6
An n-level complete binary tree embedded in Ω_8 with s as its root and the output nodes as N leaves.

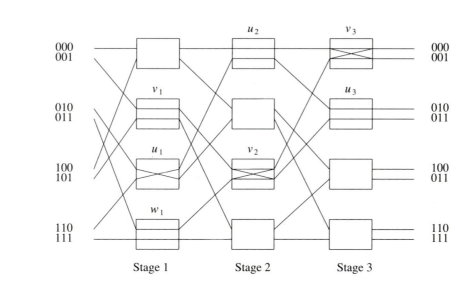

FIGURE 2.3.2.7
An illustration of the destination tag based routing algorithm: $110 \rightarrow 010$, $001 \rightarrow 001$, and $011 \rightarrow 000$.

It can be easily verified that with respect to stage k, $path(s, d)$ occupies the position

$$s_{n-k} \cdots s_2 \, s_1 \, d_n \, d_{n-1} \cdots d_{n-k+2} \, s_{n-k+1}$$

as its input, and

$$s_{n-k} \cdots s_2 \, s_1 \, d_n \, d_{n-1} \cdots d_{n-k+2} \, d_{n-k+1}$$

as its output, $1 \le k \le n$.

The real test of this idea comes when we try to realize two or more paths simultaneously. Referring to Fig. 2.3.2.7, it is seen that $path\,(001, 001)$ goes through switches v_1, v_2, and v_3. But $path(011, 000)$ *intersects* $path(001, 001)$ at the output of switch v_2. This is called a *collision,* and it occurs because the control bits (the second bit in 001 and 000) that decides the state of switch v_2 is the same for both paths. From this it follows that two paths entering a switch *do not* collide if and only if their control bits are mutually complementary. Figure 2.3.2.8 is an example of a permutation realized by Ω_8. Recall that BL_N does not realize the identity permutation (see Exercise 2.46).

We now move on to formalize the condition for the realizability of a permutation by Ω_N.

Let m be a factor of N. Given two non-negative integers x and y, x is said to be (m, N) congruent to y if and only if

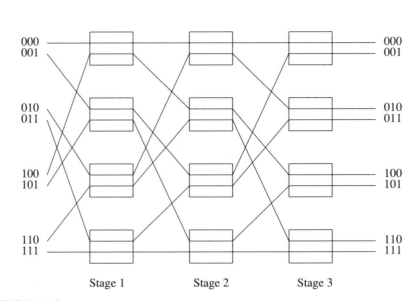

FIGURE 2.3.2.8
A routing corresponding to the identity permutation.

$$m \left\lfloor \frac{x}{m} \right\rfloor \equiv m \left\lfloor \frac{y}{m} \right\rfloor \pmod{N},$$

that is, the largest multiples of m contained in x and y are congruent mod N. We use the notation

$$x \equiv y \bmod (m, N)$$

to denote that x and y are (m, N) congruent, and

$$x \not\equiv y \bmod (m, N)$$

when they are not. As an example, let $m = 8$, $N = 16$, $x = 140$, $y = 10$, and $z = 18$. Then,

$$x \equiv y \bmod (8, 16)$$

and

$$x \not\equiv z \bmod (8, 16).$$

It can be shown (see Exercise 2.47) that if

then,
$$\left.\begin{array}{c} x \equiv y \pmod{m} \quad \text{and} \quad x \not\equiv y \pmod{N} \\ \\ x \not\equiv y \bmod (m, N). \end{array}\right\} \qquad (2.3.2.1)$$

Let

$$\pi = \{ (s_i, d_i) \mid 1 \leq i \leq N \}$$

be a permutation, where

$$s_i = s_{i,n} s_{i,n-1} \cdots s_{i,2} s_{i,1}$$

and

$$d_i = d_{i,n} d_{i,n-1} \cdots d_{i,2} d_{i,1}$$

in binary. Consider $path(s_i, d_i)$ and $path(s_j, d_j)$. The positions occupied by these paths at the output of the kth stage are given by

$$s_{i,n-k} \cdots s_{i,2} s_{i,1} d_{i,n} \cdots d_{i,n-k+1}$$

and

$$s_{j,n-k} \cdots s_{j,2} s_{j,1} d_{j,n} \cdots d_{j,n-k+1}.$$

If $m = 2^{n-k}$, since

$$s_{n-k} \cdots s_2 s_1 \equiv s \pmod{m}$$

and

$$d_n \, d_{n-1} \, \cdots \, d_{n-k+1} 00 \cdots 0 \equiv m \left\lfloor \frac{d}{m} \right\rfloor \, (\mathrm{mod}\ N),$$

it follows that $path(s_i, d_i)$ and $path(s_j, d_j)$ *intersect* at the output of the kth stage if

$$s_i \equiv s_j \, (\mathrm{mod}\ m)$$

and

$$d_i \equiv d_j \, \mathrm{mod}\ (m, N),$$

where $s_i \not\equiv s_j \, (\mathrm{mod}\ N)$. This is called path *conflict*. From this analysis, we obtain the following theorem.

Theorem 2.3.2.4. A necessary and sufficient condition for a permutation π to be realized by the omega network Ω_N is that if $s_i \not\equiv s_j \, (\mathrm{mod}\ N)$ and $s_i \equiv s_j \, (\mathrm{mod}\ m)$ then $d_i \not\equiv d_j \, \mathrm{mod}\ (m, N)$, for all pairs $i \neq j$ and for all $m = 2^{n-k}, 1 \leq k \leq n$.

Using this theorem, we now isolate a very useful subclass of permutations realized by Ω_N. Let α, β, a, and b be non-negative integers such that

$$GCD(\alpha, N) = 1 = GCD(\beta, N). \tag{2.3.2.2}$$

Define a class of permutations

$$\pi(\alpha, a, \beta, b) = \{(\alpha i + a, \beta i + b) \mid 0 \leq i < N\}, \tag{2.3.2.3}$$

where the input terminal $s_i \equiv (\alpha i + a) \, (\mathrm{mod}\ N)$ is to be connected to the output terminal $d_i \equiv (\beta i + b) \, (\mathrm{mod}\ N)$ for $0 \leq i < N$.

Applying Theorem 2.3.2.4 to (2.3.2.3), we see that a permutation in this latter class is realizable if for all $0 \leq i, j < N$, and $m = 2^{n-k}, 1 \leq k \leq n$,

$$(\alpha i + a) \not\equiv (\alpha j + a) \, (\mathrm{mod}\ N), \tag{2.3.2.4}$$

and

$$(\alpha i + a) \equiv (\alpha j + a) \, (\mathrm{mod}\ m) \tag{2.3.2.5}$$

implies

$$(\beta i + b) \not\equiv (\beta j + b) \, \mathrm{mod}\ (m, N). \tag{2.3.2.6}$$

In verifying this claim, first subtract a and then divide both sides of (2.3.2.4) by α to obtain

$$i \not\equiv j \, (\mathrm{mod}\ N). \tag{2.3.2.7}$$

Multiplying both sides of this relation by β and adding b results in

$$(\beta i + b) \not\equiv (\beta j + b) \, (\mathrm{mod}\ N). \tag{2.3.2.8}$$

Similarly, starting with (2.3.2.5), we obtain

$$(\beta i + b) \equiv (\beta j + b) \ (\text{mod} \ m). \qquad\qquad (2.3.2.9)$$

Combining (2.3.2.8) and (2.3.2.9) with (2.3.2.1), we obtain (2.3.2.6), which is to be proved.

This type of permutation often arises in conjunction with skewed storage schemes (see Exercises 2.49 and 2.50).

Thus, we obtain the following theorem.

Theorem 2.3.2.5. Under condition (2.3.2.2), the class of permutations $\pi(\alpha, a, \beta, b)$ defined in (2.3.2.3) is realizable by Ω_N.

A number of corollaries are in order whose proof is left as Exercise 2.48.

Corollary 2.3.2.6.

(a) The identity permutation $I_N = \{(i, i) \mid 0 \le i < N\}$ is realizable by Ω_N.

(b) The class $P = \{(\alpha i + a, i) \mid 0 \le i < N\}$ is realizable by Ω_N.

(c) Let $p = \{(s_i, d_i) \mid 0 \le i < N\}$ be a permutation realizable by Ω_N. Then

$$p \times \delta = \{(\, (\delta s_i) \ (\text{mod} \ N), \, d_i) \mid 0 \le i < N\}$$

is realizable by Ω_N, when δ is an odd integer.

(d) Let p be the permutation defined in (c). Then

$$p + a = \{(\, (a + s_i) \ (\text{mod} \ N), \, d_i) \mid 0 \le i < N\}$$

is realizable by Ω_N.

2.3.3 Analysis of Non-blocking Networks

Historically the first economical design of interconnection networks with $CP = 1$ but requiring fewer than N^2 switches was given by Clos. Let $N = n^2$ for some $n \ge 2$. The three-stage symmetric Clos network consists of n copies of $n \times m$ and $m \times n$ cross-bar switches in the first and third stages, where $m = 2n - 1$. The middle stage is made up of m copies of $n \times n$ cross-bar switches. Refer to Fig. 2.3.3.1 for the general schematic. The interconnections between the stages satisfy the *distributive rule*, namely, that the ith output of the jth cross-bar switch in the first (second) stage is connected to the jth input of the ith cross-bar switch in the second (third) stage. An example with $N = 4$ is given in Fig. 2.3.3.2.

To understand the basic idea of this design, recall our convention that input corresponds to processors and output to memory modules. Let the first $n - 1$ processors attached to the cross-bar switch 1 in stage 1 be connected to a set of $n - 1$ memory modules through a set S of $n - 1$ middle-stage cross-bar switches, where

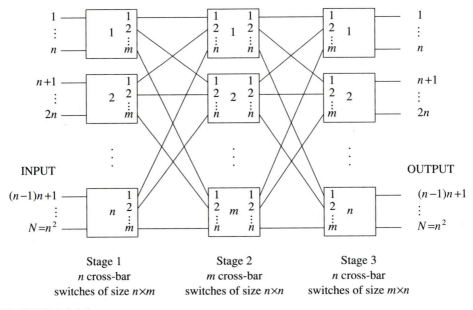

FIGURE 2.3.3.1

The three-stage Clos network with $N = n^2$ and $m = 2n - 1$.

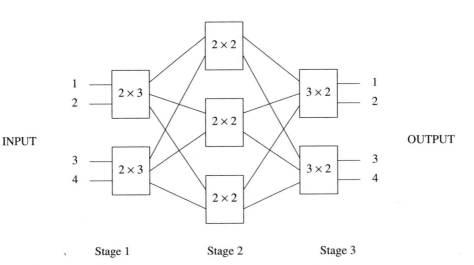

FIGURE 2.3.3.2

An example of a three-stage Clos network with $N = 4$, $n = 2$, and $m = 3$.

$S = \{s_1, s_2, s_3, \cdots, s_{n-1}\}$. Similarly, let the first $n-1$ memory modules attached to the output of the cross-bar switch 1 in stage 3 be connected to a set of $n-1$ processors through a set T of $n-1$ middle-stage cross-bar switches where $T = \{t_1, t_2, \cdots, t_{n-1}\}$. In addition, assume now that the nth processor wants to access data from the nth memory module, and let this connection be made through a single middle-stage cross-bar switch, say u. A *sufficient* condition for allowing all the above communications to progress *independently* is to require that the sets S, T and $\{u\}$ be *mutually disjoint*. Since $|S| + |T| + |\{u\}| = 2n - 1$, the middle stage of the Clos network contains $2n - 1$ cross-bar switches.

In computing the cost, observe that the first and the third stages require $n^2 m$ switches each and the middle stage requires $n^2 m$ switches as well. Thus, the total cost of an $N \times N$ (with $N = n^2$) three-stage Clos network is given by

$$C(n^2, 3) = 3n^2 m = 6N^{3/2} - 3N. \tag{2.3.3.1}$$

A comparison of this cost with that of the $N \times N$ cross-bar is given in Table 2.3.3.1. It is clear that for $N \geq 36$, the three-stage Clos network is economical compared to the single-stage cross-bar network.

It is tempting to ask if further cost reduction is possible by further increasing the number of stages. The answer is indeed yes. In fact, it is shown below that the cost of a $(2r + 1)$-stage Clos network is a decreasing function of r.

In generalizing this design, first consider a three-stage network, with $N = n^3$ and $m = 2n - 1$. The first and the third stages consist of $N^{2/3}$ copies of $n \times m$ and $m \times n$ cross-bar switches, respectively, and the middle stage consists of m copies of $N^{2/3} \times N^{2/3}$ cross-bars. The first and the third stages contain

$$2 \times N^{2/3} \times N^{1/3} \times (2N^{1/3} - 1) = 2N(2N^{1/3} - 1)$$

switches. Replacing each of the middle-stage switches of size $N^{2/3} \times N^{2/3}$ by a three-stage Clos network, using (2.3.3.1), we see that the middle stages together contain

$$(2N^{1/3} - 1)^2 \times 3N^{2/3}$$

switches. The total cost of the resulting $N \times N$ (with $N = n^3$) five-stage Clos network is

$$C(n^3, 5) = 16N^{4/3} - 14N + 3N^{2/3}. \tag{2.3.3.2}$$

An example of an 8×8 five-stage Clos network is given in Fig. 2.3.3.3.

Similarly, it can be shown (see Exercise 2.37) that a seven-stage Clos network with $N = n^4$ requires

$$C(n^4, 7) = 36N^{5/4} - 46N + 20N^{3/4} - 3N^{1/2} \tag{2.3.3.3}$$

switches and a nine-stage Clos network with $N = n^5$ requires

$$C(n^5, 9) = 76N^{6/5} - 130N + 86N^{4/5} - 26N^{3/5} + 3N^{2/5} \tag{2.3.3.4}$$

switches. We can readily generalize this trend to obtain the number of switches,

TABLE 2.3.3.1
A Comparison of Cost between Cross-bar and Three-Stage Clos Network

N	Number of Switches	
	Cross-bar N^2	3-Stage Clos Network $6N^{3/2} - 3N$
4	16	36
9	81	135
16	256	336
25	625	675
36	1,296	1,188
49	2,401	1,911
64	4,096	2,880
81	6,561	4,131
100	10,000	5,700

$C(n^{r+1}, 2r+1)$ in a $(2r+1)$-stage Clos network with $N = n^{r+1}$ (see Exercise 2.39). Instead, we derive a recursive relation for $C(n^{r+1}, 2r+1)$ by recursively defining the structure of the $(2r+1)$-stage Clos network.

Let $N = n^{r+1}$ and $m = (2n-1)$. First, design a three-stage Clos network with the first and the third stages consisting of n^r copies of $n \times m$ and $m \times n$ cross-bar switches, respectively. The middle stage consists of m copies of $n^r \times n^r$ cross-bar switches. We can now recursively replace each of the switches in the middle stage again by a three-stage Clos network. The recursion stops when the size of the middle-stage cross-bar switch reduces to n. It is readily seen that

$$C(n^{r+1}, 2r+1) = m C(n^r, 2r-1) + 2m n^{r+1}, \qquad (2.3.3.5)$$

with the boundary condition

$$C(n^2, 3) = 3n^2(2n-1). \qquad (2.3.3.6)$$

Solving this, it can be shown (see Exercises 2.40 and 2.41) that

$$C(n^{r+1}, 2r+1) = \frac{n^2(2n-1)}{n-1}\left[(5n-3)(2n-1)^{r-1} - 2n^r\right]. \qquad (2.3.3.7)$$

For large n,

$$C(n^{r+1}, 2r+1) \approx 2n^2[5n \times(2n)^{r-1} - 2n^r]$$

$$\leq 2[\frac{5}{2} \times 2^r - 2] n^{r+2},$$

that is,

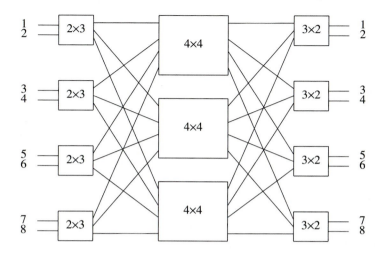

FIGURE 2.3.3.3

An 8×8 Clos network. By replacing each of the 4×4 networks with the three-stage network of Fig. 2.3.3.2, we obtain a five-stage Clos network.

$$C(N, 2r + 1) = O(N^{1 + \varepsilon}), \qquad (2.3.3.8)$$

where $\varepsilon = \dfrac{1}{r + 1} > 0$.

Thus, for $r \geq 1$, $C(N, 2r + 1)$ given above is less than N^2, the cost of the $N \times N$ cross-bar. But when compared with the lower bound ($\Omega(N \log N)$) in Theorem 2.3.1.1, it follows that the Clos network is *not* optimal. Following this lead, Benes completed the program by giving a design for the optimal network with $CP = 1$.

Let N be not a prime and $N = n \times r$. A three-stage Benes network B_N consists of r copies of $n \times n$ cross-bar switches in the first and third stages with the middle stage containing n copies of $r \times r$ cross-bar switches. The interstage interconnections satisfy the standard distributive property. An example of this network for $N = 12$, $n = 3$, and $r = 4$ is given in Fig. 2.3.3.4. By interchanging n and r, we can get another network with 12 inputs and outputs.

Like its predecessor, the Benes network admits a nice recursive structure. Let $N = 2^k$, $n = 2$, and $r = \dfrac{N}{2}$, for some $k \geq 1$. When $N = 2$, the 2×2 cross-bar switch is the single-stage Benes network B_2. Assuming that we have copies of $B_{N/2}$, we can build B_N as a three-stage network as follows: the first and the third stages consist of $\dfrac{N}{2}$ copies of 2×2 cross-bar switches, and the middle stage contains two copies of $B_{N/2}$, where the interconnections between stages satisfy the standard

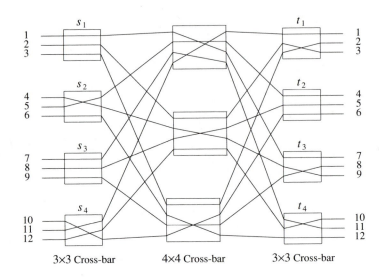

FIGURE 2.3.3.4
A three-stage Benes network with $N = 12$, $n = 3$, and $r = 4$.

distributive property. Refer to Fig. 2.3.3.5 for the structure of B_N, when $N = 2^k$, and Fig. 2.3.3.6 for examples. Clearly, when $N = 2^n$, B_N is simply a cascade of BL_N and inverse BL_N, with the last stage of BL_N and the first stage of inverse BL_N overlapping.

Let $C(N)$ be the number of 2×2 switches and $d(N)$ the number of stages in an $N \times N$ Benes network B_N, where $N = 2^k$. It follows by inspection that

$$C(N) = 2C\left(\frac{N}{2}\right) + N, \quad C(2) = 1,$$

and

$$d(N) = d\left(\frac{N}{2}\right) + 2, \quad d(2) = 1.$$

Solving these, we obtain

$$C(N) = N \log N - \frac{N}{2}$$

and

$$d(N) = 2 \log N - 1.$$

(2.3.3.9)

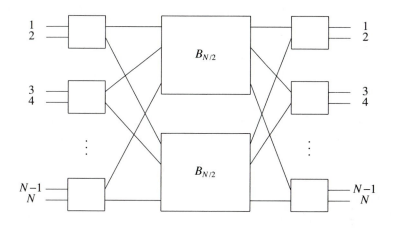

FIGURE 2.3.3.5
The recursive structure of the Benes network B_N for $N = 2^k$.

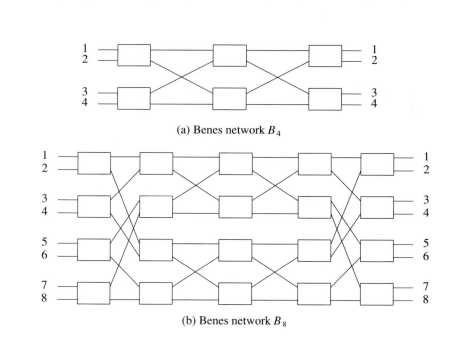

(a) Benes network B_4

(b) Benes network B_8

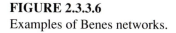

FIGURE 2.3.3.6
Examples of Benes networks.

Comparing $C(N)$ with the lower bound in Theorem 2.3.3.1, it follows that the Benes network is (cost) optimal provided we prove that this recursive structure can realize all the permutations over N objects, that is, $CP = 1$. There are at least two different methods for proving this latter claim -- one is *combinatorial* and another is *group theoretic* in nature. We present the now classical combinatorial proof. Central to this proof is Hall's theorem, which is described in Appendix B.

We now state and prove the principal result of this section.

Theorem 2.3.3.1. Let $N = nr$. Given any permutation π over N objects, there exists a setting of the switches in a three-stage $N \times N$ Benes network such that π is realizable by it.

Proof

Referring to the network in Fig. 2.3.3.7, let $s_1, s_2, \cdots, s_r$ be the r cross-bar switches of size $n \times n$ at the input stage and $t_1, t_2, \cdots, t_r$ be the r cross-bar switches of size $n \times n$ at the output stage, where $N = n \times r$. The input (output) terminals $(i-1)n + 1$ to in are incident on the ith input (output) cross-bar switch s_i (t_i), $1 \leq i \leq r$. Let

$$\pi = \begin{bmatrix} 1 & 2 & \cdots & i & \cdots & N \\ \pi(1) & \pi(2) & \cdots & \pi(i) & \cdots & \pi(N) \end{bmatrix}$$

be the permutation to be realized. Define the set

$$I = \{1, 2, 3, \cdots, r\}.$$

Let, for $1 \leq i \leq r$,

$$I_i = \{j \mid \pi(m) \in t_j \text{ for some input terminal } m \in s_i\},$$

that is, $I_i \subset I$ is the set of indices of the output cross-bar switches that carry the output terminal $\pi(m)$ corresponding to the input terminal m incident on s_i under the permutation π. Let $i_1, i_2, \cdots, i_p$ be a set of p input switches. Let

$$J = \bigcup_{x=1}^{p} I_{i_x} \tag{2.3.3.10}$$

and

$$|J| = q.$$

Clearly, the set of pn input terminals from

$$\bigcup_{x=1}^{p} s_{i_x}$$

are assigned under the permutation π to q output switches which carry a total of

$q n$ output terminals. Since no two input terminals are assigned to the same output terminal under π, we have $q n \geq p n$, that is, $q \geq p$. Combining this with (2.3.3.10), it follows that the union J of p subsets of I contains at least p distinct elements, for $1 \leq p \leq r$. Hence, by Hall's theorem (refer to Appendix B), there exists a system of distinct representatives $\{ k_1, k_2, \cdots, k_r \}$, where

$$k_i \in I_i$$

and

$$k_i \neq k_j, \qquad \text{for } i \neq j.$$

Since $| I | = r$, it follows that the mapping $\{ i \rightarrow k_i \mid 1 \leq i \leq r \}$ is a permutation. The meaning of this relation is that for every $1 \leq i \leq r$, there exists an input terminal incident on the input switch s_i such that the corresponding output terminal $\pi(m)$ is incident on the output switch t_{k_i}. In other words, Hall's theorem helps to identify a *subassignment* of π that involves exactly one terminal from every input switch to one terminal from every output switch.

Realizing this subassignment is equivalent to setting up the switches to connect the r pairs of input/output terminals involved in this subassignment. Evidently, this can be achieved by routing the subassignment through one of the middle-stage switches, say the first switch.

We are now left with an $N' \times N'$ Benes network, where $N' = (n - 1) \times r$. By repeatedly applying Hall's theorem, we can complete the realization of the permutation π.

Since π is arbitrary, it follows that the combinatorial power of B_N is 1.

We now illustrate the above theorem by an example.

Example. Let $N = 12, n = 3$, and $r = 4$, and let

$$\pi = \begin{pmatrix} 1 & 2 & 3 & 4 & 5 & 6 & 7 & 8 & 9 & 10 & 11 & 12 \\ 7 & 3 & 2 & 9 & 4 & 12 & 11 & 5 & 8 & 6 & 1 & 10 \end{pmatrix}.$$

Clearly,

$$I = \{ 1, 2, 3, 4 \}.$$

$$I_1 = \{ 3, 1, 1 \}, \quad I_2 = \{ 3, 2, 4 \}, \quad I_3 = \{ 4, 2, 3 \}, \quad \text{and} \quad I_4 = \{ 2, 1, 4 \}.$$

Select

$$k_1 = 3, \quad k_2 = 2, \quad k_3 = 4, \quad \text{and} \quad k_4 = 1$$

as the representatives of sets I_1 through I_4, respectively. These induce a subassignment consisting of the connections

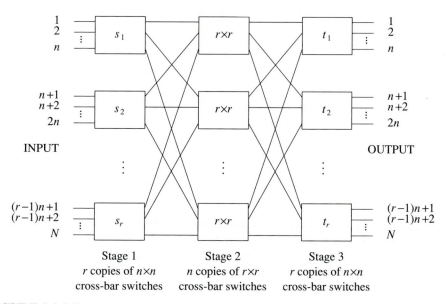

FIGURE 2.3.3.7
The structure of the three-stage Benes network used in the proof of Theorem 2.3.3.1.

$$1 \rightarrow 7, \quad 5 \rightarrow 4, \quad 7 \rightarrow 11, \quad \text{and } 11 \rightarrow 1.$$

A routing of these connections through the first cross-bar of the middle stage is shown in Fig. 2.3.3.4.

We are now left with

$$\pi' = \begin{pmatrix} 2 & 3 & 4 & 6 & 8 & 9 & 10 & 12 \\ 3 & 2 & 9 & 12 & 5 & 8 & 6 & 10 \end{pmatrix}.$$

Again

$$I = \{ 1, 2, 3, 4 \}.$$

$$I_1 = \{ 1, 1 \}, \quad I_2 = \{ 3, 4 \}, \quad I_3 = \{ 2, 3 \}, \quad \text{and} \quad I_4 = \{ 2, 4 \}.$$

Select

$$k_1 = 1, \quad k_2 = 3, \quad k_3 = 2, \quad \text{and } k_4 = 4$$

as the representatives for I_1 through I_4, respectively. The induced subassignment is given by

$$2 \rightarrow 3, \quad 4 \rightarrow 9, \quad 8 \rightarrow 5, \quad \text{and } 12 \rightarrow 10.$$

A routing of these connections through the second cross-bar switch of the middle stage is shown in Fig. 2.3.3.4.

The remaining connections in

$$\pi'' = \begin{bmatrix} 3 & 6 & 9 & 10 \\ 2 & 12 & 8 & 6 \end{bmatrix}$$

can be readily routed through the third cross-bar switch in the middle stage as shown in Fig. 2.3.3.4.

Thus, the proof of Theorem 2.3.3.1 readily suggests an algorithm for realizing any permutation by the Benes network. Detailed discussion of this algorithm and its implementation is beyond our scope, but many relevant references are cited in Section 2.4.

It should be interesting to note that the GF-11 supercomputer is built around a three-stage Benes network with $N = 576$, $n = r = 24$, using 24×24 cross-bar switches.

2.4 NOTES AND REFERENCES

Section 2.1. The monograph by Satyanarayanan [1980] gives a good introduction to shared memory multiprocessors, including C.mmp. The GF-11 project is discussed in Beetem, Denneau, and Weingarten [1985]. The Ultracomputer is described in Gottlieb et al. [1983]. Pipelined architectures including CRAY X-MP are discussed in a number of books, including Hwang and Briggs [1984]. The cosmic cube, which is typical of the parallel computers with cube architecture, is described in Seitz [1985]. The monograph by W.D. Hillis [1988] is devoted exclusively to the design of connection machines.

Section 2.2. Topological properties of base-2 cubes are described in Saad and Schultz [1985a]. A good portion of Section 2.2 is patterned after Lakshmivarahan and Dhall [1988]. Bhuyan and Agrawal [1984] describe a generalized cube which is in many ways similar to the one presented in Section 2.2. However, the main difference is that our presentation brings out the inherent recursive structure of the generalized cube. As a bonus, this recursive structure enables us to readily characterize the existence of the hierarchy and the various reconfigurations. Incomplete cubes are treated in Katseff [1988].

The conference proceedings edited by Heath [1986, 1987] contain a wealth of information on various aspects of problem solving on the hypercube. Also refer to Fox et al [1988] for methods of solving problems using a hypercube.

For a thorough discussion of binary reflected Gray codes, including the definition of $E^{(2)}$ and $D^{(2)}$, refer to the text by Reingold, Nievergelt and Deo [1977].

The theory of generalized Gray codes is developed in Barasch, Lakshmivarahan, and Dhall [1988, 1989b] (see Exercises 2.13 to 2.15).

It is well known (Garey and Johnson [1979]) that the problem of deciding if a given (source) graph is a subgraph of another given (target) graph is NP-complete. Krumme, Venkataraman, and Cybenko [1986] showed that the above problem continues to be NP-complete even if we restrict the target graph to be a base-2 cube. Wagner and Corneil [1987] proved that the embedding of general trees in a hypercube is NP-complete.

Embedding of various topologies, such as rings, one- and two-dimensional arrays, and binary trees, on a base-2 cube are discussed in Barasch, Lakshmivarahan, and Dhall [1989a], Brandenburg and Scott [1985], Ho and Johnsson [1987], Johnsson [1984, 1985], Kosaraju and Atallah [1988], Saad and Shultz [1985a], and Wu [1985]. The concept of the double-rooted tree is taken from Bhatt and Ipsen [1985] and Johnsson and Ho [1986]. Embedding of arbitrary binary trees is discussed in Bhatt and Ipsen [1985] and Bhatt, Chung, Leighton, and Rosenberg [1986].

A number of deterministic, parallel routing algorithms for the hypercube are pursued in Exercises 2.19 through 2.21. Randomized routing algorithms have been the subject of intense study by many authors -- Krizanc, Peleg, and Upfal [1988], Upfal [1984], Valiant [1982], and Valiant and Brebner [1981].

Broadcasting relates to sending the *same* packet of information to all the nodes. However, in some problems, it may be necessary to send *different* packets of information to different nodes. For example, if we want to compute the inner product of two long vectors, one strategy is to partition the vectors and send different pairs of segments to different processors. Note that the spanning tree described in Section 2.2.3 can also be used for this purpose. Once the inner products of the segments are computed, each processor using the spanning tree in the *reverse direction* fan in their partial results. The processor at the root node finally assembles the inner product. This process is often called personalized communication; refer to Johnsson and Ho [1986] and Stout and Wager [1987]. Fox and Furmanski [1987] discuss a variety of communication algorithms for convolution and matrix problems on a hypercube.

Section 2.3. The lower bound on the number of 2×2 switches needed to achieve full combinatorial power is called the *information theoretic* lower bound.

There is extensive literature on blocking networks. Baseline networks were introduced by Wu and Feng [1980a, 1980b], the indirect binary n-cube network by Pease [1977], and the omega network by Lawrie [1975]. The books by Thurber and Masson [1979], Siegel [1985], and Lipovski and Malek [1986] are devoted to the analysis and design of blocking networks. Topological equivalence of blocking networks is discussed in Kruskal and Snir [1982], and Wu and Feng [1980a, 1980b]. The discussion of the routing algorithm for the omega networks is adopted from Lawrie [1975]. The skewed storage scheme which is essential for parallel access is discussed in Budnik and Kuck [1971], Lawrie [1975], and Wijshoff and Van Leeuwen [1987].

The general class of unique path networks called Banyan networks were first introduced by Goke and Lipovski [1973]. Refer to Lipovski and Malek [1987] for further analysis of this class of networks. Patel [1981], Kruskal and Snir [1982], Kumar, Dias, and Jump [1985], and Al-Hallaq and Lakshmivarahan [1987] discuss packet switching in interconnection networks.

Networks permitting destination tag based control algorithms are also called delta networks. Agrawal [1983] provides a general graph theoretical analysis of multistage interconnection networks. For a discussion of equivalence between blocking networks, refer to Pradhan and Kodandapani [1980] and Oruc and Oruc [1986].

Non-uniform memory access patterns could create "hot spots" in the network. The effect of these hot spots and ways to mitigate it are discussed in Pfister and Norton [1985] and Rettberg and Thomas [1986].

Historically, Clos and Benes networks were developed in the context of telephone routing networks. Clos [1952] broke new ground in the design of multistage interconnection networks. Benes [1962, 1965], perfected this design by presenting optimal networks. Theorem 2.3.3.1 is often known as the Benes-Slepian-Duguid theorem. Waksman [1968] showed that $(N \log N - N + 1)$ 2×2 switches are enough to achieve full combinatorial power. A novel approach to the proof of rearrangeability is contained in Raghavendra and Varma [1986, 1987], and Kim and Prasanna Kumar [1987].

Routing algorithms for Benes type networks are described in a number of papers. Waksman [1968] and Opferman and Tsao-Wu [1970] were the earliest in this category. A number of serial and parallel routing algorithms were later developed. Refer to Nassimi and Sahni [1981a, 1982], Lenfant [1978], Lev, Pippenger, and Valiant [1981], and Lee [1985].

For reasons described in Exercise 2.45, Benes networks are often known as *rearrangeable* networks. In a series of papers, Benes [1975a, 1975b, 1975c] re-proved the rearrangeability using group theory.

2.5. EXERCISES

2.1 (Saad and Schultz [1985a]). Show that there are $n!2^n$ different ways in which the 2^n nodes of a complete $(2^n, 2, n)$ cube can be numbered so as to conform to the basic definition of the hypercube. (Without the restriction imposed by this definition there are, in fact, $(2^n)!$ different ways of numbering the nodes.)

2.2 (Saad and Schultz [1985a]). Consider a complete (N, b, k) cube and let a and b be two adjacent nodes in it. Show that the neighbors of a are in one-to-one correspondence with the neighbors of b.

2.3   (Saad and Schultz [1985a]). In a base-2 cube, define the parity of a node to be even or odd if the number of 1's in its binary label is even or odd. Clearly, neighboring nodes have opposite parity. Using this parity concept, show that there are no odd cycles in a base-2 cube.

2.4   (Saad and Schultz [1985a]). Prove that a graph $G = (V, E)$ is a complete $(2^n, 2, n)$ cube, if and only if (1) V has 2^n vertices, (2) Each vertex in V has degree n, (3) G is a connected graph, and (4) any two adjacent nodes a and b are such that the nodes that are neighbors of node a are in one-to-one correspondence with the neighbors of node b.

2.5   (a) Show that a 4×4 grid with wraparound connections is, in fact, a complete $(16, 2, 4)$ cube.

(b) Extend your result to $4 \times 4 \times 4$ grid with wrap-around connections.

2.6   (Saad and Schultz [1985a]). In Section 2.2.3, embedding of a ring of length 2^n on a complete $(2^n, 2, n)$ cube was described using binary reflected Gray codes. Describe an algorithm to embed a ring of length $4 \leq r \leq 2^n$ and r even on a complete $(2^n, 2, n)$ cube.

2.7   Consider a complete $(8, 2, 3)$ cube as shown in Fig. E2.1.

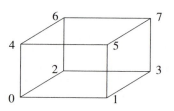

FIGURE E2.1

Define a diagonal in this cube as an edge connecting two vertices, the sum of whose labels is equal to 7. Clearly there are four diagonals in this cube.
(a) How many diagonals are there in a complete $(2^n, 2, n)$ cube? Enumerate them.
(b) If we modify a complete base-2 cube by adding all the diagonal connections, what is the resulting diameter of the modified cube?

2.8   (Bhuyan and Agrawal [1984]). A complete $(16, 4, 2)$ cube may be represented in two different ways: (a) as in Fig. 2.2.1.6 and (b) as shown in Fig. E2.2. Redraw the cubes in Fig. 2.2.1.1 through 2.2.1.5 in format(b).

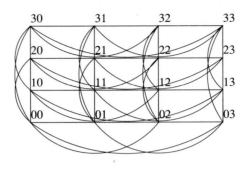

FIGURE E2.2

2.9 (Bhuyan and Agrawal [1984]). The example of Exercise 2.8 suggests the following generalization. Let $N = n_1 \times n_2 \times \cdots \times n_k$. Consider a set of N grid points with n_i points in the ith direction, $i = 1$ to k. Label a point in the grid by an ordered k tuple $x = (x_k, x_{k-1}, \cdots, x_1)$, where $0 \le x_i < n_i$; that is, the ith coordinate value x_i is an integer in the base n_i. Two grid points x and y are said to be *adjacent* if and only if x and y differ in exactly one coordinate and all the adjacent grid points are connected by an edge.

(a) Show that the above system of grid points along with the edges define an incomplete (N, b, k) cube where $b = \max_i \{ n_i \}$.

(b) Let $N = 12$. Express 12 as $4 \times 3, 6 \times 2,$ *or* $2 \times 3 \times 2$. For each way of factoring, draw the incomplete cube resulting from the above definition.

(c) Representing the integer x as $x_k x_{k-1} \cdots x_1$ in the mixed radix system where the base for the ith digit is n_i, show that

$$x = \sum_{i=1}^{k} x_i w_i,$$

where w_i is the weight of the ith digit defined by

$$w_i = \frac{n_k n_{k-1} \cdots n_1}{n_k n_{k-1} \cdots n_i} \quad \text{for } k \ge i \ge 1.$$

(d) Verify that if $n_i = b$ for all $i = 1$ to k, then the above definition naturally leads to the complete (N, b, k) cube.

2.10 (Reingold, Nievergelt, and Deo [1977]). Show that the first code word in $G^{(2)}(n)$ with exactly m 1-bits is $0^{n-m}1^m$ and the last code word is $10^{n-m}1^{m-1}$ for all $m \ge 1$ and 0^n, if $m = 0$, where 0^x1^y is a string with x zeros concatenated with y 1's.

Hint: Prove by induction.

2.11 (Reingold, Nievergelt, and Deo [1977]).

(a) Let $g(n, m)$ denote the ordered sequence of all code words in $G^{(2)}(n)$ with exactly m 1-bits. Show that the successive code words in $g(n, m)$ differ in exactly 2 bit positions.

Hint: Prove by induction.

(b) The sequence $g(n, m)$ may be recursively generated by

$$g(n, m) = \left\{ 0g(n - 1, m), \, 1g^R(n - 1, m-1) \right\},$$

where $g(n, 0) = 0^n$ and $g(n, n) = 1$. Examine this process by generating $g(4, m)$ for $0 \le m \le 4$.

2.12 Binary Gray code in general refers to a set of ordered sequence of binary strings where successive strings differ in one bit. Show (by a counterexample) that not all Gray codes have the property that successive code words with exactly m 1-bits differ in only two bits.

2.13 (Barasch, Lakshmivarahan, and Dhall [1988]). Let $N = b^k$ and $G^{(b)}(k) = \{G_0^{(b)}(k), G_1^{(b)}(k), \cdots, G_{N-1}^{(b)}(k)\}$ be the ordered set of k-digit base-b Gray code. By definition, for $0 \le i \le N - 1$,

$$h_b(G_i^{(b)}(k), G_{i+1}^{(b)}(k)) = 1.$$

$G^{(b)}(k)$ is called a base-b *cyclic* Gray code if, in addition,

$$h_b(G_0^{(b)}(k), G_{N-1}^{(b)}(k)) = 1.$$

(a) Show that the base-b reflected Gray code is cyclic if and only if b is *even*.

(b) Give examples of reflected Gray codes for $b = 3$ and $b = 5$.

2.14 (Barasch, Lakshmivarahan, and Dhall [1988]). Define σ, the *shift* operator that cyclically shifts the code words one position to the left. For example, if $G^{(5)}(1) = \{0, 1, 2, 3, 4\}$, then $\sigma[G^{(5)}(1)] = \{1, 2, 3, 4, 0\}$. Likewise, define σ_i to be a shift operator that cyclically shifts the *rightmost i* code words (recall that $G^{(b)}(k)$ is an ordered set) one position to the left. Thus, $\sigma_2[G^{(5)}(1)] = \{0, 1, 2, 4, 3\}$. Let $G^{(b)}(k)^R = \{G_{N-1}^{(b)}(k), G_{N-2}^{(b)}(k), \cdots, G_1^{(b)}(k), G_{(0)}^{(b)}(k)\}$ be the *reversal* of $G^{(b)}(k)$. Prove that the following recursive definition generates a *cyclic* Gray code for *odd* $b \ge 3$.

Step 1. $G^{(b)}(1) = \{0, 1, 2, \cdots, b - 1\}$.

Step 2. $G^{(b)}(k+1) = \{0G^{(b)}(k), 1G^{(b)}(k)^R, 2G^{(b)}(k), 3G^{(b)}(k), \cdots, (b - 3)G^{(b)}(k), (b - 2)\sigma_2[G^{(b)}(k)^R], (b - 1)\sigma[G^{(b)}(k)]\}$.

2.15 (Barasch, Lakshmivarahan, and Dhall [1988]). This exercise develops the encoding and decoding of reflected Gray codes for any b. A *fundamental ordering* α of digits in $<b>$ is a permutation, that is, $\alpha(i) = j,\ \ i,\ j \in\ <b>$, and $\alpha(i) = \alpha(j)$, if and only if $i = j$. A *reflected fundamental ordering* β of digits in $<b>$ is a permutation, where $\beta(i) = \alpha(b-i-1)$. As an example, for $b = 5$,

	0	1	2	3	4
α :	3	2	0	1	4
β :	4	1	0	2	3

Without loss of generality, in the following it is assumed that α is an identity permutation. Let

$$E : <N> \rightarrow G^{(b)}(k) \text{ where } E(i) = G_i^{(b)}(k)$$

and

$$D : G^{(b)}(k) \rightarrow <N> \text{ where } D(G_i^{(b)}(k)) = i$$

be the *encoding* and *decoding* functions, respectively, where $N = b^k$. Let $0 \le i < b^k, i = [0\ b_k\ b_{k-1}\ \cdots\ b_2\ b_1]_b$, and $G_i^{(b)}(k) = [g_k\ g_{k-1}\ \cdots\ g_2\ g_1]_b$.

Case 1. *b* even.
  Encoding:

$$g_i = f(b_i) \text{ for } i = 1, 2, \cdots, k$$

  where

$$f = \begin{cases} \alpha & \text{if } 0 \equiv b_{i+1} \pmod 2 \\ \beta & \text{if } 1 \equiv b_{i+1} \pmod 2 \end{cases}$$

  Decoding:

$$b_{k+1} = 0$$

  and

$$b_{k-i} = f^{-1}(g_{k-i}) \quad \text{for } i = 0, 1, 2, \cdots, k-1.$$

  where

$$f^{-1} = \begin{cases} \alpha & \text{if } 0 \equiv b_{k-i+1} \pmod 2 \\ \beta & \text{if } 1 \equiv b_{k-i+1} \pmod 2 \end{cases}$$

Case 2. *b* odd.
  Encoding:

$$g_i = f(b_i) \text{ for } i = 1, 2, \cdots, k$$

  where

$$
f = \begin{cases} \alpha & \text{if } 0 \equiv (\sum_{j=i+1}^{k+1} b_j) \, (\text{mod } 2) \\[2em] \beta & \text{if } 1 \equiv (\sum_{j=i+1}^{k+1} b_j) \, (\text{mod } 2) \end{cases}
$$

Decoding:

$$b_{k+1} = 0$$

and

$$b_{k-i} = f^{-1}(g_{k-i}) \quad \text{for } i = 0, 1, 2, \cdots, k-1,$$

where

$$
f^{-1} = \begin{cases} \alpha & \text{if } 0 \equiv (\sum_{j=k-i+1}^{k+1} b_j) \, (\text{mod } 2) \\[2em] \beta & \text{if } 1 \equiv (\sum_{j=k-i+1}^{k+1} b_j) \, (\text{mod } 2) \end{cases}
$$

Prove the correctness of these algorithms. Discuss both the serial and parallel implementation of these algorithms.

2.16 (Ouchark, Davis, Lakshmivarahan, and Dhall [1987]). Consider two nodes A and B at a distance d apart (recall that d is the number of edges in the path connecting A to B). The time required to send a standard packet from node A to node B may be modeled as

$$t = t_s + (d - 1)t_i + dt_c$$

where t_s is called the packet *start-up* time at the source node; t_c is the time to transmit the packet down one edge, and t_i is the time required to handle a packet at an intermediate node.

Notice that t_c is a function of the (hardware) baud rate of the channel and t_s and t_i depend on the system software associated with the message handling system.

Measure experimentally the values of the parameters t_s, t_i, and t_c if you have access to a hypercube architecture. Hence, or otherwise, compute the ratio of t_s and t_c to the time required to add/multiply two floating point numbers.

2.17 The spanning tree described in Section 2.2.3 can be readily used to broadcast a single packet from the source node (say 0000, as in Fig. 2.2.3.3(a)) to all the other nodes. Thus, referring to Fig. 2.2.3.3(a), in the first step ($j = 1$), the processor at node 0000 sends a copy of the packet to the one at node 0001. In the second step ($j = 2$), the processors at nodes 0000 and 0001 simultaneously send a copy of the same packet to processors at 0010 and 0011, respectively. Continuing in this manner, it is readily seen that in exactly four steps one processor can broadcast data to all the other 15 processors in a (16, 2, 4) cube.

Using the model of Exercise 2.16, compute the total time required to broadcast a given packet from one node to all the other nodes in an $(N, 2, k)$ cube.

2.18 Draw the minimum depth spanning tree for a (27, 3, 3) cube.

2.19 (Saad and Shultz [1985b]). Let $n >> N$, and let N divide n. Consider the problem of computing

$$x_{j+1} = Ax_j,$$

where A is an $n \times n$ matrix and x_j an $n \times 1$ vector. Given A and x_0, the problem is to compute x_j for $j = 1, 2, 3, \cdots$. A strategy for computing x_j's is as follows:

(1) Partition the matrix A and assign $\dfrac{n}{N}$ consecutive rows to each of the N processors of the $(N, 2, k)$ cube.

(2) Assign a copy of the vector x_0 to each of the N processors.

(3) Let each processor compute $\dfrac{n}{N}$ components of x_1.

(4) *Each* processor then broadcasts the $\dfrac{n}{N}$ components to *all the other* processors.

(5) Now each processor in turn assembles the vector x_1 and computes the $\dfrac{n}{N}$ components of x_2 and the cycle continues. While the computation involved in this strategy is quite routine, the strategy requires a special type of communication, where *every* processor is required to broadcast a data item to all the other processors. This is called *all-source broadcasting* (as opposed to single-source broadcasting described in Exercise 2.17). In this and the following exercises, we describe a number of algorithms for the all-source broadcast problem.

(a) Perhaps the naive solution is to repeat the one-source broadcast N times repeatedly which may be called *sequential broadcasting*. Compute the total communication time in this process.

(b) A second algorithm is to consider the cube as a ring. An obvious algorithm is as follows:

Step 1. To begin with, let each processor i send its packet to its right neighbor $(i + 1)$ synchronously.

> **Step 2.** Then processor i sends the packet it received from $(i - 1)$ in the previous step to processor $(i + 1)$ and simultaneously receives the next (new) packet from $(i - 1)$.

Thus, in $N - 1$ steps, all the processors will have all the data. This algorithm is called the *daisy chain* algorithm.

(i) Using the model in Exercise 2.16, compute the total communication time required by each method.

(ii) Implement and compare the performance of these algorithms.

2.20 (Saad and Schultz [1985b]). Another algorithm for the all-source broadcast is called the *alternate direction exchange algorithm*. Let $x = x_k x_{k-1} \cdots x_2 x_1$ be a node in an $(N, 2, k)$ cube. Let $(x \mid x_j = 1)$ be a node, the jth bit of whose label is 1.

> **Step 1.** All the nodes $(x \mid x_k = 1)$ exchange in parallel their (one) data packet with their neighbor $(x \mid x_k = 0)$. (Thus, at the end of this exchange, nodes $(x \mid x_k = 1)$ and $(x \mid x_k = 0)$ will have received each other's packet and thus have two packets.)

> **Step 2.** FOR $i = (k - 1)$ DOWNTO 1 STEP 1, DO IN PARALLEL:

> The node with label $(x \mid x_i = 1)$ exchanges all of its accumulated data packets (2^{k-i} of them) with the node $(x \mid x_i = 0)$.

Thus, in principle, in $k = \log_2 N$ stages all the nodes will have all the data packets.

If t_s and t_c are the startup time and communication time, respectively, for a packet across one channel (refer to Exercise 2.16), compute the total communication cost by this method.

2.21 (Saad and Schultz [1985b]).
(a) Let α be a standard packet of data and let $s(\alpha)$ be the source node that originally generated the packet α. (It is assumed that source information $s(\alpha)$ is contained as a part of the packet α.) An algorithm for all-source broadcasting, called *total exchange algorithm -- version 1*, is given in Fig. E2.3.

An illustration of this method for an $(8, 2, 3)$ cube is given in Table E2.1, where $s(\alpha_i) = i$. For simplicity, α_i is denoted by i in binary.

From Table E2.1, it is clear that node 3 initially has $\{\alpha_3\}$ and receives packets $\{\alpha_1, \alpha_2, \alpha_7\}$ in the first step from nodes $\{1, 2, 7\}$. Likewise, in the second step, node 3 receives $\{\alpha_0, \alpha_5\}$ from node 1, $\{\alpha_0, \alpha_6\}$ from node 2, $\{\alpha_6, \alpha_5\}$ from node 7, and so on. In other words, each node, as time passes, receives multiple copies of various packets.

FOR $i = 1$ TO k STEP 1 DO IN PARALLEL

(1) SEND from node x to node y all the packets α such that

$$h_2(s(\alpha), y) = i,$$

(2) SEND from node y to node x all the packets α such that

$$h_2(s(\alpha), x) = i,$$

where $h_2(x, y) = 1$.
END

FIGURE E2.3
Total exchange algorithm -- version 1.

TABLE E2.1
An Illustration of the Algorithm in Fig. E2.3.

Time	Node							
	000	001	010	011	100	101	110	111
0	000	001	010	011	100	101	110	111
	000	001	010	011	100	101	110	111
1	001	000	000	001	000	001	010	011
	010	011	011	010	101	100	100	110
	100	101	110	111	110	111	111	101
	000	001	010	011	100	101	110	111
	001	000	000	001	000	001	010	011
	010	011	011	010	101	100	100	110
	100	101	110	111	110	111	111	101
2	011	010	001	000	001	000	000	001
	101	100	100	101	010	011	101	010
	011	010	001	000	001	000	000	001
	110	111	111	110	111	110	011	100
	101	100	100	110	010	011	011	010
	110	111	111	101	111	110	101	100

Let $P_{x,i}$ refer to the set of all packets α received by node x at step i. Referring to Table E2.1, it follows that

$$P_{0,0} = \{\ \alpha_0\ \}$$
$$P_{0,1} = \{\ \alpha_1,\ \alpha_2,\ \alpha_4\ \}$$
$$P_{0,2} = \{\ \alpha_3,\ \alpha_5,\ \alpha_3,\ \alpha_6,\ \alpha_5,\ \alpha_6\ \},$$

etc.

Let x and y be any two adjacent nodes.

(i) Show that during time step i (≥ 2), node y sends only those packets α to x such that $\alpha \in P_{y,i-1}$ and $h_2(x, s(\alpha)) = i$.

(ii) Show that there are $\binom{k-1}{i-1}$ packets that are sent from node y to node x at step i.

(iii) Compute the total communication time required by this method.

(b) A close scrutiny of the total exchange algorithm in Exercise 2.21 reveals that it is *non-optimal* in terms of the number of data exchanges involved. In this exercise we describe a version of the algorithm that minimizes the data exchanges. To this end, first define e_i to be the binary string of length n, containing i 1's, including a 1 in the least significant position. Thus, when $n = 3$, $e_1 = 001$, $e_2 = 101$ or 011, and $e_3 = 111$. Let σ be the left (circular) shift operator. Thus, $\sigma e_1 = 010$, and $\sigma^2 e_1 = 100$. Let $N = 2^k$. The *total exchange algorithm -- version 2,* for all-source broadcasting may be stated as in Fig. E2.4. Table E2.2 illustrates the data exchanges according to this algorithm, when $n = 3$.

(i) Redo Table E2.2 with $e_2 = 101$.

(ii) Generate the table for the case of $N = 16$.

(iii) Compute the total communication time required by this method.

(iv) The inner loop of the algorithm in Fig. E2.4 assumes that the architecture permits two-way communication between two neighboring nodes u and v. Modify the algorithm for an architecture that permits only *one-way* communication.

2.22 (Bhatt, Chung, Leighton, and Rosenberg [1986]).
(a) Referring to Section 2.2.3, let $f(u) \in V_h$ and $f(v) \in V_h$ be the images of vertices $u \in V_g$ and $v \in V_g$, respectively, under an embedding f, where $G_g = (V_g, E_g)$ and $G_h = (V_h, G_h)$. Let PATH($f(u), f(v)$) be the set of all paths connecting $f(u)$ and $f(v)$ in G_h. Let the embedding f associate an edge $(u, v) \in E_g$ to a path $\rho(f(u), f(v)) \in$ PATH($f(u), f(v)$). It follows that the

The following notations are used in the algorithm:

(uv, j) denotes an edge that connects nodes u and v that differ in the jth coordinate. $s(\alpha)$ is the original source node that generated packet α. $\oplus$ is the exclusive-OR operation.

    FOR i = 1 TO k STEP 1 DO
        FOR $j \in \{1, 2, \cdots, k\}$ DO FOR ALL (uv, j) IN PARALLEL
        1. Send from node u to node v the packets α such that

$$(s(\alpha) \oplus v) \in \sigma^{j-1} e_i.$$

        2. Send from node v to node u the packets α such that

$$(s(\alpha) \oplus u) \in \sigma^{j-1} e_i.$$

        END
    END

FIGURE E2.4
Total exchange algorithm -- version 2.

TABLE E2.2
Data Exchanges According to the Algorithm in Fig. E2.4.

Nodes	$i = 1, e_1 = 001$			$i = 2, e_2 = 011$			$i = 3, e_3 = 111$
	j			j			j
	1	2	3	1	2	3	1
	$e_1 =$ 001	$\sigma e_1 =$ 010	$\sigma^2 e_1 =$ 100	$e_2 =$ 011	$\sigma e_2 =$ 110	$\sigma^2 e_2 =$ 101	$e_3 =$ 111
000	001	010	100	011	110	101	111
001	000	011	101	010	111	100	110
010	011	000	110	001	100	111	101
011	010	001	111	000	101	110	100
100	101	110	000	111	010	001	011
101	100	111	001	110	011	000	010
110	111	100	010	101	000	011	001
111	110	101	011	100	001	010	000

dilation factor D_f is the *maximum* of the path lengths of the *shortest paths* connecting $f(u)$ and $f(v)$ in G_h. Define the *load factor* $L(e_h)$ of an edge $e_h \in E_h$ as

$$L(e_h) = |\{e_g \mid (u, v) = e_g \in E_g \text{ and } e_h \in \rho(f(u), f(v))\}|.$$

The *load factor* of the embedding f is

$$L_f = \max_{e_h \in E_h} \{L(e_h)\}.$$

Compute the load factor L_f for the embeddings discussed in Section 2.2.3.

(b) Consider a seven-node complete binary tree, where the nodes are labeled 0 through 6 *in-order* as shown in Fig. E2.5(a). By mapping each node of the complete binary tree with $2^n - 1$ nodes labeled *in-order* to the nodes in the $(2^n, 2, n)$ cube (see Fig. E2.5(b)) with the corresponding address, we obtain an embedding called *in-order* embedding of a complete binary tree into the hypercube.

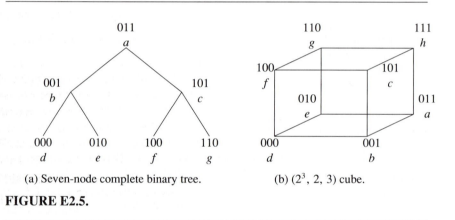

(a) Seven-node complete binary tree.   (b) $(2^3, 2, 3)$ cube.

FIGURE E2.5.

(i) Show that the *dilation D_f* equals 2 and the *load factor L_f* equals 2 for this embedding.

(ii) Compute the dilation and load factor for pre-order and post-order embeddings.

2.23 Prove that BL_N is a unique path full access network.

2.24 Prove the following relations:

(a) $\sigma_{(k)}^{-1} = \sigma_{(k)}^{k-1}$ for $1 \le k \le n$.

(b) $\sigma_{(1)} \sigma_{(2)} \cdots \sigma_{(k)} = \rho_{(k)}$. (The composition is from left to right.)

(c) $\beta_{(1)} \beta_{(2)} \cdots \beta_{(k)} = \sigma_{(k)}$.

(d) $\rho \sigma^{-1} = \sigma \rho$.

2.25   It is shown in the text that C_N can simulate an $(N, 2, n)$ cube.

     (a) In Section 2.2.3, we derived an algorithm to broadcast a message using a spanning tree in an $(N, 2, n)$ cube. How would you simulate this spanning tree in C_N? What is the total communication delay incurred?

     (b) How would you simulate an N-node ring on an N-processor parallel computer connected by the indirect binary n-cube?

2.26   (Wu and Feng [1980a, 1980b]). Prove that C_N, Ω_N, and the inverse BL_N are topologically equivalent to BL_N.

2.27   (Parker [1980]). Show that the cascade of three copies of $N \times N$ omega networks, namely $(\Omega_N)^3$, realizes the set of all permutations over N objects.

2.28   (Parker [1980]). Show that $\Omega_N^{-1} = C_N$.

2.29   Discuss the effect of connecting N processors and M memory modules on data access for $N \le M$ and $N > M$, when they are connected by

     (a) a high-speed bus
     (b) an $N \times M$ cross-bar.

2.30   Referring to Fig. 2.3.1.4(a), describe all the possible modes of interconnection obtained by independently setting the states of the switches s_{ij}, $0 \le i, j \le 1$.

2.31   Enumerate the set of all states and the corresponding permutations realized by the network in Fig. 2.3.1.5(d). Verify that $CP = 1$ for this network.

2.32   Compute the combinatorial power of the networks shown in Fig E2.6.

2.33   Consider the two-stage 4×4 network made of 2×2 switches shown in Fig. E2.7, where the four output terminals a, b, c, and d of the first stage are connected to the four input terminals A, B, C, and D of the second stage in a one-to-one fashion. This is called the *interstage* interconnection or simply the *link permutation*. Clearly, there are 4! different ways of connecting a, b, c, and d to A, B, C, and D. Compute the combinatorial power of the network resulting from each interstage interconnection.

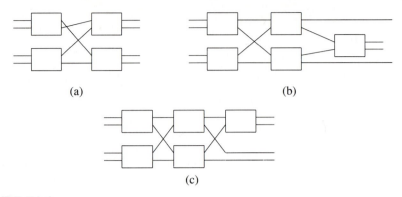

(a)   (b)

(c)

FIGURE E2.6

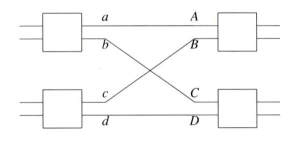

FIGURE E2.7

2.34 Discuss the effect of relabeling the input/output terminals of the networks in Figs. 2.3.1.5 (a), (b), and (c) on the combinatorial power of the network.

2.35 A 2×2 switch may be graphically represented in two complementary ways.

(1) The switch as a node and the input/output links as edges (Fig E2.8).

(2) The switch as the edges and the input/output links as nodes (Fig. E2.9).

Using these two representations, draw the graph of the networks in Figs. 2.3.1.5(a) through (d).

2.36 Prove Lemma 2.3.2.1.

2.37 Prove the relations (2.3.3.3) and (2.3.3.4).

2.38 Graphically plot and compare the cost $C(2r + 1)$ for $r = 1, 2, 3$, and 4, with the cost of a cross-bar for various values of N.

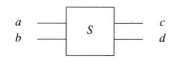

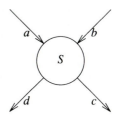

FIGURE E2.8

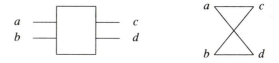

FIGURE E2.9

2.39 (Clos [1952]). Show that the number of switches in an $(s = 2r + 1)$-stage Clos network is given by

$$C(s) = 2 \sum_{k=2}^{(s+1)/2} \left\{ N^{2k/(s+1)} (2N^{2/(s+1)} - 1)^{(s+3)/2-k} \right.$$

$$\left. + N^{4/(s+1)} (2N^{2/(s+1)} - 1)^{(s-1)/2} \right\}.$$

2.40 Show that (2.3.3.7) is the solution of the recurrence in (2.3.3.5).

2.41 Let $N = n^{r+1}$. Fix N and let $r \to \infty$. Compute the limit of $C(n^{r+1}, 2r + 1)$ as $r \to \infty$.

2.42 (Clos [1952]). In the design of a $(2r + 1)$-stage Clos network, it is assumed that $N = n^{r+1}$. This simple relation between N and n may not always minimize the number of switches. To this end, let the first and third stages contain $\dfrac{N}{n}$ copies of $n \times m$ cross-bar switches and let the middle stage contain

m copies of $\dfrac{N}{n} \times \dfrac{N}{n}$ cross-bar switches. Then,

$$C(N, 3) = (2n - 1)(2N + \frac{N^2}{n^2}).$$

(a) Find the value of n that minimizes $C(N, 3)$.

(b) Extend this argument to five- and seven-stage networks and find the optimum size of switches in each case.

2.43 Derive an algorithm to realize a permutation by the three-stage Clos network.

2.44 (Waksman[1968]).
(a) By applying Hall's theorem, show that the network in Fig. E2.10 realizes all the 4! permutations.

(b) Repeat part (a) for the 8×8 network of Fig. E2.11.

(c) Extend this idea for the $N \times N$ network, where $N = 2^k$ for $k \geq 4$.

(d) Compute the number of 2×2 switches used in part (c), and compare it with that of the Benes network described in the text.

(e) Can you further reduce the number of switches in Figs. E2.10 and E2.11 without affecting the combinatorial power?

2.45 Consider the five-stage Benes network with eight inputs and outputs shown in Fig. E2.12.

Let

$$\pi = \begin{pmatrix} 1\ 2\ 3\ 4\ 5\ 6\ 7\ 8 \\ 1\ 5\ 2\ 6\ 3\ 7\ 4\ 8 \end{pmatrix}$$

and $A = \{1, 4, 6, 7, 8\}$. Let $B = \{j \mid j = \pi(i),\ i \in A\}$, that is, $B = \{1, 6, 7, 4, 8\}$. The settings of the switches connecting input terminals in A to those in B are shown in the diagram.

(a) Given this setup, verify that the remaining three connections, namely $2 \rightarrow \pi(2) = 5, 3 \rightarrow \pi(3) = 2$, and $5 \rightarrow \pi(5) = 3$, *cannot* be realized.

(b) Rearrange the connections between sets A and B to accommodate the three remaining connections.

(c) Find out how many distinct rearrangements are possible. What are the maximum number and the minimum number of rearrangements?

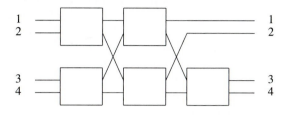

FIGURE E2.10

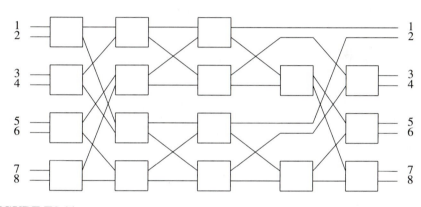

FIGURE E2.11

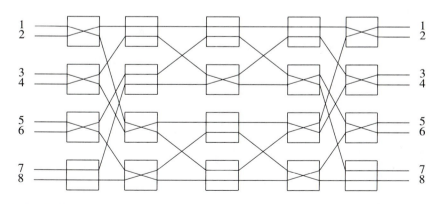

FIGURE E2.12

Note: Benes network was originally developed for telephone traffic routing. In this context, the routing shown in Fig. E2.12 connecting the terminals in set *A* to those in *B* denote the calls in progress. Given this routing, it is not possible to accommodate the new calls connecting $2 \to 5$, $3 \to 2$, and $5 \to 3$. However, we can accommodate these three new calls by rerouting or rearranging the calls from *A* to *B*. In other words, the network is *not* intrinsically blocking. For this reason, Benes referred to this class of networks as *weakly non-blocking* or *rearrangeable*. In contrast, since no such rearrangement is necessary to accommodate the new incoming calls, Clos networks is often called *strongly non-blocking*. Thus, rearrangement may be necessary while working in an asynchronous environment, such as the routing of telephone calls. However, in a synchronous parallel computing environment, since the entire permutation π to be realized by the Benes network is known *a priori*, as shown in Theorem 2.3.3.1, it can be realized *without* any rearrangement.

2.46 (a) Using the destination tag based control algorithm, show that BL_8 realizes the bit reversal permutation.

(b) Show that Ω_N does not realize the bit-reversal permutation.

2.47 Prove relation (2.3.2.1).

2.48 (Lawrie [1975]). Prove Corollary 2.3.2.6.

2.49 (Lawrie [1975]). Consider a parallel computer with N processors and L memory modules, M_0, M_1, $\cdots$, M_{L-1}, where $L \geq N$. Let $a = (a_0, a_1, \cdots , a_{N-1})$ be a row vector and s and p be two integers. Consider a storage scheme that maps element a_i, $0 \leq i < N$, to memory module M_k, where

$$k \equiv (si + p) \,(\text{mod } L)$$

Notice that the consecutive elements of the row vector a are stored in memory modules whose indices differ by s. This storage scheme is often called *s-ordered* storage.

(a) Let $N = 4$. Illustrate the *s*-order of a vector $a = (a_0, a_1, a_2, a_3)$ for $0 \leq s < 4, p = 0$, and $L = 4$ and 5.

(b) Show that a sufficient condition for an *s*-ordered vector to be accessible in parallel is that

$$L \geq N \times \text{GCD}(s, L).$$

2.50 (Lawrie [1975]). From the computational point of view, operations on matrices are conveniently expressed in terms of those on vectors, namely, rows, columns, diagonals, etc. In this exercise, we examine the conditions on the storage scheme that will permit parallel access of different cross sections of a matrix. Assume that we have L memory modules $M_0, M_1, \cdots, M_{L-1}$ each with unlimited storage and $L \geq N$. Let $A = [A_{ij}]$ be an $N \times N$ matrix with $0 \leq i, j < N$. (If the matrix is large, we can block it into submatrices of size $N \times N$ and apply the following method to each submatrix.) Let $s, t, p,$ and q be integers. Define an (s, t) skewed storage scheme that maps a_{ij} to M_k, where

$$k \equiv (si + tj) \,(\text{mod } L).$$

An example of a $(2, 3)$ storage scheme with $L = 5$ and $N = 4$ is given in the following table:

M_0	M_1	M_2	M_3	M_4
A_{00}	A_{02}	-	A_{01}	A_{03}
A_{11}	A_{13}	A_{10}	A_{12}	-
A_{22}	-	A_{21}	A_{23}	A_{20}
A_{33}	A_{30}	A_{32}	-	A_{31}

Show that the conditions

$$L \geq N \times \text{GCD}(t, L)$$
$$L \geq N \times \text{GCD}(s, L)$$
$$L \geq N \times \text{GCD}(s + t, L)$$

are sufficient for accessing rows, columns, and the principal diagonal in parallel, respectively.

Note: For further analysis of the skewed storage scheme, refer to Wijshoff and Van Leeuwen [1987].

2.51 (Kothari, Lakshmivarahan, and Peyravi [1985]). Let $N \,(> 2)$ be a non-prime integer, and $N = n_1 \times n_2 \times \cdots \times n_k$ be a *factorization of N*. Let $\mathbf{n} = (n_1, n_2, \cdots n_k)$ *be a k-vector of the factors of N.* Define two *k*-vectors $\mathbf{p} = (p_1, p_2, \cdots, p_k)$ and $\mathbf{q} = (q_1, q_2, \cdots q_k)$ *(not* necessarily distinct) as two permutations of the vector $\mathbf{n}$. Now, given $\mathbf{p}$ and $\mathbf{q}$, we can construct a k-stage, unique path, full access network, where the ith stage is made of cross-bar switches of sizes $p_i \times q_i, 1 \leq i \leq k$. Thus, by changing the number (k) of factors, and permuting the factors for a given k, we can obtain the set of all unique path, full access networks with N inputs/outputs. As an example, let $N = 16$. Thus, if $k = 1$, we obtain the single-stage cross-bar. For $k = 2$, $n_1 = n_2 = 4$. The two-stage network made of 4×4 switches is shown in Fig. E2.13. In this network, the interconnection between stages 1 and 2 is called a 4-shuffle.

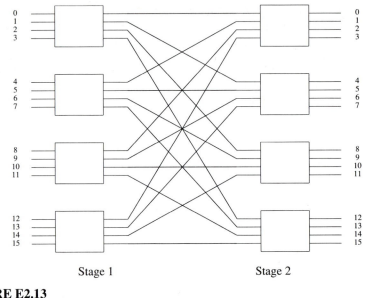

Stage 1   Stage 2

FIGURE E2.13

As another example, let $k = 3$, and $n_1 = 2, n_2 = 4$, and $n_3 = 2$, that is, $\mathbf{n} = (2, 4, 2)$. Since there are three *distinct* permutations of $\mathbf{n}$, there are *nine* distinct networks, one for each possible choice of $\mathbf{p}$ and $\mathbf{q}$. An example of a three-stage network with $\mathbf{p} = (2, 2, 4)$ and $\mathbf{q} = (2, 4, 2)$ is given in Fig. E2.14.

(a) Find the set of possible unique path, full access networks with 16 inputs/outputs.

(b) Compute the combinatorial power of each of these networks as well as their cost (measured in terms of the number of on/off switches needed).

Note: Networks of this type are called expanding and contracting SW-banyans by DeGroot [1983]. Computing the combinatorial power of these networks is *not* obvious and leads to a number of open questions.

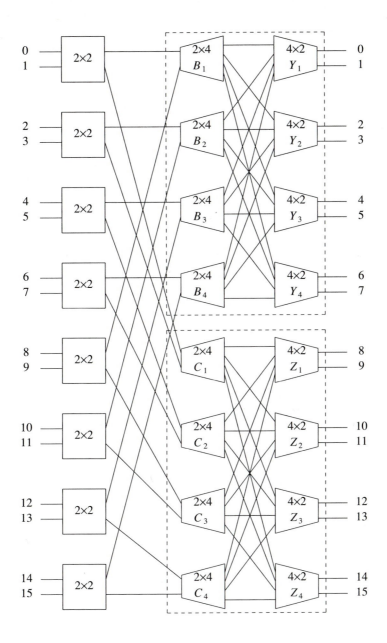

FIGURE E2.14
The example of an expanding contracting SW-banyan network with
$\mathbf{p} = (2, 2, 4)$ and $\mathbf{q} = (2, 4, 2)$.

PART 2

ARITHMETIC PROBLEMS

CHAPTER 3

BASIC ARITHMETIC OPERATIONS

3.1 INTRODUCTION

Parallelism in problem solving can be achieved in at least three different levels -- (1) procedure level, (2) expression level, and (3) basic arithmetic level. At the first two levels, the time complexity function merely indicates the number of basic (arithmetic or comparison) operations. For example, at these two levels, addition of two integers is taken as a unit (independent of the size of integers) operation. But it is common knowledge that it takes more time to add two large integers than to add two small ones. Thus, for the overall speed-up, it is necessary to use the best possible algorithms to perform these basic arithmetic operations. In this chapter we analyze the number of bit operations (such as AND and OR) needed to perform basic arithmetic operations in parallel. Since this is the lowest level at which parallelism can be achieved, it is called bit level or micro level parallelism.

Chapter 4 develops parallel algorithms for the evaluation of arithmetic expressions. Together Chapters 3 and 4 constitute Part 2 of this book and deal with parallelism in arithmetic problems. Procedure level parallelism is the topic of Part 3, which consists of Chapters 5, 6, and 7.

In Section 3.2, parallel algorithms for adding two N-bit integers are given. Parallel multiplication algorithms are described in Section 3.3. We then digress to describe the well-known algorithm for computing the discrete Fourier transform, called the fast Fourier transform (FFT). Computation of FFT in complex arithmetic is given in Section 3.4. Modulo arithmetic provides a framework for error-free computation of FFT provided we can choose a modulus large enough to support the necessary number of roots of unity. Such a choice of modulus critically depends on results from number theory described in Section 3.5. Two applications of FFT are contained in Section 3.6. The first is the classical one of computing the convolution of two vectors. The second application is to multiply two N-bit integers using the Schonhage and Strassen [1971] method. In Section 3.7, the $O(\log N)$ depth parallel algorithm due to Beame, Cook, and Hoover [1986] for the division of two N-bit numbers is described.

3.2 ANALYSIS OF PARALLEL ADDITION

Addition is the simplest of the basic arithmetic operations. Despite its simplicity, development of "optimal" parallel algorithms is far from simple and has attracted considerable attention in the literature. In this section, we present an optimal depth circuit due to Brent [1970a] for the addition of two N-bit integers. The primary reason for choosing this algorithm is that it is very general and, as shown in Chapter 4, with appropriate interpretation of operations and operands, it also leads to an optimal algorithm for the evaluation of polynomials. The conventional full-adder circuits and the ripple carry adder are described in Exercise 3.2.

3.2.1 Brent's Algorithm

Let $a = a_N\, a_{N-1} \cdots a_2\, a_1$ and $b = b_N\, b_{N-1} \cdots b_2\, b_1$ be the two integers (in binary) to be added. Let $s = (a + b) \bmod 2^N$, where $s = s_N\, s_{N-1} \cdots s_2\, s_1$. It is well known that

$$s_i = a_i \ \oplus\ b_i \ \oplus\ c_{i-1}, \qquad (3.2.1.1)$$

where $c_0 = 0$, and, for $i = 1$ to N,

$$c_i = p_i \wedge (g_i \vee c_{i-1})$$
$$p_i = a_i \vee b_i$$
$$g_i = a_i \wedge b_i$$

$$\left.\begin{array}{l} \\ \\ \\ \end{array}\right\}, \qquad (3.2.1.2)$$

where $\oplus$, $\vee$, and $\wedge$ are the logical exclusive-OR, (inclusive) OR, and AND operations, respectively. c_i is called the *carry* from the ith bit position, p_i and g_i are the carry *propagate* condition and the carry *generate* condition, respectively. Clearly, we need c_0 through c_{N-1} for computing s. (See Exercise 3.1.) Since $c_0 = 0$, by distributing p_1 in (3.2.1.2), we see that

$$c_1 = p_1 \wedge g_1$$
$$c_2 = p_2 \wedge (g_2 \vee (p_1 \wedge g_1))$$

and in general

$$c_i = p_i \wedge (g_i \vee (p_{i-1} \wedge (g_{i-1} \vee \cdots \vee (p_1 \wedge g_1) \cdots))).$$

$$\left.\begin{array}{l} \\ \\ \\ \\ \end{array}\right\} \qquad (3.2.1.3)$$

Notice that the structure of the expression for c_i is quite similar to Horner's expression that arises in the evaluation of polynomials. In view of this similarity, it is hardly surprising that the method for computing c_i can be applied to the evaluation of polynomials. (Refer to Chapter 4 for details.)

The propagate bit p_i and the generate bit g_i, for $i = 1, \cdots, N$ can be computed in parallel in unit step using a linear array of N AND gates and N OR gates with *two* inputs. Once all the carry bits are known, s_i can be computed in just two steps. Thus if $T_A(N)$ is the time required to add two N-bit binary numbers and $T_C(N-1)$ is the time to compute the $N-1$ carry bits c_1 through c_{N-1} using (3.2.1.3), then

$$T_A(N) = T_C(N-1) + 3. \qquad (3.2.1.4)$$

In the following, we derive an upper bound on $T_C(N)$. To this end, a number of intermediate results are derived.

Let $r \geq 1$ and $q \geq 1$ be integers such that $N = rq$. Define, for $i = 1, \cdots, r$,

$$P_i = p_{iq} \wedge \cdots \wedge p_{(i-1)q+1}$$
$$D_i = P_r \wedge \cdots \wedge P_{i+1}, \quad \text{and } D_r = 1$$
$$E_i = p_{iq} \wedge (g_{iq} \vee \cdots \vee (p_{(i-1)q+1} \wedge g_{(i-1)q+1}) \cdots)$$

$$\left.\begin{array}{l} \\ \\ \\ \end{array}\right\} \qquad (3.2.1.5)$$

and

$$F_i = D_i \wedge E_i.$$

The following example illustrates these quantities. Let $N = 8$, $r = 4$, and $q = 2$. Then,

$$P_1 = p_2 \wedge p_1, \quad P_2 = p_4 \wedge p_3, \quad P_3 = p_6 \wedge p_5, \quad P_4 = p_8 \wedge p_7$$

$$D_1 = P_4 \wedge P_3 \wedge P_2, \quad D_2 = P_4 \wedge P_3, \quad D_3 = P_4, \quad D_4 = 1$$

$$E_1 = p_2 \wedge (g_2 \vee (p_1 \wedge g_1))$$

$$E_2 = p_4 \wedge (g_4 \vee (p_3 \wedge g_3))$$

$$E_3 = p_6 \wedge (g_6 \vee (p_5 \wedge g_5))$$

$$E_4 = p_8 \wedge (g_8 \vee (p_7 \wedge g_7))$$

and

$$F_1 = D_1 \wedge E_1$$

$$= [P_4 \wedge P_3 \wedge P_2] \wedge [p_2 \wedge (g_2 \vee (p_1 \wedge g_1))]$$

$$= (p_8 \wedge p_7 \wedge \cdots \; p_3 \wedge p_2) \wedge (g_2 \vee (p_1 \wedge g_1))$$

$$F_2 = D_2 \wedge E_2$$

$$= [P_4 \wedge P_3] \wedge [p_4 \wedge (g_4 \vee (p_3 \wedge g_3))]$$

$$= (p_8 \wedge p_7 \wedge \cdots \wedge p_4) \wedge (g_4 \vee (p_3 \wedge g_3))$$

$$F_3 = D_3 \wedge E_3$$

$$= (p_8 \wedge p_7 \wedge p_6) \wedge (g_6 \vee (p_5 \wedge g_5))$$

$$F_4 = p_8 \wedge (g_8 \vee (p_7 \wedge g_7)).$$

Clearly, by associativity, commutativity, and distributivity,

$$c_8 = F_4 \vee F_3 \vee F_2 \vee F_1.$$

We invite the reader to redo this example with $r = 2$ and $q = 4$.

The following lemma is a generalization of this illustration and provides a framework for the parallel evaluation of c_i, for $i = 1$ to N.

Lemma 3.2.1.1.

$$p_N \wedge (g_N \vee (p_{N-1} \wedge (g_{N-1} \vee \cdots \vee (p_1 \wedge g_1) \cdots)))$$

$$= F_r \vee F_{r-1} \vee \cdots \vee F_2 \vee F_1. \qquad (3.2.1.6)$$

Proof

Let $c_N = 1$. Then there exists a j, $1 \le j \le N$, such that $g_N = g_{N-1} = \cdots = g_{j+1} = 0$, $g_j = 1$, and $p_N = p_{N-1} = \cdots = p_j = 1$. Let k be such that

$kq \geq j > (k-1)q$. From the definition $D_k = 1$, and $E_k = 1$. Thus $F_k = 1$, and the right-hand side of (3.2.1.6) is true.

Let $F_k = 1$. Then $D_k = E_k = 1$. Since $E_k = 1$, there exists j such that $kq \geq j > (k-1)q$, $g_j = 1$, and $p_{kq} = p_{kq-1} = \cdots = p_j = 1$. Also $D_k = 1$ implies that $p_N = p_{N-1} = \cdots = p_{kq+1} = 1$, and hence $c_N = 1$.

The next two lemmas characterize $T_C(N)$. In the following, unless specified otherwise, all the logarithms are to the base 2.

Lemma 3.2.1.2. Let $N = rq$. Then

$$T_C(N) \leq 1 + \lceil \log r \rceil + \max\{T_C(q), \lceil \log(r-1) \rceil + \lceil \log q \rceil \}.$$

Proof

Referring to Fig. 3.2.1.1, in view of the similarity of the functional form of E_i and c_N, it follows that E_i for $i = 1, \cdots, r$ can be computed in parallel in $T_C(q)$ steps. Simultaneously, we can compute P_i's in parallel in $\lceil \log q \rceil$ steps followed by computing D_i's in parallel in $\lceil \log(r-1) \rceil$ steps. $F_i = D_i \wedge E_i$ can be computed in parallel in *unit* step, and $c_N = F_r \vee F_{r-1} \vee \cdots \vee F_1$ can then be computed in $\lceil \log r \rceil$ steps. Since F_i can be computed only after D_i and E_i, by combining these timings, the lemma follows.

Let $N = 2^n$, and a and k be non-negative integers. Define

$$T(n) = T_C(2^n) - n. \tag{3.2.1.7}$$

Lemma 3.2.1.3.

$$T(a + kT(a) + \frac{k(k-1)}{2}) \leq k + T(a). \tag{3.2.1.8}$$

Proof

Let $N = rq$, where $r = 2^{n_1}$, $q = 2^{n_2}$, and $n_1 + n_2 = n$. From Lemma 3.2.1.2, since

$$T_C(2^{n_1 + n_2}) \leq 1 + n_1 + \max\{T_C(2^{n_2}), n_1 + n_2\},$$

we get

$$T(n_1 + n_2) \leq 1 + \max\{T_C(2^{n_2}) - n_2, n_1\}$$

$$= 1 + \max\{T(n_2), n_1\}. \tag{3.2.1.9}$$

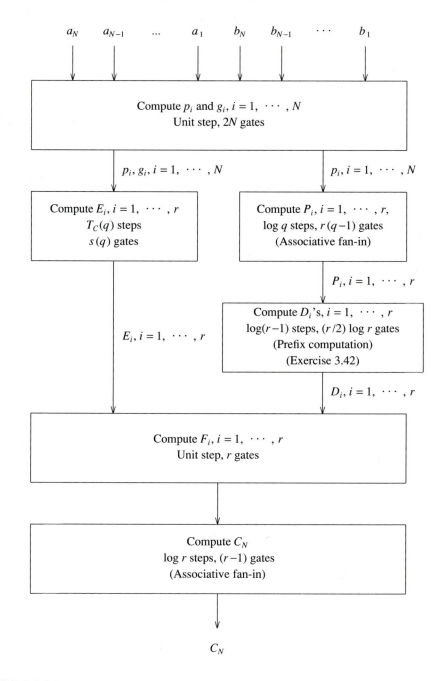

FIGURE 3.2.1.1
A parallel scheme for computing the carry.

We now prove (3.2.1.8) by induction. It is trivially true for $k = 0$. Let it be true for any k, and we now prove it for $k+1$. Let $n_1 = k + T(a)$, and $n_2 = a + kT(a) + \dfrac{k(k-1)}{2}$. Then, from (3.2.1.8),

$$T[\, a + (k+1)T(a) + \frac{k(k+1)}{2} \,]$$

$$\leq 1 + \max \left\{ T[\, a + kT(a) + \frac{k(k-1)}{2} \,], k + T(a) \right\}$$

$$\leq (1 + k) + T(a),$$

and the induction is complete.

We now state the main result of this section.

Theorem 3.2.1.4.

$$T_C(2^{k(k-1)/2}) \leq \frac{k(k+1)}{2}. \tag{3.2.1.10}$$

Proof
From (3.2.1.7), $T(0) = T_C(1) = 1$. Setting $a = 0$ in (3.2.1.8), we obtain

$$T(\frac{k(k+1)}{2}) \leq k + 1.$$

Again from (3.2.1.8),

$$T_C(2^{k(k+1)/2}) \leq (k + 1) + \frac{k(k+1)}{2} = \frac{(k+1)(k+2)}{2}.$$

By replacing k by $(k - 1)$, the theorem follows.

To extend this theorem for any N not a power of 2, find k such that

$$2^{k(k-1)/2} \geq N > 2^{(k-1)(k-2)/2}. \tag{3.2.1.11}$$

Then, since $k \approx (\lceil 2\log N \rceil)^{1/2}$,

$$T_C(N) \leq \frac{k(k+1)}{2}$$

$$= \lceil \log N \rceil + \tfrac{1}{2}(\lceil 2\log N \rceil)^{1/2} + L, \tag{3.2.1.12}$$

where L is a small positive constant. Combining this with a simple fan-in argument that c_N depends on $2N$ quantities, it follows that

TABLE 3.2.1.1

A Comparison of the Upper and Lower Bounds on $T_C(N)$

N	$\lceil \log 2N \rceil$	$\lceil \log N \rceil + \frac{1}{2}(\lceil 2\log N \rceil)^{1/2}$
4	3	3.0000
8	4	4.2247
16	5	5.4142
32	6	6.5811
64	7	7.7320
128	8	8.8708
256	9	10.0000
512	10	11.1213
1024	11	12.2360
2048	12	13.3452
4096	13	14.4495

$$\lceil \log 2N \rceil \le T_C(N) \le \lceil \log N \rceil + \frac{1}{2} (\lceil 2\log N \rceil)^{1/2} + L. \qquad (3.2.1.13)$$

Refer to Table 3.2.1.1 for a comparison of the upper and lower bounds on $T_C(N)$ for certain typical values of N. From this inequality, it follows that the above parallel algorithm is very nearly optimal. (See Exercises 3.4, 3.5, and 3.6.)

This circuit, while time-optimal, has $O(N \log N)$ size, that is, it requires $O(N \log N)$ logical elements. To our knowledge, there is no known circuit of linear size ($O(N)$ logical elements) to compute the sum of two N-bit integers in time steps satisfying (3.2.1.4) and (3.2.1.13). However, there are a number of competing designs to compute the sum in linear size but requiring a slightly larger number of steps. For example, the well-known Krapchenko [1970] adder has size $3N + 6 \times 2^n$ and depth $n + 7(2n)^{1/2} + 16$, where $n = \lceil \log N \rceil$. Another method is to consider the computation of c_i's using the formulation of the *prefix* problem. This approach is pursued in Exercises 3.42 through 3.44. A historical survey of the various results concerning the addition operation is given in Section 3.9. We invite the reader to compare the various circuits in terms of their size and depth.

3.3 PARALLEL MULTIPLICATION

Let

$$a = a_N \, a_{N-1} \, \cdots \, a_2 \, a_1$$

and

$$b = b_N \, b_{N-1} \, \cdots \, b_2 \, b_1$$

be two N bit integers. Let

$$s = a \times b = s_{2N} \, s_{2N-1} \, \cdots \, s_2 \, s_1.$$

3.3.1 Grade School Multiplication -- A Parallel Version

We first analyze the complexity of the parallel version of the grade school multiplication rule described in Fig. 3.3.1.1.

The following example illustrates this basic algorithm. Let $a = 1101$ and $b = 1101$. Then, referring to Fig. 3.3.1.1,

$$x_1 = 0001101$$

$$x_2 = 0000000$$

$$x_3 = 0110100$$

$$x_4 = 1101000.$$

Clearly,

$$x_1 + x_2 = 00001101$$

and

$$x_3 + x_4 = 10011100$$

can be computed in parallel (using the algorithm in Section 3.2) and the final result is obtained in one more addition:

$$s = (x_1 + x_2) + (x_3 + x_4) = 1\,0\,1\,0\,1\,0\,0\,1.$$

Referring to Fig. 3.3.1.1, step 1 can be completed in one unit of time using N^2 logical elements. The associative fan-in algorithm takes $\lceil \log_2 N \rceil$ stages of addition of $2N$-bit integers. Each of these latter additions can be accomplished in $O(\log N)$ steps using $O(N)$ logical elements. Thus, step 2 takes $O((\log N)^2)$ units of time using $O(N^2)$ elements. Combining these, we obtain the following theorem.

Theorem 3.3.1.1. The product of two N-bit integers can be obtained in parallel using the grade school multiplication rule using $O(N^2)$ logical elements in $O((\log N)^2)$ steps.

/* Given $a = a_N a_{N-1} \cdots a_2 a_1$ and $b = b_N b_{N-1} \cdots b_2 b_1$, find $s = a \times b = s_{2N} s_{2N-1} \cdots s_2 s_1$. */

Step 1:
Find the N partial products $x_1, x_2, \cdots, x_N$, each of which is $2N - 1$ bits long.

$x_1 = 0 \qquad 0 \qquad 0 \quad \cdots \quad 0 \qquad a_N \wedge b_1 \quad a_{N-1} \wedge b_1 \quad \cdots \quad a_2 \wedge b_1 \quad a_1 \wedge b_1$

$x_2 = 0 \qquad 0 \qquad 0 \quad \cdots \quad a_N \wedge b_2 \quad a_{N-1} \wedge b_2 \qquad \qquad \cdots \quad a_1 \wedge b_2 \qquad 0$

$x_N = a_N \wedge b_N \quad a_{N-1} \wedge b_N \quad \cdots \quad \cdots \quad \cdots \quad \cdots \quad a_1 \wedge b_N \quad \cdots \quad 0 \qquad 0$

where $a_i \wedge b_j$ is the logical AND operation.

Step 2:
Add the above set of N numbers $x_1, x_2, \cdots, x_N$ using the *associative* fan-in, where each addition is done using the $O(\log N)$ time parallel algorithm using $O(N)$ logical elements (for example, using the prefix circuit based carry look-ahead adder described in Exercise 3.42).

FIGURE 3.3.1.1
Grade school multiplication rule.

3.3.2 Ofman-Wallace Method

By cleverly exploiting the properties of the full adder, Ofman [1963] and Wallace [1964] independently developed a faster algorithm for multiplying two N-bit integers. We begin with the following basic result.

Lemma 3.3.2.1. Let x, y, z be three N-bit integers. There exist two $(N + 1)$-bit integers a and b such that

$$x + y + z = a + b, \qquad (3.3.2.1)$$

where a and b can be obtained from x, y, and z in parallel in three steps using at most $5N$ logical elements.

Proof

Let $a = a_{N+1} a_N a_{N-1} \cdots a_2 a_1$, and $b = b_{N+1} b_N b_{N-1} \cdots b_2 b_1$. Define $a_{N+1} = 0$ and $b_1 = 0$, and, for $1 \leq i \leq N$,

$$x_i + y_i + z_i = a_i + 2 \times b_{i+1}, \qquad (3.3.2.2)$$

where $+$ and $\times$ are the integer addition and multiplication respectively. Multiplying both sides of (3.3.2.2) by 2^{i-1} and adding, (3.3.2.1) follows. Further, it can be verified that a_i and b_{i+1} are obtained as the sum and the carry bit, respectively, of a full-adder circuit shown in Fig. 3.3.2.1 with x_i, y_i, and z_i as input. That is, for $1 \leq i \leq N$,

$$a_i = x_i \oplus y_i \oplus z_i$$

and

$$b_{i+1} = (x_i \wedge y_i) \vee (x_i \oplus y_i) \wedge z_i.$$

Since the computation of a_i and b_{i+1} can be done in parallel, it follows that a and b can be obtained in three steps using $5N$ logical elements.

As an example, let

$$x = 1011,$$

$$y = 0111,$$

$$z = 1101.$$

Then it can be easily verified that $a = 00001$ and $b = 11110$. Using Lemma 3.3.2.1, we can now modify step 2 of the grade school multiplication algorithm. Let $N_0 = N$ and $x_{0,1}, x_{0,2}, \cdots x_{0,N_0}$ be given, where $x_{0,i} = x_i$ is a $(2N - 1)$-bit integer obtained at the end of step 1 of the algorithm in Fig. 3.3.1.1. First form $\left\lfloor \dfrac{N_0}{3} \right\rfloor$ groups of three integers each. Applying Lemma 3.3.2.1 to each of these groups, we obtain $2 \left\lfloor \dfrac{N_0}{3} \right\rfloor$ integers $2N$ bits long. By adding a leading zero to the rest of $N_0 - 3 \left\lfloor \dfrac{N_0}{3} \right\rfloor$ integers, we now obtain

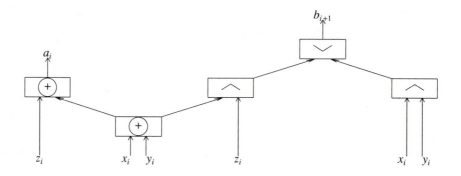

FIGURE 3.3.2.1
A circuit for computing a_i and b_{i+1} in Lemma 3.3.2.1.

$$N_1 = 2\left\lfloor\frac{N_0}{3}\right\rfloor + N_0 - 3\left\lfloor\frac{N_0}{3}\right\rfloor = N_0 - \left\lfloor\frac{N_0}{3}\right\rfloor$$

2N-bit integers. Now, form $\left\lfloor\dfrac{N_1}{3}\right\rfloor$ groups of three 2N-bit integers which by

applying Lemma 3.3.2.1 give rise to $2\left\lfloor\dfrac{N_1}{3}\right\rfloor$ integers $2N + 1$ bits long. Again, by

adding a leading zero to the rest of the $N_1 - 3\left\lfloor\dfrac{N_1}{3}\right\rfloor$ integers, we obtain

$$N_2 = 2\left\lfloor\frac{N_1}{3}\right\rfloor + N_1 - 3\left\lfloor\frac{N_1}{3}\right\rfloor = N_1 - \left\lfloor\frac{N_1}{3}\right\rfloor$$

$(2N + 1)$-bit integers. After i steps, clearly, we obtain

$$N_i = N_{i-1} - \left\lfloor\frac{N_{i-1}}{3}\right\rfloor \tag{3.3.2.3}$$

integers $2N - 1 + i$ bits long. Some typical values of the sequence N_i are given in
Table 3.3.2.1. Since for any positive integer n

$$\frac{n - 2}{3} \leq \left\lfloor\frac{n}{3}\right\rfloor \leq \frac{n}{3}, \tag{3.3.2.4}$$

from (3.3.2.3) we obtain that

$$\frac{2}{3}N_{i-1} \leq N_i \leq \frac{2}{3}N_{i-1} + \frac{2}{3}, \tag{3.3.2.5}$$

which on iterating becomes

TABLE 3.3.2.1

The Sequence $\{N_i\}$ for Different Initial Values of $N(=N_0)$

i	N_i								
0	3	4	5	6	7	8	16	32	64
1	2	3	4	4	5	6	11	22	43
2	1	2	3	3	4	4	8	15	29
3		1	2	2	3	3	6	10	20
4			1	1	2	2	4	7	14
5					1	1	3	5	10
6							2	4	7
7							1	3	5
8								2	4
9								1	3
10									2
11									1

$$(\frac{2}{3})^i N \le N_i \le (\frac{2}{3})^i N + 2. \qquad (3.3.2.6)$$

Let k be an integer such that $N_k = 2$ and $N_{k-1} = 3$. Combining this with inequality (3.3.2.6), it follows that

$$\frac{\log_2 (\frac{N}{2})}{\log_2 (\frac{3}{2})} \le k \le \frac{\log_2 N}{\log_2 (\frac{3}{2})} + 1. \qquad (3.3.2.7)$$

By Lemma 3.3.2.1, since each of the k stages takes three steps, it takes a total of $3k$ steps to reduce the N partial sums, each $2N - 1$ bits long, to two partial sums each $2N - 1 + k$ bits long. At the ith stage, to combine a group of three $(2N - 2 + i)$-bit integers to obtain two $(2N - 1 + i)$-bit integers, we need a total of $5(2N - 2 + i)$ logical elements. Since there are $\left\lfloor \dfrac{N_{i-1}}{3} \right\rfloor$ such groups, the total number of logical elements needed in all k stages is bounded by

$$\sum_{i=1}^{k} 5(2N - 2 + i) \left\lfloor \frac{N_{i-1}}{3} \right\rfloor \le \sum_{i=1}^{k} \frac{5}{3} (2N - 2 + i)\{(\frac{2}{3})^{i-1} N + 2\}$$

$$\le \frac{5}{3}(2N - 2 + k)\sum_{i=1}^{k}\{(\frac{2}{3})^{i-1} N + 2\}$$

$$\le \frac{5}{3}(2N - 2 + k)(3N + 2k) = O(N^2).$$

Let $M = 2N - 1 + k$. Now, in the last stage, the two M-bit partial sums are added using the parallel algorithm in Section 3.2.1 to obtain the product $s = a \times b$ in at most $\frac{m(m+1)}{2} + 3$ steps and using $O(M \log M)$ logical elements, where

$$2^{(m-1)(m-2)/2} \le M \le 2^{m(m-1)/2}. \tag{3.3.2.8}$$

Combining all these, the following theorem is immediate.

Theorem 3.3.2.2. The product of two N-bit integers can be obtained in

$$3k + \frac{m(m+1)}{2} + 3 = O(\log N) \tag{3.3.2.9}$$

steps using $O(N^2)$ logical elements, where k and m are defined in (3.3.2.7) and (3.3.2.8), respectively.

Proof
From the upper inequality in (3.3.2.8), it follows that

$$m \approx \frac{1}{2} + \sqrt{2 \log M},$$

and hence

$$\frac{m(m+1)}{2} \approx \log M + \sqrt{2 \log M} + O(1). \tag{3.3.2.10}$$

But from (3.3.2.7)

$$M = 2N - 1 + k$$

$$\le 2N + 1.71 \log_2 N$$

$$< 2.5 N \quad \text{for all } N \ge 2.$$

Thus

$$\log M \le \log N + O(1). \tag{3.3.2.11}$$

Combining (3.3.2.7), (3.3.2.9), and (3.3.2.10), the theorem follows.

Thus, with respect to the time required, for large N, Theorem 3.3.2.2 is an improvement over Theorem 3.3.1.1 (see Exercise 3.7).

3.3.3 Karatsuba-Ofman Algorithm

We now define a class of algorithms based on the divide-and-conquer strategy due to Karatsuba and Ofman [1963] to multiply two N-bit integers, where $N = 2^n$. First, rewrite a and b as

$$a = A_1 \times 2^{N/2} + A_0$$

$$b = B_1 \times 2^{N/2} + B_0, \qquad (3.3.3.1)$$

where A_i and B_i, $i = 0, 1$, are $\dfrac{N}{2}$-bit integers, A_0 is the remainder, and A_1 is the quotient when a is divided by $2^{N/2}$. B_0 and B_1 have similar interpretations. Define

$$r_0 = A_0 \times B_0$$
$$r_1 = (A_1 + A_0) \times (B_1 + B_0) \qquad (3.3.3.2)$$
$$r_2 = (A_1 \times B_1).$$

Then

$$a \times b = r_2 \times 2^N + (r_1 - r_2 - r_0)\, 2^{N/2} + r_0. \qquad (3.3.3.3)$$

Thus the product is obtained by performing *three* multiplications of $\dfrac{N}{2}$-bit integers (the recursive step) and a total of six additions/subtractions (of at most $2N$-bit integers). Since multiplication by 2^N and $2^{N/2}$ involves only shifting, it is assumed that these operations are performed instantaneously, requiring no time.

Let $T(N)$ be the parallel time required to perform the multiplication of a and b by this method. Notice that the multiplications in r_0, r_1, and r_2 can be performed in parallel. Further, each of the additions/subtractions in (3.3.3.2) and (3.3.3.3) can be done in parallel (using the methods of Section 3.2.1) in $O(\log N)$ steps. Combining these, we obtain

$$T(N) = T(\frac{N}{2}) + c_1 \log N, \qquad (3.3.3.4)$$

where c_1 depends on the total number of additions and the number of bits in the addends. Since $T(1) = 1$, solving (3.3.3.4), we obtain (see Exercise 3.8)

$$T(N) = O((\log N)^2). \qquad (3.3.3.5)$$

The Karatsuba-Ofman multiplication algorithm is very elegant and is naturally recursive but requires $O((\log N)^2)$ steps, which, by comparison with the grade school method modified by the Ofman-Wallace tree (Lemma 3.3.2.1 and Theorem 3.3.2.2), is quite excessive. In search of an idea to speed up this method, first refer to the recurrence (3.3.3.4). It is obvious that one direct way to reduce the overall complexity is to reduce the additive term $c_1 \log N$ in (3.3.3.4) to a constant. This cannot be done unless the time to add the integers is reduced to a constant. In other words, we need to develop a very low overhead technique for addition quite similar to the Ofman-Wallace tree of Section 3.2.1. Indeed, such a technique was developed by Mehlhorn and Preparata [1983], which is based on a clever combination of a redundant radix-4 (RR-4) representation of numbers in a modulo system for a properly chosen modulus.

3.3.4 Mehlhorn-Preparata Algorithm

Let N be an even integer, $m = 2^N + 1$, and $t = \dfrac{N}{2} + 1$. Since the arithmetic in mod m is slightly involved, we begin by collecting a number of useful facts. The residues in this modulus may be represented using N bits with the only exception that $2^N \equiv -1 \pmod{m}$, which is denoted by a special symbol, say $\bar{1}$. The computations are quite straight forward, if one or both of the operands take the value 2^N. Let $a = a_N\, a_{N-1}\, a_{N-2} \cdots a_2\, a_1$ and $b = b_N\, b_{N-1}\, b_{N-2} \cdots b_2\, b_1$ be two integers in the range $0 \le a, b < 2^N$. Let

$$s \equiv (a + b) \pmod{m},$$

where

$$s = s_N\, s_{N-1}\, s_{N-2} \cdots s_2\, s_1.$$

In computing s, let c_i, for $i = 0$ to N, be the carry bit at the position i, where $c_0 = 0$. The sum s is obtained in the usual way, except when $c_N = 1$, in which case s is to be corrected by subtracting 1 from the rightmost bit. Subtraction is quite similar to addition and is left as an exercise. (See Exercise 3.5.) Multiplication by 2^k for $0 \le k < N$ is done as follows:

$$(a_N\, a_{N-1}\, a_{N-2} \cdots a_2\, a_1) \times 2^k = ((a_{N-k}\, a_{N-k-1} \cdots a_1 0\, 0 \cdots 0)$$

$$- (0\, 0 \cdots 0\, a_N a_{N-1} \cdots a_{N-k+1})) \pmod{m}$$

When $k = N$,

$$a \times 2^N \equiv -a \pmod{m} \equiv (2^N + 1 - a) \pmod{m}.$$

The product of two integers a and b, namely, $a \times b \bmod (2^N + 1)$, is more involved and is considered in detail in Section 3.6.3 (Schonhage and Strassen method [1971]).

    We now describe the redundant radix-4 (RR-4) representation. In RR-4, the individual digits belong to the set $S = \{-3, -2, -1, 0, 1, 2, 3\}$. Let R denote the closed interval $R = [-4^t + 1, 4^t - 1]$. Let $0 \le a \le m - 1$, where

$$a = a_{t-1} \cdots a_1\, a_0,$$

where $a = \displaystyle\sum_{i=0}^{t-1} a_i\, 4^i$, $a_i \in S$ and $a \in R$. Clearly, $4m > 4^t - 1$. The process of converting an integer b to an integer $a \in R$ such that $a \equiv b \pmod{m}$ is called the RR-4 *normalization* process.

First is the *conversion* process from binary to the RR-4 representation. Let $0 \le a < m$ be represented in two's complement form using $N + 2$ bits, where

$$a = x_{N+2} \, x_{N+1} \, x_N \, \cdots \, x_3 \, x_2 \, x_1,$$

x_{N+2}, the sign bit, is zero, and $x_i \in \{0, 1\}$ for $1 \le i \le N + 1$. The conversion to RR-4 is very simple and is accomplished by inserting a zero bit to the left of x_{2i} for $i = 1$ to $\dfrac{N}{2} + 1$. Thus, comparing a in binary and RR-4, we obtain that, for $i = 0$ to $t - 1$,

$$a_i = 0 \, x_{2i+2} \, x_{2i+1}.$$

This conversion can be accomplished in parallel in constant time.

As an example, let $N = 4$, $t = 3$, and $a = 011011$ in binary. Then a is transformed into $(001)(010)(011)$, which is 123 in RR-4. Notice $a = 27$ in either case. Likewise, when $N = 8$, $t = 5$, and $b = 0110110011$, we obtain $b = (001)(010)(011)(000)(011) = 12303$ in RR-4. The value of b is 433.

We now describe the addition and subtraction of integers mod m using the RR-4 representation. Since $a = \sum\limits_{i=0}^{t-1} a_i \, 4^i$ implies $-a = \sum\limits_{i=0}^{t-1} (-a_i) \, 4^i$, we readily see that subtraction reduces to addition. Let $0 \le a, \, b < m$, with

$$a = \sum_{i=0}^{t-1} a_i \, 4^i$$

and

$$b = \sum_{i=0}^{t-1} b_i \, 4^i.$$

Let

$$
\begin{array}{cccccccc}
 & a_{t-1} & a_{t-2} & a_{t-3} & \cdots & a_2 & a_1 & a_0 \\
+ & b_{t-1} & b_{t-2} & b_{t-3} & \cdots & b_2 & b_1 & b_0 \\
\hline
 & s'_{t-1} & s'_{t-2} & s'_{t-3} & \cdots & s'_2 & s'_1 & s'_0 \\
c_t & c_{t-1} & c_{t-2} & & \cdots & c_3 & c_2 & c_1 & c_0 = 0 \\
\hline
\end{array}
$$

where $(s'_i, \, c_{i+1})$ is determined using the relation

$$s'_i + 4 \, c_{i+1} = a_i + b_i,$$

where $s'_i \in \{-2, -1, 0, 1, 2\}$ and $c_{i+1} \in \{-1, 0, 1\}$. The basic rule for addition is given in Table 3.3.4.1.

From Table 3.3.4.1, it is clear that the trick is in representing $a_i + b_i = 3$ with $s'_i = -1$ and $c_{i+1} = 1$, instead of $s'_i = 3$ and $c_{i+1} = 0$. In this way, we can pretty much localize and absorb the carry without propagating it to the next higher order position. To find the actual sum s we need to distinguish two cases.

TABLE 3.3.4.1

$a_i + b_i$	s_i'	c_{i+1}
-6	-2	-1
-5	-1	-1
-4	0	-1
-3	1	-1
-2	-2	0
-1	-1	0
0	0	0
1	1	0
2	2	0
3	-1	1
4	0	1
5	1	1
6	2	1

Case 1. $c_t = 0$. In this case,

$$s_i = s_i' + c_i \qquad \text{for } i = 0 \text{ to } t - 1,$$

where $-3 \le s_i \le 3$. It is readily seen that addition in this case takes only a constant time.

Case 2. $c_t \ne 0$. In this case, the result does not belong to the range R and a correction is needed. Thus $s_i = s_i' + c_i$ for $i = 0$ to $t - 1$, and

$$(a + b) \ (\text{mod } m) = (\sum_{i=0}^{t-1} s_i \ 4^i + c_t \ 4^t \ (\text{mod } m)) \ (\text{mod } m)$$

$$= (\sum_{i=0}^{t-1} s_i \ 4^i - 4 \ c_t) \ (\text{mod } m),$$

since $4^t = 2^{2t} = 2^{N+2} \equiv -4 \ (\text{mod } m)$.

Notice that $c_t \ 4^t$ has $000 \cdots 0(-c_t)0$ as its RR-4 representation, which needs to be added to $s = s_{t-1} s_{t-2} \cdots s_2 s_1 s_0$ to obtain the final sum. Many subcases arise. Recall that $-3 \le s_1 \le 3$ and $c_t = 1$ or -1. Thus, either $-3 \le s_1 - c_t \le 3$ or $s_1 = 3$, $c_t = -1$ or $s_1 = -3$, and $c_t = +1$. In the first case, $s_1 \ c_t \ne -3$, and in the latter two cases $s_1 \ c_t = -3$.

Case 2a. Let $s_1 \ c_t \ne -3$. In this case, the digit s_1 is replaced by $s_1^* = s_1 - c_t$, and all the other digits $s_j \ (j \ne 1)$ in s remain unchanged.

Case 2b. Let $s_1 c_t = -3$. In this case $|s_1 - c_t| = 4$ and hence the method of case 2a will not work (since in RR-4 the digits need to belong to the set S). In this case, compute $(s + c) \pmod m$, where $s = s_{t-1} s_{t-2} \cdots s_1 s_0$, and $c = 000 \cdots 0(-c_t)0$, by the same method used to find $(a + b) \pmod m$ to begin with. Using Table 3.3.4.1, the final sum $s = \bar{s}_{t-1} \bar{s}_{t-2} \cdots \bar{s}_3 \bar{s}_2 \bar{s}_1 \bar{s}_0$ is such that $\bar{s}_i = s_i$ for $i \neq 1$ and $\bar{s}_1 = -c_t$. Thus, case 2 takes constant time as well.

The following examples illustrate. Let $N = 4$, $t = 3$ and $m = 17$. Let $a = 6 = (012)_{RR-4}$ and $b = 37 = (211)_{RR-4}$. Then, $(a + b) \equiv 9 \pmod{17}$.

i	2	1	0	
a_i	0	1	2	
b_i	2	1	1	
s'_i	2	2	-1	
c_{i+1}	0	0	1	0
s_i	2	3	-1	

This corresponds to case 1, and $s = (23(-1))_{RR-4} = 43 \equiv 9 \pmod{17}$.

As a second example, let $a = 27 \equiv (123)_{RR-4}$ and $b = 45 = (231)_{RR-4}$. $(a + b) \pmod m = 4$.

i	2	1	0	
a_i	1	2	3	
b_i	2	3	1	
s'_i	-1	1	0	
c_{i+1}	1	1	1	0
s_i	0	2	0	

This corresponds to case 2a, and the corrected sum is $(010)_{RR-4} = 4$.

The third example illustrates case 2b. Let $a = 10 = (1(-1)(-2))_{RR-4}$ and $b = 27 = (2(-1)(-1))_{RR-4}$. $(a + b) \pmod m = 3$.

i	2	1	0	
a_i	1	-1	-2	
b_i	2	-1	-1	
s'_i	-1	-2	1	
c_{i+1}	1	0	-1	0
s_i	-1	-3	1	

The corrected sum is obtained by adding $((-1)(-3)(1))_{RR-4}$ and $(0(-1)0)_{RR-4}$. The sum is $((-2)01)_{RR-4} = -31 \equiv 3 \pmod{17}$.

We now turn to multiplication by 4^k for some integer k. Let $a = \sum_{i=0}^{t-1} a_i 4^i$. Then, since $4^t \equiv -4 \pmod m$,

$$a\, 4^k \pmod{m} = (a_{t-1}\, 4^{t+k-1} + \cdots + a_{t-k+1}\, 4^{t+1} + a_{t-k}\, 4^t$$

$$+ \cdots + a_1 4^{k+1} + a_0 4^k) \pmod{m}$$

$$= (\sum_{j=t}^{t+k-1} a_{j-k}\, 4^j \pmod{m} + \sum_{j=k}^{t-1} a_{j-k}\, 4^j) \pmod{m}$$

$$= (\sum_{i=0}^{k-1} a_{t-k+i}\, (-4)\, 4^i + \sum_{j=k}^{t-1} a_{j-k}\, 4^j) \pmod{m}.$$

Thus, $a4^k \pmod{m}$ is obtained by adding $(a_{t-k-1}\, a_{t-k-2} \cdots a_1\, a_0 00 \cdots 0)$ and $(00 \cdots 0(-a_{t-1})(-a_{t-2}) \cdots (-a_{t-k})0)$. This can be accomplished in the following way:

(1)   First left shift cyclically the RR-4 digits of a by k places and create two numbers

$$A_1 = (a_{t-k-1}\, a_{t-k-2} \cdots a_1\, a_0\, 000 \cdots 0)$$

and

$$A_2 = (000 \cdots 0\, a_{t-1}\, a_{t-2} \cdots a_{t-k}).$$

(2)   Change the sign of non-zero digits in A_2 and circular left shift A_2 by one place to obtain

$$A_3 = (00 \cdots 0\, (-a_{t-1})\, (-a_{t-2}) \cdots (-a_{t-k})\, 0).$$

(3)   Then $a\, 4^k \pmod{m} = (A_1 + A_3) \pmod{m}$, which can be computed by the method described above.

Since sign changes and addition can be performed in constant time, the overall time to multiply by 4^k is decided by the time required to perform the shift operation.
The following example illustrates. Let $N = 8$, $t = 5$, and $m = 257$. Let

$$a = 475 = (13123)_{RR\text{-}4} \text{ and } 475 \times 4^2 = 7600 \equiv 147 \pmod{257}.$$

In multiplying a by 4^2, we obtain $A_1 = (12300)_{RR\text{-}4}$, and $A_3 = (00(-1)(-3)0)_{RR\text{-}4}$. Adding A_1 and A_3, we find the sum to be $(12110)_{RR\text{-}4} = 404 \equiv 147 \pmod{257}$.
The division by 4^k in RR-4 representation is quite similar to the multiplication 4^k. For, $4^k = 2^q$, where $q = 2k$ and

$$4^{-k} \pmod{m} \equiv 2^{-q} \pmod{m} \equiv (2^N + 1 - 2^{N-q}) \pmod{m} \equiv -2^{N-q} \pmod{m}.$$

In other words, division by 4^k is the same as multiplication by $-2^{N-q} = -4^{(N/2-k)}$, where $k \le \dfrac{N}{2}$. We encourage the reader to develop an algorithm for division by 4^k based on elementary operations such as shifting, sign change, and addition (Exercise 3.35).
We now turn to multiplying $a = \sum_{i=0}^{t-1} a_i\, 4^i$ and $b = \sum_{i=0}^{t-1} b_i\, 4^i$. Let $r = a \times b$,

where

$$r = \sum_{i=0}^{2t-2} r_i \, 4^i$$

can be obtained by any one of the known multiplication algorithms. Then using the fact that $4^t \equiv -4 \pmod{m}$, we can readily RR-4 normalize r by techniques similar to those used in multiplying a number by a power of 4 (see Exercise 3.35).

The conversion from RR-4 to binary is quite an interesting process. Let $a = \sum_{i=0}^{t-1} a_i \, 4^i$, where some of the a_i's may be positive and others may be negative. As an example, $a = (12(-1))_{RR-4}$. Now create two new RR-4 numbers a^+ and a^- from a as follows: a^+ is obtained from a by replacing all of its negative digits with zero (called the positive part of a) and a^- is obtained from a by replacing all of its positive digits with zero (called the negative part of a). In the above example, $a^+ = 120$ and $a^- = 001$. Now convert a^+ and a^- digit by digit into the binary form. That is, $a^+ = 011000$ and $a^- = 000001$. Compute $a^* = a^+ - a^-$ by performing subtraction in binary. This subtraction can be readily accomplished in $O(\log N)$ steps by adding, say, the two's complement of a^- to a^+ (Section 3.2.1). Notice that a^* still belongs to R (why ?). Since $4m > 4^t - 1$, $a^* \pmod{m}$ can be computed by performing at most four repeated additions/subtractions of m. Continuing the above example, a^- in the two's complement is 111111, and we get $a^* = 010111$.

By combining these with the Karatsuba-Ofman algorithm, Mehlhorn and Preparata [1983] obtained the following result.

Theorem 3.3.4.1. In the RR-4 representation, two N-bit integers can be multiplied using the Karatsuba-Ofman multiplication algorithm in $O(\log N)$ steps with $O(N^{1.59})$ logical elements.

Proof
First obtain the RR-4 representation for the two N-bit integers in constant time. Then, perform the Karatsuba-Ofman algorithm on the resulting integers. During each recursive step, this latter algorithm involves only three types of operations: addition, subtraction, and multiplication by a power of 2. From the above development, it is clear that addition/subtraction in RR-4 can be done in constant time using at most $O(N)$ logical elements.

Let a be an RR-4 integer. To multiply a by 2^r, we need to consider two cases. Let r be even. Then $a \times 2^r = a \times 4^{r/2}$. If r is odd, then $a \times 2^r = a \times 2 \times 4^{\lfloor r/2 \rfloor}$. Clearly, multiplication by a power of 4 takes constant time and multiplication by 2 is the same as addition, since $2b = b + b$, which also takes constant time.

In other words, all the operations during each phase of the recursive call can be completed in constant time. Since there are only $\log N$ phases, it requires $O(\log N)$ steps to multiply two integers.

The conversion from RR-4 to binary requires $O(\log N)$ steps and $O(N)$ logical elements.

Finally, let $s(N)$ be the total number of logical elements needed by this algorithm. Clearly,

$$s(N) = 3s\left(\frac{N}{2}\right) + O(N),$$

from which it follows that $s(N) = O(N^{1.59})$. Since the conversion from RR-4 to binary takes only $O(N)$ logical elements, the theorem follows.

3.3.5 Multiplication Using Convolution

The Karatsuba-Ofman type analysis can be readily extended by splitting a and b into t (≥ 2) segments, where each segment consists of m bits and $N = tm$. Thus

$$\left.\begin{aligned} a &= A_{t-1}2^{(t-1)m} + A_{t-2}2^{(t-2)m} + \cdots + A_1 2^m + A_0, \\[2mm] b &= B_{t-1}2^{(t-1)m} + B_{t-2}2^{(t-2)m} + \cdots + B_1 2^m + B_0, \end{aligned}\right\} \qquad (3.3.5.1)$$

where A_j, $0 \leq j \leq t-1$, is an m-bit integer corresponding to the $((j-1)m+1)^{th}$ through $(jm)^{th}$ bits of a, and likewise for B_j's.

Define polynomials $p(x)$, $q(x)$, and $r(x)$, as follows:

$$p(x) = A_{t-1}x^{t-1} + A_{t-2}x^{t-2} + \cdots + A_2 x^2 + A_1 x + A_0,$$

$$q(x) = B_{t-1}x^{t-1} + B_{t-2}x^{t-2} + \cdots + B_2 x^2 + B_1 x + B_0,$$

and

$$r(x) = r_{2t-1}x^{2t-1} + r_{2t-2}x^{2t-2} + \cdots + r_2 x^2 + r_1 x + r_0.$$

Clearly,

$$a = p(2^m), \qquad b = q(2^m),$$

and

$$a \times b = r(2^m).$$

In other words, the key to finding the product $a \times b$ is to find the polynomial $r(x)$. Multiplying $p(x)$ and $q(x)$ (using distributivity) and comparing the product with $r(x)$, we obtain

$$r_0 = A_0 B_0$$

$$r_1 = A_0 B_1 + A_1 B_0$$

$$r_2 = A_0 B_2 + A_1 B_1 + A_2 B_0$$

$$\vdots$$

$$r_{t-1} = A_0 B_{t-1} + A_1 B_{t-2} + \cdots + A_{t-1} B_0$$

$$r_t = A_1 B_{t-1} + A_2 B_{t-2} + \cdots + A_{t-1} B_1$$

$$\vdots$$

$$r_{2t-2} = A_{t-1} B_{t-1}$$

and

$$r_{2t-1} = 0.$$

Define two column vectors $A = (A_0, A_1, A_2, \cdots, A_{t-1})^t$ and $B = (B_0, B_1, B_2, \cdots, B_{t-1})^t$. The above method of finding $r = (r_0, r_1, r_2, \cdots, r_{2t-1})^t$ is called the *convolution* of A and B. Direct computation of r_i's involves t^2 multiplication of m-bit integers. Since $N = tm$, this method of computing the product is *not* competitive in time. The key to reducing the computation time is to evaluate the convolution efficiently. It has been known for a long time that the convolution operation can be effectively computed using the *Fourier transform*. The basic idea is to evaluate $p(x)$ and $q(x)$ at distinct points, find the pointwise product of $p(x)$ and $q(x)$, and then interpolate or reconstruct the product polynomial $r(x)$. By properly choosing the points at which $p(.)$ and $q(.)$ are evaluated, we can develop a computationally efficient technique for computing the Fourier transform.

In Sections 3.4 and 3.5, we develop such an efficient technique for computing Fourier transforms and convolution. In Section 3.6, we then present a novel algorithm to multiply two integers.

3.4 FAST FOURIER TRANSFORM -- COMPLEX ARITHMETIC

The Fourier transform technique has been known for a long time and is very useful in solving a variety of engineering and scientific problems. In this section, we describe a version of the Fourier transform called the *discrete Fourier transform* (DFT). A fast method for computing the DFT called the *fast Fourier transform* (FFT), is then presented. We begin by reviewing many useful properties of the Nth root of unity which play a crucial role in this analysis.

3.4.1 Properties of the Nth Root of Unity

Let $N \geq 2$. The N distinct roots of the equation

$$x^N - 1 = 0 \qquad (3.4.1.1)$$

are called the N roots of unity. Define a complex number

$$\omega = e^{i2\pi/N} = \cos \frac{2\pi}{N} + i \sin \frac{2\pi}{N}, \tag{3.4.1.2}$$

where $i = \sqrt{-1}$. (In this section the lowercase i will be exclusively used to denote this unit imaginary number.) Clearly,

$$\omega \neq 1, \tag{3.4.1.3}$$

and is an Nth root of unity, because

$$\omega^N = e^{i2\pi/NN} = \cos 2\pi + i \sin 2\pi = 1. \tag{3.4.1.4}$$

Thus, $1, \omega, \omega^2, \cdots, \omega^{N-1}$ constitute the N *distinct* roots of unity, where

$$\omega^k = e^{i2\pi k/N} = \cos \frac{2\pi k}{N} + i \sin \frac{2\pi k}{N}. \tag{3.4.1.5}$$

For, if $0 \leq k_1,\ k_2 \leq N-1$, since

$$\omega^{k_1} = \omega^{k_2} \text{ only if } k_1 = k_2,$$

it follows that $\omega^0, \omega^1, \omega^2, \cdots, \omega^{N-1}$ are all distinct. Also, if $0 \leq k \leq N-1$, then from (3.4.1.4)

$$(\omega^k)^N = (\omega^N)^k = 1, \tag{3.4.1.6}$$

and hence ω^k is also an Nth root of unity. Further, from (3.4.1.4), it follows that

$$\sum_{k=0}^{N-1} \omega^k = \frac{\omega^N - 1}{\omega - 1} = \frac{1-1}{\omega - 1} = 0. \tag{3.4.1.7}$$

Let N be even. Then

$$\left. \begin{array}{c} \omega^{\frac{N}{2}} = e^{i\pi} = -1 \\ \\ \text{and} \\ \\ \omega^{\frac{N}{2}+j} = -\omega^j, \end{array} \right\} \tag{3.4.1.8}$$

that is, the pair of roots ω^j and $\omega^{N/2+j} = -\omega^j$, for $j = 1$ to $\frac{N}{2}$ are *symmetrically* located with respect to the origin. Figure 3.4.1.1 illustrates the N roots of unity for $N = 2, 3, 4$, and 8.

Given any integer m, since it can be uniquely expressed as

$$m = qN + r \quad \text{and} \quad 0 \leq r \leq N-1, \tag{3.4.1.9}$$

it follows that

$$\omega^m = \omega^{qN+r} = (\omega^N)^q \omega^r = 1^q \omega^r = \omega^r, \tag{3.4.1.10}$$

that is,

$$\omega^m = \omega^{m(\text{mod } N)}. \tag{3.4.1.11}$$

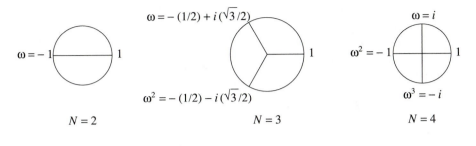

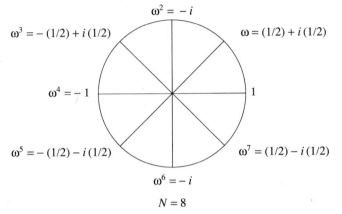

FIGURE 3.4.1.1.
Examples of the N roots of unity.

Thus, given any $0 \not\equiv m \pmod{N}$, that is, m is not a multiple of N, then it follows that

$$\sum_{j=0}^{N-1} (\omega^m)^j = 0. \tag{3.4.1.12}$$

To verify this, let $0 \neq r \equiv m \pmod{N}$. Then,

$$\sum_{j=0}^{N-1} (\omega^m)^j = \sum_{j=0}^{N-1} (\omega^r)^j = \frac{(\omega^N)^r - 1}{\omega^r - 1} = 0, \tag{3.4.1.13}$$

from which (3.4.1.12) follows.

On the other hand, if m is a multiple of N, then

$$\sum_{j=0}^{N-1} (\omega^m)^j = \sum_{j=0}^{N-1} (\omega^{qN})^j = \sum_{j=0}^{N-1} 1 = N. \tag{3.4.1.14}$$

Let α be an Nth root of unity. If α is such that $\alpha^0, \alpha^1, \alpha^2, \cdots, \alpha^{N-1}$ are distinct, and satisfy (3.4.1.11) and (3.4.1.14), then α is called a *principal N^{th}* root of unity, and N is called the *order* of α. Since the powers of α generate the set of all N distinct roots of unity, a principal root is also called a *generator* of this set. Clearly, for any $N > 1$, $\alpha = 1$ is *not* a principal N^{th} root of unity, and for any N, $\omega = e^{i2\pi/N}$ is always a principal N^{th} root of unity. We now characterize the set of all principal N^{th} roots of unity. To this end, let GCD (a, b) denote the greatest common divisor of the integers a and b. If GCD $(a, b) = 1$, then a and b are said to be *relatively prime*. Let k be such that GCD$(k, N) = 1$. Since ω is a principal N^{th} root of unity, ω^k is also a principal N^{th} root of unity. For it is well known that (see Exercises 3.10 and 3.15),

$$| \{pr \ (\text{mod } N) \mid 0 \le r \le N - 1\}| = N,$$

if and only if GCD $(p, N) = 1$. As an example, let $N = 8$. If $p = 2$, then

$$|\{2r \ (\text{mod } 8) \mid 0 \le r \le 7\}| = |\{0, 2, 4, 6\}| = 4,$$

and for $p = 3$,

$$|\{3r \ (\text{mod } 8) \mid 0 \le r \le 7\}| = 8.$$

From this it follows that ω^k is a principal N^{th} root of unity.

Given any $N \ge 2$, let $\Phi(N)$ denote the number of positive integers less than N and relatively prime to N. $\Phi(N)$ is called the *Euler's* function whose typical values are given in Table 3.4.1.1. From the above analysis, it is clear that for any N, there are $\Phi(N)$ principal roots of unity. Thus, for $N = 2$, $\omega = -1$ is the only principal root. For $N = 3$, ω and ω^2 are the only two principal roots, and for $N = 4$, ω and ω^3 are the only principal roots.

TABLE 3.4.1.1

N	2	3	4	5	6	7	8	9	10
$\Phi(N)$	1	2	2	4	2	6	4	6	4

The $N \times N$ matrices

$$\mathbf{F} = [\mathbf{F}_{kj}] = [\omega^{kj}] \tag{3.4.1.15}$$

and

$$\overline{\mathbf{F}} = [\overline{\mathbf{F}}_{kj}] = [\omega^{-kj}], \tag{3.4.1.16}$$

for $0 \le k, j \le N - 1$, play a crucial role in the sequel. For $N = 4$, since $\omega = i = \sqrt{-1}$,

$$\mathbf{F} = \begin{bmatrix} 1 & 1 & 1 & 1 \\ 1 & i & -1 & -i \\ 1 & -1 & 1 & -1 \\ 1 & -i & -1 & i \end{bmatrix} \tag{3.4.1.17}$$

and

$$\bar{\mathbf{F}} = \begin{bmatrix} 1 & 1 & 1 & 1 \\ 1 & -i & -1 & i \\ 1 & -1 & 1 & -1 \\ 1 & i & -1 & -i \end{bmatrix}.$$ (3.4.1.18)

It can be verified that

$$\mathbf{F}\,\bar{\mathbf{F}} = \bar{\mathbf{F}}\,\mathbf{F} = \begin{bmatrix} 4 & 0 & 0 & 0 \\ 0 & 4 & 0 & 0 \\ 0 & 0 & 4 & 0 \\ 0 & 0 & 0 & 4 \end{bmatrix}.$$

The following lemma generalizes this observation.

Lemma 3.4.1.1.

$$\mathbf{F}^{-1} = \frac{1}{N}\,\bar{\mathbf{F}}$$ (3.4.1.19)

Proof
Let

$$\mathbf{F}\,\mathbf{F}^{-1} = \frac{1}{N}\mathbf{F}\,\bar{\mathbf{F}} = I = [I_{kp}],$$

where

$$I_{kp} = \frac{1}{N}\sum_{j=0}^{N-1}\omega^{kj}\,\omega^{-jp} = \frac{1}{N}\sum_{j=0}^{N-1}\omega^{(k-p)j}.$$

If $k = p$, then $I_{kk} = 1$ for all $0 \le k \le N-1$. Let $m = k - p$. Since $0 \le k, p \le N-1$, for $k \ne p$, m is *not* a multiple of N, and by (3.4.1.11)

$$I_{kp} = \frac{1}{N}\sum_{j=0}^{N-1}\omega^{mj} = 0,$$

that is, I is the *identity* matrix and the lemma follows.

Computing $\mathbf{F}^{-1}$ from $\mathbf{F}$, however, is trivial as shown in the following lemma.

Lemma 3.4.1.2. Let matrix $\mathbf{F}$ be given. Then the first row of $\bar{\mathbf{F}}$ is the same as the first row of $\mathbf{F}$. The $(N-k)^{th}$ row of $\bar{\mathbf{F}}$ is the same as the kth row of $\mathbf{F}$ for $1 \le k \le N-1$.

Proof

From the definition it follows that the first rows of $\mathbf{F}$ and $\overline{\mathbf{F}}$ are the same. A typical element of the kth row of $\overline{\mathbf{F}}$ is

$$\omega^{-kj} \quad \text{for} \quad j = 0, 1, 2, \cdots, N - 1.$$

Since $\omega^{N-k} = \omega^{-k}$, it follows that

$$\omega^{-kj} = \omega^{(N-k)j} \quad \text{for} \quad j = 0, 1, 2, \cdots, N - 1.$$

Hence the lemma.

Stated in other words, $\mathbf{F}^{-1}$ is obtained by suitably permuting the rows of $\mathbf{F}$ and dividing the resulting matrix by N.

3.4.2 Fast Fourier Transform (FFT)

Let $\mathbf{a} = (a_0, a_1, a_2, \cdots, a_{N-1})^t$ be a column vector of N complex numbers. The discrete Fourier transform (DFT) of the column vector $\mathbf{a}$ is a column vector $f(\mathbf{a})$ defined as

$$f(\mathbf{a}) = \mathbf{Fa}, \tag{3.4.2.1}$$

where $\mathbf{F}$ is the $N \times N$ matrix defined in (3.4.1.15). Likewise, the inverse discrete Fourier transform of the column vector $\mathbf{a}$ is a column vector $f^{-1}(\mathbf{a})$ defined as

$$f^{-1}(\mathbf{a}) = \mathbf{F}^{-1}(\mathbf{a}), \tag{3.4.2.2}$$

where $\mathbf{F}^{-1}$ is defined in Lemma 3.4.1.1.

As an example, if $\mathbf{a} = (-1, i, 1, -i)^t$, then

$$f(\mathbf{a}) = \begin{bmatrix} 0 \\ -4 \\ 0 \\ 0 \end{bmatrix} \quad \text{and} \quad f^{-1}(f(\mathbf{a})) = \begin{bmatrix} -1 \\ i \\ 1 \\ -i \end{bmatrix}. \tag{3.4.2.3}$$

Given the column vector $\mathbf{a} = (a_0, a_1, a_2, \cdots, a_{N-1})^t$, define a polynomial $p(x)$ with elements of the vector $\mathbf{a}$ as the coefficients, that is,

$$p(x) = a_0 + a_1 x + a_2 x^2 + \cdots + a_{N-1} x^{N-1}. \tag{3.4.2.4}$$

If $f_j(\mathbf{a})$ is the jth element of $f(\mathbf{a})$, then for $0 \le j \le N - 1$,

$$f_j(\mathbf{a}) = \sum_{r=0}^{N-1} a_r \omega^{jr} = p(\omega^j), \tag{3.4.2.5}$$

that is, computing the DFT of a vector a is equivalent to evaluating the polynomial $p(x)$ at the points $1, \omega, \omega^2, \cdots, \omega^{N-1}$. Since it is well known that a polynomial of degree $N-1$ can be uniquely represented either by the set of N coefficients or by its value at N distinct points, it can be said that the DFT actually transforms the polynomial $p(x)$ from its *coefficients* representation to its *value* representation. The inverse DFT converts the value representation to the coefficient representation, as illustrated by the example in (3.4.2.3). In other words, inverse DFT is equivalent to interpolating (or recovering) the polynomial $p(x)$ from its value at the N distinct roots of unity.

By rewriting $p(x)$ in (3.4.2.4) in the form of Horner's expression as

$$p(x) = (\cdots((a_{N-1}\, x + a_{N-2})\, x + a_{N-3})\, x + \cdots + a_1)\, x + a_0,$$

it is readily seen that it takes $N-1$ multiplications and $N-1$ additions to evaluate $p(x)$ at a given point. Thus, given the column vector $\mathbf{a}$ and the set of all N roots of unity, to compute $f(\mathbf{a})$ it takes $N(N-1)$ multiplications and $N(N-1)$ additions of complex numbers. Since one complex multiplication requires four multiplications and two additions of real numbers, and one complex addition requires two additions of real numbers, computation of $f(\mathbf{a})$ requires a total of $O(N^2)$ operations. (See Exercise 3.14.)

Given N processors, as $p(\omega^j)$ for $j = 0$ to $N-1$ can be computed independently, by assigning the computation of $p(\omega^j)$ to processor j, $j = 0$ to $N-1$, it is readily seen that $f(\mathbf{a})$ can be computed in parallel in $O(N)$ time. Alternatively, since the jth component of $f(\mathbf{a})$ is the inner product of the jth row of F and the column vector $\mathbf{a}$, it readily follows that $f(\mathbf{a})$ can be computed using the associative fan-in algorithm in $O(\log N)$ steps provided N^2 processors are available. Both of these *naive* strategies require a total of $O(N^2)$ operations.

A clever method for computing $f(\mathbf{a})$ that requires a total of only $O(N \log N)$ operations is presented below. This *recursive* technique called the *fast Fourier transform* (FFT) permits evaluation of $f(\mathbf{a})$ in parallel in $O(\log N)$ steps using only $O(N)$ processors.

Let $N = 2^n$ and $n \geq 0$. Let

$$p(x) = a_0 + a_1\, x + a_2\, x^2 + \cdots + a_{N-1}\, x^{N-1}.$$

We now recursively define a binary tree of polynomials with $p(x)$ at the root defined to be at level 0. The polynomials $p_e(x)$ and $p_o(x)$ of degree $\dfrac{N}{2} - 1$ at level 1 are defined as follows:

$$p_e(x) = a_0 + a_2\, x + a_4\, x^2 + a_6\, x^3 + \cdots + a_{N-2}\, x^{N/2 - 1}$$

$$= \sum_{j=0}^{\frac{N}{2} - 1} a_{2j}\, x^j,$$

and

$$p_o(x) = a_1 + a_3\, x + a_5\, x^2 + a_7\, x^3 + \cdots + a_{N-1}\, x^{N/2 - 1}$$

$$= \sum_{j=0}^{\frac{N}{2} - 1} a_{2j+1}\, x^j.$$

Notice that $p_e(x)$ ($p_o(x)$) contains coefficients whose indices are even (odd) multiples of 2^0.

Define two polynomials $p_{ee}(x)$ and $p_{eo}(x)$ of degree ($\frac{N}{4} - 1$) as follows.

$$p_{ee}(x) = a_0 + a_4 x + a_8 x^2 + a_{12} x^3 + \cdots + a_{N-4} x^{N/4-1}$$

$$= \sum_{j=0}^{\frac{N}{4} - 1} a_{4j} x^j,$$

and

$$p_{eo}(x) = a_2 + a_6 x + a_{10} x^2 + a_{14} x^3 + \cdots + a_{N-2} x^{N/4-1}$$

$$= \sum_{j=0}^{\frac{N}{4} - 1} a_{4j+2} x^j,$$

that is, $p_{ee}(x)$ ($p_{eo}(x)$) contains coefficients whose indices are even (odd) multiples of 2^1. Likewise, define

$$p_{oe}(x) = \sum_{j=0}^{\frac{N}{4} - 1} a_{4j+1} x^j$$

and

$$p_{oo}(x) = \sum_{j=0}^{\frac{N}{4} - 1} a_{4j+3} x^j.$$

$p_{ee}(x)$, $p_{eo}(x)$, $p_{oe}(x)$, and $p_{oo}(x)$ constitute the four polynomials at level 2. At the ith level, there are 2^i polynomials, each of degree ($\frac{N}{2^i} - 1$). The leaves of this tree at level n contain the polynomials of degree 0 which is obtained by simply permuting the input data. An example of this tree of polynomials for $N = 16$ is given in Fig. 3.4.2.1.

To obtain the specific permutation of the input at the leaves, first define

$$\rho : \{0, 1\}^n \rightarrow \{0, 1\}^n,$$

where

$$\rho (b_n b_{n-1} \cdots b_2 b_1) = b_1 b_2 \cdots b_{n-1} b_n,$$

that is, ρ is called the *bit-reversal* permutation. Thus, if $0 \leq x \leq 2^n - 1$, then $0 \leq \rho(x) \leq 2^n - 1$, where the binary expansion for $\rho(x)$ is obtained by reversing that of x. As an example, if $x = (1\ 0\ 1\ 0)_2 = 10$, then $\rho(x) = (0\ 1\ 0\ 1)_2 = 5$.

Now, label the 2^n leaves of the polynomial tree in the natural order starting with 0 at the leftmost leaf. Then it can be easily verified that the ith leaf gets the input $a_{\rho(i)}$ for $i = 0, \cdots, N - 1$.

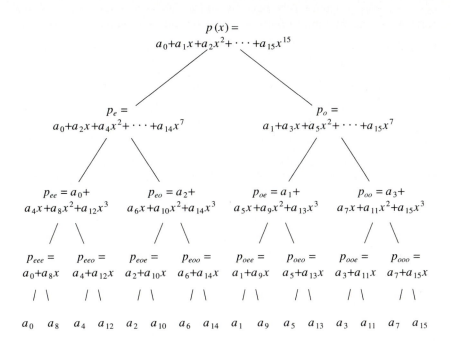

FIGURE 3.4.2.1
An illustration of the recursive tree of polynomials for $N = 16$.

From the above definition of the tree of polynomials, we obtain the following crucial relation between $p(x)$, $p_e(x)$ and $p_o(x)$:

$$p(x) = p_e(x^2) + x\, p_o(x^2)$$

$$p(-x) = p_e(x^2) - x\, p_0(x^2).$$

(3.4.2.6)

This relation immediately suggests the following scheme. First evaluate the two $(\frac{N}{2} - 1)^{th}$-degree polynomials $p_e(x)$ and $p_o(x)$ at the point ω^{2j} for $j = 1$ to $\frac{N}{2}$. Then, the values of the $(N-1)^{th}$-degree polynomial $p(x)$ at the symmetric pair of points ω^j and $\omega^{N/2+j} = -\omega^j$ can be obtained in one multiplication, one addition, and one subtraction. Since

$$p_e(x) = p_{ee}(x^2) + x\, p_{eo}(x^2),$$

$$p_e(-x) = p_{ee}(x^2) - x\, p_{eo}(x^2),$$

(3.4.2.7)

it follows that the values of $p_e(x)$ at the symmetric pair of roots, ω^{2j} and

$\omega^{N/2+2j} = -\omega^{2j}$, can be obtained by evaluating $p_{ee}(x)$ and $p_{eo}(x)$ at ω^{4j} and performing one multiplication, one addition, and one subtraction. This recursive process can likewise be applied to $p_o(x)$ and $p_o(-x)$.

Thus, in general, the values of the 2^k polynomials each of degree $(\frac{N}{2^k} - 1)$ (at level k) at the symmetric pair of points $\omega^{2^k j}$ and $\omega^{N/2 + 2^k j} = -\omega^{2^k j}$ can be obtained by evaluating 2^{k+1} polynomials of degree $(\frac{N}{2^{k+1}} - 1)$ (at level $k+1$) at $\omega^{2^{k+1} j}$ for $j = 0, 1, 2, \cdots, \frac{N}{2^{k+1}}$. Refer to Table 3.4.2.1 for an illustration of this strategy.

We now characterize the performance of this class of algorithms. Let $M(N)$ be the total number of complex multiplications and $A(N)$ be the total number of complex additions/subtractions needed to compute $f(\mathbf{a})$ by this algorithm. Since the algorithm is recursive, by analyzing the computations at level 0, it follows that

$$M(N) = 2M(\frac{N}{2}) + \frac{N}{2},$$

and

$$A(N) = 2A(\frac{N}{2}) + N,$$

where $M(1) = A(1) = 0$. Solving these, we obtain that

TABLE 3.4.2.1

Level	Degree	Evaluations
0	$N - 1 = 15$	$p(x)$ at $\{ 1, \omega, \omega^2, \omega^3, \omega^4, \omega^5, \omega^6, \omega^7, -1,$ $-\omega, -\omega^2, -\omega^3, -\omega^4, -\omega^5, -\omega^6, -\omega^7$
1	$N/2 - 1 = 7$	$p_e(x)$ and $p_o(x)$ at $\{1, \omega^2, \omega^4, \omega^6, -1, -\omega^2, -\omega^4, -\omega^6 \}$
2	$N/4 - 1 = 3$	$p_{ee}(x), p_{eo}(x), p_{oe}(x), p_{oo}(x)$ at $\{ 1, \omega^4, -1, -\omega^4 \}$
3	$N/8 - 1 = 1$	$p_{eee}(x), p_{eeo}(x), p_{eoe}(x), p_{eoo}(x), p_{oee}(x), p_{oeo}(x),$ $p_{ooe}(x), p_{ooo}(x)$ at $\{ 1 = \omega^{16}, -1 = \omega^8 \}$
4	$N/16 - 1 = 0$	Each of the given coefficients constitute the polynomial of degree 0. Permute the coefficients according to bit reversal permutation.

$$M(N) = \frac{N}{2} \log N,$$

and

$$A(N) = N \log N.$$

Since one complex multiplication is equivalent to four real multiplications and two real multiplications, and one complex addition is equivalent to two real additions, it is readily seen that this algorithm requires a total of $2N \log N$ real multiplications and $3N \log N$ real additions.

Now, given $N = 2^n$ processors, disregarding the communication time, the computations can be arranged in such a way that each processor performs uniformly one complex multiplication and one complex addition, in parallel, at each level. Thus, in all, the entire scheme requires a total of $O(\log N)$ time.

Lemma 3.4.1.2 helps to simplify the computation of the inverse Fourier transform. Let $\mathbf{a} = (a_0, a_1, a_2, \cdots, a_{N-1})^t$ be a complex vector. The inverse Fourier transform $f^{-1}(\mathbf{a})$ can be obtained as follows. First obtain the Fourier transform $f(\mathbf{a})$ of $\mathbf{a}$. Then

$$f_0^{-1}(\mathbf{a}) = \frac{1}{N} f_0(\mathbf{a})$$

and, for $1 \le k \le N - 1$,   (3.4.2.8)

$$f_k^{-1}(\mathbf{a}) = \frac{1}{N} f_{N-k}(\mathbf{a}),$$

where $f_j(\mathbf{a})$ and $f_j^{-1}(\mathbf{a})$ are the jth elements of the vectors $f(\mathbf{a})$ and $f^{-1}(\mathbf{a})$, respectively. Computationally, it takes an additional N complex divisions to obtain the inverse Fourier transform. We summarize the above analysis in the following theorem.

Theorem 3.4.2.1. Let $N = 2^n$ and $\mathbf{a} = (a_0, a_1, a_2, \cdots, a_{N-1})^t$ be a complex vector. Given N processors, both the Fourier transform $f(\mathbf{a})$ and the inverse Fourier transform $f^{-1}(\mathbf{a})$ can individually be computed in $O(\log N)$ parallel steps requiring a total of $O(N \log N)$ operations.

3.5 FAST FOURIER TRANSFORM -- MODULO ARITHMETIC

From a practical point of view, there is often the desire to perform error-free computation of FFT. This can in principle be done by performing all the computations in modulo arithmetic. Our first task is to develop the concept of roots of unity in modulo arithmetic.

3.5.1 Roots of Unity in Modulo Arithmetic

Let $m \geq 2$ be an integer. The set CRS $= \{0, 1, 2, \cdots, m-1\}$ of all distinct *residues* under mod m is called the *complete residue system* (CRS). The set

$$\text{RRS} = \left\{ x \mid x \in \text{CRS and GCD}(x, m) = 1 \right\}$$

of all residues which are relatively prime to m is called the *reduced residue system* (RRS). Let $\Phi(m)$ be the number of positive integers less than m and relatively prime to m. Clearly, $\Phi(m) = |\text{RRS}| < |\text{CRS}| = m$, for all $m > 1$. (Refer to Table 3.4.1.1.) For example, if $m = 6$, RRS $= \{1, 5\}$, and for $m = 5$, RRS $= \{1, 2, 3, 4\}$. (See Exercise 3.15.) The following lemma is quite basic.

Lemma 3.5.1.1 *(Fermat's Little Theorem).* If p is a prime and $1 < a < p$, then

$$1 \equiv a^{p-1} \pmod{p} \tag{3.5.1.1}$$

Proof
Since GCD$(a, p) = 1$, $y \equiv ax \pmod{p} \in$ RRS if $x \in$ RRS. Let $x_i = 1, 2, \cdots, p-1$ be an enumeration of the elements of RRS. Thus,

$$\prod_{i=1}^{p-1} y_i \equiv \left(\prod_{i=1}^{p-1} (ax_i) \right) \pmod{p}. \tag{3.5.1.2}$$

Since

$$\prod_{i=1}^{p-1} y_i = \prod_{i=1}^{p-1} x_i,$$

the lemma follows by canceling these terms in (3.5.1.2).

The following lemma is an extension of the above result to non-prime moduli and is known as *Euler's theorem* (see Exercise 3.16).

Lemma 3.5.1.2. If GCD$(a, m) = 1$ and $m > 1$, then

$$1 \equiv a^{\Phi(m)} \pmod{m}. \tag{3.5.1.3}$$

In analogy with (3.4.1.1), it is readily seen from (3.5.1.3) that a is the $\Phi(m)^{th}$ root of unity modulus m. In the following, we develop a number of facts from elementary number theory that are germane to the study of roots of unity in modulo arithmetic.

Lemma 3.5.1.3. Let a and m be two positive integers with $a < m$. Then in order that there exists an integer t such that $a^t \equiv 1 \pmod{m}$, it is necessary and sufficient that GCD$(a, m) = 1$.

Proof

By Euler's theorem $t = \Phi(m)$ if a and m are relatively prime. Now let $GCD(a, m) = d > 1$ and $a^t \equiv 1 \pmod{m}$ for some $t \geq 1$. Then d divides a, a^t, and m. But, from $a^t = mk + 1$ for some k, it follows that d also divides 1, which is a contradiction. Hence $d = 1$ and the lemma follows.

Stated in other words, the tth root of unity modulus m is always relatively prime to m.

It t is the smallest positive integer such that $a^t \equiv 1 \pmod{m}$ then t is called the *order of* $a \pmod{m}$ and is denoted by ord_m^a.

Lemma 3.5.1.4. If $t = \text{ord}_m^a$, then a, a^2, a^3, $\cdots$, a^t are all distinct $\pmod{m}$.

Proof

Let $1 \leq s < r \leq t$. Then

$$a^s \equiv a^r \pmod{m}$$

would imply that m divides $a^s (a^{r-s} - 1)$. Since $GCD(a, m) = 1$, it follows that $GCD(a^s, m) = 1$. Combining these, we obtain that m divides $a^{r-s} - 1$, that is, $a^{r-s} \equiv 1 \pmod{m}$ and $0 < r - s < t$. This is in contradiction with the definition of t, and the lemma follows.

A number of interesting conclusions are contained in the following:

Corollary 3.5.1.5.

(a) If $a^k \equiv 1 \pmod{m}$, then ord_m^a divides k.

(b) ord_m^a divides $\Phi(m)$.

(c) For any s, $a^s \equiv a^r \pmod{m}$, where $s = q \, \text{ord}_m^a + r$, $0 \leq r < \text{ord}_m^a$, that is, the *exponent* or the *index* of the powers of a under mod m is to be computed under mod $t = \text{ord}_m^a$.

Let $m \geq 3$. If g is an integer such that $GCD(g, m) = 1$ and if $\text{ord}_m^g = \Phi(m)$, then g is called the *primitive* $\Phi(m)^{th}$ *root of unity modulus* m or simply *primitive root of* m. It can be seen that such a g, if it exists, is always greater than unity. From Lemma 3.5.1.4, it follows that g, g^2, g^3, $\cdots$, $g^{\Phi(m)}$ are all *distinct* $\pmod{m}$. In other words, $\{g, g^2, g^3, \cdots , g^{\Phi(m)}\}$ constitutes the RRS for mod m. Let $1 \leq x < \Phi(m)$. From

$$(g^x + (m - 1)) (1 + g^x + g^{2x} + g^{3x} + \cdots + g^{[\Phi(m) - 2]x} + g^{[\Phi(m) - 1]x})$$

$$= m(1 + g^x + g^{2x} + \cdots + g^{[\Phi(m) - 1]x})$$

$$\equiv 0 \ (\text{mod } m),$$

since $(g^x + (m - 1)) \not\equiv 0 \ (\text{mod } m)$, it readily follows that

$$(1 + g^x + g^{2x} + \cdots + g^{[\Phi(m) - 1]x}) \equiv 0 \ (\text{mod } m). \tag{3.5.1.4}$$

Further, if x is a multiple of $\Phi(m)$, then, clearly,

$$1 + g^x + g^{2x} + \cdots + g^{[\Phi(m) - 1]x} = \Phi(m). \tag{3.5.1.5}$$

(See Exercise 3.19.) From (3.5.1.4), we also see that the sum of the elements in RRS is zero (mod m), and g satisfies all the properties of ω, the root of unity, described in (3.4.1.9) through (3.4.1.14).

As an example, 5 is the only primitive root of $m = 6$, since $\Phi(m) = 2$, $5^2 \equiv 1 \ (\text{mod } 6)$, and $5 + 5^2 = 30 \equiv 0 \ (\text{mod } 6)$. For $m = 8$, $\Phi(m) = 4$. Since $a^2 \equiv 1 \ (\text{mod } 8)$ for all $a \in \{3, 5, 7\}$, it follows that $\text{ord}_8^a = 2 < 4 = \Phi(4)$. That is, there is no primitive root of 8.

The question now is, which of the positive integers have primitive roots and how many of these are there? The following lemma provides the key to the answer.

Lemma 3.5.1.6. If $\text{ord}_m^a = t$, then $\text{ord}_m^{a^n} = \dfrac{t}{d}$, where $\text{GCD}(t, n) = d$.

Proof
Let $s = \text{ord}_m^{a^n}$. From

$$1 \equiv a^t \ (\text{mod } m) \equiv (a^t)^{n/d} \ (\text{mod } m) \equiv (a^n)^{t/d} \ (\text{mod } m),$$

and Corollary 3.5.1.5(a), it follows that s divides $\dfrac{t}{d}$. Also from

$$1 \equiv (a^n)^s \ (\text{mod } m) \equiv a^{ns} \ (\text{mod } m),$$

it follows that t divides ns. Thus $\dfrac{t}{d}$ divides $\left(\dfrac{ns}{d}\right)$. Since $\text{GCD}\left(\dfrac{t}{d}, \dfrac{n}{d}\right) = 1$, from this it follows that $\dfrac{t}{d}$ divides s. Combining these, we obtain that $t = sd$, and the lemma follows.

Stated in other words,

$$\text{ord}_m^a = \text{ord}_m^{a^n} = t \quad \text{if} \quad \text{GCD}(t, n) = 1. \tag{3.5.1.6}$$

From Corollary 3.5.1.5(c), we need to consider only $n < t$. Since there are only $\Phi(t)$ numbers with these properties, the following lemma is immediate.

Lemma 3.5.1.7. If $\mathrm{ord}_m^a = t$, then there are exactly $\Phi(t)$ distinct elements with the same order t.

Specializing Lemma 3.5.1.6 to the primitive roots, we obtain the following:

Corollary 3.5.1.8. If there exists a primitive root of m, then there are exactly $\Phi(\Phi(m))$ primitive roots of m.

Table 3.5.1.1 lists the primitive roots of m in the range 2 to 10. Thus, if $m = p$ is a prime, then there are $\Phi(p - 1)$ primitive roots of p.

As another example, let $m = 17$. Then $\Phi(m) = 16$ and $\Phi(16) = 8$. From Table 3.5.1.2, it follows that 3, 5, 6, 7, 10, 11, 12, and 14 are primitive roots of 17. Since $6^2 \equiv 2 \pmod{17}$, $6^4 \equiv 4 \pmod{17}$, and $6^8 \equiv 16 \pmod{17}$, it follows that $\mathrm{ord}_{17}^2 = 8$, $\mathrm{ord}_{17}^4 = 4$, and $\mathrm{ord}_{17}^{16} \equiv 2$, which verifies Lemma 3.5.1.6.

The 16 roots of unity generated by $g = 6$ are symmetrically displayed in Fig. 3.5.1.1. Thus, under mod 17, we can have a system of either two roots of unity $\{1, 16\}$, four roots of unity $\{1, 4, 16, 13\}$, eight roots of unity $\{1, 2, 4, 8, 16, 15, 13, 9\}$, or 16 roots of unity as given in Fig. 3.5.1.1.

From the above development, it is clear that the concept of primitive roots of m provides a natural framework for computing FFT in modulo arithmetic. In fact, given N, if we can find an m such that

---

TABLE 3.5.1.1

m	$\Phi(m)$	$\Phi(\Phi(m))$	Primitive Roots of m
2	1	1	1
3	2	1	2
4	2	1	3
5	4	2	2, 3
6	2	1	5
7	6	2	3, 5
8	4	2	None
9	6	2	2, 5

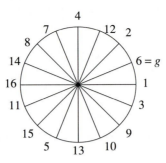

FIGURE 3.5.1.1

Examples of the 16 roots of unity mod 17 generated by the primitive root $g = 6$.

TABLE 3.5.1.2

Values of x^i (mod 17)

i	x										
	2	3	4	5	6	7	10	11	12	14	16
1	2	3	4	5	6	7	10	11	12	14	16
2	4	9	16	8	2	15	15	2	8	9	1
3	8	10	13	6	12	3	14	5	11	7	
4	16	13	1	13	4	4	4	4	13	13	
5	15	5		14	7	11	6	10	3	12	
6	13	15		2	8	9	9	8	2	15	
7	9	11		10	14	12	5	3	7	6	
8	1	16		16	16	16	16	16	16	16	
9		14		12	11	10	7	6	5	3	
10		8		9	15	2	2	15	9	8	
11		7		11	5	14	3	12	6	10	
12		4		4	13	13	13	13	4	4	
13		12		3	10	6	11	7	14	5	
14		2		15	9	8	8	9	15	2	
15		6		7	3	5	12	14	10	11	
16		1		1	1	1	1	1	1	1	

$$\Phi(m) = N,$$

then we can find all the Nth roots of unity mod m by taking the powers of a primitive root of m (see Exercise 3.20). However, there are a number of difficulties. $\Phi(m)$ as a function of m is *not* one-to-one ($\Phi(7) = \Phi(9) = 6$). Hence, the recovery of m from N is a difficult task. Even if one manages to find such an m, it may *not* possess primitive roots. (It is known that if $m = 2^k$, $k \geq 3$, then there are no primitive roots for m.) However, it may be argued that even if a modulus m does not have primitive roots, it does indeed support roots of unity. For example, mod 8 supports two roots of unity, namely $\{1, 7\}$. In fact, given any m, if

$$t = \max \left\{ \operatorname{ord}_m^a \mid \operatorname{GCD}(a, m) = 1 \right\},$$

then we can study the t roots of unity. For example, from Table 3.5.1.2, it is clear that 2 is not a primitive root of 17, yet it can generate the eight roots of unity; likewise, 4 can generate the four roots of unity and 16 can generate the two roots of unity. While such an observation can lead to an ad hoc approach to the problem of finding the value of m given N, it must be observed that the primitive root approach has some inherent "maximal" properties. Since ord_m^a divides $\Phi(m)$, the primitive root approach, wherever applicable, generates the maximum number of roots of unity for a given m. Thus, using an ad hoc approach one might end up having too few roots of unity for a given m or too large a value of m to support a given number roots of unity. We now describe an approach to the problem of choice of m for a given N.

Let $N = 2^n$, for some $n \geq 1$, be given. Pick an integer $\alpha = 2^k$ for some $k \geq 1$. Define

$$m = \alpha^{N/2} + 1 = 2^{k2^{n-1}} + 1. \tag{3.5.1.7}$$

Since α is even and m is odd, $\operatorname{GCD}(\alpha, m) = 1$, and hence $\alpha \in \operatorname{RRS} \pmod{m}$. Also, since $\operatorname{GCD}(N, m) = 1$, there exists a unique integer N^{-1}, $1 < N^{-1} < m$, called the *inverse* or the *reciprocal* of N such that $NN^{-1} \equiv 1 \pmod{m}$. From (3.5.1.7), since

$$-1 \equiv \alpha^{N/2} \pmod{m}, \tag{3.5.1.8}$$

we obtain that

$$1 \equiv \alpha^N \pmod{m}. \tag{3.5.1.9}$$

Since N is the *smallest* integer (why ?) with this property, it follows from the definition that

$$\operatorname{ord}_m^\alpha = N. \tag{3.5.1.10}$$

Consequently, $\alpha, \alpha^2, \cdots, \alpha^N$ are all distinct and

$$\sum_{i=1}^{N} \alpha^{ix} \equiv \begin{cases} 0 \pmod{m}, & \text{if } 1 \leq x < N, \\ \\ N \pmod{m}, & \text{if } x \text{ is a multiple of } N. \end{cases}$$

(See Exercise 3.19.) Further, since $N = 2^n$, from (3.5.1.9), we obtain that

$$N^{-1} \equiv 2^{-n} \equiv 2^{Nk-n} \pmod{m}. \tag{3.5.1.11}$$

In other words, the value of m given in (3.5.1.7) is sufficient to support the N roots of unity which are obtained as the powers of α.

As an example, if $N = 4$ and $\alpha = 4$, then $m = 17$, and the four roots of unity are obtained from the column with $x = 4$ in Table 3.5.1.2. If $N = 8$, and $\alpha = 2$, then again $m = 17$, and the eight roots of unity are obtained from the column with $x = 2$ in Table 3.5.1.2.

An immediate consequence of the above development is that it provides a simple algorithm for computing $x \pmod{m}$ for any given integer x.

Let $L = \dfrac{N}{2}$. Then $m = \alpha^L + 1 = 2^{kL} + 1$. Let

$$x = x_t \, x_{t-1} \, \cdots x_2 \, x_1, \tag{3.5.1.12}$$

where $0 \le x_i < \alpha^L$ for $i = 1$ to t, that is, x is a t-"digit" base-α^L integer. Notice that each x_i needs $\dfrac{N}{2} \log \alpha = kL$ bits. Then

$$x = \sum_{j=1}^{t} x_j \, \alpha^{L(j-1)}. \tag{3.5.1.13}$$

Using (3.5.1.8), we obtain

$$x \pmod{m} = (\sum_{j=1}^{t} (-1)^{j-1} \, x_j \,) \pmod{m}. \tag{3.5.1.14}$$

Thus, $x \pmod{m}$ can be computed by alternately adding and subtracting x_i's, that is,

$$x \pmod{m} = (x_1 - x_2 + x_3 - x_4 + \cdots (-1)^{t-1} x_t) \pmod{m}.$$

As an example, let $\alpha = 2$ ($k = 1$), and $L = 4$. Then $m = 17$. Let

$$x = 0000100101010111.$$

Then,

$$x_1 = 0111 = 7, \quad x_2 = 0101 = 5, \quad x_3 = 1001 = 9, \text{ and } x_4 = 0000 = 0.$$

Thus $x_1 - x_2 + x_3 - x_4 \equiv 11 \pmod{17}$. Since $x = 2391 = 140 \times 17 + 11$, the claim is verified.

The following lemma is immediate.

Lemma 3.5.1.9. $x \pmod{m}$ can be computed in $O(\log N)$ bit operations if t (the number of base α "digits" used in x) is fixed *a priori*.

Proof
From the associative fan-in algorithm, using (3.5.1.14), it follows that

$x \pmod{m}$ can be computed in $\lceil \log t \rceil$ stages. Each of the x_i's are $L \log \alpha = Lk$ bits long and from Section 3.2, it follows that $O(\log (Lk)) = O(\log N)$ bit operations are needed to add/subtract any two of the x_i's. Since t is fixed, the lemma follows.

3.5.2 Fast Fourier Transform

Let $\mathbf{a} = (a_0, a_1, a_2, \cdots, a_{N-1})^t$ be a column vector of integers. Replacing the complex root ω by α defined in (3.5.1.7), it is readily seen that the definition of DFT and its computation using the FFT algorithm *verbatim* carries over to this case as well, provided all the computations are performed modulo m. It is from here we see that by proper choice of m, we can perform all the computations in FFT free of error. In view of this close relationship, in the following we merely illustrate the key features.

We first quantify the number of bit operations required to compute the FFT and its inverse.

Let $N = 2^n$, $\alpha = 2^k$, $L = \dfrac{N}{2}$. Define

$$m = \alpha^L + 1 = 2^{kL} + 1.$$

Any residue mod m requires $B = kL + 1$ bits. The first step is to illustrate the computation of $\alpha^j \pmod{m}$ for $0 \le j < N$. This is equivalent to multiplying α by $\alpha^{j-1} = 2^{k(j-1)}$. Since α is B bits long, α^j is almost $B + k(j-1) \le B + k(N-2) < 3B - 2$ bits long.

Now using Lemma 3.5.1.9, the powers of α can be computed in parallel in no more than $O(\log N)$ steps.

As an example, let $N = 4$, $\alpha = 4$, and $m = 17$. Then $B = 5$ and $\alpha = 00100$. To compute α^2, left shift α two places to obtain $\alpha^2 \equiv 10000 \equiv 16 \pmod{17}$. To compute α^3, left shift α by four places to obtain $\alpha^3 = 001000000$. Considering α^3 as a base-$\alpha^L (= 2^4)$ integer, we obtain that

$$\alpha^3 = x_3 \, x_2 \, x_1,$$

where

$$x_3 = 0000, \quad x_2 = 0100, \quad \text{and } x_1 = 0000.$$

From (3.5.1.14)

$$\alpha^3 \pmod{m} \equiv (x_1 - x_2 + x_3) \pmod{17} \tag{3.5.2.1}$$

$$\equiv -4 \bmod 17 \equiv 13 \pmod{17}.$$

From the definition,

$$F = \left[\alpha^{qj} \ (\text{mod } m) \right] = \left[\alpha^{(qj) \ (\text{mod } N)} \right], \tag{3.5.2.2}$$

and

$$F^{-1} = \left[\alpha^{-qj} \ (\text{mod } m) \right] N^{-1} \ (\text{mod } m)$$

$$= \left[\alpha^{(N - q)j \ (\text{mod } N)} \right] N^{-1} \ (\text{mod } m), \tag{3.5.2.3}$$

where $0 \le q, \ j \le N - 1$.

Thus, when $N = 4$, $\alpha = 4$, and $m = 17$, the four roots of unity are given in Fig. 3.5.2.1, and

$$F = \begin{bmatrix} 1 & 1 & 1 & 1 \\ 1 & 4 & 16 & 13 \\ 1 & 16 & 1 & 16 \\ 1 & 13 & 16 & 4 \end{bmatrix}. \tag{3.5.2.4}$$

Since $13 \equiv 4^{-1} \ (\text{mod } 17)$

$$F^{-1} = \begin{bmatrix} 13 & 13 & 13 & 13 \\ 13 & 16 & 4 & 1 \\ 13 & 4 & 13 & 4 \\ 13 & 1 & 4 & 16 \end{bmatrix}. \tag{3.5.2.5}$$

We now state and prove the main result of this section, which is the analog of Theorem 3.4.2.1.

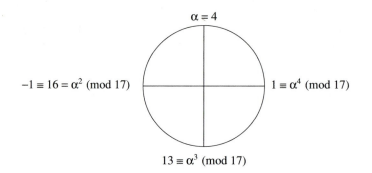

FIGURE 3.5.2.1.
The four roots of unity when $N = 4$, $\alpha = 4$, and $m = 17$.

Theorem 3.5.2.1. Let $N = 2^n$, $\alpha = 2^k$, $L = \dfrac{N}{2}$, and $m = \alpha^L + 1$. Let $\mathbf{a} = (a_0, a_1, a_2, \cdots, a_{N-1})^t$ be a vector where $0 \le a_i < m$ for $i = 0$ to $N - 1$. Then the parallel time required to compute the Fourier transform $f(\mathbf{a})$ and the inverse transform $f^{-1}(\mathbf{a})$, measured in units of t_b, is $O((\log N)^2)$, where t_b is the time required to perform a standard bit operation (such as logical AND or OR).

Proof

The computation of FFT using the algorithm in Section 3.4.2 needs addition mod m and multiplication mod m.

Since a residue mod m can be represented as $B = kL + 1$ bit integers, each addition of two B-bit integers (mod m) (by Section 3.2.1) takes $O(\log B) = O(\log N)$ steps in units of t_b.

Multiplication of a B-bit integer by $\alpha^j = 2^{kj}$, $0 \le j < N$, is done by shifting it to the left by kj places and segmenting the resulting integers into chunks of kL bits. Since $B + kj \le B + k(N-1) < 3B - 2$, as in (3.5.2.1), there are no more than three such chunks. Now applying (3.5.1.14), we obtain the residue mod m of the product which by Lemma 3.5.1.9 takes $O(\log N)$ steps in units of t_b.

The parallel computation of FFT involves $\log N$ stages, and in each stage there is one addition (mod m). Combining this with the above analysis, the first part of the theorem is proved.

Since the computation of the inverse Fourier transform is quite similar, we merely indicate the major differences. In this process, multiplication of a B-bit integer by $\alpha^{-jk} = \alpha^{(N-j)k}$, $0 \le j < N$, involves a left shift by $(N-j)k$ positions. Since $B + (N-j)k < 3B - 2$, by the above analysis, the residue under this product can be computed in $O(\log N)$ steps in units of t_b.

From (3.5.1.11), multiplication by N^{-1} (mod m) is equivalent to left shifting by $kN - n$ places. Since $B + kN - n < 3B - 2$, again the residue under the multiplication by N^{-1} (mod m) can be obtained in $O(\log N)$ steps in units of t_b.

Now, by combining this with the fact that there are $\log N$ stages with each stage consisting of an addition mod m and multiplication mod m, the second half of this theorem is proved.

3.6 TWO APPLICATIONS OF FAST FOURIER TRANSFORMS

In this section, we describe two applications of the fast Fourier transform technique. The first application is the classical one for computing the convolution of two vectors and its role in finding the *product of polynomials*. The second application is relatively new and results in a fast algorithm for *multiplying* two N-bit integers.

Since both of these applications depend critically on an operation called *convolution* of vectors, we begin by describing the latter.

3.6.1 Convolution of Vectors

Let

$$\mathbf{a} = (a_0, a_1, a_2, \cdots, a_{N-1})^t$$

and

$$\mathbf{b} = (b_0, b_1, b_2, \cdots, b_{N-1})^t$$

(3.6.1.1)

be two column vectors. The convolution of $\mathbf{a}$ and $\mathbf{b}$ denoted by $\mathbf{CON(a, b)}$ is a column vector

$$\mathbf{CON\ (a,\ b)} = \mathbf{r} = (r_0, r_1, r_2, \cdots, r_{2N-1})^t,$$

(3.6.1.2)

where for $0 \leq m < N$

$$r_m = \sum_{j=0}^{m} a_j\, b_{m-j},$$

and

$$a_h = b_h = 0, \quad \text{for all } h \geq N.$$

Thus,

$$r_0 = a_0\, b_0$$

$$r_1 = a_0\, b_1 + a_1\, b_0$$

$$r_2 = a_0\, b_2 + a_1\, b_1 + a_2\, b_0$$

$$\vdots$$

$$r_{N-1} = a_0\, b_{N-1} + a_1 b_{N-2} + \cdots + a_{N-1}\, b_0$$

$$r_N = a_1\, b_{N-1} + a_2\, b_{N-2} + \cdots + a_{N-1}\, b_1$$

$$\vdots$$

$$r_{2N-3} = a_{N-1}\, b_{N-2} + a_{N-2}\, b_{N-1}$$

$$r_{2N-2} = a_{N-1}\, b_{N-1},$$

and

$$r_{2N-1} = 0$$

is included for symmetry. It can be seen that

$$r_m = \sum_{\substack{t+s=m \\ (0 \le t,\, s \le N-1)}} a_t \, b_s. \tag{3.6.1.3}$$

The above definition of the convolution of two N-vectors as a $2N$-vector is motivated by its application to finding the product of two $(N-1)$-degree polynomials. However, there is often a need, as will be seen in Section 3.6.3, for defining the convolution of two N-vectors as an N-vector. There are at least two different ways. Let **a** and **b** be two N-vectors as given in (3.6.1.1). The *positive folded* convolution, denoted by **PCON** (**a**, **b**) is a column vector

$$\textbf{PCON (a, b)} = \mathbf{r} = (r_0, r_1, r_2, \cdots, r_{N-1})^t, \tag{3.6.1.4}$$

where, for $0 \le m < N$,

$$r_m = \sum_{j=0}^{m} a_j \, b_{m-j} + \sum_{j=m+1}^{N-1} a_j \, b_{N+m-j}.$$

Thus,

$$r_0 = a_0 \, b_0 + a_1 \, b_{N-1} + a_2 \, b_{N-2} + \cdots + a_{N-1} \, b_1$$

$$r_1 = a_0 \, b_1 + a_1 \, b_0 + a_2 \, b_{N-1} + \cdots + a_{N-1} \, b_2$$

$$r_2 = a_0 \, b_2 + a_1 \, b_1 + a_2 \, b_0 + a_3 \, b_{N-1} + \cdots + a_{N-1} \, b_3$$

$$\vdots$$

$$r_{N-1} = a_0 \, b_{N-1} + a_1 b_{N-2} + a_2 \, b_{N-3} + \cdots + a_{N-1} \, b_0.$$

It can be verified that

$$r_m = \sum_{\substack{t+s \equiv (\bmod N) \\ 0 \le t,\, s < N}} a_t \, b_s. \tag{3.6.1.5}$$

Likewise, the *negative folded* convolution denoted by **NCON** (**a**, **b**) is a column vector

$$\textbf{NCON (a, b)} = \mathbf{r} = (r_0, r_1, r_2, \cdots, r_{N-1})^t, \tag{3.6.1.6}$$

where, for $0 \le m < N$,

$$r_m = \sum_{j=0}^{m} a_j \, b_{m-j} - \sum_{j=m+1}^{N-1} a_j \, b_{N+m-j}.$$

Thus,

$$r_0 = a_0 \, b_0 - a_1 \, b_{N-1} - a_2 \, b_{N-2} - \cdots - a_{N-1} \, b_1$$

$$r_1 = a_0 \, b_1 + a_1 \, b_0 - a_2 \, b_{N-1} - a_3 \, b_{N-2} - \cdots - a_{N-1} \, b_2$$

$$r_2 = a_0 \, b_2 + a_1 \, b_1 + a_2 \, b_0 - a_3 \, b_{N-1} - \cdots - a_{N-1} \, b_3$$

$$\vdots$$

$$r_{N-1} = a_0 \, b_{N-1} + a_1 b_{N-2} + a_2 \, b_{N-3} + \cdots + a_{N-1} \, b_0$$

3.6.2 Product of Polynomials

Let $p(x)$ and $q(x)$ be two polynomials of degree $N-1$, where

$$p(x) = \sum_{t=0}^{N-1} a_t \, x^t,$$

and

$$q(x) = \sum_{t=0}^{N-1} b_t \, x^t. \qquad (3.6.2.1)$$

Then, the product polynomial $r(x)$ is given by

$$r(x) = p(x) \, q(x) = \sum_{t=0}^{2N-1} r_t \, x^t, \qquad (3.6.2.2)$$

where $r_{2N-1} = 0$ and

$$r_m = \sum_{j=0}^{m} a_j \, b_{m-j}. \qquad (3.6.2.3)$$

Comparing (3.6.2.3) with (3.6.1.2), it follows that the coefficients of the product polynomial can be readily obtained as the convolution of the vectors $\mathbf{a}$ and $\mathbf{b}$ where for $0 \le j < N$, a_j and b_j are the coefficients of the jth-degree term in $p(x)$ and $q(x)$, respectively.

Recall that (see Section 3.4.2) if $\mathbf{a}$ is a vector of the coefficients of the polynomial $p(x)$, then the Fourier transform $f(\mathbf{a})$ of the vector $\mathbf{a}$ denotes the vector consisting of the values of the polynomial $p(x)$ evaluated at the N roots of unity. Likewise, $f(\mathbf{b})$ denotes the values of $q(x)$ at the N roots of unity. Since the inverse Fourier transform *reconstructs* the polynomial (in coefficient form) from its values at the N roots of unity, by taking the inverse Fourier transform of the componentwise product of vectors $f(\mathbf{a})$ and $f(\mathbf{b})$, we can obtain $r(x)$ in the coefficient form. There is, however, a small difficulty. A well-known result from the theory of polynomials states that to reconstruct a unique polynomial of degree m we need its values at $m + 1$ distinct points. The componentwise product of f (**a**) and f (**b**) provides the values of $r(x)$ at only N points but $r(x)$ is a polynomial of degree $2N - 2$. This problem is remedied by extending $p(x)$ and $q(x)$ artificially to the $(2N - 1)^{th}$ degree by adding *zero* coefficients for the terms with degree N through $2N - 1$, and evaluating them at the $2N$ roots of unity. Thus, define

$$\underline{a} = (a_0, a_1, a_2, \cdots, a_{N-1}, 0, 0, \cdots, 0)^t$$

and

$$\underline{b} = (b_0, b_1, b_2, \cdots, b_{N-1}, 0, 0, \cdots, 0)^t.$$

$$(3.6.2.4)$$

Let $f(\underline{a})$ and $f(\underline{b})$ be the Fourier transform of $\underline{a}$ and $\underline{b}$, that is, $f(\underline{a})$ and $f(\underline{b})$ consist of values of $p(x)$ and $q(x)$ at the $2N$ distinct roots of unity.

Let

$$\textbf{CON} (\underline{a}, \underline{b}) = (r_0, r_1, r_2, \cdots r_{2N-2}, r_{2N-1})^t. \qquad (3.6.2.5)$$

The following theorem formalizes this idea.

Theorem 3.6.2.1. If **a** and **b** are two vectors given in (3.6.2.4), then

$$\textbf{CON} (\underline{a}, \underline{b}) = f^{-1}(f(\underline{a}) \times f(\underline{b})), \qquad (3.6.2.6)$$

where $\times$ denotes the componentwise multiplication of vectors.

Proof
As $a_j = b_j = 0$ for $N \le j \le 2N - 1$, we have, by definition, the kth component $f_k(\underline{a})$ of $f(\underline{a})$ given by

$$f_k(\underline{a}) = \sum_{t=0}^{N-1} a_t \, \omega^{kt}.$$

Similarly,

$$f_k(\underline{b}) = \sum_{s=0}^{N-1} b_s \, \omega^{ks}.$$

Thus, from (3.6.2.6) and the definition of the inverse Fourier transform (see Section 3.4.2), we have

$$r_m = \frac{1}{2N} \sum_{k=0}^{2N-1} f_k(\underline{a}) f_k(\underline{b}) \, \omega^{-mk} \qquad (3.6.2.7)$$

$$= \frac{1}{2N} \sum_{k=0}^{2N-1} \sum_{t=0}^{N-1} \sum_{s=0}^{N-1} a_t \, b_s \, \omega^{k(t+s-m)}$$

$$= \sum_{t=0}^{N-1} \sum_{s=0}^{N-1} a_t \, b_s \left\{ \frac{1}{2N} \sum_{k=0}^{2N-1} \omega^{k(t+s-m)} \right\}. \tag{3.6.2.8}$$

From (3.4.1.11) and (3.4.1.14) it follows that the term inside the brackets is *unity* when $t + s = m$ and *zero* when $t + s \neq m$. Thus,

$$r_m = \sum_{\substack{t+s=m \\ 0 \leq t, \, s < N}} a_t \, b_s$$

and the theorem follows.

The computation of the positive folded convolution **PCON** (**a, b**) of two vectors **a** and **b** given in (3.6.1.1) is very similar and is summarized in the following corollary.

Corollary 3.6.2.2. Let **a** and **b** be two vectors given in (3.6.1.1). Then

$$\textbf{PCON (a, b)} = f^{-1}(f(\textbf{a}) \times f(\textbf{b})),$$

where $\times$ is the componentwise vector multiplication.

Proof
From (3.6.1.4), the definition, it follows that

$$r_m = \sum_{t=0}^{N-1} \sum_{s=0}^{N-1} a_t \, b_s \left\{ \frac{1}{N} \sum_{k=0}^{N-1} \omega^{k(t+s-m)} \right\}.$$

The term in the brackets is *unity* if $t + s \equiv m \pmod{N}$ and *zero* if $t + s \not\equiv m \pmod{N}$. Hence

$$r_m = \sum_{\substack{t+s \equiv m \pmod{N} \\ 0 \leq t, \, s < N}} a_t \, b_s.$$

Comparing this with (3.6.1.5), the corollary follows.

The computation of negative folded convolution **NCON** (**a, b**), however, is slightly more complicated and is pursued in the following. Let ω and β be the principal N^{th} and $2N^{th}$ roots of unity, respectively, that is, $\omega = e^{i2\pi/N}$, $\beta = e^{i\pi/N}$, and $\beta^2 = \omega$. Further, $\beta^N = -1$ and $\beta^{N+k} = -\beta^k$ for $0 \leq k < N$. Given the vectors **a** and **b**, as in (3.6.1.1), define

$$\underline{\textbf{a}} = (a_0, \, \beta \, a_1, \, \beta^2 \, a_2, \, \cdots \, \beta^{N-1} \, a_{N-1})^t$$

and

$$\underline{\textbf{b}} = (b_0, \, \beta \, b_1, \, \beta^2 \, b_2, \, \cdots \, \beta^{N-1} \, b_{N-1})^t. \tag{3.6.2.9}$$

Let

$$\textbf{NCON} \, (\underline{\textbf{a}}, \, \underline{\textbf{b}}) = \textbf{r} = (r_0, \, \beta \, r_1, \, \beta^2 \, r_2, \, \cdots, \, \beta^{N-1} \, r_{N-1})^t. \tag{3.6.2.10}$$

The following corollary is immediate.

Corollary 3.6.2.3. If $\underline{a}$ and $\underline{b}$ are as given in (3.6.2.9), then

$$\textbf{NCON}\,(\underline{a},\,\underline{b}) = f^{-1}\,(f(\underline{a}) \times f(\underline{b})), \qquad (3.6.2.11)$$

where $\times$ denotes the componentwise multiplication.

Proof
Clearly the kth component of $f(\underline{a})$ is given by

$$f_k(\underline{a}) = \sum_{t=0}^{N-1} \beta^t \, a_t \, \omega^{kt}.$$

Similarly,

$$f_k(\underline{b}) = \sum_{s=0}^{N-1} \beta^t \, b_s \, \omega^{ks}.$$

Then, from (3.6.2.11)

$$\beta^h \, r_h = \sum_{t=0}^{N-1} \sum_{s=0}^{N-1} \beta^{t+s} \, a_t \, b_s \left\{ \frac{1}{N} \sum \omega^{k(t+s-h)} \right\}$$

$$= \sum_{\substack{t+s \equiv h \,(\mathrm{mod}\,N) \\ 0 \le t,\, s < N}} \beta^{t+s} \, a_t b_s.$$

Since $\beta^{N+k} = -\beta^k$ for $0 \le k < N$,

$$\beta^h \, r_h = \sum_{j=0}^{h} \beta^h \, a_j \, b_{h-j} - \sum_{j=h+1}^{N-1} \beta^h \, a_j \, b_{N+h-j}. \qquad (3.6.2.12)$$

Comparing this with (3.6.1.6), the corollary follows by canceling β^h on both sides of (3.6.2.12).

A number of observations are in order. Since the N roots of unity can be defined either in the complex domain (as in Section 3.4) or in modulo arithmetic (as in Section 3.5), the convolution Theorem 3.6.2.1 and Corollaries 3.6.2.2 and 3.6.2.3 hold true in both cases. However, in the case of modulo arithmetic, care must be taken to see that β is well defined. For, if $N = 4$, $\alpha = 2$ (recall that in our notation ω is the principal N^{th} root of unity in the complex case, and α is the Nth root of unity mod m), and $m = 2^{N/2} + 1 = 5$, then there exists no $\beta \in \{0, 1, 2, 3, 4\}$ such that $\beta^2 \equiv 2 \,(\mathrm{mod}\,5)$. Likewise, if $N = 6$, $\alpha = 2$, and $m = 2^{N/2} + 1 = 9$, there is no $\beta \in \{0, 1, 2, \cdots, 8\}$ such that $\beta^2 \equiv 2 \,(\mathrm{mod}\,9)$. However, if $N = 8$, $\alpha = 2$ and $m = 2^{N/2} + 1 = 17$, then $\beta = 6$, since $6^2 \equiv 2 \,(\mathrm{mod}\,17)$.

In general if $x^2 \equiv a \,(\mathrm{mod}\,m)$, then a is a perfect square or quadratic residue modulo m, and x is the (integer) square root of $a \,(\mathrm{mod}\,m)$. From the above examples, it follows that 2 is *not* a perfect square in (mod 5) and (mod 9) but is a perfect square in (mod 17) with 6 as its square root. A number of interesting properties of quadratic residues are pursued in Exercise 3.23. From part (b) of this exercise, it follows that when $m = 2^{N/2} + 1$ is a prime, a primitive root of mod m cannot be used in computing the negative folded convolution.

We shall illustrate the computation of **NCON** $(\mathbf{a}, \mathbf{b})$ by an example. Let $\alpha = 4$, $N = 4$, and $m = 17$. Then $\beta = 2$. Let $\mathbf{a} = (1, 1, 2, 3)^t$ and $\mathbf{b} = (1, 2, 3, 1)^t$. From (3.6.2.9), we obtain $\underline{\mathbf{a}} = (1, 2, 8, 7)^t$ and $\underline{\mathbf{b}} = (1, 4, 12, 8)^t$. Using (3.5.2.2), it can be seen that $f(\underline{\mathbf{a}}) = (1, 7, 0, 13)^t$ and $f(\underline{\mathbf{b}}) = (8, 7, 1, 5)^t$. Thus $f(\underline{\mathbf{a}}) \times f(\underline{\mathbf{b}}) = (8, 15, 0, 14)^t$. Again using (3.5.2.4), **NCON** $(\underline{\mathbf{a}}, \underline{\mathbf{b}}) = f^{-1}(f(\underline{\mathbf{a}}) \times f(\underline{\mathbf{b}})) = (5, 1, 16, 3)^t$. It can be seen that $\beta^{-1} \equiv 9 \pmod{17}$, $\beta^{-2} \equiv 13 \pmod{17}$, and $\beta^{-3} \equiv 15 \pmod{17}$. Combining (3.6.2.11) and (3.6.2.10), we see that

$$(1, \beta^{-1}, \beta^{-2}, \beta^{-3})^t \times \textbf{NCON}\,(\underline{\mathbf{a}}, \underline{\mathbf{b}}) = \textbf{NCON}\,(\mathbf{a}, \mathbf{b}).$$

Thus,

$$(1, 9, 13, 15)^t \times (5, 1, 16, 3)^t = (5, 9, 4, 11)^t.$$

In concluding this section, we state the following theorem.

Theorem 3.6.2.4. Given two vectors $\mathbf{a} = (a_0, a_1, a_2, \cdots, a_{N-1})^t$ and $\mathbf{b} = (b_0, b_1, b_2, \cdots, b_{N-1})^t$, it takes $O(\log N)$ arithmetic operations or $O((\log N)^2)$ bit operations to compute **CON** $(\mathbf{a}, \mathbf{b})$, **PCON** $(\mathbf{a}, \mathbf{b})$, or **NCON** $(\mathbf{a}, \mathbf{b})$.

Proof

The proof follows by combining Theorem 3.6.2.1, Corollaries 3.6.2.2 and 3.6.2.3, Theorem 3.4.2.1, and Theorem 3.5.2.1.

3.6.3 Multiplication of Integers -- Schonhage-Strassen Method

In this section, we describe a novel integer multiplication algorithm based on Fourier transform techniques that was alluded to at the end of Section 3.3. Given two N-bit integers a and b, this recursive method due to Schonhage and Strassen [1971] computes $a \times b (\bmod(2^N + 1))$ in $O(\log N)$ steps (measured in units of t_b, the time taken to compute a typical Boolean operation such as logical OR or AND). This method is based on two mathematical results: (1) computation of convolution using the FFT algorithm described in Section 3.6.2, and (2) the *Chinese Remainder Theorem*. We begin by describing the latter.

Let $m_1, m_2, \cdots, m_t$ be a set of integers with the property that for all $i \neq j$,

$$\text{GCD}(m_i, m_j) = 1. \tag{3.6.3.1}$$

Let

$$m = \prod_{i=1}^{t} m_i. \tag{3.6.3.2}$$

Given any integer a, let

$$a_i \equiv a \ (\text{mod } m_i). \tag{3.6.3.3}$$

The t-tuple $(a_1, a_2, \cdots, a_t)$ is often called the *modular* representation of the integer a.

The following lemma is quite basic.

Lemma 3.6.3.1. For every integer $0 \le a < m$, there exists a unique modular representation $(a_1, a_2, \cdots, a_t)$ and vice versa.

Proof

The existence of the unique modular representation for every integer $0 \le a < m$ is obvious. (Refer to Exercise 3.26 for an algorithm.) To prove the converse, since there are exactly m distinct t-tuples and m distinct integers $0 \le a < m$, it is sufficient to show that to each tuple there corresponds *at most* one integer. Let $0 \le a < b < m$ be two integers corresponding to the same t-tuple $(a_1, a_2, \cdots, a_t)$. Thus, $(a - b) \equiv 0 \ (\text{mod } m_i)$ for $i = 1$ to t. From this and (3.6.3.1), it follows that $(a - b) \equiv 0 \ (\text{mod } m)$. But $0 \le a < b < m$, hence it is impossible that $a - b$ is a multiple of m, and the lemma follows.

Let $(a_1, a_2, \cdots, a_t)$ and $(b_1, b_2, \cdots, b_t)$ be the modular representations of two integers a and b respectively. Let $o \in \{+, -, \times\}$. Then $(a_1 \ o \ b_1, a_2 \ o \ b_2, \cdots, a_t \ o \ b_t)$ is the modular representation of $a \ o \ b$. That is, addition, subtraction, and multiplication of integers in modular representation can be done component by component. In other words, there is no carryover in arithmetic with modular representation. The problem of division, however, is more complicated, as the following example illustrates.

Let $m_1 = 3$, $m_2 = 5$, $m_3 = 7$. Then $m = 105$. Let $a = 25$ and $b = 7$. Then $(a_1, a_2, a_3) = (1, 0, 4)$ and $(b_1, b_2, b_3) = (4, 2, 0)$. It is readily verified that the modular representation of $a + b = 32$ is $(2, 2, 4)$, the representation for $a - b = 18$ is $(0, 3, 4)$ and that of $a \times b = 175$ is $(1, 0, 0)$. Now with respect to division in general, it is not necessary that a/b is an integer as in this case of $25/7$. Even when it is an integer, as in $a = 25$ and $b = 5$, there are problems. The modular expansion for 5 is $(2, 0, 5)$. If we define the modular expansion for a/b as $(\frac{a_1}{b_1} \ (\text{mod } m_1), \frac{a_2}{b_2} \ (\text{mod } m_2), \frac{a_3}{b_3} \ (\text{mod } m_3))$, we see that $\frac{a_2}{b_2} \ (\text{mod } m_2)$ is of the form $\frac{0}{0} \ (\text{mod } 5)$, which is clearly undefined.

The converse problem of recovering the value of a (knowing that it lies in the interval $1 \le a < m$) from its modular representation $(a_1, a_2, \cdots, a_t)$ is not only important in application but also of intrinsic interest in itself. We are in fact looking for a *mixed radix* representation of the form

$$a = r_t m_1 m_2 \cdots m_{t-1} + r_{t-1} m_1 m_2 \cdots m_{t-2}$$

$$+ \cdots + r_3 m_1 m_2 + r_2 m_1 + r_1, \tag{3.6.3.4}$$

where, r_j is the jth mixed radix digit (with r_1 the least significant and r_t the most significant). Recall that (3.6.3.4) is a direct extension of the concept of positional number system. In this framework, the problem of recovering a reduces to one of finding r_j's, $j = 1$ to t, from a_i's for $i = 1$ to t.

To this end, first define a set of integers M_{kj} as

$$M_{kj} m_k \equiv 1 \pmod{m_j}. \tag{3.6.3.5}$$

That is, M_{kj} is the multiplicative inverse of $m_k \pmod{m_j}$. The least significant digit r_1 is such that

$$r_1 \equiv a \pmod{m_1} \equiv a_1 \pmod{m_1}. \tag{3.6.3.6}$$

Now, since $a \pmod{m_2} \equiv a_2$

$$r_2 \equiv (\frac{a - r_1}{m_1}) \pmod{m_2} \equiv (a_2 - r_1) M_{12} \pmod{m_2}. \tag{3.6.3.7}$$

Likewise, as $a \pmod{m_3} \equiv a_3$,

$$r_3 \equiv (((\frac{a - r_1}{m_1}) - r_2) \frac{1}{m_2}) \pmod{m_3}$$

$$\equiv ((a_3 - r_1) M_{13} - r_2) M_{23} \pmod{m_3}. \tag{3.6.3.8}$$

Continuing this process, we have essentially proved the following result:

Lemma 3.6.3.2. Let $0 \le a < m$. The mixed radix representation (3.6.3.4) for a is

$$r_1 \equiv a_1 \pmod{m_1},$$

and, for $2 \le k \le t$,

$$r_k \equiv (\cdots ((a_k - r_1) M_{1k} - r_2) M_{2k} - \cdots - r_{k-1}) M_{k-1,k} \pmod{m_k}, \tag{3.6.3.9}$$

where the t-tuple $(a_1, a_2, \cdots, a_t)$ is the modular representation for a.

A classical method for recovering a from its modular representation is given in Exercise 3.27.

We now illustrate this process by an example. Let $m_1 = 7$, $m_2 = 13$, $m_3 = 17$, and $m_4 = 29$. Then

$$M_{12} = 2,$$

$$M_{13} = 5, \quad M_{23} = 4,$$

$$M_{14} = 25, \quad M_{24} = 9, \quad M_{34} = 12.$$

$$m_1 m_2 = 91, \quad m_1 m_2 m_3 = 1547, \quad m_1 m_2 m_3 m_4 = 44863.$$

Let $a = 107$. Then the modular representation for 107 is (2, 3, 5, 20). It can be verified that $r_1 = 2$, $r_2 = 2$, $r_3 = 1$, and $r_4 = 0$.

In our analysis, a special form of this lemma will be used, and for purposes of later reference we now state it in the following corollary.

Corollary 3.6.3.3. Let $m_1 = 2^{k_1} + 1$ and $m_2 = 2^{k_2}$, where $k_1 > k_2$. Then $M_{12} \equiv 1 \pmod{m_2}$, and

$$a = a_1 + m_1 ((a_2 - a_1) \bmod m_2), \tag{3.6.3.10}$$

where $0 \le a < m_1 m_2$ and $a_i \equiv a \pmod{m_i}$, $i = 1, 2$.

Clearly, a_1 is $k_1 + 1$ bits long and a_2 is a k_2-bit integer. If $x = (a_2 - a_1) \pmod{m_2}$, then x is a k_2-bit integer. $(2^{k_1} + 1) x$ is obtained by first shifting x to the left by k_1 places and *adding* x to it, giving a result of an at most $(k_1 + k_2 + 1)$-bit integer. Finally a is obtained by adding a $(k_1 + k_2 + 1)$-bit integer with a $(k_1 + 1)$– bit integer. By using the algorithms in Section 3.2, it can be seen that computation of a takes $O(\log (k_1 + k_2)) = O(\log \log m)$ steps and requires no more than $O((k_1 + k_2)) = O(\log m))$ bit operations.

As an example, let $m_1 = 2^{10} + 1 = 1025$ and $m_2 = 2^5 = 32$. Let $a = 3472$. Then $a_1 = 397$, $a_2 = 16$, and $(a_2 - a_1) \pmod{32} \equiv -381 \pmod{32} \equiv 3$. Clearly, $397 + 1025 \times 3 = 3472$.

With all the basic tools in place, we now begin to shape the integer multiplication algorithm.

Let $N = 2^n$ and $0 \le a, b \le 2^N$ be the two $(N + 1)$-bit integers to be multiplied. Let

$$s = (a \times b) \pmod{(2^N + 1)}. \tag{3.6.3.11}$$

The special cases first. Since

$$2^N \equiv -1 \pmod{(2^N + 1)},$$

when $a = 2^N$,

$$s \equiv (2^N + 1 - b) \pmod{(2^N + 1)}, \tag{3.6.3.12}$$

and likewise, when $b = 2^N$, s is obtained by replacing b with a in (3.6.3.12). In view of this, in the following it will be assumed that $0 \le a, b < 2^N$.

If all the $2N$ bits of the product $a \times b$ are desired, first extend a and b to $2N$ bits by padding leading zeros and compute $a \times b \pmod{2^{2N} + 1}$.

Let

$$a = a_N\, a_{N-1}\, a_{N-2}\ \cdots\ a_2\, a_1,$$

$$b = b_N\, b_{N-1}\, b_{N-2}\ \cdots\ b_2\, b_1.$$

Let

$$N = tm,$$

where

$$t = 2^{\left\lfloor \frac{n}{2} \right\rfloor} = O(N^{\frac{1}{2}}),$$

$$m = 2^{\left\lceil \frac{n}{2} \right\rceil} = O(N^{\frac{1}{2}}).$$

Thus, $m \geq t$ and t divides m. The first step is to partition a and b into t groups of m bits each, that is,

$$a = \sum_{k=0}^{t-1} A_k\, 2^{m_k},$$

and

$$b = \sum_{k=0}^{t-1} B_k\, 2^{m_k},$$

where, for $0 \leq k \leq t-1$,

$$A_k = a_{(k+1)m}\, a_{(k+1)m-1}\ \cdots\ a_{km+1},$$

$$B_k = b_{(k+1)m}\, b_{(k+1)m-1}\ \cdots\ b_{km+1}.$$

Define polynomials $p(.)$ and $q(.)$ as follows:

$$p(x) = \sum_{k=0}^{t-1} A_k\, x^k,$$

$$q(x) = \sum_{k=0}^{t-1} B_k\, x^k.$$

Clearly,

$$a = p(2^m)$$

and

$$b = q(2^m).$$

Define

$$r(x) = p(x) q(x) = \sum_{j=0}^{2t-1} r_j x^j,$$

where (refer to Section 3.3)

$$r_0 = A_0 B_0$$

$$r_1 = A_0 B_1 + A_1 B_0$$

$$r_2 = A_0 B_2 + A_1 B_1 + A_2 B_0$$

$$\vdots$$

$$r_{t-1} = A_0 B_{t-1} + A_1 B_{t-2} + \cdots + A_{t-1} B_0$$

$$r_t = A_1 B_{t-1} + A_2 B_{t-2} + \cdots + A_{t-1} B_1$$

$$\vdots$$

$$r_{2t-2} = A_{t-1} B_{t-1}$$

and

$$r_{2t-1} = 0.$$

Thus, by computing $r(x)$ using the convolution Theorem 3.6.2.1, we can, in fact, recover all the $2N$ bits of $a \times b$ by evaluating $r(2^m)$. While we can readily recover $a \times b \pmod{(2^N + 1)}$ from this $r(2^m)$, this process requires $2t$ multiplications in the transformed domain.

The question is, can we compute $a \times b \pmod{(2^N + 1)}$ directly, which would require a smaller number of multiplications in the transformed domain? The answer is indeed yes and is naturally related to the concept of negative folded convolution described in Sections 3.6.1 and 3.6.2.

Since $N = tm$ for $t > \beta \geq 0$,

$$2^{m(\alpha t + \beta)} \equiv \begin{cases} -1 \pmod{(2^N + 1)} & \text{if } \alpha > 0 \\ \\ 2^{m\beta} \pmod{(2^N + 1)} & \text{if } \alpha = 0. \end{cases} \tag{3.6.3.13}$$

Then, from the definition of $r(x)$ and (3.6.3.13), we obtain

$$r(2^m) \pmod{(2^N + 1)} = D_{t-1} 2^{(t-1)m} + D_{t-2} 2^{(t-2)m}$$

$$+ \cdots + D_2 2^{2^m} + D_1 2^m + D_0, \tag{3.6.3.14}$$

where, for $0 \leq j \leq t-1$,

$$D_j = r_j - r_{t+j}$$

$$= \sum_{h=0}^{j} A_h B_{j-h} - \sum_{h=j+1}^{t-1} A_h B_{t+j-h}.$$

Comparing with (3.6.1.6), it follows that $r(2^m) \pmod{(2^N + 1)}$ can be computed using the version of the convolution theorem given in Corollary 3.6.2.3. This latter corollary requires *only* t multiplications in the transformed domain, which is one of the principal reasons for computing $a \times b \pmod{(2^N + 1)}$ (see Exercise 3.28).

There is, however, one last problem. If we directly apply the negative folded convolution using $\pmod{(2^N + 1)}$, then each of the resulting t multiplications in the transformed domain involves $(N + 1)$-bit integers, that is, we would have created t new problems each of the same size as the original problem -- a disaster. A little reflection immediately reveals that while we must take advantage of the t multiplications resulting from the application of negative folded convolution, we must also necessarily reduce the size of the integers involved in these multiplications and use this algorithm recursively. This is done by clever analysis of the magnitude of D_j's and by invoking the Chinese remainder theorem. First, we take up the analysis of the magnitude of D_j's.

As A_i and B_j are m-bit integers, the product $A_i B_j$ is a $2m$-bit integer, that is, $0 \le A_i B_j < 2^{2m}$. Since r_j is the sum of $j + 1$ such products, we obtain that

$$0 \le r_j < (j + 1)2^{2m},$$

and likewise,

$$0 \le r_{t+j} < (t - j - 1)2^{2m}.$$

Hence

$$-(t - j - 1)\, 2^{2m} < D_j < (j + 1)2^{2m},$$

and

$$0 \le |D_j| < t2^{2m}.$$

In other words, the range of D_j has $t2^{2m}$ distinct values. Since

$$t2^{2m} = 2^{\lfloor n/2 \rfloor} 2^{2^{(\lceil n/2 \rceil + 1)}} < 2^{2^n} < 2^N + 1,$$

we can compute $D_j \pmod{(2^N + 1)}$ by actually computing $D_j \pmod{t2^{2m}}$. It is in this latter computation that we exploit the Chinese remainder theorem, especially Lemma 3.6.3.2.

Since t is a power of 2, define

$$\left. \begin{aligned} E_j &\equiv D_j \pmod{(2^{2m} + 1)} \\[2mm] \text{and} \qquad\qquad & \\[2mm] F_j &\equiv D_j \pmod{t}. \end{aligned} \right\} \qquad\qquad (3.6.3.15)$$

Thus, knowing E_j and F_j, using Corollary 3.6.3.3 (with $m_1 = 2^{2m} + 1$ and $m_2 = t$), we can, in fact, recover D_j using

$$D_j = E_j + (2^{2m} + 1)\left[(F_j - E_j) \pmod{t}\right]. \tag{3.6.3.16}$$

We now compute F_j. To this end, define

$$\left.\begin{array}{l} \overline{A}_h \equiv A_h \pmod{t} \\[2em] \overline{B}_h \equiv B_h \pmod{t}. \end{array}\right\} \tag{3.6.3.17}$$

and

Let $q = \lfloor n/2 \rfloor$. Then, since $t = 2^q$, $\overline{A}_h$ and $\overline{B}_h$ are q-bit integers. Define $\overline{0}$ to be a string of q zeros, and construct two new integers $\overline{A}$ and $\overline{B}$, each $3tq$ bits long:

$$\overline{A} = \overline{0}\,\overline{0}\,\overline{A}_{t-1}\,\overline{0}\,\overline{0}\,\overline{A}_{t-2}\,\overline{0}\,\overline{0}\cdots\overline{0}\,\overline{0}\,\overline{A}_1\,\overline{0}\,\overline{0}\,\overline{A}_0,$$

and

$$\overline{B} = \overline{0}\,\overline{0}\,\overline{B}_{t-1}\,\overline{0}\,\overline{0}\,\overline{B}_{t-2}\,\overline{0}\,\overline{0}\cdots\overline{0}\,\overline{0}\,\overline{B}_1\,\overline{0}\,\overline{0}\,\overline{B}_0,$$

where

$$\overline{A} = \sum_{h=0}^{t-1} \overline{A}_h\, 2^{(3q)h}$$

and

$$\overline{B} = \sum_{h=0}^{t-1} \overline{B}_h\, 2^{(3q)h}.$$

Since $\overline{A}_h \overline{B}_h$ is $2q$ bits long, in the product $\overline{A}\,\overline{B}$ all the cross product terms $\overline{A}_h\,\overline{B}_k$ for all $h, k = 0, 1, 2, \cdots, t-1$, are confined to successive blocks of $3q$ bits. In other words, all the cross product terms can be easily read off from the product $\overline{A}\,\overline{B}$. Let

$$\overline{r} = \overline{A}\,\overline{B} = \sum_{h=0}^{2t-1} \overline{r}_j\, 2^{(3q)h},$$

where

$$\overline{r}_j = \sum_{h=0}^{j} \overline{A}_h \overline{B}_{j-h}. \tag{3.6.3.18}$$

Thus r_j's can be readily computed. Now combining (3.6.3.14) through (3.6.3.18), we see that

$$F_j \equiv D_j \pmod{t}$$

$$\equiv (\overline{r}_j - \overline{r}_{t+j}) \pmod{t}$$

$$\equiv \left[\sum_{h=0}^{j} \overline{A}_h \overline{B}_h - \sum_{h=j+1}^{t-1} \overline{A}_h \overline{B}_{t+j-h}\right] \pmod{t} \tag{3.6.3.19}$$

can be computed readily from the product $\overline{A}\,\overline{B}$.

Using the methods of Section 3.3, the product $\overline{A}\,\overline{B}$ can be found in $O(\log 3qt) = O(\log N)$ steps using at most $(3tq)^{1.6} = O(N \log N)$ bit operations.

The computation of $E_j \equiv D_j \pmod{(2^{2m}+1)}$ is actually done invoking the negative folded convolution.

Let $\alpha = 2^{4m/t}$ and $M = 2^{2m} + 1$. Since $M = \alpha^{t/2} + 1$, from Section 3.5 it follows that $\alpha, \alpha^2, \alpha^3, \cdots, \alpha^t$ define the t roots of unity mod M. Define $\beta = 2^{2m/t}$, where $\beta^2 = \alpha$, that is, β is the $2t^{th}$ root of unity mod M. Define

$$\overline{A} = (A_0, \beta A_1, \beta^2 A_2, \cdots, \beta^{t-1} A_{t-1}),$$

$$\overline{B} = (B_0, \beta B_1, \beta^2 B_2, \cdots, \beta^{t-1} B_{t-1}),$$

and

$$\overline{E} = (E_0, \beta E_1, \beta^2 E_2, \cdots, \beta^{t-1} E_{t-1}).$$

Then

$$\overline{E} = \textbf{NCON}\,(\overline{A}, \overline{B}) = f^{-1}(f(\overline{A}) \times f(\overline{B})).$$

By Theorem 3.6.2.4, the computation of the Fourier transform of $\overline{A}$ and $\overline{B}$ and that of the inverse transform each require $O(\log t) = O(\log N)$ steps and $O(tm \log t) = O(N \log N)$ operations. The t multiplications can be done in parallel by the recursive call. E_j can be recovered by multiplying $\beta^j E_j$ by $\beta^{-j} \pmod{(2^{2m}+1)}$. By Lemma 3.5.1.9, the latter operations can be done in parallel in $O(\log N)$ steps and $O(N \log N)$ operations.

After computing the actual values of D_j from (3.6.3.16), we can now compute $r(2^m) \pmod{(2^N + 1)}$ by multiplying D_j by 2^{jm}, adding and computing $\pmod{(2^N + 1)}$. All of these computations by Lemma 3.5.1.9 require $O(\log N)$ steps and $O(N \log N)$ bit operations.

The overall algorithm is summarized in Figure 3.6.3.1. Let $T(N)$ be the parallel time and $s(N)$ be the total number of operations required by this algorithm. Now combining all the above analysis, we obtain that

$$T(N) = T(2m) + O(\log N), \tag{3.6.3.20}$$

and

$$s(N) = t \times s(2m) + O(N \log N). \tag{3.6.3.21}$$

Since $m \leq 2\sqrt{N}$, it can be shown by induction that $T(N) = O(\log N)$. To solve for $s(N)$, define $s'(N) = \dfrac{s(N)}{N}$. Then, for large N, (3.6.3.21) becomes

$$s'(N) \leq 2s'(2m) + c \, \log N, \tag{3.6.3.22}$$

for some constant c. It can be readily verified that $s'(N) = O((\log N)(\log \log N))$ from which we obtain that $s(N) = O(N (\log N) \log \log N)$.

We conclude this section by summarizing the above analysis in the following theorem.

/* Given $a = a_N \, a_{N-1} \, a_{N-2} \, \cdots \, a_2 \, a_1$ and $b = b_N \, b_{N-1} \, b_{N-2} \, \cdots \, b_2 \, b_1$,
find $s = a \times b \pmod{(2^N + 1)}$. */

Step 1. Set $t = 2^{\lfloor n/2 \rfloor}$ and $m = 2^{\lceil n/2 \rceil}$. Partition the bits of a into t groups A_k, $k = 0$ to $t - 1$, where $A_k = a_{(k+1)m} \, a_{(k+1)m-1} \, \cdots \, a_{km+1}$. Likewise, define B_k for $k = 0$ to $t - 1$. Let $A = (A_0, A_1, A_2, \cdots, A_{t-1})$, $B = (B_0, B_1, B_2, \cdots, B_{t-1})$. Define $D = (D_0, D_1, D_2, \cdots, D_{t-1})$ as in (3.6.3.14).

Step 2. Compute $F_j \equiv D_j \pmod{t}$ using (3.6.3.19).

Step 3. Compute $E_j \equiv D_j \pmod{(2^{2m} + 1)}$. This step involves computing the negative folded convolution and a parallel recursive call of the Schonhage-Strassen algorithm.

Step 4. Using (3.6.3.16) (the Chinese remainder theorem), compute D_j.

Step 5. Compute $a \times b \pmod{(2^N + 1)} = r(2^m) \pmod{(2^N + 1)}$ using (3.6.3.14).

FIGURE 3.6.3.1
The Schonhage-Strassen multiplication algorithm.

Theorem 3.6.3.4. The product of two N-bit integers $\pmod{(2^N + 1)}$ can be obtained using the Schonhage-Strassen algorithm in $O(\log N)$ steps using $O(N (\log N) \log \log N)$ logical elements.

3.7 PARALLEL DIVISION

The problem of division is more involved than addition and multiplication, since given two integers, their ratio $\dfrac{a}{b}$, in general, is not an integer. Often, it *cannot* be expressed in a finite number of digits. Accordingly, we reconcile ourselves to computing the N-bit approximation to ab^{-1}, where a and b are themselves N-bit integers. Since the special cases of $a = 0$ and $b = 1$ are easily handled, let $0 < a < 2^N$ and $2 \le b < 2^N$. In the following, we first concentrate on computing the N-bit approximation to b^{-1}.

3.7.1 A Classical Algorithm

Let $b = b_N\, b_{N-1}\, b_{N-2} \cdots b_2\, b_1$ in binary, with $b_N = 1$. Let

$$b^{-1} = r = \sum_{i=1}^{\infty} r_i\, 2^{-i}. \tag{3.7.1.1}$$

From $b_N = 1$, we obtain that $b \geq 2^{N-1}$ and $b^{-1} \leq 2^{-(N-1)}$, that is, $r_j = 0$ for $j = 1$ to $N - 2$. Let $\underline{b}^{-1}$ be N-bit approximation to b^{-1}, that is, let

$$\underline{b}^{-1} = \sum_{j=0}^{N-1} r_{(N-1)+j}\, 2^{-((N-1)+j)}.$$

Thus,

$$b^* = 2^{2N-2}\, \underline{b}^{-1} = r_{N-1}\, r_{N-2} \cdots r_{2N-2} \tag{3.7.1.2}$$

in the standard binary expansion. In other words, computing the N-bit approximation to b^{-1} is equivalent to computing the N-bit integer b^*.

Let

$$c = 2^{-N} b.$$

Clearly (recall that $b_N = 1$),

$$\tfrac{1}{2} \leq c < 1,$$

and b^* is an N-bit approximation to $2^{N-2}\, c^{-1}$. Define

$$c = 1 - d,$$

where

$$0 < d \leq \tfrac{1}{2}.$$

Then,

$$c^{-1} = \frac{1}{1-d}$$

$$= \frac{1}{1-d} \times \frac{1+d}{1+d} \times \frac{1+d^2}{1+d^2} \times \frac{1+d^{2^2}}{1+d^{2^2}} \times \cdots \times \frac{1+d^{2^{k-1}}}{1+d^{2^{k-1}}}$$

$$= \frac{P_k(d)}{1-d^{2^k}},$$

where

$$P_k(d) = (1+d)(1+d^2)(1+d^{2^2}) \cdots (1+d^{2^{k-1}}) = \frac{1-d^{2^k}}{1-d}. \tag{3.7.1.3}$$

Since

$$0 \leq |P_k(d) - c^{-1}| \leq \frac{d^{2^k}}{1-d} < 2 \times 2^{-2^k}, \tag{3.7.1.4}$$

it follows that for suitably large k, $P_k(d)$ is a "good" approximation to c^{-1}.

The above analysis constitutes the basis for the now *classical* method due to Anderson, Earle, Goldschmidt, and Powers [1967]. It consists of first finding suitable approximations to d^{2^j} for $j = 0$ to $k - 1$, forming the sum $1 + d^{2^j}$, and then finding suitable approximations to the product on the right-hand side of (3.7.1.3). Before proceeding further, let us introduce some simplifying notations. Let

$$d_j = d^{2^j}.$$

Then

and

$$\left. \begin{array}{c} d_{j+1} = d_j^{\,2} \\[2em] P_k(d) = \displaystyle\prod_{j=0}^{k-1} (1 + d_j). \end{array} \right\} \qquad (3.7.1.5)$$

Let $\underline{d_j}$ be the t-bit approximation obtained by retaining the t most significant (just to the right of the binary point) bits of d_j. Let $\varepsilon = 2^{-t}$. Then as a result of truncation d_0 and $\underline{d_0}$ satisfy

$$d_0 - \varepsilon \le \underline{d_0} \le d_0. \qquad (3.7.1.6)$$

We now estimate as to how good an approximation $\underline{d_j}$ is to d_j for $j > 0$.

Lemma 3.7.1.1. For $0 \le j \le k - 1$,

$$d_j - 2\varepsilon \le \underline{d_j} \le d_j. \qquad (3.7.1.7)$$

Proof
As the basis of induction, when $j = 0$, (3.7.1.6) implies (3.7.1.7). Let it be true for $j = 0, 1, \cdots, s$. Now

$$\underline{d_{s+1}} \ge \underline{d_s}^{\,2} - \varepsilon, \qquad (\text{ by truncation })$$

$$\ge (d_s - 2\varepsilon)^2 - \varepsilon, \qquad (\text{ by inductive hypothesis })$$

$$\ge d_s^{\,2} - 4\varepsilon d_s - \varepsilon$$

$$\ge d_s^{\,2} - 2\varepsilon, \qquad (\text{ since } d_s \le \frac{1}{4} \text{ for } s \ge 1)$$

$$= d_{s+1} - 2\varepsilon.$$

The upper equality in (3.7.1.7) is trivially true and the lemma follows.

The importance of the above lemma is that the error in the t-bit approximation to d_j is independent of j. This is primarily due to the fact that the truncation errors do not grow during the squaring operation as is evident from the proof of Lemma 3.7.1.1.

Let

$$e_j(d) = 1 + \underline{d}_j, \quad \text{for } j = 0, 1, 2, \cdots, k - 1 \tag{3.7.1.8}$$

be the $(t + 1)$-bit approximation to $1 + d_j$ with 1 to the left of the binary point and t binary bits of $\underline{d}_j$ to the right of the binary point. Clearly, $\prod_{s=0}^{j} e_s(d)$ is an approximation to $p_j(d)$. The quality of this approximation is settled in the following lemma.

Lemma 3.7.1.2. For $1 \leq j \leq k$,

$$p_j(d) - \varepsilon_j(d) \leq \prod_{i=0}^{j-1} e_i(d) \leq p_j(d), \tag{3.7.1.9}$$

where

$$\varepsilon_i(d) = \varepsilon(3i - 2) \frac{1 - d_{i-1}}{1 - d_0}. \tag{3.7.1.10}$$

Proof

For $j = 1$, $\varepsilon_0(d) = \varepsilon$ and $e_0(d) = 1 + \underline{d}_0$. Since the error in $p_1(d)$ is limited to truncation, the basis for the induction is established. Let it be true for $j = 1, 2, \cdots, s - 1$. Then,

$$\prod_{i=0}^{s} e_i(d) \geq \left\{ \prod_{i=0}^{s-1} e_i(d) \right\} e_s(d) - \varepsilon \quad (\text{truncation})$$

$$\geq (p_s(d) - \varepsilon_s(d))(1 + \underline{d}_s) - \varepsilon \quad (\text{by hypothesis})$$

$$\geq (p_s(d) - \varepsilon_s(d))(1 + d_s - 2\varepsilon) - \varepsilon \quad (\text{by Lemma 3.7.1.1})$$

$$\geq P_{s+1}(d) - \varepsilon_s(d)(1 + d_s) - 2\varepsilon\, p_s(d) - \varepsilon. \tag{3.7.1.11}$$

Since

$$d_s < d_{s-1} \quad \text{and} \quad d_{s-1}^2 = d_s,$$

we obtain that

$$\varepsilon_s(d)\,(1+d_s) + 2\varepsilon p_s(d) = \varepsilon\,(3s-2)\frac{1-d_{s-1}}{1-d_0}\,(1+d_s) + 2\varepsilon\frac{1-d_s}{1-d_0}$$

$$\leq \varepsilon\,(3s-2)\,\frac{1-d_s}{1-d_0} + 2\varepsilon\,\frac{1-d_s}{1-d_0}$$

$$= \varepsilon\,3s\,\frac{1-d_s}{1-d_0}. \tag{3.7.1.12}$$

Further, as $d_s \leq d_0$,

$$\varepsilon \leq \varepsilon\,\frac{1-d_s}{1-d_0}. \tag{3.7.1.13}$$

Combining (3.7.1.11) through (3.7.1.13), we obtain that

$$\prod_{i=0}^{s} e_i(d) \geq P_{s+1}(d) - \varepsilon\,(3s-1)\,\frac{1-d_s}{1-d_0}$$

$$= P_{s+1}(d) - \varepsilon\,(3(s+1)-2)\,\frac{1-d_s}{1-d_0},$$

from which the left inequality in (3.7.1.9) follows. The right inequality in (3.7.1.9) is trivially true and the lemma follows.

Now, for the final phase of choosing t and k to guarantee the N-bit approximation we seek. To this end, consider

$$\left|\,\prod_{j=0}^{k-1} e_j(d) - c^{-1}\,\right| = \left|\,\prod_{j=0}^{k-1} e_j(d) - P_k(d) + P_k(d) - c^{-1}\,\right|$$

$$\leq \left|\,\prod_{j=0}^{k-1} e_j(d) - P_k(d)\,\right| + |\,P_k(d) - c^{-1}\,|. \tag{3.7.1.14}$$

By Lemma 3.7.1.2,

$$\left|\,\prod_{j=0}^{k-1} e_j(d) - P_k(d)\,\right| \leq \varepsilon_k(d)$$

$$\leq \varepsilon\,(3k-2)\,\frac{1-d_{k-1}}{1-d_0}$$

$$\leq \varepsilon\,\frac{3k-2}{1-d_0}$$

$$\leq (3k-2)\,2 \times 2^{-t},\text{ since } d_0 \leq \tfrac{1}{2} \text{ and } \varepsilon \leq 2^{-t}. \tag{3.7.1.15}$$

Combining (3.7.1.15) and (3.7.1.4) with (3.7.1.14), we get

$$| \prod_{j=0}^{k-1} e_j(d) - c^{-1} | \leq (3k-2) \, 2^{-t+1} + 2 \times 2^{-2^k}. \tag{3.7.1.16}$$

To guarantee N-bit approximation to c^{-1} with one bit to the left and $N-1$ bits to the right of the binary point, choose t and k such that

$$(3k-2) \, 2^{-t+1} + 2 \times 2^{-2^k} \leq 2^{-N+1}. \tag{3.7.1.17}$$

A sufficient condition for (3.7.1.17) is to pick

$$k = \lceil \log N \rceil + 1 \text{ and } t = N + 2 + \lceil \log k \rceil. \tag{3.7.1.18}$$

The following theorem summarizes the above development.

Theorem 3.7.1.3. Given two N-bit integers a and b, an N-bit approximation to ab^{-1} can be obtained by the above algorithm in $O((\log N)^2)$ steps using $O(N^2 \log N)$ logical elements.

Proof

Finding $d = 1 - 2^{-N}b$ involves one subtraction, which takes $O(\log N)$ steps and $O(N)$ logical elements. Computation of $\underline{d}_j$, $j = 0, 1, \cdots, k-1$, involves $k-1$ multiplications of t-bit numbers. Likewise, computing $\prod_{j=0}^{k-1} e_j(d)$ involves $k-1$ multiplications of $(t+1)$-bit numbers. Finally, there is one multiplication of a and b^{-1}. Thus, there is a total of $2k-1$ multiplications of $O(N)$-bit numbers (recall that $t = O(N)$ and $k = O(\log N)$). Using the grade school method of multiplication modified by the Ofman-Wallace tree approach (Section 3.3.2), it takes a total of $O((\log N)^2)$ steps and $O(N^2 \log N)$ logical elements.

We invite the reader to explore the possibilities of speeding up the computations of $\underline{d}_j$ and $\prod_{j=0}^{k-1} e_j(d)$ (Exercise 3.30).

3.7.2 Beame-Cook-Hoover Algorithm

We now describe another method due to Beame, Cook, and Hoover [1986]. Let a and b be two N-bit integers, and we want to compute $\lfloor a/b \rfloor$ to N bits. Let $0 < a < 2^N$, and $2 \leq b < 2^N$. Let $s \geq 2$ be an integer such that

$$2^{s-1} \leq b < 2^s,$$

and define

$$x = 1 - 2^{-s}b, \tag{3.7.2.1}$$

where $0 < x \le \frac{1}{2}$. Then,

$$b^{-1} = 2^{-s}(1-x)^{-1} = 2^{-s}\sum_{i=0}^{\infty} x^i. \tag{3.7.2.2}$$

Let

$$\underline{b}^{-1} = 2^{-s}\sum_{i=0}^{N-1} x^i. \tag{3.7.2.3}$$

Then,

$$b^{-1} - \underline{b}^{-1} = 2^{-s}\sum_{i=N}^{\infty} x^i$$

$$= 2^{-s} x^N \sum_{i=0}^{\infty} x^i$$

$$\le 2^{-s-N+1} \quad \text{(since } x \le \frac{1}{2}\text{)},$$

$$< 2^{-N} \quad \text{(since } s \ge 2\text{)}. \tag{3.7.2.4}$$

Clearly,

$$b^{-1} - 2^{-N} \le \underline{b}^{-1} \le b^{-1}.$$

Now, compute

$$q = a\underline{b}^{-1}, \tag{3.7.2.5}$$

which is an approximation to $\lfloor a/b \rfloor$ with error less than 1 (see Exercise 3.31).

It is clear from both the methods that the division process involves repeated multiplications and/or powering. As shown in Exercise 3.32, the problem of powering can be reduced to the division problem. In view of this intimate relation between the powering and the division, in the following we concentrate on developing an asymptotically faster algorithm (Beame, Cook, and Hoover [1986]) for the powering problem.

We begin by establishing a number of elementary facts involving operations with small integers which are crucial to the faster powering algorithms. For further discussion of these techniques refer to McKenzie [1984], Beame, Cook, and Hoover [1986], and Wegener [1987].

Lemma 3.7.2.1. Let a be an N-bit integer and $m \le N$. Then $a \pmod{m}$ can be computed in $O(\log N)$ steps.

Proof

Given N, we can precompute

$$b_i \equiv 2^{i-1} \pmod{m}$$

and have a table of (i, m) ready as the input to the algorithm. Notice that a can be as large as $2^N - 1$, but the value of the modulus is bounded by N. Thus, we are dealing with residue computation with comparatively small modulus. From

$$x = \sum_{i=1}^{N} x_i \, 2^{i-1},$$

we get

$$x \pmod{m} = \left(\sum_{i=1}^{N} (x_i \, b_i) \right) \pmod{m}.$$

As $x_i = 0$ or 1, the product $x_i b_i$ can be computed in one step and the sum

$$s = \sum_{i=1}^{N} x_i \, b_i$$

can be obtained in $O(\log N)$ steps using the Ofman-Wallace tree method (see Section 3.3.2). Now (using, say, the Schonhage-Strassen method of Section 3.6.3), compute the products $j\,m$ for $j = 1$ to $N - 1$, in parallel in $O(\log N)$ steps. For $j = 0$ to $N - 1$, compute $d_j = s - j\,m$ in parallel in $O(\log N)$ steps. Then, obtain a binary vector $c = (c_0, c_1, c_2, \cdots, c_{N-1})$, where

$$c_j = \begin{cases} 1 & \text{if } 0 \le d_j < m \\ \\ 0 & \text{otherwise,} \end{cases}$$

by comparing d_j with zero and m, in $O(\log N)$ steps (see Exercise 3.33). Since $x \pmod{m}$ is unique, there exists a unique k such that $c_k = 1$ and $c_i = 0$ for $i \ne k$. The index k can be obtained in $O(\log N)$ steps, using which we can recover $a \pmod{m}$.

Combining the above results the lemma follows.

Before stating the next Lemma, for purposes of self-contained exposition, we collect together a number of important facts from elementary number theory. Let p be an odd prime number. Then, there exists a primitive root g (see Section 3.5) of p such that $\{g^i \mid i = 1 \text{ to } p - 1\}$ constitutes the reduced residue system $RRS = \{1, 2, 3, \cdots, p - 1\}$. Thus, g is called the generator of the RRS. In other words, given any integer $b \in RRS$, there exists a unique integer $1 \le h \le p - 1$ such that

$$b = g^h.$$

The integer h is called the *discrete logarithm* or the *index* of b with respect to g and is denoted by $I_g(b)$, that is, $b = g^{I_g(b)}$. Further, the arithmetic of indices can be done in mod $(p - 1)$ (refer to Corollary 3.5.1.5).

Given an odd prime p, tables of discrete logarithms or indices can be computed. Refer to Table 3.7.2.1 for some typical examples. We now state a number of properties (without proof) of discrete logarithms. Let a and b be such that $GCD(a, p) = GCD(b, p) = 1$, and let g be the primitive root of p. $GCD(a, p) = 1$ ensures that $a \not\equiv 0 \pmod{p}$ and hence $I_g(a)$ is well defined. Likewise, for b.

(I1) $I_g(ab) = (I_g(a) + I_g(b)) \pmod{(p - 1)}$

(I2) $I_g(a^k) = (k \times I_g(a)) \pmod{(p - 1)}$.

(I3) $I_g(1) = 0$ and $I_g(g) = 1$.

(I4) $I_g(-1) = \dfrac{p - 1}{2}$.

(I5) If g_1 and g_2 are primitive roots of p, then

$$I_{g_1}(a) \equiv (I_{g_2}(a) \times I_{g_1}(g_2)) \pmod{(p - 1)}.$$

(I6) If $a\,x \equiv b \pmod{p}$, then

$$I_g(a) + I_g(x) \equiv I_g(b) \pmod{(p - 1)}.$$

The next lemma provides a fast algorithm to compute the product of integers with respect to a small prime modulus p by exploiting the properties of indices of residues of mod p.

Lemma 3.7.2.2. Let $a_1, a_2, a_3, \cdots, a_N$ be N N-bit integers such that $0 \le a_i < p$ for $i = 1$ to N, where p is a prime integer and $p \le N$. The product

$$z = \prod_{i=1}^{N} a_i \pmod{p}$$

can be computed in $O(\log N)$ steps.

Proof

Since p is known *a priori,* we can precompute the table of indices of elements $1 \le b \le p - 1$ and take it as input to the algorithm. First, test in parallel if any of the a_i's is zero, in which case $z = 0$. Clearly, such a test can be done in at most $O(\log N)$ steps by parallel comparison (see Exercise 3.33). Otherwise, by table lookup,[1] we can obtain the indices of a_i denoted by $I(a_i)$ in parallel in $O(\log N)$ steps. Now compute the sum

---

[1] The table lookup circuit is essentially a *decoder* or *multiplexer tree.* (See Kuck [1978].)

TABLE 3.7.2.1
Values of $I_g(b)$, Where $b = g^{I_g(b)}$ (mod p)

b	$p = 3,$ $g = 2$	$p = 5,$ $g = 2$	$p = 7,$ $g = 3$	$p = 11,$ $g = 2$	$p = 13,$ $g = 2$
1	0	0	0	0	0
2	1	1	2	1	1
3		3	1	8	4
4		2	4	2	2
5			5	4	9
6			3	9	5
7				7	11
8				3	3
9				6	8
10				5	10
11					7
12					6

$$I = \sum_{i=1}^{N} I(a_i)$$

in $O(\log N)$ steps using the Ofman-Wallace tree method (Section 3.3.2). Since $0 \le I < Np$, compute

$$I^* = I(\text{mod } (p-1))$$

by subtracting multiples of $(p-1)$ from I in parallel as in Lemma 3.7.2.1, in $O(\log N)$ steps. Clearly,

$$z = \prod_{i=1}^{N} a_i \ (\text{mod } p)$$

$$= g^{(\sum_{i=1}^{N} I_g(a_i)) \ (\text{mod } (p-1))}$$

$$= g^{I^*}.$$

Thus z can be obtained by one more table lookup, which takes $O(\log N)$ steps. Combining all these, the lemma follows.

A generalization of Lemma 3.7.2.2 is pursued in Exercises 3.37 and 3.38.

We now turn to computing the product of N integers. Let $a_1, a_2, a_3, \cdots, a_N$ be a set of N-bit integers, and $a = \prod_{i=1}^{N} a_i$. Let

$$M = (2^N - 1)^N. \qquad (3.7.2.6)$$

Since $0 \leq a_i \leq 2^N - 1$, we have $0 \leq a < M$. The value of a is computed using arithmetic modulo small integers described in Lemmas 3.7.2.1 and 3.7.2.2 and using the Chinese remainder theorem (see Section 3.6.3) for properly chosen modulus. To this end, we now introduce a sequence $\{ M_k \}$ called the *good* modulo sequence.

Let $h(k)$ and $g(k)$ be two polynomials in k, such that $\{ M_k \}$ satisfy the following two properties:

(P1) $(2^{\sqrt{k}} - 1)^{\sqrt{k}} < M_k \leq 2^{h(k)}$.

(P2) If p is a prime and p^t divides M_k for some $t \geq 1$, then $p^t \leq g(k)$.

Property P2 dictates that M_k does not have overly large prime factors. The role of the upper bound in property P1 is obvious from the following lemma.

Lemma 3.7.2.3. Let $0 \leq x, y < M_k$. Then $x + y$ and xy can be computed in $O(\log k)$ steps.

Proof

Residues mod M_k require at most $h(k)$ bits. Hence, using the algorithm in Section 3.2.1 and Section 3.3 (or 4.6), $x + y$ and xy can be computed in $O(\log h(k)) = O(\log k)$ steps.

Since $h(k^2)$ is also a polynomial in k, it readily follows that $x + y$ and xy can be computed in $O(\log k)$ steps even if $0 \leq x, y \leq M_{k^2}$.

We now show that there is an easy method for constructing the sequence $\{M_k\}$. Let $2 = p_1, p_2, \cdots, p_k$ be the first k primes. From the prime number theorem, it follows that (Hardy and Wright [1960]),

$$p_n = O(n \log n).$$

(See Exercise 3.40). Thus, trivially,

$$2^k \leq \prod_{j=1}^{k} p_j, \qquad (3.7.2.7)$$

and

$$\prod_{j=1}^{k} p_j = 2 \prod_{j=2}^{k} p_j$$

$$\le c \prod_{j=2}^{k} j \log j \qquad \text{for some constant } c > 0$$

$$\le (c \log k) \, k\,!$$

$$= 2^{O(k \log k)}. \tag{3.7.2.8}$$

Combining (3.7.2.7) and (3.7.2.8), it follows that the good modulo sequence $\{\, M_k \,\}$ can be obtained as the product of properly chosen primes. Admittedly, the range of values that M_k can take is quite large and one possible choice is $M_k = \prod_{j=1}^{k} p_j$. Since

$$M_{N^2} > M \ge a,$$

we can compute the product $\prod_{i=1}^{N} a_i$ using mod M_{N^2} and recover the value of a exactly. However, to take advantage of the arithmetic modulo small integers, we invoke the Chinese remainder theorem.

To this end, find the least positive integer t and the set of primes $m_1, m_2, \cdots, m_t$ such that

and

$$\left.\begin{array}{c} \max\{m_1, m_2, \cdots, m_t\} \le N \\[2em] M_{N^2} = \displaystyle\prod_{i=1}^{t} m_i > M. \end{array}\right\} \tag{3.7.2.9}$$

Since $m_i \ge 2$, it is clear that $t \le N^2$.

Since N is fixed *a priori*, we can precompute m_i's, $i = 1$ to t, and consider them as input to the algorithm.

As an example, consider $N = 4$. Then $M = (2^4 - 1)^4 = 15^4 = 50,625$. Thus, we can pick $50,625 < M_{N^2} \le 2^{16} = 65,536$. Hence, $t = 16$ and $m_i = 2$ for $i = 1$ to 16 is one possible choice.

We now turn to the long awaited algorithm. As a first step in the algorithm, compute, for all $1 \le i \le N$ and $1 \le j \le t$,

$$a_{ij} \equiv a_i \;(\text{mod } m_j). \tag{3.7.2.10}$$

Recall that a_i is an N-bit integer with $m_j \le N$. Hence, by Lemma 3.7.2.1, we can compute a_{ij}'s in parallel in $O(\log N)$ steps.

The next step is to compute

$$b_j \equiv \prod_{i=1}^{N} a_{ij} \equiv a_i \;(\text{mod } m_j),$$

for $1 \le j \le t$, in parallel using Lemma 3.7.2.2 in $O(\log N)$ steps.

The last step is to reconstruct a from b_j's by using a version of the Chinese remainder theorem (see Exercise 3.27 for another version). For $j = 1$ to t, define

$$\underline{m}_j = \frac{m}{m_j}, \tag{3.7.2.11}$$

where

$$m = \prod_{j=1}^{t} m_j \quad (= M_{N^2}) \text{ from } (3.7.2.9). \tag{3.7.2.12}$$

Compute n_j such that

$$n_j \, \underline{m}_j \equiv 1 \pmod{m_j}, \tag{3.7.2.13}$$

that is, n_j is the inverse of $\underline{m}_j \pmod{m_j}$. Using these, compute (the interpolation constants)

$$r_j = n_j \, \underline{m}_j. \tag{3.7.2.14}$$

It is easily verified that $r_j \equiv 1 \pmod{m_j}$ and $r_i \equiv 0 \pmod{m_j}$ for $i \neq j$. Since m_j's are known to begin with, the quantities $\underline{m}_j$, n_j, and r_j for $j = 1$ to t can be precomputed and are taken as the input to the algorithm.

Compute

$$b = \sum_{j=1}^{t} b_j \, r_j. \tag{3.7.2.15}$$

Notice that

$$0 \le b_j < m_j \le N$$

and

$$0 \le r_j < m \le 2^{h(N^2)}$$

for some polynomial $h(.)$. Thus, r_j is at most $h(N^2)$ bits long and b_j is $O(\log N)$ bits long. By Lemma 3.7.2.3, the product $b_j \, r_j$ can be computed in parallel in $O(\log h(N^2)) = O(\log N)$ steps. There exists another polynomial $h'(N)$ such that

$$0 \le b_j \, r_j \le Nm \le 2^{h'(N)}.$$

Thus, the number of bits in each of the summands in (3.7.2.15) is bounded by a polynomial in N. Further, the number t of such summands in (3.7.2.15) is also polynomially bounded, since $t \le N^2$. Hence using the Ofman-Wallace tree method (Section 3.3.2) the sum b can be computed in at most $O(\log N)$ steps.

To compute

$$a \equiv b \pmod{m} \tag{3.7.2.16}$$

we need to estimate the largest multiple of m contained in b. To this end, rewrite

$$b = \sum_{j=1}^{t} b_j \, r_j \ = \ \sum_{j=1}^{t} \frac{b_j \, n_j}{m_j} \, m.$$

Compute

$$u_j = q \, b_j \, n_j \tag{3.7.2.17}$$

in parallel for $j = 1$ to t, where $q = 2^{\lceil \log t \rceil}$. Thus,

$$b = \sum_{j=1}^{t} \frac{u_j}{q m_j} \, m.$$

Now, compute

$$v_j = \left\lfloor \frac{u_j}{m_j} \right\rfloor \quad \text{in parallel for } j = 1 \ \text{ to } N, \tag{3.7.2.18}$$

and let

$$v = \sum_{j=1}^{t} v_j. \tag{3.7.2.19}$$

Let

$$\alpha = \left\lfloor \frac{v}{q} \right\rfloor, \tag{3.7.2.20}$$

that is, α is obtained by truncating the right $\lceil \log t \rceil$ bits of v. From

$$\left\lfloor \frac{u_j}{m_j} \right\rfloor \leq \frac{u_j}{m_j} \leq \left\lfloor \frac{u_j}{m_j} \right\rfloor + 1,$$

we obtain

$$0 \leq b - (\frac{v}{q}) \, m = \sum_{j=1}^{t} (\frac{u_j}{q m_j} - \frac{1}{q} \left\lfloor \frac{u_j}{m_j} \right\rfloor) \, m$$

$$< \sum_{j=1}^{t} \frac{1}{q} \, m$$

$$\leq \frac{t}{2^{\lceil \log t \rceil}} \, m$$

$$\leq m.$$

Thus,

$$0 \le b - \alpha m = b - \left\lfloor \frac{v}{q} \right\rfloor m < 2m.$$

The value of a is now given by

$$a = \begin{cases} b - \alpha m & \text{if } 0 \le b - \alpha m < c \\ \\ b - (\alpha + 1)\, m & \text{otherwise.} \end{cases} \tag{3.7.2.21}$$

Now we compute the total time required to compute a from b. First, the computation of u_j in (3.7.2.17). Recall that

$$0 \le b_j,\ n_j < m_j \le N,$$

and

$$q = 2^{\lceil \log t \rceil} \le 2^{\lceil \log N^2 \rceil}$$

$$\le 2^{1 + \log N^2}$$

$$= 2N^2,$$

that is, q, b_j's, n_j's are $O(\log N)$-bit integers. Hence

$$0 \le u_j < 2N^4,$$

that is, u_j's are $O(\log N)$-bit integers and u_j's can be computed in parallel in much less than $O(\log N)$ steps using the multiplication algorithms given in Section 3.3.

Likewise, computing v_j's involves division of $O(\log N)$-bit integers by $O(\log N)$-bit integers. Thus, using any algorithm (such as the one due to Anderson, Earle, Goldschmidt, and Powers [1967] described at the beginning of this section), v_j's can be computed in much less than $O(\log N)$ steps. Since

$$0 \le v_j < 2N^3,$$

each of the v_j's is also $O(\log N)$ bits long. Thus, v is obtained by adding at most N^2 integers each of $O(\log N)$ bits. Again, by the Ofman-Wallace tree method, the sum v can be obtained in $O(\log N)$ steps. Notice that

$$0 \le v < 2N^5.$$

Hence v and α are $O(\log N)$-bit integers and α is obtained from v in one step. m is an $h(N)$-bit integer for some polynomial $h(.)$. (Typically, $h(N) = N^2$.) From (3.7.2.21), computation of a involves multiplications (finding αm, $(\alpha + 1)\, m$), comparisons and subtractions. From the sizes of b, α, and m, it follows that all of these operations can be performed in $O(\log N)$ steps.

We summarize the above development in the following theorem.

Theorem 3.7.2.4. Given a set of integers $a_1, a_2, \cdots, a_N$ each of N bits, the product $a = \prod_{i=1}^{N} a_i$ can be obtained in $O(\log N)$ steps.

Since finding the products/powers of integers constitute the crucial part of the division algorithm, we state the principal result of this section.

Theorem 3.7.2.5. There exists an $O(\log N)$ time algorithm to divide two N-bit integers.

The number of logical elements needed in the implementation of this algorithm is quite large. Beame, Cook, and Hoover [1986] estimate the number of logical elements to be ($O(N^5 \log^2 N)$). A tantalizing open question is to reduce the number of logical operations while keeping the overall depth at its present level.

3.8 NOTES AND REFERENCES

Section 3.1. There are a number of treatises devoted to computer arithmetic, among them Hwang [1979] and Waser and Flynn [1982]. Knuth's Volume 2 (Knuth [1969]) contains a wealth of information on algorithms for basic arithmetic operations. The survey by Karp and Ramachandran [1988] contains a good summary of fast algorithms for addition, multiplication and division. We do not discuss the issues in implementing arithmetic operations in VLSI. For a good discussion on this topic, refer to Brent and Kung [1982], Carlson and Sugla [1985], Han, Carlson, and Levitan [1987], Mehlhorn and Preparata [1983], and Thompson [1979]. Alt [1984] is a good reference for the computation of arithmetic functions using Boolean circuits.

Section 3.2. The method of *ripple carry adder* of Exercise 3.2 corresponds to the grade school method of addition. This method requires linear depth but has *optimal* size. Proving optimality of the sizes for Boolean circuits is beyond the scope of this book and we refer the reader to Savage [1987] and Wegener [1987]. Sklansky [1960a, 1960b] described adder circuits called *conditional-sum-adders* (CSA) with depth $1 + 2 \log N$ and size $3N \log N + 10N - 6$. Ofman [1963] was the first to describe the *carry lookahead* circuits of depth $O(\log N)$ and size $O(N)$. Our development in Section 3.2 follows closely Brent [1970a].

Since the expression for c_i given in (3.2.1.3) corresponds to Horner's expression, this method is readily applicable to the evaluation of polynomials which is pursued in Chapter 4. For a description of Krapchenko's [1970] algorithm, refer to the books by Savage [1987] and Wegener [1987].

Design of carry-lookahead adders based on *prefix* computation is given in Exercises 3.42 to 3.44. The parallel computation of prefixes has been extensively studied in the literature -- see Brent and Kung [1982], Fich [1983], Ladner and Fischer [1980], Lakshmivarahan, Yang, and Dhall [1987], Kruskal, Rudolph, and Snir [1985], Gajski [1980, 1981], Bilgory and Gajski [1986], Bilardi and Preparata [1987], and Schwartz [1980]. For a comprehensive treatment of parallel computation of prefixes, refer to the forthcoming monograph by Lakshmivarahan and Dhall [1989].

Since subtraction can be converted to addition by considering, say, the two's complement, we do not explicitly describe algorithms for subtraction.

Winograd [1965, 1967] and Spira [1969] have derived lower bounds on the time required for addition and multiplication. See Exercises 3.45 and 3.46.

Section 3.3. The method of Lemma 3.3.2.1 that speeds up the addition of N-bit binary integers is called the *carry-save-adder* and is due to Ofman [1963] and Wallace [1964]. It is also known as the Ofman-Wallace tree. The redundant radix-4 representation due to Mehlhorn and Preparata [1983] speeds up the Karatsuba-Ofman [1963] multiplication algorithm in much the same way as the Ofman-Wallace tree speeded up the grade school method. In addition, Mehlhorn and Preparata [1983] describe a whole variety of optimal design of multipliers suitable for VLSI implementation. The relation between integer arithmetic and polynomial arithmetic is quite intrinsic, refer to Chapter 8 of Aho, Hopcroft, and Ullman [1974], for details.

Sections 3.4 to 3.6. The fast Fourier transform algorithm is due to Cooley and Tukey [1965]. For a derivation of the FFT algorithm when N is not a power of 2, refer to Kronsjo [1987] and Winograd [1980]. Among other interesting results, Gentleman and Sande [1966] provide an analysis of errors in the computation of FFT. Morgenstern [1973] contains a discussion of lower bound on the time to compute FFT.

For further elaboration of results from modulo arithmetic and elementary number theory refer to Le Veque [1961], Uspensky [1948], and Vinogradov [1961]. A discussion of folded convolution is contained in Aho, Hopcroft, and Ullman [1974].

For an extensive discussion of the multiplicative complexity of convolution, Fourier transform, and other related problems, refer to Winograd [1980] and Heideman [1988].

Lemma 3.6.3.2 is due to Garner [1959]. Recently, the Schonhage-Strassen [1971] algorithm to multiply integers has been used extensively in the computation of a million digits of π, by Salamin [1976], Brent [1976], Bailey [1988a].

Section 3.7. The grade school method of division requires $O(N \log N)$ depth and $O(N^2)$ size. The first conceptual breakthrough in obtaining a faster division algorithm is due to Reif [1986] and has $O(\log N \log \log N)$ depth. The $O(\log N)$ depth circuit described in Section 3.7 was developed by Beame, Cook, and Hoover [1986]. This circuit, while optimal, requires an excessively large number of logical elements to implement. Purdy and Purdy [1987] describe a VLSI-implementable division circuit with linear depth and bounded fan-in.

3.9 EXERCISES

3.1   Let

$$a = a_N\, a_{N-1} \,\cdots\, a_2\, a_1,$$

$$b = b_N\, b_{N-1} \,\cdots\, b_2\, b_1,$$

and

$$s \equiv (a + b) \bmod 2^N,$$

where $s = s_N\, s_{N-1} \,\cdots\, s_2\, s_1$, $c_0 = 0$ and $s_i = a_i \oplus b_i \oplus c_i$, for $i = 1$ to N. Show that c_i for $i = 1$ to N, can be expressed in any one of the following forms:

(a) $c_i = (\overline{a_i} \wedge b_i \wedge c_{i-1}) \vee (a_i \wedge \overline{b_i} \wedge c_{i-1}) \vee (a_i \wedge b_i \wedge \overline{c_{i-1}}) \vee (a_i \wedge b_i \wedge c_{i-1})$

(b) $c_i = (a_i \wedge b_i) \vee (a_i \wedge c_{i-1}) \vee (b_i \wedge c_{i-1})$

(c) $c_i = (a_i \wedge b_i) \vee (a_i \vee b_i) \wedge c_{i-1}$

(d) $c_i = (a_i \wedge b_i) \vee (a_i \oplus b_i) \wedge c_{i-1}$, and

(e) $c_i = (a_i \vee b_i) \wedge ((a_i \wedge b_i) \vee c_{i-1})$

3.2   Consider Fig. E3.1, a graph of the circuit that computes s_i and c_i using form (d) in Exercise 3.1. The circuit is called a *full adder (FA)*. According to this graph, the computation of s_i and c_i takes *three* stages and *five* logical elements.

(a) Show that a total of $5N - 3$ logical elements and $2N - 1$ stages are needed to compute s using the scheme of Fig. E3.2, called the *ripple carry* adder.

(b) Draw the graph of the full-adder using formulas (c) and (e) of Exercise 3.1. In each case, compute the total number of logical elements and stages needed. Compare all the three realizations of the circuit to compute $s \equiv (a + b) \bmod 2^N$.

(c) How would you modify these circuits to compute $s = a + b$ instead of $s \equiv (a + b) \bmod 2^N$?

3.3   Referring to Fig. 3.2.1.1, show that the total number of logical elements needed to compute the sum of two N-bit integers using Theorem 3.2.1.4 is $O(N \log N)$.

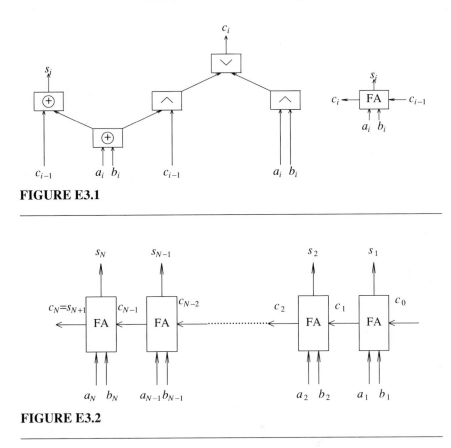

FIGURE E3.1

FIGURE E3.2

3.4 (Brent [1970a]). Theorem 3.2.1.4 was proved using logical circuits made of elements admitting *two* inputs (fan-in = 2) and which compute a logical function of their inputs in unit step. This proof carries over verbatim to addition of integers mod 2^N using circuits made of logical elements admitting $f (\geq 2)$ inputs (fan-in ≥ 2), and which computes a logical function of their input in unit step.

(a) Show that for any $k \geq 1$ and $f \geq 2$

$$T_C(f^{k(k-1)/2}) \leq \frac{k(k + 1)}{2}.$$

(b) Show that when $k = 2$ and $f = 3$ (fan-in = 3), c_3 can be computed in two steps instead of three.

3.5 Develop circuits for the subtraction operation.

Hint: Subtraction is equivalent to addition if we represent negative integers in, say, one's complement or two's complement form.

3.6   Draw the entire circuits corresponding to Theorem 3.2.1.4 for $N = 8$ and $N = 16$.

3.7   Find the break point where Theorem 3.3.2.2 provides an improvement over Theorem 3.3.1.1 in the time required to multiply two N-bit integers.

3.8   (a) Solve recurrence (3.3.3.4).

(b) Let $s(N)$ be the number of logical elements required to compute the product of two N-bit integers using the Karatsuba-Ofman algorithm (refer to 3.3.3.1 to 3.3.3.3). Show that $s(N)$ is the solution of the recurrence

$$s(N) = 3s(\frac{N}{2}) + c_2 N$$

for some constant $c_2 > 0$, where $s(1) = 1$. Show that $s(N) = O(N^{1.59})$, where $1.59 \cdots = \log_2 3$.

(c) Using this method, compute the product of $a = 10101010$ and $b = 10011001$.

3.9   Let $N = 8$. Referring to Fig. 3.4.1.1,

(1)   Let $\alpha = -\frac{1}{\sqrt{2}} + i \frac{1}{\sqrt{2}}$.   Compute α^j for $j = -7, -6, \cdots -1, 0, 1, 2, \cdots 7$.

(2) Let $\beta = -1$. Compute β^j for $j = -7, -6, \cdots, -1, 0, 1, 2, \cdots, 7$.

(3) Is β a principal 8th root of unity? Find all the principal 8th roots of unity.

3.10   Show that $|\{p \times r \pmod N\} \mid 0 \le r \le N - 1\}| = N$ if and only if $GCD(p, N) = 1$.

3.11   Prove or disprove: If ω^k is a principal N^{th} root of unity, then so is ω^{-k}.

3.12   Let N be even and α be a generator of the set of all N^{th} roots of unity. Show that α^2 is a generator of the set of all $(\frac{N}{2})^{th}$ roots of unity.

3.13   Given α, the Nth principal root of unity, find a parallel method for computing α^j for $j = 0, 1, 2, \cdots, N-1$, using N processors. What is the total number of operations required by your algorithm?

3.14   Let $z_1 = a + i b$ and $z_2 = c + i d$ be two complex numbers. Let $z = x + i y$ be the product of z_1 and z_2. Since $x = ac - bd$ and $y = ad + bc$, it takes *four* multiplications and *two* additions/subtractions of real numbers to compute z.

Alternatively, x and y can be computed as

$$x = (a + b)c - b(d + c),$$

$$y = (a + b)c + a(d - c),$$

which requires *three* real multiplications and *five* additions of real numbers.

(a) Investigate the practical implications of computing $z = z_1 z_2$ by these two different techniques.

(b) Discuss the relative merits of using these two complex multiplication schemes to compute $f(\mathbf{a})$ and $f^{-1}(\mathbf{a})$.

3.15 Show that if $\text{GCD}(a, m) = 1$ and as x runs through the elements of CRS (mod m), then for any integer b, $(ax + b) \pmod m$ also runs through CRS (mod m), perhaps in different order. That is, let $A = \{z \mid z = (ax + b \bmod m, \text{GCD}(a, m) = 1\}$, then $A = \text{CRS} \pmod m$, if $x \in \text{CRS} \pmod m$. Repeat for RRS in place of CRS.

3.16 Prove Lemma 3.5.1.2.

3.17 Show that the converse of Fermat's theorem is *not* true, that is, "if $\text{GCD}(a, m) = 1$ and $a^{m-1} \equiv 1 \pmod m$, then m is a prime" is not true.

Hint: Try $m = 15$ and $a = 4$ or $m = 91$ and $a = 3$.

3.18 (Primality Testing) Given $m > 1$, if there is an a such that $a^{m-1} \equiv 1 \pmod m$ and $a^{(m-1)/p} \not\equiv 1 \pmod m$, then m is a prime where p is a prime divisor of $m - 1$.

3.19 Let $\text{ord}^a_m = t$. Then show that

$$\sum_{i=1}^{t} a^{ix} = \begin{cases} 0 \pmod m & \text{if } 1 \le x < t \\ \\ t \pmod m & \text{if } x \text{ is a multiple of } t. \end{cases}$$

Hint: Mimic the proof of (3.5.1.4) and (3.5.1.5).

3.20 Show that

(a) $\Phi(n)$ is even for $n > 2$.

(b) If $n = m_1 m_2$ and $\text{GCD}(m_1, m_2) = 1$, then $\Phi(n) = \Phi(m_1) \Phi(m_2)$.

(c) If $n = p^k$ where p is a prime and $k \ge 1$, then $\Phi(n) = p^k - p^{k-1} = n(1 - p^{-1})$.

(d) $\Phi(n) \leq n - 1$ with the equality holding if and only if n is a prime.

(e) If $n = p_1^{k_1} p_2^{k_2} \cdots p_t^{k_t}$, where p_i's are prime and $k_i \geq 1$, then

$$\Phi(n) = n (1 - p_1^{-1}) (1 - p_2^{-1}) \cdots (1 - p_t^{-1}).$$

3.21 Let $a \in CRS$ (mod m). Show that

(a) $\displaystyle\sum_{i=0}^{N-1} a^i = \prod_{i=1}^{k-1} (1 + a^{2^i})$, where $N = 2^k$.

(b) Hence show that $\displaystyle\sum_{i=1}^{N} \alpha^{ix} \equiv 0$ (mod m), where α and m are defined in (3.5.1.7).

3.22 Compute the DFT of $a = (1, 4, 2, 3)$ using the FFT algorithm by generating the four roots of unity using $N = 4$, $\alpha = 4$, and $m = 7$. Verify your result by explicitly computing Fa, where F is given by (3.5.2.2).

3.23 (Le Veque [1961]). Let p be an odd prime and a be relatively prime to p.

(a) Show that a is a quadratic residue of modulo p if and only if

$$a^{(p-1/2)} \equiv 1 \ (\text{mod } p).$$

(b) If g is the primitive root of p then show that g cannot be a quadratic residue of p.

Note: Thus there exists no β in the range $0 < \beta < p$ such that $\beta^2 \equiv g$ (mod p). Hence if $m = 2^{N/2} + 1$ is a prime, g cannot be used in the computation of negative folded convolution.

(c) If $x^2 \equiv a$ (mod p), then $(p - x)^2 \equiv a$ (mod p).

Note: Thus, if x is a square root of a (mod p), then so is $p - x$.

3.24 Let $\beta^2 \equiv \alpha$ (mod m), where m, N, and α are related as in (3.5.1.7). Since $GCD (\alpha, m) = 1$, show that $GCD (\beta^k, m) = 1$ for all $1 \leq k \leq N - 1$.

Note: This permits us to divide both sides of (3.6.2.12) by β^r to obtain (3.6.1.6) while computing **NCON (a, b)** in modulo arithmetic.

3.25 Let $\mathbf{a} = (1, 1, 2, 3)^t$ and $\mathbf{b} = (1, 2, 3, 1)^t$.

(a) Compute **CON (a, b)** using Theorem 3.6.2.1 in modulo arithmetic. (Since $N = 4$, choose $\alpha = 2$ and $m = 5$).

(b) Compute **PCON (a, b)** using Corollary 3.6.2.2 in modulo arithmetic.

3.26 Let m_j, for $j = 1$ to $t = 2^q$, be a set of pairwise relatively prime integers. Let a be the given integer whose modular representation is sought. The following recursive algorithm is useful.

Define

$$i : j = m_i \, m_{i+1} \, \cdots \, m_j$$

and

$$a_{01} = a.$$

Let

$$a_{11} = a_{01} \bmod (1 : \frac{t}{2})$$

$$a_{12} = a_{01} \bmod (\frac{t}{2} + 1 : t)$$

$$a_{21} = a_{11} \bmod (1 : \frac{t}{4})$$

$$a_{22} = a_{11} \bmod (\frac{t}{4} + 1 : \frac{t}{2})$$

$$a_{23} = a_{12} \bmod (\frac{t}{2} + 1 : \frac{3t}{4})$$

$$a_{24} = a_{12} \bmod (\frac{3t}{4} + 1 : t)$$

and so on.

(a) Continuing this way, show that $(a_{q1}, a_{q2}, \cdots, a_{qt})$ is the required modular representation.

(b) Find the serial and parallel complexities of this algorithm.

3.27 Let $m_1, m_2, \cdots, m_t$, be a set of integers relatively prime in pairs. Given any integer a, let $a_i \equiv a \pmod{m_i}$. Let $m = \prod_{i=1}^{t} m_i$. Define

$$\bar{m}_j = (\frac{m}{m_j})^{\Phi(m_j)}$$

where $\Phi(.)$ is the Euler function, for some integer $k > 0$, $\Phi(k)$ denotes the number of integers less than k and relatively prime to k.

(a) Show that

$$a = (a_1 \bar{m}_1 + a_2 \bar{m}_2 + \cdots + a_t \bar{m}_t) \bmod m.$$

Hint: Use Euler's theorem (Lemma 3.5.1.2).

(b) Compare the above representation of a with the process of expressing a in mixed radix notation as in (3.6.3.4).

Note: Another version of the Chinese remainder theorem is given in Section 3.7 in the context of parallel division.

3.28 Discuss   the   effects   of   computing $a \times b \pmod{2^N}$ instead   of $a \times b \pmod{2^N + 1}$ in the Schonhage-Strassen multiplication rule.

3.29 Solve recurrences (3.6.3.20) and (3.6.3.21).

3.30 (a) How fast can you compute d^{2^j} (in (3.7.1.3)) and $\prod_{i=0}^{j-1} e_i(d)$ (in 3.7.1.8) for $j = 1, 2, \cdots, k$?

(b) Instead of the grade school method, use the Schonhage-Strassen method to multiply numbers in the proof of Theorem 3.7.1.3 and estimate the time and number of logical elements needed.

3.31 Compute $\dfrac{22}{b}$ for $1 < b \le 31$ using

(a) the classical method of Anderson, Earle, Goldschmidt, and Powers [1967] given in Section 3.7.1, and

(b) the method of Beame, Cook, and Hoover [1986] given in Section 3.7.2.

3.32 (Beame, Cook, and Hoover [1986]) Let a be an N-bit integer. The following algorithm shows that the problem of computing the powers of a namely $a^0, a^1, a^2, \cdots, a^N$ reduces to integer division problem.

(1) Compute $x = 2^{2N^3 + 2N^2}$ and $y = 2^{2N^2} - x$.

(2) Evaluate $z = \left\lfloor \dfrac{x}{y} \right\rfloor$ using a $(2N^3 + 2N^2)$-bit division circuit.

(a) Show that

$$\frac{x}{y} = \frac{2^{2N^3 + 2N^2}}{2^{2N^2} - x} = \sum_{i=0}^{\infty} 2^{2N^2(N-i)} x^i$$

and

$$\sum_{i=N+1}^{\infty} 2^{2N^2(N-i)} x^i < 1.$$

(b) Hence or otherwise, show that a^{N-i} can be read off as the bits in position $2N^2 i$ to $2N^2(i+1) - 1$ from the right in z where the position zero contains the low order bit. (In other words, the problem has been so scaled that none of the powers of a overlap in the resulting binary expansion for z.)

3.33 (Savage [1987]). Let $a = a_N \, a_{N-1} \, a_{N-2} \cdots a_2 \, a_1$ and $b = b_N \, b_{N-1} \, b_{N-2} \cdots b_2 \, b_1$, in binary. Show that $a \geq b$, $a > b$, $a = b$ can be tested in parallel in $O(\log N)$ steps using $O(N)$ logical elements.

3.34 Discuss the effect of different choices for $M \geq (2^N - 1)^N$ used in the powering algorithm in Section 3.7.

3.35 (Mehlhorn and Preparata [1983]). (a) Derive a simple algorithm to divide a number in RR-4 representation by a power of 4.

(b) If $r = \sum_{i=0}^{2t-2} r_i \, 4^i$, find an algorithm for the RR-4 normalization of r.

3.36 (a) Let $N = 2^n$ and $n \geq 3$. Show that the RRS $(\mathrm{mod} \ 2^n)$ can be generated by $(-1)^x \, 5^y$, where $x = 0, 1, \ 0 \leq y < 2^{n-2}$, and $-1 \equiv (2^n - 1) \, (\mathrm{mod} \ 2^n)$. As an example, let $N = 8$. Then $0 \leq y < 2$ and $5^0 \equiv 3 \, (\mathrm{mod} \ 8)$, $5^1 \equiv 5 \, (\mathrm{mod} \ 8)$, $-5^0 \equiv 7 \, (\mathrm{mod} \ 8)$, and $-5^1 \equiv 3 \, (\mathrm{mod} \ 8)$. Thus, using this representation, we can generate a table of x and y for various elements in RRS as in Table E3.1. Compute the Table of Indices for $N = 32$.

TABLE E3.1
Table of Indices mod 8

a $a \in$ RRS $(\mathrm{mod} \ 8)$	x	y
1	0	0
5	0	1
7	1	0
3	1	1

Note. For $N = 2^n$ and $n \geq 3$, these tables are to be used in lieu of the table of discrete logarithms. This is primarily due to the fact that there is *no* primitive root for mod 2^n, $n \geq 3$, and the discrete logarithms are usually defined using the primitive root.

(b) Let $a_1 = (-1)^{x_1} 5^{y_1}$ and $a_2 = (-1)^{x_2} 5^{y_2}$. Then show that $a = a_1 a_2 = (-1)^x 5^y$, where $x \equiv (x_1 + x_2) \pmod 2$ and $y \equiv (y_1 + y_2) \pmod{2^{n-2}}$.

3.37 (Beame, Cook, and Hoover [1986]). This exercise is an extension of Lemma 3.7.2.2. Let $a_1, a_2, \cdots, a_N$ be a set of N N-bit integers such that $0 \le a_i < p^n$ for all $i = 1$ to N, p is a prime, and $p^n \le N$. Assume that either p is an *odd* prime or $p^n = 2$ *or* 4. From Exercise 3.20, it follows that $\Phi(p^n) = p^n - p^{n-1}$. Let g be the primitive root of p^n, that is, $\{g^i \mid i = 1 \text{ to } \Phi(p^n)\}$ constitutes the RRS $\pmod{p^n}$. Since N and p^n are known, g and its powers can be computed *a priori* and used as input to the algorithm. Let

$$z = \prod_{i=1}^{N} a_i \pmod{p^n}.$$

(a) Show that the following algorithm computes z in $O(\log N)$ steps.

(**S1**) Compute in parallel the largest power of p, say p^{k_i}, that divides a_i for $i = 1$ to N.

(**S2**) Compute $b_i = \dfrac{a_i}{p^{k_i}}$ in parallel for $i = 1$ to N.

Note: $GCD(b_i, p^n) = 1$.

(**S3**) Let $k = \sum_{i=1}^{N} k_i$. Then,

$$\prod_{i=1}^{N} a_i = p^k \prod_{i=1}^{N} b_i \pmod{p^n}$$

(**S4**) From the table of discrete logarithms (roman mod p^n), find $I(b_i)$, the index of b_i for $i = 1$ to N.

(**S5**) Compute $I = \sum_{i=1}^{N} I(b_i)$.

(**S6**) Calculate $I^* = I \pmod{(p^n - p^{n-1})}$.

(**S7**) From the table of discrete logarithms (mod p^n), find g^{I^*} and compute

$$z = g^{I^*} p^k \pmod{p^n}.$$

(b) Illustrate the above algorithm for $N = 25$.

3.38 (Exercise 3.37 continued). When $p^n = 2^n$ for $n \ge 3$, steps (S4) through (S7) in Exercise 3.37 need to be modified to accommodate the fact that in this case the

RRS (mod 2^n) is generated by $(2^n - 1)^x 5^y$, where $x = 0, 1$, and $0 \le y < 2^{n-2}$ (see Exercise 3.36).

(a) Show that the algorithm in Exercise 3.37 with steps (S4) through (S7) modified as follows computes z in $O(\log N)$ steps.

    (**S4′**) Find the (x_i, y_i) pair from the table for RRS (mod 2^n), such that

$$b_i = (-1)^{x_i} 5^{y_i}$$

    in parallel for $i = 1$ to N.

    (**S5′**) Compute

$$x = \sum_{i=1}^{N} x_i \quad \text{and} \quad y = \sum_{i=1}^{N} y_i$$

    (**S6′**) Calculate (using the table for RRS (mod 2^n))

$$x^* \equiv x \ (\text{mod } 2) \quad \text{and} \quad y^* \equiv y \ (\text{mod } 2^{n-2})$$

    (**S7′**) From the table of indices (mod 2^n), find

$$\prod_{i=1}^{N} b_i = (-1)^{x^*} 5^{y^*} \ (\text{mod } 2^n)$$

    and compute

$$z = p^k \prod_{i=1}^{N} b_i \ (\text{mod } 2^n).$$

(b) Illustrate the above algorithm for $N = 32$.

3.39 (Beame, Cook, and Hoover [1986]). Let a and b be two N-bit integers. Show that a^b (mod m) can be computed in $O(\log N)$ steps where $m \le N$.

Hint: Let $m = \prod_{i=1}^{k} p^{n_i}$ be a prime factorization for m. Since m is small, such factors can be easily obtained and taken as inputs to the algorithms. First compute a^b (mod p^{n_i}) using the discrete logarithms and then use the Chinese remainder theorem.

3.40 (Hardy and Wright [1960]). Show that the value of the nth prime $p_n = O(n \log n)$.

3.41 Show that $(k!) \log k = 2^{O(k \log k)}$.

3.42   This exercise relates the carry computation to the *prefix* problem.

Let A be a set and o be an associative, *binary* operation defined over the elements of A and that A is *closed* under o. (A, o) is called a *semigroup* (Birkoff and Bartee [1970]). Let $\mathbf{d} = (d_1, d_2, \cdots, d_N)^t$, where $d_i \in A$ for $1 \leq i \leq N$. Let $x_i = x_{i-1} \text{ o } d_i$, where $x_1 = d_1$. Since $x_i = d_1 \text{ o } d_2 \text{ o } \cdots \text{ o } d_i$, the problem of computing x_i is called the *prefix* problem.

From Exercise 3.1, we can write the carry c_i as

$$c_i = h_i \wedge c_{i-1} \vee g_i = f_i(c_{i-1}),$$

where $g_i = a_i \wedge b_i$ and $h_i = a_i \oplus b_i$. If o denotes the *composition* of functions, namely,

$$f_k \text{ o } f_{k+1}(c_{k-1}) = f_{k+1}(f_k(c_{k-1})),$$

then, it can be seen that

$$c_i = f_1 \text{ o } f_2 \text{ o } \cdots \text{ o } f_i(c_0).$$

Since the composition of function is *associative,* it follows that c_i's can be computed as prefixes.

(a) If

$$f_i \text{ o } f_j(x) = f_j(f_i(x)) = h \wedge x \vee g,$$

then compute h and g as a function of g_i, g_j, h_i, and h_j.

(b) Draw a Boolean circuit for computing $f_i \text{ o } f_j(x)$. Compute its depth and size.

3.43   In this exercise we develop a typical circuit for computing prefixes. Let

$$\mathbf{d} = (d_1, d_2, \cdots, d_N)^t$$

and $i : j = d_i \text{ o } d_{i+1} \text{ o } \cdots \text{ o } d_j$, for $i \leq j$. Let a two-input prefix circuit be denoted as in Fig. E3.3. Let $N = 2^n$ and define recursively the N-input prefix circuit P_N as in Fig. E3.4.

(a) Draw circuits P_4, P_8, and P_{16}.

(b) Show that the depth of P_N is $\log N$ and the size of $P_N = O(N \log N)$.

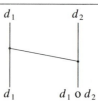

$d_1 \qquad\qquad d_2$

$d_1 \qquad\qquad d_1 \text{ o } d_2$

FIGURE E3.3

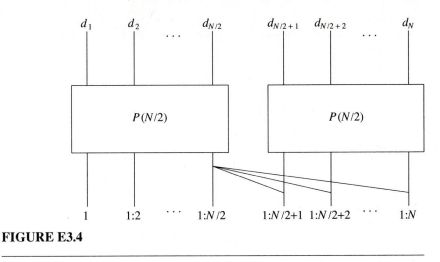

FIGURE E3.4

3.44 (Ladner and Fischer [1980]). An N-input Ladner-Fischer circuit $LF_k(N)$, where $0 \leq k \leq \lceil \log N \rceil$, is recursively defined as in Figs. E3.5 through E3.7. Let $s_k(N)$ and $d_k(N)$ be the size and depth of $LF_k(N)$.

(a) Show that

$$d_k(N) \leq \lceil \log N \rceil + k$$

and

$$s_k(N) \leq 2N(1 + \frac{1}{2^k}) - F(5 + \log N - k) - k + 1,$$

where $F(y)$ is the yth Fibonacci number.

(b) Tabulate $s_k(N)$ and $d_k(N)$ for $N = 2^n$ for $1 \leq n \leq 20$, $0 \leq k \leq \lceil \log N \rceil$, and compare it with the size and depth of P_N in Exercise 3.43.

Note: Thus, $LF_k(N)$ exhibits a natural *depth* vs. size trade-off. Snir [1986] proved that for any N-input parallel prefix circuit (size + depth) $\geq 2N - 2$. For optimal designs of prefix circuits, refer to Snir [1986] and Lakshmivarahan, Yang, and Dhall [1987].

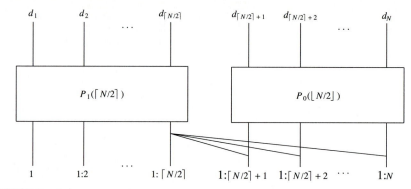

FIGURE E3.5
Ladner-Fischer parallel prefix circuit $P_0(N)$.

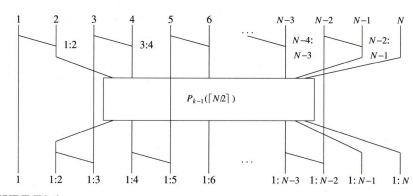

FIGURE E3.6
Ladner-Fischer parallel prefix circuit $P_k(N)$ -- N odd.

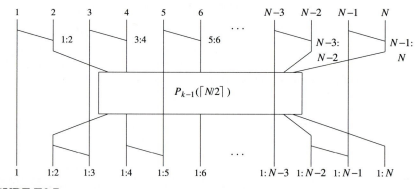

FIGURE E3.7
Ladner-Fischer parallel prefix circuit $P_k(N)$ -- N even.

CHAPTER
4

PARALLELISM IN ARITHMETIC EXPRESSIONS

4.1 INTRODUCTION

We now move on to describing parallel algorithms for the evaluation of arithmetic expressions. These algorithms are useful in the design of compilers for computers with multifunctional units.

4.1.1 Motivation and Statement of Problem

In this chapter we present parallel methods for evaluating different types of arithmetic expressions involving combinations of operators $+, -, \times, /$. The expressions considered may contain balanced *nested* parentheses. The standard method for measuring the *depth, d,* of nesting is to assign a count to each parenthesis. The leftmost parenthesis is assigned a count 1, and in the left-to-right scan, the count of each left parenthesis is increased by 1 and that of each right parenthesis is decreased by 1. The following expression E has depth $d = 2$ nesting. It is assumed that there are no redundant parenthesis pairs.

$$E = a (b + c (d + e) + f (g + h))$$
$$\quad\quad 1\quad\quad 2\quad\quad 1\quad 2\quad\quad 1\ 0$$

It is readily seen that in an expression E with N atoms, the depth $d < \left\lfloor \dfrac{N}{2} \right\rfloor$.

Since nested parentheses impose a strict sequencing of operations, they often inhibit parallel evaluation. For example, in the above expression $d + e$ must be computed before multiplying by c, and so on.

We now introduce some standard concepts and conventions. An *atom* is a single variable or a constant. The subtraction operation is not explicitly considered, since, without loss of generality, it can often be subsumed at the variable or constant level. For example, $a - (b + c)$ is replaced by $a + ((-b) + (-c))$, where the sign change operation can be done in parallel at the input stage. Let $E(N)$ denote an expression with *at most* N atoms, and $E(N, d)$ refer to an expression with at most N atoms and parenthesis nesting of depth d. The actual number of atoms in an expression is denoted by $|E|$. A well-formed arithmetic expression has one or more parse trees. Since the operations in question are all binary, the parse trees are all binary trees. Figure 4.1.1.1 provides two parse trees corresponding to the expression

$$E = a (b + c (d + e (f + g \times h))).$$

One proven technique for inducing parallelism in the evaluation of arithmetic expressions is to exploit the properties of associativity, commutativity, and distributivity of the arithmetic operators.[1] It will be shown that if an expression contains nested parentheses, then the use of associativity and commutativity alone is *not* helpful in obtaining speed-up in evaluation. In such cases, the use of distributivity is necessary to bring about speed-up. While explicit algorithms for restructuring the expressions are *not* given, since the methods described are all constructive in nature, one could readily incorporate these into the design of compilers for computers with multifunctional units.

In Section 4.2, we first prove the necessity of distributivity in obtaining speed-up in the evaluation of nested expressions. A variety of parallel algorithms for the evaluation of polynomials which exploit associativity, distributivity, and commutativity are described in Section 4.3. We conclude that section by deriving a lower bound on the parallel time to evaluate Horner's expression using a fixed

---

[1] Recall that in floating point arithmetic under finite precision, these properties may not hold. To simplify the analysis, we therefore assume ideal conditions.

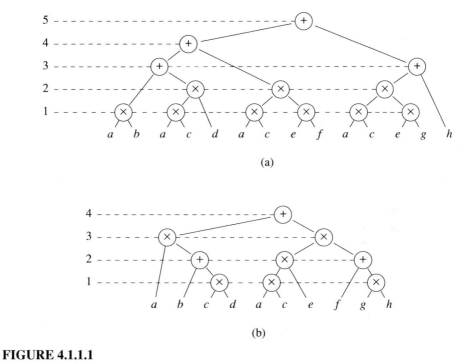

(a)

(b)

FIGURE 4.1.1.1
Two different parse trees for the expression $E = a\,(b + c\,(d + e\,(f + gh)))$.

number of processors. Under this set-up, optimality of certain evaluation strategies is proved. Section 4.4 is divided into two subsections. In the first subsection, we derive upper bounds on the parallel time to evaluate general arithmetic expressions *without* involving the division operation. The second subsection derives similar results for general arithmetic expressions involving the division operation as well. Except for the use of the division operation, the expressions considered in Section 4.4 may contain nested parentheses, and the upper bounds are derived by exploiting associativity, commutativity, and distributivity.

4.2 EVALUATION OF EXPRESSIONS WITH NESTED PARENTHESES

In this section, we consider parallel evaluation of arithmetic expressions involving + (addition), × (multiplication), and / (division) operators, and *nested* parentheses. It is well known that nested parentheses in arithmetic expressions often induce a strict precedence relation, which in turn impedes parallelism. It is shown that there exist nested (Horner's type) expressions whose evaluation cannot be speeded up by the use of associativity and commutativity. This result is fundamental and, in a sense, establishes the necessity for using the distributive property of operators. In fact, all the methods used in Sections 4.3 and 4.4 exploit all three properties -- associativity, commutativity, and distributivity of arithmetic operators -- in obtaining faster methods for evaluation.

4.2.1 Associativity and Commutativity Are Not Enough for Speed-up

Recall that $E(N, d)$ denotes an expression with at most N atoms and parenthesis nesting of *depth d*. Let T_E be a parse tree for E. Define mh(T_E) to be the *minimum height* of all the parse trees for E obtained using associativity and commutativity. The *effective length, e (E)*, of an arithmetic expression E is defined as $e(E) = 2^{\text{mh}(T_E)}$. Thus, if $E = a/(b + c)$, then mh$(T_E) = 2$ and $e(E) = 4$. If $E = a(b + c(f + g))$, then mh$(T_E) = 4$ and $e(E) = 16$. As a last example, if $E = a + b + c \times f$, then mh$(T_E) = 2$ and $e(E) = 4$. Thus $|E| \le e(E)$. Given any $E(N, d)$, we can construct a *related* expression $E'(e(E), 1)$ with $e(E)$ atoms, and *all* nested only at one level such that the height of the minimum height tree for $E(N, d)$ is never greater than $\log e(E)$, which is the minimum height of the parse tree $T_{E'}$ for $E'(e(E), 1)$.

    If the last operation to be performed in evaluating an expression is +, then that expression is called a *factor;* otherwise it is called a *term*. For example, $x + y$, $(x + y) + (n/m + t)$ are factors and $(x + y)/(z \times (a + b))$, $(\frac{a}{b}) \times (\frac{z}{x})$ are terms. It is assumed that multiplication and division have the same precedence and the association of operations is from left to right. Accordingly,

$$x \times y / m / n \times a = (((x \times y) / m) / n) \times a = \frac{xya}{mn}.$$

Define

$$E(N) = \overset{N}{\underset{i=1}{\Gamma}} a_i,$$

where

$$\overset{N}{\underset{i=1}{\Gamma}} a_i = a_{11}\, a_{12} \cdots a_{1\,t_1} / a_{21} / a_{22} / \cdots / a_{2\,t_2}$$

$$\cdots\; a_{s-1,1}\, a_{s-1,2} \cdots a_{s-1,t_{s-1}} / a_{s1} / a_{s2} / \cdots / a_{s\,t_s}$$

$$= \frac{a_{11}\, a_{12} \cdots a_{1\,t_1} \cdots a_{s-1,1}\, a_{s-1,2} \cdots a_{s-1,t_{s-1}}}{a_{21}\, a_{22} \cdots a_{2\,t_2} \cdots a_{s1}\, a_{s2} \cdots a_{s\,t_s}},$$

and $\sum_{i=1}^{s} t_i = N$, that is, Γ refers to a sequence of products and quotients. Thus, we can rewrite $E(N)$ as

$$E(N) = \prod_{i=1}^{N} a_i = \frac{E_1(m)}{E_2(N-m)}, \qquad (4.2.1.1)$$

for some $0 < m < N$.

Our first step is to quantify the minimum height for certain types of arithmetic expressions. To this end, we begin by developing a number of useful lemmas.

Lemma 4.2.1.1. For any integers N and s,

$$\left\lceil \frac{N}{2^s} \right\rceil = \left\lceil \cdots \left\lceil \left\lceil \frac{N}{2} \right\rceil_1 \frac{1}{2} \right\rceil_2 \cdots \frac{1}{2} \right\rceil_s$$

where $\lceil . \rceil_i$ refers to the ith ceiling.

Proof

The lemma is trivial for $s = 1$. Hence let $s \geq 2$. Assume that

$$N = N_m 2^m + N_{m-1} 2^{m-1} + \cdots + N_{t+1} 2^{t+1} + N_t 2^t + \cdots + N_0 2^0 \quad (4.2.1.2)$$

in binary. It is convenient to consider two cases.

    Case 1. Let $r \equiv N \pmod{2^t}$, where $2^t > r > 0$ and $t \geq 2$. Then,

$$N = N_m 2^m + N_{m-1} 2^{m-1} + \cdots + N_t 2^t + r \qquad (4.2.1.3)$$

and

$$\left\lceil \frac{N}{2^t} \right\rceil = N_m 2^{m-t} + \cdots + N_t + 1.$$

Thus,

$$\left\lceil \left\lceil \frac{N}{2^t} \right\rceil \frac{1}{2} \right\rceil = \left\lceil N_m 2^{m-t-1} + \cdots + N_{t+1} + \frac{N_t + 1}{2} \right\rceil$$

$$= N_m 2^{m-t-1} + \cdots + N_{t+1} + 1.$$

Also, from (4.2.1.3), it follows that

$$\left\lceil \frac{N}{2^{t+1}} \right\rceil = N_m \, 2^{m-t-1} + \cdots + N_{t+1} + 1,$$

and this case is proved.

Case 2. Let $0 \equiv N \pmod{2^t}$. Then from (4.2.1.3) with $r = 0$, we obtain

$$\left\lceil \frac{N}{2^t} \right\rceil = N_m \, 2^{m-t} + \cdots + N_t.$$

Thus,

$$\left\lceil \left\lceil \frac{N}{2^t} \right\rceil \frac{1}{2} \right\rceil = N_m \, 2^{m-t-1} + \cdots + N_{t+1} + \left\lceil \frac{N_t}{2} \right\rceil.$$

Also from (4.2.1.2), we obtain that

$$\left\lceil \frac{N}{2^{t+1}} \right\rceil = N_m \, 2^{m-t-1} + \cdots + N_{t+1} + \left\lceil \frac{N_t}{2} \right\rceil,$$

and the lemma is proved.

In the following, unless specified otherwise, all the logarithms are to the base 2.

Lemma 4.2.1.2.

(a) For any real x and integer a,

$$\left\lceil \log \left(\lceil x \rceil + a \right) \right\rceil = \left\lceil \log \left(x + a \right) \right\rceil.$$

(b) For any integers m and n, if $b = 2^m$, then

$$\lceil \log nb \rceil = \log b + \lceil \log n \rceil.$$

Proof

Given a real x and an integer a, let k be such that

$$2^{k-1} < x + a \le 2^k. \tag{4.2.1.4}$$

Then since $x \le 2^k - a$ and 2^k and a are integers, it follows that $\lceil x \rceil \le 2^k - a$. Thus, $\lceil x \rceil + a \le 2^k$. From this and (4.2.1.4), part (a) follows.

To prove part (b), let $n = 2^t + r$, where $r < 2^t$. Then,

$$\lceil \log nb \rceil = \left\lceil \log 2^m (2^t + r) \right\rceil$$

$$= \left\lceil \log 2^m + \log (2^t + r) \right\rceil$$

$$= \begin{cases} m + t + 1 & \text{if } r > 0 \\ m + t & \text{if } r = 0. \end{cases}$$

Since

$$\log b + \lceil \log n \rceil = \begin{cases} m + t + 1 & \text{if } r > 0 \\ m + t & \text{if } r = 0, \end{cases}$$

claim (b) follows.

Lemma 4.2.1.3. Let a_i, P_i, and S_i, $i = 1, \cdots, t$, denote a set of atoms, terms, and factors respectively. Then the upper bounds on the minimum tree heights for certain combinations of atoms, terms, and factors, using associativity and commutativity, are given below:

(a) If $E = \sum_{i=1}^{m} a_i$, $\prod_{i=1}^{m} a_i$, or $\Gamma_{i=1}^{m} a_i$, then

$$mh(T_E) = \lceil \log m \rceil.$$

(b) Let $E = \sum_{i=1}^{m} P_i$, then

$$mh(T_E) \le \left\lceil \log \left(\sum_{i=1}^{m} e(P_i) \right) \right\rceil.$$

(c) Let $E = \Gamma_{i=1}^{m} (S_i)$, then

$$\mathrm{mh}(T_E) \le \left\lceil \log \left(\sum_{i=1}^{m} e(S_i) \right) \right\rceil .$$

Proof

If $E(m) = \sum_{i=1}^{m} a_i$ or $\prod_{i=1}^{m} a_i$, then $\mathrm{mh}(E) = \lceil \log m \rceil$ follows from the associative fan-in argument. Now, it follows from (4.2.1.1) that there exist r_1 and r_2 such that $1 \le r_1, r_2 \le m - 1$, $r_1 + r_2 = m$, and

$$E(m) = \frac{E'(r_1)}{E''(r_2)} = \frac{b_1 \, b_2 \; \cdots \; b_{r_1}}{c_1 \, c_2 \; \cdots \; c_{r_2}}.$$

In this case, by extending the idea illustrated in the example in Fig. 4.2.1.1, it follows that $\mathrm{mh}(E) = \lceil \log m \rceil$. This completes the proof of part (a).

To prove part (b), let $P_i = P_i \, (\mid P_i \mid, \, d_i)$ be a term with $\mid P_i \mid$ atoms nested at depth d_i. Define the corresponding expression $P_i' = P_i' \, (e(P_i), 1)$, with $e(P_i)$

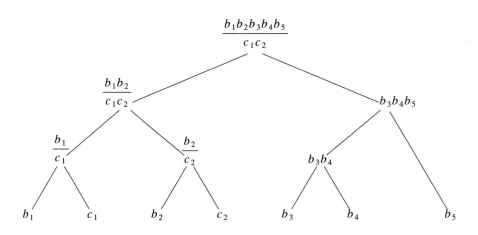

FIGURE 4.2.1.1

An evaluation of $E = \dfrac{b_1 b_2 b_3 b_4 b_5}{c_1 c_2}$ in three steps, where $r_1 = 5$, $r_2 = 2$.

atoms all nested at one level. Let T_{P_i} and $T_{P_i'}$ be the minimum height parse trees for P_i and P_i', where $\mathrm{mh}(T_{P_i}) \leq \mathrm{mh}(T_{P_i'}) = \log e(P_i)$, $i = 1$ to m. Let

$$T = \{T_{P_i} \mid i = 1 \text{ to } m\}, \quad \text{and} \quad T' = \{T_{P_i'} \mid i = 1 \text{ to } m\}.$$

Now partition T' into t $(t \leq m)$ groups in terms of the height of the trees. Let there be m_i trees of height $\log e_i$, where $\sum_{i=1}^{t} m_i = m$, $\sum_{i=1}^{t} e_i m_i = \sum_{i=1}^{m} e(P_i)$, and $e_1 < e_2 < \cdots < e_t$.

Now combine the m_1 trees of least height $\log e_1$ pairwise to obtain $\left\lceil \dfrac{m_1}{2} \right\rceil$ trees of height $1 + \log e_1$. Repeat this process $k_1 = \log(e_2/e_1)$ times (since e_i is a power of 2, k_1 is an integer > 0), to obtain

$$\alpha_1 = \left\lceil \quad \cdots \quad \left\lceil \left\lceil \frac{m_1}{2} \right\rceil_1 \frac{1}{2} \right\rceil_2 \quad \cdots \quad \right\rceil_{k_1} = \left\lceil \frac{m_1}{2^{k_1}} \right\rceil$$

trees of height $\log e_2$. We now have $\alpha_1 + m_2$ trees of height $\log e_2$. These trees are now combined $k_2 = \log\left(\dfrac{e_3}{e_2}\right)$ times to obtain

$$\alpha_2 = \left\lceil \frac{\alpha_1 + m_2}{2^{k_2}} \right\rceil$$

trees of height $\log e_3$. Continuing in this fashion, in the last stage we obtain $\alpha_{t-1} + m_t$ trees of height $\log e_t$. These trees are now combined pairwise to obtain the final tree $T_{E'}$ for E', where

$$\mathrm{mh}(T_{E'}) = \log e_t + \left\lceil \log(\alpha_{t-1} + m_t) \right\rceil \tag{4.2.1.5}$$

$$= \log e_t + \left\lceil \log\left(\left\lceil \frac{\alpha_{t-2} + m_{t-1}}{2^{k_{t-1}}} \right\rceil + m_t\right) \right\rceil .$$

Using Lemma 4.2.1.2,

$$\mathrm{mh}(T_{E'}) = \log e_t + \left\lceil \log\left(\left(\frac{\alpha_{t-2} + m_{t-1}}{2^{k_{t-1}}}\right) + m_t\right) \right\rceil .$$

Since e_t is a power of 2, again using Lemma 4.2.1.2,

$$\mathrm{mh}(T_{E'}) = \left\lceil \log\left(\frac{e_t}{2^{k_{t-1}}} (\alpha_{t-2} + m_{t-1}) + e_t m_t\right) \right\rceil .$$

By definition $e_i = e_{i-1} 2^{k_{i-1}}$, for $i = 1, 2, \cdots, t$. Using this,

$$\mathrm{mh}(T_{E'}) = \left\lceil \log(e_{t-1} \alpha_{t-2} + e_{t-1} m_{t-1} + e_t m_t) \right\rceil . \tag{4.2.1.6}$$

Rewrite

$$e_{t-1}\, \alpha_{t-2} + e_{t-1}\, m_{t-1} + e_t\, m_t = e_{t-1}\, (\alpha_{t-2} + \beta_{t-1}), \qquad (4.2.1.7)$$

where

$$\beta_{t-1} = m_{t-1} + \frac{e_t}{e_{t-1}}\, m_t = m_{t-1} + 2^{k_{t-1}}\, m_t. \qquad (4.2.1.8)$$

Using (4.2.1.7) in (4.2.1.6) from Lemma 4.2.1.2,

$$\text{mh}(T_{E'}) = \log e_{t-1} + \left\lceil \log (\alpha_{t-2} + \beta_{t-1}) \right\rceil, \qquad (4.2.1.9)$$

which is quite similar to (4.2.1.5). By iterating these computations, we obtain

$$\text{mh}(T_{E'}) = \left\lceil \log (e_2\, \alpha_1 + \sum_{i=2}^{t} e_i\, m_i) \right\rceil$$

$$= \log e_2 + \left\lceil \log \left(\left\lceil \frac{m_1}{2^{k_1}} \right\rceil + \beta_2 \right) \right\rceil, \qquad (4.2.1.10)$$

where,

$$\beta_2 = \frac{1}{e_2} \sum_{i=2}^{t} e_i\, m_i.$$

Using Lemma 4.2.1.2, we finally obtain

$$\text{mh}(T_{E'}) = \left\lceil \log (\sum_{i=1}^{t} e_i\, m_i) \right\rceil = \left\lceil \log (\sum_{i=1}^{m} e(P_i)) \right\rceil.$$

Starting from set T, if we now combine the trees in it to obtain a tree T_E, since $\text{mh}(T_{P_i}) \leq \text{mh}(T_{P_i'})$, it is seen that

$$\text{mh}(T_E) \leq \text{mh}(T_{E'}),$$

from which part (b) follows.

The proof of part (c) is similar to that of part (b), and we merely indicate the major steps. As in part (a), we can rewrite

$$E = \prod_{i=1}^{m} (S_i)$$

as

$$E = \frac{(F_1)(F_2) \cdots (F_{r_1})}{(G_1)(G_2) \cdots (G_{r_2})},$$

where $r_1 + r_2 = m$ and $F_i, G_j \in \{S_1, S_2, \cdots, S_m\}$, for $i = 1$ to r_1 and $j = 1$ to r_2. Let F_i' be an expression related to F_i with $e(F_i)$ atoms nested at one level, for $i = 1$ to r_1. Likewise, define G_j' for $j = 1$ to r_2 and E'. As in part (b), the claim of the lemma follows if we can show that

$$E' = \frac{(F'_1)\,(F'_2)\,\cdots\,(F'_{r_1})}{(G'_1)\,(G'_2)\,\cdots\,(G'_{r_2})}$$

can be evaluated in $\left\lceil \log \sum_{i=1}^{m} e(S_i) \right\rceil$ steps. To this end, partition the set of minimum height parse trees for F'_i and G'_j into t sets of equal heights. In the process of pairing parse trees, we can either pair parse trees (of equal heights) corresponding to two factors F'_{i_1} and F'_{i_2} by the $\times$ operation, or two factors G'_{j_1} and G'_{j_2}, by the $\times$ operation, or one F'_{i_3}, and one G'_{j_3} by the $/$ operation. Evidently, this process leads to a final tree for E' such that

$$\mathrm{mh}(T_{E'}) = \left\lceil \log \left(\sum_{i=1}^{m} e(S_i) \right) \right\rceil.$$

This completes the proof of Lemma 4.2.1.3.

We now prove the principal result of this section.

Theorem 4.2.1.4. Given any arbitrary arithmetic expression $E(N, d)$, using commutativity and associativity, we can evaluate $E(N, d)$ in parallel in $T(E(N, d))$ steps, where

$$T(E(N, d)) \le 1 + 2d + \lceil \log N \rceil,$$

by using at most $\left\lceil \dfrac{N - 2d}{2} \right\rceil$ processors.

Proof

The proof is by induction on d and is independent of N. Let a_{ij} be atoms,

$$E(N, 0) = \sum_{i=1}^{m} R_i \quad \text{and} \quad R_i = \prod_{j=1}^{t_i} a_{ij},$$

where R_i's do not contain any parenthesis, and $\sum_{i=1}^{m} t_i = N$. By part (b) of Lemma 4.2.1.3, we readily see that

$$\mathrm{mh}(T_{E(N,\,0)}) \le \left\lceil \log \left(\sum_{i=1}^{m} e(R_i) \right) \right\rceil. \tag{4.2.1.11}$$

But, by part (a) of the same lemma,

$$\mathrm{mh}(T_{R_i}) = \left\lceil \log t_i \right\rceil.$$

Thus,

$$e(R_i) = 2^{\mathrm{mh}(T_{R_i})} = 2^{\lceil \log t_i \rceil} < 2^{\log 2t_i} = 2t_i.$$

Combining this with (4.2.1.11), it follows that

$$\mathrm{mh}(T_{E(N, \, 0)}) \le \left\lceil \log \left(\sum_{i=1}^{m} 2t_i \right) \right\rceil$$

$$\le \left\lceil 1 + \log \sum_{i=1}^{m} t_i \right\rceil = 1 + \lceil \log N \rceil \, .$$

Since the height of the parse tree determines the parallel time and at most $\left\lceil \dfrac{N}{2} \right\rceil$ processors are needed to achieve this time, the theorem follows for $d = 0$.

Assume that Theorem 4.2.1.4 is true for $d \le k$. Let $R_{ij} = R_{ij} \, (N_{ij}, d_{ij})$ be any arithmetic expression with $d_{ij} \le k$ and assume that

$$T(R_{ij}) = \mathrm{mh}(T_{R_{ij}}) \le 1 + 2d_{ij} + \left\lceil \log N_{ij} \right\rceil \, ,$$

using at most $\left\lceil \dfrac{N - 2d}{2} \right\rceil$ processors. Thus,

$$e(R_{ij}) \le 2^{(1 + 2d_{ij})} \times 2^{\lceil \log N_{ij} \rceil} < 2^{(1 + 2d_{ij})} \times 2^{\log 2N_{ij}} = N_{ij} \, 2^{2(1 + d_{ij})}. \quad (4.2.1.12)$$

Now consider

$$E(N, \, k+1) = \sum_{i=1}^{m} Q_i \quad \text{and} \quad Q_i = \prod_{j=1}^{t_i} (R_{ij}),$$

where at least one of the R_{ij}'s has nested parentheses of depth $d_{ij} = k$. By part (b) of Lemma 4.2.1.3,

$$\mathrm{mh}(T_{E(N, \, k+1)}) \le \left\lceil \log \sum_{i=1}^{m} e(Q_i) \right\rceil. \quad (4.2.1.13)$$

Again, by part (c) of the Lemma 4.2.1.3, and the induction hypothesis,

$$\mathrm{mh}(T_{Q_i}) \le \left\lceil \log \left(\sum_{j=1}^{t_i} e(R_{ij}) \right) \right\rceil$$

$$\le \left\lceil \log \left(\sum_{j=1}^{t_i} N_{ij} \, 2^{2(1 + d_{ij})} \right) \right\rceil$$

$$< \log \left(2^{3 + 2k} \sum_{j=1}^{t_i} N_{ij} \right),$$

from which we obtain that

$$e(Q_i) = 2^{\text{mh}(T_{Q_i})} < 2^{3+2k} \sum_{j=1}^{t_i} N_{ij}. \tag{4.2.1.14}$$

Combining (4.2.1.13) and (4.2.1.14),

$$\text{mh}(T_{E(N,\ k+1)}) = \left\lceil \log 2^{(3+2k)} \sum_{i=1}^{m} \sum_{j=1}^{t_i} N_{ij} \right\rceil$$

$$= \lceil 3 + 2k + \log N \rceil$$

$$= 1 + 2(k+1) + \lceil \log N \rceil,$$

from which we obtain the upper bound on the parallel time.

To derive the processor bound, if $d = k + 1$, at least two atoms appear at a level of parenthesis nesting that did not exist when $d = k$. The maximum number of processors required when $d = k + 1$ is one less than that at $d = k$, that is, it is $\left\lceil \dfrac{n - 2k}{2} \right\rceil - 1$. But, since

$$\left\lceil \frac{n - 2(k+1)}{2} \right\rceil = \left\lceil \frac{n - 2k}{2} - 1 \right\rceil = \left\lceil \frac{n - 2k}{2} \right\rceil - 1,$$

the proof of this theorem is now complete.

In the following, we show the existence of nested arithmetic expressions whose parallel evaluation *cannot* be speeded up by use of commutativity and associativity. This is proved by showing that the upper bound given in Theorem 4.2.1.4 is quite sharp. To this end, define the class of expressions known as Horner's expression with $2k + 1$ atoms nested to a depth k:

$$H\,(2k + 1,\ k) = ((\ \cdots\ ((a_k\,b_{k-1} + a_{k-1})\,b_{k-2} + a_{k-2})\,b_{k-3}$$

$$+ \cdots\ )\,b_1 + a_1)\,b_0 + a_0.$$

It is easily proved by induction that, using associativity and commutativity,

$$\text{mh}(T_{H\,(N,\ d)}) = 2 \left\lfloor \frac{N}{2} \right\rfloor,$$

where $d = \left\lfloor \dfrac{N}{2} \right\rfloor$, that is, a Horner's expression with N atoms and nested to a depth $d = \left\lfloor \dfrac{N}{2} \right\rfloor$ requires $2 \left\lfloor \dfrac{N}{2} \right\rfloor$ steps for its evaluation. Now consider the ratio

$$\frac{\mathrm{mh}(T_{E_H (N, d)})}{1 + 2d + \lceil \log N \rceil} = \frac{2 \left\lfloor \dfrac{N}{2} \right\rfloor}{1 + 2 \left\lfloor \dfrac{N}{2} \right\rfloor + \lceil \log N \rceil}$$

$$\rightarrow 1 \text{ as } N \rightarrow \infty.$$

In other words, the upper bound given by Theorem 4.2.1.4 is very nearly optimal. This result establishes the necessity of using distributivity to speed up the evaluation of arithmetic expressions. In fact, in the rest of this chapter, all three properties, namely, associativity, commutativity, and distributivity are used.

4.3 PARALLEL ALGORITHMS FOR POLYNOMIAL EVALUATION

Let

$$p(x) = a_N x^N + a_{N-1} x^{N-1} + \cdots + a_2 x^2 + a_1 x + a_0$$

be a given polynomial. The optimal serial method for computing the value of a polynomial at a point is the well-known Horner's method, which may be described as follows. Let

$$p_N = a_N,$$

and for $i = N-1, N-2, \cdots, 2, 1, 0,$

$$p_i = p_{i+1} x + a_i.$$

Thus,

$$p_0 = p(x).$$

The above relation in p_i is known as a first-order linear recurrence. The general methods for evaluating first-order linear recurrences in parallel are discussed in Chapter 5. Horner's method clearly requires N multiplications and N additions. In the following, we describe a number of parallel methods for evaluating a polynomial.

4.3.1 Dorn's n^{th}-Order Horner's Method

Let $p(x)$ be a polynomial of degree N and n (≥ 2) be the number of processors. Define n polynomials (in x^n) of degree at most $\left\lfloor \dfrac{N}{n} \right\rfloor$ as follows:

$$p_0(x^n) = a_0 + a_n x^n + a_{2n} x^{2n} + \cdots + a_{n\lfloor N/n \rfloor} x^{n \left\lfloor \frac{N}{n} \right\rfloor}$$

$$p_1(x^n) = a_1 + a_{n+1} x^n + a_{2n+1} x^{2n} + \cdots$$

$$p_2(x^n) = a_2 + a_{n+2} x^n + a_{2n+2} x^{2n} + \cdots$$

$$\vdots$$

$$p_{n-1}(x^n) = a_{n-1} + a_{2n-1} x^n + a_{3n-1} x^{2n} + \cdots$$

Then, clearly

$$p(x) = p_0(x^n) + p_1(x^n) x + p_2(x^n) x^2 + \cdots + p_{n-1}(x^n) x^{n-1}.$$

The above relations immediately suggest a three-step process called *Dorn's algorithm*. First compute $x, x^2, x^3, \cdots, x^n$ using $\frac{n}{2}$ processors in $\lceil \log n \rceil$ units of time (refer to Chapter 1). Then compute $p_i(x^n)$ for $i = 0, 1, 2, \cdots, n-1$, using Horner's method in parallel (with n processors) in at most $2 \left\lfloor \dfrac{N}{n} \right\rfloor$ steps. In the last step, multiply $p_i(x^n)$ by x^i for $i = 0, 1, 2, \cdots, n-1$ in one step and add them up using the associative fan-in algorithm in $\lceil \log n \rceil$ steps. Let $T(N, n)$ be the time to compute $p(x)$ of degree N using n processors by this method. Then

$$T(N, n) = 2 \lceil \log n \rceil + 2 \left\lfloor \frac{N}{n} \right\rfloor + 1. \tag{4.3.1.1}$$

When $n = 1$, this method reduces to the regular Horner's method and

$$T(N, 1) = 2N. \tag{4.3.1.2}$$

Likewise, if $n \geq N + 1$, this method reduces to finding x^j for $j = 1, 2, \cdots, N$, multiplying a_i with x^i, and adding them using associative fan-in. Thus, in this case,

$$T(N, k) = T(N, N+1) = \lceil \log N \rceil + \lceil \log (N+1) \rceil + 1, \tag{4.3.1.3}$$

for all $k \geq N+1$.

In the following, we analyze the properties of $T(N, n)$. As shown in Table 4.3.1.1, as a function of n, it is *not* monotonically non-increasing. This clearly indicates that we must exercise extreme caution in picking the number of processors for this method.

Define $T^*(N)$ as

$$T^*(N) = \min_{1 \leq n \leq N+1} T(N, n), \tag{4.3.1.4}$$

that is, $T^*(N)$ represents the minimum number of steps required to evaluate $p(x)$ using n^{th}-order Horner's method. The following result is immediate.

TABLE 4.3.1.1
Typical Values of $T(N, n)$

n	N																		
	2	3	4	5	6	7	8	9	10	11	12	13	14	15	16	17	18	19	20
1	4	6	8	10	12	14	16	18	20	22	24	26	28	30	32	34	36	38	40
2		5	7	7	9	9	11	11	13	13	15	15	17	17	19	19	21	21	23
3		7	7	7	9	9	9	11	11	11	13	13	13	15	15	15	17	17	17
4		5	7	7	7	7	9	9	9	9	11	11	11	11	13	13	13	13	15
5			6	9	9	9	9	9	11	11	11	11	11	13	13	13	13	13	15
6				7	9	9	9	9	9	9	11	11	11	11	11	11	13	13	13
7					7	9	9	9	9	9	9	9	11	11	11	11	11	11	11
8						7	9	9	9	9	9	9	9	9	11	11	11	11	11
9							8	11	11	11	11	11	11	11	11	11	13	13	13
10								9	11	11	11	11	11	11	11	11	11	11	13
11									9	11	11	11	11	11	11	11	11	11	11
12										9	11	11	11	11	11	11	11	11	11
13											9	11	11	11	11	11	11	11	11
14												9	11	11	11	11	11	11	11
15													9	11	11	11	11	11	11
16														9	11	11	11	11	11
17															9	13	13	13	13
18																11	13	13	13
19																	11	13	13
20																		11	13

Lemma 4.3.1.1.

$$T^*(N) = T(N, N+1) = \lceil \log N \rceil + \lceil \log(N+1) \rceil + 1.$$

Proof

Combining (4.3.1.1) through (4.3.1.3), it is seen that the lemma will follow if we show that

$$2\lceil \log n \rceil + 2\left\lfloor \frac{N}{n} \right\rfloor + 1 \geq 2\lceil \log(N+1) \rceil + 1,$$

that is,

$$\lceil \log n \rceil + \left\lfloor \frac{N}{n} \right\rfloor \geq \lceil \log(N+1) \rceil.$$

Let $N = 2^g + t$ for $1 \leq t \leq 2^g$ and $n = 2^k + s$ for $1 \leq s \leq 2^k$.

Case 1. $g = k$. Since $t \geq s$, $\lceil \log n \rceil = g + 1 = k + 1$,

$$(g + 1) \leq \lceil \log(N + 1) \rceil \leq g + 2,$$

and

$$\left\lfloor \frac{N}{n} \right\rfloor = \left\lfloor \frac{2^g + t}{2^g + s} \right\rfloor = 1.$$

Hence $\lceil \log n \rceil + \left\lfloor \frac{N}{n} \right\rfloor = g + 2 \geq \lceil \log(N+1) \rceil$.

Case 2. $g > k$ and $1 \leq t < 2^g$. Then

$$\lceil \log(N + 1) \rceil = g + 1, \quad \lceil \log n \rceil = k + 1,$$

and

$$\left\lfloor \frac{N}{n} \right\rfloor = \left\lfloor \frac{2^g + t}{2^k + s} \right\rfloor \geq 2^{g-k-1}.$$

Thus,

$$\lceil \log n \rceil + \left\lfloor \frac{N}{n} \right\rfloor \geq k + 1 + 2^{g-k-1} \geq (g + 1),$$

since $2^z \geq 2z$ for all positive integers z.

Case 3. $g > k$ and $t = 2^g$. Then

$$\lceil \log(N + 1) \rceil = g + 2, \qquad \lceil \log n \rceil = k + 1,$$

$$\left\lfloor \frac{N}{n} \right\rfloor = \left\lfloor \frac{2^{g+1}}{2^k + t} \right\rfloor \geq 2^{g-k}.$$

Thus,

$$\lceil \log n \rceil + \left\lfloor \frac{N}{n} \right\rfloor = (k + 1) + 2^{g-k} \geq (g + 2),$$

since $2^z \geq z + 1$ for all positive integers z. Hence the lemma.

The following lemma characterizes the minimum number of processors needed to compute $p(x)$ in the minimum time.

Lemma 4.3.1.2. Let $n = n^*$ be such that

$$T(N, n^*) = T^*(N)$$

and $g = \lfloor \log N \rfloor$. Then,

    (a) $n^* = N + 1$ if $N = 2^g$.

    (b) $n^* = \left\lceil \dfrac{N + 1}{3} \right\rceil$ if $2^g < N < 2^g + 2^{g-1}$.

    (c) $n^* = \left\lceil \dfrac{N + 1}{2} \right\rceil$ if $2^g + 2^{g-1} \leq N < 2^{g+1}$.

Proof

(a) From (4.3.1.3), it is known that if $n = N + 1$ then $T(N, N + 1) = T^*(N)$. We now show that if $n \leq n^* - 1$ (that is, $n \leq N$), then

$$T(N, n) > T^*(N).$$

In this case

$$T^*(N) = 2g + 2.$$

Let $n = 2^k + p$, where $k < g$, and $1 \leq p < 2^k$. Now, from (4.3.1.1),

$$T(N, n) = 2k + 3 + 2 \left\lfloor \frac{2^g}{2^k + p} \right\rfloor \geq 2k + 3 + 2 \left\lfloor 2^{g-k-1} \right\rfloor.$$

Since $g > k$, we obtain

$$T(N, n) \geq 2k + 3 + 2^{g-k}.$$

Then,

$$T(N, n) - T^*(N) = 2^{g-k} - 2(g - k) + 1 > 0,$$

since $2^z \geq 2z - 1$ for all $z \geq 0$. In other words, $N + 1$ is the least number of processors that are required to evaluate a polynomial of degree N when $N = 2^g$.

(b) In this case, we shall first evaluate $T(N, n)$ at $n = \left\lceil \dfrac{N + 1}{3} \right\rceil$. Since $2^g < N < 2^g + 2^{g-1}$,

$$T^*(N) = 2g + 3, \qquad \frac{N + 1}{3} \leq 2^{g-1},$$

and

$$\left\lceil \log \left\lceil \frac{N + 1}{3} \right\rceil \right\rceil = g - 1. \tag{4.3.1.5}$$

Let

$$\left\lceil \frac{N + 1}{3} \right\rceil = k, \quad \text{for some } k \geq 3.$$

Then,

$$N = 3k - p - 1, \text{ for } p \leq 2,$$

and

$$\left\lfloor \frac{N}{\left\lceil \frac{N + 1}{3} \right\rceil} \right\rfloor = \left\lfloor \frac{3k - p - 1}{k} \right\rfloor = 2, \tag{4.3.1.6}$$

since $0 \leq \dfrac{p + 1}{k} \leq 1$. Now combining (4.3.1.1), (4.3.1.5), and (4.3.1.6), we obtain

$$T(N, \left\lceil \frac{N + 1}{3} \right\rceil) = T^*(N) = 2g + 3. \tag{4.3.1.7}$$

For $k < 3$, refer to Table 4.3.1.1.

To complete the proof, we have to show if $n < \left\lceil \dfrac{N + 1}{3} \right\rceil$,then

$$T(N, n) > T^*(N). \tag{4.3.1.8}$$

Consider two cases:

(1) $2^i < n \le 2^{i+1}$ when $i + 1 \le g - 2$ and

(2) $2^{g-2} < n < \left\lceil \dfrac{N+1}{3} \right\rceil$.

Case 1. Let $g - 2 = i + 1 + j$ for $j \ge 0$. Then

$$\lceil \log n \rceil = i + 1 = g - 2 - j,$$

and since $2^g < N < 2^g + 2^{g-1}$,

$$\left\lfloor \frac{N}{n} \right\rfloor \ge 2^{g-i-1} = 2^{2+j}.$$

Thus,

$$2\lceil \log n \rceil + 2 \left\lfloor \frac{N}{n} \right\rfloor + 1 \ge 2(g - 2 - j) + 2^{3+j} + 1.$$

From this and (4.3.1.7), we obtain (4.3.1.8) if $2^{(j+3)} \ge 2(j + 3)$, which is always true for $j \ge 0$.

Case 2. When

$$2^{g-2} < n < \left\lceil \frac{N+1}{3} \right\rceil,$$

write

$$n = \left\lceil \frac{N+1}{3} \right\rceil - q = k - q > 0, \text{ for some } q \ge 1.$$

It can be shown that

$$2\lceil \log n \rceil + 2 \left\lfloor \frac{N}{n} \right\rfloor + 1 = 2(g - 1) + 2 \left\lfloor \frac{3k - p - 1}{k - q} \right\rfloor + 1.$$

From this and (4.3.1.7), we obtain (4.3.1.8) if

$$k + 2q - p - 1 > 0. \tag{4.3.1.9}$$

Since $k > q$, (4.3.1.9) is true if $3q - p - 1 > 0$. This latter inequality is true since $q \ge 1$ and $p \le 2$, and claim (b) follows.

The proof of claim (c) in Lemma 4.3.1.2 can be shown along similar lines and is left as an exercise (see Exercise 4.1).

The values of n^* for various values of N are given in Table 4.3.1.2.

TABLE 4.3.1.2

N	n^*	N	n^*	N	n^*	N	n^*
3	2	15	8	27	14	39	14
4	5	16	17	28	15	40	14
5	2	17	6	29	15	41	14
6	4	18	7	30	16	42	15
7	4	19	7	31	16	43	15
8	9	20	7	32	33	44	15
9	4	21	8	33	12	45	16
10	4	22	8	34	12	46	16
11	4	23	8	35	12	47	16
12	7	24	13	36	13	48	25
13	7	25	13	37	13	49	25
14	8	26	14	38	13	50	26

4.3.2 A Divide-and-Conquer Strategy

Let $p(x)$ be a polynomial of degree $N = 2^n - 1$ for some $n \geq 1$. First express

$$p(x) = q(x) x^{\lfloor N/2 \rfloor + 1} + r(x),$$

where

$$q(x) = a_N x^{\lfloor N/2 \rfloor} + a_{N-1} x^{\lfloor N/2 \rfloor - 1} + \cdots + a_{\lfloor N/2 \rfloor + 1},$$

and

$$r(x) = a_{\lfloor N/2 \rfloor} x^{\lfloor N/2 \rfloor} + a_{\lfloor N/2 \rfloor - 1} x^{\lfloor N/2 \rfloor - 1} + \cdots + a_1 x + a_0.$$

Since $\lfloor N/2 \rfloor = 2^{n-1} - 1$, we can likewise express $q(x)$ and $r(x)$ as follows:

$$q(x) = q_1(x) x^{\lfloor N/2^2 \rfloor + 1} + q_2(x),$$

and

$$r(x) = r_1(x) x^{\lfloor N/2^2 \rfloor + 1} + r_2(x),$$

and so on. Thus, the computation $p(x)$ may be expressed in the form of a binary tree as shown in the example in Fig. 4.3.2.1.

Given enough processors (how many?), it is readily seen that $p(x)$ can be computed in exactly $2\lceil \log N \rceil$ steps provided all the powers $x^2, x^4, x^8, \cdots$ are also available without delay whenever they are needed (see Exercise 4.2).

This divide-and-conquer strategy based algorithm due to Estrin [1960] is known as the method of *binary splitting*. Algorithmically, computations proceed from bottom up and the maximum parallelism occurs at the leaf level of the binary tree. The algorithm is given in Fig. 4.3.2.2.

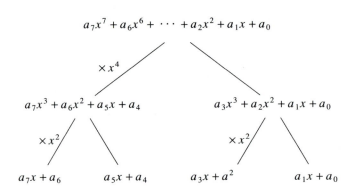

FIGURE 4.3.2.1
An illustration of the divide-and-conquer strategy for $N = 7$.

/* Define $p_i^{(0)}(x) = a_{i+1}x + a_i$ for $i = 0, 2, 4, \cdots 2^n-2$. */

FOR $j = 1$ TO $n - 1$ STEP 1

    FOR $i \in \{0, 2^{j+1}, 2 \times 2^{j+1}, \cdots 2^n - 2^{j+1} \}$ DO IN PARALLEL

        $p_i^{(j)}(x) = p_i^{(j-1)}(x) + x^{2^j} \times p_{i+2^j}^{(j-1)}(x)$

    END

END

$p(x) = p_0^{(n-1)}(x).$

FIGURE 4.3.2.2
Estrin's binary splitting algorithm.

An alternative to the binary splitting is to split the polynomial using the well-known *golden ratio,* due to Muraoka [1971], which provides measurable improvement in the performance of the parallel algorithm. (Actually, Muraoka calls this the *folding* method.)

Let $p(x)$ be a polynomial of degree $N = F_{t+1} - 1$, where F_i is the ith Fibonacci number defined as $F_0 = 1$, $F_1 = 1$, and for $i \geq 2$

$$F_i = F_{i-1} + F_{i-2}.$$

Refer to Table 4.3.2.1.

TABLE 4.3.2.1

i	0	1	2	3	4	5	6	7	8	9	10
F_i	1	1	2	3	5	8	13	21	34	55	89

It can be shown that (Reingold, Nievergelt, and Deo [1977])

$$F_i = \frac{1}{\sqrt{5}} \left(\frac{1 + \sqrt{5}}{2} \right)^{i+1} - \frac{1}{\sqrt{5}} \left(\frac{1 - \sqrt{5}}{2} \right)^{i+1}.$$

$$\approx \frac{1}{\sqrt{5}} \left(\frac{1 + \sqrt{5}}{2} \right)^{i+1}.$$

The number

$$\frac{F_{i+1}}{F_i} = \frac{1 + \sqrt{5}}{2} \approx 1.618$$

is known as the *golden ratio.*

Let

$$p(x) = a_{F_{t+1} - 1}\, x^{F_{t+1} - 1} + a_{F_{t+1} - 2}\, x^{F_{t+1} - 2} + \cdots + a_1 x + a_0.$$

Rewrite $p(x)$ as

$$p(x) = p_1(x) \times x^{F_t} + p_2(x),$$

where $p_2(x)$ is a polynomial of degree $F_t - 1$ and $p_1(x)$ is a polynomial of degree $F_{t-1} - 1$. Now, $p_1(x)$ can be expressed as

$$p_1(x) = p_{11}(x)\, x^{F_{t-2}} + p_{12}(x),$$

where $p_{12}(x)$ is a polynomial of degree $F_{t-2} - 1$ and $p_{11}(x)$ is of degree $F_{t-3} - 1$. Likewise, $p_2(x)$ can be expressed in a similar manner, and so on. Refer to Figs. 4.3.2.3 and 4.3.2.4 for illustration.

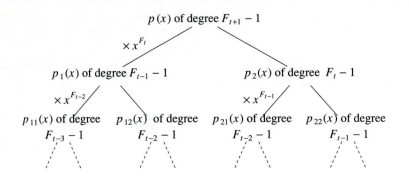

FIGURE 4.3.2.3
An illustration of splitting of polynomials using the golden ratio.

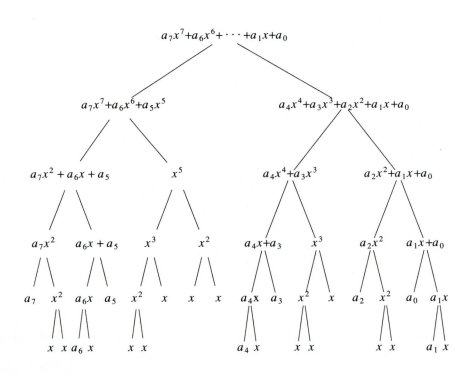

FIGURE 4.3.2.4
An example of parallel evaluation of polynomials using the method of golden ratio due to Muraoka.

The reader is invited to develop a parallel algorithm quite similar to the one in Fig. 4.3.2.2 for computing $p(x)$ using the method of golden ratio splitting (see Exercise 4.3).

From the above discussion, it is readily seen that if enough processors (how many ?) are available, then $p(x)$ of degree N where $F_t \leq N < F_{t+1}$ can be computed in just $t + 1$ steps. Since

$$F_t \approx \frac{1}{\sqrt{5}} (\frac{1+\sqrt{5}}{2})^{t+1},$$

we obtain that

$$t + 1 \approx 1.44 \log_2 F_t \leq 1.44 \log_2 N.$$

Table 4.3.2.2 illustrates this relation between parallel time and degrees of polynomials that can be evaluated using this method. It is clear that division by golden ratio is better than binary splitting.

TABLE 4.3.2.2

Number of Steps	Degrees of Polynomials	Number of Steps	Degrees of Polynomials
3	2	13	233 - 376
4	3 - 4	14	377 - 609
5	5 - 7	15	610 - 986
6	8 - 12	16	987 - 1,596
7	13 - 20	17	1,597 - 2,583
8	21 - 33	18	2,584 - 4,180
9	34 - 54	19	4,181 - 6,764
10	55 - 88	20	6,765 - 10,945
11	89 - 143	21	10,946 - 17,710
12	144 - 232	22	17,711 - 28,656

4.3.3 Method of Multiple Folding

The method of folding described in the previous section is essentially dependent on splitting the polynomial into two parts -- based on either binary splitting or the golden ratio. In this section, we describe a class of algorithms called *multiple folding methods,* wherein the given polynomial is split into more than two parts, which results in a marked improvement in performance.

Let $N(t)$ be the largest degree polynomial that can be computed in time t. Define

$$D_{s,i} = \frac{s(s+1)}{2} + i,$$

where $s \geq 2$ and $-1 \leq i \leq s-1$.

Typical values of $D_{s,i}$ are given in Table 4.3.3.1.

TABLE 4.3.3.1

s	$D_{s,i}$							
	$i = -1$	0	1	2	3	4	5	6
2	2	3	4					
3	5	6	7	8				
4	9	10	11	12	13			
5	14	15	16	17	18	19		
6	20	21	22	23	24	25	26	
7	27	28	29	30	31	32	33	34

The following lemma is fundamental.

Lemma 4.3.3.1. If an unlimited number of processors are available, then

$$N(D_{s,i}) \geq 2^{D_{s-1,i}}.$$

Proof

The proof is by induction. Let $s = 2$. Then $D_{2,i} = 3 + i$, $i = -1, 0, 1$, and

$$N(3 + i) \geq 2^{1+i}.$$

It can be easily verified that polynomials of degree 1, 2, and 4 can be evaluated in 2, 3, and 4 units of time, respectively. Hence the lemma is true for $s = 2$. Assume that the lemma is true for $s = k$. That is, all polynomials of degree less than or equal to $2^{D_{k-1,i}}$ can be computed in $D_{k,i}$ steps. Also notice that all the powers of x up to and including $x^{2^{D_{k,i}}}$ can be made available, in parallel, in this time period (since an unlimited number of processors are available). A polynomial $p(x)$ of degree less than or equal to $2^{D_{k,i}}$ can be expressed as

$$p(x) = \sum_{j=0}^{2^k - 1} Q_j(x)\, x^{j 2^{D_{k-1,\,i}}}, \tag{4.3.3.1}$$

where each $Q_j(x)$ is a polynomial of degree less than $2^{D_{k-1,\,i}}$. By inductive hypothesis, since all the terms on the right hand side of (4.3.3.1) are available on or before step $D_{k-1,\,i}$, it only requires $k+1$ steps to compute $p(x)$ as above (one multiplication and k addition steps using the associative fan-in algorithm). As

$$D_{k+1,i} - D_{k,i} = (k+1),$$

$p(x)$ will indeed be available at time $D_{k+1,i}$ and hence the lemma.

Let

$$t = \frac{s(s+1)}{2} + i. \tag{4.3.3.2}$$

Then from Lemma 4.3.3.1 it follows that a polynomial of degree 2^{t-s} can be computed in t steps. From (4.3.3.2) we obtain that

$$s \approx -\frac{1}{2} + \sqrt{2(t-i)}.$$

Since $i = O(t^{1/2})$, it follows that

$$s \approx -\frac{1}{2} + \sqrt{2t}.$$

That is, a polynomial of degree as large as $\sqrt{2}\, 2^{t - \sqrt{2t}}$ can be computed in t units of time. The following theorem readily follows from this discussion.

Theorem 4.3.3.2. A polynomial of degree N can be evaluated in

$$T(N) \le \log N + \sqrt{2\log N} + O(1)$$

steps using unlimited parallelism.

We now present a method that achieves this bound. Let $p(x)$ be a polynomial of degree N, where $n = \lceil \log(N+1) \rceil$, that is, $N \le 2^n - 1$. Define

$$d_m = \frac{1}{2}\, m(m+1) + 1. \tag{4.3.3.3}$$

Let n be such that

$$d_{m-1} < n \le d_m. \tag{4.3.3.4}$$

Table 4.3.3.2 illustrates the relation between m, n, and N for some typical values of m.

TABLE 4.3.3.2

m	Bounds on n	Bounds on N
0	$n = 1$	$N = 1$
1	$1 < n \leq 2$	$2 \leq N \leq 3$
2	$2 < n \leq 4$	$4 \leq N \leq 15$
3	$4 < n \leq 7$	$16 \leq N \leq 127$
4	$7 < n \leq 11$	$128 \leq N \leq 2047$
5	$11 < n \leq 16$	$2048 \leq N \leq 65{,}535$
6	$16 < n \leq 22$	$2^{16} \leq N \leq 2^{22} - 1$
7	$22 < n \leq 29$	$2^{22} \leq N \leq 2^{29} - 1$
8	$29 < n \leq 37$	$2^{29} \leq N \leq 2^{37} - 1$

Let $k = n - m$. Then we can express $p(x)$ as

$$p(x) = p_0(x) + p_1(x) x^{2^k} + p_2(x) x^{2 \times 2^k} + \cdots + p_{2^m - 1}(x) x^{(2^m - 1)2^k}. \quad (4.3.3.5)$$

Refer to Fig. 4.3.3.1 for an example. (Also see Exercise 4.5.)

If $p(x)$ is a polynomial of degree N, then (4.3.3.5) implies that (see Exercise 4.4)

$$\max_{i=0 \text{ to } 2^m - 1} \{ \text{degree of } p_i(x) \} < 2^{n-m}. \quad (4.3.3.6)$$

Thus, if $p_i(x)$ and $x^{i \times 2^k}$ for $i = 0$ to $2^m - 1$ are available, then $p(x)$ using (4.3.3.5) can be computed in just $m + 1$ steps (one multiplication and m additions using associative fan-in algorithm). (See Exercise 4.6.)

We now prove by induction that $p(x)$ can be computed in $n + m + 1$ steps.

As the basis, when $N = 1$, we obtain $n = 1$ and $m = 0$. Since $a_0 + a_1 x$ can be computed in two steps, the basis is true. Now, let the claim be true for all polynomials of degree less than N. In particular, since the maximum of the degree of $p_i(x)$ is $2^{n-m} - 1$, from (4.3.3.4) we obtain

$$d_{m-2} < n - m \leq d_{m-1},$$

that is, by hypothesis, $p_i(x)$ is computable in $(n - m) + (m - 1) + 1 = n$ steps. Since x^i, $1 \leq i \leq 2^n$, can be computed in n steps, using (4.3.3.5) $p(x)$ can be computed in $n + m + 1$ steps, and the claim follows.

From (4.3.3.4), we obtain that $m \approx (2n)^{1/2}$. Thus, if $T(N)$ is the time required to evaluate $p(x)$ by this method, then

$$T(N) = n + m + 1 = \log N + (2 \log N)^{1/2} + O(1). \quad (4.3.3.7)$$

Typical values of N vs. $T(N)$ are given in Table 4.3.3.3. Comparing this with Table 4.3.2.2, it follows that for polynomials of low degree Fibonacci splitting is better.

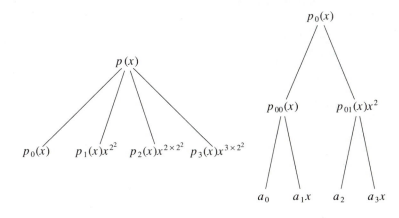

FIGURE 4.3.3.1

$p(x)$ is a polynomial of degree $N = 15$. $n = 4$, $m = 2$, $n - m = 2$. Each $p_i(x)$ is of degree 3. The process is repeated on each of the $p_i(x)$ as shown for $p_0(x)$.

TABLE 4.3.3.3

The maximum degree N polynomial that can be computed in $T(N)$ steps

$T(N) = n + m + 1$	Degree N	$T(N) = n + m + 1$	Degree N
4	3	14	511
5	3	15	1,023
6	7	16	2,047
7	15	17	2,047
8	15	18	4,095
9	31	19	8,191
10	63	20	16,381
11	127	21	32,763
12	127	22	65,527
13	255	23	131,055

4.3.4 A Lower Bound on Polynomial Evaluation --
Unbounded Parallelism

In this section we derive a lower bound, due to Kosaraju [1986], on the time required to evaluate a polynomial under unbounded parallelism. Consider a polynomial

$$p(x) = \sum_{i=0}^{n-1} a_i x^{k_i}, \tag{4.3.4.1}$$

such that a_i's are non-zero and real and k_i's are *distinct, non-negative* integers. The number n of (non-zero) coefficients is called the *size* of the polynomial $p(x)$, and $N = \max_{0 \le i \le n-1} \{k_i\}$ is called the *degree* of the polynomial $p(x)$. Clearly, $n \le N$.

Let $mh(T_p)$ be the minimum height of the tree T_p used in the evaluation of $p(x)$. Define

$$T(n) = \min_{\{p(x) \mid size = n\}} \{mh(T_p)\}. \tag{4.3.4.2}$$

The following observations are quite useful.

(P1) If $p(x)$ is of degree m, then

$$mh(T_p) \ge \log m. \tag{4.3.4.3}$$

(P2) Let $p_1(x)$ and $p_2(x)$ be two polynomials. If the term x^s does not exist in $p_1(x)$ and $p_2(x)$, then x^s does not exist in $p_1(x) + p_2(x)$.

(P3) In any evaluation tree of $p(x)$, if $p_1(x) \times p_2(x)$ is a subtree, then at least one of $p_1(x)$ and $p_2(x)$ must be a *monomial* (which is a term of the type x^s for some $s > 0$), and one of $p_1(x)$ and $p_2(x)$ has the same size as $p_1(x) \times p_2(x)$.

With these preliminaries, we now state and prove a fundamental result due to Kosaraju [1986].

Theorem 4.3.4.1. For any n,

$$T(n) \ge \log n + \sqrt{2 \log n} - (\log n)^{1/4} - c, \tag{4.3.4.4}$$

for some constant $c > 0$, where $T(n)$ is defined in (4.3.4.2).

Proof
The proof is by induction on the size n. For small n, the basis of the induction can be verified by properly choosing the constant c. (We encourage the reader to verify this for n up to 8.) Assume that the theorem is true for all polynomials of size less than n. Consider

$$p(x) = \sum_{i=0}^{n-1} a_i \, x^{k_i}$$

of size n. Since k_i's are non-negative and distinct, there are *at most* $n/\log n$ distinct values of k_i in the range $0 \le k_i < n/\log n$. In other words, there are at least $(n - n/\log n)$ values of i with

$$k_i \ge \frac{n}{\log n}. \qquad (4.3.4.5)$$

Consider any restructured tree T_p of $p(x)$. In this tree, the internal nodes correspond to *either* the multiplication operation, $\times$, *or* the addition operation, $+$. Let $p_1, p_2, \cdots, p_t$ be the t internal nodes in T_p with the property that each of these nodes corresponds to $\times$ *and* each of them has no ancestor node which is $\times$. Let d_i be the depth of the node p_i measured by the number of edges in the path from the root of T_p to p_i, which is the same as the number of ancestors of p_i. Since no p_i is an ancestor of another p_j, it follows that (Exercise 4.30)

$$\sum_{i=1}^{t} 2^{-d_i} \le 1. \qquad (4.3.4.6)$$

Let D_i be the degree of the polynomial computed by the subtree T_{p_i} rooted at p_i.

Case 1. From some $1 \le i \le t$, let

$$d_i \ge \sqrt{2 \log n}$$

and

$$D_i \ge \frac{n}{\log n}.$$

From observation (P1), it follows that the minimum height of T_{p_i} is $\log(\frac{n}{\log n}) = \log n - \log \log n$. Since p_i itself is at depth d_i, combining these,

$$T(n) \ge \log n + \sqrt{2 \log n} - \log \log n.$$

Since $\log x \le x^{1/4}$, it follows that

$$T(n) \ge \log n + \sqrt{2 \log n} - (\log n)^{1/4} - C,$$

for properly chosen constant $C \ge 0$.

Case 2. If for any $1 \le i \le t$,

$$d_i \ge \sqrt{2 \log n},$$

then

$$D_i < \frac{n}{\log n}.$$

By observation (P2), no subtree rooted at an internal node '+' can realize a term

x^s that is missing in both of its subtrees. Consequently, each of the $n - (n/\log n)$ terms of the form $a_s \, x^s$ with

$$k_s \geq \frac{n}{\log n} \tag{4.3.4.7}$$

has to come from those subtrees T_{p_j} with

$$d_j < \sqrt{2 \log n}. \tag{4.3.4.8}$$

Consider the tree T_{p_j} satisfying (4.3.4.7) and (4.3.4.8). Let v_j be the number of terms with degree k_s satisfying (4.3.4.7). If

$$v_j < (n - \frac{n}{\log n}) \, 2^{-d_i}, \tag{4.3.4.9}$$

then the total number v of terms with degree k_s satisfying (4.3.4.7) realized by the entire tree T_p is such that

$$v = \sum_{j=1}^{t} v_j$$

$$< \sum_{j=1}^{t} (n - \frac{n}{\log n}) \, 2^{-d_j}$$

$$< (n - \frac{n}{\log n}), \quad \text{by (4.3.4.6)}.$$

Combining this with (4.3.4.5), it follows that there exists a p_l, $1 \leq l \leq t$, such that

$$d_l < \sqrt{2 \log n} \tag{4.3.4.10}$$

and T_{p_l} realizes at least

$$v_l = (n - \frac{n}{\log n}) \, 2^{-d_l}$$

terms with degree k_s satisfying (4.3.4.7). From observation (P3), one of the two subtrees of T_{p_l} realizes *at least* v_l terms. The subtrees of T_{p_l} are at depth $d_l + 1$. Combining these facts, we obtain

$$T(n) \geq 1 + d_l + T(v_l). \tag{4.3.4.11}$$

Since $v_l < n$, apply the inductive hypothesis to evaluate $T(v_l)$.

Let $x = \dfrac{1}{\log n}$. Then

$$- \log (1 - x) = \sum_{k=1}^{\infty} \frac{x^k}{k}$$

$$= \sum_{k=1}^{\infty} \frac{1}{k (\log n)^k}$$

$$= c_n, \quad \text{say.}$$

To get an idea of the value of c_n, consider

$$c_4 = \sum_{k=1}^{\infty} \frac{1}{k \, 2^k} \leq \sum_{k=1}^{\infty} \frac{1}{2^k} = 1.$$

Thus, c_n is positive and bounded by a (small) constant, say, δ, and $c_n \to 0$ as n becomes large. Now, from

$$v_l = n (1 - x) \, 2^{-d_l},$$

we obtain

$$\log v_l = \log n + \log (1 - x) - d_l$$

$$\geq (\log n) - (\delta + d_l). \tag{4.3.4.12}$$

Since $d_l < \sqrt{2 \log n}$, it follows that

$$(2 \log v_l)^{1/2} \geq (2 \log n)^{1/2} - \delta_1, \tag{4.3.4.13}$$

for some constant $\delta_1 > 0$.

From $v_l < n$, we have

$$(\log v_l)^{1/4} < (\log n)^{1/4}. \tag{4.3.4.14}$$

Combining (4.3.4.11) through (4.3.4.14) with the induction hypothesis, we obtain (4.3.4.4), and the theorem follows.

The following corollary follows from combining Theorems 4.3.3.2 and 4.3.4.1.

Corollary 4.3.4.2. The multifolding method for the parallel evaluation of polynomial described in Section 4.3.3 is optimal.

4.3.5 Optimal Evaluation of Polynomials -- Fixed Parallelism

In this section we derive a lower bound and an upper bound on the speed-up achievable in evaluating polynomials using a fixed number, p, of processors. We begin by defining a Horner's expression

$$H_{2N+1} = (\, \cdots \, ((a_N \, b_{N-1} + a_{N-1}) \, b_{N-2} + a_{N-2}) \, b_{N-3}$$

$$+ \, \cdots \, + a_1) \, b_0 + a_0 \tag{4.3.5.1}$$

for $N \geq 1$, where $a_0, a_1, a_2, \cdots , a_N, b_0, b_1, \cdots , b_{N-1}$ are $2N + 1$ variables. If

$b_i \equiv x$, then H_{2N+1} is, in fact, a polynomial in x of degree N. First, the upper bound.

H_{2N+1} can be expressed in the form of a first-order linear recurrence as follows. Let $X_N = a_N$ and

$$X_i = b_i X_{i+1} + a_i \qquad (4.3.5.2)$$

for $i = N-1, N-2, \cdots, 2, 1, 0$. Rewrite (4.3.5.2) in the matrix form as

$$\mathbf{y}_i = \mathbf{A}_i \mathbf{y}_{i+1}, \qquad (4.3.5.3)$$

where

$$\mathbf{A}_i = \begin{bmatrix} b_i & a_i \\ 0 & 1 \end{bmatrix} \qquad (4.3.5.4)$$

and

$$\mathbf{y}_i = \begin{pmatrix} X_i \\ 1 \end{pmatrix}. \qquad (4.3.5.5)$$

By iterating (4.3.5.3), it follows that

$$\mathbf{y}_0 = \left[\prod_{i=0}^{N-1} \mathbf{A}_i \right] \mathbf{y}_N, \qquad (4.3.5.6)$$

where

$$\prod_{i=0}^{N-1} \mathbf{A}_i = \mathbf{A}_0 \mathbf{A}_1 \cdots \mathbf{A}_{N-2} \mathbf{A}_{N-1}. \qquad (4.3.5.7)$$

Split the computations on the right-hand side of (4.3.5.6) into two groups:

$$\mathbf{B} = \prod_{i=0}^{N-k-1} \mathbf{A}_i \qquad (4.3.5.8)$$

and

$$\mathbf{y} = \left[\prod_{i=N-k}^{N-1} \mathbf{A}_i \right] \mathbf{y}_N, \qquad (4.3.5.9)$$

where k is a parameter to be fixed.

Let $p - 1$ processors compute $\mathbf{B}$ in T_B steps and the remaining one processor compute $\mathbf{y}$ in T_y steps. To quantify T_B, recall that each matrix $\mathbf{A}_i$ is of the form

$$\begin{bmatrix} \times & \times \\ 0 & 1 \end{bmatrix}, \qquad (4.3.5.10)$$

where $\times$ denotes non-zero elements. It is readily seen that when two matrices of this type are multiplied, the resulting matrix is also of the same form. Thus, it takes only three operations (two multiplications and one addition) to multiply two of these matrices. Let

$$s = \left\lceil \frac{N-k}{p-1} \right\rceil. \tag{4.3.5.11}$$

First compute

$$
\begin{aligned}
\mathbf{B}_1 &= \mathbf{A}_0 \, \mathbf{A}_1 \,, \ldots, \, \mathbf{A}_{s-1} \\
\mathbf{B}_2 &= \mathbf{A}_s \, \mathbf{A}_{s+1} \,, \ldots, \, \mathbf{A}_{2s-1} \\
\mathbf{B}_3 &= \mathbf{A}_{2s} \, \mathbf{A}_{2s+1} \,, \ldots, \, \mathbf{A}_{3s-1} \\
&\quad \cdot \\
&\quad \cdot \\
&\quad \cdot \\
\mathbf{B}_{p-1} &= \mathbf{A}_{(p-2)s} \, \mathbf{A}_{(p-2)s+1} \,, \ldots, \, \mathbf{A}_{N-k-1}
\end{aligned}
\tag{4.3.5.12}
$$

in $3(s-1)$ steps using $p-1$ processors. Then compute $\mathbf{B}$ from $\mathbf{B}_1, \mathbf{B}_2, \cdots, \mathbf{B}_{p-1}$ using the associative fan-in algorithm in $3\lceil \log(p-1) \rceil$ steps. Thus

$$T_B = 3 \left((s-1) + \lceil \log(p-1) \rceil \right). \tag{4.3.5.13}$$

To quantify T_y, observe that the product

$$
\begin{bmatrix} \times & \times \\ 0 & 1 \end{bmatrix}
\begin{bmatrix} \times \\ 1 \end{bmatrix}
$$

takes only two (one multiplication and one addition) operations. Thus, $\mathbf{y}$ can be computed serially in

$$T_y = 2k \tag{4.3.5.14}$$

steps. Since $\mathbf{B}$ and $\mathbf{y}$ are computed in parallel, it readily follows that

$$T = \max\{ T_B, \, T_y \} + 2, \tag{4.3.5.15}$$

where the two steps are needed to compute

$$\mathbf{y}_0 = \mathbf{B} \, \mathbf{y}.$$

It can be shown that (see Exercise 4.16) if $p < N$ and

$$k = \left\lceil \frac{3N}{2p+1} \right\rceil,$$

then

$$\max\{ T_B, \, T_y \} \le \left\lceil \frac{3}{p+\frac{1}{2}} \right\rceil N + O(\log p).$$

Thus,

$$T \le \left\lceil \frac{3}{p + \frac{1}{2}} \right\rceil N + O(\log p). \tag{4.3.5.16}$$

We now turn to deriving a fundamental lower bound relating to the evaluation of H_{2N+1}. To this end, we first define the structure of a class of algorithms for evaluating H_{2N+1} in the form of layered arithmetic circuits or, equivalently, by a directed (acyclic) graph as follows. The indegree of nodes is either zero or 2. Nodes with indegree zero are called *input* nodes. All the other nodes perform the binary arithmetic operations + (addition) and × (multiplication). The outdegree of the only *output* node is zero, and that of all the other nodes is greater than or equal to unity. The nodes which are neither input nodes nor output nodes are called *internal* nodes. Associated with each node is a number called the *value* of the node. The value of an input node is defined to be one of the input numbers. The value of a non-input node is obtained by performing the operation corresponding to that node on the two inputs to the node. Consequently, the value of the output node is the value of H_{2N+1}. Refer to Fig. 4.3.5.1 for an example.

The nodes in the graph (or circuit) are arranged in layers (or levels) $L_0, L_1, \cdots, L_T$ where all the input nodes are at the layer L_0. Further, input to the nodes at layer L_i is fed from the output of nodes at any level L_j for $j = i-1, i-2, \cdots, 1, 0$. In other words, the two *predecessors* of any node at level L_i are from levels L_j, and L_k, where $k, j \in \{0, 1, \cdots, i-1\}$. If $|L_i|$ denotes the number of nodes at level i, then it is required that $|L_i| > 0$ for all $i = 0, 1, \cdots, T$. Clearly, the output node is the only one node at level L_T. It is readily seen that the depth, which is the length of the longest path in this graph, is T, which is the time taken by the parallel algorithm (defined by the graph) to evaluate H_{2N+1}. Define

$$W = \max_{1 \le i \le T} \{|L_i|\}$$

as the *width* of the circuit and

$$S = \sum_{i=1}^{T} |L_i|$$

as the *size* of the circuit. Notice that W indicates the maximum parallelism in the algorithm. Thus, the algorithm is serial if $W = 1$.

We now establish a number of useful properties of these graphs.

Property 1. In H_{2N+1}, if a pair of variables (a_j, b_{j-1}) are assigned real values for some $1 \le j \le N$, then H_{2N+1} reduces to H_{2N-1}.

This relates to the reproducing property of the Horner's expressions under substitution of values to the associated pair of variables a_j and b_{j-1}. This can be easily seen through the recurrence relation (4.3.5.2), as shown below.

Let $a_j = p$ and $b_{j-1} = q$, where p and q are real numbers. Then X_i, for $i = N-1$ to $j+1$ and $i = j-2$ to 0, are as defined in (4.3.5.2). X_j is eliminated and X_{j-1} is

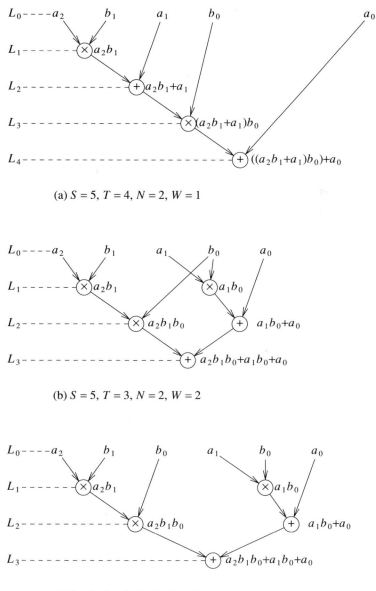

(a) $S = 5$, $T = 4$, $N = 2$, $W = 1$

(b) $S = 5$, $T = 3$, $N = 2$, $W = 2$

(c) $S = 5$, $T = 3$, $N = 2$, $W = 2$

FIGURE 4.3.5.1
Examples of layered graph for evaluating H_5.

replaced by

$$X_{j-1} = b'_j X_{j+1} + a'_{j-1},$$

where $b'_j = a\, b_{j+1}$ and $a'_{j-1} = pq + a_{j-1}$.

From Section 4.2, it follows that the nested structure of H_{2N+1} often inhibits parallelism. The only way to introduce parallelism in the evaluation of H_{2N+1} is to remove the nesting. Mathematically, removing nesting is equivalent to distributing multiplication with respect to addition. For example, in

$$H_5 = (a_2\, b_1 + a_1)b_0 + a_0,$$

distributing the multiplication by b_0, we obtain

$$H_5 = a_2\, b_1\, b_0 + a_1\, b_0 + a_0.$$

In Fig. 4.3.5.1, the graph (a) corresponds to the nested expression H_5 and those in (b) and (c) correspond to H_5, resulting from the distribution of b_0. The effect of distribution of b_0 is that it is required in the evaluation of more than one subexpression. This requirement can be satisfied either by fanning out b_0 to wherever it is required as in Fig. 4.3.5.1(b), or simply by introducing as many input nodes with label b_0 as the number of subexpressions in which it occurs, as in Fig. 4.3.5.1(c). These observations naturally lead to the following property.

Property 2. Consider a directed graph that evaluates H_{2N+1}. If the outdegree of each input node in this graph is unity and if there are exactly $2N + 1$ nodes, one for each of $a_0, a_1, \cdots, a_N, b_0, b_1, \cdots, b_{N-1}$, then there is only one node at level L_1, and its value is $a_N\, b_{N-1}$.

Proof

To prove this property, let v be the value of a node at level L_1. Then, clearly

$$v = a_i\, \Delta\, b_j \quad \text{or} \quad b_i\, \Delta\, b_j \quad \text{or} \quad a_i\, \Delta\, a_j,$$

for some i and j, where Δ is either the addition or the multiplication operation.

Consider the case when $v = a_i\, \Delta\, b_j$. Since each input node has outdegree unity, and there is only one node for each of the $2N + 1$ inputs $a_0, a_1, \cdots, a_N, b_0, b_1 \cdots, b_{N-1}$, it follows that the value V of the output node is a function of v, a_p, and b_q for $p \neq i$ and $q \neq j$. Now, comparing the coefficients of a_i and b_j in H_{2N+1} and V, it would readily follow that $v = a_N\, b_{N-1}$, and this is the value of the only node at L_1. The proof for the other cases, when $v = b_i\, \Delta\, b_j$ or $a_i\, \Delta\, a_j$, is similar and is left as an exercise (Exercise 4.17).

The following is an extension of the above property, and its proof is omitted.

Property 3. In addition to the assumptions stated in Property 2, if the only node at level L_1 has outdegree unity, then there is only one node at L_2.

We are now ready to prove the following fundamental result.

Theorem 4.3.5.1. For any algorithm that evaluates H_{2N+1}, the following inequality relating the size S, time T and input size N is true:

$$S + \frac{T}{2} \geq 3N. \qquad (4.3.5.17)$$

Proof

The proof of this theorem critically depends on the reproducing property of the Horner's expression (Property 1) under substitution of values to the variables. This property immediately suggests a class of algorithms called reduction algorithms (Hyfil and Kung [1977]) for the evaluation of H_{2N+1} and is given in Fig. 4.3.5.2. Using this algorithm, we now analyze the evaluation process. Illustrations of this process are given in Figs. 4.3.5.3 and 4.3.5.4.

/* Given $2N + 1$ real variables $a_0, a_1, \cdots a_N, b_0, b_1, \cdots, b_{N-1}$. */

Initialize the evaluation process by substituting the value of the variable a_0 in H_{2N+1}. Define $I = \{1, 2, \cdots, N\}$, the index set.

Step 1: If the conditions of Property 2 are satisfied, then let j be the smallest integer in set I and go to step 3.

Step 2: Since the conditions of Property 2 are not satisfied, there exists j such that a_j or b_j appears either in more than one input node or in an input node with outdegree greater than unity.

Step 3: Now substitute $a_j = p$ and $b_{j-1} = q$, where p and q are real numbers.

Step 4: Find the node, say Z, at the highest level that receives a numerical value resulting from the above substitution. Reduce the graph by removing all the predecessor nodes of Z and their associated directed arcs.

Step 5: $I = I - \{j\}$. If $I = \varnothing$, the null set, then stop, otherwise go to step 1.

FIGURE 4.3.5.2
Hyafil and Kung reduction algorithm.

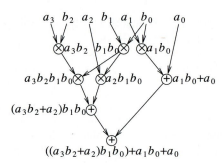

(a) A graph for H_7

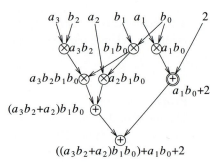

(b) In (a), the variable a_0 is assigned a value 2.

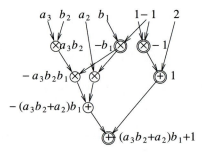

(c) In graph (b) the associated pair (a_1, b_0) is assigned values $(1, -1)$.

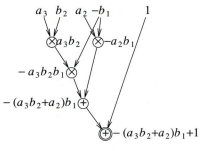

(d) The reduced graph obtained from (c).

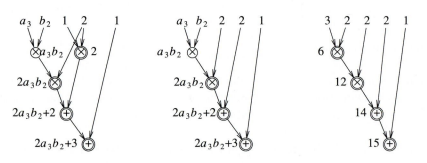

(e) In graph (d) the associated pair (a_2, b_1) is assigned $(1, -2)$.

(f) Reduced graph obtained from (e).

(g) The associated pair (a_3, b_2) is assigned $(3, 2)$.

FIGURE 4.3.5.3

Illustration of evaluation of H_{2N+1} using the recursion process. The activated nodes resulting from assignment of values are denoted by double circles.

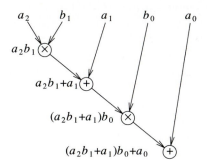

(a) The graph of H_5.

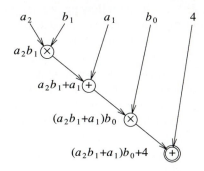

(b) Initialized by assigning 4 to a_0.

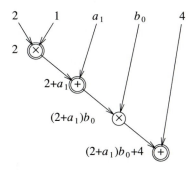

(c) The associated pair (a_2, b_1)
is assigned (2, 1).

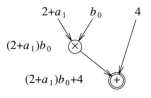

(d) The reduced graph resulting from (c).

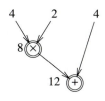

(e) The associated pair (a_1, b_0) is assigned (2,2).

FIGURE 4.3.5.4
Another illustration of evaluation of H_{2N+1} using the reduction process.

In the following, we say a binary operation is *activated* if at least one of its operands receives a numerical value resulting from the assignment (step 3 of the algorithm). Since we are interested in counting the number of operations needed in evaluating H_{2N+1}, whenever an operation is activated, we flag that operation after counting it. All the flagged nodes are denoted by double circles in the illustrations in Figs. 4.3.5.3 and 4.3.5.4.

Clearly, while initializing, only one operation is activated. After initialization, the algorithm loops N times to eliminate all the pairs (a_j, b_{j-1}), $j = 1, 2, \cdots, N$. Let N_1 be the number of times that Property 2 is *not* satisfied and N_2 be the number of times it is satisfied, where

$$N = N_1 + N_2.$$

(1) If conditions of Property 2 are *not* satisfied (step 2), then from the structure of the graph it follows that at least *three* operations are activated. Since this process is repeated N_1 times, there are at least $3N_1$ operations activated in this way. Refer to graphs (c) and (e) of Fig. 4.3.5.3 for illustration.

(2) If conditions of Property 2 are satisfied, then we may consider two subcases.

Case 2A. In addition to Property 2, if Property 3 is also satisfied, then during the reduction phase the depth of the graph reduces by at least 2. Further, at least *two* operations are activated if $|I| \geq 2$, and *one* operation is activated if $|I| = 1$. See Fig. 4.3.5.4 for an illustration of this case.

Case 2B. If Property 3 is *not* satisfied, then the outdegree of the only node at level L_1 is at least 2. Hence, a minimum of *three* operations are activated if $|I| \geq 2$, and only *two* operations are activated if $|I| = 1$. Further, this process leads to the reduction in depth at least by *unity*.

Let N_{2A} and N_{2B} be the number of times the conditions for case 2A and case 2B are satisfied, where $N_2 = N_{2A} + N_{2B}$. Now, when $|I| = 1$, either case 2A or case 2B will hold, but not both. Assume first that case 2A holds. The total contribution to the operation count from case 2A is $2(N_{2A} - 1) + 1 = 2N_{2A} - 1$. Likewise case 2B contributes $3N_{2B}$ toward the total count. On the other hand, if case 2B holds, when $|I| = 1$, then we obtain a contribution of $2N_{2A}$ and $3N_{2B} - 1$ operations toward the total count from case 2A and case 2B, respectively.

Combining all these, and from the definition of S and T, it follows that

$$S \geq 3N_1 + 2N_{2A} + 3N_{2B} = 3N - N_{2A} \tag{4.3.5.18}$$

and

$$T \geq 2N_{2A} + N_{2B}. \tag{4.3.5.19}$$

Again from these two inequalities, we obtain

$$S \geq 3N - \frac{T}{2} + \frac{N_{2B}}{2}. \tag{4.3.5.20}$$

Since $N_{2B} \geq 0$, this completes the proof of Theorem 4.3.5.1, and the equality (4.3.5.20) is possible only if $N_{2B} = 0$.
Theorem 4.3.5.1 has a number of consequences.

Corollary 4.3.5.2. For any algorithm that evaluates H_{2N+1}, if $T < 2N$, then $S > 2N$.

Since the serial algorithm for evaluating H_{2N+1} takes 2N steps, the preceding corollary implies that if a parallel algorithm is to be faster than the serial algorithm, then it must necessarily perform more operations than the serial algorithm. In other words, Theorem 4.3.5.1 presents a trade-off between the total number of operations (also called size) and the time or depth.

Applying the above trade-off result to the problem of evaluating H_{2N+1}, using p processors, we readily see that

$$pT \geq S. \tag{4.3.5.21}$$

Now combining (4.3.5.17) and (4.3.5.21), we obtain

$$\frac{T}{2} \geq 3N - S \geq 3N - pT,$$

$$T \geq \left\lceil \frac{3}{p + \frac{1}{2}} \right\rceil N. \tag{4.3.5.22}$$

From this inequality, we obtain an upper bound on the speed-up S_p, in evaluating H_{2N+1} using p processors as

$$S_p \leq \frac{2}{3}p + \frac{1}{3}. \tag{4.3.5.23}$$

Further, combining (4.3.5.16) and (4.3.5.22), we get

$$\left\lceil \frac{3}{p + \frac{1}{2}} \right\rceil N \leq T \leq \left\lceil \frac{3}{p + \frac{1}{2}} \right\rceil N + O(\log p). \tag{4.3.5.24}$$

Thus for a fixed p, as $N \to \infty$, the upper and the lower bounds are nearly the same. This in turn implies that the parallel method for the evaluation of H_{2N+1} described at the beginning of this section is optimal with respect to this trade-off. Also notice that when $p = 1$, the bound (4.3.5.22) is sharp. (See Exercise 4.18.)

Some of the conclusions transcend the boundaries of the problem of evaluation of polynomials. Since evaluation of H_{2N+1} is equivalent to solving a first-order linear recurrence of the type (4.3.5.2), it readily follows that the upper bound on the speed-up given in (4.3.5.23) applies to the evaluation of linear recurrences as well. Chapters 5 and 6 deal with algorithms for solving linear recurrences of various types.

4.4 PARALLEL EVALUATION OF GENERAL ARITHMETIC EXPRESSIONS

Throughout this section we consider general arithmetic expressions with *distinct* atoms called *primitive* expressions. Thus, $E(N)$ refers to an expression with at most N distinct atoms. Let $E(N, x)$ denote an expression with at most $N + 1$ distinct atoms, one of which is x. Because of this condition of distinctiveness of the atoms, expressions such as $a + x\,(b + x\,(c + d))$ or x^{10} are excluded from consideration. This is, however, not a serious restriction, since the analysis below readily provides an upper bound on the parallel time required to evaluate expressions of the type $a + x_1\,(b + x_2\,(c + d))$ or $x_1\,x_2\,\cdots\,x_{10}$, etc. (See Exercise 4.19.)

4.4.1 A Basic Lemma

The (parse) tree corresponding to an expression E is denoted by T_E. Let $|T_E|$ denote the number of leaves in T_E. We say that two trees T_1 and T_2 (with roots θ_1 and θ_2, respectively) are joined together to form a tree T (with root θ) if each of the roots θ_1 and θ_2 is joined to θ by an edge as demonstrated in Fig. 4.4.1.1. Such a tree T is denoted by $T_1\,\theta\,T_2$. The trees T_1 and T_2 are known as the (maximal) subtrees of T. Likewise T_1 and T_2 may contain subtrees each of which is considered a subtree of T. Clearly, the leaves of tree T are also subtrees of T.

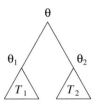

FIGURE 4.4.1.1
The tree T obtained by joining two subtrees T_1 and T_2. T is denoted by $T_1\,\theta\,T_2$.

The following lemma is fundamental and is repeatedly used in the sequel.

Lemma 4.4.1.1. Let $1 \le m \le N$ and let T_E be a parse tree of an expression $E(N)$. Let x be a leaf node of the tree T_E. Then

(a) There exists a subtree T_{E_1} of T_E such that $T_{E_1} = T_{E_L}\,\theta\,T_{E_R}$, where

$$| T_{E_1} | = | T_{E_L} | + | T_{E_R} | \geq m, \quad | T_{E_L} | < m, \quad \text{and } | T_{E_R} | < m$$

and $\theta \in \{+, \times, /\}$.

(b) There exists a subtree $T_{E_1} = T_{E_L} \theta T_{E_R}$ of T_E, such that $| T_{E_1} | \geq m$ and either (1) x is a leaf node in T_{E_L} with $| T_{E_L} | < m$ and $| T_{E_R} | \leq m - 1$ or (2) x is a leaf node in T_{E_R} with $| T_{E_R} | < m$ and $| T_{E_L} | \leq m - 1$.

Proof

Let $T = T_E = T_1^{(1)} \theta_1 T_2^{(1)}$. If $| T_i^{(1)} | < m$ for $i = 1, 2$, then the lemma follows. Without loss of generality, let $| T_1^{(1)} | > m$ and let $T_1^{(1)} = T_1^{(2)} \theta_2 T_2^{(2)}$. Continuing in this way, eventually we end up finding a subtree $T_1^{(j)} = T_1^{(j+1)} \theta_{j+1} T_2^{(j+1)}$ such that

$$| T_1^{(j)} | = | T_1^{(j+1)} | + | T_2^{(j+1)} | \geq m$$

$$| T_1^{(j+1)} | < m \quad \text{and} \quad | T_2^{(j+1)} | < m$$

Clearly $T_{E_1} = T_1^{(j)}$, $T_{E_L} = T_1^{(j+1)}$, and $T_{E_R} = T_2^{(j+1)}$, and part (a) of the lemma follows. The proof of part (b) is quite similar and is omitted.

4.4.2 Arithmetic Expressions Without Division

In this section we derive upper bounds on the parallel time required to evaluate general arithmetic expressions involving only addition and multiplication operations, using associativity, commutativity, and distributivity. (Recall that if the expression involves only addition or multiplication, then the associative fan-in algorithm of Chapter 1 provides the solution.) Accordingly, in this section $E(N)$ will denote a general arithmetic expression involving at most N distinct atoms and using addition and multiplication. Let $T(E(N))$ be the time required to evaluate $E(N)$ with these properties. Using the basic fan-in arguments, it follows that

$$T(E(N)) \geq \lceil \log N \rceil . \tag{4.4.2.1}$$

The following lemma is quite basic and is repeatedly used in the sequel.

Lemma 4.4.2.1. Let $E(N, x)$ be an arithmetic expression. Then using only the associative, commutative, and distributive properties of $\{+, \times\}$, $E(N, x)$ can be regrouped in the form

$$E_1(N, x) = A(N) x + B(N),$$

where $A(N)$ and $B(N)$ contain at most N atoms.

Proof

Let T_E be a parse tree of E, as shown in Fig. 4.4.2.1, where it is assumed without loss of generality that the variable x and a subtree T_1 of T_E are joined by the operator θ_1 to form a new subtree $(x\ \theta_1\ T_1)$. Let this subtree in turn be joined to a subtree T_2 of T_E by the operator θ_2. Continuing in this way, let θ_r be the root of the tree T_E. Let $I = \{i \mid 1 \le i \le r$ and $\theta_i = \times$, the multiplication operator $\}$. If E_i is the subexpression corresponding to a subtree T_i, then $A\,(N)$ is obtained by *distributing* all the appropriate E_i's, that is,

$$A\,(N) = \prod_{i \in I} E_i.$$

In other words, $A\,(N)$ is the product of the subexpressions corresponding to the subtrees attached to $\times$ nodes on the path from the parent of x to the root of the overall tree.

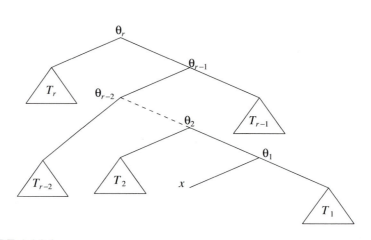

FIGURE 4.4.2.1
A parse tree T_E used in Lemma 4.4.2.1.

Excluding x, as there are at most N atoms, $A\,(N)$ contains at most N atoms.

Now, to obtain $B\,(N)$, let t be the smallest index of the $+$ operator, that is, $\theta_i = \times$ for $i = 1$ to $t-1$, and $\theta_t = +$. If $t > 1$, first delete the subtree corresponding to $E_{t-1} \times E_{t-2} \times \cdots \times E_2 \times x \times E_1$ from the T_E, and the expression corresponding to the remaining portion of the tree is in fact $B\,(N)$. On the other hand, if $t = 1$, then $B\,(N)$ is obtained by removing x from T_E. In either case, $B\,(N)$ contains at most N atoms.

This process of restructuring $E\,(N,\ x)$ is called expansion of E with respect to x.

The example in Fig. 4.4.2.2 illustrates this lemma. Notice that $B\,(N)$ is obtained by setting $x = 0$ in T_E.

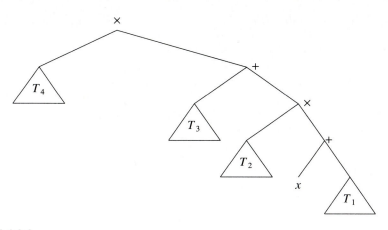

FIGURE 4.4.2.2

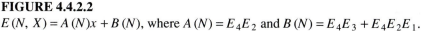

$E(N, X) = A(N)x + B(N)$, where $A(N) = E_4 E_2$ and $B(N) = E_4 E_3 + E_4 E_2 E_1$.

The following is one of the principal results of this section.

Theorem 4.4.2.2. Let $N = 2^n$ and $n \geq 3$. Using associativity, commutativity, and distributivity, any arithmetic expression $E(N)$ involving only $+$ and $\times$ operations can be evaluated in $T(E(N)) = 3n - 4$ parallel steps using at most $4^{n-2} = \dfrac{1}{16} N^2$ processors.

Proof
The proof is by induction. As the basis, for $n = 3$, it is readily seen that $E(8)$ can be evaluated in at most five steps. (Referring to Fig. 4.1.1.1, it is seen that an expression $E(N) = a (b + c (d + e (f + g \times h)))$ can be evaluated in five steps under full distribution. But using only a partial distribution, the same expression may be evaluated in four steps.)

Now assume that $E(2^n)$ can be evaluated in $3n - 4$ steps.

Let T_E be a parse tree of $E(2^{n+1})$ and let $m = 2^n$. Using Lemma 4.4.1.1, we can find (refer to part (a) of Fig. 4.4.2.3) subtrees T_{E_L} and T_{E_R} of T_E such that

$$|T_{E_L}| + |T_{E_R}| \geq m, \quad |T_{E_L}| < m, \quad \text{and} \quad |T_{E_R}| < m.$$

By inductive hypothesis, expressions E_L and E_R corresponding to T_{E_L} and T_{E_R} can be evaluated in $3n - 4$ steps. Thus $E_1 = E_L \; \theta \; E_R$ can be evaluated in $3n - 3$ steps.

Let T_{E_2} be the tree resulting from replacing the subtree T_{E_1} by a new variable, say x. (Refer to part (b) of Fig. 4.4.2.3). Since $|T_{E_1}| \geq 2^n$, it follows

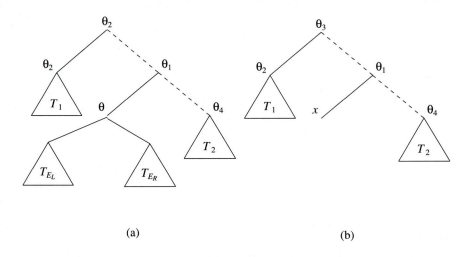

(a)   (b)

FIGURE 4.4.2.3
An illustration of the construction used in the proof of Theorem 4.4.2.2.

___

that

$$| \, T_{E_2} \, | \leq 2^{n+1} - 2^n + 1 \; = \; 2^n + 1.$$

We can write E_2 as $E_2(2^n, x)$. Now applying Lemma 4.4.2.1, let

$$E_2(2^n, x) = A(2^n) \times x + B(2^n)$$

for some expressions A and B, where $E = A \times E_1 + B$. Again by inductive hypothesis, A and B can be evaluated in $3n - 4$ steps. As E_1 is available in $3n - 3$ steps, $A \times E_1$ is available in $3n - 2$ steps and hence E is available in $3n - 1 = 3(n + 1) - 4$ steps.

When $n = 3$, referring to Fig. 4.1.1.1(b), it is immediate that four processors are sufficient. Assume that 4^{n-2} processors are sufficient to evaluate $E(2^n)$ in $3n - 4$ steps. Since the subexpressions A, B, E_L, and E_R are evaluated in parallel using four groups of 4^{n-2} processors (in $3n - 4$ steps), it is readily seen that a total of 4^{n-1} processors are enough to compute $E(2^{n+1})$ in $3n - 1$ steps. Hence the theorem.

From Theorem 4.4.2.2, it is clear that an expression with N atoms can be evaluated in

$$T(E(N)) = 3 \lceil \log N \rceil - 4$$

parallel steps. (See Exercise 4.20.)

In the following, we present an improved bound on $T(N)$. To this end, we first introduce an interesting sequence of integers as follows.

Let

$$g_0 = 1, \ g_1 = 2, \ g_2 = 3,$$

and, for $k \geq 0$,

$$g_{k+3} = g_{k+1} + g_k + 1. \tag{4.4.2.2}$$

The first few terms of this sequence are given in Table 4.4.2.1. The importance of this sequence stems from the following lemma.

Lemma 4.4.2.3. If $T(E(g_k))$ is the parallel time required to evaluate a general arithmetic expression $E(g_k)$ involving $+$ and $\times$ and using associativity, commutativity, and distributivity, then $T(E(g_k)) \leq k$.

Proof

Since the proof is similar to that of Theorem 4.4.2.2, we only indicate the major steps. The lemma is trivially true for $k = 0$. Assume that it is true for $T(g_i) \leq i$ for $i = 1, 2, \cdots, k+2$. To prove it from $i = k+3$, let T_E be a parse tree corresponding to $E(g_{k+3})$. Let $m = 1 + g_k$ and $N = g_{k+3}$. Then there exist subtrees T_L and T_R satisfying the conditions of Lemma 4.4.1.1. Since $|T_L| \leq m - 1 = g_k$, it follows that E_L can be evaluated in k steps and similarly for T_R. Let $E_1 = E_L \ \theta \ E_R$. If T_{E_2} is the tree resulting from replacing $T_L \ \theta \ T_R$ by a variable x, then (since $|E_1| \geq m = 1 + g_k$)

TABLE 4.4.2.1

k	g_k	h_k	k	g_k	h_k
0	1	0.945	10	36	35.745
1	2	1.667	11	48	47.768
2	3	2.624	12	64	63.694
3	4	3.892	13	85	84.791
4	6	5.572	14	113	112.739
5	8	7.796	15	150	149.760
6	11	10.749	16	199	198.803
7	15	14.648	17	264	263.770
8	20	19.819	18	350	349.832
9	27	26.670	19	464	463.838

$$| E_2 | \le g_{k+3} + 1 - | E_1 | \le g_{k+3} - g_k = 1 + g_{k+1}.$$

Hence by Lemma 4.4.2.1,

$$E_2(g_{k+1}, x) = A(g_{k+1}) x + B(g_{k+1}).$$

Since, by hypothesis both A and B can be evaluated in $k + 1$ steps, E can be evaluated in $k + 3$ steps. Hence the lemma follows by induction.

To obtain the general solution of this recurrence in (4.4.2.2), consider the related characteristic equation

$$\lambda^3 - \lambda - 1 = 0. \tag{4.4.2.3}$$

The method of solving cubic equations of this type is of intrinsic interest, and in the following we outline the major steps. Setting $\lambda = u + v$, (4.4.2.3) becomes

$$u^3 + v^3 + (3uv - 1)(u + v) - 1 = 0. \tag{4.4.2.4}$$

Requiring

$$u v = \frac{1}{3}, \tag{4.4.2.5}$$

it follows that the solution of (4.4.2.2) can be obtained by solving

$$u^3 + v^3 = 1 \quad \text{and} \quad u^3 v^3 = \frac{1}{27}. \tag{4.4.2.6}$$

In view of the symmetry of (4.4.2.6) with respect to the unknowns, both u^3 and v^3 are obtained as the solution of the following quadratic equation:

$$s^2 - s + \frac{1}{27} = 0. \tag{4.4.2.7}$$

Let

$$u^3 = \frac{1}{2} + \sqrt{\frac{1}{4} - \frac{1}{27}} \approx 0.9615$$

and

$$v^3 = \frac{1}{2} - \sqrt{\frac{1}{4} - \frac{1}{27}} \approx 0.0385.$$

Let $\alpha = (0.9615)^{1/3} = 0.9870$ be one of the roots of 0.9615. Then the three possible values of u are given by

$$u = \alpha, \quad \omega\alpha \quad \text{and} \quad \omega^2\alpha, \tag{4.4.2.8}$$

where

$$\omega = \frac{-1 + i\sqrt{3}}{2}$$

is the cube root of unity and $i = \sqrt{-1}$, the imaginary constant.

Likewise, if $\beta = (0.0385)^{1/3} = 0.3377$, then the three possible values of v are

$$v = \beta, \quad \omega\beta \quad \text{and} \quad \omega^2\beta. \tag{4.4.2.9}$$

Since $uv = \dfrac{1}{3}$, the associated pair of values u_i and v_i, for $i = 1, 2, 3$, are given by

$$u_1 = \alpha \qquad v_1 = \beta,$$

$$u_2 = \omega\alpha \qquad v_2 = \omega^2\beta,$$

and

$$u_3 = \omega^2\alpha \qquad v_3 = \omega\beta.$$

From this, the solution of equation (4.4.2.2) is obtained as

$$\left.\begin{array}{l} \lambda_1 = \alpha + \beta = 1.3247 \\[4pt] \lambda_2 = \omega\alpha + \omega^2\beta = -\tfrac{1}{2}(\lambda_1 + i(3\lambda_1{}^2 - 4)^{1/2}) \\[8pt] \lambda_3 = \omega^2\alpha + \omega\beta = -\tfrac{1}{2}(\lambda_1 - i(3\lambda_1{}^2 - 4)^{1/2}) \end{array}\right\} \tag{4.4.2.10}$$

where $|\lambda_2| = |\lambda_3| = (\lambda_1)^{-1/2}$.

Using the method of generating functions, the general solution to the linear recurrence (4.4.2.2) may be expressed as

$$g_k = \sum_{i=1}^{3} c_i \lambda_i^k - 1. \tag{4.4.2.11}$$

From the boundary conditions $g_0 = 1$, $g_1 = 2$, and $g_2 = 3$, we obtain for $i = 1, 2, 3$ that

$$c_i = \frac{3\lambda_i{}^2 + 4\lambda_i + 2}{2\lambda_i + 3} \tag{4.4.2.12}$$

and

$$|c_2| = |c_3| = \left[\frac{\lambda_1{}^2 + \lambda_1 - 3}{4\lambda_1{}^2 - 6\lambda_1 + 5}\right]^{1/2}. \tag{4.4.2.13}$$

Define

$$h_k = c_1\lambda_1{}^k - 2|c_2| - 1, \tag{4.4.2.14}$$

where $c_1 = 2.2496$ and $|c_2| = |c_3| = 0.14004$.

Now, using (4.4.2.10), it follows from (4.4.2.11) that

$$g_k \geq c_1\lambda_1{}^k - 2|c_2|\lambda_1{}^{-k/2} - 1. \tag{4.4.2.15}$$

Since $\lambda_1{}^{-1/2} = 0.8688$, it follows that

$$g_k \geq h_k. \tag{4.4.2.16}$$

The values of h_k are given in Table 4.4.2.1.

The following theorem due to Brent, Kuck, and Maruyama [1973] provides an improved bound alluded to above.

Theorem 4.4.2.4. For any $N \geq 2$,

$$T(E(N)) = 2.4699 \log N + O(1).$$

Proof

Given N (≥ 2), let k be such that

$$g_{k-1} < N \leq g_k.$$

From this and (4.4.2.16) it follows that

$$N \geq g_{k-1} + 1 \geq c_1 \lambda_1^{k-1} - 2|c_2|,$$

that is,

$$aN + b \geq \lambda_1^k,$$

where $a = \dfrac{\lambda_1}{c_1} \approx 0.5956$ and $b = \dfrac{2|c_2|\lambda_1}{c_1} \approx 0.1665$. Thus,

$$k \leq \log_{\lambda_1}(aN + b) = 2.4699 \log N + O(1).$$

Having succeeded in reducing the upper bound from $3\lceil \log N \rceil - 4$ to $2.4699 \log N + O(1)$, the question is: is further reduction possible? While there is no known lower bound (except perhaps for the one due to Kosaraju [1986] for polynomial evaluation given in Theorem 4.3.4.1) on the parallel time required to evaluate general arithmetic expressions, a number of improved designs with better upper bounds have been reported in the literature. For division-free arithmetic expressions, Preparata and Muller [1975] first reduced the upper bound to $2.1507 \log N + O(1)$ (see Exercise 4.33). Almost simultaneously, they showed (Preparata and Muller [1976]) that, by exploiting dual distributivity, Boolean expressions with N distinct literals involving AND and OR operations can be evaluated in at most $1.81 \log N$ steps. Shortly thereafter, Muller and Preparata [1976] developed algorithms for restructuring expressions *with* and *without* division operations. For division-free expressions in particular, they showed that $2.08 \log N + O(1)$ steps are sufficient for parallel evaluation. Very recently, Kosaraju [1986] showed, among other things, that $2 \log N + O(1)$ steps are sufficient to evaluate division-free expressions in parallel. We conclude this section with a description of Kosaraju's algorithm.

We begin by introducing some useful concepts. A tree T is said to be *composed* of subtrees T_i, $1 \leq i \leq t$, if *every leaf of T is a leaf of some subtree T_i, $1 \leq i \leq t$.*

Given a tree T_E corresponding to expression E, the *effective size* of T_E, $ES(T_E)$, is said to be m, if E can be restructured into an expression $\hat{E}$ such that the *depth* of $T_{\hat{E}}$ is *bounded above* by $2 \log m + c$ for some constant $c > 0$. Recall that $|T_E|$ denotes the *size* of E (also denoted by $|E|$), measured in terms of the number of leaves (which are assumed to be distinct) in T_E. Our principal aim is to prove that if E is a division-free arithmetic expression and $|T_E| = N$, then $ES(T_E) = N$.

Our first result characterizes the effective size of a tree T_E in terms of the effective sizes of the constituent subtrees T_{E_i}, $1 \le i \le t$. Let T_{E_1} and T_{E_2} be two trees with

$$ES(T_{E_i}) = \alpha_i N, \qquad (4.4.2.17)$$

for some $0 < \alpha_i < 1$, $i = 1, 2$. Let $T_E = T_{E_1} \theta T_{E_2}$. Let $\alpha = \max\{\alpha_1, \alpha_2\}$. Then

$$ES(T_E) = \sqrt{2} \, \alpha N, \qquad (4.4.2.18)$$

since

$$2 \log (\sqrt{2} \, \alpha N) + c = 1 + 2 \log (\alpha N) + c.$$

Referring to Fig. 4.4.2.4, notice that both the roots of the subtrees T_{E_1} and T_{E_2} are at depth $d = 1$, measured from the root of T_E. Thus, $ES(T_E)$ is obtained by adding $d \,(= 1)$ to the maximum of the depths of T_{E_1} and T_{E_2}, which is the same as multiplying the maximum of $ES(T_{E_1})$ and $ES(T_{E_2})$ by $\sqrt{2}$.

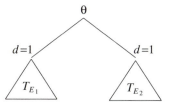

FIGURE 4.4.2.4
$T_E = T_{E_1} \theta T_{E_2}$. The roots of T_{E_1} and T_{E_2} are at depth 1 from the root of T_E.

A generalization of this fact is the following lemma, whose proof is left to the reader. (See Exercise 4.22.)

Lemma 4.4.2.5. If a tree T_E is restructured into a tree $T_{\hat{E}}$ such that $T_{\hat{E}}$ is composed of subtrees $T_{E_1}, T_{E_2}, \cdots, T_{E_t}$, where

$$ES\,(T_{E_i}) = \alpha_i\,N, \quad 0 < \alpha_i < 1,$$

and the root of T_{E_i} is at depth d_i from the root of $T_{\hat{E}}$ for $i = 1$ to t, then

$$ES(T_E) = \max\{(\sqrt{2})^{d_i}\,\alpha_i\,N \mid i = 1 \text{ to } t\}. \tag{4.4.2.19}$$

We now digress to establish two lemmas which are useful in the proof of the main result.

Lemma 4.4.2.6. Let $E = E_1 \times E_2 \times \cdots \times E_t$, where $\mid E \mid \leq N$, $\mid E_1 \mid \leq \dfrac{N}{2}$, and $\mid E_i \mid \leq \dfrac{N}{2\sqrt{2}}$, for $i = 2$ to t. Then

(a) There exist expressions F_i, for $i = 1$ to 3, or G_j, for $j = 1$ to 4, such that E can be restructured as $\hat{E}$, where

$$\hat{E} = F_1 \times (F_2 \times F_3)$$

or

$$\hat{E} = G_1 \times (G_2 \times (G_3 \times G_4)),$$

and

(b) If $\mid E_i \mid = \alpha_i\,N$ implies $ES(T_{E_i}) = \alpha_i N$ for $i = 1$ to t, and $\alpha_i \leq \frac{1}{2}$, then $ES(T_{\hat{E}}) = \dfrac{N}{\sqrt{2}}.$

Proof

If E_i and E_j are such that $\mid E_i \times E_j \mid \leq \dfrac{N}{2\sqrt{2}}$, then E_i and E_j are replaced by a single term $E_i \times E_j$. In this way, repeatedly combine any *two* product terms into *one* until no such combination is possible. Likewise, repeatedly combine any term E_j with E_1 if the resulting term $E_1 \times E_j$ is such that $\mid E_1 \times E_j \mid \leq \dfrac{N}{2}$, until no such combination is possible. In view of this possibility, we could assume without loss of generality that

$$\mid E_1 \mid \geq \mid E_2 \mid \geq \cdots \geq \mid E_t \mid.$$

The first conclusion is

$$\mid E_{t-1} \mid > \dfrac{N}{4\sqrt{2}},$$

for otherwise E_{t-1} and E_t could be combined into one term, since

$$| E_t | \le | E_{t-1} | \le \frac{N}{4\sqrt{2}}.$$

The second conclusion is $t \le 4$ for if $t \ge 5$, then, since

$$| E_1 | + | E_t | > \frac{N}{2}$$

$$| E_2 | + | E_3 | > \frac{N}{2\sqrt{2}}$$

$$| E_{t-1} | > \frac{N}{4\sqrt{2}},$$

we have

$$| E | \ge \frac{N}{2} + \frac{N}{2\sqrt{2}} + \frac{N}{4\sqrt{2}} > N,$$

a contradiction. Further, from $| E_1 | \le \frac{N}{2}$, $| E_2 | \le \frac{N}{2\sqrt{2}}$, we obtain that $t \ge 3$. Now, restructure E as

$$\hat{E} = \begin{cases} E_1 \times (E_2 \times E_3) & \text{if } t = 3 \\ \\ E_1 \times (E_2 \times (E_3 \times E_4)) & \text{if } t = 4. \end{cases}$$

Clearly, the choices of F_i's and G_j's is obvious and part (a) is proved.

To prove part (b), let $t = 3$. In the parse tree for $\hat{E}$, T_{E_1} is at depth 1 and T_{E_2} and T_{E_3} are at depth 2. Hence, by Lemma 4.4.2.5,

$$ES(T_{\hat{E}}) = \max\{\sqrt{2} \times \frac{N}{2}, (\sqrt{2})^2 \times \frac{N}{2\sqrt{2}}\} = \frac{N}{\sqrt{2}}.$$

Let $t = 4$. From $| E_1 | + | E_4 | > \frac{N}{2}$ and $| E_2 | \ge | E_3 |$, it follows that

$$| E_3 | \le \frac{| E_2 | + | E_3 |}{2} \le \frac{1}{2}(N - \frac{N}{2}) = \frac{N}{4}.$$

Hence, $| E_4 | \le | E_3 | \le \frac{N}{4}$. In addition, $| E_1 | \le \frac{N}{2}$ and $| E_2 | \le \frac{N}{2\sqrt{2}}$. Further, in the parse tree of $T_{\hat{E}}$, T_{E_1} is at depth 1, T_{E_2} is at depth 2 and T_{E_3} and T_{E_4} are depth three. Combining these facts, from Lemma 4.4.2.5, we obtain

$$ES(T_{\hat{E}}) = \max\{\sqrt{2} \times \frac{N}{2}, (\sqrt{2})^2 \times \frac{N}{2\sqrt{2}}, (\sqrt{2})^3 \times \frac{N}{4}\} = \frac{N}{\sqrt{2}},$$

which completes the proof of part (b).

Lemma 4.4.2.7. Let $E = D \times E_1 \times E_2 \times \cdots \times E_t$ in which $ES(T_D) = \dfrac{N}{2\sqrt{2}}$, $|E| \le \dfrac{N}{2}$, $|E_i| \le \dfrac{N}{2\sqrt{2}}$ for $2 \le i \le t$, and $|E_1 \times E_2 \times \cdots \times E_t| \le \dfrac{N}{\sqrt{2}}$. Then

(a) There exist expressions F_1, F_2, or G_1, G_2, G_3 such that E can be restructured as $\hat{E}$, where $\hat{E} = F_1 \times (D \times F_2)$ or $G_1 \times (D \times (G_2 \times G_3))$, and

(b) If $|E_i| = \alpha_i N$ implies $ES(T_{E_i}) = \alpha_i N$ for $i = 1$ to t, and $\alpha_i \le \frac{1}{2}$, then $ES(T_{\hat{E}}) = \dfrac{N}{\sqrt{2}}$.

Proof

Assume without loss of generality that

$$|E_1| \ge |E_2| \ge \cdots \ge |E_t|$$

(for otherwise, we can repeatedly invoke the recombination process described in Lemma 4.4.2.6), and

$$E = D \times E_1 \times E_2 \times \cdots \times E_t.$$

If $t \ge 4$, from

$$|E_1| + |E_t| > \frac{N}{2} \quad \text{and} \quad |E_2| + |E_3| > \frac{N}{2\sqrt{2}},$$

we obtain,

$$|E_1 \times E_2 \times \cdots \times E_t| \ge \frac{N}{2} + \frac{N}{2\sqrt{2}} > \frac{N}{\sqrt{2}},$$

a contradiction to the assumption. Restructuring E as

$$\hat{E} = \begin{cases} E_1 \times (D \times E_2) & \text{if } t = 2, \\ \\ E_1 \times (D \times (E_2 \times E_3)) & \text{if } t = 3, \end{cases}$$

part (a) follows.

To prove (b), let $t = 2$. In the parse tree for $\hat{E}$, the subtree for E_1 is at depth 1 and those for D and E_2 are at depth 2. Combining these, from Lemma 4.4.2.5 it follows that

$$ES(T_{\hat{E}}) = \max\{\sqrt{2} \times \frac{N}{2}, (\sqrt{2})^2 \times \frac{N}{2\sqrt{2}}\} = \frac{N}{\sqrt{2}}.$$

If $t = 3$, from $|E_1| + |E_3| > \dfrac{N}{2}$, we obtain

$$| E_2 | < \frac{N}{\sqrt{2}} - \frac{N}{2} < \frac{N}{4}.$$

Hence, $| E_3 | \leq | E_2 | < \frac{N}{4}$. Now, in the parse tree $T_{\hat{E}}$, the subtree for E_1 is at depth 1, that for D is at depth 2 and those for E_2 and E_3 are at depth 3. Combining this with Lemma 4.4.2.5, we have

$$ES(T_{\hat{E}}) = \max\{\sqrt{2} \times \frac{N}{2}, (\sqrt{2})^2 \times \frac{N}{2\sqrt{2}}, (\sqrt{2})^3 \times \frac{N}{4}\} = \frac{N}{\sqrt{2}},$$

which completes part (b).

Lemma 4.4.2.8. Let $E = E_L + E_R$, where $| E | \geq N(1 - \frac{1}{\sqrt{2}})$ and $| E_L | < | E_R | \leq N(1 - \frac{1}{\sqrt{2}})$. Assume further that if an expression is of size αN; for $\alpha < 1$, then its effective size is αN. Then E can be restructured into

$$E = G + F,$$

where

$$ES(T_G) = \frac{N}{2\sqrt{2}}$$

and

$$| F | \leq | E | - N(1 - \frac{1}{\sqrt{2}}).$$

Proof

Applying Lemma 4.4.1.1 to the subtree T_{E_R}, we can find a subtree T_D in T_{E_R} where (refer to Fig. 4.4.2.5)

$$\frac{N}{2\sqrt{2}} \geq | T_D | \geq \frac{N}{4\sqrt{2}},$$

$$| T_{D_L} | \leq | T_{D_R} | < \frac{N}{4\sqrt{2}}.$$

Case 1. Let $| T_{D_R} | \leq \frac{N}{8}$. Using a variation of Lemma 4.4.2.1, we can express E_R as

$$E_R = J_1 \times (D_L \theta D_R) + J_2.$$

Observe that

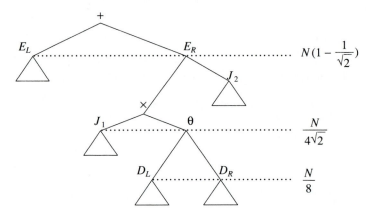

FIGURE 4.4.2.5
$E = E_L + E_R$, $E_R = J_1 \times D + J_2$, $D = D_L \, \theta \, D_R$.

$$| J_1 | \leq | E_R | - | D_L \, \theta \, D_R | = N(1 - \frac{1}{\sqrt{2}}) - \frac{N}{4\sqrt{2}} < \frac{N}{8},$$

and likewise

$$| J_2 | < \frac{N}{8}.$$

Two subcases arise.

Case 1a. Let $| E_L | \leq \frac{N}{4\sqrt{2}}$. Define

$$E = G = J_1 \times (D_L \, \theta \, D_R) + (E_L + J_2)$$

and

$$F = 0.$$

Since $| T_{D_L} | \leq | T_{D_R} | \leq \frac{N}{8}$ and $| E_L | \leq \frac{N}{4\sqrt{2}}$, from Lemma 4.4.2.5 we obtain that

$$ES\,(T_{E_L + J_2}) = \frac{N}{4},$$

$$ES\,(T_{J_1 \times (D_L \,\theta\, D_R)}) = \frac{N}{4},$$

and

$$ES\,(T_G) = \frac{N}{2\sqrt{2}}.$$

Case 1b. Let $\dfrac{N}{4\sqrt{2}} < |\,E_L\,| < N(1 - \dfrac{1}{\sqrt{2}})$. Define

$$G = J_1 \times (D_L \,\theta\, D_R) + E_L$$

and

$$F = J_2.$$

Note that

$$|\,F\,| = |\,J_2\,| \le |\,E_R\,| - |\,D_L \,\theta\, D_R\,|$$

$$\le |\,E\,| - |\,E_L\,| - \frac{N}{4\sqrt{2}}$$

$$= |\,E\,| - \frac{N}{4\sqrt{2}} - \frac{N}{4\sqrt{2}}$$

$$= |\,E\,| - N(1 - \frac{1}{\sqrt{2}}).$$

The proof of $ES\,(T_G) = \dfrac{N}{2\sqrt{2}}$ follows from case 1.1.

Case 2. Let $\dfrac{N}{8} < |\,T_{D_R}\,| < \dfrac{N}{4\sqrt{2}}$. Using a variation of Lemma 4.4.2.1, express E_R as

$$E_R = \hat{A} \times D_R + \hat{B},$$

where

$$\hat{A} = \begin{cases} J_1 & \text{if } \theta = + \\[2mm] J_1 \, D_L & \text{if } \theta = \times, \end{cases}$$

and

$$\hat{B} = \begin{cases} J_1 D_L + J_2 & \text{if } \theta = + \\ \\ J_2 & \text{if } \theta = \times. \end{cases}$$

Case 2a. Let $| E_L | \le \dfrac{N}{4\sqrt{2}}$. Define

$$G = \hat{A} \times D_R + (\hat{B} + E_L)$$

and

$$F = 0.$$

Observe that

$$| \hat{A} | = | E_R | - | D_R | \le N(1 - \frac{1}{\sqrt{2}}) - \frac{N}{4\sqrt{2}} < \frac{N}{8}.$$

Likewise,

$$| \hat{B} | < \frac{N}{8}.$$

Combining these as in case 1a, it follows that

$$ES(T_G) = \frac{N}{2\sqrt{2}}.$$

Case 2b. Let $\dfrac{N}{4\sqrt{2}} < | E_L | < N(1 - \dfrac{1}{\sqrt{2}})$. Define

$$G = \hat{A} \times D_R + E_L,$$

and

$$F = \hat{B}.$$

Notice that

$$| \hat{B} | \le | E_R | - | D_R | \le | E | - | E_L | - \frac{N}{8}$$

$$< | E | - \frac{N}{4\sqrt{2}} - \frac{N}{8}$$

$$< | E | - N(1 - \frac{1}{\sqrt{2}}).$$

The proof of $ES(T_G) = \dfrac{N}{2\sqrt{2}}$ is quite similar to the previous cases, and the proof of the lemma is now complete.

We now prove the main result.

Theorem 4.4.2.9. Any division-free arithmetic expression E of size N can be restructured, using associativity, commutativity, and distributivity, into an expression $\hat{E}$ such that $ES(T_{\hat{E}})$ is N, that is, $\hat{E}$ is of depth less than or equal to $2 \log N + c$ for some constant $c > 0$.

Proof

The proof is by induction on N. For small N, the theorem can be verified by proper choice of the constant c. (Refer to Fig. 4.1.1.1 for an example with $N = 8$.) Let the theorem be true for all expressions of size less than or equal to $N - 1$.

Consider the expression E of size N. Applying Lemma 4.4.1.1, identify a subtree T_{E_1} of T_E such that $T_{E_1} = T_{E_L} \theta T_{E_R}$; $N \geq |T_{E_1}| \geq \dfrac{N}{2}$, $|T_{E_L}| \leq |T_{E_R}| < \dfrac{N}{2}$, $\theta \in \{+, \times\}$, and $E = A \times E_1 + B$.

Case 1. Let $|T_{E_R}| \leq \dfrac{N}{2\sqrt{2}}$. By using a variation of Lemma 4.4.2.1 (with E_1 in place of x in it), we can express E as (refer to Fig. 4.4.2.6(a))

$$E = A \times (E_L \theta E_R) + B \qquad (4.4.2.20)$$

in which $|A| \leq \dfrac{N}{2}$, $|B| \leq \dfrac{N}{2}$, and $|E_R| \leq \dfrac{N}{(\sqrt{2})^3}$. Referring to Fig. 4.4.2.7(a) for the depth of the subtrees, and applying Lemma 4.4.2.5, it follows that

$$ES(T_E) = \max\left\{ \sqrt{2} \times \dfrac{N}{2}, (\sqrt{2})^2 \times \dfrac{N}{2}, (\sqrt{2})^3 \times \dfrac{N}{(\sqrt{2})^3} \right\} = N.$$

Case 2. $\dfrac{N}{2\sqrt{2}} < |T_{E_R}| < \dfrac{N}{2}$ and $\theta = +$. Referring to Fig. 4.4.2.6(a), we can express E as

$$E = A \times |E_R| + (A \times E_L + B), \qquad (4.4.2.21)$$

in which $|A| \leq \dfrac{N}{2}$ and $|E_L| < \dfrac{N}{2}$. Notice that $(A \times E_L + B)$ is obtained from E by replacing E_1 (found at the beginning of the inductive step) by E_L. Thus,

$$|B'| = |A \times E_L + B| = |E| - |E_R| < N - \dfrac{N}{2\sqrt{2}} < \dfrac{N}{\sqrt{2}}.$$

From Fig. 4.4.2.7(b), and applying Lemma 4.4.2.5, we obtain

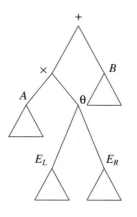

(a) $E = A \times E_1 + B$ and $E_1 = E_L \, \theta \, E_R$

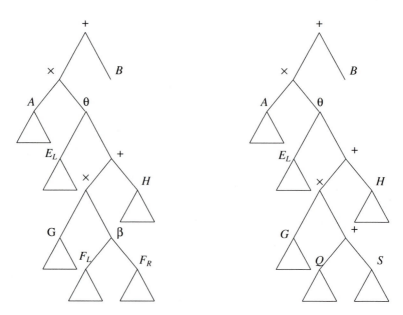

(b) $E = A \times E_1 + B$; $E_1 = E_L \, \theta \, E_R$;   (c) Case 3.3 of Theorem 4.4.2.9
$E_R = G \times F + H$, and $F = F_L \, \beta \, F_R$

FIGURE 4.4.2.6
A restructuring of E used in the proof of Theorem 4.4.2.9.

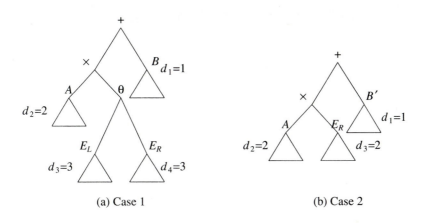

(a) Case 1   (b) Case 2

FIGURE 4.4.2.7
Structures used in the proof of Theorem 4.4.2.9.

$$ES\,(T_E) = \max\{\sqrt{2} \times \frac{N}{\sqrt{2}}, \ (\sqrt{2})^2 \times \frac{N}{2}\} \ = \ N.$$

Case 3. $\dfrac{N}{2\sqrt{2}} < |\,T_{E_R}\,| < \dfrac{N}{2}$, and $\theta = \times$. Using Lemma 4.4.1.1, we can

find a subtree $T_F = T_{F_L}\,\beta\,T_{F_R}$ of T_{E_R} such that $|\,T_F\,| \geq N(1 - \dfrac{1}{\sqrt{2}})$,

$|\,T_{F_L}\,| \leq |\,T_{F_R}\,| < N(1 - \dfrac{1}{\sqrt{2}})$, and $\beta \in \{+,\times\}$. Using this, we can express

(refer to Fig. 4.4.2.6(b))

$$E_R = G \times F + H = G \times (F_L\,\beta\,F_R) + H.$$

Three subcases arise.

Case 3a. Let $\beta = \times$. Using a variation of Lemma 4.4.2.1 (with F_R replacing x in it), we can express E as (refer to Fig. 4.4.2.6(b))

$$E = \hat{A} \times F_R + \hat{B}, \tag{4.4.2.22}$$

where

$$\hat{A} = A \times E_L \times G \times F_L$$

and   (4.4.2.23)

$$\hat{B} = A \times E_L \times H + B,$$

from which it follows that

$$| \hat{B} | \le | E | - | F_R | < N - N(1 - \frac{1}{\sqrt{2}}) = \frac{N}{\sqrt{2}}. \qquad (4.4.2.24)$$

Referring to Fig. 4.4.2.6(b), it follows that the sizes of the subexpressions E_L, G, F_L, F_R are bounded by $\dfrac{N}{2\sqrt{2}}$ and that of A is bounded by $\dfrac{N}{2}$. Combining this with the inductive hypothesis and Lemma 4.4.2.6, it follows that

$$ES(T_{\hat{A} \times F_R}) = \frac{N}{\sqrt{2}}. \qquad (4.4.2.25)$$

Again, combining (4.4.2.24), the inductive hypothesis, (4.4.2.25), and Lemma 4.4.2.5, we obtain

$$ES(T_E) = N.$$

Case 3b. Let $\beta = +$ and $| F_R | \le \dfrac{N}{4}$. Using a variation of Lemma 4.4.2.1 (with F replacing x in it), we have

$$E = \hat{A} \times (F_L + F_R) + \hat{B}, \qquad (4.4.2.26)$$

where

$$\hat{A} = A \times E_L \times G$$

and

$$\hat{B} = A \times E_L \times H + B,$$

from which it follows that

$$| \hat{B} | = | E | - | F | \le N - N(1 - \frac{1}{\sqrt{2}}) = \frac{N}{\sqrt{2}}. \qquad (4.4.2.27)$$

Since $| F_L | \le | F_R | \le \dfrac{N}{4}$, by the inductive hypothesis

$$ES(T_F) = \sqrt{2} \times \frac{N}{4} = \frac{N}{2\sqrt{2}}.$$

Referring to Fig. 4.4.2.6(b), $\hat{A}$ is the product of terms in which $| E_L | \le \dfrac{N}{2\sqrt{2}}$, $| G | \le \dfrac{N}{2\sqrt{2}}$, and $| A | \le \dfrac{N}{2}$. Further, from (4.4.2.26), we have

$$| \hat{A} | = | E | - | F | \le N - N(1 - \frac{1}{\sqrt{2}}) \le \frac{N}{\sqrt{2}}.$$

Combining these with Lemma 4.4.2.7, it follows that

$$ES(T_{\hat{A} \times F}) = \frac{N}{\sqrt{2}}. \qquad (4.4.2.28)$$

Now from (4.4.2.26) to (4.4.2.28), the inductive hypothesis, and Lemma 4.4.2.5, we have

$$ES(T_E) = N.$$

Case 3c. Let $\beta = +$ and $\frac{N}{4} < |T_{F_R}| \leq N(1 - \frac{1}{\sqrt{2}})$. Using Lemma 4.4.2.8, we can restructure $F_L + F_R$ as

$$F_L + F_R = Q + S,$$

in which

$$ES(T_Q) = \frac{N}{2\sqrt{2}}$$

and

$$|S| \leq |F| - N(1 - \frac{1}{\sqrt{2}}).$$

Using this restructuring, we can now express E as (refer to Fig. 4.4.2.6(c))

$$E = \hat{A} \times Q + \hat{B},$$

where

$$\hat{A} = A \times E_L \times G$$

and

$$\hat{B} = A \times E_L \times (G \times S + H) + B.$$

Further,

$$|\hat{B}| \leq |E| - |F_L + F_R| = N - N(1 - \frac{1}{\sqrt{2}}) = \frac{N}{\sqrt{2}},$$

and from Lemma 4.4.2.7 and the inductive hypothesis, we obtain that

$$ES(T_{\hat{A} \times Q}) = \frac{N}{\sqrt{2}}.$$

Combining these and the inductive hypothesis, it follows that

$$ES(T_E) = N,$$

and the proof is complete.

It can be shown that the number of processors needed to compute $E(N)$ by the best known algorithm implicit in Theorem 4.4.2.9 is $O(N^{1+\varepsilon})$ for some $\varepsilon > \frac{1}{2}$ (see Exercise 4.36).

Theorems 4.4.2.2, 4.4.2.4, and 4.4.2.9 establish upper bounds on $T(E(N))$ using $O(N^{1+\varepsilon})$ processors $(\varepsilon > \frac{1}{2})$. In Theorem 4.4.2.10, another upper bound on $T(E(N))$ using only $O(N)$ processors is derived. The derivation of this new bound is also quite similar to that in Theorem 4.4.2.2.

Theorem 4.4.2.10. Let E be an arithmetic expression with N distinct atoms and using $+$ and $\times$ operations (with any level of parenthesis nesting). Define

$$n = \begin{cases} N+2 & \text{if } N \leq 3 \\ \lceil 4\log(N-1) \rceil & \text{if } N \geq 4. \end{cases} \qquad (4.4.2.29)$$

Let

$$Q_1(N) = 2(N-1) \qquad \text{and} \qquad Q_2(N) = \max\{0, 2(N-2)\}.$$

Then, using associativity, commutativity, and distributivity,

(a) E can be evaluated in $n-3$ steps using at most $Q_1(N)$ operations and $O(N)$ processors, and

(b) If $E = A\,x + B$, where x is an atom of E and A and B do not involve x (it might happen that A may be 1 and that B may be 0), then A and B can be evaluated in parallel in at most n steps using at most $Q_2(N)$ operations and $O(N)$ processors.

Proof

It follows from the definition that $n \geq N+2$ for all $N \leq 7$. Since $E(N)$ can be evaluated in $N-1$ steps using one processor, part (a) holds good for $N \leq 7$. Likewise, part (b) also holds for $N \leq 7$, since, using two processors, A and B can be evaluated in at most $N-2$ steps using at most $2(N-2)$ operations. This constitutes the basis for the induction proof.

Assume that the theorem is true for all $N < M$, where $M \geq 8$. We now prove it for $N = M$. It follows from (4.4.2.29) that $N \geq 4$, $N \leq 2^{n/4} + 1$. Let $T_{E_1} = T_{E_L} \theta T_{E_R}$ be a subtree of T_E satisfying Lemma 4.4.1.1, with $m = \left\lceil \dfrac{7N+5}{12} \right\rceil$. If T_{E_2} is the resulting tree when T_{E_1} is replaced by an atom, say, x, then

$$|E_2| = N + 1 - |E_1|$$

$$\leq \frac{5(N-1)}{12} + 1 \quad \leq \quad 2^{(n-5)/4} + 1$$

and

$$\left\lceil 4 \log \left(| E_2 | - 1 \right) \right\rceil \leq n - 5.$$

Likewise,

$$| E_L | \leq \frac{7N + 5}{12} \leq 2^{(n-3)/4} + 1.$$

Thus,

$$\left\lceil 4 \log \left(| E_L | - 1 \right) \right\rceil \leq n - 3,$$

and, similarly

$$\left\lceil 4 \log \left(| E_R | - 1 \right) \right\rceil \leq n - 3.$$

Applying the induction hypothesis to $E_2 = A_1 \times E_1 + B_1$, it follows that A_1 and B_1 can be evaluated in $n - 5$ steps using $O(| E_2 |)$ processors and at most $Q_2(| E_2 |)$ operations. Similarly, E_L and E_R can be evaluated in $(n - 3) - 3 = n - 6$ steps using $O(| E_L |) + O(| E_R |)$ processors and $Q_1(| E_L |) + Q_1(| E_R |)$ operations. Finally (using one more processor), $E_1 = E_L \theta E_R$ is obtained in $n - 5$ steps and $E_2 = A_1 E_1 + B_1$ is obtained in $n - 3$ steps.

The total number of processors required is bounded by

$$1 + O(| E_2 | + O(| E_L |) + O(| E_R |) = O(N).$$

If $E_1 \neq E$, then the number of operations needed is at most

$$3 + Q_2(| E_2 |) + Q_1(| E_L |) + Q_1(| E_R |)$$

$$= 3 + 2(| E_2 | - 2) + 2(| E_L | - 1) + 2(| E_R | - 1)$$

$$= 3 + 2\{(| E_2 | + | E_L | + | E_R |) - 4 \}$$

$$\leq 2N - 5 \ \leq \ 2(N - 1).$$

On the other hand, if $E_1 = E$, then $E = E_L \theta E_R$ can be evaluated in at most

$$1 + Q_1(| E_L |) + Q_1(| E_R |) = 1 + 2(| E_L | + | E_R | - 2)$$

$$= 2N - 3 \ < \ 2(N - 1)$$

operations. This completes the proof of the first half.

Now, let x be an atom of E. Let $T_{E_1} = T_{E_L} \theta T_{E_R}$ be a subtree of T_E satisfying the second part of Lemma 4.4.1.1, with $m = \left\lceil \dfrac{N + 1}{2} \right\rceil$. Without loss of generality, let x be an atom of E_L. If E_2 is the expression resulting from E by replacing E_1 by an atom, then

$$| E_2 | = N + 1 - | E_1 | \le \frac{N+1}{2} \le 2^{(n-4)/4} + 1.$$

By inductive hypothesis, $E_2 = A_2 E_1 + B_2$, and A_2 and B_2 can be evaluated in $n-4$ steps using $Q_2(| E_2 |)$ operations and $O(| E_2 |)$ processors. Similarly, $E_L = A_3 x + B_3$, where A_3 and B_3 are evaluated in $n-4$ (since $| E_L | \le 2^{(n-4)/4} + 1$) steps using $Q_2(| E_L |)$ operations and $O(| E_L |)$ processors. Finally, since $| E_R | \le N - 1$, it follows from the hypothesis that $| E_R |$ can be evaluated in $n-3$ steps, with $Q_1(| E_R |)$ operations and $O(| E_R |)$ processors. Thus,

$$E_2 = A_2 E_1 + B_2$$

$$= A_2 (E_L \; \theta \; E_R) + B_2$$

$$= A_2 ((A_3 x + B_3) \; \theta \; E_R) + B_2$$

$$= \begin{cases} (A_2 A_3) x + (A_2 (B_3 + E_R) + B_2) & \text{if } \theta = + \\ (A_2 A_3 E_R) x + ((A_2 B_3) E_R + B_2) & \text{if } \theta = \times \end{cases}$$

In either case, from the above discussion, it can be easily verified that E_2 can be calculated using $Q_2(N)$ operations and using $O(N)$ processors.

From the point of application, the following corollary is a simpler version of Theorem 4.4.2.10.

Corollary 4.4.2.11. If E is an arithmetic expression using $+$ and $\times$ (with any depth of parenthesis nesting), then E can be evaluated in at most $4 \log | E |$ steps using at most $O(| E |)$ processors and at most $2(| E | - 1)$ operations.

An application of this result consists in deriving the upper bound on $T_p(E(N))$ when only a fixed number, p, of processors are available. To this end, the following lemma is crucial.

Lemma 4.4.2.12. If a set $E_1, E_2, \cdots, E_r$ of arithmetic expressions can be evaluated in parallel in t steps using Q operations and q processors, then $E_1, E_2, \cdots, E_r$ can be evaluated in at most $t + \dfrac{Q-t}{p}$ steps using only p processors, where $p < q$.

Proof
Let s_i be the number of operations that are performed in step $i = 1, 2, \cdots, t$, where $Q = \sum\limits_{i=1}^{t} s_i$. Using only p processors, step i clearly takes $\left\lceil \dfrac{s_i}{p} \right\rceil$ steps to

complete. Hence, since $\left| \dfrac{x}{y} \right| \leq \dfrac{x-1}{y} + 1$, the total time needed to complete the computation of $E_1, E_2, \cdots, E_r$ using only p processors is given by

$$\sum_{i=1}^{t} \left\lceil \frac{s_i}{p} \right\rceil \leq (1 - \frac{1}{p}) t + \sum_{i=1}^{t} \frac{s_i}{p} = t + \frac{Q-t}{p}.$$

Hence the lemma.

The following theorem is immediate.

Theorem 4.4.2.13. Let E be an arithmetic expression using $+$ and $\times$ (with any level of parenthesis nesting). If p processors capable of performing $+$ and $\times$ are available, then E can be evaluated in at most $4 \log N + \dfrac{2(N-1)}{p}$ steps, where $|E| = N$.

Proof
Since this result can be verified for $N < 4$, let $N \geq 4$. Combining Corollary 4.4.2.11 and Lemma 4.4.2.12, we see that $t = 4 \log N$ and $Q = 2(N-1)$, and hence

$$T_p(E(N)) = (1 - \frac{1}{p}) 4 \log_2 N + \frac{2(N-1)}{p} \leq 4 \log_2 N + \frac{2(N-1)}{p},$$

and the proof is complete.

Define

$$\Phi(N, p) = \max\{\log N, \frac{N-1}{p}\}. \tag{4.4.2.30}$$

It can be easily verified that (Exercise 4.21)

$$(4 \log N + 2 \frac{N-1}{p}) \leq 6 \, \Phi(N, p). \tag{4.4.2.31}$$

To evaluate expressions of the type $\sum_{i=1}^{N} x_i$ or $\prod_{i=1}^{N} x_i$, it takes at least $\log N$ steps. Also since $N - 1$ operations are involved in evaluating these latter expressions, it takes a minimum of $\dfrac{N-1}{p}$ steps if only p processors are available. From these, it immediately follows that

$$\Phi(N, p) \leq T_p(E(N)) \leq 6\Phi(N, p). \tag{4.4.2.32}$$

In other words, Theorem 4.4.2.13 is optimal within a constant factor (Exercise 4.22).

4.4.3 Arithmetic Expressions With Division

In this Section we extend the analysis of parallel evaluation of arithmetic expressions to include the division operation. The method involves restructuring the given general expression into a *rational* form. The numerator and the denominator expressions (not involving division) are first evaluated and the value of the expression is computed in the end by a single division. (Refer to Section 4.2 for examples.) The principal result of this section is contained in the following theorem.

Theorem 4.4.3.1. Let E be an arithmetic expression with N distinct atoms using $+$, $\times$, and $/$ operations, and with any level of parenthesis nesting. Let

$$P_1(N) = 3(N-1), \qquad Q_1(N) = \max\{0,\, 10N - 9\},$$

$$P_2(N) = \max\{0,\, 3N - 4\}, \qquad Q_2(N) = \max\{0,\, 10N - 29\},$$

and

$$n = \begin{cases} N + 1 & \text{if } N \le 2 \\ \lceil 4 \log (N-1) \rceil & \text{if } N \ge 3. \end{cases} \tag{4.4.3.1}$$

Then, using associativity, commutativity, and distributivity,

(a) If $E = \dfrac{F}{G}$, then F and G can be evaluated in parallel in $n-2$ steps using $P_1(N)$ processors and $Q_1(N)$ operations, and

(b) if x is any atom of E, then $E = \dfrac{Ax + B}{Cx + D}$, where the expressions A, B, C, and D not containing x and can be evaluated in parallel in n steps with $P_2(N)$ processors and $Q_2(N)$ operations.

Proof

For $N \le 7$, the theorem can be verified by exhausting all possibilities. Assume that the theorem is true for all $N < N^*$, where $N^* \ge 7$.

To prove it for $N = N^*$, let $T_{E_1} = T_{E_L} \theta T_{E_R}$ be a subtree of T_E satisfying Lemma 4.4.1.1, with $m = \left\lceil \dfrac{N+1}{2} \right\rceil$. From (4.4.3.1), it follows that $N \le 2^{n/4} + 1$. Also $|T_{E_L}| \le \dfrac{N}{2} < 2^{(n-4)/4} + 1$, and likewise for T_{E_R}. By part (a) of the hypothesis, $E_L = \dfrac{F_L}{G_L}$ and $E_R = \dfrac{F_R}{G_R}$, where F_L, F_R, G_L, and G_R can be evaluated in parallel in $(n-4)-2 = n-6$ steps using $P_1(|E_L|) + P_1(|E_R|)$ processors in $Q_1(|E_L|) + Q_1(|E_R|)$ operations. Let

$$E_1 = E_L \, \theta \, E_R = \left[\frac{F_L}{G_L}\right] \theta \left[\frac{F_R}{G_R}\right] = \frac{F_1}{G_1},$$

where

$$F_1 = F_L\,G_R + F_R\,G_L, \quad G_1 = G_L\,G_R \quad \text{if } \theta = +$$
$$F_1 = F_L\,F_R, \quad\quad\quad G_1 = G_L\,G_R \quad \text{if } \theta = \times$$
$$F_1 = F_L\,G_R, \quad\quad\quad G_1 = G_L\,F_R \quad \text{if } \theta = /.$$

Hence F_1 and G_1 can be computed in two more steps, that is, in $n-4$ steps.

If T_{E_2} is the tree resulting by replacing T_{E_1} by an atom $\times$, then

$$|E_2| = N + 1 - |E_1| \ < \ \frac{N+1}{2} = 2^{(n-4)/4} + 1.$$

Applying part (b) of the hypothesis to E_2, we can write

$$E_2 = \frac{A_1 x + B_1}{A_2 x + B_2},$$

where $A_1, A_2, B_1,$ and B_2 can be evaluated in $n-4$ steps using $P_2(|E_2|)$ processors and $Q_2(|E_2|)$ operations. Since

$$E_1 = \frac{F_1}{G_1}, E_2 = \frac{A_1 F_1 + B_1 G_1}{A_2 F_1 + B_1 G_1} = \frac{F}{G}.$$

Thus F and G can be evaluated in two more steps, that is, in $n-2$ steps.

In calculating $F_L, G_L, F_R, G_R, A_1, A_2, B_1,$ and B_2, during the first $n-6$ steps, $P_1(|E_L|) + P_1(|E_R|) + P_2(|E_2|)$ processors are active. From $n-6$ to $n-4$ time steps, compute F and G, and finish computing $A_1, B_1, A_2,$ and B_2, using $2 + P_2(|E_2|)$ processors. In the last phase of $n-4$ to $n-2$ compute F and G using four processors. Thus, the number of processors needed is given by P^*, where

$$P^* = \max\{P_1(|E_L|) + P_1(|E_R|) + P_2(|E_2|), \ 2 + P_2(|E_2|), \ 4\}$$

$$\leq \max\{3(|E_L| + |E_R| + |E_2|) - 10, \ 3(|E_L| + |E_R|) - 6, 3|E_2| - 2, 4\}.$$

Since $|E_L| + |E_R| + |E_2| \leq N + 1$, $|E_L| + |E_R| \leq N$, and $|E_2| < \frac{N+1}{2}$,

$$P^* \leq \max\{3N - 7, \ 3N - 6, \ \frac{3(N+1)}{2} - 2, \ 4\}$$

$$< \ 3(N-1) = P_1(N).$$

Computation of F_1 and G_1 takes four operations, and that of F and G takes six more operations. Thus, the total number of operations, Q^*, is given by

$$Q^* = 10 + Q_1(|E_L|) + Q_1(|E_R|) + Q_2|E_2|)$$

$$= 10(\mid E_L \mid + \mid E_R \mid + \mid E_2 \mid) - 47$$

$$< Q_1(N).$$

To prove part (b), let x be an atom of E. Apply Part (b) of Lemma 4.4.1.1 with $m = \left\lceil \dfrac{N+1}{2} \right\rceil$ to a subtree $T_{E_1} = T_{E_L} \theta T_{E_R}$ of T_E. Let x be a part of E_L. Let T_{E_2} be the tree resulting from replacing T_{E_1} by an atom. Then

$$\mid E_2 \mid = N + 1 - \mid E_1 \mid \le 2^{(n-4)/4} + 1.$$

By part (b) of the inductive hypothesis, we can rewrite E_2 as

$$E_2 = \frac{A_1 E_1 + B_1}{A_2 E_1 + B_2}, \tag{4.4.3.2}$$

where A_1, A_2, B_1, and B_2 can be evaluated in $n-4$ steps using $P_2(\mid E_2 \mid)$ processors and $Q_2(\mid E_2 \mid)$ operations. Likewise,

$$E_L = \frac{A_3 x + B_3}{A_4 x + B_4},$$

where A_3, B_3, A_4 and B_4 can be evaluated in $n-4$ steps using $P_2(\mid E_L \mid)$ processors and $Q_2(\mid E_L \mid)$ operations. Similarly, express $E_R = \dfrac{F}{G}$, where F and G can be calculated in $n-6$ steps using $P_1(\mid E_R \mid)$ processors and $Q_1(\mid E_R \mid)$ operations. Let us now compute E_2 in the form

$$E_2 = \frac{Ax + B}{Cx + D}.$$

If $\theta = +$, substituting $E_L + E_R$ for E_1 in (4.4.3.2), we obtain that

$$\left. \begin{aligned} A &= (A_1 A_3 + B_1 A_4)G + A_1 A_4 F \\ B &= (A_1 B_3 + B_1 B_4)G + A_1 B_4 F \\ C &= (A_2 A_3 + B_2 A_4)G + A_2 A_4 F \\ D &= (A_2 A_3 + B_2 A_4)G + A_2 A_4 F \end{aligned} \right\}. \tag{4.4.3.3}$$

All these computations take four steps in parallel using 12 processors and 28 operations. Thus, A, B, C and D can be computed in n steps. Similar expressions can be derived if $\theta = \times$ or $/$.

The number of processors P^* needed to complete this computation may be estimated as follows. In the first $n-4$ steps $P_2(\mid E_2 \mid) + P_2(\mid E_L \mid) + P_1(\mid E_R \mid)$ processors are needed. Assuming that the computations of A, B, C, and D in (4.4.3.3) are done after the $(n-4)^{th}$ step to the nth step, we obtain that

$$P^* = \max\{P_2(\mid E_2 \mid) + P_2(\mid E_L \mid) + P_1(\mid E_R \mid), \ 12\}$$

$$= \max\{3(|\,E_2\,| + |\,E_L\,| + |\,E_R\,|) - 11, \ 12\}$$

$$= \max\{3N - 8, \ 12\}$$

$$= 3N - 8 \ < \ 3N - 4 = P_2(N).$$

The number of operations Q^* needed to compute E can be obtained as follows:

$$Q^* = 28 + Q_2(|\,E_2\,|) + Q_2(|\,E_L\,|) + Q_1(|\,E_R\,|)$$

$$= 10(|\,E_2\,| + |\,E_L\,| + |\,E_R\,|) - 49$$

$$= 10N - 39 \ < \ Q_2(N).$$

This completes the proof of the theorem.

The following theorem is an immediate corollary.

Theorem 4.4.3.2. Let E be an arithmetic expression with N distinct atoms and using $+$, $\times$, and $/$, with any level of parenthesis nesting. If only p processors are available, then E can be computed using associativity, commutativity, and distributivity in at most $T_p(E(N)) = 4 \log N + \dfrac{10(N-1)}{p}$ steps.

Proof
Since this is true for $N \le 3$, let $N \ge 4$. From Theorem 4.4.3.1, it follows that E can be evaluated in at most $t = 4 \log N$ steps using at most $10(N-1)$ operations and $O(N)$ processors. From Lemma 4.4.2.12, it follows that

$$T_p(E(N)) = (1 - \frac{1}{p}) 4 \log N + \frac{10(N-1)}{p}$$

$$\le 4 \log N + \frac{10(N-1)}{p}.$$

Hence the theorem.

Using (4.4.2.30), it also follows that

$$\Phi(N, p) \le T_p(E(N)) \le 14\Phi(N, p). \qquad (4.4.3.4)$$

While it is true that the preceding upper bound can be improved, it is apparent that the result of Theorem 4.4.3.1 is optimal within a multiplicative constant (Exercise 4.21.)

We conclude this chapter by deriving an improved upper bound due to Muller and Preparata [1976] on the parallel time needed to evaluate a general arithmetic expression involving addition, multiplication, and division operations using $O(N^{1+\varepsilon})$ processors for $\varepsilon > 0$. We distinguish two types of variables: *atomic variables* $a_1, a_2, \cdots, a_N$ and *free* variables $x_1, x_2, \cdots, x_t$. An expression E is called *primitive* if each variable occurs only once. In the following, $|E|$ denotes the *number of atomic* variables in E. During an evaluation process, free variables can be replaced by subexpressions in atomic variables.

Any general expression E can be expressed in a *rational* form as

$$E = \frac{P_1}{P_2}, \qquad (4.4.3.5)$$

where P_1 and P_2 are polynomials in the variables and have no common factors, that is, P_1 and P_2 are relatively prime. Refer to Section 4.2 for examples. In particular, if E is primitive, then each of the variables in P_1 and P_2 occurs in its first degree (that is, no powers of the variables are allowed). Let P_1 and P_2 be expressed in a series in the free variables as follows:

$$P_1 = \sum_{i=1}^{t} A_i \lambda_i$$

and $\qquad\qquad\qquad\qquad\qquad\qquad\qquad\qquad\qquad\qquad\qquad$ (4.4.3.6)

$$P_2 = \sum_{i=1}^{t} B_i \lambda_i$$

where

(1)   Each λ_i is either 0 or 1 or product of *distinct free variables,* and

(2)   the coefficients A_i and B_i are either 0 or 1 or expressions, in *atomic variables* that do not involve any division operation.

As an example,

$$P_1 = a_1 + 1(x_2\, x_3) + (a_2 + a_3)\, x_4\, x_1$$

and

$$P_2 = b_1 + 0(x_2\, x_3) + b_2\, x_4\, x_1.$$

If E contains any free variable at all (that is, $t > 1$), then computing E is equivalent to computing the coefficient expressions in P_1 and P_2. Let $T(A_i)$ and $T(B_j)$ be the *minimum* time needed to compute A_i and B_j, respectively, for all i and j. Since A_i's and B_j's can be evaluated in parallel, define

$$T(P_1) = \max_{1 \le i \le t} \{T(A_i)\}$$

and

$$T(P_2) = \max_{1 \le j \le t} \{T(B_j)\}.$$

Let

$$\hat{T}(E) = \max\{T(P_1), T(P_2)\}. \tag{4.4.3.7}$$

Since P_1 and P_2 are unique except for the ordering of atoms, it follows that $\hat{T}(E)$ is unique for a given E.

Let $T(E)$ be the time required to compute E. If E does not involve any free variables (that is, $t = 1$), then the numerical value of E is obtained by dividing P_1 by P_2, in one more step. In other words,

$$T(E) = 1 + \hat{T}(E). \tag{4.4.3.8}$$

We now introduce a basic operation called the *composition* of expressions. Let E_1 and E_2 be two primitive expressions with different sets of variables. Let x be a free variable in E_1. The process of substituting expression E_2 for x in E_1 is called the composition of E_1 with E_2 and is denoted by $E_1 : x : E_2$. Clearly, the resulting expression is primitive if E_1 and E_2 are. As an example, let

$$E_1 = \frac{a_1 + a_2\,y\,z}{b_1 + (b_3 + b_2)\,y\,z}$$

and

$$E_2 = \frac{c_1}{c_2}.$$

Then

$$E_1 : y : E_2 = \frac{a_1\,c_2 + a_1\,c_1\,z}{b_1\,c_2 + (b_3 + b_2)\,c_1\,z}.$$

The following lemma characterizes the time required to perform some standard operations on primitive expressions.

Lemma 4.4.3.3. Let E_1 and E_2 be two primitive expressions (in rational form) with distinct sets of variables. Assume that there exist restructuring algorithms using which E_i can be evaluated in time T_i, that is, $\hat{T}(E_i) \le T_i$, $i = 1, 2$. Let $T^* = \max\{T_1, T_2\}$. Then

(a) $\hat{T}(E) \le 2 + T^*$, where $E = E_1 : x : E_2$,

(b) $\hat{T}(E_1 \pm E_2) \le 2 + T^*$,

(c) $\hat{T}\left(\dfrac{E_1}{E_2}\right) \le 1 + T^*$, and

(d) $\hat{T}(E_1 \times E_2) \le 1 + T^*$.

Proof
Let

$$E_1 = \frac{P_1}{P_2} \quad \text{and} \quad E_2 = \frac{Q_1}{Q_2},$$

where

$$P_1 = \sum_{i=1}^{t} A_i \lambda_i, \quad Q_1 = \sum_{i=1}^{s} C_i \mu_i,$$

$$P_2 = \sum_{i=1}^{t} B_i \lambda_i, \quad Q_2 = \sum_{i=1}^{s} D_i \mu_i.$$

Let x be a free variable in E_1, and let λ_u and λ_v be the products in the rational form for E_1 such that $\lambda_u = x\lambda_v$. Then

$$P_1 = (A_u x + A_v)\lambda_v + \sum_{k \neq u,\, v} A_k \lambda_k,$$

and

$$P_2 = (B_u x + B_v)\lambda_v + \sum_{k \neq u,\, v} B_k \lambda_k.$$

Let

$$E = \frac{R_1}{R_2}.$$

Then

$$R_1 = (A_u Q_1 + A_v Q_2)\lambda_v + Q_2 \sum_{k \neq u,\, v} A_k \lambda_k$$

$$= \sum_{i=1}^{s} (A_u C_i + A_v D_i)\mu_i \lambda_v + \sum_{i=1}^{s} \sum_{k \neq u,\, v} (A_k D_i) \mu_i \lambda_k.$$

Likewise,

$$R_2 = (B_u Q_1 + B_v Q_2)\lambda_v + Q_2 \sum_{k \neq u,\, v} B_k \lambda_k$$

$$= \sum_{i=1}^{s} (B_u C_i + B_v D_i)\mu_i \lambda_v + \sum_{i=1}^{s} \sum_{k \neq u,\, v} (B_k D_i) \mu_i \lambda_k.$$

Now, the computation of the coefficient expressions, such as $(A_u C_i + A_v D_i)$ in R_1 and $(B_u C_i + B_v D_i)$ in R_2, in parallel requires two steps (one multiplication and one addition). Combining this with the definitions of T_1 and T_2, claim (a) follows. The proof of the other claims (b) to (d) is quite similar and is left as an exercise (see Exercise 4.37).

We now state without proof a useful variation of Lemma 4.4.1.1 which plays a crucial role in the following development.

Lemma 4.4.3.4. Let E be a primitive expression with $|\, E\, | = N > 1$, and let r be a real number such that $1 < r \leq N$. Then there exists a restructuring algorithm using which E can be rewritten as

$$E = A : x : (B \; \theta \; C),$$

where

(a) A, B, and C are primitive expressions with no common variables.

(b) x is a free variable in A and is the only variable in A, B, and C that does not appear in E.

(c) $\theta \in \{+, \times, /\}$, and

(d) $| B | \leq | C | < r$ and $| B \; \theta \; C | \geq r$.

As a final preparation before stating the principal result, consider the following equation (which is, in fact, the characteristic equation related to the recurrence relation that defines the Fibonnaci sequence):

$$Z^2 - Z - 1 = 0.$$

The two roots of this equation are

$$\alpha = 1.618 \qquad \text{and} \qquad \beta = -0.618.$$

As will be seen below, the positive root α plays a crucial role in the analysis. (We encourage the reader to compare this with the developments in Lemma 4.4.2.3 and Theorem 4.4.2.4.)

The following is the main result.

Theorem 4.4.3.5. If E is a primitive expression with $| E | = N > 1$, then there exists a restructuring algorithm for evaluating E such that

$$\hat{T}(E) \leq \frac{2 \log N}{\log \alpha}. \tag{4.4.3.9}$$

Proof

For $N \leq 4$, this claim is trivially verified. Let (4.4.3.9) be true for all $| E | < N$ for some $N > 4$. Consider the case when $| E | = N$. Define

$$r = \alpha^{-2} N.$$

From $\alpha = 1.618$ and $N > 4$, it is readily verified that $1 < r < N$. For this value of r, we now restructure E using Lemma 4.4.3.4, as

$$E = A : x : (B \; \theta \; C) \tag{4.4.3.10}$$

where

$$| B | \leq | C | < \alpha^{-2} N \quad \text{and} \quad | B \; \theta \; C | \geq \alpha^{-2} N$$

Since C is primitive and $| C | < N$, by the inductive hypothesis,

$$\hat{T}(C) \leq \frac{2 \log | C |}{\log \alpha}$$

$$\leq \frac{2 \log (\alpha^{-2} N)}{\log \alpha}$$

$$= 2 \left[\frac{\log N}{\log \alpha} - 2 \right]. \tag{4.4.3.11}$$

As $|B| \leq |C|$, the same bound also applies to $\hat{T}(B)$. Recall that B and C are primitive expressions with $\theta \in \{+, \times, /\}$. Hence, using Lemma 4.4.3.3, we can compute $(B \theta C)$, in

$$\hat{T}(B \hat{\theta} C) \leq 2 \left[\frac{\log N}{\log \alpha} - 1 \right]. \tag{4.4.3.12}$$

Further,

$$|A| = |E| - |B| - |C|$$

$$< N - \alpha^{-2} N$$

$$= N \alpha^{-1}, \quad \text{since } \alpha^2 = \alpha + 1.$$

By the inductive hypothesis,

$$\hat{T}(A) \leq 2 \frac{\log |A|}{\log \alpha}$$

$$\leq 2 \frac{\log (\alpha^{-1} N)}{\log \alpha}$$

$$= 2 \left[\frac{\log N}{\log \alpha} - 1 \right]. \tag{4.4.3.13}$$

As the last step, substituting $B \theta C$ for the free variable x in A and combining (4.4.3.10), (4.4.3.12), (4.4.3.13) with Lemma 4.4.3.3, we obtain that

$$\hat{T}(A : x : (B \theta C)) \leq \frac{2 \log N}{\log \alpha}$$

from which the theorem follows.

The following final result is immediate.

Theorem 4.4.3.6. If E is a primitive expression containing *no free variable,* then E can be restructured in such a way that

$$T(E) \leq 2.88 \log N + 1.$$

Proof
If E is primitive and has no free variable, then from (4.4.3.8)

$$T(E) = \hat{T}(E) + 1. \qquad (4.4.3.14)$$

Since E having no free variable is a special case of Theorem 4.4.3.5, combining (4.4.3.9), (4.4.3.14), and $(\log_2 \alpha)^{-1} = 1.44 \cdots$, the theorem follows.

4.5 NOTES AND REFERENCES

Section 4.2. In 1969 Baer and Bovet ([1969]) gave a comprehensive survey of algorithms for the parallel evaluation of arithmetic expressions using associativity and commutativity. They also presented a new class of parallel algorithms which performed better than the existing algorithms. Later, Beatty [1972] presented a formal analysis of the Baer-Bovet algorithm. The development in Section 4.2 is essentially patterned after Kuck and Muraoka [1974].

Section 4.3. The polynomial evaluation problem has attracted the attention of a number of researchers. For the optimality of the serial Horner's method, refer to Ostrowski [1954], Motzkin [1955], Pan [1966], and Borodin and Munro [1975]. The nth-order Horner's method is due to Dorn [1962]. Our exposition of this method follows Muraoka [1971]. The method of binary splitting (also called the folding method) is due to Estrin [1960] and Muraoka [1971]. Multifolding methods developed independently by Munro and Patterson [1973] and Maruyama [1973] provide a sharp upper bound. Similar upper bounds are also known for the parallel evaluation of Horner's type Boolean expressions, such as those occurring in the evaluation of carry bits while adding integers in binary (Brent [1970a]). (Refer to Section 3.2.) The lower bound in Theorem 4.3.4.1 is due to Kosaraju [1986]. Section 4.3.5 follows closely Hyafil and Kung [1977]. Results in this section carry over to the linear first order recurrences as well.

Exercises 4.7 through 4.15 develop many interesting algorithms for polynomial evaluation.

Section 4.4. This section provides a comprehensive summary of the *restructuring* algorithms used in the parallel evaluation of general arithmetic expressions. For further details refer to Brent [1973, 1974], Brent, Kuck, and Maruyama [1973], Preparata and Muller [1975, 1976], Muller and Preparata [1976], Winograd [1975], and Kosaraju [1986]. A number of special cases (such as when the number of parentheses or number of division operators is known) are given in Kuck and Maruyama [1975] and are developed in Exercises 4.24 to 4.29. Brent [1973] also proves the numerical stability of the algorithms implicit in Theorem 4.4.2.5. It should be interesting to develop similar stability analysis for the method of Theorem 4.4.3.1. The method of solving cubic equations given in Section 4.4.2 is adapted from Uspensky [1948], who attributes this technique to an Italian mathematician Cardan (A.D.1501 - 1576).

4.6 EXERCISES

4.1   Prove claim (c) in Lemma 4.3.1.2.

4.2   Compute the minimum number of processors needed to complete Estrin's binary splitting algorithm in $2\lceil \log N \rceil$ steps. Also describe a schedule of computations and compute the speed-up and redundancy for this algorithm.

4.3   (Muraoka [1971]). Let $p_k(x)$ refer to a (dense) polynomial of degree k. Then the method of golden ratio splitting (also called the folding method) may be stated in the following form.

Given that the polynomial $p_{t-1}(x)$ can be computed in $h - 1$ steps, $p_i(x)$ for $t \le i < s-1$ are computed in h steps, and $p_s(x)$ can be computed in $h + 1$ steps, then show that all $p_j(x)$ for $s \le j \le s + t - 1$ can be computed in $h + 1$ steps and that $p_{s+t}(x)$ can be computed in $h + 2$ steps.

4.4   Prove inequality (4.3.3.6).

4.5   Derive a recurrence relation for the parallel time required to compute $p(x)$ using (4.3.3.5).

4.6   Illustrate the method of (4.3.3.5) for polynomials of degree 31 and 511.

4.7   (Munro and Patterson [1973]). The following algorithm is very useful when the number of processors, k, is small compared to N, the degree of the polynomial.

Step 1:   Compute $p_i = a_{2i} + a_{2i+1} x$, for $i = 0, 1, 2, \cdots, \left\lfloor \dfrac{N}{2} \right\rfloor$, and $x^2, x^4, x^6 \cdots, x^{2k-2}$, and x^{2k}.

Step 2: Using processor j $(j = 1, 2, \cdots, k)$, compute

$$p_j^* = \sum_{i=0}^{\lfloor N/2k \rfloor} p_{ik+j-1} (x^{2k})^i$$

using Horner's method.

Step 3: Evaluate $p(x) = \sum_{j=1}^{k} p_j^* x^{2(j-1)}$.

Analyze this algorithm by computing the total number of operations required. Compute the shortest possible schedule of these computations by exploiting all possible overlap in computation.

4.8 (Yao [1976]). It is well known that for any integer $i > 0$, x^i can be computed from x with at most $2\lfloor \log i \rfloor$ multiplications. Using this as a basis, we now describe an algorithm due to Yao [1976] for computing x^m for any $0 < m \le n$ from $\{x, x^2, x^4, \cdots x^{2\lfloor \log m \rfloor}\}$ as follows:

Define $k = \left\lceil \dfrac{\log \log n}{2} \right\rceil$, $d = 2^k$ and $t = \lfloor \log_d n \rfloor$. Let the d-ary expansion of m be

$$m = a_t \, a_{t-1} \cdots a_1 \, a_0,$$

where $m = \sum\limits_{i=0}^{t} a_i d^i$ and $0 \le a_i \le d - 1$, for $i = 0, 1, 2, \cdots t$.

Define a partition $\mathbf{P}(0)$, $\mathbf{P}(1)$, $\cdots$,$\mathbf{P}(d-1)$, of $\{0, 1, \cdots , t\}$ as follows:

$$\mathbf{P}(i) = \{j \mid a_j = i\}, \quad \text{for } i = 0, 1, 2, \cdots , d-1,$$

where $\sum\limits_{i=0}^{d-1} |\,\mathbf{P}(i)\,| = t + 1$.

Let $m_i = \sum\limits_{j \in \mathbf{P}(i)} d^j$. Then, $m = \sum\limits_{i=1}^{d-1} i\, m_i$. Thus,

$$x^m = \prod\limits_{i=1}^{d-1} (x^{m_i})^i$$

and

$$x^{m_i} = \prod\limits_{j \in \mathbf{P}(i)} x^{d^j}.$$

The algorithm for computing x^m thus becomes:

Step 1: For $i = 1, 2, 3, \cdots , d - 1$

    (a) Compute x^{m_i} (in at most $|\,\mathbf{P}(i)\,|$ multiplications).

    (b) Compute $(x^{m_i})^i$ (in at most $2\lfloor \log i \rfloor$ multiplications).

Step 2: Compute x^m using just $d - 2$ multiplications.

(a) Using this algorithm show that x^m can be calculated in time $c\dfrac{\log n}{\log \log (n + 2)}$ for some constant $c > 0$. Find a *good* estimate of the constant c.

(b) Show that given any set of positive integers $\{n_1, n_2, \cdots , n_k\}$, $\{x^{n_1}, x^{n_2}, \cdots , x^{n_k}\}$ is computable from x in at most $\log N + c \sum\limits_{i=1}^{k} \dfrac{\log n_i}{\log \log (n_i + 2)}$ multiplications, where $N = \max\limits_{1 \le i \le k} \{n_i\}$.

(c) How can you parallelize the above algorithm for computing $\{x^{n_1}, x^{n_2}, \cdots, x^{n_k}\}$?

4.9 Let $p(x) = a_n x^{i_n} + a_{n-1} x^{i_{n-1}} + \cdots + a_1 x^{i_1}$ be a sparse polynomial where $a_i \neq 0$ for $i = 1$ to n and $i_n > i_{n-1} > i_{n-2} > \cdots > i_1 \geq 0$. Horner's method can be extended to this sparse case as follows.

$$p = 0, i_0 = 0.$$
FOR $j = n$ TO 1 STEP -1 DO
$$p = (p + a_j) \times x^{(i_j - i_{j-1})}.$$
END.

(a) Using the method in Exercise 4.8, show that this evaluation needs only $n + O(\log i_n)$ multiplications.

(b) Devise parallel methods for evaluating special classes of sparse polynomials.

4.10 Let

$$p(x) = a_N x^N + a_{N-1} x^{N-1} + \cdots + a_2 x^2 + a_1 x + a_0$$

and

$$s = \left\lfloor \frac{N}{2} \right\rfloor \quad \text{and} \quad t = \left\lceil \frac{N}{2} \right\rceil.$$

Rewrite $p(x)$ as

$$p(x) = p_e(x^2) + x \, p_o(x^2),$$

where

$$p_e(x^2) = (\cdots ((a_{2s} x^2 + a_{2s-2})x^2 + a_{2s-4})x^2 + \cdots + a_2)x^2 + a_0$$

and

$$p_o(x^2) = (\cdots ((a_{2t-1} x^2 + a_{2t-3})x^2 + a_{2t-5})x^2 + \cdots + a_3)x^2 + a_1.$$

Clearly,

$$p(y) = p_e(y^2) + y \, p_o(y^2)$$

and

$$p(-y) = p_e(y^2) - y \, p_o(y^2).$$

Applying this recursively, compute the total operations needed to compute $p(y)$ and $p(-y)$ for some y.

4.11 Let $p_n(x) = b_0 x^n + b_1 x^{n-1} + \cdots + b_{n-1} x + b_n$ for $n = 0, 1, 2, \cdots, N$.
Define $y_n = \dfrac{dp_n(x)}{dx}$.

(a) Show that y_n satisfies the recurrence for $n = 1, 2, 3, \cdots, N,$

$$y_n - 2x\, y_{n-1} + x^2\, y_{n-2} = b_{n-1}.$$

(b) Using this recurrence, find an algorithm to compute y_n.

4.12 If $p(x) = a_N x^N + a_{N-1} x^{N-1} + \cdots + a_2 x^2 + a_1 x + a_0$, then it is well known that the following linear first-order recurrence in p_i computes $p(x)$:

$$If \quad p_N = a_N \quad and \quad p_i = p_{i+1}\, x + a_i \ for \ i = N-1, N-2, \cdots, 1, 0,$$

$$then \quad p_0 = p(x).$$

(a) Show that the following linear recurrence in q_i's computes the first derivative of p(x):

Let

$$q_N = 0$$

and

$$q_i = q_{i+1}\, x + p_{i+1} \ for \ i = N-1, N-2, \cdots, 1, 0.$$

Then

$$q_0 \equiv \frac{dp(x)}{dx} = Na_N x^{N-1} + (N-1)a_{N-1}x^{N-2} + \cdots + 2a_2 x + a_1.$$

(b) Likewise define

$$r_N = 0$$

and

$$r_i = r_{i+1}\, x + q_{i+1}.$$

Show that $2r_0$ is the second derivative of $p(x)$.

(c) Derive a recurrence for computing $\dfrac{1}{k!}\dfrac{d^k p(x)}{dx^k}$, where $p(x)$ is a polynomial.

(d) Derive a parallel algorithm for computing the polynomial and k of its first derivatives at a given point.

4.13 Let $p(x) = a_N x^N + a_{N-1}x^{N-1} + \cdots + a_1 x + a_0$ be a polynomial with real coefficients. If $z = x + iy$, then show that $p(z)$ can be calculated using the following system:

Let

$$r = x + y \quad and \quad s = x^2 + y^2.$$

Define

$$p_N = a_N, \qquad q_N = a_{N-1},$$

and

$$p_j = q_{j+1} + rp_{j+1}, \quad q_j = a_{j-1} - sp_{j+1} \text{ for } j = N-1, N-2, \cdots, 1.$$

Then prove that $p(z) = zp_1 + q_1$. Also compute the total number of operations required by this algorithm. How would you parallelize this method?

4.14 Let (x_i, y_i) for $i = 1$ to N, be given. Define a polynomial $p_j^L(x)$ of degree $(j-1)$, where

$$p_j^L(x) = \sum_{i=1}^{j} \left[\prod_{j \neq i} \left(\frac{x - x_j}{x_i - x_j} \right) \right] y_i, \quad j = 1, 2, \cdots, N.$$

Then $p_N^L(x_i) = y_i$ for all $i = 1$ to N. (Vacuous products are taken to be unity.) This *sum of products* form is called the *Lagrangian interpolation formula*.

(a) Compute the total number of operations involved in constructing $p(x)$ in the *coefficient* form as $p(x) = a_{N-1}x^{N-1} + a_{N-2}x^{N-2} + \cdots + a_1 x + a_0$.

(b) Discuss the suitability of the sum of product form and the coefficient form for repeated evaluation of $p(x)$ at M points, where M is large compared to N.

4.15 Another equivalent interpolation formula due to Newton is slightly better in the sense that if we have an interpolation of N points, then it can be easily extended to $N + 1$ points as follows.

Let $p_j^N(x)$ be the interpolation for j points (x_k, y_k), $1 \leq k \leq j$. Then $p_{j+1}^N(x)$ for $j+1$ points (x_k, y_k), $1 \leq k \leq j+1$, can be iteratively found as follows:

Let $p_1^N(x) = y_1$ and let $D_j(x) = (x - x_1)(x - x_2) \cdots (x - x_j)$. Then define

$$p_{j+1}^N(x) = \left[y_{j+1} - p_j^N(x_{j+1}) \right] \frac{D_j(x)}{D_j(x_{j+1})} + p_j^N(x).$$

(a) Show that $p_j^L(x) = p_j^N(x)$.

(b) Compute the total number of operations required in constructing $p_N^N(x)$ and compare it with that of $p_N^L(x)$.

(c) Discuss the suitability of this formulation for repeated evaluation of polynomials at M points.

4.16 Check the validity of inequality (4.3.5.16).

4.17 Verify Property 2 in Section 4.3.5, when $v = b_i \Delta b_j$ and $v = a_i \Delta a_j$ where Δ is either the multiplication or the addition operation.

4.18 In the graph model leading to the Hyafil and Kung reduction process, it is assumed that the inputs to nodes at level L_i are fed from the outputs of nodes at level L_j, $j = 0, 1, \cdots, i-1$. We call this an *unrestricted layered graph*. We now define a *restricted layered graph* as follows: One of the two inputs to a node at level L_i is from an output of a node at level L_{i-1}, and the other input could be from the output of a node at level L_j, $j = 0, 1, 2, \cdots, i-1$.

(a) Prove an analog of Theorem 4.3.5.1 for the evaluation of H_{2N+1} using the restricted layered graph model. Give examples.

(b) If there is only one node at level L_1 of a restricted layered graph, then show that it degenerates to the serial algorithm.

4.19 Enumerate the set of all arithmetic expressions using $+$ and $\times$ and involving at most eight distinct atoms. Verify that each of these expressions can be evaluated in parallel in at most five steps. Find the maximum number of processors to achieve this time bound.

4.20 (Brent, Kuck and Maruyama [1973]).
(a) Show that the number of processors needed to evaluate $E(N)$ in $3 \lceil \log N \rceil - 4$ steps in Theorem 4.4.2.2 can be improved to $O(3^n) = O(N^{1.58})$.

(b) Likewise, show that the number of processors required to achieve the time bound given in Theorem 4.4.2.4 is $O(N^{1.71})$, where $\log_{\lambda_1} (\dfrac{1 + \sqrt{5}}{2}) = 1.71$ and $\lambda_1 = 1.3247$.

4.21 Verify (4.4.2.31) and (4.4.3.4). In each case, find a better upper bound on $T_p(E(N))$.

4.22 Show that a better lower bound on $T_p(E(N))$ is

$$T_p(E(N)) \geq \left\lfloor \frac{N}{p} \right\rfloor - 1 + \lceil \log p \rceil.$$

4.23 Find examples of arithmetic expressions whose parallel evaluation times match those given by Theorems 4.4.2.2 and 4.4.3.1.

4.24 (Kuck and Maruyama [1975]). Let $E[N|p]$ denote an arithmetic expression with at most N distinct atoms and with at most p pairs of parentheses. Likewise, let $E[N|q]$ denote arithmetic expressions with at most N atoms and with at most q division operations. Given any expression E, let $PAR(E)$

and $DIV(E)$ denote the actual number of parenthesis pairs and division operators, respectively, in E. Notice that $E[N|p]$ and $PAR(E)$ do not provide any information regarding the level of nesting of the parentheses. For example, $E_1 = a(b + c(d + e))$ and $E_2 = x(a + b) + y(d + e)$ each have two pairs of parentheses, but the depth of nesting in E_1 is 2 and that in E_2 is 1. Let $PAR(E(N)) = p$ and $DIV(E(N)) = q$. Prove the following analog of Lemma 4.4.1.1.

There exists a subexpression E_1 of $E(N)$ such that $E_1 = E_L \theta E_R$, $\theta \in \{+, -, \times, /\}$, and

(a) For any $p \geq m \geq 0$,
$$PAR(E_L) \leq m, \quad PAR(E_R) \leq m, \quad \text{and} \quad PAR(E_1) \geq m.$$

(b) For any atom x in E_1, and $p \geq m \geq 0$, with $PAR(E_1) \geq m$, either x is in E_L and $PAR(E_L) \leq m$, or x is in E_R and $PAR(E_R) \leq m$.

(c) For any $q \geq m \geq 0$,
$$DIV(E_L) \leq m, \quad DIV(E_R) \leq m, \quad \text{and} \quad DIV(E_1) \geq m.$$

(d) For any atom x in E_1 and $q \geq m \geq 0$ with $PAR(E_1) \geq m$, either x is in E_L and $DIV(E_L) \leq m$ or x is in E_R and $PAR(E_R) \leq m$.

4.25 (Kuck and Maruyama [1975]). Let $E[N|p]$ be an arithmetic expression with up to N distinct atoms, p pairs of parentheses and *no* division operation. Let $T(E[N|p])$ denote the parallel time to evaluate $E[N|p]$. From the first principles, prove the following:

(a) $T(E[N|0]) \leq \lceil \log N \rceil + 1$.

(b) $T(E[N|k]) \leq \lceil \log N \rceil + k + 2$, for $k = 1, 2, 3$.

4.26 (Kuck and Maruyama [1975]). Let $p_0 = 1$, $p_1 = 2$, $p_2 = 3$, and for $t \geq 0$
$$p_{t+3} = p_{t+1} + p_t.$$

(a) Show that for any arithmetic expression involving no division $T(E[N|p_t]) = \log N + t + O(1)$, where p_t is the number of parenthesis pairs.

Hint: Prove by induction as in Lemma 4.4.2.3.

(b) Hence, or otherwise, show that for any arithmetic expression $E[N|p]$, with *no* division operation,
$$T(E[N|p]) = \log N + 2.465 \log p + O(1).$$

Hint: Prove as in Theorem 4.4.2.4.

4.27 (Kuck and Maruyama [1975]). Let $E[N|p]$ be as defined in Exercise 4.24, with *one* division operation. Then $E[N|p]$ can be readily expressed as either

$$E[N|p] = \frac{G}{H},$$

where the subexpressions G and H do not involve any division operation, or

$$E[N|p] = \frac{Ax+B}{Cx+D},$$

where x is any atom in $E[N|p]$ and each of A, B, C, and D as subexpressions does not involve a division operation. Prove that

$$T(E[N|p]) = \lceil \log N \rceil + 4 \lceil \log p \rceil + O(1).$$

Hint: Prove by induction. Show that G and H can be evaluated in $\lceil \log N \rceil + 4 \lceil \log p \rceil + 3$ steps. Also show that A, B, C, and D can be evaluated in $\lceil \log N \rceil + 4 \lceil \log p \rceil + 5$ steps.

4.28 (Kuck and Maruyama [1975]). A continued fraction $CF(N)$ of degree N is an arithmetic expression with $2N + 1$ distinct atoms defined as

$$CF(N) = a_0 \, \theta_1 \, (b_1 \, \theta_2 \, (a_1 \, \theta_3 \, (b_2 \, \theta_4 \, \cdots \, \theta_{2N-1} \, (b_N \, \theta_{2N} \, a_N) \cdots))),$$

where $\theta_{2k} = /$, the division operation, and $\theta_{2k-1} \in \{+, -\}$, for $k = 1, 2, \cdots, N$. As an example,

$$CF(2) = a_0 - (b_1/(a_1 + (b_2/a_2)))$$

$$= a_0 - \cfrac{b_1}{a_1 + \cfrac{b_2}{a_2}}.$$

Let x be an arbitrary arithmetic expression. Define $CF[N|x]$ to be the continued fraction of degree N resulting by replacing a_N in $CF(N)$ by x.

(a) Let y be an atom. Then show that $CF[N|y]$ can be written in the form $(Ay+B)/(Cy+D)$, where A, B, C, D, as subexpressions, do not involve division.

(b) Prove that if $4N$ processors are available, then $CF(N)$ can be evaluated in

$$T(CF(N)) = 2 \lceil \log N \rceil + O(1)$$

steps requiring a total of at most $24N$ operations, at most one of which is the division operation.

Remark: This result is an improvement over an earlier result due to Stone [1973b] for the parallel evaluation of a continued fraction.

4.29 (Kuck and Maruyama [1975]). A polynomial form $PF(N)$ of degree N is an arithmetic expression of the type

$$PF(N) = ((\cdots (a_N \, \theta_{2N} \, x_N \, \theta_{2N-1} \, a_{N-1}) \, \theta_{2N-2} \, x_{N-1} \, \theta_{2N-3} a_{N-2})$$

$$\cdots \theta_3 \, a_1) \, \theta_2 \, x_1 \, \theta_1 \, a_0,$$

where $\theta_{2k} \in \{\times, /\}$, and $\theta_{2k-1} \in \{+, -\}$, for $k = 1, 2, \cdots, N$. Notice that $PF(N)$ is an extension of the Horner's expression H_{2N-1} discussed in Section 4.3.4. Define

$$x_1 \, \theta_1 \, x_2 \, \theta_2 \, \cdots \, \theta_{t-1} \, x_t = \begin{cases} \displaystyle\sum_{i=1}^{t}{}^{*} x_i & \text{if } \theta_i \in \{+, -\} \\[2em] \displaystyle\prod_{i=1}^{t}{}^{*} x_i & \text{if } \theta_i \in \{\times, /\} \end{cases}.$$

Clearly,

$$PF(N) = \sum_{i=1}^{N}{}^{*} a_i \, X(i) \pm a_0,$$

where $X(i) = \displaystyle\prod_{k=1}^{i}{}^{*} x_k$.

(a) Show that $\displaystyle\sum_{i=1}^{t}{}^{*} x_i$ and $\displaystyle\prod_{i=1}^{t}{}^{*} x_i$ can be individually computed in $\lceil \log t \rceil$ steps using $\left\lfloor \dfrac{t}{2} \right\rfloor$ processors.

(b) Let $N(t)$ be the degree of the polynomial form $PF(N(t))$ which can be evaluated in t steps. Show that under unlimited parallelism

$$N(t) \geq 2^{d_{t-1}},$$

where $d_t = \dfrac{t(t+1)}{2}$.

(c) Prove that any polynomial form $PF(N)$ can be evaluated in $\log N + \sqrt{2} \log N + O(1)$ steps using $2N$ processors, where $N = d_t$ for some $t > 0$.

Remark: This is an extension of the multifolding method described in Section 4.3.3.

4.30 Consider a binary tree T with $n \, (> 1)$ nodes. Pick a subset $V = \{a_1, a_2, \cdots, a_k\}$ of $k < n$ nodes such that no node in V is an ancestor of any other node in it. Let d_i be the depth of node a_i measured from the root of the tree T, where $d_i \geq 1$ for $i = 1$ to k. Show that

$$\sum_{i=1}^{k} 2^{-d_i} \le 1.$$

This is called the *Kraft inequality* (Abramson [1963]).

4.31 (Kosaraju [1986]). Let E be an arithmetic expression involving $\times$ and $+$ (that is, E is division-free). E is said to be a *simple arithmetic expression* (SAE) if one of the operands for every $\times$ node in the parse tree T_E of E is a leaf.

(a) If T_E is a parse tree of an SAE E, then show that (1) every subtree of T_E corresponds to an SAE and (2) replacing a subtree of T_E by 0 (zero) results in an SAE.

(b) Draw the parse tree for

$$E = b \left((a_1 + (a_2 + a_3)) \, a_4 + (a_5 + (a_6 + a_7) \, a_8) \, a_9\right)$$

and verify part (a).

(c) Show that in any parse tree T_E of an SAE E, if the nodes of T_E are partitioned into trees T_{E_i}, $i = 1$ to t, then

$$E = \sum_{i=1}^{t} p_{i_i} \times E'_i.$$

where p_{i_i} is the product of the subexpressions attached to the $\times$ nodes on the path from the root of T_{E_i} to the root of T_E and E'_i is obtained from E_i by replacing all of its subtrees by 0 (zero).

Note: This is an extension of Lemma 4.4.2.1.

(d) Thus, if p_{i_i} and E'_i are known, then E can be computed first by multiplying p_{i_i} and E'_i in parallel and then adding the products using the associative fan-in algorithm. Let n be the size of E and

$$n^* = \max_{1 \le i \le t} \{ \text{ size of } E'_i \}.$$

(1) Show that each of the p_{i_i}'s can be computed in at most $\log n$ steps.

(2) If $T(n)$ is the number of steps needed to compute E, then show that

$$T(n) \le 1 + \lceil \log t \rceil + \max\{\log n, \; T(n^*)\}.$$

(3) Express E given in part (b) using the restructuring result given in part (c).

4.32 (Kosaraju [1986]). In any parse tree of an expression, let the *size* of the parse tree denote the number of leaves in it.

(a) Let T_E be a parse tree of an SAE E of size n. Let $2 \le k < n$. Show that a set of k edges of T_E can be selected such that their removal results in a forest of at most k trees in which each tree is of size less than or equal to $\dfrac{2n}{k-1}$.

Hint: Repeatedly apply Lemma 4.4.1.1 with $m = \dfrac{n}{k-1}$.

(b) Hence or otherwise show that every SAE can be evaluated in parallel in at most $\log n + 2(\log n)^{1/2} + O(1)$ steps.

Hint: Prove by induction using $k = 2^{2\sqrt{\log N}}$ (part (a)) and combine it with part (c) of Exercise 4.30.

(c) Compute the number of processors needed to achieve this time bound.

4.33 (Preparata and Muller [1975]). Define a sequence $\{ u_j \}$ of integers as follows. $u_i = i + 1$ for $i = 0, 1, 2, 3$, and, for $i \geq 4$,

$$u_i = u_{i-1} + u_{i-4} + 1.$$

(a) Show that the largest positive (real) root of the characteristic equation associated with this recurrence is $\alpha \approx 1.3802$. Hence, or otherwise, estimate the rate of growth of u_i with i.

(b) Compare the rate of growth of u_i with that of g_i defined in (4.4.2.2).

(c) Prove (by induction) that

(1) $u_k - 2u_{k-1} + u_{k-3} \leq 0$ for $k \geq 3$, and

(2) $u_k - 2u_{k-3} - u_{k-4} - 2 \leq 0$ for $k \geq 4$.

4.34 (Preparata and Muller [1975]).
(a) Let E be a division-free arithmetic expression. Let $T(E)$ be the number of steps needed to evaluate E, where $u_{k-1} + 1 \leq |E| \leq u_k$. Then prove (by induction) that the following algorithm evaluates E, where

$$T(E) \leq k.$$

Step 0: Find a subexpression $X_1 = L_1 \, \theta_1 \, R_1$ of E, where $|X_1| \geq m_1$, $|L_1| < m_1$, $|R_1| < m_1$, and $|L_1| \leq |R_1|$, $\theta_1 \in \{+, \times\}$, and

$$m_1 = u_{k-1} - u_{k-2} + u_{k-4} + 1 \leq u_{k-2} + 1.$$

Rewriting $E = A_1 X_1 + B_1$, show that

$$|A_1| \leq u_{k-2} \quad \text{and} \quad |B_1| \leq u_{k-2}.$$

Note: This is made possible by Lemma 4.4.1.1.

Step 1: If $|R_1| \leq u_{k-3}$, then E can be restructured as

$$E = A_1 (L_1 \, \theta_1 \, R_1) + B_1.$$

Step 2: Otherwise $(u_{k-3} < \mid R_1 \mid \leq u_{k-2})$, let $\theta_1 = +$. Then E can be restructured as

$$E = A_1 \, R_1 + (A_1 \, L_1 + B_1).$$

(Notice that $A_1 \, L_1 + B_1$ is obtained from E by replacing X_1 by L_1. This is a major point of departure from the proof used in Section 4.4.1.) Show that $T(A_1 \, R_1) \leq k - 1$ and $T(A_1 \, L_1 + B_1) \leq k - 1$.

Step 3: Let $\theta_1 = \times$. Let $X_2 = L_2 \, \theta_2 \, R_2$ be a subexpression of R_1, where

$$\mid X_2 \mid \geq m_2, \quad \mid L_2 \mid < m_2, \quad \mid R_2 \mid < m_2, \quad \theta_2 \in \{ +, \times \}, \quad m_2 \geq u_{k-4} + 1.$$

Now restructure R_1 using X_2 as

$$R_1 = A_2 \, X_2 + B_2.$$

Show that

$$T(X_2) \leq k - 3 \quad \text{and} \quad T(A_2) \leq k - 4.$$

Note: This step is made possible by Lemma 4.4.1.1.

Step 3a: If $\mid L_1 \mid \leq u_{k-4}$, then express E as

$$E = (A_1 \, L_1 \, B_2 + B_1) + A_1(X_2(L_1 \, A_2)).$$

Step 3b: If $u_{k-4} < \mid L_1 \mid \leq u_{k-3}$, then set E as

$$E = (A_1 \, L_1 \, B_2 + B_1) + (A_1 \, L_1) \, (X_2 \, A_2).$$

Step 3c: If $u_{k-3} < \mid L_1 \mid \leq u_{k-2}$, then restructure E as

$$E = (A_1 \, L_1 \, B_2 + B_1) + (L_1(X_2(A_1 \, A_2))).$$

(Note that $A_1 \, L_1 \, B_2 + B_1$ is obtained by replacing X_1 in the original parse tree of E with $L_1 \, B_2$, and B_2 is obtained by replacing X_2 by 0 in R_1.)

(a) Show that $T(A_1 \, L_1 \, B_2 + B_1) \leq k - 1$. Show likewise that $A_1(X_2(L_1 \, A_2))$, $(A_1 \, L_1)(X_2 \, A_2)$, and $L_1(X_2(A_1 \, A_2))$ in each of the three cases can be computed in $k - 1$ steps.

(b) From $u_k \geq c \, \alpha^k$ for some constant $c > 0$ (where $\alpha = 1.3802$, obtained from Exercise 4.32), prove that

$$T(E) = 2.1507 \log_2 \mid E \mid + O(1).$$

Note: This is an improvement over Theorem 4.4.2.4 due to Brent, Kuck, and Maruyama [1973].

(c) Compute the number of processors needed to achieve this time bound.

4.35 (Preparata and Muller [1976]). Let E be a Boolean expression with n literals. (A *literal* is either a variable or its complement. In this way all the

complement operations are limited to single variables and are taken care of at
the input stage.) E is said to be *primitive* if all the literals in it are distinct.
Consider the problem of evaluating a primitive Boolean expression with N
literals involving only two types of operations $\lor$ (OR) and $\land$ (AND).

(a) Show that $\alpha = 1.4666$ is the positive, real root of the cubic equation
$z^3 = z^2 + 1$.

(b) Prove by induction that the following algorithm can be used to evaluate a
primitive Boolean expression E with N literals in time $T(E(N))$, where

$$T(E(N)) \le \frac{\log N}{\log \alpha} = 1.81 \log N.$$

Step 1: Let $m = N\alpha^{-3}$. Find the subexpression $X = B\ \theta^*\ C$ of E, where
$\theta^* \in \{\lor, \land\}$, $|X| \ge m$, and $|B| \le |C| < m$. (This is made
possible by Lemma 4.4.1.1.) Let A be an expression obtained from E
by replacing $B\ \theta^*\ C$ by an indeterminate y. Now, A can be expressed
in either of the two forms:

$$A = (A_1 \lor y) \land A_2 \quad or \quad A = (A_3 \land y) \lor A_4.$$

Replacing y by $B\ \theta^*\ C$, we obtain

$$E = (A_1 \lor (B\ \theta^*\ C)) \lor A_2 \quad or \quad E = (A_3 \land (B\ \theta^*\ C)) \lor A_4.$$

Step 2: Define recursively the path from the root of T_E to the root of the
subtree T_X corresponding to the subexpression X found in step 1 as
follows:

Let $T_0 = E$, for $i = 0, 1, 2, \cdots, r - 1$,

$$T_i = L_{i+1}\ \theta_i\ T_{i+1},$$

where $\theta_i \in \{\lor, \land\}$, $|L_{i+1}| \le |T_{i+1}|$, and $T_r = T_X$. Define

$$s_1 = \sum_{\{\theta_i = \lor\ |\ i = 0\ \text{to}\ r-1\}} |L_{i+1}|$$

and

$$s_2 = \sum_{\{\theta_i = \land\ |\ 0\ \text{to}\ r-1\}} |L_{i+1}|.$$

Then

$$E = \begin{cases} (A_1 \lor (B\ \theta^*\ C)) \land A_2 & \text{if } s_1 \le s_2 \\ \\ (A_3 \land (B\ \theta^*\ C)) \lor A_4 & \text{otherwise.} \end{cases}$$

Note: This algorithm exploits the dual distributivity of Boolean operators $\lor$
and $\land$.

4.36 Show that the number of processors needed by the algorithm implicit in Theorem 4.4.2.9 is $O(N^{1.82})$.

4.37 Complete the proof of parts (b) to (d) of Lemma 4.4.3.3.

4.38 (Muller and Preparata [1976]). Show that the number of processors needed to achieve the time bound in Theorem 4.4.3.6 is $O(N^{1.44})$.

4.39 (Muller and Preparata [1976]). (a) Show that the time bound given in (4.4.3.9) remains unaltered if the value of r used in the proof of Theorem 4.4.3.5 is allowed to be in the range $\alpha^{-2}N \le r \le \alpha^{-1}N$.

(b) If any integer $M > 0$, we can find a constant $C > 0$ such that

$$\hat{T}(E) \le \frac{\log |E|}{\log \alpha} - C,$$

where $\alpha^{-2}M \le |E| < M$, then show that the inductive proof of Theorem 4.4.3.5 can be extended to establish the above upper bound for $|E| \ge M$.

(c) Write a computer program to generate various forms of general arithmetic expressions E and analyze the time for evaluation when $|E| \le k$ for some small k.

4.40 (Muller and Preparata [1976]). Define a sequence of primitive expressions recursively as follows:

(1) $E_0 = a$, $E_1 = b$, where a and b are atomic variables.

(2) Define

$$E_k = E_{k-2} + \frac{a_k}{b_k + E_{k-1}},$$

where the atomic variables in E_{k-1}, E_{k-2} are distinct.

(a) Show that $|E_k| \le 2.18 \, \alpha^k$, where $\alpha = 1.618$ is the positive root of the equation $z^2 = z + 1$.

(b) Prove or disprove the conjecture that the time to evaluate the expression E_k defined above is bounded below by

$$2.18 \log |E_k| - C$$

for some constant $C > 0$.

PART 3

MATRIX PROBLEMS

CHAPTER
5

LINEAR
RECURRENCE
AND
TRIDIAGONAL
SYSTEMS

5.1 INTRODUCTION

Chapters 5, 6, and 7 are devoted to matrix problems and constitute Part 3 of this book. This chapter begins with a coverage of parallel algorithms for solving linear recurrences in Section 5.2. It is followed by a comprehensive discussion of algorithms for solving linear tridiagonal systems. To emphasize the basic ideas, and for added convenience in presentation, the scalar tridiagonal case is covered in Section 5.3 and the block tridiagonal case in Section 5.4. Our treatment includes mapping of algorithms into a hypercube architecture and a detailed stability analysis. While the main body of the chapter deals with the direct technique, various iterative methods are developed in exercises.

5.2 FIRST-ORDER LINEAR RECURRENCE

5.2.1 Statement and Motivation

Stated in its generic form, the *first-order* linear recurrence system of size N, LR[N, 1], is given by

$$x_1 = d_1$$
$$x_i = a_i x_{i-1} + d_i, \quad i = 2, \cdots, N. \tag{5.2.1.1}$$

The problem is to compute x_i, $1 \le i \le N$, where $\mathbf{a} = (a_1, a_2, \cdots, a_N)^t$, $a_1 = 0$, and $\mathbf{d} = (d_1, d_2, \cdots, d_N)^t$ are given and t denotes the transpose. Stated in matrix form, (5.2.1.1) becomes

$$\mathbf{Ax} = \mathbf{d}, \tag{5.2.1.2}$$

where $\mathbf{x} = (x_1, x_2, \cdots, x_N)^t$, and

$$\mathbf{A} = \begin{bmatrix} 1 & 0 & 0 & 0 & \cdots & & \cdot & \cdot \\ -a_2 & 1 & 0 & 0 & \cdots & & \cdot & \cdot \\ 0 & -a_3 & 1 & 0 & \cdots & & \cdot & \cdot \\ 0 & 0 & -a_4 & 1 & \cdots & & \cdot & \cdot \\ \cdot & \cdot & \cdot & \cdot & \cdots & & \cdot & \cdot \\ \cdot & \cdot & \cdot & \cdot & \cdots & & & \\ \cdot & \cdot & \cdot & \cdot & \cdots & & & \\ 0 & 0 & 0 & 0 & \cdots & & -a_N & 1 \end{bmatrix} \tag{5.2.1.3}$$

is called a *banded matrix of bandwidth* 2, or simply a *bidiagonal* matrix.

The importance of the linear recurrence system of type (5.2.1.1) and the interest in solving it are primarily due to the fact that it manifests itself in a number of application areas.

A. The Problem of Computing Prefixes. If $a_i = 1$ for $2 \le i \le N$, then (5.2.1.1) reduces to computing all the partial sums, that is, computing the sum $d_1 + d_2 + \cdots + d_i$ for all $i = 1$ to N. In general if o represents an *associative binary* operation, then computing $d_1 \circ d_2 \circ \cdots \circ d_i$ for all i is called the *prefix* problem. This problem arises naturally in computing the sum of two N-bit integers. Refer to Exercises 3.42 to 3.44 in Chapter 3 for a treatment of the prefix problem.

B. Polynomial Evaluation Using Horner's Method. Let

$$p(x) = a_0 x^N + a_1 x^{N-1} + \cdots + a_{N-1} x + a_N. \tag{5.2.1.4}$$

The well-known Horner's method for evaluating $p(.)$ at any point x is given by expressing the computations in the form of a first-order linear recurrence $L(N, 1)$ as follows.

Define

$$p = a_0$$

and compute

$$p = px + a_i, \quad 1 \le i \le N. \tag{5.2.1.5}$$

Clearly, in the end, the value of p is that of $p(x)$. Parallel algorithms for computing Horner's expression are given in Chapter 4.

C. Automatic Vectorization of Serial Programs. During the past four decades, huge investments have been made in developing very efficient application software for running on the serial machines. However, an efficient piece of software fine-tuned for a given serial architecture may not run efficiently on a parallel architecture. With the coming in of a variety of newer architectures and the attendant interest in parallel processing, the application software industry has been faced with the tough (and expensive) question of developing special-purpose software for these newer architectures. Since software development continues to be very expensive, in the interest of protecting the huge investments in the serial software, an intermediate solution to this problem was proposed. This consists in automatically translating an existing serial program into a version that will readily map onto a given architecture. In fact, considerable experience has been gained with respect to the translation of serial programs for machines with *pipelined* arithmetic. This experience has shown that the innermost do-loops are the prime targets for this automatic vectorization process. Often, these innermost do-loops involve computation of recurrence systems, and hence any class of efficient parallel methods for solving linear recurrences would have a definite impact on program transformation.

D. Solution of Tridiagonal Systems. The now classical Gaussian elimination algorithm for solving linear tridiagonal systems naturally leads to the solution of first-order recurrence systems. This topic is pursued in depth in Section 5.3.

Motivated by these applications, we describe four methods for solving (5.2.1.1).

5.2.2 The Cyclic Elimination Scheme

Let $N = 2^n$. Consider the first-order linear recurrence

$$\begin{aligned} x_1 &= d_1 \\ x_i &= a_i x_{i-1} + d_i, \quad 2 \le i \le N. \end{aligned} \tag{5.2.2.1}$$

By iterating (5.2.2.1) once and substituting back, we obtain

$$x_i = (a_i a_{i-1}) x_{i-2} + (a_i d_{i-1} + d_i), \quad i = 2, \cdots, N. \tag{5.2.2.2}$$

Define

$$a_i^{(0)} = a_i \ ; \ d_i^{(0)} = d_i, \qquad i = 1, \ \cdots, N,$$

and

$$a_i^{(1)} = a_i^{(0)} a_{i-1}^{(0)}; \ d_i^{(1)} = a_i^{(0)} d_{i-1}^{(0)} + d_i^{(0)}, \ i = 2, \ \cdots, N.$$

$$(5.2.2.3)$$

Using these definitions, (5.2.2.1) and (5.2.2.2) can be expressed as

$$x_i = a_i^{(0)} x_{i-2^0}^{(0)} + d_i^{(0)}, \qquad 2 \le i \le N,$$

and

$$x_i = a_i^{(1)} x_{i-2^1} + d_i^{(1)}, \tag{5.2.2.4}$$

respectively. Iterating (5.2.2.4) once again, and substituting back, we obtain

$$x_i = (a_i^{(1)} a_{i-2}^{(1)}) x_{i-2^2} + (a_i^{(1)} d_{i-2}^{(1)} + d_i^{(1)}). \tag{5.2.2.5}$$

Again, defining

$$a_i^{(2)} = a_i^{(1)} a_{i-2}^{(1)}; \quad d_i^{(2)} = a_i^{(1)} d_{i-2}^{(1)}, + d_i^{(1)}$$

(5.2.2.5) becomes

$$x_i = a_i^{(2)} x_{i-2^2} + d_i^{(2)}. \tag{5.2.2.6}$$

Generalizing this trend, we obtain

$$x_i = a_i^{(j)} x_{i-2^j} + d_i^{(j)}, \tag{5.2.2.7}$$

where

$$a_i^{(j)} = a_i^{(j-1)} a_{i-2^{j-1}}^{(j-1)}$$

and

$$d_i^{(j)} = a_i^{(j-1)} d_{i-2^{j-1}}^{(j-1)} + d_i^{(j-1)},$$

$$(5.2.2.8)$$

where $1 \le i \le N$ and $j = 1, \ \cdots, n = \log N$, and any quantity with subscript outside the range 1 to N is taken to be zero. Thus, when $j = n$, we obtain the solution

$$x_i = d_i^{(n)}, \quad 1 \le i \le N. \tag{5.2.2.9}$$

Before organizing these computations in the form of a parallel algorithm, it is instructive to illustrate this process in matrix form.

Let $N = 8$. Then (5.2.2.7) can be expressed in matrix form:

$$A^{(j)} x = d^{(j)},$$

where

$$
\mathbf{A}^{(0)} = \begin{bmatrix}
1 & 0 & 0 & 0 & 0 & 0 & 0 & 0 \\
-a_2^{(0)} & 1 & 0 & 0 & 0 & 0 & 0 & 0 \\
0 & -a_3^{(0)} & 1 & 0 & 0 & 0 & 0 & 0 \\
0 & 0 & -a_4^{(0)} & 1 & 0 & 0 & 0 & 0 \\
0 & 0 & 0 & -a_5^{(0)} & 1 & 0 & 0 & 0 \\
0 & 0 & 0 & 0 & -a_6^{(0)} & 1 & 0 & 0 \\
0 & 0 & 0 & 0 & 0 & -a_7^{(0)} & 1 & 0 \\
0 & 0 & 0 & 0 & 0 & 0 & -a_8^{(0)} & 1
\end{bmatrix}
$$

$$
\mathbf{d}^{(0)} = \left[d_1^{(0)}, d_2^{(0)}, d_3^{(0)}, d_4^{(0)}, d_5^{(0)}, d_6^{(0)}, d_7^{(0)}, d_8^{(0)} \right]^t
$$

$$
\mathbf{A}^{(1)} = \begin{bmatrix}
1 & 0 & 0 & 0 & 0 & 0 & 0 & 0 \\
0 & 1 & 0 & 0 & 0 & 0 & 0 & 0 \\
-a_3^{(1)} & 0 & 1 & 0 & 0 & 0 & 0 & 0 \\
0 & -a_4^{(1)} & 0 & 1 & 0 & 0 & 0 & 0 \\
0 & 0 & -a_5^{(1)} & 0 & 1 & 0 & 0 & 0 \\
0 & 0 & 0 & -a_6^{(1)} & 0 & 1 & 0 & 0 \\
0 & 0 & 0 & 0 & -a_7^{(1)} & 0 & 1 & 0 \\
0 & 0 & 0 & 0 & 0 & -a_8^{(1)} & 0 & 1
\end{bmatrix}
$$

$$
\mathbf{d}^{(1)} = \left[d_1^{(1)}, d_2^{(1)}, d_3^{(1)}, d_4^{(1)}, d_5^{(1)}, d_6^{(1)}, d_7^{(1)}, d_8^{(1)} \right]^t
$$

$$
\mathbf{A}^{(2)} = \begin{bmatrix}
1 & 0 & 0 & 0 & 0 & 0 & 0 & 0 \\
0 & 1 & 0 & 0 & 0 & 0 & 0 & 0 \\
0 & 0 & 1 & 0 & 0 & 0 & 0 & 0 \\
0 & 0 & 0 & 1 & 0 & 0 & 0 & 0 \\
-a_5^{(2)} & 0 & 0 & 0 & 1 & 0 & 0 & 0 \\
0 & -a_6^{(2)} & 0 & 0 & 0 & 1 & 0 & 0 \\
0 & 0 & -a_7^{(2)} & 0 & 0 & 0 & 1 & 0 \\
0 & 0 & 0 & -a_8^{(2)} & 0 & 0 & 0 & 1
\end{bmatrix}
$$

$$
\mathbf{d}^{(2)} = \left[d_1^{(2)}, d_2^{(2)}, d_3^{(2)}, d_4^{(2)}, d_5^{(2)}, d_6^{(2)}, d_7^{(2)}, d_8^{(2)} \right]^t
$$

and

$$\mathbf{A}^{(3)} = \mathbf{I},$$

where $\mathbf{I}$ is the identity matrix, and

$$\mathbf{d}^{(3)} = (d_1^{(3)}, d_2^{(3)}, \cdots, d_8^{(3)})^t = (x_1, x_2, \cdots, x_8)^t.$$

A schematic representation of the computations in (5.2.2.8) for $N = 8$ is given in Fig. 5.2.2.1. This figure clearly brings out the parallelism inherent in cyclic elimination. The same set of computations in vector form is expressed in algorithm form in Fig. 5.2.2.2, where SHIFTR($\mathbf{x}, \alpha$) denotes a vector obtained by shifting $\mathbf{x}$ to the right by α places ($\alpha \geq 0$). Thus, if $\mathbf{x} = (x_1, x_2, \cdots, x_N)$, then

$$\text{SHIFTR}(\mathbf{x}, \alpha) = (0, 0, \cdots, 0, x_1, x_2, \cdots, x_{N-\alpha}).$$

The time and processor bounds for this algorithm are given in the next theorem.

$j = 0$	$j = 1$	$j = 2$
$a_2^{(0)}$		
$a_3^{(0)}$	$a_3^{(1)}$	
$a_4^{(0)}$	$a_4^{(1)}$	
$a_5^{(0)}$	$a_5^{(1)}$	$a_5^{(2)}$
$a_6^{(0)}$	$a_6^{(1)}$	$a_6^{(2)}$
$a_7^{(0)}$	$a_7^{(1)}$	$a_7^{(2)}$
$a_8^{(0)}$	$a_8^{(1)}$	$a_8^{(2)}$

$j = 0$	$j = 1$	$j = 2$	$j = 3$
$d_1^{(0)} = x_1$			
$(a_2^{(0)}, d_2^{(0)})$	$d_2^{(1)} = x_2$		
$(a_3^{(0)}, d_3^{(0)})$	$(a_3^{(1)}, d_3^{(1)})$	$d_3^{(2)} = x_3$	
$(a_4^{(0)}, d_4^{(0)})$	$(a_4^{(1)}, d_4^{(1)})$	$d_4^{(2)} = x_4$	
$(a_5^{(0)}, d_5^{(0)})$	$(a_5^{(1)}, d_5^{(1)})$	$(a_5^{(2)}, d_5^{(2)})$	$d_5^{(3)} = x_5$
$(a_6^{(0)}, d_6^{(0)})$	$(a_6^{(1)}, d_6^{(1)})$	$(a_6^{(2)}, d_6^{(2)})$	$d_6^{(3)} = x_6$
$(a_7^{(0)}, d_7^{(0)})$	$(a_7^{(1)}, d_7^{(1)})$	$(a_7^{(2)}, d_7^{(2)})$	$d_7^{(3)} = x_7$
$(a_8^{(0)}, d_8^{(0)})$	$(a_8^{(1)}, d_8^{(1)})$	$(a_8^{(2)}, d_8^{(2)})$	$d_8^{(3)} = x_8$

FIGURE 5.2.2.1
A schematic representation of the computations in cyclic elimination.

/* In the following +, ×, and = are componentwise addition, multiplication, and assignment of vectors, respectively. **x** is initialized to **d**. $N = 2^n$. **a** is the vector of coefficients. */

> FOR $j = 1$ TO n STEP 1 DO
>> $\mathbf{x} = \mathbf{x} + \mathbf{a} \times$ SHIFTR $(\mathbf{x}, \ 2^{j-1})$
>> $\mathbf{a} = \mathbf{a} \times$ SHIFTR $(\mathbf{a}, \ 2^{j-1})$
> END

FIGURE 5.2.2.2
Cyclic elimination -- vector form.

Theorem 5.2.2.1. The cyclic elimination algorithm requires a total of $3N \log N$ operations and takes

$$T_N(N) \ = \ 3 \log N$$

steps to complete using N processors.

Proof
From (5.2.2.8), it is clear that for each i and j, there are three arithmetic operations. The theorem follows from the fact that for each $1 \le j \le \log N$, the computations in $i = 1$ to N can be done in parallel.

From this theorem it follows that this method requires $\Omega(\log N)$ processors to attain a speed-up greater than unity.

The same algorithm can be expressed as a row-oriented operation on the augmented matrix **A**, obtained by adding **d** as the $(N + 1)^{th}$ column. This version of the algorithm is given in Fig. 5.2.2.3. The analysis of this version of the algorithm is left as Exercise 5.1.

/* In the following, the operations −, ×, and = are componentwise subtraction, multiplication, and assignment of vectors, respectively. Let **A** be augmented with the **d**-vector as the $(N + 1)^{th}$ column. At the end the $(N + 1)^{th}$ column contains the **x**-values. */

> FOR $k = 1$ STEP k UNTIL $N - 1$ DO
>> FOR $i \in \{1, 2, \cdots, N\}$ DO IN PARALLEL
>>> $row(i) = row(i) - \dfrac{a_{i,i-k}}{a_{i-k,i-k}} \times row(i - k)$
>> END
> END

FIGURE 5.2.2.3
A version of cyclic elimination -- row-oriented operation.

5.2.3 The Cyclic Reduction Algorithm

This method is very closely related to cyclic elimination but admits only limited parallelism. It requires fewer scalar operations but does so at the expense of elapsed time. In fact, this method is to be preferred if the number of processors is limited and is independent of the size of the problem.

Given $N = 2^n$, and x_1, let

$$-a_i x_{i-1} + x_i = d_i, \quad \text{for } i = 2, 3, 4, \cdots, N. \qquad (5.2.3.1)$$

First eliminating all the *odd-indexed* terms in (5.2.3.1), we obtain

$$-a_i^{(1)} x_{i-2} + x_i = d_i^{(1)}, \quad \text{for } i = 2, 4, \cdots, N, \qquad (5.2.3.2)$$

where $a_i^{(1)}$ and $d_i^{(1)}$ are the same as given in (5.2.2.3). It is readily seen that $x_2 = d_2^{(1)}$. Eliminating terms with indices that are *odd multiples of* 2 in (5.2.3.2), we get

$$-a_i^{(2)} x_{i-2^2} + x_i = d_i^{(2)}, \quad \text{for } i = 4, 8, 12, \cdots, N. \qquad (5.2.3.3)$$

Again, it can be seen that $x_4 = d_4^{(2)}$. After iterating j times, it can be shown that

$$-a_i^{(j)} x_{i-2^j} + x_i = d_i^{(j)}, \quad \text{for } i = 2^j, 2\times2^j, 3\times2^j, \cdots, 2^{n-j}\times2^j, \qquad (5.2.3.4)$$

where $a_i^{(j)}$ and $d_i^{(j)}$ are given in (5.2.2.8) and

$$x_{2^j} = d_{2^j}^{(j)}.$$

Thus, when $j = n = \log N$, from

$$-a_i^{(n)} x_{i-2^n} + x_i = d_i^{(n)}, \quad i = 2^n,$$

since all the quantities with subscripts outside the range 1 to N are taken to be zero, it follows that

$$x_N = d_N^{(n)}. \qquad (5.2.3.5)$$

Now, x_{2^j}, for $j = 0, 1, 2, \cdots, n$, are known, and the rest of the x_i's can be obtained by a suitable *fill-in* or *back-substitution* process using the following formula:

$$x_i = \frac{x_{i+2^r} - d_{i+2^r}^{(r)}}{a_{i+2^r}^{(r)}}, \qquad (5.2.3.6)$$

for all i starting from $2^r + 2^{r+1}$ increasing in steps of 2^{r+1} up to (but not including) N, and for all r starting from $n-2$ decreasing in steps of 1 to 0 (including).

An example illustrating these computations for $N = 16$ is given in Fig. 5.2.3.1.

For purposes of analysis, this algorithm may be viewed as consisting of two parts. Part 1 consists of $n = \log N$ iterations. During iteration j, a new equation relating x_i to x_{i-2^j}, for $i = 2^j, 2\times2^j, 3\times2^j, \cdots, 2^{(n-j)}\times2^j$, is obtained by eliminating terms with indices that are odd multiples of 2^{j-1}. Thus, at the jth step, 2^{n-j} variables are eliminated and each such elimination requires three operations. Hence, the total number of scalar operations required by this computational scheme in part 1 is given by

$d_1^{(0)}=x_1$							
$(a_2^{(0)},d_2^{(0)})$	$(a_2^{(1)},\ d_2^{(1)}=x_2)$						
$(a_3^{(0)},d_3^{(0)})$							x_3
$(a_4^{(0)},d_4^{(0)})$	$(a_4^{(1)},d_4^{(1)})$	$(a_4^{(2)},\ d_4^{(2)}=x_4)$					
$(a_5^{(0)},d_5^{(0)})$							x_5
$(a_6^{(0)},d_6^{(0)})$	$(a_6^{(1)},d_6^{(1)})$					x_6	
$(a_7^{(0)},d_7^{(0)})$							x_7
$(a_8^{(0)},d_8^{(0)})$	$(a_8^{(1)},d_8^{(1)})$	$(a_8^{(2)},d_8^{(2)})$	$(a_8^{(3)},\ d_8^{(3)}=x_8)$				
$(a_9^{(0)},d_9^{(0)})$							x_9
$(a_{10}^{(0)},d_{10}^{(0)})$	$(a_{10}^{(1)},d_{10}^{(1)})$					x_{10}	
$(a_{11}^{(0)},d_{11}^{(0)})$							x_{11}
$(a_{12}^{(0)},d_{12}^{(0)})$	$(a_{12}^{(1)},d_{12}^{(1)})$	$(a_{12}^{(2)},d_{12}^{(2)})$			x_{12}		
$(a_{13}^{(0)},d_{13}^{(0)})$							x_{13}
$(a_{14}^{(0)},d_{14}^{(0)})$	$(a_{14}^{(1)},d_{14}^{(1)})$					x_{14}	
$(a_{15}^{(0)},d_{15}^{(0)})$							x_{15}
$(a_{16}^{(0)},d_{16}^{(0)})$	$(a_{16}^{(1)},d_{16}^{(1)})$	$(a_{16}^{(2)},d_{16}^{(2)})$	$(a_{16}^{(3)},d_{16}^{(3)})$	$(a_{16}^{(4)},\ d_{16}^{(4)}=x_{16})$			

FIGURE 5.2.3.1

An illustration of the computation in cyclic reduction.

$$3\sum_{j=1}^{n} 2^{n-j} = 3(2^n - 1) = 3(N-1).$$

Now, given $\dfrac{N}{2}$ processors, it is readily seen that the first iteration in part 1 takes three steps, and the rest of the iterations in part 1 require only two time units (why?), and part 1 in its entirety requires a total of $2n + 1 = 1 + 2\log N$ units of time.

In part 2, using the known x_{2^s}, $s = 0, 1, \cdots$, $\log N$, the rest of the x_i's are computed. At the rth step, $2^{n-r-1} - 1$ variables are computed using (5.2.3.4), and each such computation takes two operations. The total scalar operations in part 2 are given by

$$2 \sum_{r=0}^{n-2} (2^{n-r-1}-1) = 2(N - \log N - 1). \tag{5.2.3.7}$$

Again, given $\dfrac{N}{2}$ processors, part 2 takes a total of $2(\log N - 1)$ units of time. Combining these, we obtain the following theorem.

Theorem 5.2.3.1. The cyclic reduction algorithm requires a total of $5N - 2 \log N - 5$ scalar operations and takes

$$T_{N/2}(N) = 4 \log N - 1$$

steps to complete using $\dfrac{N}{2}$ processors.

Since this algorithm only requires $O(N)$ operations, it is highly recommended when only a small but fixed number of processors are available. (See Exercise 5.2.)

5.2.4 A Divide-and-Conquer Method

The solution to the linear first-order recurrence (5.2.1.1) in closed form is given by

$$x_i = \sum_{j=1}^{i} \left[\prod_{s=j+1}^{i} a_s \right] d_j. \tag{5.2.4.1}$$

In this section, we describe a divide-and-conquer method for computing (5.2.4.1). To this end, we introduce two functions $A[u, v]$ of a_i's and $Y[s, t]$ of a_i's and d_i's. Let

$$A[u,v] = \prod_{r=u+1}^{v} a_r, \tag{5.2.4.2}$$

where vacuous products are taken to be unity, and let

$$Y[s,t] = \sum_{j=s}^{t} A[j,t] \, d_j, \quad \text{for } t \geq s. \tag{5.2.4.3}$$

A number of useful properties of the functions $A[.,.]$ and $Y[.,.]$ are developed in the following lemmas.

Lemma 5.2.4.1. The function $A[u, v]$ satisfies the following:

(a) $A[u, v] = 1$ for all $u \geq v$.
(b) $A[u, v + m] = A[u, v] A[v, v + m]$ for any integer $m > 0$.

Proof

The proof of this lemma is straightforward and is left as an exercise.

Lemma 5.2.4.2. The function $Y[s, .]$ also satisfies the recurrence of type (5.2.1.1), that is,

$$Y[s, t] = a_t\, Y[s, t-1] + d_t. \tag{5.2.4.4}$$

Proof

Rewriting (5.2.4.3), we readily obtain

$$Y[s, t] = \sum_{j=s}^{t-1} A[j, t]\, d_j + A[t, t]\, d_t.$$

Since $A[t, t] = 1$, and $A[j, t] = a_t\, A[j, t-1]$, the lemma follows.

Lemma 5.2.4.3. $x_t = Y[1, t]$ for $1 \leq t \leq N$.

Proof

The proof follows from the definitions.

The following lemma, which is a generalization of Lemma 5.2.4.2, provides the basis for this algorithm.

Lemma 5.2.4.4. If $t \geq s$, then for $i > 0$,

$$Y[s, t+i] = A[t, t+i]\, Y[s, t] + Y[t+1, t+i]. \tag{5.2.4.5}$$

Proof

From equation (5.2.4.3), it follows that

$$Y[s, t+i] = \sum_{j=s}^{t+i} A[j, t+i]\, d_j$$

$$= \sum_{j=s}^{t} A[j, t+i]\, d_j + \sum_{j=t+1}^{t+i} A[j, t+i]\, d_j. \tag{5.2.4.6}$$

It is readily seen from equation (5.2.4.3) that the second term is in fact $Y[t+1, t+i]$. From Lemma 5.2.4.1(b),

$$A[j, t+i] = A[j, t]\, A[t, t+i]. \tag{5.2.4.7}$$

Substituting (5.2.4.7) in the first term of (5.2.4.6), the lemma follows.

Let $N = 2mp$, $p = 2^k$, where $m \geq 1$ and $k \geq 1$. In the following a function of p will denote the number of processors. Let $1 \leq s \leq k$, and $0 \leq g \leq 2^{k-s-1}$. The algorithm for solving (5.2.1.1) consists of two parts: (1) a parallel algorithm A for computing $A[u, v]$ and (2) a parallel algorithm Y for computing $Y[s, t]$, given in Figs. 5.2.4.1 and 5.2.4.2. In fact, Algorithm A computes all those $A[u, v]$ which are needed in the computation of $Y[s, t]$. Since these two algorithms are working in parallel, the total number of processors is equal to the sum of the processors used in both the algorithms, but the time is the maximum of the time needed by the two algorithms. Algorithm Y uses p processors $P_0, P_1, \cdots, P_{p-1}$, and Algorithm A uses q processors $Q_0, Q_1, \cdots, Q_{q-1}$, where $q = \dfrac{p}{2}$.

In stage 1 of Algorithm A in Fig. 5.2.4.1, a total of $2qm$ of the $A[., .]$ functions are updated using q processors. Each update involves one multiplication. This stage takes $\dfrac{N}{p}$ units of time.

In stage 2, a total of $2m(q-1)$ of $A[., .]$ functions are updated using $q-1$ processors. This stage also takes $\dfrac{N}{p}$ units of time.

In stage 3, in any step s, there are $2^{k-s} - 1$ groups of computations, and within each group $2ms$ $A[., .]$ functions are updated. Since $2ms(2^{k-s} - 1) \leq 2m(q-1)$, using no more than $q-1$ processors, each of the above steps can be completed in no more than $\dfrac{N}{p}$ units of time.

Thus the entire Algorithm A, using q processors, does not take more than $\dfrac{N}{p}(2 + \log p)$ units of time.

In each of stages 1 and 2 of the Algorithm Y in Fig. 5.2.4.2, a total of $\dfrac{N}{2}$ $Y[., .]$ functions are updated using p processors. Since each update requires two operations (a multiplication and an addition), each of the above stages takes $\dfrac{N}{p}$ units of time.

It is readily seen that at any step s in stage 3, Algorithm Y identifies 2^{n-s} groups indexed by g and within each group there are 2^s processors working in parallel. Thus within each group $2^s m$ $Y[., .]$ functions are updated. It readily follows that computations in each group take the same amount of time equal to $\dfrac{N}{p}$ units. Thus the entire stage 3 takes $\dfrac{N}{p} \log p$ units of time.

For the correct functioning of Algorithm Y, the values of

$$A[\, 2^s m(1+2g), \; 2^s m(1+2g) + i \,],$$

for $0 \leq g < 2^{k-s}$ and $1 \leq i \leq k$, must be made available for each $1 \leq s \leq k$. In fact, these functions are generated in parallel by Algorithm A. A close scrutiny reveals that all the values of the $A[., .]$ functions that are needed in stage 3 of Algorithm Y are in fact generated by Algorithm A at least one step ahead of time. Thus, the overall time for solving for x_i's in (5.2.1.1) is decided by the running time of Algorithm Y.

Stage 1. Each processor Q_j, $0 \leq j \leq q - 1$, computes the following.

> FOR $i = 1$ TO $2m$ STEP 1 DO
>   FOR $j \in \{ 0, 1, 2, \cdots, q - 1 \}$ DO IN PARALLEL
>   COMPUTE $A[2m(1 + 2j), 2m(1 + 2j) + i]$
>   END
> END

Stage 2. Each processor Q_j, $0 \leq j \leq q - 2$, computes the following.

> FOR $i = 1$ TO $2m$ STEP 1 DO
>   FOR $j \in \{ 0, 1, 2, \cdots, q - 2 \}$ DO IN PARALLEL
>   COMPUTE $A[4m(1 + j), 4m(1 + j) + i]$
>   END
> END

Stage 3.

> FOR $s = 1$ TO $k - 1$ STEP 1 DO
>   FOR $j \in \{ 0, 1, 2, \cdots, 2^{k-s} - 2\}$ DO IN PARALLEL
>   LET $h_j = 6m \, 2^{s-1} + 2^{s+1} mj$
>   FOR $i = 1$ TO $2ms$ DO
>   COMPUTE $A[h_j - 2^s m, h_j + i]$
>   END
>   END
> END

FIGURE 5.2.4.1
Algorithm A.

Before stating the main result of this section, we illustrate Algorithms Y and A through an example.

Example 5.2.4.1. Let $p = 8$, $q = 4$, $k = 3$, $m = 4$, $N = 64$. The various stages of Algorithm Y are shown in Fig. 5.2.4.3. In Fig. 5.2.4.4, further details of the computations in stage 3 of Algorithm Y are given. Figure 5.2.4.5 illustrates various stages of Algorithm A. Comparing Figs. 5.2.4.4 and 5.2.4.5, it follows that the values of the $A[.,.]$ function are made available at least one step ahead of the time they are needed in Algorithm Y.

Stage 1. /* Each processor P_i, $0 \leq i \leq p-1$, computes the following. */

        FOR $j = 0$ TO $m - 1$ STEP 1 DO

            FOR $i \in \{0, 1, 2, \cdots, p - 1\}$ DO IN PARALLEL

              COMPUTE $Y[\, 2im+1, \, 2im+1+j \,] =$
                  $a_{2im+1+j} \, Y[\, 2im+1, \, 2im+j] + d_{2im+1+j}$

            END

        END

Stage 2. /* Each processor P_i, $0 \leq i \leq p-1$, computes the following. */

        FOR $j = 0$ TO $m - 1$ STEP 1 DO

            FOR $i \in \{0, 1, 2, \cdots, p - 1\}$ DO IN PARALLEL

            COMPUTE $Y[\, 2im+1, \, (2i+1)m+1+j] =$
                  $a_{(2i+1)m+1+j} \, Y[2im+1,(2i+1)m+j] + d_{(2i+1)m+1+j}$

            END

        END

Stage 3. FOR $s = 1$ TO k STEP 1 DO

            FOR $g \in \{0, 1, 2, \cdots, 2^{k-s} - 1\}$ DO IN PARALLEL

            $h_g = 2^s m(1 + 2g)$

            FOR $i = 1$ TO $m \, 2^s$ DO

              COMPUTE $Y[h_g - 2^s m + 1, \, h_g + i] =$
                  $A[\, h_g, \, h_g + i \,] \, Y[\, h_g - 2^s m + 1, \, h_g \,] + Y[\, h_g + 1, \, h_g + i \,]$

            END

            END

        END

FIGURE 5.2.4.2
Algorithm Y.

Stage 1	Stage 2	Stage 3		
$0 \le j \le 3$	$0 \le j \le 3$	$s = 1$ $1 \le i \le 8$	$s = 2$ $1 \le i \le 16$	$s = 3$ $1 \le i \le 32$
$P_0 : Y[1, 1+j]$				
	$P_0 : Y[1, 5+j]$			
$P_1 : Y[9, 9+j]$		$P_0 - P_1$		
	$P_1 : Y[9, 13+j]$	$Y[1, 8+i]$		
$P_2 : Y[17, 17+j]$				
	$P_2 : Y[17, 21+j]$		$P_0 - P_3$	
$P_3 : Y[25, 25+j]$		$P_2 - P_3$	$Y[1, 16+i]$	
	$P_3 : Y[25, 29+j]$	$Y[17, 24+i]$		
$P_4 : Y[33, 33+j]$				
	$P_4 : Y[33, 37+j]$			
$P_5 : Y[41, 41+j]$		$P_4 - P_5$		
	$P_5 : Y[41, 45+j]$	$Y[33, 40+i]$		$P_0 - P_7$
$P_6 : Y[49, 49+j]$				$Y[1, 32+i]$
	$P_6 : Y[49, 53+j]$.		$P_4 - P_7$	
$P_7 : Y[57, 57+j]$		$P_6 - P_7$	$Y[33, 48+i]$	
	$P_7 : Y[57, 61+j]$	$Y[49, 56+i]$		

FIGURE 5.2.4.3

Various stages of Algorithm Y, $N = 64$, $p = 8$, $m = 4$.

$$s = 1, \ 1 \le i \le 8$$

$$g = 0: Y[1, \ 8 + i] = A[8, \ 8 + i]Y[1, \ 8] + Y[9, \ 8 + i]$$

$$g = 1: Y[17, \ 24 + i] = A[24, \ 24 + i]Y[17, \ 24] + Y[25, \ 24 + i]$$

$$g = 2: Y[33, \ 40 + i] = A[40, \ 40 + i]Y[33, \ 40] + Y[41, \ 40 + i]$$

$$g = 3: Y[49, \ 56 + i] = A[56, \ 56 + i]Y[49, \ 56] + Y[57, \ 56 + i]$$

$$s = 2, \ 1 \le i \le 16$$

$$g = 0: Y[1, \ 16 + i] = A[16, \ 16 + i]Y[1, \ 16] + Y[17, \ 16 + i]$$

$$g = 1: Y[33, \ 48 + i] = A[48, \ 48 + i]Y[33, \ 48] + Y[49, \ 48 + i]$$

$$s = 3, \ 1 \le i \le 32$$

$$g = 0: Y[1, \ 32 + i] = A[32, \ 32 + i]Y[1, \ 32] + Y[33, \ 32 + i]$$

FIGURE 5.2.4.4
Details of the stage 3 computation for Algorithm Y. $N = 64$, $p = 8$, and $m = 4$.

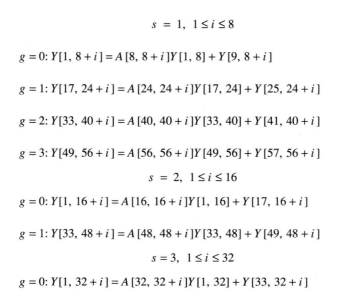

Stage 1	Stage 2	Stage 3	
$1 \le i \le 8$	$1 \le i \le 8$	$s = 1$ $1 \le i \le 8$	$s = 2$ $1 \le i \le 16$
$Q_0 : A[8, \ 8 + i]$			
	$Q_0 : A[16, \ 16 + i]$		
$Q_1 : A[24, \ 24 + i]$		$Q_0 : A[16, \ 24 + i]$	
	$Q_1 : A[32, \ 32 + i]$		
$Q_2 : A[40, \ 40 + i]$		$Q_1 : A[32, \ 40 + i]$	
	$Q_2 : A[48, \ 48 + i]$		$Q_0 - Q_1$
$Q_3 : A[56, \ 56 + i]$		$Q_2 : A[48, \ 56 + i]$	$A[32, \ 48 + i]$

FIGURE 5.2.4.5
Various stages of Algorithm A. $N = 64$, $m = 4$, and $p = 8$.

We now state the main result of this section.

Theorem 5.2.4.5. Using a total of $\frac{3}{2}p$ processors, Algorithms Y and A compute $Y[1, t]$ for $1 \le t \le N$ in $\frac{N}{p}(2 + \log p)$ units of time.

Proof
At the end of stage 1 of Algorithm Y, $Y[1, t]$ for $1 \le t \le m$, and at the end of stage 2, $Y[1, t]$ for $1 \le t \le 2m$ are computed. In stage 3, at the end of each step $s = i$, $Y[1, t]$ for $1 \le t \le 2^{i+1}m$ are computed. Thus the entire sequence of $Y[1, t]$ for $1 \le t \le N$ is available at the end of stage 3. This proves the correctness of Algorithm Y.

Of the $\frac{3}{2}p$ processors, Algorithm Y uses p and Algorithm A uses $\frac{p}{2}$. Further, since Algorithms A and Y are acting in parallel and Algorithm Y takes a longer time than Algorithm A, the total time is that of Algorithm Y. It is readily seen from the description of the algorithms that Algorithm Y takes $\frac{N}{p}(2 + \log p)$ units of time, and the theorem follows. (See Exercise 5.3.)

5.2.5 Recursive Doubling Algorithm

The recursive doubling algorithm is obtained from Lemma 5.2.4.4. By setting $s = 1$ and $t = i$, (5.2.4.5) becomes

$$Y[1, 2i] = A[i, 2i]Y[1, i] + Y[i+1, 2i].\qquad(5.2.5.1)$$

The recursive doubling algorithm based on this relation is given in Fig. 5.2.5.1.

```
/*    N = 2^n : d = (d_1, d_2, ··· , d_N), a = (0, a_2, ··· , a_N) */
        FOR i = 1 STEP i UNTIL N/2 DO
            FOR j ∈ {i+1, i+2, ··· , N}, DO IN PARALLEL
            d_j = d_j + a_j × d_{j-i}
            a_j = a_j × a_{j-i}
            END
        END
```

FIGURE 5.2.5.1
The recursive doubling algorithm.

This Algorithm is astonishingly similar to the cyclic elimination (Exercise 5.4). The interesting feature of this recursive doubling algorithm is that its derivation is quite the same as that of the divide-and-conquer Algorithm in Section 5.2.4, but its mechanics are quite akin to that of cyclic elimination in Section 5.2.2. Thus, our analysis brings out the unity among these four methods of computing the solution of a linear recurrence system in parallel.

5.2.6 General First-Order Recurrence

In this section, we present a generalization of the above methods to a class of first-order recurrences, not necessarily linear. (See Exercise 5.5.) Given x_1, the initial value, let

$$x_i = f(\alpha_i, x_{i-1}), \qquad (5.2.6.1)$$

where α_i, for each i, is a set of parameters; x_i, $i > 0$, are (real) scalars, and $f(., .)$ is a function with appropriately defined domain and codomain. The function $f(., .)$ is called the *recurrence* function. The following are some examples.

(a)
$$\left.\begin{array}{l} x_1 = b_1 \\ x_i = a_i\, x_{i-1} + b_i, \qquad N \geq i \geq 2 \\ \alpha_i = (a_i, b_i). \end{array}\right\} \qquad (5.2.6.2)$$

This is the standard first-order linear recurrence.

(b)
$$\left.\begin{array}{l} x_1 = b_1 \\ x_i = b_i\, x_{i-1}^{a_i}, \qquad N \geq i \geq 2 \\ \alpha_i = (a_i, b_i). \end{array}\right\} \qquad (5.2.6.3)$$

This is a non-linear recurrence.

(c)
$$\left.\begin{array}{l} x_1 = \dfrac{a_1}{c_1} \\[2mm] x_i = \dfrac{a_i + b_i\, x_{i-1}}{c_i + d_i\, x_{i-1}}, \qquad N \geq i \geq 2 \\[2mm] \alpha_i = (a_i, b_i, c_i, d_i). \end{array}\right\} \qquad (5.2.6.4)$$

This is a recurrence involving a rational function.

(d)
$$x_1 = b_1$$

$$x_i = b_i + \frac{a_i}{x_{i-1}}, \quad N \geq i \geq 2 \tag{5.2.6.5}$$

$$\alpha_i = (a_i, b_i).$$

This is the continued fraction expansion.

If $a_i \equiv 1$, then (5.2.6.2) becomes

$$x_i = f(\alpha_i, x_{i-1}) = b_i + x_{i-1},$$

where the recurrence function, $f(., .)$ is clearly *associative,* and in this case the *associative fan-in* algorithm in Chapter 1 can be readily applied to compute x_i's in parallel. But if the a_i's are not identically equal to unity in (5.2.6.2), then in general $f(., .)$ is not associative, that is,

$$f(\alpha, f(\beta, x)) \neq f(f(\alpha, \beta), x). \tag{5.2.6.6}$$

Notice that $f(\alpha, \beta)$ may not even be defined. (See Exercise 5.6.) Thus, in general, when the function $f(., .)$ does satisfy (5.2.6.6), parallel algorithms for computing x_i's are not obvious at all.

In the following, we develop a set of sufficient conditions on $f(., .)$ with which parallel algorithms for computing x_i's can be derived. This sufficient condition is expressed in terms of another function $g(., .)$, related to $f(., .)$, which is defined as follows. The recurrence function $f(., .)$ is said to have a *companion* function $g(., .)$ (Kogge [1973, 1974], Kogge and Stone [1973]) if for all the values of the parameters α_1 and α_2

$$f(\alpha_1, f(\alpha_2, x)) = f(g(\alpha_1, \alpha_2), x). \tag{5.2.6.7}$$

In the following, we first derive the companion function for the four examples given above in the same order.

(a)
$$\begin{aligned} x_i &= a_i x_{i-1} + b_i \\ &= (a_i a_{i-1}) x_{i-2} + (a_i b_{i-1} + b_i) \\ g(\alpha_i, \alpha_{i-1}) &= \alpha_i^{(1)} \\ &= (a_i a_{i-1}, a_i b_{i-1} + b_i) \end{aligned} \tag{5.2.6.8}$$

(b)
$$\begin{aligned} x_i &= b_i x_{i-1}^{a_i} \\ &= b_i b_{i-1}^{a_i} x_{i-2}^{a_i a_{i-1}} \\ g(\alpha_i, \alpha_{i-1}) &= \alpha_i^{(1)} \\ &= (a_i a_{i-1}, b_i b_{i-1}^{a_i}) \end{aligned} \tag{5.2.6.9}$$

(c)
$$\left. \begin{aligned} x_i &= \frac{a_i + b_i\, x_{i-1}}{c_i + d_i\, x_{i-1}} \\ &= \frac{(a_i\, c_{i-1} + b_i\, a_{i-1}) + (a_i\, d_{i-1} + b_i\, b_{i-1})\, x_{i-2}}{(c_i\, c_{i-1} + d_i\, a_{i-1}) + (c_i\, d_{i-1} + d_i\, b_{i-1})\, x_{i-2}} \\ g(\alpha_i, \alpha_{i-1}) &= \alpha_i^{(1)} \\ &= (a_i c_{i-1} + b_i a_{i-1},\ a_i d_{i-1} + b_i b_{i-1}, \\ &\qquad c_i c_{i-1} + d_i a_{i-1},\ c_i d_{i-1} + d_i b_{i-1}) \end{aligned} \right\} \qquad (5.2.6.10)$$

(d)
$$x_i = b_i + \frac{a_i}{x_{i-1}}. \qquad (5.2.6.11)$$

Rewriting x_i as

$$x_i = \frac{a_i + b_i\, x_{i-1}}{x_{i-1}}, \qquad (5.2.6.12)$$

it is readily seen that this is a special case of (c), with $c_i = 0$ and $d_i = 1$.

The following theorem is fundamental and essentially follows from (5.2.6.7).

Theorem 5.2.6.1. If a recurrence function $f(.,.)$ has an associated companion function $g(.,.)$, satisfying (5.2.6.7), then for $\alpha_1, \alpha_2, \alpha_3$, and x,

$$f(g(\alpha_1, g(\alpha_2, \alpha_3)), x) = f(g(g(\alpha_1, \alpha_2), \alpha_3), x).$$

That is, $g(.,.)$ is associative with respect to $f(.,.)$.

Proof
It follows from the definition that

$$f(\alpha_1, f(\alpha_2, f(\alpha_3, x))) = f(\alpha_1, f(g(\alpha_2, \alpha_3), x))$$

$$= f(g(\alpha_1, g(\alpha_2, \alpha_3)), x). \qquad (5.2.6.13)$$

On the other hand, we can also get

$$f(\alpha_1, f(\alpha_2, f(\alpha_3, x))) = f(g(\alpha_1, \alpha_2), f(\alpha_3, x))$$

$$= f(g(g(\alpha_1, \alpha_2), \alpha_3), x). \qquad (5.2.6.14)$$

Combining (5.2.6.13) and (5.2.6.14), the theorem follows.

To understand the importance of this theorem, consider the following:

$x_5 = f(\alpha_5, x_4)$

$= f(\alpha_5, f(\alpha_4, x_3))$

$= f(\alpha_5, f(\alpha_4, f(\alpha_3, x_2)))$

$= f(\alpha_5, f(\alpha_4, f(\alpha_3, f(\alpha_2, x_1))))$

$= f(\alpha_5, f(\alpha_4, f(g(\alpha_3, \alpha_2), x_1)))$

$= f(\alpha_5, f(g(\alpha_4, g(\alpha_3, \alpha_2)), x_1))$

$= f(g(\alpha_5, g(\alpha_4, g(\alpha_3, \alpha_2))), x_1)$

$= f(g(g(\alpha_5, \alpha_4), g(\alpha_3, \alpha_2)), x_1)$ (by Theorem 5.2.6.1).

Refer to Fig. 5.2.6.1 for an illustration. This illustration readily suggests a parallel algorithm for computing x_i, $i = 1 \cdots N$. See Exercises 5.7 and 5.8.

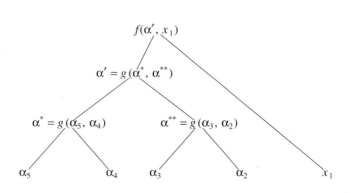

FIGURE 5.2.6.1
An illustration of Theorem 5.2.6.1.

5.3 LINEAR TRIDIAGONAL SYSTEM

In this section, we focus our attention on the problem of solving a linear tridiagonal system, where the individual elements of the tridiagonal matrix are scalars, that is, real or complex numbers. The case when the individual elements of this matrix are themselves matrices is called the *block* tridiagonal system and is considered in the next section. The methods described here are called parallel *direct* methods. A number of parallel *iterative* techniques for solving tridiagonal systems are developed in the exercises. Here again, we discuss four different algorithms for solving this problem. These methods are very similar to the ones discussed in Section 5.2. A number of other parallel methods are pursued in the exercises. We also analyze the communication complexity of mapping these algorithms on hypercube-based architectures. Since these algorithms are generalizations of the ones given in Section 5.2, the communication complexity results presented in this section are also applicable to parallel algorithms for solving linear recurrences.

Tridiagonal systems of both the scalar and block types occur naturally in solving a variety of partial differential equations using finite difference schemes. A discussion of the finite difference schemes is beyond the scope of our book, and we refer the reader to Hockney [1965], Buzbee, Golub, and Nielson [1970], and Varga [1962].

5.3.1 The Cyclic Reduction Algorithm

Let $M = N - 1$ and $N = 2^n$. Consider a linear tridiagonal system

$$\mathbf{Ax} = \mathbf{d}, \tag{5.3.1.1}$$

where

$$\mathbf{A} = \begin{bmatrix} b_1 & c_1 & 0 & 0 & 0 & \cdots & 0 & 0 & 0 \\ a_2 & b_2 & c_2 & 0 & 0 & \cdots & 0 & 0 & 0 \\ 0 & a_3 & b_3 & c_3 & 0 & \cdots & 0 & 0 & 0 \\ . & . & . & . & . & \cdots & . & . & . \\ . & . & . & . & . & \cdots & . & . & . \\ . & . & . & . & . & \cdots & . & . & . \\ 0 & 0 & 0 & 0 & 0 & \cdots & a_{M-1} & b_{M-1} & c_{M-1} \\ 0 & 0 & 0 & 0 & 0 & \cdots & 0 & a_M & b_M \end{bmatrix}, \tag{5.3.1.2}$$

$$\mathbf{x} = (x_1, x_2, \cdots, x_M)^t,$$

and

$$\mathbf{d} = (d_1, d_2, \cdots, d_M)^t.$$

To bring out the basic idea of this type of algorithm, consider the following set of three consecutive equations, centered around $i = 2, 4, 6, 8, \cdots, M - 1$, where

$$a_i^{(0)} = a_i, \quad b_i^{(0)} = b_i, \quad c_i^{(0)} = c_i, \quad \text{and } d_i^{(0)} = d_i,$$

$$a_{i-1}^{(0)} x_{i-2} + b_{i-1}^{(0)} x_{i-1} + c_{i-1}^{(0)} x_i = d_{i-1}^{(0)}, \tag{5.3.1.3}$$

$$a_i^{(0)} x_{i-1} + b_i^{(0)} x_i + c_i^{(0)} x_{i+1} = d_i^{(0)}, \tag{5.3.1.4}$$

$$a_{i+1}^{(0)} x_i + b_{i+1}^{(0)} x_{i+1} + c_{i+1}^{(0)} x_{i+2} = d_{i+1}^{(0)}. \tag{5.3.1.5}$$

Let

$$e_i = -\frac{a_i^{(0)}}{b_{i-1}^{(0)}} \tag{5.3.1.6}$$

and

$$f_i = -\frac{c_i^{(0)}}{b_{i+1}^{(0)}}. \tag{5.3.1.7}$$

Multiplying (5.3.1.3) with e_i and (5.3.1.5) with f_i and adding them to (5.3.1.4), we eliminate x_{i-1} and x_{i+1}, resulting in

$$a_i^{(1)} x_{i-2} + b_i^{(1)} x_i + c_i^{(1)} x_{i+2} = d_i^{(1)}, \tag{5.3.1.8}$$

where

$$e_i^{(1)} = -\frac{a_i^{(0)}}{b_{i-1}^{(0)}}$$

$$f_i^{(1)} = -\frac{c_i^{(0)}}{b_{i+1}^{(0)}}$$

$$a_i^{(1)} = e_i^{(1)} a_{i-1}^{(0)}$$

$$c_i^{(1)} = f_i^{(1)} c_{i+1}^{(0)}$$

$$b_i^{(1)} = b_i^{(0)} + e_i^{(1)} c_{i-1}^{(0)} + f_i^{(1)} a_{i+1}^{(0)}$$

$$d_i^{(1)} = d_i^{(0)} + e_i^{(1)} d_{i-1}^{(0)} + f_i^{(1)} d_{i+1}^{(0)},$$

for $i = 2, 4, 6, \cdots, M - 1$. The cyclic reduction algorithm consists of two phases: (a) the *reduction phase,* during which selective elimination of variables is done and (b) the *back-substitution phase,* during which the values of the eliminated x_i's are recovered.

    (a) *The Reduction Phase:* In this phase, in the first step all the odd-indexed variables $x_1, x_3, x_5, \cdots, x_{2^n-1}$ are eliminated, resulting in $2^{n-1} - 1$ equations. In the second step, variables with indices that are odd multiples of 2, that is, $x_2, x_6, x_{10}, \cdots, x_{2(2^{n-1}-1)},$ are eliminated, resulting in $2^{n-2} - 1$ equations. At the jth step, all the variables with indices that are odd multiples of 2^{j-1}, that is $x_{2^{j-1}}, x_{3 \times 2^{j-1}}, x_{5 \times 2^{j-1}}, \cdots, x_{(2^{n-j+1}-1) \times 2^{j-1}},$ are eliminated, resulting in $2^{(n-j)} - 1$ equations. Thus, after the $(n-1)^{th}$ step, $x_{2^{n-2}}$ and $x_{3 \times 2^{n-2}}$ are eliminated, leaving behind only one equation in the unknown $x_{2^{n-1}}$.

Let $h = 2^{j-1}$. Define

$$
\left.
\begin{aligned}
e_i^{(j)} &= -\frac{a_i^{(j-1)}}{b_{i-h}^{(j-1)}} \\[6pt]
f_i^{(j)} &= -\frac{c_i^{(j-1)}}{b_{i+h}^{(j-1)}} \\[6pt]
a_i^{(j)} &= e_i^{(j)}\, a_{i-h}^{(j-1)} \\[4pt]
c_i^{(j)} &= f_i^{(j)}\, c_{i+h}^{(j-1)} \\[4pt]
b_i^{(j)} &= b_i^{(j-1)} + e_i^{(j)}\, c_{i-h}^{(j-1)} + f_i^{(j)}\, a_{i+h}^{(j-1)} \\[4pt]
d_i^{(j)} &= d_i^{(j-1)} + e_i^{(j)}\, d_{i-h}^{(j-1)} + f_i^{(j)}\, d_{i+h}^{(j-1)}.
\end{aligned}
\right\}
\qquad (5.3.1.9)
$$

for $i = 2 \times 2^{j-1},\, 4 \times 2^{j-1},\, 6 \times 2^{j-1},\, \cdots ,\, (2^{n-j+1} - 2) \times 2^{j-1}$. Let

$$
p_i^{(j)} = (a_i^{(j)},\, b_i^{(j)},\, c_i^{(j)},\, d_i^{(j)}\,), \qquad (5.3.1.10)
$$

where

$$
p_i^{(j)} = (0,\, 1,\, 0,\, 0), \quad \text{for } i \le 0 \text{ and } i \ge N,
$$

and

$$
x_i = 0, \quad \text{for } i \le 0 \text{ and } i \ge N.
$$

The algorithm for the reduction phase is given in Fig. 5.3.1.1.

FOR $j = 1$ TO $n - 1$ DO
    FOR $i \in \{\, 2^j,\, 2 \times 2^j,\, 3 \times 2^j,\, \cdots ,\, 2^n - 2^j \,\}$ DO IN PARALLEL
        COMPUTE $p_i^{(j)}$ using (5.3.1.9)
    END
  END

FIGURE 5.3.1.1
Reduction phase of the cyclic reduction algorithm.

The interaction between various parallel computations for $M = 15$ are graphically represented in Fig. 5.3.1.2. In this graph, the quantities $p_i^{(j)}$ and x_i are associated with node i. The labels of the edges correspond to the computation step of the reduction phase. Notice that the computation of $p_i^{(j)}$ in node i involves (a) $p_i^{(j-1)}$ in node i, (b) $p_{i-h}^{(j-1)}$ from node $i-h$, and (c) $p_{i+h}^{(j-1)}$ from node $i+h$. This fact is denoted by the directed edges from node $i+h$ and $i-h$ to node i with label j. Since this graph describes only the logical connections needed between various interacting computations, we refer to these graphs as *communication* graphs.

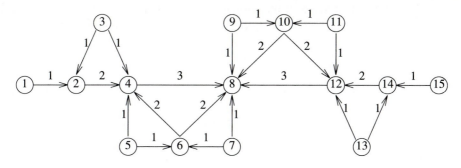

FIGURE 5.3.1.2
Communication graph of the reduction phase. $M = 15$.

(b) *The Back-Substitution Phase:* This phase is initialized by first computing x_{2^n-1} using

$$x_{2^n-1} = \frac{d_{2^{n-1}}^{(n-1)}}{b_{2^{n-1}}^{(n-1)}}. \qquad (5.3.1.11)$$

The rest of this phase consists of $(n-1)$ steps, and for convenience we number steps starting from $(n-1)$ to 1 in steps of -1.

At the $(n-1)^{th}$ step, two variables with indices that are odd multiples of 2^{n-2}, that is, $x_{2^{n-2}}$ and $x_{3 \times 2^{n-2}}$, are recovered. In general, at the $(n-j)^{th}$ step, 2^j variables with indices that are odd multiples of 2^{n-j-1}, that is, $x_{2^{n-j-1}}, x_{3 \times 2^{n-j-1}}, \cdots, x_{(2^{j+1}-1) \times 2^{n-j-1}}$, are recovered. At step 1, 2^{n-1} variables with odd indices, that is, $x_1, x_3, x_5, \cdots, x_{2^n-1}$, are all recovered. These computations are arranged in the form of an algorithm given in Fig. 5.3.1.3.

FOR $k = n - 1$ TO 1 STEP $- 1$ DO

FOR $i \in \{ 2^{k-1}, 3 \times 2^{k-1}, 5 \times 2^{k-1}, \cdots, 2^n - 2^{k-1} \}$ DO IN PARALLEL
  $h = 2^{k-1}$

  COMPUTE $x_i = \dfrac{d_i^{(k-1)} - a_i^{(k-1)} x_{i-h} - c_i^{(k-1)} x_{i+h}}{b_i^{(k-1)}}$

  END
END

FIGURE 5.3.1.3
Back-substitution phase of the cyclic reduction algorithm.

The interaction between the various parallel computations for $M = 15$ is again graphically illustrated in Fig. 5.3.1.4. Comparing the two graphs in Figs. 5.3.1.2 and 5.3.1.4, it is clear that the communication requirements of the reduction and the back-substitution phases are similar in the sense that one graph is obtained from the other by simply reversing the direction of the edges. Henceforth, in view of this similarity, the communication graphs of the two phases are combined to give a labeled undirected graph. Further, in the following, we restrict our attention to the reduction phase. All the results would immediately apply to the back-substitution phase as well. Examples of the (undirected) communication graph of the cyclic reduction of $M = 15$ and $M = 31$ are given in Figs. 5.3.1.5 and 5.3.1.6.

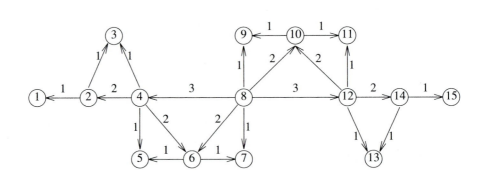

FIGURE 5.3.1.4
Communication graph of the back-substitution phase. $M = 15$.

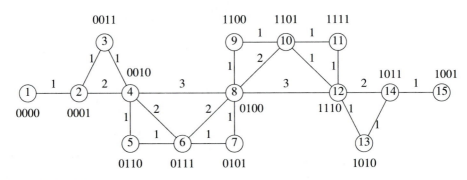

FIGURE 5.3.1.5
Communication graph of the cyclic reduction. $M = 15$.

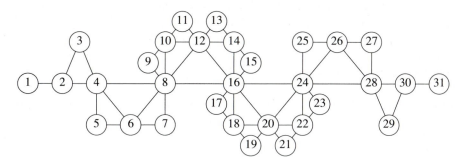

FIGURE 5.3.1.6
Communication graph of the cyclic reduction. $M = 31$.

The processor and time bounds for this algorithm are contained in the following theorem.

Theorem 5.3.1.1. The linear tridiagonal system in (5.3.1.1) can be solved using the cyclic reduction algorithm in $O(\log N)$ steps using $O(N)$ processors, and the algorithm performs a total of $O(N)$ operations.

Proof
Excluding the sign change, (5.3.1.9) requires 12 operations. Thus, from Fig. 5.3.1.1, the reduction phase requires a total of

$$12 \sum_{j=1}^{n-1} (2^{n-j} - 1) = 12[N - \log N - 1]$$

operations. Similarly, the back-substitution phase requires no more than

$$5 \sum_{j=1}^{n} 2^{n-j} = 5(N - 1)$$

operations. Clearly, both the phases take $O(\log N)$ steps using $O(N)$ processors and the theorem follows.

Since the degree of parallelism varies from step to step, we encourage the reader to develop a schedule of computations that will utilize as many processors as possible.

We now discuss the problem of mapping this algorithm onto a hypercube architecture.[1] The following result due to Johnsson [1984] on the mapping of the

---

[1] In the rest of this section, a working knowledge of the standard properties of the hypercube interconnection and the role of the Gray codes in mapping standard graphs into hypercubes is assumed. Refer to Chapter 2 for details.

communication graph onto the base-2 cube is fundamental. If the computation of $p_i^{(j)}$ is assigned to a node in a base-2 cube whose label (in binary) corresponds to the $(i-1)^{th}$ code word in the binary reflected Gray code (Chapter 2), then all the communications in any step of the reduction phase are restricted to processors that are at a distance (Hamming distance in a base-2 cube) no more than 2 apart. In Fig. 5.3.1.5, such an assignment is shown by the binary label outside of each node. As an example, the label outside of node 1 is 0000, since the latter is the 0th code word in the set of binary reflected Gray codes of length 4. Likewise, since 1110 is the eleventh code word, the label outside of node 12 is 1110. In other words, under this mapping the nodes that are *logically adjacent* (in the communication graph) are *not* mapped onto processors that are *physically adjacent* in the base-2 cube. Counting the cost of one communication between processors at *d distance* apart as *d units,* it can be shown (Johnsson [1984]) that the total communication cost of the reduction phase resulting from the above mapping is $2n - 3$. While this is of the same order of magnitude as the computational complexity, since communication in the contemporary architectures is many times more expensive than basic arithmetic operations (Ouchark, Davis, Lakshmivarahan, and Dhall [1987]) it is interesting to ask if there exists a mapping of the reduction phase with still lower communication cost. Recall that the absolute minimum for the communication cost is equal to the number of steps in the reduction phase. This discussion immediately leads to the following.

A. Mapping Cyclic Reduction onto a Hypercube. A mapping of the cyclic reduction algorithm onto a base-2 cube is said to be *desirable* if it achieves the minimum communication cost. Notice that under desirable mapping, the communications are restricted to physically adjacent processors, that is, the *dilation factor* for desirable mapping is unity (refer to Chapter 2).

Our first result of this section relates to *non-existence* of a *desirable* mapping of the cyclic reduction on the base-2 cube.

Theorem 5.3.1.2. In any mapping of the reduction phase onto an N-node base-2 cube, it is necessary that at least $\dfrac{n}{2} - 1$ steps of the reduction phase involve communication between processors that are at distance 2 or more apart.

Proof
Consider an arbitrary mapping of the reduction phase onto an N-node base-2 cube. Let m be the label of a nodal processor that is responsible for the computation of $p_{2^n-1}^{(j)}$. It is clear from the communication graph that this nodal processor must communicate with two distinct processors in *each* of the $n - 1$ steps of the reduction phase. If each of these communications is to be restricted to processors that are at *unit* distance from m, then clearly this designated nodal

processor m must necessarily have $2(n-1)$ neighbors. But, in an N-node $(N = 2^n)$ base-2 cube there are only n neighbors to each node. Thus, the nodal processor m must communicate with at least $n - 2$ processors that are at distance 2 or more. Since each step involves a pair of processors, the theorem follows.

The following corollary is immediate.

Corollary 5.3.1.3. The mapping of the cyclic reduction onto an N-node base-2 cube based on the binary reflected Gray code is very nearly optimal.

Proof

At most $\dfrac{n}{2}$ steps can be restricted to processors at unit distance apart. Since the rest of the $\dfrac{n}{2} - 1$ steps should involve communication between processors at distance 2 or more apart, clearly the reduction requires a minimum of $\dfrac{n}{2} + 2(\dfrac{n}{2} - 1) = \dfrac{3}{2}n - 2$ communication steps. Since Johnsson's method (Johnsson [1984]) requires a total of only $2n - 3$ unit communication steps, it is very nearly optimal (up to a constant of multiplication).

We now turn to analyze the existence of *desirable* mapping of the reduction phase onto an N-node base-b cube for $N \geq b > 2$. Recall that the basic requirement of the desirable mapping is to consider the logical neighbors of the communication graph as physical neighbors as well. From this consideration, the following theorem is rather immediate.

Theorem 5.3.1.4. There exists a desirable mapping of the reduction phase onto the complete $(M, M, 1)$ cube.

Proof

The complete $(M, M, 1)$ cube is a complete graph on M nodes. Since the nodes in this cube are numbered 0 through $M - 1$, by assigning $p_i^{(j)}$ and x_i to node $i - 1$ of this cube, we readily obtain a desirable mapping of the reduction phase.

Since the complete $(M, M, 1)$ cube is too expensive to be practical, in the following we analyze complete (L, b, k) cubes with $2 < b < N$ and $k \geq 2$. In this cube, any node x has a label $x = x_k x_{k-1} \cdots x_1$, where $x_i \in \; <b>$ for all $i = 1, \cdots, k$. The following lemma is fundamental to our analysis.

Lemma 5.3.1.5. Any three-node graph connected in a triangle can be mapped onto three mutually adjacent nodes (say with labels x, y, and z) on a complete (L, b, k) cube if and only if x, y, and z differ in the same base-b digit position, that is, x, y, and z belong to the same basic projection.

Proof

Let $G = (V, E)$, with $V = \{a, b, c\}$ and $E = \{(a, b), (b, c), (c, a)\}$, be the given three-node (undirected) graph. Let f be a mapping such that $f(a) = x$, $f(b) = y$, and $f(c) = z$. Clearly x and y are neighbors if and only if

$$x = x_k \, x_{k-1} \, \cdots \, x_{j-1} \, x_j \, x_{j+1} \, \cdots \, x_1$$

and

$$y = x_k \, x_{k-1} \, \cdots \, x_{j+1} \, y_j \, x_{j-1} \, \cdots \, x_1, \qquad x_j \neq y_j.$$

Let $z = z_k \, z_{k-1} \, \cdots \, z_1$, where $z_q \neq x_q$ and $z_i = x_i$ for all $i \neq q$, that is, z is a neighbor of x. But, clearly, both $h_b(x, z)$ and $h_b(y, z)$ are unity if and only if $q = j$, and $z_q \neq y_j \neq x_j$. Hence the lemma.

The following corollary is widely applicable.

Corollary 5.3.1.6. Consider a set of four nodes a, b, c, and d connected in the form of two triangles with a common edge as in Fig. 5.3.1.7. Under the desirable mapping, the fourth node (say d) belongs to the same projection as the first three nodes (a, b, c) do.

Proof

Let a, b, and c be assigned to nodes x_a, x_b, and x_c in a cube that differs in, say, the first base-b digit position. Notice that unless d is mapped onto a node x_d that differs from nodes x_b and x_c in the first digit position, d cannot be simultaneously the neighbor of x_b and x_c. Hence the corollary.

To appreciate the relevance of Lemma 5.3.1.5, observe that the basic (structural) building block of the communication graphs given in Figs. 5.3.1.5 and 5.3.1.6 is a triangle or a (simple) cycle of length 3. From the lemma, it is clear that any desirable mapping must map the three nodes of every simple cycle of length 3 onto the same basic projection. Since there are no odd cycles in a base-2 cube, this lemma further *seconds* the conclusion of Theorem 5.3.1.2. A base-4 cube, on the other hand, admits a variety of odd cycles (including cycles of length 3; refer to Chapter 2 for details). This observation might lead one to suspect the existence of desirable mapping onto the base-4 cube. However, the following theorem implies that for $N \geq 16$, there does *not* exist a desirable mapping on a base-4 cube either.

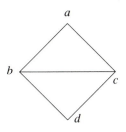

FIGURE 5.3.1.7
The four-node graph used in Corollary 5.3.1.6.

Theorem 5.3.1.7. There does not exist a desirable mapping of the reduction phase onto a complete (L, b, k) cube where $L \geq N$, $k \geq 2$, and $2 < b < N$ unless $b \geq \dfrac{N}{4} + 1$.

Proof

It would be helpful to understand this proof using the examples in Figs. 5.3.1.5 and 5.3.1.6.

Consider the portion of the communication graph between nodes 2^{n-2} and 2^{n-1} given in Fig. 5.3.1.8. Clearly nodes 2^{n-2}, $2^{n-2} + 2^{n-3}$, and 2^{n-1} form a triangle and hence under the desirable mapping must be in the same basic projection, that is, they must be mapped onto three nodes on the cube whose labels differ in the same digit position, which we assume without loss of generality to be the first base-b digit position.

Now referring to Fig. 5.3.1.8 again, we find that nodes 2^{n-2}, $2^{n-2} + 2^{n-4}$, and $2^{n-2} + 2^{n-3}$ form a triangle and so do the nodes $2^{n-2} + 2^{n-3}$, $2^{n-2} + 2^{n-3} + 2^{n-4}$, and 2^{n-1}. Further these two triangles share a common side with the triangle of the above paragraph. Hence, by Corollary 5.3.1.6, all nodes 2^{n-2}, $2^{n-2} + 2^{n-4}$, $2^{n-2} + 2^{n-3}$, $2^{n-2} + 2^{n-3} + 2^{n-4}$, and 2^{n-1}, under the desirable mapping, must belong to the same basic projection.

Continuing along this line, we can readily see that all the $2^{n-2} + 1$ nodes, 2^{n-2}, $2^{n-2} + 1$, $2^{n-2} + 2$, $\cdots$, 2^{n-1}, must belong to the same basic projection. Since a basic projection in a base-b cube contains exactly b nodes, it is necessary that $b \geq 2^{n-2} + 1 = \dfrac{N}{4} + 1$. Hence the theorem.

Notice that this theorem only provides a necessary condition for the existence of desirable maps. The actual map, if it exists, still has to be found by other means. To further understand the importance of this theorem, recall that a

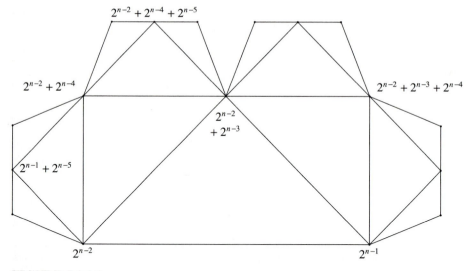

FIGURE 5.3.1.8

The basic structure of the portion of the communication graph between 2^{n-2} and 2^{n-1}.

complete $(L, \frac{N}{4} + 1, 2)$ cube has $L = (\frac{N}{4} + 1)^2$ nodes and $\frac{N}{4}(\frac{N}{4} + 1)^2$ edges. The complete $(M, M, 1)$, cube on the other hand, has M nodes and $\frac{M(M-1)}{2}$ edges, where $M = N - 1$ and $N = 2^n$. Thus, when $N = 16$, a complete $(15, 15, 1)$ cube has 15 nodes and 105 edges. But a complete $(L, 5, 2)$ cube has $L = 25$ nodes and 100 edges. An example of a desirable map on the $(25, 5, 2)$ cube for $M = 15$ is given in Fig. 5.3.1.9. Notice that this latter cube, at the cost of *five* edges, needs *ten* more nodal processors.

But for $N > 16$, since the complete $(L, \frac{N}{4} + 1, 2)$ cube has more nodes and edges than the $(M, M, 1)$ cube, it is obvious that the complete $(M, M, 1)$ cube is the most economical of the cubes on which desirable mapping of the reduction phase exists.

B. Stability Analysis. We conclude this section by discussing an inherent advantage of the reduction phase in the cases when the matrix **A** is *diagonally dominant*. To this end, following Hockney and Jesshope [1981], define the diagonal dominance μ of **A** as

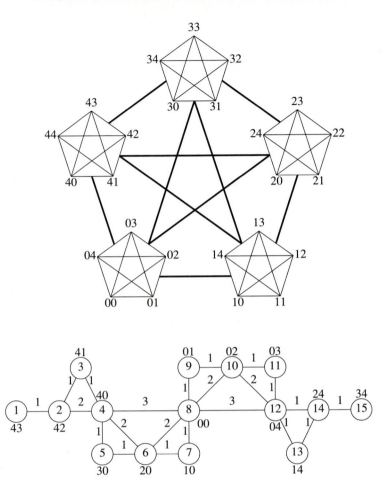

FIGURE 5.3.1.9

An example of an embedding of the reduction phase onto a complete (25, 5, 2) cube for $M = 15$. For example, node 8 of the communication graph is assigned to node 00 of the cube, 1 to 43 of the cube, etc.

$$\mu = \min_{i}\{ \, | \frac{b_i}{a_i} |, \, | \frac{b_i}{c_i} | \, \}. \tag{5.3.1.12}$$

Let $\mu = \dfrac{b}{a}$ and consider the system

$$a \, x_{i-1} + b \, x_i + a \, x_{i+1} = d_i, \tag{5.3.1.13}$$

for $i = 1, 2, \cdots, M$. It follows that the original system (5.3.1.1) is at least as diagonally dominant as (5.3.1.13), which in turn implies that the former system can be solved at least as accurately as the latter one. In light of this observation, we move on to solving (5.3.1.13).

Let $a^{(0)} \equiv a$ and $b^{(0)} \equiv b$. Now, specializing (5.3.1.9) to this case, we obtain

$$
\left.
\begin{aligned}
a^{(j)} &= -\frac{(a^{(j-1)})^2}{b^{(j-1)}} \\[2mm]
b^{(j)} &= b^{(j-1)} - \frac{2(a^{(j-1)})^2}{b^{(j-1)}} \\[2mm]
d_i^{(j)} &= d_i^{(j-1)} - \frac{a^{(j-1)}}{b^{(j-1)}}(d_{i-h}^{(j-1)} + d_{i+h}^{(j-1)}).
\end{aligned}
\right\}
\tag{5.3.1.14}
$$

System (5.3.1.13), after j steps of the reduction, becomes

$$
a^{(j)}\, x_{i-h} + b^{(j)}\, x_i + a^{(j)}\, x_{i+h} = d_i^{(j)},
\tag{5.3.1.15}
$$

where $h = 2^j$ and $i = 2^j,\, 2 \times 2^j,\, 3 \times 2^j,\, \cdots,\, (2^n - 2^j)$. Thus,

$$
x_i = \frac{d_i^{(j)}}{b^{(j)}} - \frac{a^{(j)}}{b^{(j)}}\,[x_{i-h} + x_{i+h}].
\tag{5.3.1.16}
$$

To understand the effect of diagonal dominance on the solution, define

$$
\mu^{(j)} = \left|\frac{b^{(j)}}{a^{(j)}}\right|,
\tag{5.3.1.17}
$$

where $\mu^{(0)} = \left|\dfrac{b}{a}\right|$. Rewriting (5.3.1.16), we obtain

$$
\left| x_i - \frac{d_i^{(j)}}{b^{(j)}}\right| = \frac{|x_{i-h} + x_{i+h}|}{\mu^{(j)}}.
\tag{5.3.1.18}
$$

Now, from (5.3.1.14), we obtain

$$
\mu^{(j)} = |(\mu^{(j-1)})^2 - 2|.
\tag{5.3.1.19}
$$

Thus, if $\mu^{(0)} = \mu > 2$, then

$$
\mu^{2^{j-1}} < \mu^{(j)} \le \mu^{2^j}.
\tag{5.3.1.20}
$$

Refer to Table 5.3.1.1 for some typical values of $\mu^{(j)}$.

If it is known *a priori* that x_i's are uniformly bounded and n is large, since $\mu^{(j)}$ grows exponentially, one could find a $j^* < n - 1$ such that the term on the right-hand side of (5.3.1.18) is negligible. In other words, we could terminate the reduction process after j^* steps and recover the eliminated variable by the back-substitution process. Such a truncated reduction process could result in enormous saving in time. Thus, if ε is the allowed relative error in the solution, and if the x_i's are bounded by unity, then from (5.3.1.18)

TABLE 5.3.1.1
$\mu^{(0)} = \mu$

j	$\mu = 2.5$ $\mu^{(j)}$	$\mu = 3.5$ $\mu^{(j)}$	$\mu = 4$ $\mu^{(j)}$
1	4.25	10.25	14.0
2	16.06	103.06	194.0
3	2.56×10^2	1.06×10^4	3.76×10^4
4	6.55×10^4	1.13×10^8	1.42×10^9
5	4.30×10^9	1.27×10^{16}	2.00×10^{18}
6	1.85×10^{19}	1.62×10^{32}	4.02×10^{36}

$$\frac{|\,(x_{i-h} + x_{i+h})\,|}{\mu^{(j)}} \le \frac{2}{\mu^{(j)}} \le \varepsilon,$$

that is,

$$\mu^{(j)} \ge 2\,\varepsilon^{-1}.$$

From (5.3.1.20), a sufficient condition for this to be true is

$$\mu^{2^{j^*-1}} = 2\,\varepsilon^{-1},$$

that is,

$$j^* = 1 + \log \left\{ \frac{\log 2\varepsilon^{-1}}{\log \mu} \right\}. \tag{5.3.1.21}$$

As an example, if $\varepsilon = 2^{-20} \approx 10^{-6}$ and $\mu = 4$, then $j^* = 4.3928$, that is, five iterations are needed. Clearly, for this analysis to be useful, it is necessary that $j^* < n$, where $N = 2^n - 1$.

5.3.2 The Cyclic Elimination Scheme

Let

$$\mathbf{Ax} = \mathbf{d} \tag{5.3.2.1}$$

be a tridiagonal system of the type (5.3.1.1), except that $\mathbf{A}$ is a tridiagonal matrix of size $N = 2^n$. The cyclic elimination scheme is given in Fig. 5.3.2.1. The proof of the following theorem on time and processor bounds is left as an exercise.

FOR $j = 1$ TO n STEP 1 DO

    FOR $i \in \{ 1, 2, 3, \cdots, N \}$ DO IN PARALLEL

        COMPUTE $p_i^{(j)}$ USING (5.3.1.9)

    END

END

FOR $i \in \{ 1, 2, 3, \cdots, N \}$ DO IN PARALLEL

    COMPUTE $x_i = \dfrac{d_i^{(n)}}{b_i^{(n)}}$

END

FIGURE 5.3.2.1
The Cyclic Elimination scheme.

Theorem 5.3.2.1. The linear tridiagonal system in (5.3.2.1) can be solved using the cyclic elimination scheme in $O(\log N)$ steps using $O(N)$ processors, with a total of $O(N \log N)$ operations.

The communication graphs for this algorithm for $N = 8$ and 16 are given in Fig. 5.3.2.2. From these graphs, it is clear that each node communicates with *no more than two* distinct (logical) neighbors in a given step and that the maximum degree of a node is $2n - 1$. Since there are only n neighbors to a node in a base-2 cube, the following analog of Theorem 5.3.1.2 and Corollary 5.3.1.3 is immediate.

Theorem 5.3.2.2. In any mapping of the cyclic elimination onto a base-2 cube, it is necessary that at least $\dfrac{n}{2} - 1$ steps involve communication between processors that are at distance 2 or more apart. Further, the mapping based on binary reflected Gray code is also very nearly optimal for cyclic elimination.

Comparing the algorithm for the reduction phase of cyclic reduction with the cyclic elimination, it follows that the communication graph for the reduction phase is a subgraph of that of the cyclic elimination. The following theorem is a direct analog of Theorem 5.3.1.7 for the cyclic reduction.

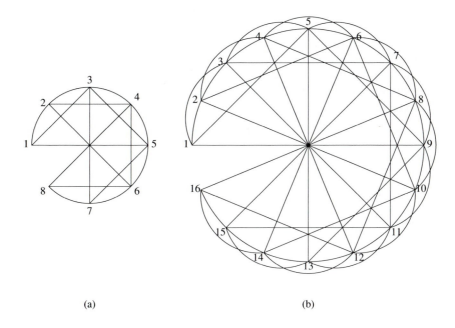

(a)   (b)

FIGURE 5.3.2.2
Communication graph of the cyclic elimination algorithm.

Theorem 5.3.2.3. There does not exist a desirable mapping of the cyclic elimination onto a complete (L, b, k) cube where $L \geq N$, $k \geq 1$, and $2 < b \leq N$, unless $b = N$, $k = 1$, and $L = N$.

Proof
The proof is very similar to that of Theorem 5.3.1.7 and essentially follows by repeated application of Lemma 5.3.1.5 and Corollary 5.3.1.6.

Thus for all $N \geq 2$, the complete $(N, N, 1)$ cube is the most economical topology on which desirable mapping of this algorithm exists.

The modification of the cyclic elimination algorithm for the diagonally dominant case is quite straightforward. Clearly, we need to compute $p_i^{(j)}$ for $i \in \{1, 2, \cdots, N\}$ only for $j = 1, 2, \cdots, j^*$, where j^* is given by (5.3.1.21). The x_i's are then computed in parallel in one division.

5.3.3 The Recursive Doubling Algorithm

The Gaussian elimination algorithm provides the mathematical framework for both the recursive doubling due to Stone [1973b] and a new algorithm, which is a modified recursive doubling algorithm, due to Lakshmivarahan and Dhall [1986a], analyzed in the next section.

It is well known that an $N \times N$ matrix $\mathbf{A}$ can be uniquely expressed as a product of a lower triangular matrix $\mathbf{L}$ and an upper triangular matrix $\mathbf{U}$. (See Exercise 5.9 for a condition.) That is,

$$\mathbf{A} = \mathbf{LU}, \tag{5.3.3.1}$$

where

$$\mathbf{L} = \begin{bmatrix} e_1^{-1} & 0 & 0 & \cdots & 0 & 0 & 0 \\ a_2 & e_2^{-1} & 0 & \cdots & 0 & 0 & 0 \\ 0 & a_3 & e_3^{-1} & \cdots & 0 & 0 & 0 \\ \cdot & \cdot & \cdot & \cdots & \cdot & \cdot & \cdot \\ \cdot & \cdot & \cdot & \cdots & \cdot & \cdot & \cdot \\ \cdot & \cdot & \cdot & \cdots & \cdot & \cdot & \cdot \\ 0 & 0 & 0 & \cdots & a_{N-1} & e_{N-1}^{-1} & 0 \\ 0 & 0 & 0 & \cdots & 0 & a_N & e_N^{-1} \end{bmatrix} \tag{5.3.3.2}$$

and

$$\mathbf{U} = \begin{bmatrix} 1 & w_1 & 0 & \cdots & 0 & 0 \\ 0 & 1 & w_2 & \cdots & 0 & 0 \\ 0 & 0 & 1 & \cdots & 0 & 0 \\ \cdot & \cdot & \cdot & \cdots & \cdot & \cdot \\ \cdot & \cdot & \cdot & \cdots & \cdot & \cdot \\ \cdot & \cdot & \cdot & \cdots & \cdot & \cdot \\ 0 & 0 & 0 & \cdots & 1 & w_{N-1} \\ 0 & 0 & 0 & \cdots & 0 & 1 \end{bmatrix} . \tag{5.3.3.3}$$

Using this decomposition, the linear system $\mathbf{Ax} = \mathbf{d}$ can be solved in two stages as

$$\mathbf{Lg} = \mathbf{d} \tag{5.3.3.4}$$

and

$$\mathbf{Ux} = \mathbf{g}. \tag{5.3.3.5}$$

Stated in the component form, (5.3.3.1), (5.3.3.4), and (5.3.3.5) reduce to a system of three recurrences given in the following order.

(a) $\qquad w_i = \dfrac{c_i}{b_i - a_i \, w_{i-1}}, \qquad$ for $2 \le i \le N-1,$ $\qquad\qquad$ (5.3.3.6)

where $w_1 = \dfrac{c_1}{b_1}$. Also, it can be shown that $e_i = \dfrac{w_i}{c_i}$ for $1 \le i \le N.$

(b) $\qquad g_i = \dfrac{d_i - a_i \, g_{i-1}}{b_i - a_i \, w_{i-1}}, \qquad$ for $2 \le i \le N,$ $\qquad\qquad$ (5.3.3.7)

with $g_1 = \dfrac{d_1}{b_1}$, and

(c) $\qquad\qquad x_i = g_i - w_i \, x_{i+1}, \qquad$ for $1 \le i \le N-1,$ $\qquad\qquad$ (5.3.3.8)

where $x_N = g_N.$

Notice that (5.3.3.6) is a first-order non-linear recurrence but (5.3.3.7) and (5.3.3.8) are first-order linear recurrences. The method of recursive doubling consists in first converting the first-order non-linear recurrence (5.3.3.6) into a first-order linear recurrence in the vector form. To this end, define

$$ w_i = \frac{y_i}{y_{i+1}}. \qquad\qquad (5.3.3.9) $$

Substituting in (5.3.3.6) and simplifying, we obtain

$$ \mathbf{V}_i = \mathbf{A}_i \, \mathbf{V}_{i-1}, \qquad \text{for } 2 \le i \le N-1, \qquad\qquad (5.3.3.10) $$

where

$$ \mathbf{V}_i = (\, y_i, \, y_{i+1} \,)^t, \qquad \mathbf{V}_1 = (\, 1, \, \frac{b_1}{c_1} \,)^t, \qquad\qquad (5.3.3.11) $$

and

$$ \mathbf{A}_i = \begin{bmatrix} 0 & 1 \\[2mm] -\dfrac{a_i}{c_i} & \dfrac{b_i}{c_i} \end{bmatrix}. \qquad\qquad (5.3.3.12) $$

(See Exercise 5.5.)

Thus, in the framework of recursive doubling, the problem of solving (5.3.1.1) reduces to one of solving the following two *generic* problems.

Problem 1. Solve for $Z_i,\ i = 2, \cdots, M,$ when

$$ Z_i = f_i \, Z_{i-1} + h_i, \qquad\qquad (5.3.3.13) $$

where $Z_1, (\, f_2, f_3, \cdots, f_M \,),$ and $(\, h_2, \cdots, h_M \,)$ are given.

Problem 2. Solve for $\mathbf{V}_i, i = 2$ to $M,$ when

$$\mathbf{V}_i = \mathbf{A}_i \, \mathbf{V}_{i-1}, \tag{5.3.3.14}$$

where $\mathbf{V}_1$ and $\mathbf{A}_2, \mathbf{A}_3, \cdots, \mathbf{A}_M$ are given.

Further, comparing (5.3.3.13) and (5.3.3.14), it readily follows that any parallel algorithm for solving (5.3.3.13) can be readily adapted to solving (5.3.3.14) by simply extending the scalar operations to compatible matrix - matrix and matrix - vector operations. Thus, in the following, we merely concentrate on analyzing the communication complexity of solving (5.3.3.13) using recursive doubling. To this end, observe that the solution to (5.3.3.13) in closed form is given by

$$Z_i = \sum_{j=1}^{i} \left[\prod_{s=j+1}^{i} f_s \right] h_j. \tag{5.3.3.15}$$

To obtain the recursive doubling algorithm for computing (5.3.3.15), define

$$A\,[u,\,v\,] = \prod_{r=u+1}^{v} f_r \tag{5.3.3.16}$$

and

$$Y\,[s,\,t\,] = \sum_{j=s}^{t} A\,[j,\,t\,]\,h_j, \quad \text{for } s < t, \tag{5.3.3.17}$$

where vacuous products are taken to be unity.

Many useful properties of $A[.,\,.]$ and $Y[.,\,.]$, stated in the following lemma are proved in Section 5.2.4.

Lemma 5.3.3.1.

(P1) $A\,[u,\,v\,] = 1$, for all $u \geq v$.

(P2) $A\,[u,\,v+m\,] = A\,[u,\,v\,]\,A\,[v,\,v+m\,]$, for $u \leq v$ and $m > 0$.

(P3) $Y[s,\,t\,] = f_t\,Y[s,\,t-1\,] + h_t$.

(P4) $Y\,[s,\,t+i\,] = A[t,\,t+i\,]\,Y\,[s,\,t\,] + Y\,[t+1,\,t+i\,]$,   for $s \leq t$ and $i > 0$.

(P5) $Z_t = Y[1,\,t\,]$,   for $1 \leq t \leq n$.

The recursive doubling algorithm, given in Fig. 5.3.3.1, is obtained by setting $s = 1$ and $t = i$ in (P4), that is, from

$$Y[1,\,2i\,] = A[i,\,2i\,]\,Y[1,\,i\,] + Y[i+1,\,2i\,].$$

The communication graphs of this algorithm for $N = 8$ and 16 are given in Fig. 5.3.3.2. Now comparing the graphs in Fig. 5.3.3.2 with those in Fig. 5.3.2.2, it is readily seen that the communication pattern of this recursive doubling algorithm is astonishingly similar to that of cyclic elimination. Thus, all the conclusions of Section 5.3.2 are directly applicable to the recursive doubling algorithm.

Step 1: FOR $j = 1$ TO N STEP 1 DO

    $Y_j = h_j$

    $m_j = f_j$

    END

Step 2: FOR $i = 1$ STEP i UNTIL $\dfrac{N}{2}$ DO

        FOR $j \in \{ i+1, i+2, \cdots, N \}$ DO IN PARALLEL

        $Y_j = Y_j + m_j \times Y_{j-i}$

        $m_j = m_j \times m_{j-i}$

      END

    END

FIGURE 5.3.3.1

Recursive doubling algorithm.

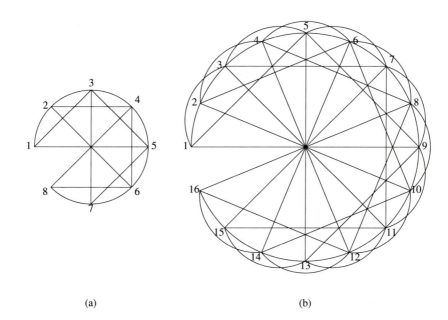

           (a)   (b)

FIGURE 5.3.3.2

Communication graph of the recursive doubling algorithm.

5.3.4 Modified Recursive Doubling Algorithm

Following the developments in Section 5.2.4, an algorithm for computing Z_i's in (5.3.3.13) can be derived again from Lemma 5.3.3.1. Let $N = 2^n$, $p = 2^k$, and $N = 2mp$, for some $m \geq 1$. Let $1 \leq s \leq k$ and $0 \leq g \leq 2^{k-s} - 1$. The algorithm consists of two parts: (a) Algorithm Y, which computes $Y[s, t]$ and (b) Algorithm A, which computes only those $A[u, v]$ that are needed by $Y[s, t]$. These two algorithms work in parallel and are described in Section 5.2.4. In the following, we merely concentrate on analyzing the communication complexity.

The communication graphs of Algorithm Y for $N = 8$ and $N = 16$ are given in Fig. 5.3.4.1. It can be shown that, in general, node $\dfrac{N}{2}$ of these graphs has the maximum degree of $\dfrac{N}{2} + n - 1$. Clearly, there does not exist any desirable mapping of Algorithm A on a base-2 cube. Another peculiarity of this algorithm is that even under binary reflected Gray code mapping on a base-2 cube, the maximum distance between communicating processors is *not* limited to 2. In fact, under any coding on a base-2, this maximum distance is equal to the diameter of the cube. Further, using arguments similar to those in Theorem 5.3.1.7, the following result can be proved, and the proof is omitted.

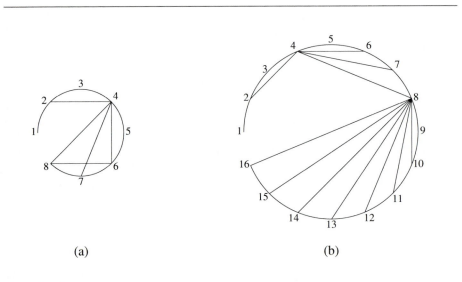

(a)   (b)

FIGURE 5.3.4.1
Communication graph of Algorithm Y.

Theorem 5.3.4.1. There does not exist a desirable mapping of the new algorithm onto a complete (L, b, k) cube, where $L \geq N$, $k \geq 1$, and $2 < b \leq N$, unless $b \geq \dfrac{N}{2} + 1$ and $k \geq 2$.

From this theorem, it readily follows that for $N \geq 2$, the complete $(N, N, 1)$ cube is the most economical cube topology permitting desirable mapping of this modified recursive doubling algorithm.

5.3.5 A Comparison

The following comments and observations relate to the four algorithms discussed above.

(1)   Except for the actual schedule of computations, both the cyclic reduction and cyclic elimination essentially follow from the same first principle, namely, elimination of variables. Likewise, both the recursive doubling and the new algorithm follow from another related first principle -- that of **LU** factorization of the given tridiagonal matrix.

(2)   In spite of the differences, it is interesting to note that the binary reflected Gray code mapping of the cyclic reduction, cyclic elimination, and recursive doubling onto a base-2 cube leads to near-optimal communication complexity. With respect to the modified recursive doubling algorithm, the binary reflected Gray code mapping is *not* optimal. Thus, the modified recursive doubling algorithm is *not* suitable for cube architecture.

(3)   Since there does not exist any desirable mapping of any of these algorithms onto a base-2 cube, the question of the relative performance between three competing algorithms -- namely, cyclic reduction, cyclic elimination, and recursive doubling -- must be settled only by actual benchmarking.

(4)   From Section 5.3.3, it is clear that the communication pattern in solving first-order linear recurrences by recursive doubling is intimately related to those that arise in solving tridiagonal systems using cyclic elimination. A special case of the first-order linear recurrence is obtained when $f_i = 1$ for all i in (5.3.3.13). This latter problem is often called the *prefix* or *cascade sum* problem. Thus, the analysis in Section 5.3.3 is directly applicable to the prefix or the cascade sum problem. (See Exercises 3.42 to 3.44.)

(5)   We encourage the reader to analyze the effect of diagonal dominance on the recursive doubling algorithm and the modified recursive doubling method. It should be interesting to compare the performance of these four algorithms in the case of diagonal dominance.

5.4 LINEAR BLOCK TRIDIAGONAL SYSTEM

5.4.1 Statement and Motivation

Consider a linear tridiagonal system

$$\mathbf{A}\mathbf{x} = \mathbf{d}, \tag{5.4.1.1}$$

where

$$\mathbf{A} = \begin{bmatrix} \mathbf{B} & \mathbf{C} & \mathbf{0} & \mathbf{0} & \cdots & \mathbf{0} & \mathbf{0} & \mathbf{0} \\ \mathbf{C} & \mathbf{B} & \mathbf{C} & \mathbf{0} & \cdots & \mathbf{0} & \mathbf{0} & \mathbf{0} \\ \mathbf{0} & \mathbf{C} & \mathbf{B} & \mathbf{C} & \cdots & \mathbf{0} & \mathbf{0} & \mathbf{0} \\ \cdot & \cdot & \cdot & & \cdots & & \cdot & \cdot \\ \cdot & \cdot & \cdot & & \cdots & & \cdot & \cdot \\ \cdot & \cdot & \cdot & & \cdots & & \cdot & \cdot \\ \mathbf{0} & \mathbf{0} & \mathbf{0} & \mathbf{0} & \cdots & \mathbf{C} & \mathbf{B} & \mathbf{C} \\ \mathbf{0} & \mathbf{0} & \mathbf{0} & \mathbf{0} & \cdots & \mathbf{0} & \mathbf{C} & \mathbf{B} \end{bmatrix} \tag{5.4.1.2}$$

is a block tridiagonal matrix with $\mathbf{B}$ and $\mathbf{C}$ square matrices of order $n \geq 2$. It is assumed that there are M such blocks along the principal diagonal of $\mathbf{A}$, and $M = 2^k - 1$, for some $k \geq 2$. Thus, $N = Mn$ denotes the order of $\mathbf{A}$. It is assumed that the vectors $\mathbf{x}$ and $\mathbf{d}$ are likewise partitioned, that is, $\mathbf{x} = (\mathbf{x}_1, \mathbf{x}_2, \cdots, \mathbf{x}_M)'$, $\mathbf{d} = (\mathbf{d}_1, \mathbf{d}_2, \cdots, \mathbf{d}_M)'$, $\mathbf{x}_i = (x_{i1}, x_{i2}, \cdots, x_{in})'$, and $\mathbf{d}_i = (d_{i1}, d_{i2}, \cdots, d_{in})'$, for $i = 1, 2, \cdots, M$. It is further assumed that the blocks $\mathbf{B}$ and $\mathbf{C}$ are *symmetric* and *commute*, that is,

$$\mathbf{B}\,\mathbf{C} = \mathbf{C}\,\mathbf{B}. \tag{5.4.1.3}$$

Equations of this type are known to arise in discretizing a certain class of partial differential equations of the elliptic type, using the idea of separation of variables (Buzbee, Golub, and Nielson [1970]).

5.4.2 The Block Odd - Even Reduction Algorithm

On rewriting, (5.4.1.1) becomes

$$\left.\begin{aligned} \mathbf{B}\,\mathbf{x}_1 + \mathbf{C}\,\mathbf{x}_2 &= \mathbf{d}_1 \\ \mathbf{C}\,\mathbf{x}_{j-1} + \mathbf{B}\,\mathbf{x}_j + \mathbf{C}\,\mathbf{x}_{j+1} &= \mathbf{d}_j, \quad j = 2, 3, \cdots, M-1, \\ \mathbf{C}\,\mathbf{x}_{M-1} + \mathbf{B}\,\mathbf{x}_M &= \mathbf{d}_M. \end{aligned}\right\} \tag{5.4.2.1}$$

Consider a set of three consecutive equations centered around $\mathbf{x}_i$ for $i = 2, 4, 6, \cdots, M-1$. It is assumed that $\mathbf{x}_i$ and $\mathbf{d}_i$ are $\mathbf{0}$ for $i < 1$ and $i > M$.

$$
\left.
\begin{aligned}
\mathbf{C}\,x_{i-2} + \mathbf{B}\,x_{i-1} + \mathbf{C}\,x_i &= d_{i-1} \\
\mathbf{C}\,x_{i-1} + \mathbf{B}\,x_i + \mathbf{C}\,x_{i+1} &= d_i \\
\mathbf{C}\,x_i + \mathbf{B}\,x_{i+1} + \mathbf{C}\,x_{i+2} &= d_{i+1}.
\end{aligned}
\right\}
\qquad (5.4.2.2)
$$

Multiplying the second of these equations by $-\mathbf{B}$ and the first and the third by $\mathbf{C}$ and adding the three resulting equations, we obtain

$$
\mathbf{C}^2\,x_{i-2} + (2\mathbf{C}^2 - \mathbf{B}^2)\,x_i + \mathbf{C}^2\,x_{i+2} = \mathbf{C}\,d_{i-1} - \mathbf{B}\,d_i + \mathbf{C}\,d_{i+1}. \qquad (5.4.2.3)
$$

Notice that in this process, we have eliminated x_{i-1} and x_{i+1}, the *odd-indexed* subvectors.

This constitutes the first step of the reduction process, after which the given system (5.4.1.1) is split into two subsystems -- one for odd-indexed and another for even-indexed terms -- as follows:

$$
\begin{bmatrix}
(2\mathbf{C}^2 - \mathbf{B}^2) & \mathbf{C}^2 & 0 & \cdots & 0 & 0 & 0 \\
\mathbf{C}^2 & (2\mathbf{C}^2 - \mathbf{B}^2) & \mathbf{C}^2 & \cdots & 0 & 0 & 0 \\
\cdot & \cdot & \cdot & \cdots & \cdot & \cdot & \cdot \\
\cdot & \cdot & \cdot & \cdots & \cdot & \cdot & \cdot \\
\cdot & \cdot & \cdot & \cdots & \cdot & \cdot & \cdot \\
0 & 0 & 0 & \cdots & \mathbf{C}^2 & (2\mathbf{C}^2 - \mathbf{B}^2) & \mathbf{C}^2 \\
0 & 0 & 0 & \cdots & 0 & \mathbf{C}^2 & (2\mathbf{C}^2 - \mathbf{B}^2)
\end{bmatrix}
\begin{bmatrix}
x_2 \\ x_4 \\ \cdot \\ \cdot \\ \cdot \\ x_{M-3} \\ x_{M-1}
\end{bmatrix}
$$

$$
=
\begin{bmatrix}
\mathbf{C}\,d_1 - \mathbf{B}\,d_2 + \mathbf{C}\,d_3 \\
\mathbf{C}\,d_3 - \mathbf{B}\,d_4 + \mathbf{C}\,d_5 \\
\cdot \\
\cdot \\
\cdot \\
\mathbf{C}\,d_{M-2} - \mathbf{B}\,d_{M-1} + \mathbf{C}\,d_M
\end{bmatrix}
\qquad (5.4.2.4)
$$

and

$$
\begin{bmatrix}
\mathbf{B} & 0 & 0 & \cdots & 0 & 0 \\
0 & \mathbf{B} & 0 & \cdots & 0 & 0 \\
\cdot & \cdot & \cdot & \cdots & \cdot & \cdot \\
\cdot & \cdot & \cdot & \cdots & \cdot & \cdot \\
\cdot & \cdot & \cdot & \cdots & \cdot & \cdot \\
0 & 0 & 0 & \cdots & \mathbf{B} & 0 \\
0 & 0 & 0 & \cdots & 0 & \mathbf{B}
\end{bmatrix}
\begin{bmatrix}
x_1 \\ x_3 \\ \cdot \\ \cdot \\ \cdot \\ x_{M-2} \\ x_M
\end{bmatrix}
=
\begin{bmatrix}
d_1 - \mathbf{C}\,x_2 \\
d_3 - \mathbf{C}\,x_2 - \mathbf{C}\,x_4 \\
\cdot \\
\cdot \\
\cdot \\
d_{M-2} - \mathbf{C}\,x_{M-3} - \mathbf{C}\,x_{M-1} \\
d_M - \mathbf{C}\,x_{M-1}
\end{bmatrix}
\qquad (5.4.2.5)
$$

(5.4.2.4) is called the *reduced* system, and (5.4.2.5) is called the *eliminated* system. Thus, solving (5.4.1.1) is equivalent to solving (5.4.2.4) for $x_2, x_4, \cdots, x_{M-1}$ and then solving for $x_1, x_3, \cdots, x_M$ in parallel using (5.4.2.5).

The reduced system (5.4.2.4) has the same structure as (5.4.1.1). Applying the reduction process to (5.4.2.4), we can eliminate variables with indices that are odd multiples of 2, that is, $x_2, x_6, x_{10}, \cdots, x_{M-1}$. To express the resulting reduced and eliminated systems, we introduce the following notations.

Let

$$\mathbf{B}(0) = \mathbf{B}, \quad \mathbf{C}(0) = \mathbf{C}, \quad \text{and} \quad \mathbf{d}_i(0) = \mathbf{d}_i, \tag{5.4.2.6}$$

for $i = 1, 2, \cdots, M$. Define, for $i = 2, 4, 6, \cdots, M - 1$,

$$\left. \begin{aligned} \mathbf{B}(1) &= 2\mathbf{C}^2(0) - \mathbf{B}^2(0) \\ \mathbf{C}(1) &= \mathbf{C}^2(0) \\ \mathbf{d}_i(1) &= \mathbf{C}(0)[\mathbf{d}_{i-1}(0) + \mathbf{d}_{i+1}(0)] - \mathbf{B}(0)\,\mathbf{d}_i(0). \end{aligned} \right\} \tag{5.4.2.7}$$

Using this notation, (5.4.2.4) can be written as

$$\begin{bmatrix} \mathbf{B}(1) & \mathbf{C}(1) & 0 & \cdots & 0 & 0 & 0 \\ \mathbf{C}(1) & \mathbf{B}(1) & \mathbf{C}(1) & \cdots & 0 & 0 & 0 \\ \cdot & \cdot & \cdot & \cdots & \cdot & \cdot & \cdot \\ \cdot & \cdot & \cdot & \cdots & \cdot & \cdot & \cdot \\ \cdot & \cdot & \cdot & \cdots & \cdot & \cdot & \cdot \\ 0 & 0 & 0 & \cdots & \mathbf{C}(1) & \mathbf{B}(1) & \mathbf{C}(1) \\ 0 & 0 & 0 & \cdots & 0 & \mathbf{C}(1) & \mathbf{B}(1) \end{bmatrix} \begin{bmatrix} x_2 \\ x_4 \\ \cdot \\ \cdot \\ \cdot \\ x_{M-3} \\ x_{M-1} \end{bmatrix} = \begin{bmatrix} d_2(1) \\ d_4(1) \\ \cdot \\ \cdot \\ \cdot \\ d_{M-3}(1) \\ d_{M-1}(1) \end{bmatrix}, \tag{5.4.2.8}$$

that is, for $i = 2, 4, 6, \cdots, M - 1$,

$$\left. \begin{aligned} \mathbf{B}(1)\,x_2 + \mathbf{C}(1)\,x_4 &= \mathbf{d}_2(1) \\ \mathbf{C}(1)\,x_{i-2} + \mathbf{B}(1)\,x_i + \mathbf{C}(1)\,x_{i+2} &= \mathbf{d}_i(1) \\ \mathbf{C}(1)\,x_{M-3} + \mathbf{B}(1)\,x_{M-1} &= \mathbf{d}_{M-1}(1). \end{aligned} \right\} \tag{5.4.2.9}$$

Now consider a set of three consecutive equations centered around x_i for $i = 4, 8, 12, \cdots, M - 3$:

$$\left. \begin{aligned} \mathbf{C}(1)\,x_{i-4} + \mathbf{B}(1)\,x_{i-2} + \mathbf{C}(1)\,x_i &= \mathbf{d}_{i-2}(1) \\ \mathbf{C}(1)\,x_{i-2} + \mathbf{B}(1)\,x_i + \mathbf{C}(1)\,x_{i+2} &= \mathbf{d}_i(1) \\ \mathbf{C}(1)\,x_i + \mathbf{B}(1)\,x_{i+2} + \mathbf{C}(1)\,x_{i+4} &= \mathbf{d}_{i+2}(1). \end{aligned} \right\} \tag{5.4.2.10}$$

Multiplying the second equation by $-\mathbf{B}(1)$, the first and the last by $\mathbf{C}(1)$, and adding, we obtain

$$\mathbf{C}^2(1)\,\mathbf{x}_{i-2^2} + [2\mathbf{C}^2(1) - \mathbf{B}^2(1)]\,\mathbf{x}_i + \mathbf{C}^2(1)\,\mathbf{x}_{i+2^2}$$

$$= \mathbf{C}(1)\,[\mathbf{d}_{i-2}(1) + \mathbf{d}_{i+2}(1)] - \mathbf{B}(1)\,\mathbf{d}_i(1). \quad (5.4.2.11)$$

That is, in this process we have eliminated $\mathbf{x}_{i-2}$ and $\mathbf{x}_{i+2}$, the subvectors with indices that are *odd multiples* of 2. Define

$$\left.\begin{aligned}
&\mathbf{B}(2) = 2\mathbf{C}^2(1) - \mathbf{B}^2(1) \\
&\mathbf{C}(2) = \mathbf{C}^2(1) \\
&\mathbf{d}_i(2) = \mathbf{C}(1)\,[\mathbf{d}_{i-2}(1) + \mathbf{d}_{i+2}(1)] - \mathbf{B}(1)\,\mathbf{d}_i(1),
\end{aligned}\right\} \quad (5.4.2.12)$$

for $i = 4,\ 8,\ 12,\ \cdots,\ M-3$.

Using (5.4.2.12), we can represent the reduced system after two steps as follows.

$$\begin{bmatrix}
\mathbf{B}(2) & \mathbf{C}(2) & \mathbf{0} & \cdots & \mathbf{0} & \mathbf{0} & \mathbf{0} \\
\mathbf{C}(2) & \mathbf{B}(2) & \mathbf{C}(2) & \cdots & \mathbf{0} & \mathbf{0} & \mathbf{0} \\
\cdot & \cdot & \cdot & \cdots & \cdot & \cdot & \cdot \\
\cdot & \cdot & \cdot & \cdots & \cdot & \cdot & \cdot \\
\cdot & \cdot & \cdot & \cdots & \cdot & \cdot & \cdot \\
\mathbf{0} & \mathbf{0} & \mathbf{0} & \cdots & \mathbf{C}(2) & \mathbf{B}(2) & \mathbf{C}(2) \\
\mathbf{0} & \mathbf{0} & \mathbf{0} & \cdots & \mathbf{0} & \mathbf{C}(2) & \mathbf{B}(2)
\end{bmatrix}
\begin{bmatrix}
\mathbf{x}_4 \\ \mathbf{x}_8 \\ \cdot \\ \cdot \\ \cdot \\ \mathbf{x}_{M-7} \\ \mathbf{x}_{M-3}
\end{bmatrix}
=
\begin{bmatrix}
\mathbf{d}_4(2) \\ \mathbf{d}_8(2) \\ \cdot \\ \cdot \\ \cdot \\ \mathbf{d}_{M-7}(2) \\ \mathbf{d}_{M-3}(2)
\end{bmatrix}
\cdot \quad (5.4.2.13)$$

The eliminated system, after two steps, becomes

$$\begin{bmatrix}
\mathbf{B}(1) & \mathbf{0} & \mathbf{0} & \cdots & \mathbf{0} & \mathbf{0} \\
\mathbf{0} & \mathbf{B}(1) & \mathbf{0} & \cdots & \mathbf{0} & \mathbf{0} \\
\cdot & \cdot & \cdot & \cdots & \cdot & \cdot \\
\cdot & \cdot & \cdot & \cdots & \cdot & \cdot \\
\cdot & \cdot & \cdot & \cdots & \cdot & \cdot \\
\mathbf{0} & \mathbf{0} & \mathbf{0} & \cdots & \mathbf{B}(1) & \mathbf{0} \\
\mathbf{0} & \mathbf{0} & \mathbf{0} & \cdots & \mathbf{0} & \mathbf{B}(1)
\end{bmatrix}
\begin{bmatrix}
\mathbf{x}_2 \\ \mathbf{x}_6 \\ \cdot \\ \cdot \\ \cdot \\ \mathbf{x}_{M-5} \\ \mathbf{x}_{M-1}
\end{bmatrix}$$

$$= \begin{bmatrix} \mathbf{d}_2(1) - \mathbf{C}(1)\,\mathbf{x}_4 \\ \mathbf{d}_6(1) - \mathbf{C}(1)\,\mathbf{x}_4 - \mathbf{C}(1)\,\mathbf{x}_8 \\ \cdot \\ \cdot \\ \cdot \\ \mathbf{d}_{M-5}(1) - \mathbf{C}(1)\,\mathbf{x}_{M-7} - \mathbf{C}(1)\,\mathbf{x}_{M-3} \\ \mathbf{d}_{M-1}(1) - \mathbf{C}(1)\,\mathbf{x}_{M-3} \end{bmatrix} . \qquad (5.4.2.14)$$

Solving (5.4.2.4) is equivalent to solving (5.4.2.13) for $\mathbf{x}_4$, $\mathbf{x}_8$, $\mathbf{x}_{12}$, $\cdots$, $\mathbf{x}_{M-3}$ and then solving in parallel $\mathbf{x}_2$, $\mathbf{x}_6$, $\mathbf{x}_{10}$, $\cdots$, $\mathbf{x}_{M-1}$ using (5.4.2.14).

To generalize this reduction process, define

$$\left. \begin{aligned} &\mathbf{B}(j) = 2\mathbf{C}^2(j-1) - \mathbf{B}^2(j-1) \\[2mm] &\mathbf{C}(j) = \mathbf{C}^2(j-1) \\[2mm] &\mathbf{d}_i(j) = \mathbf{C}(j-1)\,[\mathbf{d}_{i-h}(j-1) + \mathbf{d}_{i+h}(j-1)] - \mathbf{B}(j-1)\,\mathbf{d}_i(j-1), \end{aligned} \right\} \qquad (5.4.2.15)$$

where $h = 2^{j-1}$, $i = 2^j$, 2×2^j, 3×2^j, $\cdots$, $(2^{k-j} - 1)\,2^j$, and $j = 1, 2, \cdots , k$.

After the jth step, the reduced system becomes

$$\mathbf{R}(j)\,\mathbf{U}(j) = \mathbf{V}(j), \qquad (5.4.2.16)$$

where

$$\mathbf{R}(j) = \begin{bmatrix} \mathbf{B}(j) & \mathbf{C}(j) & 0 & \cdots & 0 & 0 & 0 \\ \mathbf{C}(j) & \mathbf{B}(j) & \mathbf{C}(j) & \cdots & 0 & 0 & 0 \\ \cdot & \cdot & \cdot & \cdots & \cdot & \cdot & \cdot \\ \cdot & \cdot & \cdot & \cdots & \cdot & \cdot & \cdot \\ \cdot & \cdot & \cdot & \cdots & \cdot & \cdot & \cdot \\ 0 & 0 & 0 & \cdots & \mathbf{C}(j) & \mathbf{B}(j) & \mathbf{C}(j) \\ 0 & 0 & 0 & \cdots & 0 & \mathbf{C}(j) & \mathbf{B}(j) \end{bmatrix}$$

is a matrix of order $2^{k-j} - 1$,

$$\mathbf{U}(j) = \begin{bmatrix} \mathbf{x}_t \\ \mathbf{x}_{2t} \\ \cdot \\ \cdot \\ \cdot \\ \mathbf{x}_{it} \\ \cdot \\ \cdot \\ \cdot \\ \mathbf{x}_{(2^{k-j}-1)t} \end{bmatrix}, \qquad \mathbf{V}(j) = \begin{bmatrix} \mathbf{d}_t(j) \\ \mathbf{d}_{2t}(j) \\ \cdot \\ \cdot \\ \cdot \\ \mathbf{d}_{it}(j) \\ \cdot \\ \cdot \\ \cdot \\ \mathbf{d}_{(2^{k-j}-1)t}(j) \end{bmatrix},$$

and $t = 2^j$. The reader can easily verify that (5.4.2.16) reduces to (5.4.2.13) and (5.4.2.8) for $j = 2$ and 1, respectively.

The eliminated system after the jth step can likewise be written as

$$\mathbf{E}(j)\,\mathbf{w}(j) = \mathbf{y}(j), \qquad (5.4.2.17)$$

where

$$\mathbf{E}(j) = \begin{bmatrix} \mathbf{B}(j-1) & \mathbf{0} & \mathbf{0} & \cdots & \mathbf{0} & \mathbf{0} \\ \mathbf{0} & \mathbf{B}(j-1) & \mathbf{0} & \cdots & \mathbf{0} & \mathbf{0} \\ \cdot & \cdot & \cdot & \cdots & \cdot & \cdot \\ \cdot & \cdot & \cdot & \cdots & \cdot & \cdot \\ \cdot & \cdot & \cdot & \cdots & \cdot & \cdot \\ \mathbf{0} & \mathbf{0} & \mathbf{0} & \cdots & \mathbf{B}(j-1) & \mathbf{0} \\ \mathbf{0} & \mathbf{0} & \mathbf{0} & \cdots & \mathbf{0} & \mathbf{B}(j-1) \end{bmatrix},$$

$$\mathbf{w}(j) = \begin{bmatrix} \mathbf{x}_{t-s} \\ \mathbf{x}_{2t-s} \\ \cdot \\ \cdot \\ \cdot \\ \mathbf{x}_{it-s} \\ \cdot \\ \cdot \\ \cdot \\ \mathbf{x}_{2^{k-j}t-s} \end{bmatrix},$$

and

$$y(j) = \begin{bmatrix} \mathbf{d}_{t-s}(j-1) - \mathbf{C}(j-1)\,\mathbf{x}_t \\ \mathbf{d}_{2t-s}(j-1) - \mathbf{C}(j-1)\,[\mathbf{x}_{2t} - \mathbf{x}_t] \\ \cdot \\ \cdot \\ \cdot \\ \mathbf{d}_{it-s}(j-1) - \mathbf{C}(j-1)\,[\mathbf{x}_{it} + \mathbf{x}_{(i-1)t}] \\ \cdot \\ \cdot \\ \cdot \\ \mathbf{d}_{2^{k-j}t-s}(j-1) - \mathbf{C}(j-1)\,\mathbf{x}_{(2^{k-j}-1)t} \end{bmatrix},$$

where $t = 2s = 2^j$.

The components of $\mathbf{w}(j)$ can be solved in parallel using (5.4.2.17) after solving the reduced system (5.4.2.16).

After $k - 1$ steps, we are left with

$$\mathbf{C}(k-1)\,\mathbf{x}_{i-2^{k-1}} + \mathbf{B}(k-1)\,\mathbf{x}_i + \mathbf{C}(k-1)\,\mathbf{x}_{i+2^{k-1}} = \mathbf{d}_i(k-1),$$

for $i = 2^{k-1}$. Since $\mathbf{x}_j = 0$ for $j \le 0$ and $j \ge M$, we obtain

$$\mathbf{B}(k-1)\,\mathbf{x}_{2^{k-1}} = \mathbf{d}_{2^{k-1}}(k-1). \qquad (5.4.2.18)$$

Thus,

$$\mathbf{R}(k-1) = \mathbf{B}(k-1), \quad \mathbf{U}(k-1) = \mathbf{x}_{2^{k-1}}, \quad \text{and} \quad \mathbf{V}(k-1) = \mathbf{d}_{2^{k-1}}(k-1).$$

Now solving (5.4.2.18) for $\mathbf{x}_{2^{k-1}}$, and using the eliminated system, we can repeatedly recover the $\mathbf{x}_i$'s in a binary tree fashion. As an example, when $k = 4$, first $\mathbf{x}_8$ is obtained. Then $\mathbf{x}_4$ and $\mathbf{x}_{12}$ are computed. In the third step $\mathbf{x}_2$, $\mathbf{x}_6$, $\mathbf{x}_{10}$, and $\mathbf{x}_{14}$ are recovered. In the last step, $\mathbf{x}_1$, $\mathbf{x}_3$, $\mathbf{x}_5$, $\cdots$, $\mathbf{x}_{13}$, and $\mathbf{x}_{15}$ are computed.

While (5.4.2.18) can be solved by the standard Gaussian elimination, namely, the **L U** factorization, we describe another method also based on factoring the matrix $\mathbf{B}(k-1)$. To this end, we first analyze the form of the matrix $\mathbf{B}(k-1)$.

Recall that $\mathbf{B}(0) = \mathbf{B}$ and $\mathbf{B}(1) = 2\mathbf{C}^2 - \mathbf{B}^2$. Consider a sequence of polynomials, where $p_0(a, t) = -2$ and $p_1(a, t) = -2t \cos \theta$. Let

$$p_2(a, t) = 2t^2 - a^2. \qquad (5.4.2.19)$$

Since $p_2(\mathbf{B}, \mathbf{C}) = \mathbf{B}(1)$, and $\mathbf{B}$ and $\mathbf{C}$ commute, we concentrate on factoring $p_2(a, t)$. For $t \ne 0$, change the variables using

$$a = -2t \cos \theta. \qquad (5.4.2.20)$$

Using (5.4.2.20),

$$p_2(a, t) = -2t^2\,[-1 + 2\cos^2 \theta] = -2t^2 \cos 2\theta.$$

Consequently,

$$p_2(a, t) = 0$$

if

$$\cos \theta = \pm \frac{1}{\sqrt{2}},$$

that is,

$$\frac{a}{2t} = -\cos\left(\frac{2j-1}{2^2}\right)\pi, \quad j = 1, 2. \tag{5.4.2.21}$$

Thus,

$$p_2(a, t) = -\prod_{j=1}^{2}\left[a + 2t \cos\left(\frac{2j-1}{2^2}\right)\pi\right]. \tag{5.4.2.22}$$

Using this, we obtain a factorization for $\mathbf{B}(1)$, namely,

$$\mathbf{B}(1) = -\prod_{j=1}^{2}\left[\mathbf{B} + 2\mathbf{C} \cos\left(\frac{2j-1}{2^2}\right)\pi\right],$$

that is,

$$\mathbf{B}(1) = -(\mathbf{B} + \sqrt{2}\,\mathbf{C})(\mathbf{B} - \sqrt{2}\,\mathbf{C}) = 2\mathbf{C}^2 - \mathbf{B}^2, \tag{5.4.2.23}$$

since, by (5.4.1.3), $\mathbf{B}$ and $\mathbf{C}$ commute.

Generalizing this development, we see that (Exercise 5.20)

$$\mathbf{B}(r) = p_{2^r}(\mathbf{B}, \mathbf{C}), \tag{5.4.2.24}$$

where

$$p_{2^r}(a, t) = \sum_{i=0}^{2^r-1} q_{2i}\, a^{2i}\, t^{2^r - 2i} \tag{5.4.2.25}$$

and $q_{2^r} = -1$.

From the definition of $\mathbf{B}(r)$ in (5.4.2.15), it follows that (Exercise 5.21)

$$p_{2^{r+1}}(a, t) = 2t^{2^{r+1}} - [p_{2^r}(a, t)]^2. \tag{5.4.2.26}$$

Now, changing the variable using (5.4.2.20), it can be shown (Exercise 5.22) that

$$p_{2^r}(a, t) = -2t^{2^r} \cos 2^r \theta. \tag{5.4.2.27}$$

$-p_{2^r}(a, 1)$ is known as the Chebyshev polynomial of the first kind and degree 2^r (Sweet [1988]).

Clearly,

$$p_{2^r}(a, t) = 0$$

if

$$\frac{a}{2t} = -\cos\left(\frac{2j-1}{2^{r+1}}\right)\pi, \quad j = 1, 2, \cdots, 2^r. \tag{5.4.2.28}$$

Combining these, we obtain the following factorization for $p_{2^r}(a, t)$ and $\mathbf{B}(r)$ (Exercises 5.23 and 5.24):

$$p_{2^r}(a,\ t) = -\prod_{j=1}^{2^r} (a + 2t \cos \theta_j(r)),$$

$$\mathbf{B}(r) = -\prod_{j=1}^{2^r} \mathbf{H}_j(r), \qquad\qquad (5.4.2.29)$$

where

$$\theta_j(r) = (\frac{2j-1}{2^r+1})\pi,$$

and the matrix

$$\mathbf{H}_j(r) = [\mathbf{B} + 2\,\mathbf{C} \cos \theta_j(r)].$$

We now return to solving (5.4.2.18), which may be rewritten as follows.

$$[\mathbf{H}_1(k-1)\,\mathbf{H}_2(k-1) \cdots \mathbf{H}_{2^{k-1}}(k-1)]\,\mathbf{x}_{2^{k-1}} = -\mathbf{d}_{2^{k-1}}(k-1). \qquad (5.4.2.30)$$

Define

$$\mathbf{Z}_0 = -\mathbf{d}_{2^{k-1}}(k-1),$$

and for $i = 1, 2, \cdots, 2^{k-1}$, solve

$$\mathbf{H}_i(k-1)\mathbf{Z}_i = \mathbf{Z}_{i-1} \qquad\qquad (5.4.2.31)$$

repeatedly for $\mathbf{Z}_i$. Clearly,

$$\mathbf{x}_{2^{k-1}} = \mathbf{Z}_{2^{k-1}}.$$

Since the matrix of the eliminated systems in (5.4.2.17) depends only on $\mathbf{B}(j)$'s, we can use the same factorizations to solve these systems as well. The overall algorithm is given in Fig. 5.4.2.1. We encourage the reader to compute the complexity of this algorithm when $\mathbf{B}$ is tridiagonal and $\mathbf{C} = \mathbf{I}$, the identity matrix (Exercise 5.26).

The method of recovering $\mathbf{x}_{2^{k-1}}$ described above is inherently sequential, and parallelism in this approach is limited to solving the system (5.4.2.31). This is a major bottleneck to achieving speed-up and is a direct consequence of the (multiplicative) factorization of $\mathbf{B}(r)$ in (5.4.2.29). This can be remedied to a large extent by using an alternative approach due to Sweet [1988] in which $\mathbf{B}(r)$ is expressed additively using the partial fraction expansion.

We illustrate this idea using an example, and the generalization is obvious. From (5.4.2.22), it can be shown that

$$\frac{2\sqrt{2}\,t}{p_2(a,\ t)} = \frac{1}{a + \sqrt{2}\,t} - \frac{1}{a - \sqrt{2}\,t}, \qquad\qquad (5.4.2.32)$$

and

$$[\mathbf{B}(1)]^{-1} = [p_2(\mathbf{B},\ \mathbf{C})]^{-1}$$

/*   **A** is a block tridiagonal matrix of order Mn partitioned into blocks of size $n(\geq 2)$ and $M = 2^k - 1$ for some $k \geq 2$. $\mathbf{d} = (\mathbf{d}_1, \mathbf{d}_2, \cdots, \mathbf{d}_M)$ is a partitioned vector where $\mathbf{d}_i = (d_{i1}, d_{i2}, \cdots, d_{in})$. */

Let **B**(0) = **B**,   **C**(0) = **C**,   and $\mathbf{d}_i(0) = \mathbf{d}_i$. $\mathbf{x} = (\mathbf{x}_1, \mathbf{x}_2, \cdots, \mathbf{x}_M)^t$,   where $\mathbf{x}_i = (x_{i1}, x_{i2}, \cdots, x_{in})^t$.

/*   Reduction Phase   */

FOR $j = 1$ TO $k - 1$ STEP 1 DO IN PARALLEL
     COMPUTE **B**(j), **C**(j), $\mathbf{d}_i(j)$ using (5.4.2.15).
END

SOLVE FOR $\mathbf{x}_{2^{k-1}}$ using the factorization method given in (5.4.2.30) and (5.4.2.31).

/*   Back-Substitution Phase   */

FOR $j = k - 1$ TO 1 STEP -1 DO IN PARALLEL
     SOLVE the eliminated system (5.4.2.17) using the factorization method given in (5.4.2.30) and (5.4.2.31).
END

FIGURE 5.4.2.1 A version of the block cyclic reduction algorithm.

$$= \frac{\mathbf{C}^{-1}}{2\sqrt{2}} \{ (\mathbf{B} + \sqrt{2}\,\mathbf{C})^{-1} - (\mathbf{B} - \sqrt{2}\,\mathbf{C})^{-1} \}. \qquad (5.4.2.33)$$

Generalizing this idea, from Exercise 5.38, we obtain

$$\mathbf{x}_{2^{k-1}} = -[p_{2^{k-1}}(\mathbf{B}, \mathbf{C})]^{-1} \mathbf{d}_{2^{k-1}}(k-1)$$

$$= \sum_{j=1}^{2^{k-1}} f_j(\mathbf{C})[\mathbf{B} + 2\mathbf{C} \cos \theta_j(r)]^{-1} \mathbf{d}_{2^{k-1}}(k-1). \qquad (5.4.2.34)$$

Since all the matrices on the right-hand side depend only on the input and can be precomputed, the matrix - vector product on the right-hand side can be computed in parallel and the resulting set of vectors can then be added using the associative fan-in algorithm.

The reader is encouraged to compare the performance of the approaches in (5.4.2.31) and (5.4.2.34). Another approach for approximating $[\mathbf{B}(r)]^{-1}$ is pursued in Exercise 5.39.

5.4.3 Stability Analysis of Block Cyclic Reduction

In the case of numerically oriented problems, the practical usefulness of a parallel algorithm critically depends on the level of accuracy or the relative error it can guarantee for the solution. It turns out that the block cyclic reduction algorithm, while suitable for parallel computation, does *not* possess good control over the round-off errors. In this section, we identify the main source of these errors, and in the next section we present modified versions of the cyclic reduction algorithms with better error-control features.

As will become evident, the main source of round-off error lies in the computation of $\mathbf{d}_i(r + 1)$, especially in $\mathbf{B}(r)\,\mathbf{d}_i(r)$ in (5.4.2.15). To this end, first consider the sequence of polynomials $p_s(a, t)$ defined in (5.4.2.27), when $|a| < 2t$, namely,

$$p_s(a, t) = -2t^s \cos (s\theta), \qquad (5.4.3.1)$$

where

$$p_0(a, t) = -2, \qquad p_1(a, t) = -2t \cos \theta,$$

and, for $t \neq 0$,

$$\frac{a}{t} = -2 \cos \theta.$$

This polynomial can be recursively computed as follows.

$$p_s(a, t) = -a p_{s-1}(a, t) - t^2 p_{s-2}(a, t). \qquad (5.4.3.2)$$

For, substituting (5.4.3.1) in the right-hand side of (5.4.3.2), we obtain

$$2t^{s-1}[a \cos (s-1)\theta + t \cos (s-2)\theta] = 2t^s[-2 \cos \theta \cos (s-1)\theta + \cos (s-2)\theta]$$

$$= -2t^s \cos s\theta,$$

$$= p_s(a, t).$$

For purposes of later analysis, when $|a| \geq |2t|$, we may also rewrite $p_s(a, t)$ using the hyperbolic functions as

$$p_s(a, t) = -2t^s \cosh (s\phi), \qquad (5.4.3.3)$$

with

$$p_0(a, t) = -2,$$

$$p_1(a, t) = -2t \cosh \phi,$$

$$p_s(a, t) = -ap_{s-1}(a, t) - t^2 p_{s-2}(a, t),$$

and, for $t \neq 0$,

$$\frac{a}{t} = -2 \cosh \phi,$$

Hyperbolic functions satisfy identities which are very similar to those satisfied by trigonometric functions, and we refer the reader to Salas and Hille [1982] for details. Again combining (5.4.3.3) and (5.4.3.2), we can readily verify the validity of the recursive definition of $p_s(a, t)$, using these hyperbolic functions.

Using this recursive definition,

$$\mathbf{B}(r) \, \mathbf{d}_i(r) = p_{2^r}(\mathbf{B}, \mathbf{C}) \, \mathbf{d}_i(r)$$

can be computed as follows.

Let

$$\eta_0 = -2\mathbf{d}_i(r),$$

$$\eta_1 = \mathbf{B} \, \mathbf{d}_i(r),$$

and, for $s = 2, 3, 4, \cdots, 2^r$,

$$\eta_s = -\mathbf{B} \, \eta_{s-1} - \mathbf{C}^2 \, \eta_{s-2}. \qquad (5.4.3.4)$$

Thus,

$$\eta_{2^r} = p_{2^r}(\mathbf{B}, \mathbf{C}) \, \mathbf{d}_i(r) = \mathbf{B}(r) \, \mathbf{d}_i(r).$$

In practice, due to round-off errors, we are actually computing a related sequence given by

$$\overline{\eta}_0 = -2\mathbf{d}_i(r),$$

$$\overline{\eta}_1 = \mathbf{Bd}_i(r) + \delta_0,$$

and

$$\overline{\eta}_s = -\mathbf{B} \, \overline{\eta}_{s-1} - \mathbf{C}^2 \, \overline{\eta}_{s-2} + \delta_{s-1}, \qquad (5.4.3.5)$$

where δ_j is the round-off error resulting in the computation of η_{j+1}.

Since it is known that $\mathbf{B}$ and $\mathbf{C}$ commute and are symmetric, from the theory of matrices (Chapter 4, Bellman [1960]), it is well known that there exists an orthogonal matrix $\mathbf{Q}$ that diagonalizes $\mathbf{B}$ and $\mathbf{C}$ simultaneously, that is,

$$\mathbf{B} = \mathbf{Q}\Lambda\mathbf{Q}^t \quad \text{and} \quad \mathbf{C} = \mathbf{Q}\Omega\mathbf{Q}^t, \qquad (5.4.3.6a)$$

where

$$\Lambda = \begin{bmatrix} \lambda_1 & 0 & 0 & \cdots & 0 \\ 0 & \lambda_2 & 0 & \cdots & 0 \\ 0 & 0 & \lambda_3 & \cdots & 0 \\ \cdot & \cdot & \cdot & & \cdot \\ \cdot & \cdot & \cdot & & \cdot \\ \cdot & \cdot & \cdot & & \cdot \\ 0 & 0 & 0 & \cdots & \lambda_n \end{bmatrix} \qquad (5.4.3.6b)$$

and

$$\Omega = \begin{bmatrix} \omega_1 & 0 & 0 & \cdots & 0 \\ 0 & \omega_2 & 0 & \cdots & 0 \\ 0 & 0 & \omega_3 & \cdots & 0 \\ \cdot & \cdot & \cdot & & \cdot \\ \cdot & \cdot & \cdot & & \cdot \\ \cdot & \cdot & \cdot & & \cdot \\ 0 & 0 & 0 & \cdots & \omega_n \end{bmatrix}, \qquad (5.4.3.6c)$$

are diagonal matrices of eigenvalues of $\mathbf{B}$ and $\mathbf{C}$, respectively. (It is also assumed that the eigenvalues of $\mathbf{B}$ and $\mathbf{C}$ are distinct.)

Without loss of generality, it is assumed that the columns of $\mathbf{Q}$ are normalized eigenvectors of $\mathbf{B}$ and $\mathbf{C}$. Further, it is well known that $\mathbf{Q}^t = \mathbf{Q}^{-1}$ and $\mathbf{Q}\,\mathbf{C}^2\,\mathbf{Q}^t = \Omega^2$, where

$$\Omega^2 = \begin{bmatrix} \omega_1^2 & 0 & 0 & \cdots & 0 \\ 0 & \omega_2^2 & 0 & \cdots & 0 \\ 0 & 0 & \omega_3^2 & \cdots & 0 \\ \cdot & \cdot & \cdot & & \cdot \\ \cdot & \cdot & \cdot & & \cdot \\ \cdot & \cdot & \cdot & & \cdot \\ 0 & 0 & 0 & \cdots & \omega_n^2 \end{bmatrix} \cdot$$

Combining these with (5.4.3.5) and (5.4.3.6), we obtain

$$\left. \begin{aligned} \xi_0 &= -2\overline{\mathbf{d}}_i(r) \\ \xi_1 &= -\frac{1}{2}\Lambda\xi_0 + \psi_0 \\ \xi_s &= -\Lambda\,\xi_{s-1} - \Omega^2\,\xi_{s-2} + \psi_{s-1}, \end{aligned} \right\} \qquad (5.4.3.7)$$

where

$$\begin{matrix} \xi_s = Q^t \, \bar{\eta}_s \\ \bar{d}_i(r) = Q^t \, d_i(r) \\ \psi_s = Q^t \, \delta_s. \end{matrix} \Bigg\} \tag{5.4.3.8}$$

Exploiting the diagonal nature of Λ and Ω, we can write (5.4.3.7) in component form as

$$\xi_{j,s+1} + \lambda_j \, \xi_{j,s} + \omega_j^2 \, \xi_{j,s-1} = \psi_{j,s}, \tag{5.4.3.9}$$

where $j = 1, 2, \cdots, n$. To obtain the solution for this recurrence, consider its characteristic equation

$$m^2 + \lambda_j m + \omega_j^2 = 0. \tag{5.4.3.10}$$

Let

$$\mu_j = \frac{-\lambda_j + \sqrt{\lambda_j^2 - 4\omega_j^2}}{2} \quad \text{and} \quad v_j = \frac{-\lambda_j - \sqrt{\lambda_j^2 - 4\omega_j^2}}{2}$$

be the two roots of (5.4.3.10).

Case 1. $\mu_j \neq v_j$. It can be shown (Exercise 5.28) that

$$\xi_{j,s} = \frac{\mu_j^s - v_j^s}{\mu_j - v_j} \, \xi_{j,1} - \mu_j \, v_j \frac{\mu_j^{s-1} - v_j^{s-1}}{\mu_j - v_j} \, \xi_{j,0}$$

$$+ \sum_{t=1}^{s-1} \frac{\mu_j^{s-t} - v_j^{s-t}}{\mu_j - v_j} \, \psi_{j,t}. \tag{5.4.3.11}$$

From (5.4.3.7), since

$$\xi_{j,0} = -2\bar{d}_{j,0}(r)$$

and

$$\xi_{j,1} = -\frac{1}{2}\lambda_j \, \xi_{j,0} + \psi_{j,0},$$

we obtain

$$\xi_{j,s} = (\frac{\mu_j^s - v_j^s}{\mu_j - v_j} \, \lambda_j + \mu_j \, v_j \frac{\mu_j^{s-1} - v_j^{s-1}}{\mu_j - v_j}) \, \bar{d}_{j,0}(r)$$

$$+ \sum_{t=0}^{s-1} \frac{\mu_j^{s-t} - v_j^{s-t}}{\mu_j - v_j} \, \psi_{j,t}. \tag{5.4.3.12}$$

From (5.4.3.10), it follows that μ_j and v_j are complex conjugates if $|\lambda_j| < |2\omega_j|$ and are real if $|\lambda_j| > |2\omega_j|$. Let

$$-\left|\frac{\lambda_j}{2\omega_j}\right| = \begin{cases} \cos\theta_j, & \text{if } |\lambda_j| < |2\omega_j| \\ \cosh\phi_j, & \text{if } |\lambda_j| > |2\omega_j|. \end{cases} \quad \text{(5.4.3.13)}$$

Case 1a. $|\lambda_j| < |2\omega_j|$ and μ_j and ν_j are complex conjugates. In this case $\mu_j \neq \nu_j$ and

$$\mu_j = \omega_j\,(\cos\theta_j + i\,\sin\theta_j) = \omega_j\,e^{i\theta_j}$$

$$\left.\vphantom{\begin{array}{c}a\\a\end{array}}\right\} \quad \text{(5.4.3.14)}$$

$$\nu_j = \omega_j\,(\cos\theta_j - i\,\sin\theta_j) = \omega_j e^{-i\theta_j},$$

where $i = \sqrt{-1}$. Substituting (5.4.2.14) into (5.4.2.12) and simplifying, we obtain

$$\xi_{j,s} = (\lambda_j\,\omega_j^{s-1}\,\frac{\sin s\theta_j}{\sin\theta_j} + 2\omega_j^s\,\frac{\sin(s-1)\theta_j}{\sin\theta_j})\,\bar{d}_{j,0}(r)$$

$$+ \sum_{t=0}^{s-1} \omega_j^{s-t-1}\,\frac{\sin(s-t)\theta_j}{\sin\theta_j}\,\psi_{j,t}.$$

Combining this with $\lambda_j = -2\,\omega_j\,\cos\theta_j$ and simplifying, we obtain

$$\xi_{j,s} = -2\,\bar{d}_{j,0}(r)\,\omega_j^s\,\cos(s\theta_j) + \sum_{t=0}^{s-1} \omega_j^{s-t-1}\,\frac{\sin(s-t)\,\theta_j}{\sin\theta_j}\,\psi_{j,t}. \quad \text{(5.4.3.15)}$$

Case 1b. $|\lambda_j| > |2\omega_j|$ and μ_j and ν_j are real and distinct. In this case,

$$\mu_j = \omega_j\,(\cosh\phi_j + \sinh\phi_j) = \omega_j\,e^{\phi_j}$$

$$\left.\vphantom{\begin{array}{c}a\\a\end{array}}\right\} \quad \text{(5.4.3.16)}$$

$$\nu_j = \omega_j\,(\cosh\phi_j - \sinh\phi_j) = \omega_j\,e^{-\phi_j}.$$

Substituting (5.4.3.16) into (5.4.3.12) and simplifying, we obtain

$$\xi_{j,s} = (\lambda_j\,\omega_j^{s-1}\,\frac{\sinh(s\phi_j)}{\sinh\phi_j} + 2\,\omega_j^s\,\frac{\sinh(s-1)\phi_j}{\sinh\phi_j})\,\bar{d}_{j,0}(r)$$

$$+ \sum_{t=0}^{s-1} \omega_j^{s-t-1}\,\frac{\sinh(s-t)\phi_j}{\sinh\phi_j}\,\psi_{j,t}. \quad \text{(5.4.3.17)}$$

Combining this with $\lambda_j = -2\omega_j\,\cosh\phi_j$ and simplifying, we obtain

$$\xi_{j,s} = -2\bar{d}_{j,0}(r)\,\omega_j^s\,\cosh(s\phi_j) + \sum_{t=0}^{s-1} \omega_j^{s-t-1}\,\frac{\sinh(s-t)\phi_j}{\sinh\phi_j}\,\psi_{j,t}. \quad \text{(5.4.3.18)}$$

Let $\mathbf{p}_s(\Lambda, \Omega)$ be a matrix, where

$$[\mathbf{p}_s(\Lambda, \Omega)]_{jl} = \begin{cases} p_s(\lambda_j, \omega_j), & \text{if } j = l, \\ 0, & \text{if } j \neq l, \end{cases} \quad \text{(5.4.3.19)}$$

where, from (5.4.3.1) and (5.4.3.3)

$$p_s(\lambda_j, \omega_j) = -2\omega_j^s \times \begin{cases} \cos(s\theta_j), & \text{if } |\lambda_j| < |2\omega_j|, \\ \cosh(s\phi_j), & \text{if } |\lambda_j| > |2\omega_j|. \end{cases} \qquad (5.4.3.20)$$

From (5.4.3.6), we obtain

$$p_s(\mathbf{B}, \mathbf{C}) = \mathbf{Q}\, p_s(\Lambda, \Omega)\, \mathbf{Q}^t. \qquad (5.4.3.21)$$

Similarly, define a matrix $\mathbf{R}(q)$ where

$$[\mathbf{R}(q)]_{jl} = \omega_j^{q-1} \times \begin{cases} \dfrac{\sin q\theta_j}{\sin \theta_j}, & \text{if } j = l \text{ and } |\lambda_j| < |2\omega_j|, \\[2ex] \dfrac{\sinh q\phi_j}{\sin \phi_j}, & \text{if } j = l \text{ and } |\lambda_j| > |2\omega_j|, \end{cases} \qquad (5.4.3.22)$$

and

$$[\mathbf{R}(q)]_{jl} = 0, \quad \text{if } j \neq l,$$

that is, $\mathbf{R}(q)$ is a diagonal matrix.

Using (5.4.3.19) and (5.4.3.22), we can express ξ_j in matrix-vector form as

$$\xi_s = p_s(\Lambda, \Omega)\, \overline{\mathbf{d}}_i(r) + \sum_{t=0}^{s-1} \mathbf{R}(s-t)\, \psi_t. \qquad (5.4.3.23)$$

From (5.4.3.19) and (5.4.3.21), we can rewrite (5.4.3.23) as

$$\overline{\eta}_s = \mathbf{Q}\, \xi_s = p_s(\mathbf{B}, \mathbf{C})\, \mathbf{d}_i(r) + \sum_{t=0}^{s-1} [\mathbf{Q}\, \mathbf{R}(s-t)\, \mathbf{Q}^t]\, \delta_t. \qquad (5.4.3.24)$$

A major source of error occurs, if $\phi_n > \phi_1$, when $\left| \dfrac{\lambda_j}{2\omega_j} \right| > 1$. In this case, from (5.4.3.18), it can be seen that for large s, $\xi_{n,s}$ could be very large compared to $\xi_{1,s}$. Since $\overline{\eta}_s = \mathbf{Q}\, \xi_s$, the effect of $\xi_{1,s}$ may be lost in rounding.

As an example, consider the case when

$$\mathbf{B} = \begin{bmatrix} -4 & 1 & 0 & \cdots & 0 & 0 & 0 \\ 1 & -4 & 1 & \cdots & 0 & 0 & 0 \\ \cdot & \cdot & \cdot & & \cdot & \cdot & \cdot \\ \cdot & \cdot & \cdot & & \cdot & \cdot & \cdot \\ \cdot & \cdot & \cdot & & \cdot & \cdot & \cdot \\ 0 & 0 & 0 & \cdots & 1 & -4 & 1 \\ 0 & 0 & 0 & \cdots & 0 & 1 & -4 \end{bmatrix}_{n \times n} \qquad (5.4.3.25)$$

$$\mathbf{C} = \mathbf{I}_n, \text{ the identity matrix of order } n. \qquad (5.4.3.26)$$

This type of matrices occur in discretizing Poisson's equation with Dirichlet's boundary condition (Buzbee, Golub, and Nielson [1970]). In this case (Exercise 5.27),

$$\left. \begin{array}{l} \lambda_j = -4 + 2\cos\left(\dfrac{j\pi}{n+1}\right) \\[2em] \omega_j = 1. \end{array} \right\} \qquad (5.4.3.27)$$

Further, it can be shown (Buzbee [1973]) that the orthonormal matrix $\mathbf{Q} = [Q_{ij}]$ of eigenvectors of $\mathbf{B}$ is given by

$$Q_{ij} = \sqrt{\frac{2}{n+1}} \, \sin\left(\frac{i\,j\,\pi}{n+1}\right). \qquad (5.4.3.28)$$

The eigenvalues λ_i and the matrix $\sqrt{\dfrac{n+1}{2}}\,\mathbf{Q}$ are given in Tables 5.4.3.1 and 5.4.3.2, respectively.

Table 5.4.3.3 gives values of $\cosh(s\phi_j)$, for $s = 1, 5, 10, 20,$ and 31. As $\omega_j = 1$, from (5.4.3.20), it follows that by multiplying each column in Table 5.4.3.3 by -2, we obtain the diagonal elements of $\mathbf{p}_s(\Lambda, \Omega)$ for $s = 1, 5, 10, 20,$ and 31, respectively. It is evident from this table that even for moderate values of s, $\xi_{n,s}$ could be very large compared to $\xi_{1,s}$, causing round-off errors.

Case 2. $\mu_j = \nu_j = -\dfrac{\lambda_j}{2}$. This can happen only when $\lambda_j^2 = 4\omega_j^2$. In this case, it can be shown (Exercise 5.28) that

$$\xi_{j,s} = s\mu_j^{s-1}\xi_{j,1} - (s-1)\,\mu_j^s\,\xi_{j,0} + \sum_{t=1}^{s-1}(s-t)\,\mu_j^{s-t-1}\psi_{j,t}. \qquad (5.4.3.29)$$

Using (5.4.3.7) and $\lambda_j = \nu_j = -\dfrac{\lambda_j}{2}$ in (5.4.3.29), we obtain

$$\xi_{j,s} = -\left(-\frac{\lambda_j}{2}\right)^s d_{j,0} + \sum_{t=0}^{s-1}(s-t)\left(-\frac{\lambda_j}{2}\right)^{s-t-1}\psi_{j,t}. \qquad (5.4.3.30)$$

It can be easily verified that, when $\mathbf{B}$ and $\mathbf{C}$ are as given in (5.4.3.25) and (5.4.3.26), $\lambda_j^2 \neq 4\omega_j^2$. However, the analysis of numerical stability for this case is left to the reader (Exercise 5.29).

TABLE 5.4.3.1

Eigenvalue λ_j in (5.4.3.27) for $n = 8$. $\phi_j = \cosh^{-1}(\dfrac{-\lambda_j}{2\omega_j})$

j	λ_j	$-\lambda_j/2$	ϕ_j
1	−2.12	1.06	0.3447
2	−2.4679	1.2339	0.6713
3	−3.0	1.50	0.9624
4	−3.6527	1.8264	1.2104
5	−4.3473	2.1737	1.4119
6	−5.0	2.50	1.5668
7	−5.5321	2.7661	1.6762
8	−5.8794	2.9397	1.7412

TABLE 5.4.3.2

The Elements of the Matrix $\sqrt{\dfrac{n+1}{2}}$ Q for $n = 8$

i	j							
	1	2	3	4	5	6	7	8
1	0.3420	0.6428	0.866	0.9848	0.9848	0.866	0.6428	0.3420
2	0.6428	0.9848	0.866	0.3420	−0.3420	−0.866	−0.9848	−0.6428
3	0.866	0.866	0	−0.866	−0.866	0	0.866	0.866
4	0.9848	0.3420	−0.866	−0.6428	0.6428	−0.866	−0.3420	−0.9848
5	0.9848	−0.3420	−0.866	0.6428	0.6428	−0.866	−0.3420	0.9848
6	0.866	−0.866	0	0.866	−0.866	0	0.866	−0.866
7	0.6428	−0.9848	0.866	−0.342	−0.342	0.866	−0.9848	0.6428
8	0.342	−0.6428	0.866	−0.9848	0.9848	−0.866	0.6428	−0.3420

TABLE 5.4.3.3

ϕ_j	cosh (s ϕ_j)				
	$s = 1$	$s = 5$	$s = 10$	$s = 20$	$s = 31$
0.3447	1.06	2.8913	15.7189	493.17	2.19×10^4
0.6713	1.2339	14.36	411.52	3.38×10^5	5.45×10^8
0.9624	1.50	61.49	7561.7	1.14×10^8	4.53×10^{12}
1.2104	1.8264	212.48	90296.4	1.63×10^{10}	9.88×10^{15}
1.4119	2.1737	581.93	6.77×10^5	9.17×10^{11}	5.1×10^{18}
1.5668	2.50	1262.5	3.19×10^6	2.03×10^{13}	6.21×10^{20}
1.6762	2.7661	2181.7	9.52×10^6	1.81×10^{14}	1.84×10^{22}
1.7412	2.9397	3019.5	1.82×10^7	6.65×10^{14}	1.38×10^{23}

5.4.4 A Stable Version of Cyclic Reduction -- Buneman's Algorithm

Having proved that block cyclic reduction is *not* numerically stable, in this section, we seek to rearrange the computation so as to induce stability. The idea of this reorganization is due to Buneman [1969], and our exposition follows Buzbee, Golub, and Nielson [1970]. The difference principally lies in the way in which the elements $d_i(j)$ on the right-hand side of the reduced system are computed.

Consider the special case of (5.4.1.2), when $C = I_n$, the unit matrix of order n. In this case, after the first step of the reduction phase, we obtain from (5.4.2.3), for $i = 2, 4, 6, \cdots, M - 1$,

$$\mathbf{x}_{i-2} + \mathbf{B}(1)\, \mathbf{x}_i + \mathbf{x}_{i+2} = \mathbf{d}_i(1), \tag{5.4.4.1}$$

where

$$\mathbf{B}(1) = (2\mathbf{I}_n - \mathbf{B}^2), \tag{5.4.4.2}$$

$$\mathbf{d}_i(1) = \mathbf{d}_{i-1} + \mathbf{d}_{i+1} - \mathbf{B}\mathbf{d}_i, \tag{5.4.4.3}$$

and $\mathbf{x}_i = 0$ for $i < 1$ or $> M$.

The *trick* lies in rewriting the right-hand side of (5.4.4.3) by adding and subtracting $2\mathbf{B}^{-1}\, \mathbf{d}_i$ to it. Thus,

$$\mathbf{d}_i(1) = \mathbf{d}_{i-1} + \mathbf{d}_{i+1} - \mathbf{B}\, \mathbf{d}_i$$

$$= \mathbf{B}(1) \, \mathbf{B}^{-1} \, \mathbf{d}_i + \mathbf{d}_{i-1} + \mathbf{d}_{i+1} - 2\mathbf{B}^{-1} \, \mathbf{d}_i$$

$$= \mathbf{B}(1) \, \alpha_i(1) + \beta_i(1), \tag{5.4.4.4}$$

where

$$\alpha_i(1) = \mathbf{B}^{-1} \, \mathbf{d}_i$$

$$\left.\begin{array}{c} \\ \\ \end{array}\right\} \tag{5.4.4.5}$$

$$\beta_i(1) = \mathbf{d}_{i-1} + \mathbf{d}_{i+1} - 2\alpha_i(1).$$

Now considering a system of three consecutive equations centered around $i = 4$, 8, 12, $\cdots$, $M - 3$, analogous to (5.4.2.10), we obtain

$$\mathbf{x}_{i-2^2} + [2\mathbf{I}_n - \mathbf{B}^2(1)] \, \mathbf{x}_i + \mathbf{x}_{i+2^2} = \mathbf{d}_i(2), \tag{5.4.4.6}$$

where

$$\mathbf{d}_i(2) = \mathbf{d}_{i-2}(1) + \mathbf{d}_{i+2}(1) - \mathbf{B}(1) \, \mathbf{d}_i(1). \tag{5.4.4.7}$$

In rewriting (5.4.4.7), first substitute (5.4.4.4) into it to obtain

$$\mathbf{d}_i(2) = \mathbf{B}(1) \, [\alpha_{i-2}(1) + \alpha_{i+2}(1) - \beta_i(1) \,]$$

$$+ \beta_{i-2}(1) + \beta_{i+2}(1) - \mathbf{B}^2(1) \, \alpha_i(1). \tag{5.4.4.8}$$

Adding and subtracting $2\alpha_i(1)$, since $\mathbf{B}(2) = 2\mathbf{I}_n - (\mathbf{B}(1))^2$, it becomes

$$\mathbf{d}_i(2) = \mathbf{B}(2) \, \alpha_i(1) + \mathbf{B}(1) \, [\alpha_{i-2}(1) + \alpha_{i+2}(1) - \beta_i(1)]$$

$$+ \beta_{i-2}(1) + \beta_{i+2}(1) - 2\alpha_i(1). \tag{5.4.4.9}$$

Again, adding and subtracting

$$2(\mathbf{B}(1))^{-1} \, [\alpha_{i-2}(1) + \alpha_{i+2}(1) - \beta_i(1)],$$

we get

$$\mathbf{d}_i(2) = \mathbf{B}(2) \, \alpha_i(2) + \beta_i(2), \tag{5.4.4.10}$$

where

$$\alpha_i(2) = \alpha_i(1) - (\mathbf{B}(1))^{-1} \, [\alpha_{i-2}(1) + \alpha_{i+2}(1) - \beta_i(1)]$$

$$\left.\begin{array}{c} \\ \\ \end{array}\right\} \tag{5.4.4.11}$$

$$\beta_i(2) = \beta_{i-2}(1) + \beta_{i+2}(1) - 2\alpha_i(2).$$

To better understand the structure of the new terms $\alpha_i(j)$ and $\beta_i(j)$, we now state the initial conditions:

$$\left.\begin{array}{l} \alpha_i(0) = \mathbf{0} \\[1.5em] \beta_i(0) = \mathbf{d}_i \end{array}\right\}, \quad i = 1, 2, \cdots, M. \tag{5.4.4.12}$$

Continuing in this way, after $t + 1$ steps for $t = 0, 1, 2, \cdots$, of the reduction phase, we obtain

$$\mathbf{d}_i(t + 1) = \mathbf{B}(t+1)\,\alpha_i(t+1) + \beta_i(t + 1) \tag{5.4.4.13}$$

and

$$\left.\begin{array}{l} \alpha_i(t+1) = \alpha_i(t) - (\mathbf{B}(t))^{-1}\,[\alpha_{i-h}(t) + \alpha_{i+h}(t) - \beta_i(t)] \\[1.5em] \beta_i(t + 1) = \beta_{i-h}(t) + \beta_{i+h}(t) - 2\alpha_i(t+1), \end{array}\right\} \tag{5.4.4.14}$$

for $i = l(\,2^{t+1}), \quad l = 1, 2, \cdots, 2^{k-t-1} - 1, \quad$ and $\quad h = 2^t$.

As the first variation in computing the solution, rewrite the first equation in (5.4.4.14) as

$$\mathbf{B}(t)\,[\alpha_i(t) - \alpha_i(t+1)] = \alpha_{i-h}(t) + \alpha_{i+h}(t) - \beta_i(t). \tag{5.4.4.15}$$

Since $\alpha_i(j)$'s and $\beta_i(j)$'s are known, $\alpha_i(t+1)$ is obtained by solving (5.4.4.15) by exploiting the factorization for $\mathbf{B}(t)$ as in (5.4.2.29) through (5.4.2.31).

After $k - 1$ steps of the reduction phase (since $M = 2^k - 1$), we obtain a single reduced system given by (refer to (5.4.2.18)),

$$\mathbf{B}(k-1)\,\mathbf{x}_{2^{k-1}} = \mathbf{B}(k-1)\,\alpha_{2^{k-1}}(k - 1) + \beta_{2^{k-1}}(k - 1). \tag{5.4.4.16}$$

Hence

$$\mathbf{x}_{2^{k-1}} = \alpha_{2^{k-1}}(k - 1) + (\mathbf{B}(k-1))^{-1}\,\beta_{2^{k-1}}(k - 1). \tag{5.4.4.17}$$

Once again, we use the factorization of $\mathbf{B}(k-1)$ to compute the second term of the right-hand side of (5.4.4.17).

To recover the other components of the vector $\mathbf{x}$ in (5.4.1.1), consider the equation

$$\mathbf{x}_{i-2^r} + \mathbf{B}(r)\,\mathbf{x}_i + \mathbf{x}_{i+2^r} = \mathbf{B}(r)\,\alpha_i(r) + \beta_i(r), \tag{5.4.4.18}$$

from which we obtain

$$\mathbf{B}(r)\,[\mathbf{x}_i - \alpha_i(r)] = \beta_i(r) - (\mathbf{x}_{i-2^r} + \mathbf{x}_{i+2^r}). \tag{5.4.4.19}$$

For $i = 2^r, 3 \times 2^r, 5 \times 2^r, \cdots, 2^k - 2^r$, and $r = k - 2, k - 3, \cdots, 2, 1, 0$, solve (5.4.4.19) for $\mathbf{x}_i$ using the factorization for $\mathbf{B}(r)$. The entire algorithm is stated in Fig. 5.4.4.1.

For another variation of Buneman's algorithm, refer to Exercise 5.32.

Combining the original governing equation,

$$\mathbf{x}_{i-1} + \mathbf{B}\,\mathbf{x}_i + \mathbf{x}_{i+1} = \mathbf{d}_i,$$

/*   Given $\alpha_i(0) = 0$ and $\beta_i(0) = \mathbf{d}_i$, $i = 1, 2, \cdots, M$, where $M = 2^k - 1$. */

    FOR $r = 1$ TO $k - 1$ STEP 1 DO
        FOR $i \in \{2^r, 2 \times 2^r, 3 \times 2^r, \cdots, 2^k - 2^r\}$ DO IN PARALLEL
            COMPUTE $\alpha_i(r)$ and $\beta_i(r)$ from (5.4.4.14) using factorization for $\mathbf{B}(r)$.
        END
    END

    SOLVE FOR $\mathbf{x}_{2^{k-1}}$ from (5.4.4.17) using factorization for $\mathbf{B}(r)$.

    FOR $r = k - 2$ TO 0 STEP -1 DO
        FOR $i \in \{2^r, 3 \times 2^r, 5 \times 2^r, \cdots, 2^k - 2^r\}$ DO IN PARALLEL
            COMPUTE $\mathbf{x}_i$ from (5.4.4.19) using factorization for $\mathbf{B}(r)$.
        END
    END

FIGURE 5.4.4.1
Buneman's algorithm.

with (5.4.4.5), we can express the $\alpha_i(1)$'s and $\beta_i(1)$'s in terms of the $\mathbf{x}_i$'s as follows:

$$\alpha_i(1) = \mathbf{x}_i + \mathbf{B}^{-1}(\mathbf{x}_{i-1} + \mathbf{x}_{i+1}) \tag{5.4.4.20}$$

and

$$\beta_i(1) = \mathbf{x}_{i-2} + \mathbf{x}_{i+2} - \mathbf{B}^{-1}\,\mathbf{B}(1)\,[\mathbf{x}_{i-1} + \mathbf{x}_{i+1}]. \tag{5.4.4.21}$$

Combining these with (5.4.4.11) and simplifying, we obtain

$$\alpha_i(2) = \mathbf{x}_i - \mathbf{B}^{-1}(1)\,\mathbf{B}^{-1}\,(\mathbf{x}_{i-3} + \mathbf{x}_{i-1}) - \mathbf{B}^{-1}(1)\,\mathbf{B}^{-1}\,(\mathbf{x}_{i+1} + \mathbf{x}_{i+3})$$

$$= \mathbf{x}_i - \mathbf{S}(2) \sum_{j=1}^{2} [\mathbf{x}_{i-(2j-1)} + \mathbf{x}_{i+(2j-1)}], \tag{5.4.4.22}$$

where $\mathbf{B}(0) = \mathbf{B}$ and

$$\mathbf{S}(2) = (\mathbf{B}(0)\,\mathbf{B}(1))^{-1}. \tag{5.4.4.23}$$

Likewise,

$$\beta_i(2) = \mathbf{x}_{i-4} + \mathbf{x}_{i+4} + \mathbf{S}(2)\,\mathbf{B}(2) \sum_{j=1}^{2} [\mathbf{x}_{i-(2j-1)} + \mathbf{x}_{i+(2j-1)}]. \tag{5.4.4.24}$$

Generalizing this, it can be shown (Exercise 5.30) that

$$\alpha_i(r) = \mathbf{x}_i + (-1)^{r+1} \, \Delta_i(r)$$

$$\left.\begin{matrix} \\ \\ \\ \end{matrix}\right\} \qquad (5.4.4.25)$$

$$\beta_i(r) = \mathbf{x}_{i-2^r} + \mathbf{x}_{i+2^r} + (-1)^r \, \mathbf{B}(r) \, \Delta_i(r),$$

where

$$\Delta_i(r) = \mathbf{S}(r) \sum_{j=1}^{2^{r-1}} [\mathbf{x}_{i-(2j-1)} + \mathbf{x}_{i+(2j-1)}] \qquad (5.4.4.26)$$

and (see Exercise 5.31)

$$\mathbf{S}(r) = [\mathbf{B}(0) \, \mathbf{B}(1) \cdots \mathbf{B}(r-1)]^{-1}. \qquad (5.4.4.27)$$

We conclude this section by proving the stability of this modified algorithm. To establish formal results, many standard definitions and properties related to matrices are needed which we now quote without proof. For details refer to Bellman [1960] and Varga [1972]. (See Exercise 5.35.)

Let $\mathbf{u} = (u_1, u_2, \cdots, u_N)^t$ and $\mathbf{v} = (v_1, v_2, \cdots, v_N)^t$ be two vectors with real or complex elements. Then, the Euclidean norm $\| \mathbf{u} \|$ of the vector is defined to be

$$\| \mathbf{u} \| = (\sum_{i=1}^{N} |u_i|^2)^{\frac{1}{2}},$$

where $|u_i|$ denotes the absolute value of u_i. Let α be a non-zero real or complex number. The Euclidean vector norm satisfies the following properties.

(V1) $\| \mathbf{u} \| = 0$, only if $u_i = 0$ for all $i = 1, 2, \cdots, n$.

(V2) $\| \alpha \mathbf{u} \| = |\alpha| \, \| \mathbf{u} \|$.

(V3) $\| \mathbf{u} + \mathbf{v} \| \leq \| \mathbf{u} \| + \| \mathbf{v} \|$.

Let $\mathbf{A}$ be an $N \times N$ matrix of real elements. Let λ_i, $i = 1, 2, \cdots, n$, be the eigenvalues of $\mathbf{A}$. Then

$$\rho(\mathbf{A}) = \max_{1 \leq i \leq N} \{ |\lambda_i| \}$$

is called the *spectral radius of the matrix* $\mathbf{A}$. *The spectral norm* $\| \mathbf{A} \|$ of the matrix $\mathbf{A}$ is defined by

$$\| \mathbf{A} \| = \sup_{\mathbf{u} \neq 0} \frac{\| \mathbf{A} \mathbf{u} \|}{\| \mathbf{u} \|} = \sup_{\| \mathbf{u} \| = 1} \| \mathbf{A} \mathbf{u} \|.$$

The following properties of the matrix norm are standard. Let $\mathbf{A}$ and $\mathbf{B}$ be two $N \times N$ matrices, and $\mathbf{u}$ an N vector.

(M1) $\| \mathbf{A} \| > 0$ unless $\mathbf{A}$ is a null matrix.

(M2) $\| \mathbf{A} + \mathbf{B} \| \leq \| \mathbf{A} \| + \| \mathbf{B} \|$.

(M3) $\| \mathbf{A} \mathbf{B} \| \leq \| \mathbf{A} \| \, \| \mathbf{B} \|$.

(M4) $\| \mathbf{A} \, \mathbf{u} \| \leq \| \mathbf{A} \| \, \| \mathbf{u} \|.$

(M5) $\| \mathbf{A} \| \geq \rho(\mathbf{A}).$

(M6) Let $\mathbf{A}$ be a real matrix. Then

$$\| \mathbf{A} \| = (\rho(\mathbf{A}^t \mathbf{A}))^{\frac{1}{2}},$$

where $\mathbf{A}^t$ is the transpose of $\mathbf{A}$. Consequently,

$$\| \mathbf{A} \| = \rho(\mathbf{A}) \quad \text{if} \quad \mathbf{A} \ \text{is symmetric,}$$

and

$$\| \mathbf{A} \| = 1 \quad \text{if} \quad \mathbf{A} \ \text{is orthogonal (since} \ \mathbf{A}^t = \mathbf{A}^{-1}).$$

(M7) If $\mathbf{Q}$ is an orthogonal matrix, then

$$\| \mathbf{A} \| = \| \mathbf{Q} \, \mathbf{A} \| = \| \mathbf{A} \, \mathbf{Q} \|,$$

that is, the spectral norm is *orthogonal invariant.*

(M8) Let λ be an eigenvalue of a matrix $\mathbf{A}$. If $\mathbf{A}$ is non-singular and $\lambda \neq 0$, then λ^{-1} is an eigenvalue of $\mathbf{A}^{-1}$.

(M9) Let $\mathbf{A}$ be a real symmetric matrix of order N with distinct eigenvalues, and $\mathbf{Q}$ be an orthogonal matrix of its eigenvectors. Then $\mathbf{A} = \mathbf{Q} \, \mathbf{D} \, \mathbf{Q}^t$, where $\mathbf{D}$ is the diagonal matrix of eigenvalues $\lambda_1, \lambda_2, \cdots, \lambda_n$ of $\mathbf{A}$. Clearly, $\mathbf{A}^{-1} = \mathbf{Q} \mathbf{D}^{-1} \mathbf{Q}^t$ and

$$\| \mathbf{A}^{-1} \| = \| \mathbf{D}^{-1} \| = \max_i \{ | \lambda_i^{-1} | \}.$$

(M10) Let $q(x)$ be a polynomial with real coefficients. If $\mathbf{A}$ is symmetric, then $q(\mathbf{A})$ is symmetric and

$$\| q(\mathbf{A}) \| = \rho(q(\mathbf{A})) = \max_{1 \leq i \leq N} \{ | q(\lambda_i) | \},$$

and

$$\| (q(\mathbf{A}))^{-1} \| = \max_{1 \leq i \leq N} \{ | (q(\lambda_i))^{-1} | \}.$$

With these preliminaries, we once again analyze the properties of the polynomial in (5.4.3.20),

$$p_s(a, t) = -2t^s \begin{cases} \cos(s\theta), & \text{when } | a | < | 2t | \\[2mm] \cosh s\phi, & \text{when } | a | \geq | 2t |, \end{cases} \tag{5.4.4.28}$$

where

$$-\left|\frac{a}{2t}\right| = \begin{cases} \cos\theta, & \text{when } |a| < |2t| \\ \\ \cosh\phi, & \text{when } |a| \geq |2t|. \end{cases}$$

Let $\psi = -\dfrac{a}{2}$ and

$$\psi = \begin{cases} \cos\theta & \text{when } |\psi| < 1 \\ \\ \cosh\phi & \text{when } |\psi| \geq 1. \end{cases} \tag{5.4.4.29}$$

When $t = 1$, we rewrite the polynomial as

$$p_s(a) = p_s(a, 1) = \begin{cases} -2\cos(s\cos^{-1}\psi) & \text{if } |\psi| < 1 \\ \\ -2\cosh(s\cosh^{-1}\psi) & \text{if } |\psi| \geq 1. \end{cases} \tag{5.4.4.30}$$

Since $\mathbf{C} = \mathbf{I}_n$, combining (5.4.2.24) and (5.4.4.30), we obtain

$$\mathbf{B}(j) = p_{2^j}(\mathbf{B}),$$

where $\mathbf{B}$ is real and symmetric. From (5.4.4.27) and the properties of the spectral norm, we obtain (see Exercise 5.39)

$$\|\mathbf{S}(r)\| \leq \prod_{j=0}^{r-1} \|(\mathbf{B}(j))^{-1}\| \leq \prod_{j=0}^{r-1} \max_{\lambda_i}\{|(p_{2^j}(\lambda_i))^{-1}|\},$$

where λ_i's are the eigenvalues of $\mathbf{B}$. When $\mathbf{B}$ is such that $|\lambda_i| \geq 2$ (this happens when $\mathbf{B}$ is of the type given in (5.4.3.25)), from (5.4.4.29) and (5.4.4.30) it follows that

$$\left.\begin{aligned} |\psi| &= \left|-\frac{\lambda_i}{2}\right| > 1 \\ \\ \phi_i &= \cosh^{-1}\left(-\frac{\lambda_i}{2}\right), \end{aligned}\right\} \tag{5.4.4.31}$$

and

$$\|\mathbf{S}(r)\| \leq 2^{-r} \prod_{j=0}^{r-1} \max_{\phi_i}\{(\cosh(2^j\phi_i))^{-1}\}. \tag{5.4.4.32}$$

Likewise, when $|\lambda_i| \geq 2$,

$$\|\mathbf{B}(r)\,\mathbf{S}(r)\| \leq 2^{-r+1} \max_{\phi_i}\left\{\cosh(2^r\phi_i)\prod_{j=0}^{r-1}(\cosh(2^j\phi_j))^{-1}\right\}. \tag{5.4.4.33}$$

From (5.4.3.27) and (5.4.4.31),

$$-\frac{\lambda_i}{2} = 2 - \cos \frac{i\,\pi}{n+1} = \cosh \phi_i, \tag{5.4.4.34}$$

and $\phi_i > 1$ for all i.

Let ϕ^* be such that (Exercise 5.33)

$$(\cosh 2^j \, \phi^*)^{-1} = \max_{\phi_i} \left\{ (\cosh 2^j \, \phi_i)^{-1} \right\}. \tag{5.4.4.35}$$

Further, since

$$(\cosh Z)^{-1} = \frac{2\,e^{-Z}}{1 + e^{-2Z}} \le 2\,e^{-Z}, \tag{5.4.4.36}$$

combining these with (5.4.4.32), we get

$$\|S(r)\| \le \frac{e^{-(2^r - 1)\phi^*}}{\displaystyle\prod_{j=0}^{r-1}(1 + e^{-2^{(j+1)}\phi^*})} \le e^{-(2^r - 1)\,\phi^*}. \tag{5.4.4.37}$$

Let

$$\|x\|^* = \sum_{j=1}^{M} \| \, x_j \, \|. \tag{5.4.4.38}$$

Then, from (5.4.4.25),

$$\|\alpha_i(r) - x_i\| \le \|\Delta_i(r)\|$$

$$\le \|S(r)\| \, \|x\|^*$$

$$\le \|x\|^* \, e^{-(2^r - 1)\,\phi^*}, \tag{5.4.4.39}$$

that is, for large r, $\alpha_i(r)$ is a good approximation to x_i.

Similarly, from (5.4.4.33) and (5.4.4.36),

$$\|B(r)\,S(r)\| \le 2 \max_{\phi_i} \left\{ \frac{(e^{2^r \phi_i} + e^{-2^r \phi_i})}{2} \, e^{-(2^r - 1)\,\phi_i} \right\}$$

$$\le 2 \max_{\phi_i} \left\{ e^{2^r \phi_i} \, e^{-(2^r - 1)\phi_i} \right\}$$

$$\le 2e^{\phi_n}, \tag{5.4.4.40}$$

since from (5.4.4.31) that e^{ϕ_i} is maximum when $\phi_i = \phi_n$. Hence,

$$\|\beta_i(r) - (x_{i-2^r} + x_{i+2^r})\| \le 2e^{\phi_n} \, \|x\|^*, \tag{5.4.4.41}$$

that is, $\beta_i(r)$ remains bounded throughout the computations. In other words, Buneman's variation leads to a numerically stable algorithm.

5.4.5 A Matrix Decomposition Method

This method, due to Buzbee, Golub, and Nielson [1970], begins with the system (5.4.2.1) reproduced here for convenience:

$$
\left.
\begin{aligned}
&\mathbf{B}\,\mathbf{x}_1 + \mathbf{C}\,\mathbf{x}_2 = \mathbf{d}_1 \\
&\mathbf{C}\,\mathbf{x}_{j-1} + \mathbf{B}\,\mathbf{x}_j + \mathbf{C}\,\mathbf{x}_{j+1} = \mathbf{d}_j \\
&\mathbf{C}\,\mathbf{x}_{M-1} + \mathbf{B}\,\mathbf{x}_M = \mathbf{d}_M,
\end{aligned}
\right\}
\qquad (5.4.5.1)
$$

for $j = 2, 3, 4, \cdots, M-1$, where the matrices $\mathbf{B}$ and $\mathbf{C}$ satisfy (5.4.1.3), $\mathbf{x}_i = (x_{1i}, x_{2i}, \cdots, x_{ni})^t$, and $\mathbf{d}_i = (d_{1i}, d_{2i}, \cdots, d_{ni})^t$. Using the matrix $\mathbf{Q}$ defined in (5.4.3.6a), the above system can be transformed as follows:

$$
\left.
\begin{aligned}
&\mathbf{\Lambda}\,\overline{\mathbf{x}}_1 + \mathbf{\Omega}\,\overline{\mathbf{x}}_2 = \overline{\mathbf{d}}_1 \\
&\mathbf{\Omega}\,\overline{\mathbf{x}}_{j-1} + \mathbf{\Lambda}\,\overline{\mathbf{x}}_j + \mathbf{\Omega}\,\overline{\mathbf{x}}_{j+1} = \overline{\mathbf{d}}_j \\
&\mathbf{\Omega}\,\overline{\mathbf{x}}_{n-1} + \mathbf{\Lambda}\,\overline{\mathbf{x}}_n = \overline{\mathbf{d}}_n,
\end{aligned}
\right\}
\qquad (5.4.5.2)
$$

for $j = 2, 3, 4, \cdots, M-1$, where $\mathbf{\Lambda}$ and $\mathbf{\Omega}$ are defined in (5.4.3.6b) and (5.4.3.6c),

$$
\left.
\begin{aligned}
&\overline{\mathbf{x}}_i = \mathbf{Q}^t\,\mathbf{x}_i \\
&\overline{\mathbf{d}}_i = \mathbf{Q}^t\,\mathbf{d}_i,
\end{aligned}
\right\}
\qquad (5.4.5.3)
$$

$i = 1, 2, 3, \cdots, M$,

$$
\overline{\mathbf{x}}_i = (\overline{x}_{1i}, \overline{x}_{2i}, \cdots, \overline{x}_{ni})^t \quad \text{and} \quad \overline{\mathbf{d}}_i = (\overline{d}_{1i}, \overline{d}_{2i}, \cdots, \overline{d}_{ni})^t.
$$

First, collect all the equations involving λ_i and ω_i from (5.4.5.2):

$$
\left.
\begin{aligned}
&\lambda_i\,\overline{x}_{i1} + \omega_i\,\overline{x}_{i2} = \overline{d}_{i1} \\
&\omega_i\,\overline{x}_{i,j-1} + \lambda_i\,\overline{x}_{ij} + \omega_i\,\overline{x}_{i,j+1} = \overline{d}_{ij} \\
&\omega_i\,\overline{x}_{i,M-1} + \lambda_i\,\overline{x}_{iM} = \overline{d}_{iM},
\end{aligned}
\right\}
\qquad (5.4.5.4)
$$

for $j = 2, 3, \cdots, M-1$, and $i = 1, 2, \cdots, n$. Define

$$\Gamma_i = \begin{bmatrix} \lambda_i & \omega_i & 0 & \cdots & 0 & 0 & 0 \\ \omega_i & \lambda_i & \omega_i & \cdots & 0 & 0 & 0 \\ \cdot & \cdot & \cdot & & \cdot & \cdot & \cdot \\ \cdot & \cdot & \cdot & & \cdot & \cdot & \cdot \\ \cdot & \cdot & \cdot & & \cdot & \cdot & \cdot \\ 0 & 0 & 0 & \cdots & \omega_i & \lambda_i & \omega_i \\ 0 & 0 & 0 & \cdots & 0 & \omega_i & \lambda_i \end{bmatrix} \qquad (5.4.5.5)$$

a symmetric tridiagonal matrix of order M with constants along the non-zero diagonals and

$$\left. \begin{aligned} \hat{\mathbf{x}}_i &= (\bar{x}_{i1}, \bar{x}_{i2}, \cdots, \bar{x}_{iM})^t \\[2em] \hat{\mathbf{d}}_i &= (\bar{d}_{i1}, \bar{d}_{i2}, \cdots, \bar{d}_{iM})^t. \end{aligned} \right\} \qquad (5.4.5.6)$$

and

Using these, (5.4.5.4) can be rewritten as

$$\Gamma_i \hat{\mathbf{x}}_i = \hat{\mathbf{d}}_i, \qquad (5.4.5.7)$$

for $i = 1, 2, \cdots, n$.

The effect of the above transformation is to decouple (5.4.5.1) and express it as a system of n independent tridiagonal systems (5.4.5.7). The parallel algorithm based on the above analysis is given in Fig. 5.4.5.1.

Since $\mathbf{Q}$ is known, steps 2 and 4, in general, involve inner product computations. But in the special case when

$$\mathbf{B} = \begin{bmatrix} -4 & 1 & 0 & \cdots & 0 & 0 & 0 \\ 1 & -4 & 1 & \cdots & 0 & 0 & 0 \\ \cdot & \cdot & \cdot & & \cdot & \cdot & \cdot \\ \cdot & \cdot & \cdot & & \cdot & \cdot & \cdot \\ \cdot & \cdot & \cdot & \cdots & \cdot & \cdot & \cdot \\ 0 & 0 & 0 & \cdots & 1 & -4 & 1 \\ 0 & 0 & 0 & & 0 & 1 & -4 \end{bmatrix}$$

and

$$\mathbf{C} = \mathbf{I}_n,$$

it can be shown (Buzbee [1973]) that the matrix $\mathbf{Q}$ of eigenvectors is given by

---

/* Given the system (5.4.5.1) */

Step 1. COMPUTE the eigenvalues λ_i and ω_i, $i = 1, 2, \cdots, n$, of matrices **B** and **C** and the matrix **Q** of eigenvectors of matrix **B**.

Step 2. COMPUTE $\overline{\mathbf{d}}_j = \mathbf{Q}^t \, \mathbf{d}_j$ for $j = 1, 2, \cdots, M$ IN PARALLEL.

Step 3. SOLVE the tridiagonal system

$$\Gamma_i \, \hat{\mathbf{x}}_i = \hat{\mathbf{d}}_i \quad \text{for } i = 1, 2, \cdots, n$$

IN PARALLEL using any method of Section 5.4.3.

Step 4. COMPUTE $\mathbf{x}_j = \mathbf{Q} \, \overline{\mathbf{x}}_j$ for $j = 1, 2, \cdots, M$ IN PARALLEL.

Note. $\overline{\mathbf{x}}_j$ can be readily constructed from $\hat{\mathbf{x}}_i$ be reassembling the components.

FIGURE 5.4.5.1
A matrix decomposition algorithm.

$$\mathbf{Q} = [Q_{ij}] = \sqrt{\frac{2}{n+1}} \, \sin \frac{ij\pi}{n+1}.$$

In this case $\overline{\mathbf{d}}_j$ in step 2 is defined as the discrete *sine transform* of $\mathbf{d}_j$. Since the sine transform is a special case of the FFT algorithm given in Chapter 3 (Swarztrauber [1982]), we can exploit the FFT algorithm to further speed up the computations in steps 2 and 4. See Exercise 5.34 for a variation of this algorithm for the case when **B** and **C** do not commute.

5.4.6 The Block Gaussian Algorithm

Consider a general block tridiagonal system

$$\mathbf{A} \, \mathbf{x} = \mathbf{d}, \tag{5.4.6.1}$$

where

$$A = \begin{bmatrix} B_1 & C_1 & 0 & \cdots & 0 & 0 & 0 \\ A_2 & B_2 & C_2 & \cdots & 0 & 0 & 0 \\ \cdot & \cdot & \cdot & & \cdot & \cdot & \cdot \\ \cdot & \cdot & \cdot & & \cdot & \cdot & \cdot \\ \cdot & \cdot & \cdot & & \cdot & \cdot & \cdot \\ 0 & 0 & 0 & \cdots & A_{M-1} & B_{M-1} & C_{M-1} \\ 0 & 0 & 0 & \cdots & 0 & A_M & B_M \end{bmatrix}, \qquad (5.4.6.2)$$

with

$$\mathbf{x} = (x_1, x_2, \cdots, x_M)^t,$$

$$\mathbf{d} = (d_1, d_2, \cdots, d_M)^t,$$

where A_i, B_i, and C_i are $n \times n$ block matrices and $\mathbf{x}_i$ and $\mathbf{d}_i$ are n-vectors. The crux of this method consists in expressing A as the product of lower triangular and upper triangular block matrices L and U.

$$L = \begin{bmatrix} L_1 & 0 & 0 & \cdots & 0 & 0 & 0 \\ A_2 & L_2 & 0 & \cdots & 0 & 0 & 0 \\ 0 & A_3 & L_3 & \cdots & 0 & 0 & 0 \\ \cdot & \cdot & \cdot & & \cdot & \cdot & \cdot \\ \cdot & \cdot & \cdot & & \cdot & \cdot & \cdot \\ \cdot & \cdot & \cdot & & \cdot & \cdot & \cdot \\ 0 & 0 & 0 & \cdots & A_{M-1} & L_{M-1} & 0 \\ 0 & 0 & 0 & \cdots & 0 & A_M & L_M \end{bmatrix},$$

$$U = \begin{bmatrix} I & U_1 & 0 & \cdots & 0 & 0 \\ 0 & I & U_2 & \cdots & 0 & 0 \\ \cdot & \cdot & \cdot & & \cdot & \cdot \\ \cdot & \cdot & \cdot & & \cdot & \cdot \\ \cdot & \cdot & \cdot & & \cdot & \cdot \\ 0 & 0 & 0 & \cdots & I & U_{M-1} \\ 0 & 0 & 0 & \cdots & 0 & I \end{bmatrix},$$

where L_i, U_j, and I are $n \times n$ block matrices. From

$$A = L U,$$

we can compute L_i and U_j, using the following:

$$L_1 = B_1, \qquad U_1 = L_1^{-1} C_1,$$

and for $j = 2, 3, \cdots, M$,   (5.4.6.3)

$$L_j = B_j - A_j U_{j-1}, \qquad U_j = L_j^{-1} C_j.$$

(Since $C_M = 0$, the null matrix, there is no need to compute L_M^{-1}.) The above computation is intrinsically serial in j. However, depending on the size and the structure of the block matrices A_i, B_i, and C_i, one could very cleverly exploit parallelism in the standard matrix vector operations. For a systematic development of these ideas, refer to Berry and Sameh [1988].

Given the factors L and U, we now solve (5.4.6.1) by the standard forward elimination and back-substitution process.

(a) **Forward Elimination Phase:** Here, we solve for $L y = d$ as follows:

$$y_1 = L_1^{-1} d_1,$$

and, for $j = 2, 3, \cdots, M$,

$$y_j = L_j^{-1} (d_j - A_j y_{j-1}). \qquad (5.4.6.4)$$

(b) **Back-Substitution Phase:** We recover the components of the vector x as follows:

$$x_n = y_n,$$

and, for $j = n - 1, n - 2, \cdots, 2, 1$,

$$x_j = y_j - U_j x_{j+1}. \qquad (5.4.6.5)$$

These computations can be efficiently implemented on a multivector architecture such as the Alliant FX/8, and we refer the reader to Berry and Sameh [1988], and Dowers, Lakshmivarahan, and Dhall [1987, 1989] for details of implementations.

For this algorithm to be numerically stable, we need some kind of a bound on the pivotal growth, that is,

$$\max_i \{\|L_i\|, \|U_j\|\} \leq k, \qquad (5.4.6.6)$$

where $\|.\|$ is a matrix norm. (See Exercise 5.35 for various choices for the matrix norms.) When $n = 1$, that is, in the scalar case (see Section 5.3.1), this is ensured by the diagonal dominance condition (5.3.1.12). In the following, we develop a similar dominance condition for the block case.

The block tridiagonal matrix A in (5.4.6.2) is said to be *block diagonally dominant* (Varah [1972]) with respect to the chosen norm $\| . \|$ if

$$\|B_i^{-1}\| (\| A_i \| + \| C_i \|) \leq 1. \qquad (5.4.6.7)$$

It is tacitly assumed that the diagonal blocks are non-singular. In addition, it is assumed that $C_i \neq 0$, for all i, for if $C_j = 0$ for some j, the system could be decoupled. With these observations, we now state a preparatory lemma.

Lemma 5.4.6.1. Let R be a matrix with $\| R \| < 1$. Then $I - R$ is non-singular, and

$$\| (I - R)^{-1} \| \leq (1 - \| R \|)^{-1}. \qquad (5.4.6.8)$$

Proof

Let Z be a non-null vector. Then

$$\| (I - R)\, Z \| = \| Z - R\, Z \|$$

$$\geq \| Z \| - \| R\, Z \|$$

$$\geq \| Z \| (1 - \| R \|)$$

$$> 0, \qquad \text{since } \| R \| < 1.$$

That is, for every non-null vector Z, the product $(I - R)\, Z$ is also a non-null vector. Since $(I - R)\, Z = 0$ has a non-null solution if and only if $(I - R)$ is singular, combining this with the above fact, it follows that $(I - R)$ is non-singular.

Now from

$$(I - R)\,(I - R)^{-1} = I,$$

we obtain

$$(I - R)^{-1} = I + R(I - R)^{-1}.$$

Hence

$$\| (I - R)^{-1} \| \leq \| I \| + \| R \| \| (I - R)^{-1} \|,$$

and the lemma follows.

We now state a key lemma that guarantees the pivotal growth condition (5.4.6.6).

Lemma 5.4.6.2. If the matrix A in (5.4.6.1) satisfies the block diagonal dominance condition (5.4.6.7), then $\| L_i^{-1} \| \leq \dfrac{1}{\| C_i \|}$.

Proof

The proof is by induction. From (5.4.6.3) and (5.4.6.7), we obtain

$$\| \mathbf{L}_1^{-1} \| = \| \mathbf{B}_1^{-1} \| \leq \frac{1}{\| \mathbf{C}_1 \|},$$

from which the basis follows. Let it be true for $i = 1, 2, \cdots, j - 1$. Clearly, from (5.4.6.3),

$$\mathbf{L}_j = \mathbf{B}_j - \mathbf{A}_j \mathbf{U}_{j-1}$$

$$= \mathbf{B}_j - \mathbf{A}_j \mathbf{L}_{j-1}^{-1} \mathbf{C}_{j-1}$$

$$= \mathbf{B}_j (\mathbf{I} - \mathbf{B}_j^{-1} \mathbf{A}_j \mathbf{L}_{j-1}^{-1} \mathbf{C}_{j-1})$$

$$= \mathbf{B}_j (\mathbf{I} - \mathbf{R}),$$

where

$$\mathbf{R} = \mathbf{B}_j^{-1} \mathbf{A}_j \mathbf{L}_{j-1}^{-1} \mathbf{C}_{j-1}.$$

Then

$$\| \mathbf{R} \| \leq \| \mathbf{B}_j^{-1} \| \| \mathbf{A}_j \|, \quad \text{by the induction hypothesis}$$

$$\leq (1 - \| \mathbf{B}_j^{-1} \| \| \mathbf{C}_j \|), \quad \text{by (5.4.6.7)}.$$

Thus, using Lemma 5.4.6.1, we obtain

$$\| \mathbf{L}_j^{-1} \| \leq \| (\mathbf{I} - \mathbf{R})^{-1} \| \| \mathbf{B}_j^{-1} \|$$

$$\leq \frac{1}{\| \mathbf{C}_j \|},$$

which completes the proof.

In view of Lemma 5.4.6.2, from (5.4.6.3) we obtain that

$$\| \mathbf{U}_j \| \leq \| \mathbf{L}_j^{-1} \| \| \mathbf{C}_j \| \leq 1, \tag{5.4.6.9}$$

and

$$\| \mathbf{L}_j \| \leq \| \mathbf{B}_j \| + \| \mathbf{A}_j \| \| \mathbf{U}_{j-1} \|$$

$$\leq \| \mathbf{B}_j \| + \| \mathbf{A}_j \|. \tag{5.4.6.10}$$

In other words, if matrix $\mathbf{A}$ in (5.4.6.1) is diagonally dominant, then the block $\mathbf{L}\,\mathbf{U}$ decomposition in (5.4.6.3) is numerically stable and the resulting block matrices $\mathbf{L}_i$ and $\mathbf{U}_i$ satisfy (5.4.6.9) and (5.4.6.10).

For a further discussion of the stability and complexity of this method, refer to Varah [1972]. (Also refer to Exercise 5.36.)

5.5 NOTES AND REFERENCES

Section 5.1. For a discussion of the role of linear recurrences in automatic vectorization of serial programs, refer to Kuck [1976].

Section 5.2. The methods of cyclic reduction and elimination were developed by Golub and Hockney and are reported in Hockney [1965] and Hockney and Jesshope [1981]. They are also known as odd-even reduction and elimination, respectively. Also refer to Buzbee, Golub, and Nielson [1970] and Buzbee [1973]. The method of recursive doubling and the use of companion functions are described in Kogge and Stone [1973], Kogge [1973, 1974], and Stone [1973b, 1975]. The divide-and-conquer method is from Lakshmivarahan and Dhall [1985a, 1985b]. It is a generalization of the method of recursive doubling and has the advantage of being adaptable for a wide range of processors. Also refer to Heller [1976], Kuck [1978], Karp, Miller, and Winograd [1967], Gajski [1980, 1981], and Wimp [1984] for methods of solving recurrences. Dhall, Lakshmivarahan, and Seshacharyulu [1985] report the performance of some of these algorithms on the HEP multiprocessor.

Section 5.3. The coverage of the parallel methods for solving linear tridiagonal systems is standard (Hockney [1965], Stone [1973b, 1975], Heller [1978], Lakshmivarahan and Dhall [1986a]). The use of Gray codes in mapping cyclic reduction algorithm into a cube is due to Johnsson [1984]. For a discussion of Gray codes, refer to Chapter 2 and Reingold, Nievergelt, and Deo [1977]. The discussion of the communication complexity of solving linear tridiagonal systems on cube-based architecture, especially the hierarchy of cubes, is adopted from Lakshmivarahan and Dhall [1986b]. Also refer to Johnsson [1984, 1985] for further discussion of the solution of linear tridiagonal systems on tree architecture, shuffle-connected architectures, etc. A number of parallel iterative methods for solving tridiagonal systems are given in the exercises. Lambiotte and Voigt [1975] and Stone [1975] present a thorough analysis of the implementation of various techniques for solving tridiagonal systems on CDC STAR-100, the forerunner of Cyber-205. For further discussion of parallel iterative techniques refer to Ortega [1988], Gentzsch [1983] and Schendel [1984]. Dowers, Lakshmivarahan, and Dhall [1987] contains a comparison of the performance of cyclic reduction and elimination on the Alliant.

Section 5.4. There is an extensive literature on parallel methods for solving linear block tridiagonal systems. Our exposition in Sections 5.4.1 through 5.4.5 is patterned after Buzbee, Golub, and Nielson [1970]. The discussion of block Gaussian elimination and its stability analysis is adapted from Varah [1972].

Swarztrauber [1974] describes an extension of the block cyclic reduction for the case when the matrix **A** in (5.4.1.2) is of the form

$$
A = \begin{bmatrix}
B_1 & C_1 & 0 & \cdots & 0 & 0 & 0 \\
A_2 & B_2 & C_2 & \cdots & 0 & 0 & 0 \\
\cdot & \cdot & \cdot & \cdots & \cdot & \cdot & \cdot \\
\cdot & \cdot & \cdot & \cdots & \cdot & \cdot & \cdot \\
\cdot & \cdot & \cdot & \cdots & \cdot & \cdot & \cdot \\
0 & 0 & 0 & \cdots & A_{M-1} & B_{M-1} & C_{M-1} \\
0 & 0 & 0 & \cdots & 0 & A_M & B_M
\end{bmatrix}.
$$

This type of general block tridiagonal matrix arises in discretizing separable elliptic equations

$$ a(x)f_{xx} + b(x)f_x + c(x)f + d(y)f_{yy} + e(y)f_y + g(y)f = -h(x, y), $$

where f_x (f_y) and f_{xx} (f_{yy}) are the first and second partial derivatives, respectively, of $f = f(x, y)$ with respect to $x(y)$ using Dirichlet or Neumann boundary condition and the standard five-point stencil. When $a(x) \equiv d(y) \equiv 1$ and $b(x) \equiv c(x) \equiv e(y) \equiv g(y) \equiv 0$, then we obtain the standard Poisson equation. The matrix in (5.4.1.2) arises in discretizing this latter equation. Buzbee and Dorr [1974] deal with the solution of Poisson's equations with irregular region.

In his review paper, Swarztrauber [1977] analyzes the second variation of Buneman's algorithm described in Exercise 5.32 for the case when $C = I$ in (5.4.1.2). This variation requires nearly half as much storage at the expense of a slight increase in the number of operations compared to the first variant described in Section 5.4.4. In addition, Swarztrauber [1977] compares the matrix decomposition method (which he calls the Fourier method) of Section 5.4.5 with the second variation of Buneman's algorithm and shows that a clever combination of these two methods has a lesser operation count than either method alone.

Very recently, Swarztrauber [1987] developed a class of *approximate* block cyclic reduction algorithms which result in a considerable saving in time. See Exercise 5.39 for details.

Sweet [1974, 1977] extends the block cyclic reduction algorithm to the case when M (the number of blocks along the principal diagonal of the block tridiagonal matrix A in (5.4.1.2)) is *not* of the form $2^k - 1$. Very recently, Sweet [1988] proposed a parallel variant of the cyclic reduction algorithm which is pursued in Exercise 5.38.

Heller [1976] proved that the cyclic reduction is equivalent to the Gaussian elimination on the permuted system (see Exercise 5.40). In Section 5.3.1, it was shown that if the (scalar) tridiagonal matrix is diagonally dominant, then we can safely terminate the reduction phase earlier without compromising accuracy. Heller [1976] extended this result to the diagonally dominant block tridiagonal matrix.

For an experimental comparison of the performance of the cyclic reduction and block Gaussian elimination on the Alliant, refer to Dowers, Lakshmivarahan, and Dhall [1989] and Berry and Sameh [1988]. Geist and Romine [1988] and many of the references in it, describe an implementation of the **LU** factorization algorithm on a hypercube architecture.

For a comprehensive coverage of the techniques for solving partial differential equations on vector and parallel computers, refer to the survey by Ortega and Voigt [1985].

5.6 EXERCISES

5.1 Analyze the version of the cyclic elimination algorithm given in Fig. 5.2.2.3, and compare it with that given in Fig. 5.2.2.2.

5.2 Compute the redundancy factor for the cyclic reduction, and find the minimum number of processors necessary to perform better than the serial algorithm when using this method.

5.3 Compute the speed-up and the redundancy factor for the divide-and-conquer method of Section 5.2.4 as a function of p, $2 \leq p \leq \dfrac{N}{2}$.

5.4 Compare the cyclic elimination and recursive doubling algorithms.

5.5 The parallel methods for solving linear recurrences may be readily extended to a number of non-linear recurrences. In the following, we describe some useful transformations for converting certain classes of non-linear recurrences into linear recurrences.

Let

$$x_i = \frac{a_i}{c_i + d_i \, x_{i-1}}$$

be the given *first-order non-linear recurrence*. If $y_i = \dfrac{1}{x_i}$, then clearly

$$y_i = A_i + \frac{B_i}{y_{i-1}}$$

where $A_i = \dfrac{c_i}{a_i}$ and $B_i = \dfrac{d_i}{a_i}$ which is again a *first-order non-linear recurrence*. Now, define $y_i = \dfrac{z_i}{z_{i-1}}$. Then we obtain an equivalent linear, second-order recurrence in z as follows:

$$z_i = A_i \, z_{i-1} + B_i \, z_{i-2}.$$

Again, define $V_i = (z_i, \ z_{i-1})^t$. Then, the above z recurrence is equivalent to a first-order linear matrix recurrence in V_i,

$$V_i = M_i \, V_{i-1}, \quad \text{where } M_i = \begin{bmatrix} A_i & B_i \\ 1 & 0 \end{bmatrix}.$$

Obtain a closed-form solution to the x-recurrence by first solving the V-recurrence and then retracing the above steps backwards.

5.6 Let $x_1 = a_1$ and $x_i = f(a_i, x_{i-1})$, where a_i, $i \geq 1$ are reals and $f(., .)$ is a real-valued function. Check the associativity condition (5.2.6.6), when $f(., .)$ is of the form

(a) $f(a, b) = a + b$
(b) $f(a, b) = a - b$
(c) $f(a, b) = ab$
(d) $f(a, b) = b^a$
(e) $f(a, b) = |a - b|$
(f) $f(a, b) = \max(a, b)$
(g) $f(a, b) = \min(a, b)$

5.7 Describe a parallel algorithm for computing x_i, where the recurrence function $f(., .)$ in (5.2.6.1) satisfies the conditions of Theorem 5.2.6.1.

5.8 Develop parallel algorithms for solving the following recurrences.

(a) $x_i = b_i \, x_{i-1}^{a_i}$

Hint: Take logarithms.

(b) $x_n x_{n-2} = a_n \, x_{n-1}^2$

Hint: $y_n = \dfrac{x_n}{x_{n-1}}$

(c) $x_{n+1} = 2 \, x_n \, (1 - x_n)$

Hint: $y_n = x_n - \dfrac{1}{2}$.

(d) $x_{n+1} \, x_n + a x_{n+1} + b x_n + c = 0$

Hint: Choose $x_n = y_n + A$, where $A^2 + (a + b)A + c = 0$ and $z_n = \dfrac{1}{y_n}$.

(e) $x_n = 7 x_{n/2} + n^2$

Hint: $y_i = \dfrac{x_{2^i}}{7^i}$

5.9 Let A_k denote the leading *principal* submatrix of the tridiagonal matrix $\mathbf{A}$ given in (5.3.1.2), that is,

$$\mathbf{A}_1 = \begin{bmatrix} b_1 \end{bmatrix}, \qquad \mathbf{A}_2 = \begin{bmatrix} b_1 & c_1 \\ a_2 & b_2 \end{bmatrix},$$

$$\mathbf{A}_3 = \begin{bmatrix} b_1 & c_1 & 0 \\ a_2 & b_2 & c_2 \\ 0 & a_3 & b_3 \end{bmatrix},$$

and so on.

(a) Show that if $\mathbf{A}_k$, $k = 1, 2, \cdots, N - 1$, is non-singular, then the factorization

$$\mathbf{A} = \mathbf{L}\,\mathbf{U}$$

given in (5.3.3.1) to (5.3.3.3) is well defined.

Hint: Relate the denominator of $\mathbf{w}_k$ in (5.3.3.6) to the determinant of the matrix $\mathbf{A}_k$ for $k = 2, 3, \cdots, N - 1$.

(b) Using (5.3.3.1), compute the determinant of $\mathbf{A}$.

5.10 (Swarztrauber [1979]). Parallel Evaluation of Determinant of Tridiagonal Matrix (5.3.1.2). Define

$$b_\nu^{(\mu)} = \begin{vmatrix} b_\nu & c_\nu & 0 & \cdots & 0 & 0 & 0 \\ a_{\nu+1} & b_{\nu+1} & c_{\nu+1} & \cdots & 0 & 0 & 0 \\ \cdot & \cdot & \cdot & \cdots & \cdot & \cdot & \cdot \\ \cdot & \cdot & \cdot & \cdots & \cdot & \cdot & \cdot \\ \cdot & \cdot & \cdot & \cdots & \cdot & \cdot & \cdot \\ 0 & 0 & 0 & \cdots & a_{\mu-1} & b_{\mu-1} & c_{\mu-1} \\ 0 & 0 & 0 & \cdots & 0 & a_\mu & b_\mu \end{vmatrix}$$

where $\mu \geq \nu$. That is, $b_\nu^{(\mu)}$ is a *principal minor* determined by μ and ν. Now define

$$D_i = b_1^{(i)}.$$

Clearly, D_i is the principal minor corresponding to the first i rows and columns of $\mathbf{A}$ in (5.3.1.2).

Now expand D_i in terms of its ith row to obtain

$$D_i = b_i D_{i-1} - a_i c_{i-1} D_{i-2},$$

where $D_0 = 1$ and $D_1 = b_1$. Rewrite this recurrence in a matrix form as

$$
\begin{bmatrix} D_i \\ D_{i-1} \end{bmatrix} = \begin{bmatrix} b_i - a_i c_{i-1} & D_{i-1} \\ 1 & 0 \end{bmatrix} \begin{bmatrix} D_{i-1} \\ D_{i-2} \end{bmatrix}.
$$

Define a new variable E_i as

$$
E_i = c_i D_{i-1}.
$$

Substituting in the previous equation, the latter becomes

$$
\begin{bmatrix} D_i \\ E_i \end{bmatrix} = \begin{bmatrix} b_i - a_i & D_{i-1} \\ c_i & 0 \end{bmatrix} \begin{bmatrix} D_{i-1} \\ E_{i-1} \end{bmatrix}.
$$

Define

$$
\mathbf{Q}_i = \begin{bmatrix} b_i - a_i \\ c_i & 0 \end{bmatrix}, \quad \mathbf{W}_i = \begin{bmatrix} D_i \\ E_i \end{bmatrix}, \quad \text{and} \quad \mathbf{e} = \begin{bmatrix} 1 \\ 0 \end{bmatrix}.
$$

Thus, it is readily seen that

$$
\mathbf{W}_i = \mathbf{Q}_i \mathbf{Q}_{i-1} \cdots \mathbf{Q}_2 \mathbf{Q}_1 \mathbf{e}.
$$

(a) Using the above development, compute all the principal minors D_i, $i=1, \cdots , M$, in parallel.

(b) How fast can you compute the determinant D_n of matrix $\mathbf{A}$ in (5.3.1.2)? Analyze the speed-up and communication requirements for this computation.

Hint: See associative fan-in algorithm.

(c) Compute the sequence D_i when $a_i = c_i = 1$ for all i, and $b_i = b$. Analyze the behavior of D_i when $b = 0$, 0.5, 1.0, and 4.0

(d) Analyze the sequence D_i when $a_i = c_i = s$, $b_i = 1$ for all i, and $0 < s < \tfrac{1}{2}$, $s = \tfrac{1}{2}$, $\tfrac{1}{2} < s < 1$, $s = 1$, and $s > 1$.

5.11 (Swarztrauber [1979]). Define a quantity

$$
F_i = b_i^{(n)}.
$$

(a) Show that F_i evolves according to

$$
\begin{bmatrix} F_i \\ F_{i+1} \end{bmatrix} = \begin{bmatrix} b_i - a_{i+1} c_i \\ 1 & 0 \end{bmatrix} \begin{bmatrix} F_{i+1} \\ F_{i+2} \end{bmatrix}.
$$

(b) Define $G_i = - a_i F_{i+1}$. Show that

$$
\mathbf{Z}_i = \mathbf{Q}_i \mathbf{Z}_{i+1},
$$

where $\mathbf{Z}_i = \begin{bmatrix} F_i \\ G_i \end{bmatrix}$ and $\mathbf{Q}_i$ is as defined in Exercise 5.10.

(c) Using this formulation, compute $\mathbf{Z}_i$'s, and hence G_i's, in parallel.

5.12 Swarztrauber [1979]. Parallel Computation of Solution of (5.3.1.1) Using Cramer's rule. Define

$$S_i = \begin{vmatrix} b_1 & c_1 & 0 & \cdots & 0 & 0 & d_1 \\ a_2 & b_2 & c_2 & \cdots & 0 & 0 & d_2 \\ \cdot & \cdot & \cdot & \cdots & \cdot & \cdot & \cdot \\ \cdot & \cdot & \cdot & \cdots & \cdot & \cdot & \cdot \\ \cdot & \cdot & \cdot & \cdots & \cdot & \cdot & \cdot \\ 0 & 0 & 0 & \cdots & a_{i-1} & b_{i-1} & d_{i-1} \\ 0 & 0 & 0 & \cdots & 0 & a_i & d_i \end{vmatrix}$$

and

$$U_i = \begin{vmatrix} d_i & c_i & 0 & \cdots & 0 & 0 & 0 \\ a_{i+1} & b_{i+1} & c_{i+1} & \cdots & 0 & 0 & 0 \\ \cdot & \cdot & \cdot & \cdots & \cdot & \cdot & \cdot \\ \cdot & \cdot & \cdot & \cdots & \cdot & \cdot & \cdot \\ \cdot & 0 & 0 & \cdots & a_{n-1} & b_{n-1} & c_{n-1} \\ d_n & 0 & 0 & \cdots & 0 & a_n & b_n \end{vmatrix}$$

(a) Show that (referring to Exercise 5.10)

$$U_i = -c_i\, U_{i+1} + b_{i+1}^{(n)}\, d_i$$

and

$$S_i = -\, a_i\, S_{i-1} + D_{i-1} d_i.$$

(b) Consider the system in (5.3.1.1). Expanding by the ith row of **A**, using Cramer's rule, show that

$$x_i \;=\; D_n^{-1}\, (\, G_i\, S_{i-1} + D_{i-1}\, U_i\,).$$

Hint: Expand using Cramer's rule and use (a).

(c) Exercises 5.10 and 5.11 provide parallel methods for computing D_i's and G_i's, respectively. Referring to (a), since U_i and S_i are defined by first-order linear recurrences of the type (5.2.1.1), both U_i and S_i can be computed in parallel using any one of the methods described in Section 5.2. Hence x_i's can be computed in parallel. Using the cyclic reduction method for computing U_i and S_i, compute the total number of scalar operations and speed-up for various degrees of parallelism for this method.

(d) Compare the above parallel method with those given in Section 5.3.

5.13 (Traub [1973]). Let

$$\mathbf{Ax = d}$$

be an $N \times N$ tridiagonal system, where all the diagonal elements of the matrix **A** are normalized to unity. Let

$$A = \begin{bmatrix} 1 & c_1 & 0 & \cdots & 0 & 0 & 0 \\ a_2 & 1 & c_2 & \cdots & 0 & 0 & 0 \\ \cdot & \cdot & 1 & \cdots & \cdot & \cdot & \cdot \\ \cdot & \cdot & \cdot & \cdots & \cdot & \cdot & \cdot \\ \cdot & \cdot & \cdot & \cdots & \cdot & \cdot & \cdot \\ 0 & 0 & 0 & \cdots & a_{N-1} & 1 & c_{N-1} \\ 0 & 0 & 0 & \cdots & 0 & a_N & 1 \end{bmatrix}.$$

The **LU** decomposition and the Gaussian elimination derived at the beginning of Section 5.3.3 may be expressed in matrix form as follows. Let

$$A = A_l + I + A_r = LU,$$

$$L = A_l + D, \quad U = I + W,$$

where A_l (A_r) is a matrix whose only non-zero elements are those along the first sub (super) diagonal, which is, in fact, the first sub (super) diagonal of **A**. Likewise, **W** is a matrix whose only non-zeros are along the super diagonal. Let

$$L = \begin{bmatrix} e_1^{-1} & 0 & 0 & \cdots & 0 & 0 & 0 \\ a_2 & e_2^{-1} & 0 & \cdots & 0 & 0 & 0 \\ 0 & a_3 & e_3^{-1} & \cdots & 0 & 0 & 0 \\ \cdot & \cdot & \cdot & \cdots & \cdot & \cdot & \cdot \\ \cdot & \cdot & \cdot & \cdots & \cdot & \cdot & \cdot \\ \cdot & \cdot & \cdot & \cdots & \cdot & \cdot & \cdot \\ 0 & 0 & 0 & \cdots & a_{N-1} & e_{N-1}^{-1} & 0 \\ 0 & 0 & 0 & \cdots & 0 & a_N & e_N^{-1} \end{bmatrix},$$

$$U = \begin{bmatrix} 1 & w_1 & 0 & \cdots & 0 & 0 \\ 0 & 1 & w_2 & \cdots & 0 & 0 \\ 0 & 0 & 1 & \cdots & 0 & 0 \\ \cdot & \cdot & \cdot & \cdots & \cdot & \cdot \\ \cdot & \cdot & \cdot & \cdots & \cdot & \cdot \\ \cdot & \cdot & \cdot & \cdots & \cdot & \cdot \\ 0 & 0 & 0 & \cdots & 1 & w_{N-1} \\ 0 & 0 & 0 & \cdots & 0 & 1 \end{bmatrix},$$

$$
\mathbf{W} = \begin{bmatrix}
0 & w_1 & 0 & \cdots & 0 & 0 \\
0 & 0 & w_2 & \cdots & 0 & 0 \\
0 & 0 & 0 & \cdots & 0 & 0 \\
\cdot & \cdot & \cdot & \cdots & \cdot & \cdot \\
\cdot & \cdot & \cdot & \cdots & \cdot & \cdot \\
\cdot & \cdot & \cdot & \cdots & \cdot & \cdot \\
0 & 0 & 0 & \cdots & w_{N-2} & 0 \\
0 & 0 & 0 & \cdots & 0 & w_{N-1} \\
0 & 0 & 0 & \cdots & 0 & 0
\end{bmatrix},
$$

and

$$
\mathbf{D} = \begin{bmatrix}
e_1^{-1} & 0 & 0 & \cdot & 0 & 0 \\
0 & e_2^{-1} & 0 & \cdot & 0 & 0 \\
0 & 0 & e_3^{-1} & \cdot & 0 & 0 \\
\cdot & \cdot & \cdot & \cdot & \cdot & \cdot \\
\cdot & \cdot & \cdot & \cdot & \cdot & \cdot \\
\cdot & \cdot & \cdot & \cdot & \cdot & \cdot \\
0 & 0 & 0 & \cdot & e_{N-1} & 0 \\
0 & 0 & 0 & \cdot & 0 & e_N^{-1}
\end{bmatrix}.
$$

(a) Show that

$$\mathbf{A}_l \, \mathbf{W} \text{ is a diagonal matrix,}$$

$$\mathbf{D} + \mathbf{A}_l \, \mathbf{W} = \mathbf{I}, \text{ the unit matrix,}$$

$$(\mathbf{I} - \mathbf{A}_l \mathbf{W})\mathbf{W} = \mathbf{A}_r.$$

and

$$\mathbf{DW} = \mathbf{A}_r.$$

(b) Rewrite $\mathbf{Ax} = \mathbf{d}$ using the factored form as

$$(\mathbf{A}_l + \mathbf{D})\,(\mathbf{I} + \mathbf{W})\mathbf{x} = \mathbf{d}.$$

Let $\mathbf{g}$ be such that $(\mathbf{I} + \mathbf{W})\,\mathbf{x} = \mathbf{g}$, and

$$(\mathbf{A}_l + \mathbf{D})\,\mathbf{g} = \mathbf{d}.$$

Show that

$$(\mathbf{I} + \mathbf{A}_l\,(\mathbf{I} - \mathbf{W})\,)\,\mathbf{g} = \mathbf{d}.$$

5.14 (Traub [1973]). A Parallel Iterative Algorithm for **LU** Factorization. Let $\mathbf{W}^{(0)}$ be the given initial estimate for $\mathbf{W}$. Then iteratively define $\mathbf{W}^{(i)}$ using

$$(\mathbf{I} - \mathbf{A}_l \, \mathbf{W}^{(i-1)}) \, \mathbf{W}^{(i)} = \mathbf{A}_r, \quad i = 1, 2, \cdots, k$$

and

$$\mathbf{D} = \mathbf{I} - \mathbf{A}_l \, \mathbf{W}^{(k)},$$

where $\mathbf{W}^{(0)}$ is assumed to be given and k is a positive integer.

Stated in component form, let the non-zero elements of $\mathbf{W}^{(i)}$ be $w_j^{(i)}$, $j = 1, \cdots, N-1$. Then, given $w_j^{(0)}$, $j = 1, \cdots, N-1$, define

$$w_1^{(i)} = c_1, \quad \text{for} \quad i = 0, \cdots, k,$$

$$w_j^{(i)} = \frac{c_i}{1 - a_i \, w_{j-1}^{(i-1)}}, \quad \text{for} \quad i = 1, \cdots, k, \quad \text{and} \quad j = 2, \cdots, N-1,$$

$$e_1^{-1} = 1,$$

and

$$e_j^{-1} = 1 - a_j \, w_{j-1}^{(k)}, \quad j = 2, \cdots, N.$$

Notice that for each i, there is a parallelism in j.

The method described in Section 5.3.3 for computing the factors $\mathbf{L}$ and $\mathbf{U}$ is called the *direct* method. Compare the direct method with the above *iterative* method for finding the factors. More specifically, compare their implementation on a multivector machine (Alliant FX/8) and hypercube architecture.

5.15 (Traub [1973]). Let $\mathbf{y} = (y_1, y_2, \cdots, y_N)^t$ and $\mathbf{B} = [b_{ij}]_{N \times N}$. Define the norm (see Exercise 5.35) of $\mathbf{y}$ and $\mathbf{B}$ as

$$\| \mathbf{y} \|_\infty = \max_{i = 1 \text{ to } N} \{ \, |y_i| \, \},$$

and

$$\| \mathbf{B} \|_\infty = \max_{i = 1 \text{ to } N} \{ \sum_{j=1}^{N} |b_{ij}| \, \}.$$

Then, clearly

$$\| \mathbf{A}_r \|_\infty = c^* = \max\{ \, |c_1|, |c_2|, \cdots, |c_{N-1}| \, \}$$

$$\| \mathbf{A}_l \|_\infty = a^* = \max\{ \, |a_2|, |a_3|, \cdots, |a_N| \, \}.$$

Since the matrix $\mathbf{A}$ in Exercise 5.13 is tridiagonal, it follows that $a^* c^* > 0$. Let the roots r_1 and r_2 of the quadratic equation

$$f(z) = a^* z^2 - z + c^* = 0$$

be such that

$$r_1 = \frac{1 - \sqrt{1 - 4a^* c^*}}{2a^*},$$

$$r_2 = \frac{1 + \sqrt{1 - 4a^* c^*}}{2a^*}.$$

If $a^* + c^* < 1$, then show that r_1 and r_2 are real, distinct, and

(a) $0 < c^* < r_1 < a^* + c^* < 1 < r_2$.
(b) $a^* < r_2^{-1} < a^* + c^* < 1$.
(c) $a^* c^* < r_1 r_2^{-1} < (a^* + c^*)^2 < 1$.

5.16 (Traub [1973]). Analysis of Convergence of Parallel Iterative Factorization of Exercise 5.14. Let $4a^* c^* < 1$. Then show that

(a) $0 < c^* < r_1 < 2c^* < r_2$.

(b) $a^* < r_2^{-1} < 2a^*$.

(c) $a^* c^* < r_1 r_2^{-1} < 4a^* c^* < 1$.

(d) If $\| W^{(0)} \| < r_1$, then

$$\| \mathbf{W}^{(i)} - \mathbf{W} \| < r_1 r_2^{-1} \| \mathbf{W}^{(i-1)} - \mathbf{W} \|.$$

Notice that since $r_1 r_2^{-1} < 1$, clearly the $\mathbf{W}$ iteration is norm-reducing.

5.17 (Traub [1973]). Parallel Iterative Gaussian Algorithm. Let $\mathbf{W}^{(0)}$, $\mathbf{g}^{(0)}$, and $\mathbf{x}^{(0)}$ be given. Let k_1, k_2, k_3 be positive integers. Then define

(a) $(\mathbf{I} - \mathbf{A}_l \mathbf{W}^{(i-1)}) \mathbf{W}^{(i)} = \mathbf{A}_r, \quad i = 1, 2, \cdots, k_1$.

(b) $(\mathbf{I} - \mathbf{A}_l \mathbf{W}^{(k_1)}) \mathbf{g}^{(i)} = \mathbf{d} - \mathbf{A}_l \mathbf{g}^{(i-1)}, \quad i = 1, 2, \cdots, k_2$.

(c) $\mathbf{x}^{(i)} = \mathbf{g}^{(k_2)} - \mathbf{W}^{(k_1)} \mathbf{x}^{(i-1)}, \quad i = 1, 2, \cdots, k_3$.

Compare this parallel iterative method with the direct method described in Section 5.3.3. Implement this parallel iterative method, and compare its performance with that of the direct method on an Alliant FX/8 and hypercube architecture.

Note: The proof of convergence of this parallel iterative method is the content of Theorems 3.3 through 3.9 in Traub [1973].

5.18 (Traub [1973]). In the parallel iterative method of Exercise 5.17, while the individual iterations may be done in parallel, there is a serial dependence in the sense that the iterations (a), (b), and (c) must be completed in that order. The following is a version of the parallel iterative method which permits the above three iterations to be performed independently.

(a) $(\mathbf{I} - \mathbf{A}_l \, \mathbf{W}^{(i-1)}) \, \mathbf{W}^{(i)} = \mathbf{A}_r, \quad i = 1, 2, \cdots, k.$

(b) $(\mathbf{I} - \mathbf{A}_l \, \mathbf{W}^{(i)}) \, \mathbf{g}^{(i)} = \mathbf{d} - \mathbf{A}_l \, \mathbf{g}^{(i-1)}, \quad i = 1, 2, \cdots, k.$

(c) $\mathbf{x}^{(i)} = \mathbf{g}^{(i)} - \mathbf{W}^{(i)} \, \mathbf{g}^{(i-1)}, \quad i = 1, 2, \cdots, k.$

Compare these two iterative methods by implementing them on an Alliant FX/8 and hypercube architectures.

5.19 (Traub [1973]). Parallel Algorithms Based on Additive Splitting of the Matrix **A**. Let **A x = d** be a linear tridiagonal system where **A** is an $N \times N$ matrix with all the diagonal elements normalized to 1. Let

$$\mathbf{A} = \mathbf{A}_l + \mathbf{I} + \mathbf{A}_r,$$

where $\mathbf{A}_l$ and $\mathbf{A}_r$ are as defined in Exercise 5.13. Let $\mathbf{x}^{(0)}$ be an initial guess for the solution. (1) *Jacobi's Algorithm* This algorithm iteratively refines the solution using the following scheme:

$$\mathbf{x}^{(i)} = -(\mathbf{A}_l + \mathbf{A}_r)\, \mathbf{x}^{(i-1)} + \mathbf{d}.$$

In this algorithm and in all three that follow, the parallelism is in **x**.

(2) *Jacobi's Over-relaxation (JOR) Algorithm.* In this case, define

$$\mathbf{x}^{(i)} = [(1 - \alpha)\mathbf{I} - \alpha(\mathbf{A}_l + \mathbf{A}_r)]\, \mathbf{x}^{(i-1)} + \alpha \mathbf{d},$$

for some real $\alpha > 0$.

(3) *Gauss-Seidel Algorithm.*
(i) Define first $\mathbf{x}^{(i)}$ using the iteration

$$(\mathbf{I} + \mathbf{A}_r)\, \mathbf{x}^{(i)} = -\mathbf{A}_l \, \mathbf{x}^{(i-1)} + \mathbf{d}.$$

Notice that the matrix - vector product and the vector addition on the right-hand side of this relation admits parallelism. Clearly $\mathbf{x}^{(i)}$ is obtained as the solution of a bi-diagonal system

$$(\mathbf{I} + \mathbf{A}_r)\, \mathbf{y} = \mathbf{Z},$$

where

$$\mathbf{Z} = -\mathbf{A}_l \, \mathbf{x}^{(i-1)} + \mathbf{d} \quad \text{and} \quad \mathbf{y} = \mathbf{x}^{(i)}.$$

(ii) Now define iteratively the solution of the above bidiagonal system as

$$\mathbf{y}^{(j)} = \mathbf{Z} - \mathbf{A}_r \mathbf{y}^{(j-1)}.$$

Notice that this is the Jacobi iteration for the solution of the bidiagonal system. (i) is called the *outer* and (ii) is called the *inner* iteration.

Note: Recall that a bidiagonal system corresponds to a linear first-order recurrence. The above bidiagonal system may be solved in parallel by any one of the methods of Section 5.2, as well.

(4) Parallel Successive Over-relaxation (SOR).

(i) Let

$$(I + \alpha A_r) x^{(i)} = [(1 - \alpha) I - \alpha A_l] x^{(i-1)} + \alpha d,$$

for some $\alpha > 0$. Define

$$Z_\alpha = [(1 - \alpha) I - \alpha A_l] x^{(i-1)} + \alpha d$$

and

$$y_\alpha = x^{(i)}.$$

Notice that y_α is defined as the solution of the bidiagonal system

$$(I + \alpha A_r) y_\alpha = Z_\alpha,$$

which in turn is solved by the following iterative procedure.

(ii) Define

$$y_\alpha^{(j)} = Z_\alpha - \alpha A_r y_\alpha^{(j-1)}.$$

Analyze the performance of these four algorithms on the linear tridiagonal system with the following $N \times N$ matrix:

$$A = \begin{bmatrix} 1 & a & 0 & \cdots & 0 & 0 & 0 \\ a & 1 & a & \cdots & 0 & 0 & 0 \\ 0 & a & 1 & \cdots & 0 & 0 & 0 \\ . & . & . & \cdots & . & . & . \\ . & . & . & \cdots & . & . & . \\ . & . & . & \cdots & . & . & . \\ 0 & 0 & 0 & \cdots & a & 1 & a \\ 0 & 0 & 0 & \cdots & 0 & a & 1 \end{bmatrix},$$

where $0 < a < \frac{1}{2}$, by implementing them on a multivector machine such as the Alliant FX/8.

5.20 Compute the polynomials $p_{2^r}(a, t)$ defined in (5.4.2.25) for $r = 2, 3,$ and 4.

5.21 Verify the recursive relation (5.4.2.26).

5.22 Derive (5.4.2.27) from (5.4.2.26).

5.23 Show that (5.4.2.28) defines the zeros of $p_{2^{r+1}}(a, t)$.

5.24 For $r = 2, 3,$ and 4, compute the factors of $B(r)$.

5.25   Solve (5.4.1.1) when

$$B = \begin{bmatrix} -4 & 1 & 0 & \cdots & 0 & 0 & 0 \\ 1 & -4 & 1 & \cdots & 0 & 0 & 0 \\ & \cdot & \cdot & \cdots & \cdot & \cdot & \cdot \\ \cdot & \cdot & \cdot & \cdots & \cdot & \cdot & \cdot \\ \cdot & \cdot & \cdot & \cdots & \cdot & \cdot & \cdot \\ 0 & 0 & 0 & \cdots & 1 & -4 & 1 \\ 0 & 0 & 0 & \cdots & 0 & 1 & -4 \end{bmatrix}$$

and

$$C = I, \text{ the identity matrix.}$$

5.26   Compute the overall complexity of the algorithm in Fig. 5.4.2.1, when **B** is tridiagonal and **C** is an identity matrix, and calculate the number of processors needed to achieve your bound.

5.27   Compute the eigenvalues of the matrix **B** in Exercise 5.25.

5.28   Prove from first principles that $\xi_{j,s}$ given in (5.4.3.11) and (5.4.3.29) are the solution of the linear second-order recurrence (5.4.3.9).

5.29   Analyze the numerical stability of case 2 in (5.4.3.30).

5.30   Derive (5.4.4.25) and (5.4.4.26).

5.31   Prove or disprove that

(a) $\mathbf{B}(0)\,\mathbf{B}(1) \cdots \mathbf{B}(j) = \mathbf{B}(j)\,\mathbf{B}(j-1) \cdots \mathbf{B}(1)\,\mathbf{B}(0)$.

(b) $\mathbf{B}(r)\,\mathbf{S}(r) = \mathbf{S}(r)\,\mathbf{B}(r)$.

5.32   **Another Variation of Buneman's Algorithm.** From the second equation in (5.4.4.14), we obtain

$$\alpha_i(t+1) = \frac{1}{2}\,[\beta_{i-2g}(t) + \beta_{i+2g}(t) - \beta_i(t+1)\,], \qquad (*)$$

where $g = 2^{t-1}$. Substituting this in the first equation in (5.4.4.14), we obtain the following:

$$\beta_i(t+1) = \beta_{i-2g}(t) - \beta_{i-g}(t-1) + \beta_i(t) - \beta_{i+g}(t-1) + \beta_{i+2g}(t)$$

$$+ [\mathbf{B}(t)]^{-1}\{\beta_{i-3g}(t-1) - \beta_{i-2g}(t) + \beta_{i-g}(t-1) - 2\beta_i(t)$$

$$+ \beta_{i+g}(t-1) - \beta_{i+2g}(t) + \beta_{i+3g}(t-1)\} \tag{**}$$

where $\beta_i = 0$ for $i < 1$ or $i > M$, $\beta_i(0) = \mathbf{d}_i$ for $i = 1, 2, \cdots, M$, and

$$\beta_i(1) = \mathbf{d}_{i-1} + \mathbf{d}_{i+1} - 2\mathbf{B}^{-1}\mathbf{d}_i,$$

for $i = 2, 4, 6, \cdots, M - 1$.

Combining (*) with (5.4.4.19),

$$\mathbf{x}_i = \alpha_i(t) - [\mathbf{B}(t)]^{-1}\{\mathbf{x}_{i-2g} + \mathbf{x}_{i+2g} - \beta_i(t)\}$$

$$= \frac{1}{2}\{\beta_{i-g}(t-1) + \beta_{i+g}(t-1) - \beta_i(t)\}$$

$$- [\mathbf{B}(t)]^{-1}\{\mathbf{x}_{i-2g} + \mathbf{x}_{i+2g} - \beta_i(t)\}. \tag{***}$$

From these we have the following algorithm:

Step 1. Compute the sequence $\{\beta_i(t)\}$ using (**) for $t = 1, 2, \cdots, k - 1$.

Step 2. Back-solve for $\mathbf{x}_i$ using (***).

Show that this variation requires half the storage and nearly twice as many additions as the algorithm in Fig. 5.4.4.1.

5.33 Given n, find ϕ^* satisfying (5.4.4.35).

5.34 The matrix decomposition method in Section 5.4.5 exploits the commutativity of $\mathbf{B}$ and $\mathbf{C}$. In cases when $\mathbf{BC} \neq \mathbf{CB}$, we need a slightly different approach. Let $\mathbf{B}$ be symmetric and $\mathbf{C}$ be symmetric and positive-definite. It is well-known (Bellman [1960]) that there exists a decomposition

$$\mathbf{C} = \mathbf{P}\,\mathbf{P}^t$$

and

$$\mathbf{B} = \mathbf{P}\,\Delta\,\mathbf{P}^t,$$

where Δ is a diagonal matrix of eigenvalues $\{\delta_1, \delta_2, \cdots, \delta_n\}$ of $\mathbf{C}^{-1}\mathbf{B}$, and $(\mathbf{P}^{-1})^t$ is a matrix of eigenvectors of $\mathbf{C}^{-1}\mathbf{B}$. The new algorithm (similar to the one given in Fig. 5.4.5.1) may be stated as follows:

Step 1. Compute the eigenvalues and eigenvectors of $\mathbf{C}^{-1}\mathbf{B}$.

Step 2. Compute $\overline{\mathbf{d}}_j = \mathbf{P}^{-1}\mathbf{d}_j$ for $j = 1, 2, \cdots, M$ in parallel.

Step 3. Solve $\Gamma_i\,\hat{\mathbf{x}}_i = \hat{\mathbf{d}}_i$ for $i = 1, 2, \cdots, n$ in parallel, where

$$
\Gamma_i = \begin{bmatrix}
\delta_i & 1 & \cdots & 0 & 0 \\
1 & \delta_i & \cdots & 0 & 0 \\
\cdot & \cdot & \cdots & \cdot & \cdot \\
\cdot & \cdot & \cdots & \cdot & \cdot \\
\cdot & \cdot & \cdots & \cdot & \cdot \\
0 & 0 & \cdots & \delta_i & 1 \\
0 & 0 & \cdots & 1 & \delta_i
\end{bmatrix}.
$$

Step 4. Compute $\mathbf{x}_j = (\mathbf{P}^{-1})^t \overline{\mathbf{x}}_j$.

(a) Develop a method of finding the eigenvalues of $\mathbf{C}^{-1}\mathbf{B}$ by rewriting it as

$$\mathbf{By} = \delta\mathbf{Cy}.$$

Note: This problem is known as the *generalized eigenvalue problem,* and we refer the reader to the papers by Peters and Wilkinson [1970] and Stewart [1973].

(b) Compute the number of operations required by this method.

5.35 (Golub and Van Loan [1983]). In Section 5.4.4, we used the *Euclidean norm* for the vectors and the *spectral norm* for matrices. We now define other vector and matrix norms. Let $\mathbf{u} = (u_1, u_2, \cdots, u_N)^t$ be a vector and $\mathbf{A} = [a_{ij}]$ be an $N \times N$ matrix.

(1) For a vector $\mathbf{u}$, $\| \mathbf{u} \|_p = [\sum_{i=1}^{N} | u_i |^p]^{1/p}$ for some integer $p \geq 1$ is called the p-norm. In particular,

$$\| \mathbf{u} \|_1 = | u_1 | + | u_2 | + \cdots + | u_N |,$$

$$\| \mathbf{u} \|_2 = (u_1^2 + u_2^2 + \cdots + u_N^2)^{1/2}, \text{ the Euclidean norm},$$

and

$$\| \mathbf{u} \|_\infty = \max_i \{ | u_i | \},$$

are often used.

(a) Show that the vector p-norm satisfies properties (V1) to (V3) given in Section 5.4.4.

(2) For matrices,

$$\| \mathbf{A} \|_F = [\sum_{i=1}^{N} \sum_{j=1}^{N} | a_{ij} |^2]^{1/2},$$

called the *Frobenius norm,* and

$$\| A \|_p = \sup_{u \neq 0} \frac{\| A u \|_p}{\| u \|_p},$$

called the *p-norm*, are very useful. Notice that the matrix *p*-norm is defined using the vector *p*-norm.

(b) Show that $\|\cdot\|_F$ and $\|\cdot\|_p$ satisfy properties (M1) to (M4) in Section 5.4.4.

(c) (Faddeeva [1959]). Show that

$$\| A \|_1 = \max_j \{ \sum_{i=1}^{N} | a_{ij} | \},$$

$$\| A \|_\infty = \max_i \{ \sum_{j=1}^{N} | a_{ij} | \},$$

and

$$\| A \|_2 = (\rho(A^t A))^{\frac{1}{2}}.$$

(d) If **R** and **S** are orthogonal matrices, then show that

$$\| RAS \|_F = \| A \|_F$$

and

$$\| RAS \|_2 = \| A \|_2.$$

Note: While there is great flexibility in defining norms, caution must be exercised in the choice of matrix norms. For, if we define

$$\| A \| = \max\{ | a_{ij} | \},$$

the inequality (M3), namely, $\| A B \| \leq \| A \| \, \| B \|$, does not hold when all the elements in **A** and **B** are unity, for example,

$$A = B = \begin{bmatrix} 1 & 1 \\ 1 & 1 \end{bmatrix}.$$

For further discussion of norms, refer to Householder [1964] and Stewart [1973].

5.36 Let **A** be a general block tridiagonal matrix as given in (5.4.6.2). Let $A = \overline{L}\,\overline{U}$, where

$$
\overline{L} = \begin{bmatrix}
I & 0 & 0 & \cdots & 0 & 0 \\
L_2 & I & 0 & \cdots & 0 & 0 \\
0 & L_3 & I & \cdots & 0 & 0 \\
\cdot & \cdot & \cdot & \cdots & \cdot & \cdot \\
\cdot & \cdot & \cdot & \cdots & \cdot & \cdot \\
\cdot & \cdot & \cdot & \cdots & \cdot & \cdot \\
0 & 0 & 0 & \cdots & I & 0 \\
0 & 0 & 0 & \cdots & L_M & I
\end{bmatrix},
$$

$$
\overline{U} = \begin{bmatrix}
U_1 & C_1 & 0 & \cdots & 0 & 0 \\
0 & U_2 & C_2 & \cdots & 0 & 0 \\
0 & 0 & U_3 & \cdots & 0 & 0 \\
\cdot & \cdot & \cdot & \cdots & \cdot & \cdot \\
\cdot & \cdot & \cdot & \cdots & \cdot & \cdot \\
\cdot & \cdot & \cdot & \cdots & \cdot & \cdot \\
0 & 0 & 0 & \cdots & U_{M-1} & C_{M-1} \\
0 & 0 & 0 & \cdots & 0 & U_M
\end{bmatrix}.
$$

(a) Find the recurrence for L_i and U_i.

(b) Under the block diagonal dominance condition (5.4.6.7), show that

$$
\| L_i \| \le \frac{\|A_i\|}{\| C_{i-1} \|} \quad \text{and} \quad \| U_i \| \le \| B_i \| + \| A_i \|.
$$

(c) Let

$$
D = \begin{bmatrix}
D_1 & 0 & 0 & \cdots & 0 \\
0 & D_2 & 0 & \cdots & 0 \\
0 & 0 & D_3 & \cdots & 0 \\
\cdot & \cdot & \cdot & \cdots & \cdot \\
\cdot & \cdot & \cdot & \cdots & \cdot \\
\cdot & \cdot & \cdot & \cdots & \cdot \\
0 & 0 & 0 & \cdots & D_M
\end{bmatrix}
$$

and

$$
\mathbf{E} =
\begin{bmatrix}
\mathbf{E}_1 & 0 & 0 & \cdots & 0 \\
0 & \mathbf{E}_2 & 0 & \cdots & 0 \\
0 & 0 & \mathbf{E}_3 & \cdots & 0 \\
\cdot & \cdot & \cdot & \cdots & \cdot \\
\cdot & \cdot & \cdot & \cdots & \cdot \\
\cdot & \cdot & \cdot & \cdots & \cdot \\
0 & 0 & 0 & \cdots & \mathbf{E}_M
\end{bmatrix}.
$$

Show that if $\mathbf{A} = \overline{\mathbf{L}}\,\overline{\mathbf{U}}$, then $\mathbf{DAE} = (\mathbf{D}\overline{\mathbf{L}})(\overline{\mathbf{U}}\mathbf{E})$.

Note: This process is called *block diagonal scaling*.

(d) Let $\mathbf{D}_i = \mathbf{B}_i^{-1}$ and $\mathbf{E}_i = e_i\mathbf{I}$ for some constant e_i. Show that $\mathbf{DAE}$ is diagonally dominant if $\mathbf{Pe} \geq 0$, where $\mathbf{e} = (e_1, e_2, \cdots, e_M)^t$ and $\mathbf{P}$ is a tridiagonal matrix,

$$
\mathbf{P} =
\begin{bmatrix}
1 & -\delta_1 & 0 & 0 & \cdots & 0 & 0 \\
-\gamma_2 & 1 & -\delta_2 & 0 & \cdots & 0 & 0 \\
0 & -\gamma_3 & 1 & -\delta_3 & \cdots & 0 & 0 \\
\cdot & \cdot & \cdot & \cdot & \cdots & \cdot & \cdot \\
\cdot & \cdot & \cdot & \cdot & \cdots & \cdot & \cdot \\
\cdot & \cdot & \cdot & \cdot & \cdots & \cdot & \cdot \\
0 & 0 & 0 & 0 & \cdots & 1 & -\delta_{M-1} \\
0 & 0 & 0 & 0 & \cdots & -\gamma_M & 1
\end{bmatrix},
$$

with $\delta_i = \|\mathbf{B}_i^{-1}\mathbf{C}_i\|$ and $\gamma_i = \|\mathbf{B}_i^{-1}\mathbf{A}_i\|$.

(e) Hence, or otherwise, prove that the **LU** factorization of **DAE** is numerically stable if the matrix

$$
\mathbf{S} =
\begin{bmatrix}
1 & \alpha_1 & 0 & 0 & \cdots & 0 & 0 \\
\alpha_1 & 1 & \alpha_2 & 0 & \cdots & 0 & 0 \\
0 & \alpha_2 & 1 & \alpha_3 & \cdots & 0 & 0 \\
\cdot & \cdot & \cdot & \cdot & \cdots & \cdot & \cdot \\
\cdot & \cdot & \cdot & \cdot & \cdots & \cdot & \cdot \\
\cdot & \cdot & \cdot & \cdot & \cdots & \cdot & \cdot \\
0 & 0 & 0 & 0 & \cdots & 1 & \alpha_{M-1} \\
0 & 0 & 0 & 0 & \cdots & \alpha_{M-1} & 1
\end{bmatrix}
$$

is positive semidefinite, where $\alpha_i = \dfrac{\delta_i + \gamma_{i+1}}{2}$.

5.37 (Evans [1980b]). Consider the linear system $\mathbf{Ax} = \mathbf{d}$, where $\mathbf{A}$ is a *(Toeplitz) tridiagonal matrix* of the type

$$\mathbf{A} = \begin{bmatrix} b+a & +a & 0 & \cdots & 0 & 0 & -a \\ -a & b & +a & \cdots & 0 & 0 & 0 \\ 0 & -a & b & \cdots & 0 & 0 & 0 \\ \cdot & \cdot & \cdot & \cdots & \cdot & \cdot & \cdot \\ \cdot & \cdot & \cdot & \cdots & \cdot & \cdot & \cdot \\ \cdot & \cdot & \cdot & \cdots & \cdot & \cdot & \cdot \\ 0 & 0 & 0 & \cdots & -a & b & a \\ +a & 0 & 0 & \cdots & 0 & -a & b \end{bmatrix}.$$

(a) Let $\mathbf{A} = \mathbf{PQ}$, $\mathbf{P} = \beta^{-1}\overline{\mathbf{P}}$, and $\mathbf{Q} = \beta^{-1}\overline{\mathbf{Q}}$.

$$\overline{\mathbf{P}} = \begin{bmatrix} 1 & 0 & 0 & \cdots & 0 & -\alpha \\ -\alpha & 1 & 0 & \cdots & 0 & 0 \\ 0 & -\alpha & 1 & \cdots & 0 & 0 \\ \cdot & \cdot & \cdot & \cdots & \cdot & \cdot \\ \cdot & \cdot & \cdot & \cdots & \cdot & \cdot \\ \cdot & \cdot & \cdot & \cdots & \cdot & \cdot \\ 0 & 0 & 0 & \cdots & 1 & 0 \\ 0 & 0 & 0 & \cdots & -\alpha & 1 \end{bmatrix}$$

and

$$\overline{\mathbf{Q}} = \begin{bmatrix} 1 & \alpha & 0 & \cdots & 0 & 0 \\ 0 & 1 & \alpha & \cdots & 0 & 0 \\ 0 & 0 & 1 & \cdots & 0 & 0 \\ \cdot & \cdot & \cdot & \cdots & \cdot & \cdot \\ \cdot & \cdot & \cdot & \cdots & \cdot & \cdot \\ \cdot & \cdot & \cdot & \cdots & \cdot & \cdot \\ 0 & 0 & 0 & \cdots & 1 & \alpha \\ \alpha & 0 & 0 & \cdots & 0 & 1 \end{bmatrix},$$

where $\alpha = \dfrac{\gamma}{\beta}$. Find β and γ and hence α in terms of a and b. Under what conditions is $|\alpha| \le 1$?

(b)   Let $\overline{\mathbf{P}}\mathbf{v} = \mathbf{g}$ and $\overline{\mathbf{Q}}\mathbf{u} = \mathbf{v}$,   where $\mathbf{u} = (u_1, u_2, \cdots, u_N)^t$, $\mathbf{v} = (v_1, v_2, \cdots, v_N)^t$, and $\mathbf{g} = (g_1, g_2, \cdots, g_N)^t$. Show that

$$v_1 = \frac{(g_1 + \alpha^{N-1}g_2 + \cdots + \alpha^2 g_{N-1} + \alpha g_N)}{(1 - \alpha^N)},$$

and, for $i = 2, 3, \cdots, N$,

$$v_i = g_i + \alpha v_{i-1}.$$

Likewise, show that

$$u_N = \frac{(-\alpha v_1 + \alpha^2 v_2 - \alpha^3 v_3 + \cdots (-\alpha)^{N-1} v_{N-1} + v_N)}{(1 + (-\alpha)^N)},$$

and, for $i = N - 1, N - 2, \cdots, 2, 1,$

$$u_i = v_i - \alpha u_{i+1}.$$

(c) Using this framework, derive a parallel algorithm to solve $\mathbf{Ax} = \mathbf{d}$, where $\mathbf{A}$ is of the type given at the beginning of the problem.

Note: Matrices of this type are known (Evans [1980b]) to arise in solving first-order partial differential equations of the type

$$\frac{\partial \mathbf{U}}{\partial t} + c \frac{\partial \mathbf{U}}{\partial x} = 0, \quad c \text{ is a constant},$$

in the domain $R = \{a \le x \le b; \ t \ge 0\}$, where $\mathbf{U}(x, 0) = f(x)$.

5.38 (Sweet [1988]).
(a) Using partial fraction expansion, show that the inverse of the matrix $\mathbf{B}(r)$ in (5.4.2.29) can be expressed as

$$\mathbf{B}(r)^{-1} = [p_{2^r}(\mathbf{B}, \mathbf{C})]^{-1} = \sum_{j=1}^{2^r} f_j(\mathbf{C})[\mathbf{B} + 2\mathbf{C} \cos \theta_j(r)]^{-1},$$

where

$$[f_j(\mathbf{C})]^{-1} = \frac{\partial}{\partial a} \{p_{2^r}(a, t)\} \Big|_{a = -2t \cos \theta_j(r)}.$$

(b) Specialize to the case when $\mathbf{C} = \mathbf{I}$, the identity matrix.

5.39 (Swarztrauber [1987]). Referring to (5.4.4.30), consider the polynomial

$$p_m(a) = -2 \cosh [m \cosh^{-1} (\frac{a}{2})], \quad \text{for } a < -2.$$

If

$$q_m(a) = -\frac{1}{2} p_m (-2 - \frac{a}{m^2}),$$

then we obtain

$$q_m(a) = \cosh [m \cosh^{-1} (1 + \frac{a}{2m^2})].$$

(a) Show that

$$\lim_{m \to \infty} q_m(a) = \cosh(\sqrt{a}).$$

Hint: Recall $\cosh^{-1}(x) = \log_e [x + (x^2 - 1)^{1/2}]$ and $\log(1 + x) \approx x$, for small x.

(b) Given an $\varepsilon > 0$, show that there exists a rational polynomial function $R(a)$ such that

$$| R(a) - \operatorname{sech}(\sqrt{a}) | \le \frac{\varepsilon}{4}.$$

Hint: Use the Taylor series for $\operatorname{sech}(x)$.

(c) Combining the results in (a) and (b), show that for any $\varepsilon > 0$, there exists an m^* such that for all $m > m^*$ and $a > 0$,

$$| p_m^{-1}(a) + 2R(-m^2(a + 2)) | \le \varepsilon,$$

that is, $-2R(-m^2(a + 2))$ is an accurate rational polynomial approximation to all rational polynomials $p_m^{-1}(a)$ for $m > m^*$.

Note: Since $[B(j)]^{-1} = [p_{2^j}(B)]^{-1}$, using the above approximation we can develop a very good approximation to $[B(j)]^{-1}$, which, when used in conjunction with Buneman's algorithm, will result in considerable saving in the number of operations. For details, refer to Swarztrauber [1987].

5.40 (Heller [1976]). Let $M = 2^k - 1$ and $\mathbf{P}$ be a permutation matrix that reorders the vector $\mathbf{x} = (1, 2, 3, \cdots, M)$ in such a way that the odd multiples of 1 are followed by the odd multiples of 2, which in turn are followed by odd multiples of 4, etc. As an example, when $k = 3$, such a $\mathbf{P}$ is of the form

$$\mathbf{P} = \begin{bmatrix} 1 & 0 & 0 & 0 & 0 & 0 & 0 \\ 0 & 0 & 1 & 0 & 0 & 0 & 0 \\ 0 & 0 & 0 & 0 & 1 & 0 & 0 \\ 0 & 0 & 0 & 0 & 0 & 0 & 1 \\ 0 & 1 & 0 & 0 & 0 & 0 & 0 \\ 0 & 0 & 0 & 0 & 0 & 1 & 0 \\ 0 & 0 & 0 & 1 & 0 & 0 & 0 \end{bmatrix},$$

and clearly, $\mathbf{Px} = (1, 3, 5, 7, 2, 6, 4)^t$.

(a) Let $\mathbf{A}$ be the tridiagonal matrix in (5.3.1.2) with $M = 7$. Compute $\mathbf{PAP}^t$.

(b) Show that $\mathbf{PAP}^t = \mathbf{LU}$, where

$$L = \left[\begin{array}{cccc|ccc}
1 & 0 & 0 & 0 & 0 & 0 & 0 \\
0 & 1 & 0 & 0 & 0 & 0 & 0 \\
0 & 0 & 1 & 0 & 0 & 0 & 0 \\
0 & 0 & 0 & 1 & 0 & 0 & 0 \\
\hline
a_2 b_1^{-1} & c_2 b_3^{-1} & 0 & 0 & 1 & 0 & 0 \\
0 & 0 & a_6 b_5^{-1} & c_6 b_7^{-1} & 0 & 1 & 0 \\
0 & a_4 b_3^{-1} & c_4 b_5^{-1} & 0 & a_4^{(1)}(b_2^{(1)})^{-1} & c_4^{(1)}(b_6^{(1)})^{-1} & 1
\end{array}\right],$$

and

$$U = \left[\begin{array}{cccc|ccc}
b_1 & 0 & 0 & 0 & c_1 & 0 & 0 \\
0 & b_3 & 0 & 0 & a_3 & 0 & c_3 \\
0 & 0 & b_5 & 0 & 0 & c_5 & a_5 \\
0 & 0 & 0 & b_7 & 0 & a_7 & 0 \\
\hline
0 & 0 & 0 & 0 & b_2^{(1)} & 0 & c_2^{(1)} \\
0 & 0 & 0 & 0 & 0 & b_6^{(1)} & a_6^{(1)} \\
0 & 0 & 0 & 0 & 0 & 0 & b_4^{(2)}
\end{array}\right],$$

where $a_i^{(j)}$, $c_i^{(j)}$, and $b_i^{(j)}$ are defined in (5.3.1.9).

Note: This exercise relates the cyclic reduction and the classical Gaussian elimination scheme.

TRIANGULAR AND BANDED LINEAR SYSTEMS

6.1 INTRODUCTION

Many of the ideas for solving the linear first-order recurrence described in Chapter 5 naturally extend to m^{th}-order linear recurrence. This chapter examines the close relation between the mth-order linear recurrences, the (lower) banded linear systems, and (lower) triangular linear systems.

6.1.1 Statement of Problem and Motivation

The general class of linear recurrence system LR[N, m] of size N and order m is given by

$$x_i = \sum_{j=i-m}^{i-1} -a_{ij} x_j + d_i, \qquad (6.1.1.1)$$

where $1 \leq i \leq N$, $1 \leq m \leq N-1$ and $x_i = 0$ for $i \leq 0$ and $i > N$. Stated in matrix form, for $N = 8$ and $m = 3$, (6.1.1.1) becomes

$$\mathbf{Ax = d} \tag{6.1.1.2}$$

where

$$\mathbf{A} = \begin{bmatrix} 1 & 0 & 0 & 0 & 0 & 0 & 0 & 0 \\ a_{21} & 1 & 0 & 0 & 0 & 0 & 0 & 0 \\ a_{31} & a_{32} & 1 & 0 & 0 & 0 & 0 & 0 \\ a_{41} & a_{42} & a_{43} & 1 & 0 & 0 & 0 & 0 \\ 0 & a_{52} & a_{53} & a_{54} & 1 & 0 & 0 & 0 \\ 0 & 0 & a_{63} & a_{64} & a_{65} & 1 & 0 & 0 \\ 0 & 0 & 0 & a_{74} & a_{75} & a_{76} & 1 & 0 \\ 0 & 0 & 0 & 0 & a_{85} & a_{86} & a_{87} & 1 \end{bmatrix}, \tag{6.1.1.3}$$

$$\mathbf{x} = (x_1, x_2, \cdots, x_8)^t, \tag{6.1.1.4}$$

and

$$\mathbf{d} = (d_1, d_2, \cdots, d_8)^t. \tag{6.1.1.5}$$

and t denotes the transpose. It follows that the mth order linear recurrence gives rise to a linear *banded lower triangular* system of *bandwidth* (defined as the number of non-zero diagonals) $m + 1$. When $m = N - 1$, $\mathbf{A}$ is called a *lower triangular* matrix.

In this chapter we first present parallel algorithms for linear lower triangular and banded lower triangular systems. These algorithms are widely applicable. For example, given a dense linear system

$$\mathbf{Bx = y}, \tag{6.1.1.6}$$

a fundamental method for solving it consists in expressing $\mathbf{B}$ as a product

$$\mathbf{B = LU}, \tag{6.1.1.7}$$

where $\mathbf{L}$ and $\mathbf{U}$ are lower and upper triangular matrices. To solve (6.1.1.6), first solve

$$\mathbf{Lz = y}, \tag{6.1.1.8}$$

and then

$$\mathbf{Ux = z}. \tag{6.1.1.9}$$

Since both $\mathbf{L}$ and $\mathbf{U}^t$ have similar structure, the methods described in this chapter are applicable to solving (6.1.1.6).

Section 6.2 deals with lower triangular systems, and banded lower triangular systems are treated in Section 6.3.

6.2 LINEAR LOWER TRIANGULAR SYSTEMS

6.2.1 Column Sweep and Wave Front Methods

Consider a lower triangular system

$$\mathbf{A}\mathbf{x} = \mathbf{d}, \tag{6.2.1.1}$$

where

$$\mathbf{A} = \begin{bmatrix} 1 & 0 & 0 & \cdots & 0 \\ a_{21} & 1 & 0 & \cdots & 0 \\ a_{31} & a_{32} & 1 & \cdots & 0 \\ \cdot & \cdot & \cdot & \cdots & \cdot \\ \cdot & \cdot & \cdot & \cdots & \cdot \\ \cdot & \cdot & \cdot & \cdots & \cdot \\ a_{N1} & a_{N2} & a_{N3} & \cdots & 1 \end{bmatrix}, \tag{6.2.1.2}$$

where

$$\mathbf{x} = (x_1, x_2, \cdots, x_N)^t \tag{6.2.1.3}$$

and

$$\mathbf{d} = (d_1, d_2, \cdots, d_N)^t. \tag{6.2.1.4}$$

The serial algorithm computes the solution as follows.

$$\left.\begin{array}{l} x_1 = d_1, \\ x_i = d_i - \sum_{j=1}^{i-1} a_{ij} x_j, \quad i = 2, 3, \cdots, N. \end{array}\right\} \tag{6.2.1.5}$$

Clearly, this algorithm takes $\frac{1}{2}N(N-1)$ additions and $\frac{1}{2}N(N-1)$ multiplications. Thus, totally there are $N(N-1)$ operations.

To understand the mechanics of the column sweep method, let us first rename (6.2.1.1) as

$$\mathbf{A}^{(1)}\mathbf{x} = \mathbf{d}^{(1)}, \tag{6.2.1.6}$$

where

$$\mathbf{A}^{(1)} = \mathbf{A}, \quad \mathbf{x}^{(1)} = \mathbf{x}, \quad \text{and} \quad \mathbf{d}^{(1)} = \mathbf{d}$$

are given in (6.2.1.2), (6.2.1.3), and (6.2.1.4), respectively.

In this method, since it is known that $x_1 = d_1$, we first eliminate x_1 from the rest of the equations, arriving at a system of $N - 1$ equations, in variables x_2 through x_N, as

$$\mathbf{A}^{(2)} \mathbf{x} = \mathbf{d}^{(2)}, \tag{6.2.1.7}$$

where

$$\mathbf{A}^{(2)} = \begin{bmatrix} 1 & 0 & 0 & \cdots & 0 \\ a_{32} & 1 & 0 & \cdots & 0 \\ a_{42} & a_{43} & 1 & \cdots & 0 \\ \cdot & \cdot & \cdot & \cdots & \cdot \\ \cdot & \cdot & \cdot & \cdots & \cdot \\ \cdot & \cdot & \cdot & \cdots & \cdot \\ a_{N2} & a_{N3} & a_{N4} & \cdots & 1 \end{bmatrix}, \tag{6.2.1.8}$$

$$\left. \begin{aligned} \mathbf{x} &= (x_2, x_3, \cdots, x_N)^t, \\[2mm] \mathbf{d}^{(2)} &= (d_2^{(2)}, d_3^{(2)}, \cdots, d_N^{(2)})^t, \end{aligned} \right\} \tag{6.2.1.9}$$

where

$$d_i^{(2)} = d_i^{(1)} - a_{i1} x_1, \quad \text{for } i = 2, 3, \cdots, N. \tag{6.2.1.10}$$

Notice that (6.2.1.7) is the same as (6.2.1.1) except for the size. We now eliminate x_2 in the same manner as we did x_1, and this elimination process can be iteratively continued until all the variables are recovered. This algorithm, called the *column sweep method,* is given in Fig. 6.2.1.1 and requires the same number of operations as the serial algorithm described above, yet it is amenable to parallel computation. The column sweep method admits of an easy implementation on pipelined vector machines.

If we assume that $N - 1$ processors are available, then the column sweep algorithm requires a total of $2(N - 1)$ steps.

A careful analysis of the column sweep algorithm reveals that on an *average* no more than 50% of the processors are utilized. We now examine the strategies for improving the processor efficiency *without* unduly increasing the elapsed time. A standard approach to increase the processor efficiency is to decrease the number of processors. Since there are a total of $N(N - 1)$ operations to be performed, if we still want to compute the solution in $2(N - 1)$ steps, as in the *column sweep algorithm,* it follows from the first principles that a minimum of $\dfrac{N}{2}$ processors are needed. By a

/* Given $\mathbf{A}^{(1)}$ and $\mathbf{d}^{(1)}$ of (6.2.1.1) */

$x_1 = d_1^{(1)}$
FOR $j = 2$ TO N STEP 1 DO
    FOR $i \in \{\, j, \ j+1, \ j+2, \ \cdots , N \,\}$ DO IN PARALLEL
    $d_i^{(j)} = d_i^{(j-1)} - a_{i,j-1}\, x_{j-1}$
    END
    $x_j = d_j^{(j)}$
END

FIGURE 6.2.1.1
Column sweep algorithm.

careful scheduling of the processors, we now describe a modified column sweep method called the *wave front* algorithm that computes the solution in $2N - 1$ steps using $\dfrac{N-1}{2} \le p < N - 1$ processors.

We illustrate the basic ideas of this method by an example. Let $N = 15$ and $p = 9$. Referring to Fig. 6.2.1.2, the entry (t, p) at the intersection of the ith row and the jth column refers to the computation of the pth processor at the tth step of the algorithm, namely

$$d_i = d_i - a_{ij}\, x_j.$$

For convenience, the method is divided into three phases.

Phase 1 consists of $j + 1$ steps, where $j = N - p - 1$. Since x_1 is known, in the first *step* of phase 1, processors $1 \le k \le p$ compute

$$d_{k+1} = d_{k+1} - a_{k+1,\,1}\, x_1$$

in parallel. In Fig. 6.2.1.2, these computations are labeled $(1,1)$, $(1,2)$, $\cdots$, $(1,9)$. Now x_2 is known, and in the *second step* processors $2 \le k \le p$ compute in parallel

$$d_{k+1} = d_{k+1} - a_{k+1,\,2}\, x_2,$$

while processor 1 computes

$$d_{p+2,\,1} = d_{p+2,\,1} - a_{p+2,\,1}\, x_1.$$

These computations are labeled $(2,1)$, $(2,2)$, $\cdots$, $(2,9)$ in Fig. 6.2.1.2. This process of *folding* or *rescheduling* continues for $j + 1$ steps. The computations of the $(j + 1)^{th}$ step are labeled $(6,1)$, $(6,2)$, $\cdots$, $(6,9)$, in this example.

In the first step of phase 2 (that is, at the $j + 2 = 7^{th}$ step), processor 6 is

1	x_1														
2	(1,1)	x_2													
3	(1,2)	(2,2)	x_3												
4	(1,3)	(2,3)	(3,3)	x_4											
5	(1,4)	(2,4)	(3,4)	(4,4)	x_5										
6	(1,5)	(2,5)	(3,5)	(4,5)	(5,5)	x_6									
7	(1,6)	(2,6)	(3,6)	(4,6)	(5,6)	(6,6)	x_7								
8	(1,7)	(2,7)	(3,7)	(4,7)	(5,7)	(6,7)	(7,7)	x_8							
9	(1,8)	(2,8)	(3,8)	(4,8)	(5,8)	(6,8)	(7,8)	(8,8)	x_9						
10	(1,9)	(2,9)	(3,9)	(4,9)	(5,9)	(6,9)	(7,9)	(8,9)	(9,9)	x_{10}					
11	(2,1)	(3,1)	(4,1)	(5,1)	(6,1)	(7,1)	(8,1)	(9,1)	(10,1)	×	x_{11}				
12	(3,2)	(4,2)	(5,2)	(6,2)	(7,2)	(8,2)	(9,2)	(10,2)	(10,9)	×	×	x_{12}			
13	(4,3)	(5,3)	(6,3)	(7,3)	(8,3)	(9,3)	(10,3)	(9,8)	(10,8)	×	×	×	x_{13}		
14	(5,4)	(6,4)	(7,4)	(8,4)	(9,4)	(10,4)	(8,7)	(9,7)	(10,7)	×	×	×	×	x_{14}	
15	(6,5)	(7,5)	(8,5)	(9,5)	(10,5)	(7,6)	(8,6)	(9,6)	(10,6)	×	×	×	×	×	x_{15}

FIGURE 6.2.1.2

An illustration of the computations in the wave front method. $N = 15$, $p = 9$. × denotes non-zero entries.

reassigned to computing $a_{15,6} x_6$. To avoid *access conflicts* with the computation of processor 5, processor 6 accumulates these partial products in a temporary location. The computations at the 7th step are labeled (7,1), (7,2), $\cdots$, (7,9). Similarly, during the time steps 8 through 10, processors 6 through 9 accumulate similar partial products. At the end of phase 2, d_{12} through d_{15} are corrected by subtracting proper partial products in parallel in *one* step.

Thus, at the beginning of phase 3, we are left with a lower triangular system of size $(N - p - 1) \leq p$. This system is solved by using the *column sweep algorithm* in Fig. 6.2.1.1. The analysis of this algorithm is left as an exercise (Exercise 6.1). A number of modifications of the column sweep algorithm have been reported in the literature, and these algorithms are covered in Exercises 6.30 and 6.31.

6.2.2 Heller's Algorithm Using the Determinant of a Hessenberg Matrix

In this section, we derive a parallel algorithm for solving (6.2.1.1) by relating its solution to the *determinants* of submatrices (more specifically, principal submatrices) of a matrix called the *lower Hessenberg* matrix **H** derived from the given lower triangular matrix **A**. To get an idea of this approach, we begin by directly evaluating the solution in explicit form using (6.2.1.5). Thus,

$$
\left.
\begin{aligned}
x_1 &= d_1, \\
x_2 &= d_2 - a_{21}\, d_1, \\
x_3 &= d_3 - a_{31}\, d_1 - a_{32}\, d_2 + a_{32}\, a_{21}\, d_1, \\
x_4 &= d_4 - a_{41}\, d_1 - a_{42}\, d_2 + a_{42}\, a_{21}\, d_1 - a_{43}\, d_3 \\
&\quad + a_{43}\, a_{31}\, d_1 + a_{43}\, a_{32}\, d_2 - a_{43}\, a_{32}\, a_{21}\, d_1,
\end{aligned}
\right\}
\tag{6.2.2.1}
$$

and so on. To explore the relation between this solution and the determinants of lower Hessenberg matrices, define the matrix

$$
\mathbf{H} =
\begin{bmatrix}
d_1 & -1 & \cdots & 0 & 0 \\
d_2 & -a_{21} & \cdots & 0 & 0 \\
d_3 & -a_{31} & \cdots & 0 & 0 \\
\cdot & \cdot & & \cdot & \cdot \\
\cdot & \cdot & & \cdot & \cdot \\
\cdot & \cdot & & \cdot & \cdot \\
d_{N-1} & -a_{N-1,\,1} & \cdots & -a_{N-1,\,N-1} & -1 \\
d_N & -a_{N,\,1} & \cdots & -a_{N,\,N-1} & -a_{N,\,N}
\end{bmatrix}.
\tag{6.2.2.2}
$$

Notice that **H** is obtained by changing the sign of each element of **A**, dropping its last column, and adding the vector $\mathbf{d} = (d_1, d_2, \cdots, d_N)^t$ as the new first column. Matrices in this form are called *normalized lower Hessenberg* matrices and have been extensively studied. (See Exercise 6.3.)

Let **H**[i:j; s:t] denote the slice of the matrix bounded by rows i through j and columns s through t. When $i = s$ and $j = t$, we denote this slice succinctly as **H**[i:j], that is, **H**[i:j] is the submatrix of **H** formed by rows i to j and columns i to j, where $i \leq j$. As an example,

$$
\mathbf{H}[2\!:\!4] =
\begin{bmatrix}
-a_{21} & -1 & 0 \\
-a_{31} & -a_{32} & -1 \\
-a_{41} & -a_{42} & -a_{43}
\end{bmatrix},
$$

and

$$\mathbf{H}[3{:}3; \, 2{:}4] = \left[\, -a_{31}, \quad -a_{32}, \quad -1 \, \right].$$

Let $\mathbf{D}[i : j]$ be the determinant of $\mathbf{H}[i : j]$. In evaluating these determinants, we follow the convention of evaluation along the last row, from right to left. Thus, we obtain

$$\mathbf{D}[1{:}\,1] = d_1,$$

$$\mathbf{D}[1{:}\,2] = \begin{vmatrix} d_1 & -1 \\ d_2 & -a_{21} \end{vmatrix} = -a_{21}\,\mathbf{D}[1{:}\,1] + d_2,$$

$$\mathbf{D}[1{:}\,3] = \begin{vmatrix} d_1 & -1 & 0 \\ d_2 & -a_{21} & -1 \\ d_3 & -a_{31} & -a_{32} \end{vmatrix} = -a_{32}\,\mathbf{D}[1{:}\,2] - a_{31}\,\mathbf{D}[1{:}\,1] + d_3,$$

$$\mathbf{D}[1{:}\,4] = \begin{vmatrix} d_1 & -1 & 0 & 0 \\ d_2 & -a_{21} & -1 & 0 \\ d_3 & -a_{31} & -a_{32} & -1 \\ d_4 & -a_{41} & -a_{42} & -a_{43} \end{vmatrix}$$

$$= -a_{43}\,\mathbf{D}[1{:}\,3] - a_{42}\,\mathbf{D}[1{:}\,2] - a_{41}\,\mathbf{D}[1{:}\,1] + d_4.$$

Generalizing this, it can be shown that

$$\mathbf{D}[1{:}\,i] = d_i - \sum_{j=1}^{i-1} a_{ij}\,\mathbf{D}[1{:}\,j], \tag{6.2.2.3}$$

where vacuous summation is taken to be zero. Comparing (6.2.2.3) with (6.2.1.5), by the uniqueness of the solution to (6.2.1.1), we obtain the following theorem.

Theorem 6.2.2.1. The solution to (6.2.1.1) is given by

$$x_i = \mathbf{D}[1{:}\,i], \tag{6.2.2.4}$$

for $i = 1$ to N.

This theorem can also be proved by applying Cramer's rule to the system (6.2.1.1) (Exercise 6.2).

If $d_i = 0$, for $2 \le i \le N$, it then follows from the above analysis that

$$x_i = d_1\,\mathbf{D}[2{:}\,i].$$

In view of this intimate relation between the solution of (6.2.1.1) and determinants of lower Hessenberg matrices, in the following we describe a parallel method for computing the latter, which is also of independent interest.

Formally, let $\mathbf{H} = [h_{ij}]$ be a lower Hessenberg matrix, where

$$h_{ij} = 0, \quad \text{for} \quad j > i + 1,$$

that is,

$$\mathbf{H} = \begin{bmatrix}
h_{11} & h_{12} & 0 & \cdots & \cdot & 0 & 0 \\
h_{21} & h_{22} & h_{23} & \cdots & \cdot & 0 & 0 \\
h_{31} & h_{32} & h_{33} & \cdots & \cdot & 0 & 0 \\
\cdot & \cdot & \cdot & \cdots & \cdot & \cdot & \cdot \\
\cdot & \cdot & \cdot & & \cdot & \cdot & \cdot \\
\cdot & \cdot & \cdot & & \cdot & \cdot & \cdot \\
h_{N-1,1} & h_{N-1,2} & h_{N-1,3} & \cdots & \cdot & h_{N-1,N-1} & h_{N-1,N} \\
h_{N,1} & h_{N,2} & h_{N,3} & \cdots & \cdot & h_{N,N-1} & h_{N,N}
\end{bmatrix} . \qquad (6.2.2.5)$$

If $\mathbf{H}$ is a lower Hessenberg matrix, then $\mathbf{H}^t$ is called an *upper Hessenberg* matrix, where t denotes the transpose. A lower Hessenberg matrix is said to be *normalized* if

$$h_{i,i+1} = -1,$$

for $i = 1, 2, \cdots, N - 1$. Define a new matrix $D = [D_{ij}]$, where

$$D_{ij} = \begin{cases}
\mathbf{D}[i:j], & \text{if } 1 \le i \le j \le N, \\
\mathbf{D}[i:i-1] = 1, & \text{if } 2 \le i \le n, \ j = i - 1, \\
0, & \text{otherwise,}
\end{cases}$$

and $\mathbf{D}[i:j]$ is the determinant of the submatrix $\mathbf{H}[i:j]$. Thus, D is the matrix of determinants of submatrices of $\mathbf{H}$, and

$$D = \begin{bmatrix}
\mathbf{D}[1:1] & \mathbf{D}[1:2] & \mathbf{D}[1:3] & \cdots & \mathbf{D}[1:N-1] & \mathbf{D}[1:N] \\
1 & \mathbf{D}[2:2] & \mathbf{D}[2:3] & \cdots & \mathbf{D}[2:N-1] & \mathbf{D}[2:N] \\
0 & 1 & \mathbf{D}[3:3] & \cdots & \mathbf{D}[3:N-1] & \mathbf{D}[3:N] \\
\cdot & \cdot & \cdot & \cdots & \cdot & \cdot \\
\cdot & \cdot & \cdot & \cdots & \cdot & \cdot \\
\cdot & \cdot & \cdot & \cdots & \cdot & \cdot \\
0 & 0 & 0 & \cdots & \mathbf{D}[N-1:N-1] & \mathbf{D}[N-1:N] \\
0 & 0 & 0 & \cdots & 1 & \mathbf{D}[N:N]
\end{bmatrix}$$

is an upper Hessenberg matrix. For consistency in notation, let

$$\mathbf{D}[1:0] = \mathbf{D}[N+1, N] = 1. \qquad (6.2.2.6)$$

Notice that

$$\mathbf{D}[1:N] = DET(\mathbf{H}).\qquad(6.2.2.7)$$

Since the whole idea hinges on the possibility of evaluation of $\mathbf{D}[i:j]$, we analyze the evaluation of $\mathbf{D}[i:j]$ through an example. Consider $\mathbf{H}[2:6]$.

$$\mathbf{H}[2:6] = \begin{bmatrix} h_{22} & h_{23} & 0 & 0 & 0 \\ h_{32} & h_{33} & h_{34} & 0 & 0 \\ h_{42} & h_{43} & h_{44} & h_{45} & 0 \\ h_{52} & h_{53} & h_{54} & h_{55} & h_{56} \\ h_{62} & h_{63} & h_{64} & h_{65} & h_{66} \end{bmatrix}.$$

Expanding along the last row from right to left, we obtain

$$\mathbf{D}[2:6] = h_{66}\,\mathbf{D}[2:5] - h_{65} \begin{bmatrix} h_{22} & h_{23} & 0 & 0 \\ h_{32} & h_{33} & h_{34} & 0 \\ h_{42} & h_{43} & h_{44} & 0 \\ h_{52} & h_{53} & h_{54} & h_{56} \end{bmatrix}$$

$$+ h_{64} \begin{bmatrix} h_{22} & h_{23} & 0 & 0 \\ h_{32} & h_{33} & 0 & 0 \\ h_{42} & h_{43} & h_{45} & 0 \\ h_{52} & h_{53} & h_{55} & h_{56} \end{bmatrix} - h_{63} \begin{bmatrix} h_{22} & 0 & 0 & 0 \\ h_{32} & h_{34} & 0 & 0 \\ h_{42} & h_{44} & h_{45} & 0 \\ h_{52} & h_{54} & h_{55} & h_{56} \end{bmatrix}$$

$$+ h_{62} \begin{bmatrix} h_{23} & 0 & 0 & 0 \\ h_{33} & h_{34} & 0 & 0 \\ h_{43} & h_{44} & h_{45} & 0 \\ h_{53} & h_{54} & h_{55} & h_{56} \end{bmatrix}$$

$$= h_{66}\,\mathbf{D}[2:5] - h_{65}\,\mathbf{D}[2:4]\,(h_{56}) + h_{64}\,\mathbf{D}[2:3]\,(h_{45}\,h_{56})$$

$$- h_{63}\,\mathbf{D}[2:2]\,(h_{34}\,h_{45}\,h_{56}) + h_{62}\,(h_{23}\,h_{34}\,h_{45}\,h_{56}).$$

Generalizing this, we obtain

$$\mathbf{D}[r:s] = \sum_{i=r}^{s} h_{si}\,\mathbf{D}[r:i-1] \prod_{k=i}^{s-1} (-h_{k,k+1}).\qquad(6.2.2.8)$$

Similarly, expanding along the first column,

$$\mathbf{D}[r:s] = \sum_{i=r}^{s} h_{ir}\,\mathbf{D}[i+1:s] \prod_{k=r}^{i-1} (-h_{k,k+1}).\qquad(6.2.2.9)$$

We now state a very useful result:

Lemma 6.2.2.2. If $1 \leq r \leq s < t \leq N$, then

$$\mathbf{D}[r:s]\,\mathbf{D}[s+1:t] + \sum_{i=s+1}^{t} \sum_{j=r}^{s} h_{ij}\,\mathbf{D}[r:j-1]\,\mathbf{D}[i+1:t] \prod_{k=j}^{i-1} (-h_{k,k+1})$$

$$= \mathbf{D}[r:s+1]\,\mathbf{D}[s+2:t]$$

$$+ \sum_{i=s+2}^{t} \sum_{j=r}^{s+1} h_{ij}\,\mathbf{D}[r:j-1]\,\mathbf{D}[i+1:t] \prod_{k=j}^{i-1} (-h_{k,k+1}). \quad (6.2.2.10)$$

Proof

From (6.2.2.9), we have

$$\mathbf{D}[s+1:t] = \sum_{i=s+1}^{t} h_{i,s+1}\,\mathbf{D}[i+1:t] \prod_{k=s+1}^{i-1} (-h_{k,k+1}).$$

Substituting this in the left hand side (LHS) expression in (6.2.2.10)

$$\text{LHS} = \sum_{i=s+1}^{t} \sum_{j=r}^{s+1} h_{ij}\,\mathbf{D}[r:j-1]\,\mathbf{D}[i+1:t] \prod_{k=j}^{i-1} (-h_{k,k+1}).$$

Split this latter double summation as

$$\sum_{i=s+2}^{t} \sum_{j=r}^{s+1} h_{ij}\,\mathbf{D}[r:j-1]\,\mathbf{D}[i+1:t] \prod_{k=j}^{i-1} (-h_{k,k+1})$$

$$+ \sum_{j=r}^{s+1} h_{s+1,j}\,\mathbf{D}[r:j-1]\,\mathbf{D}[s+2:t] \prod_{k=j}^{s} (-h_{k,k+1}). \quad (6.2.2.11)$$

Using (6.2.2.8), the second term in (6.2.2.11) can be rewritten as

$$\mathbf{D}[s+2:t]\,\mathbf{D}[r:s+1].$$

Combining these, the lemma follows.

The following result provides the key to the parallel algorithm.

Theorem 6.2.2.3. For $1 \leq r \leq s \leq t \leq N$,

$$\mathbf{D}[r:t] = \mathbf{D}[r:s]\,\mathbf{D}[s+1:t]$$

$$+ \sum_{i=s+1}^{t} \sum_{j=r}^{s} h_{ij}\,\mathbf{D}[r:j-1]\,\mathbf{D}[i+1:t] \prod_{k=j}^{i-1} (-h_{k,k+1}). \quad (6.2.2.12)$$

Proof

Since this result is obvious for $t = s$, let $t \geq s + 1$. Rewrite the right-hand side of (6.2.2.12) using Lemma 6.2.2.2 repeatedly until we obtain

$$\mathbf{D}[r:t-1]\,\mathbf{D}[t:t] + \sum_{i=t}^{t} \sum_{j=r}^{t-1} h_{ij}\,\mathbf{D}[r:j-1]\,\mathbf{D}[i+1:t] \prod_{k=j}^{i-1}(-h_{k,k+1})$$

$$= \mathbf{D}[r:t-1]\,\mathbf{D}[t:t] + \sum_{j=r}^{t-1} h_{tj}\,\mathbf{D}[r:j-1]\,\mathbf{D}[t+1:t] \prod_{k=j}^{t-1}(-h_{k,k+1}).$$

But $\mathbf{D}[t:t] = h_{tt}$ and $\mathbf{D}[t+1:t] = 1$, and vacuous products are taken to be unity. Thus, the above expression can be rewritten as

$$\sum_{j=r}^{t} h_{tj}\,\mathbf{D}[r:j-1] \prod_{k=j}^{t-1}(-h_{k,k+1}).$$

Using (6.2.2.8), this expression is in fact $\mathbf{D}[r:t]$ and the theorem is proved.

This theorem essentially provides a *doubling formula* (quite similar to those used by the recursive doubling algorithm in Chapter 5) for computing the determinants. For, if we set $s = r + k - 1$ and $t = r + 2k - 1$, then evaluation of $\mathbf{D}[r: r + 2k - 1]$, a determinant of a lower Hessenberg matrix of size $2k \times 2k$, uses only determinants of size at most k.

Before turning to the algorithm, we prove a number of important corollaries. Define

$$\left. \begin{array}{l} \mathbf{U}(r,\ s) = (\mathbf{D}[r:r-1],\ \mathbf{D}[r:r],\ \mathbf{D}[r:r+1],\ \cdots,\ \mathbf{D}[r:s-1]) \\[20pt] \mathbf{V}(s,\ t) = (\mathbf{D}[s+2:t],\ \mathbf{D}[s+3:t],\ \mathbf{D}[s+4:t],\ \cdots,\ \mathbf{D}[t+1:t])^t, \end{array} \right\} \quad (6.2.2.13)$$

two vectors of size $s - r + 1$ and $t - s$, respectively.

By definition, recall that

$$\mathbf{H}[s+1:t;r:s] = \begin{bmatrix} h_{s+1,r} & h_{s+1,r+1} & \cdots & h_{s+1,s} \\ h_{s+2,r} & h_{s+2,r+1} & \cdots & h_{s+2,s} \\ \cdot & \cdot & & \cdot \\ \cdot & \cdot & & \cdot \\ \cdot & \cdot & & \cdot \\ h_{t,r} & h_{t,r+1} & \cdots & h_{t,s} \end{bmatrix}_{(t-s)\times(s-r+1)} \quad \cdot \quad (6.2.2.14)$$

Using this, we now state the following.

Corollary 6.2.2.4. If $\mathbf{H}$ is a normalized lower Hessenberg matrix, for $1 \le r \le s \le t \le N$, then

$$\mathbf{D}[r:t] = \mathbf{D}[r:s]\,\mathbf{D}[s+1:t] + \mathbf{U}(r,\ s)\,\mathbf{H}^t[s+1:t;\ r:s]\,\mathbf{V}(s,t), \quad (6.2.2.15)$$

where t denotes the transpose and

$$\mathbf{D}[r:t] = \mathbf{U}(r,\ s+1)\ \mathbf{H}^t[s+1{:}t;\ r{:}s+1]\ \mathbf{V}(s,t). \tag{6.2.2.16}$$

Proof

Since $h_{k,k+1} = -1$ in a normalized lower Hessenberg matrix, (6.2.2.15) immediately follows from (6.2.2.12). To prove (6.2.2.16), using (6.2.2.9) and (6.2.2.10), since $h_{k,k+1} = -1$, we first express $\mathbf{D}[s+1{:}t]$ as

$$\mathbf{D}[s+1{:}t] = \sum_{i=s+1}^{t} h_{i,s+1}\ \mathbf{D}[i+1{:}t],$$

and

$$\mathbf{D}[r:s]\ \mathbf{D}[s+1{:}t] = \mathbf{D}[r:s] \sum_{i=s+1}^{t} h_{i,s+1}\ \mathbf{D}[i+1{:}t]$$

$$= \mathbf{D}[r:s]\ (h_{s+1,s+1},\ h_{s+2,s+1},\ \cdots,\ h_{t,s+1})\ \mathbf{V}(s,t).$$

Clearly, adding this to

$$\mathbf{U}(r,\ s)\ \mathbf{H}^t[s+1{:}t;\ r:s]\ \mathbf{V}(s,\ t),$$

we obtain (6.2.2.16).

The following example illustrates (6.2.2.16).

Let $N = 8$, $r = 1$, $t = 7$, and $s = 3$. Then

$$\mathbf{U}(1,\ 4) = (\ \mathbf{D}[1:0],\ \mathbf{D}[1:1],\ \mathbf{D}[1:2],\ \mathbf{D}[1:3]\ ),$$

$$\mathbf{V}(3,\ 7) = (\ \mathbf{D}[5:7],\ \mathbf{D}[6:7],\ \mathbf{D}[7:7],\ \mathbf{D}[8:7]\ )^t,$$

$$\mathbf{H}[4:7;\ 1:4] = \begin{bmatrix} h_{41} & h_{42} & h_{43} & h_{44} \\ h_{51} & h_{52} & h_{53} & h_{54} \\ h_{61} & h_{62} & h_{63} & h_{64} \\ h_{71} & h_{72} & h_{73} & h_{74} \end{bmatrix}.$$

Then

$$\mathbf{D}[1:7] = \mathbf{U}(1,\ 4)\ \mathbf{H}^t[4:7;\ 1:4]\ \mathbf{V}(3,\ 7).$$

Now if we change $s = 4$, then

$$\mathbf{U}(1,\ 5) = (\ \mathbf{D}[1:0],\ \mathbf{D}[1:1],\ \mathbf{D}[1:2],\ \mathbf{D}[1:3],\ \mathbf{D}[1:4]\ ),$$

$$\mathbf{V}(4,\ 7) = (\ \mathbf{D}[6\colon 7],\ \mathbf{D}[7\colon 7],\ \mathbf{D}[8\colon 7]\ )^t,$$

$$\mathbf{H}[5\colon 7;\ 1\colon 5] = \begin{bmatrix} h_{51} & h_{52} & h_{53} & h_{54} & h_{55} \\ h_{61} & h_{62} & h_{63} & h_{64} & h_{65} \\ h_{71} & h_{72} & h_{73} & h_{74} & h_{75} \end{bmatrix},$$

and

$$\mathbf{D}[1\colon 7] = \mathbf{U}(1,\ 5)\ \mathbf{H}^t\ [5\colon 7;\ 1\colon 5]\ \mathbf{V}(4,\ 7).$$

Thus, if $\mathbf{U}(r,\ s+1)$ and $\mathbf{V}(s,\ t)$ are known, $\mathbf{D}[r\colon t]$ involves computation of inner products in parallel.

The lower Hessenberg matrix $\mathbf{H}$ becomes a *tridiagonal* matrix if $h_{ij} = 0$ for $i > j + 1$.

Corollary 6.2.2.5. If $\mathbf{H}$ is a tridiagonal matrix, then for $1 \le r \le s \le t \le N$,

$$\mathbf{D}[r\colon t] = \mathbf{D}[r\colon s]\ \mathbf{D}[s+1\colon t]$$

$$- h_{s+1,s}\ h_{s,s+1}\ \mathbf{D}[r\colon s-1]\ \mathbf{D}[s+2\colon t]. \qquad (6.2.2.17)$$

Proof
Since $\mathbf{H}$ is tridiagonal, the terms in the double summation on the right hand side of (6.2.2.12) are non-zero only when $j = s$ and $i = s + 1$, and (6.2.2.17) follows.

We invite the reader to compare this method of computing the determinant of a tridiagonal matrix with that in Exercise 5.12 (Chapter 5).

Since any lower Hessenberg matrix can be transformed into a normalized lower Hessenberg matrix (Exercise 6.3), it is assumed that $\mathbf{H}$ is normalized. Heller's parallel algorithm for computing the determinants of normalized Hessenberg matrices is given in Fig. 6.2.2.1.

As an example, let $N = 8$. The initialization step computes the following in parallel:

$$\mathbf{D}[1\colon 0] = \mathbf{D}[2\colon 1] = \mathbf{D}[3\colon 2] = \cdots = \mathbf{D}[9\colon 8] = 1,$$

$$\mathbf{D}[r\colon r] = h_{rr}, \qquad 1 \le r \le 8,$$

$$\mathbf{D}[r\colon r + 1] = h_{rr}*h_{r+1,\ r} + h_{r+1,\ r}, \qquad 1 \le r \le N.$$

The computations involved in the main FOR loop with index i are given in Table 6.2.2.1. The FOR loop variable i takes values 1, 3, 7, 15, 31, $\cdots$, that is, $2^k - 1$ for $k = 1, 2, \cdots, n$. The determinants needed in computing $\mathbf{D}[r\colon t]$ are listed in Table 6.2.2.2. For example, computation of $\mathbf{D}[1\colon 8]$ needs $\mathbf{D}[1\colon 0]$, $\mathbf{D}[1\colon 1]$, $\mathbf{D}[1\colon 2]$, $\mathbf{D}[1\colon 3]$, $\mathbf{D}[1\colon 4]$, $\mathbf{D}[6\colon 8]$, $\mathbf{D}[7\colon 8]$, $\mathbf{D}[8\colon 8]$, and $\mathbf{D}[9\colon 8]$. Notice that the values of

---

/*   Given a normalized Hessenberg matrix H. Compute $x_i = \mathbf{D}[1:i]$ for $i = 1$ to N,
      where $N = 2^{n+1}$. */

    FOR $r \in \{2, 3, \cdots, N, N+1\}$ DO IN PARALLEL
      $\mathbf{D}[r:r-1] = 1$
    END

    FOR $r \in \{1, 2, 3, \cdots, N\}$ DO IN PARALLEL
      $\mathbf{D}[r:r] = h_{rr}$
    END

    FOR $r \in \{1, 2, 3, \cdots, N\}$ DO IN PARALLEL
      $\mathbf{D}[r:r+1] = h_{rr} \times h_{r+1,\,r} + h_{r+1,\,r}$
    END

    FOR $i = 1$ STEP $(i+1)$ TO $N-1$
      FOR $j \in \{1, 2, 3, \cdots, i+1\}$ AND
             $r \in \{1, 2, 3, \cdots, N-i-j\}$ DO IN PARALLEL
        COMPUTE $\mathbf{D}[r:r+i+j]$ using (6.2.2.16) with $s = r+i$
      END
    END

FIGURE 6.2.2.1
A parallel algorithm for computing the determinants of a normalized Hessenberg
matrix.

---

each of these determinants are available before the computation of $\mathbf{D}[1:8]$ begins,
and hence the latter can be computed in parallel. A similar observation holds good
for each of the $\mathbf{D}[r:t]$ computed by the algorithm.

From the algorithm in Fig. 6.2.2.1, it is clear that it takes n iterations to compute
$\mathbf{D}[r, t]$, $r = 1$ and $1 \leq t \leq N$, where $N = 2^{n+1}$. The vectors $\mathbf{U}(r, s+1)$ and $\mathbf{V}(s, t)$ in
(6.2.2.16) are of lengths $s - r + 2$ and $t - s$. Since $s = r + i$ and $t = r + i + j$,
computations in (6.2.2.16) involve inner products of vectors of size $i + 2$ and j,
where $1 \leq j \leq i + 1$. Thus, to compute $\mathbf{D}[r:t]$ in parallel using (6.2.2.16), it takes
two multiplications and $\lceil \log (i+2) \rceil$ and $\lceil \log j \rceil$ additions. Since $i = 2^k - 1$,

$$\lceil \log (i+2) \rceil = k + 1,$$

and

TABLE 6.2.2.1

i	j	r	Compute $\mathbf{D}[r : r + i + j]$ using (6.2.2.16) with $s = r + i$.
1	1	$\{1, 2, 3, 4, 5, 6\}$	$\mathbf{D}[1: 3]$, $\mathbf{D}[2: 4]$, $\mathbf{D}[3: 5]$ $\mathbf{D}[4: 6]$, $\mathbf{D}[5: 7]$, $\mathbf{D}[6: 8]$
	2	$\{1, 2, 3, 4, 5\}$	$\mathbf{D}[1: 4]$, $\mathbf{D}[2: 5]$, $\mathbf{D}[3: 6]$ $\mathbf{D}[4: 7]$, $\mathbf{D}[5: 8]$
3	1	$\{1, 2, 3, 4\}$	$\mathbf{D}[1: 5]$, $\mathbf{D}[2: 6]$, $\mathbf{D}[3: 7]$ $\mathbf{D}[4: 8]$
	2	$\{1, 2, 3\}$	$\mathbf{D}[1: 6]$, $\mathbf{D}[2: 7]$, $\mathbf{D}[3: 8]$
	3	$\{1, 2\}$	$\mathbf{D}[1: 7]$, $\mathbf{D}[2: 8]$
	4	$\{1, 2\}$	$\mathbf{D}[1: 8]$

$$\lceil \log j \rceil \le k.$$

Let $T(N)$ be the total time required by this algorithm. As it takes two steps to compute $\mathbf{D}[r : r+1]$, we have

$$
\left.
\begin{aligned}
T(N) &= 2 + 2n + \sum_{k=1}^{n} \left(\lceil \log (i + 2) \rceil + \log j \right) \\
&\le 2 + 2n + \sum_{k=1}^{n} (2k + 1) \\
&= n^2 + 4n + 2 = O((\log N)^2).
\end{aligned}
\right\} \tag{6.2.2.18}
$$

Combining Theorem 6.2.2.1 and Algorithm 6.2.2.1, we obtain the following theorem, proof of which is left as an exercise (Exercises 6.5 and 6.6).

Theorem 6.2.2.6 The solution of a lower triangular system can be obtained in $O((\log N)^2)$ steps using $O(N^4)$ processors.

A number of special cases are treated in the exercises. For example, the solution of the banded systems using this method is the content of Exercises 6.4 and 6.9. Lower triangular systems with constant coefficients are contained in Exercises 6.7 and 6.8. We encourage the reader to further specialize these to constant coefficient banded systems.

TABLE 6.2.2.2

(i, j)	$r:t$	s	Values of Determinants Needed in Computing $\mathbf{D}[r:t]$ Using (6.2.2.16)
(1, 1)	1:3	2	1:0, 1:1, 1:2, 4:3
	2:4	3	2:1, 2:2, 2:3, 5:4
	3:5	4	3:2, 3:3, 3:4, 6:5
	4:6	5	4:3, 4:4, 4:5, 7:6
	5:7	6	5:4, 5:5, 5:6, 8:7
	6:8	7	6:5, 6:6, 6:7, 9:8
(1, 2)	1:4	2	1:0, 1:1, 1:2, 4:4, 5:4
	2:5	3	2:1, 2:2, 2:3, 5:5, 6:5
	3:6	4	3:2, 3:3, 3:4, 6:6, 7:6
	4:7	5	4:3, 4:4, 4:5, 7:7, 8:7
	5:8	6	5:4, 5:5, 5:6, 8:8, 9:8
(3, 1)	1:5	4	1:0, 1:1, 1:2, 1:3, 1:4, 6:5
	2:6	5	2:1, 2:2, 2:3, 2:4, 2:5, 7:6
	3:7	6	3:2, 3:3, 3:4, 3:5, 3:6, 8:7
	4:8	7	4:3, 4:4, 4:5, 4:6, 4:7, 9:8
(3, 2)	1:6	4	1:0, 1:1, 1:2, 1:3, 1:4, 6:6
	2:7	5	2:1, 2:2, 2:3, 2:4, 2:5, 7:7
	3:8	6	3:2, 3:3, 3:4, 3:5, 3:6, 8:8
(3,3)	1:7	4	1:0, 1:1, 1:2, 1:3, 1:4, 6:7, 7:7, 8:7
	2:8	5	2:1, 2:2, 2:3, 2:4, 2:5, 7:8, 8:8, 9:8
(3, 4)	1:8	4	1:0, 1:1, 1:2, 1:3, 1:4, 6:8, 7:8, 8:8, 9:8

In the next section we describe an algorithm for solving lower triangular systems in $O((\log N)^2)$ steps using only $O(N^3)$ processors.

6.2.3 Sameh-Brent Algorithm-1

Consider the system (6.2.1.1) where $N = 2^n - 1$. The solution $\mathbf{x}$ may be expressed as

$$\mathbf{x} = \mathbf{A}^{-1}\,\mathbf{d}. \tag{6.2.3.1}$$

This algorithm relies on computing $\mathbf{A}^{-1}$ as a product of N *elementary* lower triangular matrices. We begin by defining this latter class of matrices.

Let $\mathbf{e}_j = (0, 0, \cdots, 0, 1, 0, \cdots, 0)^t$ be an N-vector, called the jth *unit* vector, whose j^{th} element is unity and all the other elements are zero, and let $\mathbf{a}_i = (0, 0, \cdots, 0, a_{i+1,i}, a_{i+2,i}, \cdots, a_{N,i})^t$ be a vector whose first i components are zero. Further, let $\mathbf{A}$ be a lower triangular matrix, given in (6.2.1.2). Define, for $i = 1$ to N, the set of all N elementary lower triangular matrices $\mathbf{A}_i(\mathbf{a}_i)$ as follows:

$$\mathbf{A}_i(\mathbf{a}_i) = \mathbf{I} - \mathbf{a}_i\,\mathbf{e}_i^t = \begin{bmatrix} 1 & 0 & \cdots & 0 & 0 & \cdots & 0 \\ 0 & 1 & \cdots & 0 & 0 & \cdots & 0 \\ \cdot & \cdot & \cdots & \cdot & \cdot & \cdots & \cdot \\ \cdot & \cdot & \cdots & \cdot & \cdot & \cdots & \cdot \\ \cdot & \cdot & \cdots & \cdot & \cdot & \cdots & \cdot \\ 0 & 0 & \cdots & 1 & 0 & \cdots & 0 \\ 0 & 0 & \cdots & -a_{i+1,i} & 1 & \cdots & 0 \\ \cdot & \cdot & \cdots & \cdot & \cdot & \cdots & \cdot \\ \cdot & \cdot & \cdots & \cdot & \cdot & \cdots & \cdot \\ 0 & 0 & \cdots & -a_{N,i} & 0 & \cdots & 1 \end{bmatrix}. \tag{6.2.3.2}$$

The following properties are immediate (Exercise 6.10).

Lemma 6.2.3.1. $\mathbf{A}_i^{-1}(\mathbf{a}_i) = \mathbf{A}_i(-\mathbf{a}_i)$.

Lemma 6.2.3.2.

$$
\mathbf{A}_i(\mathbf{a}_i)\,\mathbf{A}_{i+1}(\mathbf{a}_{i+1}) =
\begin{bmatrix}
1 & 0 & \cdots & 0 & 0 & \cdots & 0 \\
0 & 1 & \cdots & 0 & 0 & \cdots & 0 \\
\cdot & \cdot & \cdots & \cdot & \cdot & \cdots & \cdot \\
\cdot & \cdot & \cdots & \cdot & \cdot & \cdots & \cdot \\
\cdot & \cdot & \cdots & \cdot & \cdot & \cdots & \cdot \\
0 & 0 & \cdots & 1 & 0 & \cdots & 0 \\
0 & 0 & \cdots & -a_{i+1,i} & 1 & \cdots & 0 \\
\cdot & \cdot & \cdots & \cdot & -a_{i+2,i+1} & \cdots & \cdot \\
\cdot & \cdot & \cdots & \cdot & \cdot & \cdots & \cdot \\
\cdot & \cdot & \cdots & \cdot & \cdot & \cdots & \cdot \\
0 & 0 & \cdots & -a_{N,i} & -a_{N,i+1} & \cdots & 1
\end{bmatrix}.
$$

Lemma 6.2.3.3.

$$
\mathbf{A} = \mathbf{A}_1(\mathbf{a}_1)\mathbf{A}_2(\mathbf{a}_2)\mathbf{A}_3(\mathbf{a}_3) \;\cdots\; \mathbf{A}_N(\mathbf{a}_N),
$$

and

$$
\mathbf{A}^{-1} = \mathbf{A}_N(-\mathbf{a}_N)\mathbf{A}_{N-1}(-\mathbf{a}_{N-1}) \;\cdots\; \mathbf{A}_2(-\mathbf{a}_2)\mathbf{A}_1(-\mathbf{a}_1).
$$

An alternative approach to computing the inverse of a lower triangular matrix is pursued in Exercise 6.24.

In the following we simplify the notation by denoting $\mathbf{A}_i(-\mathbf{a}_i)$ as $\mathbf{A}_i$. Combining this with (6.2.3.1) and Lemma 6.2.3.3, we obtain that

$$
\mathbf{x} = \mathbf{A}_N\,\mathbf{A}_{N-1}\,\mathbf{A}_{n-2} \;\cdots\; \mathbf{A}_2\,\mathbf{A}_1\,\mathbf{d}. \tag{6.2.3.3}
$$

This expression readily suggests an associative fan-in algorithm given in Fig. 6.2.3.1. An illustration of this algorithm is given in Fig. 6.2.3.2.

To understand the parallelism inherent in each of the expressions involving the matrix - matrix and matrix - vector multiplications within the inner loop of the algorithm in Fig. 6.2.3.1, first consider the structure of the matrix $\mathbf{A}_i^{(j)}$, where

$$/* \ N \ = \ 2^n - 1, \quad \mathbf{A}_i^{(0)} \ = \ \mathbf{A}_i, \quad \text{for } i = 1 \ \text{ to } \ N \ */$$

FOR $j = 0$ TO $n - 2$ STEP 1 DO

    FOR $i \in \{ 1, 2, 3, ..., 2^{n-j-1} - 1 \}$ DO IN PARALLEL

        $\mathbf{A}_i^{(j+1)} \ = \ \mathbf{A}_{2i+1}^{(j)} \ \mathbf{A}_{2i}^{(j)}$

        $\mathbf{d}^{(j+1)} \ = \ \mathbf{A}_1^{(j)} \ \mathbf{d}^{(j)}$

    END

END

$$\mathbf{d}^{(n)} \ = \ \mathbf{A}_1^{(n-1)} \mathbf{d}^{(n-1)}$$

FIGURE 6.2.3.1

Sameh-Brent Algorithm-1 for computing $\mathbf{x} = \mathbf{d}^{(n)}$.

$$\mathbf{A}_i^{(j)} \ = \ \begin{bmatrix} \mathbf{I}_i^{(j)} & \mathbf{0} & \mathbf{0} \\ \mathbf{0} & \mathbf{L}_i^{(j)} & \mathbf{0} \\ \mathbf{0} & \mathbf{S}_i^{(j)} & \overline{\mathbf{I}}_i^{(j)} \end{bmatrix}, \qquad (6.2.3.4)$$

$\mathbf{I}_i^{(j)}$ is an identity matrix of order $i \, 2^j - 1$,

$\overline{\mathbf{I}}_i^{(j)}$ is an identity matrix of order $2^n - (i+1) \, 2^j$,

$\mathbf{L}_i^{(j)}$ is a lower triangular matrix of order 2^j,

and

    $\mathbf{S}_i^{(j)}$ is a matrix of order $(2^n - (i+1) \, 2^j) \times 2^j$.

Further, partition $\mathbf{S}_i^{(j)}$ as

$$\mathbf{S}_i^{(j)} \ = \ \begin{bmatrix} \mathbf{U}_i^{(j)} \\ \mathbf{V}_i^{(j)} \end{bmatrix},$$

where $\mathbf{U}_i^{(j)}$ is a square matrix of order 2^j and $\mathbf{V}_i^{(j)}$ is a matrix of order $(2^n - (i + 2) \, 2^j) \times 2^j$.

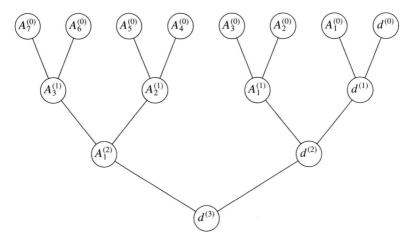

FIGURE 6.2.3.2
An illustration of the Sameh-Brent algorithm in Fig. 6.2.3.1.

Clearly, when $j = 0$ (refer to Fig. 6.2.3.3),

$$\mathbf{L}_i^{(0)} = [\, 1 \,],$$

$$\mathbf{S}_i^{(0)} = \begin{bmatrix} a_{i+1,i} \\ a_{i+2,i} \\ \cdot \quad \cdot \\ \cdot \\ \cdot \\ a_{N,i} \end{bmatrix},$$

where $\mathbf{U}_i^{(0)} = [\, a_{i+1,i} \,]$.

$\mathbf{I}_i^{(0)}$ and $\overline{\mathbf{I}}_i^{(0)}$ are two unit matrices of size $i - 1$ and $2^n - (i + 1) = N - i$. Using this information, and referring to Fig. 6.2.3.3, we obtain

$$\mathbf{A}_i^{(j+1)} = \mathbf{A}_{2i+1}^{(j)} \, \mathbf{A}_{2i}^{(j)}, \tag{6.2.3.5}$$

where

$$A_i^{(j+1)}$$

I	0	0	0
0	$L_{2i}^{(j)}$	0	0
0	$L_{2i+1}^{(j)} U_{2i}^{(j)}$	$L_{2i+1}^{(j)}$	0
0	$S_{2i+1}^{(j)} U_{2i}^{(j)} + V_{2i}^{(j)}$	$S_{2i+1}^{(j)}$	I

$$|<\text{---------------------}>|$$
$$2^{j+1}$$

$$A_{2i+1}^{(j)} \qquad\qquad A_{2i}^{(j)}$$

$=$

I	0	0	0
0	I	0	0
0	0	$L_{2i+1}^{(j)}$	0
0	0	$S_{2i+1}^{(j)}$	I

$$|<--->|\quad|<--->|$$
$$2^{j}\qquad 2^{j}$$

I	0	0	0
0	$L_{2i}^{(j)}$	0	0
0	$U_{2i}^{(j)}$	I	0
0	$V_{2i}^{(j)}$	0	I

$$|<--->|\quad|<--->|$$
$$2^{j}\qquad 2^{j}$$

FIGURE 6.2.3.3
Structure of the product $A_{2i+1}^{(j)} A_{2i}^{(j)} = A_i^{(j+1)}$.

$$L_i^{(j+1)} = \begin{bmatrix} L_{2i}^{(j)} & 0 \\ L_{2i+1}^{(j)} U_{2i}^{(j)} & L_{2i+1}^{(j)} \end{bmatrix}, \tag{6.2.3.6}$$

and

$$S_i^{(j+1)} = \begin{bmatrix} S_{2i+1}^{(j)} U_{2i}^{(j)} + V_{2i}^{(j)} & S_{2i+1}^{(j)} \end{bmatrix}. \tag{6.2.3.7}$$

Refer to Fig. 6.2.3.4 for an illustration of this process.

$$\mathbf{A}_3^{(0)} \qquad\qquad\qquad \mathbf{A}_2^{(0)}$$

$$
\mathbf{A}_3^{(0)} =
\begin{bmatrix}
1 & 0 & 0 & 0 & 0 & 0 & 0 \\
0 & 1 & 0 & 0 & 0 & 0 & 0 \\
0 & 0 & 1 & 0 & 0 & 0 & 0 \\
0 & 0 & a & 1 & 0 & 0 & 0 \\
0 & 0 & b & 0 & 1 & 0 & 0 \\
0 & 0 & c & 0 & 0 & 1 & 0 \\
0 & 0 & d & 0 & 0 & 0 & 1
\end{bmatrix}
\qquad
\mathbf{A}_2^{(0)} =
\begin{bmatrix}
1 & 0 & 0 & 0 & 0 & 0 & 0 \\
0 & 1 & 0 & 0 & 0 & 0 & 0 \\
0 & e & 1 & 0 & 0 & 0 & 0 \\
0 & f & 0 & 1 & 0 & 0 & 0 \\
0 & g & 0 & 0 & 1 & 0 & 0 \\
0 & h & 0 & 0 & 0 & 1 & 0 \\
0 & k & 0 & 0 & 0 & 0 & 1
\end{bmatrix}
$$

$$\mathbf{A}_1^{(1)}$$

$$
=
\begin{bmatrix}
1 & 0 & 0 & 0 & 0 & 0 & 0 \\
0 & 1 & 0 & 0 & 0 & 0 & 0 \\
0 & e & 1 & 0 & 0 & 0 & 0 \\
0 & ea+f & a & 1 & 0 & 0 & 0 \\
0 & eb+g & b & 0 & 1 & 0 & 0 \\
0 & ec+h & c & 0 & 0 & 1 & 0 \\
0 & ed+k & d & 0 & 0 & 0 & 1
\end{bmatrix}
$$

FIGURE 6.2.3.4
An illustration of the product $\mathbf{A}_1^{(1)} = \mathbf{A}_3^{(0)} \, \mathbf{A}_2^{(0)}$

Likewise, partition $\mathbf{d}^{(j)}$ as

$$\mathbf{d}^{(j)} = \begin{bmatrix} \mathbf{g}_1^{(j)} \\ \mathbf{g}_2^{(j)} \\ \mathbf{g}_3^{(j)} \end{bmatrix}, \tag{6.2.3.8}$$

where $\mathbf{g}_1^{(j)}$ and $\mathbf{g}_2^{(j)}$ are column vectors of size $2^j - 1$ and 2^j, respectively. Thus, $\mathbf{g}_3^{(j)}$ is of size $2^n - 2^{j+1}$. From this, it follows that

$$\mathbf{d}^{(j+1)} = \begin{bmatrix} \mathbf{g}_1^{(j+1)} \\ \mathbf{g}_2^{(j+1)} \\ \mathbf{g}_3^{(j+1)} \end{bmatrix} = \mathbf{A}_1^{(j)}\, \mathbf{d}^{(j)}, \tag{6.2.3.9}$$

where

$$\begin{rcases} \mathbf{g}_1^{(j+1)} = \mathbf{g}_1^{(j)}, \\ \mathbf{g}_2^{(j+1)} = \mathbf{L}_1^{(j)}\, \mathbf{g}_2^{(j)}, \\ \mathbf{g}_3^{(j+1)} = \mathbf{S}_1^{(j)}\, \mathbf{g}_2^{(j)} + \mathbf{g}_3^{(j)}. \end{rcases} \tag{6.2.3.10}$$

The proof of the following Lemma is left to the reader (Exercise 6.11).

Lemma 6.2.3.4. The first $2^j - 1$ components of $\mathbf{d}_i^{(j)}$ contain the $2^j - 1$ components of the solution vector $\mathbf{x}$.

Thus the entire solution is recovered in n steps of the algorithms.

In the following, we compute the minimum time required by this algorithm and an estimate of the degree of parallelism required to complete the algorithm in this time.

Referring to the algorithm in Fig. 6.2.3.1, let $t_i^{(j)}$ and $p_i^{(j)}$ be the minimum time and the number of processors required to compute $\mathbf{A}_i^{(j+1)}$. Likewise, let $r^{(j)}$ and $q^{(j)}$ be the minimum time and the number of processors required to compute $\mathbf{d}^{(j+1)}$. Then

$$T^{(j)} = \max\, \{r^{(j)}, t_i^{(j)} \mid i\ \varepsilon\ \{1, 2, \cdots, 2^{n-j-1} - 1\}\, \} \tag{6.2.3.11}$$

is the minimum time required to compute the inner loop of Algorithm 6.2.3.1 for a given j. Likewise,

$$p^{(j)} = q^{(j)} + \sum_{i=1}^{2^{n-j-1}-1} p_i^{(j)} \tag{6.2.3.12}$$

is the number of processors required to complete the above inner loop in time $T^{(j)}$. Let

$$T = r^{(n-1)} + \sum_{j=0}^{n-2} T^{(j)} \tag{6.2.3.13}$$

and (since $\sum_{i=a}^{b} x_i = 0$, if $b < a$)

$$P = \max \{ p^{(j)} \mid j = 0, 1, \cdots, n-1 \} \tag{6.2.3.14}$$

be the minimum time and the number of processors, respectively, required to complete the entire Algorithm 6.2.3.1.

Computation of $A_i^{(j)}$. From (6.2.3.4) to (6.2.3.7), it follows that computation of $A_i^{(j)}$ reduces to the following.

(a) *Compute* $L_{2i+1}^{(j)} U_{2i}^{(j)}$. Each column of this product matrix is obtained as 2^j inner products of vectors of size 2^j. Clearly, all these inner products must be computable in $1 + j$ steps (one multiplication and j additions using the associative fan-in rule). Since $L_{2i+1}^{(j)}$ is a lower triangular matrix, the number of processors required to compute a column of this product matrix is $2^{j-1} (2^j + 1)$. Hence, a total of $2^{2j-1} (2^j + 1)$ processors are needed in this computation.

(b) *Compute* $S_{2i+1}^{(j)} U_{2i}^{(j)}$. Computing each of the $2^{n+j} - (i + 1) 2^{2j+1}$ elements of this product matrix involves inner product of vectors of length 2^j. Clearly, the time required is $1 + j$ steps and the number of processors required is $(2^{n+j} - (i + 1) 2^{2j+1}) 2^j$.

(c) *Compute* $S_{2i+1}^{(j)} U_{2i}^{(j)} + V_{2i}^{(j)}$. Using the same number of processors as in (b) above, this matrix sum can be completed in parallel in just *one* step.

Notice that (a) and (b) can be computed in parallel. Now from (a) and combining (b) and (c), it follows that

$$t_i^{(j)} = 2 + j. \tag{6.2.3.15}$$

Also from (a) and (b) (since the processors in (b) can be used in (c)), it follows that

$$p_i^{(j)} = 2^{2j-1} (2^j + 1) + (2^{n+j} - (i+1) 2^{2j+1}) 2^j$$

$$= 2^{2j} (2^n + \tfrac{1}{2}) - 2^{3j} (2i + \frac{3}{2}). \tag{6.2.3.16}$$

Computation of d$^{(j)}$. From (6.2.3.8) to (6.2.3.10), it follows that computing $d^{(j)}$ reduces to the following:

(d) *Compute* $L_1^{(j)} g_2^{(j)}$. Each element of this vector can be obtained as the inner product of vectors of length 2^j. Hence this computation can be completed in $1 + j$ steps using $2^{j-1} (2^j + 1)$ processors.

(e) *Compute* $S_1^{(j)} g_2^{(j)} + g_3^{(j)}$. Each element of this vector can be obtained in $2 + j$ units of time using $(2^n - 2^{j+1}) 2^j$ processors.

From (d) and (e), it follows that

$$r^{(j)} = (2 + j) \tag{6.2.3.17}$$

and

$$q^{(j)} = 2^{j-1} (2^j + 1) + (2^n - 2^{j+1}) 2^j$$

$$= 2^j (2^n + \frac{1}{2}) - (\frac{3}{2}) 2^{2j}. \tag{6.2.3.18}$$

From (6.2.3.13), (6.2.3.15), and (6.2.3.17), it follows that

$$T = \sum_{j=0}^{n-1} (2 + j) = \frac{n(n+3)}{2} = O((\log N)^2). \tag{6.2.3.19}$$

Consider

$$p^{(j)} = q^{(j)} + \sum_{i=1}^{2^{n-j-1} - 1} p_i^{(j)}$$

$$= 2^j (2^n + \frac{1}{2}) - \frac{3}{2} 2^{2j} + \sum_{i=1}^{2^{n-j-1} - 1} [2^{2j} (2^n + \frac{1}{2}) - 2^{3j} (2i + \frac{3}{2})]$$

$$= \frac{3}{2} 2^{3j} - \frac{2^{2j}}{4} [5 \times 2^n + 8] + \frac{2^j}{4} [2^{2n} + 5 \times 2^n + 2].$$

Let $2^j = y$ and consider the function

$$f(y) = \frac{3}{2} y^3 - \frac{y^2}{4} [5 \times 2^n + 8] + \frac{y}{4} [2^{2n} + 5 \times 2^n + 2].$$

It can be shown that the maximum of this function (for $n \geq 4$) occurs approximately at $y = \frac{2^n}{8}$. Therefore, from (6.2.3.14), we have

$$P = \frac{15}{1024} 2^{3n} + \frac{8}{1024} 2^{2n} + \frac{1}{64} 2^n$$

$$= O(N^3). \tag{6.2.3.20}$$

The following is a summary of the above development.

Theorem 6.2.3.5. Using the Sameh-Brent Algorithm-1, the lower triangular linear system of size N can be solved in $O((\log N)^2)$ steps using $O(N^3)$ processors.

A careful study of the above analysis would indicate that the *maximum degree of parallelism at any step is essentially dictated* by the number of multiplications at that step. Thus, $p^{(j)}$ represents the total number of multiplications at step j of Algorithm 6.2.3.1. It would be an interesting exercise to find the total number of scalar operations required by this algorithm (Exercise 6.12). Often in practice, one may not have the luxury of $O(N^3)$ processors but have access to only a fixed number of processors (Exercise 6.31). The above algorithm in this form may not be best in such circumstances. Further, it can be shown (Exercise 6.28) that the error in the solution computed by this algorithm can be arbitrarily large, which further limits its practical applicability.

6.2.4 Sameh-Brent Algorithm-2

Consider the linear system (6.2.1.1), where $\mathbf{A}$ is a lower triangular matrix of order N (given in (6.2.2.1)), where $N = 2^n$ for some $n \geq 2$. Define $\mathbf{A}^{(0)} = \mathbf{A}$ and $\mathbf{d}^{(0)} = \mathbf{d}$. Let $\mathbf{I}^{(j)}$ be a unit matrix of order 2^j for $j = 1, 2, \cdots, n-1$. Let $\mathbf{A}_{ij}^{(0)} = [\, a_{ij} \,]_{2^0 \times 2^0}$ and $d_i^{(0)} = d_i$ for $i = 1$ to N. Define a block diagonal matrix $\mathbf{D}^{(0)}$ where

$$[\mathbf{D}^{(0)}]^{-1} = \begin{bmatrix} \mathbf{D}_1^{(0)} & 0 & 0 & \cdots & 0 \\ 0 & \mathbf{D}_2^{(0)} & 0 & \cdots & 0 \\ 0 & 0 & \mathbf{D}_3^{(0)} & \cdots & 0 \\ \cdot & \cdot & \cdot & \cdots & \cdot \\ \cdot & \cdot & \cdot & \cdots & \cdot \\ \cdot & \cdot & \cdot & \cdots & \cdot \\ 0 & 0 & \cdot & \cdots & \mathbf{D}_{N/2}^{(0)} \end{bmatrix}, \tag{6.2.4.1}$$

where, for $i = 1, 2, \cdots, \dfrac{N}{2}$,

$$\mathbf{D}_i^{(0)} = \begin{bmatrix} \mathbf{I}^{(0)} & \mathbf{0} \\ \\ \mathbf{A}_{2i,\,2i-1}^{(0)} & \mathbf{I}^{(0)} \end{bmatrix} = \begin{bmatrix} 1 & 0 \\ \\ a_{2i,\,2i-1} & 1 \end{bmatrix} \tag{6.2.4.2}$$

is a block of size 2×2. (See Exercise 6.14.)

Now define

$$\mathbf{A}^{(1)} = \mathbf{D}^{(0)} \mathbf{A}^{(0)} \tag{6.2.4.3}$$

and

$$\mathbf{d}^{(1)} = \mathbf{D}^{(0)} \mathbf{d}^{(0)}, \tag{6.2.4.4}$$

where $\mathbf{A}^{(1)}$ is a block lower triangular matrix of order $\dfrac{N}{2}$ with blocks of size 2×2, given by

$$\mathbf{A}^{(1)} = \begin{bmatrix} \mathbf{I}^{(1)} & \mathbf{0} & \mathbf{0} & \cdots & \mathbf{0} & \mathbf{0} \\ \mathbf{A}_{21}^{(1)} & \mathbf{I}^{(1)} & \mathbf{0} & \cdots & \mathbf{0} & \mathbf{0} \\ \mathbf{A}_{31}^{(1)} & \mathbf{A}_{32}^{(1)} & \mathbf{I}^{(1)} & \cdots & \mathbf{0} & \mathbf{0} \\ \cdot & \cdot & \cdot & \cdots & \cdot & \cdot \\ \cdot & \cdot & \cdot & \cdots & & \cdot \\ \cdot & \cdot & \cdot & \cdots & \cdot & \\ \mathbf{A}_{N/2,1}^{(1)} & \mathbf{A}_{N/2,2}^{(1)} & \mathbf{A}_{N/2,3}^{(1)} & \cdots & \mathbf{A}_{N/2,N/2-1}^{(1)} & \mathbf{I}^{(1)} \end{bmatrix}, \tag{6.2.4.5}$$

and, for $i = 2, 3, \cdots, \dfrac{N}{2}$, and $k = 1, 2, \cdots, \dfrac{N}{2} - 1$,

$$\mathbf{A}_{ik}^{(1)} = \begin{bmatrix} \mathbf{I}^{(0)} & \mathbf{0} \\ \\ -\mathbf{A}_{2i,\,2i-1}^{(0)} & \mathbf{I}^{(0)} \end{bmatrix} \begin{bmatrix} \mathbf{A}_{2i-1,\,2k-1}^{(0)} & \mathbf{A}_{2i-1,\,2k}^{(0)} \\ \\ \mathbf{A}_{2i,\,2k-1}^{(0)} & \mathbf{A}_{2i,\,2k}^{(0)} \end{bmatrix} . \tag{6.2.4.6}$$

Likewise, $\mathbf{d}^{(1)} = (\mathbf{d}_1^{(1)}, \mathbf{d}_2^{(1)}, \cdots, \mathbf{d}_{N/2}^{(1)})^t$ is a partitioned vector, where, for $i = 1, 2, \cdots, \dfrac{N}{2}$,

$$\mathbf{d}_i^{(1)} = \begin{bmatrix} \mathbf{I}^{(0)} & \mathbf{0} \\ \\ -\mathbf{A}_{2i,\,2i-1}^{(0)} & \mathbf{I}^{(0)} \end{bmatrix} \begin{bmatrix} \mathbf{d}_{2i-1}^{(0)} \\ \\ \mathbf{d}_{2i}^{(0)} \end{bmatrix} . \tag{6.2.4.7}$$

Now, for $j = 1, 2, \cdots, n-1$, consider

$$\mathbf{A}^{(j+1)} = \mathbf{D}^{(j)} \mathbf{A}^{(j)} \tag{6.2.4.8}$$

and

$$\mathbf{d}^{(j+1)} = \mathbf{D}^{(j)} \mathbf{d}^{(j)}, \tag{6.2.4.9}$$

where

$$\mathbf{A}^{(j)} = \begin{bmatrix} \mathbf{I}^{(j)} & \mathbf{0} & \mathbf{0} & \cdots & \mathbf{0} & \mathbf{0} \\ \mathbf{A}_{21}^{(j)} & \mathbf{I}^{(j)} & \mathbf{0} & \cdots & \mathbf{0} & \mathbf{0} \\ \mathbf{A}_{31}^{(j)} & \mathbf{A}_{32}^{(j)} & \mathbf{I}^{(j)} & \cdots & \mathbf{0} & \mathbf{0} \\ \cdot & \cdot & \cdot & \cdots & \cdot & \cdot \\ \cdot & \cdot & \cdot & \cdots & \cdot & \cdot \\ \cdot & \cdot & \cdot & \cdots & \cdot & \cdot \\ \mathbf{A}_{N/2^j,1}^{(j)} & \mathbf{A}_{N/2^j,2}^{(j)} & \mathbf{A}_{N/2^j,3}^{(j)} & \cdots & \mathbf{A}_{N/2^j,N/2^j-1}^{(j)} & \mathbf{I}^{(j)} \end{bmatrix}, \tag{6.2.4.10}$$

$$[\mathbf{D}^{(j)}]^{-1} = \begin{bmatrix} \mathbf{D}_1^{(j)} & \mathbf{0} & \mathbf{0} & \cdots & \mathbf{0} \\ \mathbf{0} & \mathbf{D}_2^{(j)} & \mathbf{0} & \cdots & \mathbf{0} \\ \mathbf{0} & \mathbf{0} & \mathbf{D}_3^{(j)} & \cdots & \mathbf{0} \\ \cdot & \cdot & \cdot & \cdots & \cdot \\ \cdot & \cdot & \cdot & \cdots & \cdot \\ \cdot & \cdot & \cdot & \cdots & \cdot \\ \mathbf{0} & \mathbf{0} & \mathbf{0} & \cdots & \mathbf{D}_{N/2}^{(j)} \end{bmatrix},$$

for $i = 1, 2, \cdots, \dfrac{N}{2^j}$,

$$\mathbf{D}_i^{(j)} = \begin{bmatrix} \mathbf{I}^{(j)} & \mathbf{0} \\ \mathbf{A}_{2i,2i-1}^{(j)} & \mathbf{I}^{(j)} \end{bmatrix}, \tag{6.2.4.11}$$

for $i = 2, 3, \cdots, \dfrac{N}{2^{j+1}}$ and $k = 1, 2, \cdots, \dfrac{N}{2^{j+1}} - 1$,

$$\mathbf{A}_{ik}^{(j+1)} = \begin{bmatrix} \mathbf{I}^{(j)} & \mathbf{0} \\ -\mathbf{A}_{2i,2i-1}^{(j)} & \mathbf{I}^{(j)} \end{bmatrix} \begin{bmatrix} \mathbf{A}_{2i-1,2k-1}^{(j)} & \mathbf{A}_{2i-1,2k}^{(j)} \\ \mathbf{A}_{2i,2k-1}^{(j)} & \mathbf{A}_{2i,2k}^{(j)} \end{bmatrix}, \tag{6.2.4.12}$$

and, for $i = 1, 2, \cdots, \dfrac{N}{2^{j+1}}$,

$$\mathbf{d}_i^{(j+1)} = \begin{bmatrix} \mathbf{I}^{(j)} & \mathbf{0} \\ -\mathbf{A}_{2i,\,2i-1}^{(j)} & \mathbf{I}^{(j)} \end{bmatrix} \begin{bmatrix} \mathbf{d}_{2i-1}^{(j)} \\ \mathbf{d}_{2i}^{(j)} \end{bmatrix} \cdot \qquad (6.2.4.13)$$

Notice that $\mathbf{A}_{ik}^{(j)}$ is a matrix of order 2^j, and $d_i^{(j)}$ is a vector of order 2^j.

It is clear from the above development that

$$\mathbf{A}^{(n)} = \mathbf{I}^{(n)}, \qquad (6.2.4.14)$$

and hence

$$\mathbf{x} = \mathbf{d}^{(n)}. \qquad (6.2.4.15)$$

An illustration of the various steps are given in Fig. 6.2.4.1 for $N = 8$. The algorithm is stated in Fig. 6.2.4.2.

Referring to the algorithm in Fig. 6.2.4.2, let $T^{(j)}$ and $p^{(j)}$ be the minimum time and degree of parallelism, respectively, required to complete the computation of $\mathbf{A}^{(j+1)}$. Let $r^{(j)}$ and $q^{(j)}$ be the minimum time and processors required to compute $\mathbf{d}^{(j+1)}$. Then clearly

$$T = \sum_{j=0}^{n-1} \max \{ T^{(j)}, r^{(j)} \}, \qquad (6.2.4.16)$$

and

$$P = \max_{j=0 \text{ to } n-1} \{ p^{(j)} + r^{(j)} \} \qquad (6.2.4.17)$$

are the total time and the total number of processors required to complete the algorithm in Fig. 6.2.4.2.

To compute $T^{(j)}$, observe, using (6.2.4.12), that

$$\mathbf{A}_{ik}^{(j+1)} = \begin{bmatrix} \mathbf{A}_{2i,\,2k-1}^{(j)} & \mathbf{A}_{2i-1,\,2k}^{(j)} \\ \mathbf{A}_{2i,\,2k-1}^{(j)} - \mathbf{A}_{2i,\,2i-1}^{(j)}\,\mathbf{A}_{2i-1,2k-1} & \mathbf{A}_{2i,\,2k}^{(j)} - \mathbf{A}_{2i,\,2i-1}^{(j)}\,\mathbf{A}_{2i-1,2k} \end{bmatrix} \cdot \qquad (6.2.4.18)$$

Clearly, the products $\mathbf{A}_{2i,\,2i-1}^{(j)} \mathbf{A}_{2i-1,2k-1}^{(j)}$ and $\mathbf{A}_{2i,\,2i-1}^{(j)} \mathbf{A}_{2i-1,2k}^{(j)}$ can be computed in $1 + j$ steps using 2^{3j+1} processors. Then, using the same number of processors, $\mathbf{A}_{ik}^{(j+1)}$ can be computed in just one more step (subtraction). Thus

$$T^{(j)} = 2 + j. \qquad (6.2.4.19)$$

Computation of $\mathbf{A}^{(j+1)}$ clearly involves

$$1 + 2 + 3 + \cdots + 2^{n-j-1} - 1 = 2^{n-j-2}\,(2^{n-j-1} - 1)$$

such matrix products. Thus

Step 0:

$$\mathbf{A}^{(0)} = \begin{bmatrix} 1 & 0 & 0 & 0 & 0 & 0 & 0 & 0 \\ a_{21} & 1 & 0 & 0 & 0 & 0 & 0 & 0 \\ a_{31} & a_{32} & 1 & 0 & 0 & 0 & 0 & 0 \\ a_{41} & a_{42} & a_{43} & 1 & 0 & 0 & 0 & 0 \\ a_{51} & a_{52} & a_{53} & a_{54} & 1 & 0 & 0 & 0 \\ a_{61} & a_{62} & a_{63} & a_{64} & a_{65} & 1 & 0 & 0 \\ a_{71} & a_{72} & a_{73} & a_{74} & a_{75} & a_{76} & 1 & 0 \\ a_{81} & a_{82} & a_{83} & a_{84} & a_{85} & a_{86} & a_{87} & 1 \end{bmatrix}$$

Step 1:

$$\left[\mathbf{D}^{(0)}\right]^{-1} = \left[\begin{array}{cc|cc|cc|cc} 1 & 0 & & & & & & \\ a_{21} & 1 & & & & & & \\ \hline & & 1 & 0 & & & & \\ & & a_{43} & 1 & & & & \\ \hline & & & & 1 & 0 & & \\ & & & & a_{65} & 1 & & \\ \hline & & & & & & 1 & 0 \\ & & & & & & a_{87} & 1 \end{array}\right]$$

$$\mathbf{A}^{(1)} = \left[\begin{array}{cc|cc|cc|cc} 1 & 0 & & & & & & \\ 0 & 1 & & & & & & \\ \hline \times & \times & 1 & 0 & & & & \\ \times & \times & 0 & 1 & & & & \\ \hline \times & \times & \times & \times & 1 & 0 & & \\ \times & \times & \times & \times & 0 & 1 & & \\ \hline \times & \times & \times & \times & \times & \times & 1 & 0 \\ \times & \times & \times & \times & \times & \times & 0 & 1 \end{array}\right] = \begin{bmatrix} \mathbf{I}^{(1)} & 0 & 0 & 0 \\ \mathbf{A}_{21}^{(1)} & \mathbf{I}^{(1)} & 0 & 0 \\ \mathbf{A}_{31}^{(1)} & \mathbf{A}_{32}^{(1)} & \mathbf{I}^{(1)} & 0 \\ \mathbf{A}_{41}^{(1)} & \mathbf{A}_{42}^{(1)} & \mathbf{A}_{43}^{(1)} & \mathbf{I}^{(1)} \end{bmatrix}$$

Step 2:

$$
\left[\mathbf{D}^{(1)}\right]^{-1} =
\begin{bmatrix}
\mathbf{I}^{(1)} & | & \mathbf{0} & | & & \\
\overline{} & | & \overline{} & | & \mathbf{0} & \\
\mathbf{A}_{21}^{(1)} & | & \mathbf{I}^{(1)} & | & & \\
\hline
& & & | & \mathbf{I}^{(1)} & | & \mathbf{0} \\
& \mathbf{0} & & | & \overline{} & | & \overline{} \\
& & & | & \mathbf{A}_{43}^{(1)} & | & \mathbf{A}^{(1)}
\end{bmatrix}
$$

$$
\mathbf{A}^{(2)} =
\begin{bmatrix}
1 & 0 & 0 & 0 & | & & & & \\
0 & 1 & 0 & 0 & | & & & & \\
0 & 0 & 1 & 0 & | & & \mathbf{0} & & \\
0 & 0 & 0 & 1 & | & & & & \\
\hline
\times & \times & \times & \times & | & 1 & 0 & 0 & 0 \\
\times & \times & \times & \times & | & 0 & 1 & 0 & 0 \\
\times & \times & \times & \times & | & 0 & 0 & 1 & 0 \\
\times & \times & \times & \times & | & 0 & 0 & 0 & 1
\end{bmatrix}
=
\begin{bmatrix}
\mathbf{I}^{(2)} & | & \mathbf{0} \\
\hline
\mathbf{A}_{21}^{(1)} & | & \mathbf{I}^{(2)}
\end{bmatrix}
$$

Step 3:

$$
\left[\mathbf{D}^{(3)}\right]^{-1} = \mathbf{A}_{21}^{(2)}, \qquad\qquad \mathbf{A}^{(3)} = \mathbf{I}
$$

FIGURE 6.2.4.1
An illustration of Sameh-Brent Algorithm-2 for $N = 8$. (Non-zero entries are denoted by $\times$.)

/* $N = 2^n$, $\mathbf{A}^{(0)}$, and $\mathbf{d}^{(0)}$ are given. */

FOR $j = 0$ TO $n - 1$ STEP 1 DO
      COMPUTE $\mathbf{A}^{(j+1)}$ and $\mathbf{d}^{(j+1)}$ using (6.2.4.8) and (6.2.4.9)
END

$\mathbf{x} = \mathbf{d}^{(n)}$

FIGURE 6.2.4.2
Sameh-Brent Algorithm-2 to solve lower triangular system.

$$p^{(j)} = 2^{2n+j-2} - 2^{n+2j-1}. \tag{6.2.4.20}$$

Likewise, since

$$\mathbf{d}_i^{(j+1)} = \begin{bmatrix} \mathbf{d}_{2i-1}^{(j)} \\ \\ \mathbf{d}_{2i}^{(j)} - \mathbf{A}_{2i,\,2i-1}^{(j)} \, \mathbf{d}_{2i-1}^{(j)} \end{bmatrix}, \tag{6.2.4.21}$$

it can be seen that

$$r^{(j)} = 2 + j \tag{6.2.4.22}$$

and

$$q^{(j)} = \frac{2^n}{2^{j+1}} \times 2^{2j} = 2^{n+j-1}. \tag{6.2.4.23}$$

Now combining (6.2.4.16), (6.2.4.19), and (6.2.4.22), it follows that

$$T = \sum_{j=0}^{n-1} (2 + j) = \frac{n(n+3)}{2} = O\,(\log N)^2. \tag{6.2.4.24}$$

From (6.2.4.17), (6.2.4.20), and (6.2.4.23), we obtain

$$P = \max_{0 \le j \le n-1} \{2^{2n+j-2} - 2^{n+2j-1} + 2^{n+j-1}\}. \tag{6.2.4.25}$$

Let $2^j = y$, and since $2^n = N$, consider the function

$$f(y) = (\frac{N^2}{4} + \frac{N}{2})\,y - \frac{N}{2}\,y^2.$$

As $f(y)$ attains its maximum at

$$y = \frac{N}{4} + \frac{1}{2},$$

it follows that P attains its maximum value of

$$P = \frac{N^3}{32} + \frac{N^2}{8} = O\,(N^3) \tag{6.2.4.26}$$

at $j = n - 2$.

Summarizing this, we obtain the following theorem.

Theorem 6.2.4.1. Using the Sameh-Brent Algorithm-2 in Fig. 6.2.4.2, the lower triangular linear system of size N can be solved in $O\,((\log N)^2)$ steps using $O\,(N^3)$ processors.

Comparing this method with that of Section 6.2.3, it readily follows that this method requires nearly double the number of processors but still requires the same time. This method is particularly useful in solving banded systems covered in the next section.

6.3 BANDED LOWER TRIANGULAR LINEAR SYSTEMS

In this section we describe two algorithms for solving banded lower triangular linear systems. The first one is similar to the algorithm in Fig. 6.2.4.2, which requires unlimited parallelism (where the number of processors is a polynomial function of the size of the problem). The second method is more suitable when only a fixed number of processors are available.

6.3.1 Sameh-Brent Algorithm-1

Let

$$\mathbf{A}\,\mathbf{x} = \mathbf{d}, \tag{6.3.1.1}$$

where

$$\mathbf{A} = [\,a_{ij}\,],$$

$$a_{ii} = 1, \text{ for } all \ i = 1, 2, \ \cdots, N,$$

$$a_{ij} \neq 0, \text{ for } j = 1, 2, \ \cdots, N-1, \ i > j \text{ and } i - j \leq m, \tag{6.3.1.2}$$

and $N = 2^n$, $m = 2^k$, and $n - k = r > 0$. Let $\mathbf{d} = (d_1, d_2, \ \cdots, d_N)^t$.

$$A = \begin{bmatrix} L_1 & 0 & 0 & 0 \\ U_1 & L_2 & 0 & 0 \\ 0 & U_2 & L_3 & 0 \\ 0 & 0 & U_3 & L_4 \end{bmatrix},$$

where

$$L_1 = \begin{bmatrix} 1 & 0 & 0 & 0 \\ a_1 & 1 & 0 & 0 \\ b_1 & a_2 & 1 & 0 \\ c_1 & b_2 & a_3 & 1 \end{bmatrix}, \qquad L_2 = \begin{bmatrix} 1 & 0 & 0 & 0 \\ a_5 & 1 & 0 & 0 \\ b_5 & a_6 & 1 & 0 \\ c_5 & b_6 & a_7 & 1 \end{bmatrix},$$

$$L_3 = \begin{bmatrix} 1 & 0 & 0 & 0 \\ a_9 & 1 & 0 & 0 \\ b_9 & a_{10} & 1 & 0 \\ c_9 & b_{10} & a_{11} & 1 \end{bmatrix}, \qquad L_4 = \begin{bmatrix} 1 & 0 & 0 & 0 \\ a_{13} & 1 & 0 & 0 \\ b_{13} & a_{14} & 1 & 0 \\ c_{13} & b_{14} & a_{15} & 1 \end{bmatrix},$$

$$U_1 = \begin{bmatrix} d_1 & c_2 & b_3 & a_4 \\ 0 & d_2 & c_3 & b_4 \\ 0 & 0 & d_3 & c_4 \\ 0 & 0 & 0 & d_4 \end{bmatrix}, \qquad U_2 = \begin{bmatrix} d_5 & c_6 & b_7 & a_8 \\ 0 & d_6 & c_7 & b_8 \\ 0 & 0 & d_7 & c_8 \\ 0 & 0 & 0 & d_8 \end{bmatrix},$$

$$U_3 = \begin{bmatrix} d_9 & c_{10} & b_{11} & a_{12} \\ 0 & d_{10} & c_{11} & b_{12} \\ 0 & 0 & d_{11} & c_{12} \\ 0 & 0 & 0 & d_{12} \end{bmatrix},$$

and 0 is a 4×4 matrix of zeros.

FIGURE 6.3.1.1
An example of a partitioned banded matrix with $m = 4$ and $N = 16$.

The first step consists in partitioning the banded matrix $\mathbf{A}$ in (6.3.1.1) into submatrices of size $\dfrac{N}{m} = 2^r$. Thus, $\mathbf{A}$ becomes

$$\mathbf{A} = \begin{bmatrix}
\mathbf{L}_1 & \mathbf{0} & \mathbf{0} & \cdots & \mathbf{0} & \mathbf{0} \\
\mathbf{U}_1 & \mathbf{L}_2 & \mathbf{0} & \cdots & \mathbf{0} & \mathbf{0} \\
\mathbf{0} & \mathbf{U}_2 & \mathbf{L}_3 & \cdots & \mathbf{0} & \mathbf{0} \\
\cdot & \cdot & \cdot & \cdots & \cdot & \cdot \\
\cdot & \cdot & \cdot & \cdots & \cdot & \cdot \\
\cdot & \cdot & \cdot & \cdots & \cdot & \cdot \\
\mathbf{0} & \mathbf{0} & \mathbf{0} & \cdots & \mathbf{L}_{N/m-1} & \mathbf{0} \\
\mathbf{0} & \mathbf{0} & \mathbf{0} & \cdots & \mathbf{U}_{N/m-1} & \mathbf{L}_{N/m}
\end{bmatrix}, \tag{6.3.1.3}$$

where $\mathbf{L}_i$ is a lower triangular matrix of order m and $\mathbf{U}_i$ is an upper triangular matrix of order m.

Partition $\mathbf{d}$ as

$$\mathbf{d}^t = (\, \overline{\mathbf{d}}_1^{\,t}, \, \overline{\mathbf{d}}_2^{\,t}, \, \cdots, \, \overline{\mathbf{d}}_{N/m}^{\,t} \,)^t, \tag{6.3.1.4}$$

where

$$\overline{\mathbf{d}}_i^{\,t} = (\, d_{(i-1)m+1}, \, \cdots, \, d_{im} \,).$$

Define a diagonal matrix $\mathbf{D}$ such that

$$\mathbf{D}^{-1} = \begin{bmatrix}
\mathbf{L}_1 & \mathbf{0} & \mathbf{0} & \cdot & \cdots & \mathbf{0} \\
\mathbf{0} & \mathbf{L}_2 & \mathbf{0} & \cdot & \cdots & \mathbf{0} \\
\mathbf{0} & \mathbf{0} & \mathbf{L}_3 & \cdot & \cdots & \mathbf{0} \\
\cdot & \cdot & \cdot & \cdot & \cdots & \cdot \\
\cdot & \cdot & \cdot & \cdot & \cdots & \cdot \\
\cdot & \cdot & \cdot & \cdot & \cdots & \cdot \\
\mathbf{0} & \mathbf{0} & \mathbf{0} & \cdot & \cdots & \cdot \\
\mathbf{0} & \mathbf{0} & \mathbf{0} & \cdot & \cdots & \mathbf{L}_{N/m}
\end{bmatrix}. \tag{6.3.1.5}$$

Consider

$$\mathbf{A}^{(0)}\mathbf{x} = \mathbf{d}^{(0)}, \tag{6.3.1.6}$$

where

$$
A^{(0)} = DA = \begin{bmatrix}
I^{(0)} & 0 & 0 & \cdots & 0 & 0 \\
U_1^{(0)} & I^{(0)} & 0 & \cdots & 0 & 0 \\
0 & U_2^{(0)} & I^{(0)} & \cdots & 0 & 0 \\
\cdot & \cdot & \cdot & \cdots & \cdot & \cdot \\
\cdot & \cdot & \cdot & \cdots & \cdot & \cdot \\
\cdot & \cdot & \cdot & \cdots & \cdot & \cdot \\
0 & 0 & 0 & \cdots & I^{(0)} & 0 \\
0 & 0 & 0 & \cdots & U_{N/m-1}^{(0)} & I^{(0)}
\end{bmatrix} , \tag{6.3.1.7}
$$

$$
d^{(0)} = Dd = \begin{bmatrix}
\overline{d}_1^{(0)} \\
\overline{d}_2^{(0)} \\
\cdot \\
\cdot \\
\cdot \\
\overline{d}_{N/m}^{(0)}
\end{bmatrix} , \tag{6.3.1.8}
$$

and $I^{(0)}$ is an identity matrix of order $m2^j$, and

$$
\left.\begin{aligned}
U_i^{(0)} &= L_{i+1}^{-1} U_i, & i = 1, 2, \cdots, \frac{N}{m} - 1 \\[2mm]
\overline{d}_i^{(0)} &= L_i^{-1} \overline{d}_i, & i = 1, 2, \cdots, \frac{N}{m}.
\end{aligned}\right\} \tag{6.3.1.9}
$$

These are the initial conditions for the algorithm to be described below.
Define a sequence, for $j = 0, 1, \cdots, r-1$,

$$
\left.\begin{aligned}
A^{(j+1)} &= D^{(j)} A^{(j)} \\[2mm]
d^{(j+1)} &= D^{(j)} d^{(j)},
\end{aligned}\right\} \tag{6.3.1.10}
$$

where $D^{(j)}$ is defined as below.

$$
\left[\mathbf{D}^{(j)} \right]^{-1} =
\begin{bmatrix}
\mathbf{D}_1^{(j)} & 0 & \cdots & & 0 \\
0 & \mathbf{D}_2^{(j)} & \cdots & & 0 \\
\cdot & \cdot & \cdots & & \cdot \\
\cdot & \cdot & \cdots & & \cdot \\
\cdot & \cdot & \cdots & & \cdot \\
0 & 0 & \cdots & & \mathbf{D}_{N/2^{j+1}m}^{(j)}
\end{bmatrix},
\tag{6.3.1.11}
$$

and

$$
\left[\mathbf{D}_i^{(j)} \right]^{-1} =
\begin{bmatrix}
\mathbf{I}^{(j)} & 0 \\
-U_{2i-1}^{(j)} & \mathbf{I}^{(j)}
\end{bmatrix}
\tag{6.3.1.12}
$$

is a matrix of order $m2^{j+1}$. Since

$$
\mathbf{A}^{(j)} =
\begin{bmatrix}
\mathbf{I}^{(j)} & 0 & 0 & \cdots & 0 & 0 \\
U_1^{(j)} & \mathbf{I}^{(j)} & 0 & \cdots & 0 & 0 \\
0 & U_2^{(j)} & \mathbf{I}^{(j)} & \cdots & 0 & 0 \\
\cdot & \cdot & \cdot & \cdots & \cdot & \cdot \\
\cdot & \cdot & \cdot & \cdots & \cdot & \cdot \\
\cdot & \cdot & \cdot & \cdots & \cdot & \cdot \\
0 & 0 & 0 & \cdots & \mathbf{I}^{(j)} & 0 \\
0 & 0 & 0 & \cdots & U_{N/2^j m-1}^{(j)} & \mathbf{I}^{(j)}
\end{bmatrix},
\tag{6.3.1.13}
$$

it follows that, for $i = 1, 2, \cdots, \dfrac{N}{2^{j+1}m} - 1$,

$$
U_i^{(j+1)} =
\begin{bmatrix}
0 & U_{2i}^{(j)} \\
0 & -U_{2i+1}^{(j)} U_{2i}^{(j)}
\end{bmatrix}.
\tag{6.3.1.14}
$$

Likewise, since $\mathbf{d}^{(j)} = (\overline{\mathbf{d}}_1^{(j)}, \overline{\mathbf{d}}_2^{(j)}, \cdots, \overline{\mathbf{d}}_{N/2^j m}^{(j)})$, for $i = 1, 2, \cdots, \dfrac{N}{2^{j+1}m}$,

$$
\overline{\mathbf{d}}_i^{(j+1)} =
\begin{bmatrix}
\overline{\mathbf{d}}_{2i-1}^{(j)} \\
-U_{2i-1}^{(j)} \overline{\mathbf{d}}_{2i-1}^{(j)} + \overline{\mathbf{d}}_{2i}^{(j)}
\end{bmatrix}.
\tag{6.3.1.15}
$$

It immediately follows (Exercise 6.15) from the above development that

$$\left.\begin{array}{c} \mathbf{A}^{(r)} = \mathbf{I} \\[1em] \mathbf{x} = \mathbf{d}^{(r)}. \end{array}\right\}$$

and   **(6.3.1.16)**

Thus, this algorithm consists of two phases: The initial phase consists of obtaining (6.3.1.6) from (6.3.1.1), and the second phase consists of computing $\mathbf{A}^{(j+1)}$ and $\mathbf{d}^{(j+1)}$ according to (6.3.1.10).

We now derive an estimate of the minimum time required to complete the above set of computations. From (6.3.1.6) and (6.3.1.9), it follows that the initial phase essentially consists of solving lower triangular systems

$$\left.\begin{array}{cc} \mathbf{L}_{i+1}\,\mathbf{U}_i^{(0)} = \mathbf{U}_i & i = 1, 2, \cdots, \dfrac{N}{m} - 1 \\[1.5em] \mathbf{L}_i\,\overline{\mathbf{d}}_i^{(0)} = \overline{\mathbf{d}}_i & i = 1, 2, \cdots, \dfrac{N}{m}. \end{array}\right\}$$

and   (6.3.1.17)

Since the matrices involved in these systems are all of order $m \times m$, using the algorithm in Fig. 6.2.4.2, all of these systems can be solved in parallel in

$$t_{in} = \frac{1}{2}(\log m)^2 + \frac{3}{2}\log m \tag{6.3.1.18}$$

steps, using a "sufficient" number of processors.

During the second phase, it can be shown (by exploiting the structure of the matrices involved in the computation) that the computations of $\mathbf{U}_i^{(j+1)}$ and $\mathbf{d}_i^{(j+1)}$ in (6.3.1.14) and (6.3.1.15) can be completed in

$$t_j = 2 + \log m \tag{6.3.1.19}$$

steps, using a "sufficiently" large number of processors.

Thus, the total time required is given by

$$T = t_{in} + \sum_{j=0}^{r-1} t_j$$

$$= \frac{1}{2}(\log m)^2 + \frac{3}{2}\log m + (2 + \log m)\,r$$

$$= (2 + \log m)\log N - \frac{1}{2}(1 + \log m)\log m \tag{6.3.1.20}$$

This development leads to the following theorem.

Theorem 6.3.1.1. A banded lower triangular linear system of order N and bandwidth $m + 1$ can be solved in T steps, where T is given in (6.3.1.20) using $\frac{1}{2} m^2 N + O(mN)$ processors.

Computing the degree of parallelism required to achieve this time bound is left to the reader (Exercise 6.16).

6.3.2 Sameh-Brent Algorithm-2 -- Limited Number of Processors

In this section, we describe a method of solving a linear banded lower triangular system

$$\mathbf{A}\,\mathbf{x} = \mathbf{d} \qquad (6.3.2.1)$$

of bandwidth $m + 1$ using only p processors, where $\mathbf{A}$ is an $N \times N$ matrix, with unity all along the principal diagonal. Let $N = 2^n$, $m = 2^t$, and $p = km$, for some $k \geq 2$. Let $s = \dfrac{N}{k}$, and $s \geq m + 1$. Let $\mathbf{I}_r$ be an identity matrix of order r.

Partition $\mathbf{A}$ in the form

$$\mathbf{A} = \begin{bmatrix} \mathbf{L}_1 & \mathbf{0} & \mathbf{0} & \cdots & \mathbf{0} & \mathbf{0} & \mathbf{0} \\ \mathbf{U}_1 & \mathbf{L}_2 & \mathbf{0} & \cdots & \mathbf{0} & \mathbf{0} & \mathbf{0} \\ \mathbf{0} & \mathbf{U}_2 & \mathbf{L}_3 & \cdots & \mathbf{0} & \mathbf{0} & \mathbf{0} \\ . & . & . & \cdots & . & . & . \\ . & . & . & \cdots & . & . & . \\ . & . & . & \cdots & . & . & . \\ \mathbf{0} & \mathbf{0} & \mathbf{0} & \cdots & \mathbf{U}_{k-2} & \mathbf{L}_{k-1} & \mathbf{0} \\ \mathbf{0} & \mathbf{0} & \mathbf{0} & \cdots & \mathbf{0} & \mathbf{U}_{k-1} & \mathbf{L}_k \end{bmatrix}, \qquad (6.3.2.2)$$

where $\mathbf{L}_i$ is a lower triangular matrix of bandwidth $m + 1$ and order s; $\mathbf{U}_i$ is an upper triangular matrix

$$\mathbf{U}_i = \begin{bmatrix} u^i_{\alpha\beta} \end{bmatrix}, \qquad (6.3.2.3)$$

where

$$u^i_{\alpha\beta} \neq 0, \text{ if and } only \text{ if } \beta - \alpha \geq s - m.$$

Since $s \geq m + 1$, it follows that the first $s - m$ columns of $\mathbf{U}_i$ contain all zeros. Refer to Fig. 6.3.2.1 for an example of this partition. $\mathbf{U}_i$ is an upper triangular matrix of order s.

$$
\mathbf{A} = \begin{bmatrix}
1 & 0 & 0 & 0 & 0 & 0 & 0 & 0 & 0 & 0 & 0 & 0 & 0 & 0 & 0 & 0 \\
x & 1 & 0 & 0 & 0 & 0 & 0 & 0 & 0 & 0 & 0 & 0 & 0 & 0 & 0 & 0 \\
x & x & 1 & 0 & 0 & 0 & 0 & 0 & 0 & 0 & 0 & 0 & 0 & 0 & 0 & 0 \\
x & x & x & 1 & 0 & 0 & 0 & 0 & 0 & 0 & 0 & 0 & 0 & 0 & 0 & 0 \\
x & x & x & x & 1 & 0 & 0 & 0 & 0 & 0 & 0 & 0 & 0 & 0 & 0 & 0 \\
0 & x & x & x & x & 1 & 0 & 0 & 0 & 0 & 0 & 0 & 0 & 0 & 0 & 0 \\
0 & 0 & x & x & x & x & 1 & 0 & 0 & 0 & 0 & 0 & 0 & 0 & 0 & 0 \\
0 & 0 & 0 & x & x & x & x & 1 & 0 & 0 & 0 & 0 & 0 & 0 & 0 & 0 \\
0 & 0 & 0 & 0 & x & x & x & x & 1 & 0 & 0 & 0 & 0 & 0 & 0 & 0 \\
0 & 0 & 0 & 0 & 0 & x & x & x & x & 1 & 0 & 0 & 0 & 0 & 0 & 0 \\
0 & 0 & 0 & 0 & 0 & 0 & x & x & x & x & 1 & 0 & 0 & 0 & 0 & 0 \\
0 & 0 & 0 & 0 & 0 & 0 & 0 & x & x & x & x & 1 & 0 & 0 & 0 & 0 \\
0 & 0 & 0 & 0 & 0 & 0 & 0 & 0 & x & x & x & x & 1 & 0 & 0 & 0 \\
0 & 0 & 0 & 0 & 0 & 0 & 0 & 0 & 0 & x & x & x & x & 1 & 0 & 0 \\
0 & 0 & 0 & 0 & 0 & 0 & 0 & 0 & 0 & 0 & x & x & x & x & 1 & 0 \\
0 & 0 & 0 & 0 & 0 & 0 & 0 & 0 & 0 & 0 & 0 & x & x & x & x & 1
\end{bmatrix} = \begin{bmatrix} \mathbf{L}_1 & 0 \\ & \\ \mathbf{U}_1 & \mathbf{L}_2 \end{bmatrix}
$$

FIGURE 6.3.2.1
An example illustrating the partitions $N = 16$, $m = 4$, $p = 8$, $s = 8$. Notice that the first $s - m = 4$ columns of $\mathbf{U}_1$ are zero. (x denotes non-zero elements.)

Likewise, partition **d** and **x** as follows:

$$\mathbf{d} = (\,\overline{\mathbf{d}}_1^t, \ \overline{\mathbf{d}}_2^t, \ \cdots, \ \overline{\mathbf{d}}_k^t\,)^t, \text{ with } \overline{\mathbf{d}}_i^t = (\,d_{(i-1)\,s+1}, \ d_{(i-1)\,s+2}, \ \cdots, d_{is}\,),$$

and

$$\mathbf{x} = (\,\overline{\mathbf{x}}_1^t, \ \overline{\mathbf{x}}_2^t, \ \cdots, \ \overline{\mathbf{x}}_k^t\,)^t, \text{ with } \overline{\mathbf{x}}_i^t = (\,x_{(i-1)\,s+1}, \ x_{(i-1)\,s+2}, \ \cdots, x_{is}\,).$$

We now describe the algorithm.

Step 1: Let **D** be a diagonal matrix such that

$$\mathbf{D}^{-1} = \begin{bmatrix} \mathbf{L}_1 & \mathbf{0} & \mathbf{0} & \cdots & \mathbf{0} \\ \mathbf{0} & \mathbf{L}_2 & \mathbf{0} & \cdots & \mathbf{0} \\ \mathbf{0} & \mathbf{0} & \mathbf{L}_3 & \cdots & \mathbf{0} \\ . & . & . & \cdots & . \\ . & . & . & \cdots & . \\ . & . & . & \cdots & . \\ \mathbf{0} & \mathbf{0} & \mathbf{0} & \cdots & . \\ \mathbf{0} & \mathbf{0} & \mathbf{0} & \cdots & \mathbf{L}_k \end{bmatrix} \cdot \tag{6.3.2.4}$$

Compute (in partitioned form)

$$\mathbf{A}^{(0)}\mathbf{x} = \mathbf{d}^{(0)}, \tag{6.3.2.5}$$

where

$$\mathbf{A}^{(0)} = \mathbf{D}\mathbf{A} = \begin{bmatrix} \mathbf{I}_s & \mathbf{0} & \mathbf{0} & \cdots & \mathbf{0} & \mathbf{0} \\ \mathbf{U}_1^{(0)} & \mathbf{I}_s & \mathbf{0} & \cdots & \mathbf{0} & \mathbf{0} \\ \mathbf{0} & \mathbf{U}_2^{(0)} & \mathbf{I}_s & \cdots & \mathbf{0} & \mathbf{0} \\ . & . & . & \cdots & . & . \\ . & . & . & \cdots & . & . \\ . & . & . & \cdots & . & . \\ \mathbf{0} & \mathbf{0} & \mathbf{0} & \cdots & \mathbf{I}_s & \mathbf{0} \\ \mathbf{0} & \mathbf{0} & \mathbf{0} & \cdots & \mathbf{U}_{k-1}^{(0)} & \mathbf{I}_s \end{bmatrix}, \tag{6.3.2.6}$$

and, for $i = 1, 2, \cdots, k-1$,

$$\mathbf{L}_{i+1} \mathbf{U}_i^{(0)} = \mathbf{U}_i. \tag{6.3.2.7}$$

Likewise,

$$\mathbf{d}^{(0)} = \mathbf{D}\mathbf{d} = \begin{bmatrix} \overline{\mathbf{d}}_1^{(0)} \\ \overline{\mathbf{d}}_2^{(0)} \\ . \\ . \\ . \\ \overline{\mathbf{d}}_k^{(0)} \end{bmatrix}, \tag{6.3.2.8}$$

and, for $i = 1, 2, \cdots, k$,

$$\mathbf{L}_i\overline{\mathbf{d}}_i^{(0)} = \overline{\mathbf{d}}_i. \tag{6.3.2.9}$$

Step 2. Observe that the first $s - m$ columns of $\mathbf{U}_i^{(0)}$ are zero, since the same set of columns in $\mathbf{U}_i$ is zero. Further, partition $\mathbf{U}_i^{(0)}$ in the form

$$\mathbf{U}_i^{(0)} = \begin{bmatrix} 0 & \mathbf{M}_i \\ 0 & \mathbf{H}_i \end{bmatrix}, \tag{6.3.2.10}$$

where $\mathbf{H}_i$ is a square matrix of order m. Similarly, partition

$$\overline{\mathbf{d}}_i^{(0)} = \begin{bmatrix} \mathbf{u}_i \\ \mathbf{v}_i \end{bmatrix} \tag{6.3.2.11}$$

and

$$\overline{\mathbf{x}}_i = \begin{bmatrix} \mathbf{y}_i \\ \mathbf{z}_i \end{bmatrix}, \tag{6.3.2.12}$$

where $\mathbf{v}_i$ and $\mathbf{z}_i$ are m vectors.

To solve (6.3.2.5), consider $\mathbf{A}^{(0)}$, $\mathbf{x}$, and $\mathbf{d}^{(0)}$ in the new partitioned form

$$\mathbf{A}^{(0)} = \begin{bmatrix}
\mathbf{I}_{s-m} & 0 & 0 & 0 & \cdots & 0 & 0 & 0 \\
0 & \mathbf{I}_m & 0 & 0 & \cdots & 0 & 0 & 0 \\
0 & \mathbf{M}_1 & \mathbf{I}_{s-m} & 0 & \cdots & 0 & 0 & 0 \\
0 & \mathbf{H}_1 & 0 & \mathbf{I}_{s-m} & \cdots & 0 & 0 & 0 \\
0 & 0 & 0 & \mathbf{M}_2 & \cdots & 0 & 0 & 0 \\
0 & 0 & 0 & \mathbf{H}_2 & \cdots & 0 & 0 & 0 \\
\cdot & \cdot & \cdot & \cdot & \cdots & \cdot & \cdot & \cdot \\
\cdot & \cdot & \cdot & \cdot & \cdots & \cdot & \cdot & \cdot \\
\cdot & \cdot & \cdot & \cdot & \cdots & \cdot & \cdot & \cdot \\
0 & 0 & 0 & 0 & \cdots & 0 & 0 & 0 \\
0 & 0 & 0 & 0 & \cdots & \mathbf{I}_{s-m} & 0 & 0 \\
0 & 0 & 0 & 0 & \cdots & \mathbf{M}_{k-1} & \mathbf{I}_{s-m} & 0 \\
0 & 0 & 0 & 0 & \cdots & \mathbf{H}_{k-1} & 0 & \mathbf{I}_m
\end{bmatrix} \tag{6.3.2.13}$$

$$
\mathbf{x} = \begin{bmatrix} \mathbf{y}_1 \\ \mathbf{z}_1 \\ \mathbf{y}_2 \\ \mathbf{z}_2 \\ . \\ . \\ . \\ \mathbf{y}_k \\ \mathbf{z}_k \end{bmatrix} \quad \text{and} \quad \mathbf{d}^{(0)} = \begin{bmatrix} \mathbf{u}_1 \\ \mathbf{v}_1 \\ \mathbf{u}_2 \\ \mathbf{v}_2 \\ . \\ . \\ . \\ \mathbf{u}_k \\ \mathbf{v}_k \end{bmatrix} \cdot \qquad (6.3.2.14)
$$

Now it follows that solving (6.3.2.5) is equivalent to solving the following linear recurrence.

Step 2a. Solve

$$
\mathbf{z}_1 = \mathbf{v}_1 \quad \text{and} \quad \mathbf{z}_{i+1} = -\mathbf{H}_i \mathbf{z}_i + \mathbf{v}_{i+1}, \qquad (6.3.2.15)
$$

for $i = 1, 2, \cdots, k-1$.

Step 2b. Evaluate

$$
\mathbf{y}_1 = \mathbf{u}_1 \quad \text{and} \quad \mathbf{y}_i = \mathbf{u}_i - \mathbf{M}_{i-1} \mathbf{z}_{i-1}, \qquad (6.3.2.16)
$$

for $i = 2, 3, \cdots, k$.

Let t_{1a} and t_{1b} be the times required to solve (6.3.2.7) and (6.3.2.8) and let t_{2a} and t_{2b} be the times required to complete step 2a and step 2b.

Since $s - m$ columns of $\mathbf{U}_i$ are zero, solving (6.3.2.7) reduces to solving

$$
\mathbf{L}_{i+1} \overline{\mathbf{U}}_i^{(0)} = \overline{\mathbf{U}}_i, \qquad i = 1, 2, \cdots, k-1, \qquad (6.3.2.17)
$$

where $\overline{\mathbf{U}}_i$ and $\overline{\mathbf{U}}_i^{(0)}$ consist of only the m non-zero columns of $\mathbf{U}_i$ and $\mathbf{U}_i^{(0)}$, respectively. This is equivalent to solving a total of $m(k-1)$ linear systems of the type

$$
\mathbf{L}\, \alpha = \beta,
$$

where $\mathbf{L}$ is a lower (banded) triangular matrix. Using only one processor for each of these systems (recall there are mk processors available), (6.3.2.17) and hence (6.3.2.7) can be solved in

$$
t_{1a} = \frac{2Nm^2}{p} - m(m+1) \qquad (6.3.2.18)
$$

units of time.

Now using m processors to solve each of the systems in (6.3.2.9), using the column sweep method of Section 6.2.1, it readily follows that

$$t_{1b} = 2(s - 1) = 2(\frac{Nm}{p} - 1).$$ (6.3.2.19)

We can rewrite (6.3.2.15) as a banded lower triangular system of size $p = km$:

$$\begin{bmatrix} \mathbf{I}_m & & & & & \\ \mathbf{H}_1 & \mathbf{I}_m & & & & \\ & \mathbf{H}_2 & & & & \\ & & \cdot & & & \\ & & & \cdot & & \\ & & & & \cdot & \\ & & & & \mathbf{I}_m & \\ & & & & \mathbf{H}_{k-1} & \mathbf{I}_m \end{bmatrix} \begin{bmatrix} \mathbf{z}_1 \\ \mathbf{z}_2 \\ \\ \cdot \\ \cdot \\ \cdot \\ \mathbf{z}_{k-1} \\ \mathbf{z}_k \end{bmatrix} = \begin{bmatrix} \mathbf{v}_1 \\ \mathbf{v}_2 \\ \\ \cdot \\ \cdot \\ \cdot \\ \mathbf{v}_{k-1} \\ \mathbf{v}_k \end{bmatrix} \cdot$$ (6.3.2.20)

This can be solved using the method of Section 6.3.1 using only p processors in

$$t_{2a} = (m^2 + m + 1) \log (\frac{p}{m}) - m^2$$ (6.3.2.21)

steps (Exercise 6.17).

The solution vector $\mathbf{x}$ can be obtained by computing $\mathbf{y}_i$'s in (6.3.2.16) in

$$t_{2b} = (\frac{Nm}{p} - m) (2 + \log m)$$

steps. Thus the total time required by this algorithm

$$T = t_{1a} + t_{1b} + t_{2a} + t_{2b}$$

$$= \frac{Nm}{p}[4 + 2m + \log m] + (m^2 + m + 1) \log (\frac{p}{4m}) - m \log 2m.$$ (6.3.2.22)

It must be interesting to specialize this algorithm when $m = 1$ (Exercise 6.18). Another interesting special case when $\mathbf{A}$ is a lower triangular Toeplitz banded matrix is treated in Exercise 6.29.

6.4 TRIANGULAR DECOMPOSITION

It is well known that the linear system $\mathbf{Ax} = \mathbf{d}$ can be solved by first factoring $\mathbf{A} = \mathbf{LU}$, where $\mathbf{L}$ is unit lower triangular and $\mathbf{U}$ is upper triangular, and then solving the triangular systems $\mathbf{Ly} = \mathbf{d}$ and $\mathbf{Ux} = \mathbf{y}$, in that order. In this section, we describe two algorithms for factoring the given non-singular matrix $\mathbf{A}$. First is the classical $\mathbf{LU}$ decomposition algorithm in Section 6.4.1, which admits a variety of parallel implementations on different architectures, and the second is a parallel version based on the Givens transformation (Section 6.4.2).

6.4.1 The LU Decomposition

The key idea behind the **LU** decomposition algorithm relates to the ability to annihilate components of a vector. Let $\mathbf{z} = (z_1, z_2, \cdots, z_N)^t$, and define a matrix

$$\mathbf{M}_i = \mathbf{I} - \mathbf{m}\mathbf{e}_i^t, \tag{6.4.1.1}$$

where $\mathbf{e}_i$ is the ith unit vector, $\mathbf{I}$ is the identity matrix,

$$\mathbf{m} = (0, 0, \cdots, m_{i+1}, m_{i+2}, \cdots, m_N)^t,$$

and

$$m_r = \frac{z_r}{z_i}, \quad \text{for } r = i+1 \text{ to } N.$$

It can be verified that

$$\mathbf{M}_i\mathbf{z} = (z_1, z_2, \cdots, z_i, 0, \cdots, 0)^t \tag{6.4.1.2}$$

As an example,

$$\begin{bmatrix} 1 & 0 & 0 \\ -z_2/z_1 & 1 & 0 \\ -z_3/z_1 & 0 & 1 \end{bmatrix} \begin{bmatrix} z_1 \\ z_2 \\ z_3 \end{bmatrix} = \begin{bmatrix} z_1 \\ 0 \\ 0 \end{bmatrix}.$$

If the vector $\mathbf{z}$ denotes the ith column of a matrix $\mathbf{A}$, then

$$\mathbf{M}_i\mathbf{A} = \mathbf{A} - \mathbf{m}\mathbf{e}_i^t\mathbf{A} \tag{6.4.1.3}$$

is a matrix whose j^{th} row is obtained by subtracting m_i times the ith row of $\mathbf{A}$ from the jth row of $\mathbf{A}$. Consequently, all the elements below the principal diagonal of the ith column of the matrix $\mathbf{M}_i\mathbf{A}$ are zero. Thus, by properly designing the sequence $\mathbf{M}_1, \mathbf{M}_2, \cdots, \mathbf{M}_{N-1}$ of matrices, we obtain a sequence

$$\mathbf{A}^{(i)}\mathbf{x} = \mathbf{d}^{(i)}, \tag{6.4.1.4}$$

where $\mathbf{A}^{(0)} = \mathbf{A}$, $\mathbf{d}^{(0)} = \mathbf{d}$, and, for $1 \leq i \leq N - 1$,

$$\left. \begin{aligned} \mathbf{A}^{(i)} &= \mathbf{M}_i\mathbf{A}^{(i-1)} \\[2ex] \mathbf{d}^{(i)} &= \mathbf{M}_i\mathbf{d}^{(i-1)}. \end{aligned} \right\} \tag{6.4.1.5}$$

Clearly

$$\mathbf{U} = \mathbf{A}^{(N-1)}, \qquad \mathbf{y} = \mathbf{d}^{(N-1)}, \tag{6.4.1.6}$$

and

$$\mathbf{L} = \mathbf{M}_{N-1}^{-1} \mathbf{M}_{N-2}^{-1} \cdots \mathbf{M}_2^{-1}\mathbf{M}_1^{-1}. \tag{6.4.1.7}$$

Properties of matrices $\mathbf{M}_i$ are contained in Lemmas 6.2.3.1 to 6.2.3.3.

The algorithm for computing **U** in component form is given in Fig. 6.4.1.1. By appending the right-hand side **d** as the $(N + 1)^{th}$ column of **A**, we can obtain $\mathbf{y} = \mathbf{d}^{(N-1)}$ at the same time as **U** (Exercise 6.33). Parallel implementations as well as extensions of this basic algorithm are pursued in Exercises 6.33 through 6.38.

/* Given the matrix **A** */

FOR $k = 1$ TO $N - 1$
    FOR $i = k + 1$ *TO N*
$$m_{ik} = \frac{a_{ik}}{a_{kk}}$$
      FOR $j = k + 1$ *TO N*
$$a_{ij} = a_{ij} - m_{ik}a_{kj}$$
      END
    END
END

FIGURE 6.4.1.1
LU decomposition algorithm.

If a_{kk} is very small for any k, then the algorithm in Fig. 6.4.1.1 may be subjected to large round-off errors. This can be mitigated to a large extent by permuting the rows and columns of **A** (equivalently by renaming the variables) in such a way that a_{kk} is as large as possible for all k. This process is called *pivoting*. Pivoting in general inhibits parallelism but often may be necessary to guarantee the quality of the solution. For a comprehensive discussion of the need and the effect of pivoting, refer to Forsythe and Moler [1967], Stewart [1973], Golub and Van Loan [1983], and Wilkinson [1965].

6.4.2 The QR Decomposition

The major difficulty with the **LU** decomposition is that except in special cases such as when **A** is diagonally dominant, it needs pivoting, which invariably limits the speed-up. This can be circumvented by resorting to annihilation schemes based on *orthogonal* transformations. In this approach, the decomposition problem is reformulated as follows. Given **A**, find an orthogonal matrix **Q** such that

$$\mathbf{QA} = \mathbf{R} \qquad (6.4.2.1)$$

is an upper triangular matrix. The matrix **Q** is expressed as a product of simple orthogonal matrices called *Givens transformations*. We begin by describing this latter class of matrices. Define a class of matrices $G(i, j)$, $1 \le i, j \le N$,

$$
G(i, j) = \begin{bmatrix}
1 & 0 & \cdots & 0 & . & \cdots & . & 0 & \cdots & 0 \\
0 & 1 & \cdots & 0 & . & \cdots & . & 0 & \cdots & 0 \\
. & . & \cdots & . & . & \cdots & . & . & \cdots & . \\
. & . & \cdots & . & . & \cdots & . & . & \cdots & . \\
. & . & \cdots & . & . & \cdots & . & . & \cdots & . \\
0 & 0 & \cdots & c_{ii} & . & \cdots & . & s_{ij} & \cdots & 0 \\
. & . & \cdots & . & 1 & \cdots & . & . & \cdots & . \\
. & . & \cdots & . & . & \cdots & 1 & . & \cdots & . \\
0 & 0 & \cdots & -s_{ji} & . & \cdots & . & c_{jj} & \cdots & 0 \\
. & . & \cdots & . & . & \cdots & . & . & \cdots & . \\
. & . & \cdots & . & . & \cdots & . & . & \cdots & . \\
. & . & \cdots & . & . & \cdots & . & . & \cdots & . \\
0 & 0 & \cdots & 0 & 0 & \cdots & . & 0 & \cdots & 1
\end{bmatrix} .
\tag{6.4.2.2}
$$

Let $\mathbf{x} = (x_1, x_2, \cdots, x_N)^t$, $\mathbf{y} = (y_1, y_2, \cdots, y_N)^t$, and

$$
\mathbf{y} = G(i, j)\mathbf{x}.
\tag{6.4.2.3}
$$

Then it follows that $y_k = x_k$, for $k \ne i, j$, and

$$
\left. \begin{aligned}
y_i &= c_{ii}x_i + s_{ij}x_j \\[2mm]
y_j &= -s_{ji}x_i + c_{jj}x_j.
\end{aligned} \right\}
\tag{6.4.2.4}
$$

Choosing

$$
\left. \begin{aligned}
c_{ii} = c_{jj} = c &= \frac{x_i}{r} \\[4mm]
s_{ji} = s_{ij} = s &= \frac{x_j}{r} \\[4mm]
r &= (x_i^2 + x_j^2)^{1/2},
\end{aligned} \right\}
\tag{6.4.2.5}
$$

and

it can be seen that $y_i = r$ and $y_j = 0$, that is, $G(i, j)$ annihilates x_j (Exercise 6.40). If (i, j) and (m, l) are two disjoint pairs of indices, then multiplying $\mathbf{x}$ (on the left) by $G(i, j)$ and $G(m, l)$ annihilates x_j and x_l. Thus, using the Givens transformations, we can annihilate a maximum of $\left\lfloor \dfrac{N}{2} \right\rfloor$ components of a vector simultaneously.

We can readily extend the annihilating property of $\mathbf{G}(i, j)$ to matrices. Let $\mathbf{A}$ and $\mathbf{B}$ be two matrices such that

$$\mathbf{B} = \mathbf{G}(i, j)\mathbf{A}. \tag{6.4.2.6}$$

Then

$$b_{pq} = a_{pq} \quad \text{for } p \neq i \quad \text{and } q \neq j,$$

and, for $1 \leq k \leq N$,

$$\left. \begin{array}{l} b_{ik} = c_{ii}a_{ik} + s_{ij}a_{jk} \\ \\ b_{jk} = -s_{ji}a_{ik} + c_{jj}a_{jk}. \end{array} \right\} \tag{6.4.2.7}$$

If, for any $1 \leq l \leq N$,

$$\left. \begin{array}{l} c_{ii} = c_{jj} = c = \dfrac{a_{il}}{r} \\ \\ s_{ji} = s_{ij} = s = \dfrac{a_{jl}}{r} \\ \\ r = (a_{il}^2 + a_{jl}^2)^{1/2}, \end{array} \right\} \tag{6.4.2.8}$$

and

then we obtain $b_{il} = r$ and $b_{jl} = 0$ (Exercise 6.41).

In transforming a matrix $\mathbf{A}$ into an upper triangular form, we need to annihilate all the $\dfrac{N(N-1)}{2}$ elements of $\mathbf{A}$ that are below the principal diagonal. Since two rows always get affected by this transformation, at most $\left\lfloor \dfrac{N}{2} \right\rfloor$ annihilations can be done in parallel. However, great care must be exercised in choosing the annihilation pattern to prevent the previously eliminated elements from reappearing later.

The first algorithm for parallel annihilation, due to Sameh and Kuck [1978], is given in Fig. 6.4.2.1.

It is convenient to represent the annihilation pattern defined by this algorithm in the form of a lower triangular matrix. Refer to Fig. 6.4.2.2 for an illustration with $N = 12$. If the $(i, j)^{th}$ entry is k, then a_{ij} is annihilated in step k of the algorithm. Thus, the element $a_{12,1}$ is annihilated in the first step ($k = 1$). Also, elements $a_{11,4}$, $a_{9,3}, a_{7,2}$, and $a_{5,1}$ are all annihilated in step 8.

The property of this algorithm is summarized in the following theorem.

Theorem 6.4.2.1. The Sameh-Kuck algorithm in Fig. 6.4.2.1 takes $2N - 3$ steps using $O(N^2)$ processors.

/* In the following, $\delta(k) = 0$ or 1, when k is odd or even, respectively. */

FOR $k = 1$ TO $N - 1$ STEP 1 DO
    FOR $(i, j) \in \{(N - k + 1, 1), (N - k + 3, 2), (N - k + 5, 3), \cdots ,$
            $(N - \delta(k), \lceil k/2 \rceil)\}$ DO IN PARALLEL
      COMPUTE $\mathbf{G}(i, j)\mathbf{A}$
  END
END

FOR $k = N$ TO $2N - 3$ STEP 1 DO
    FOR $(i, j) \in \{(k - N + 3, k - N + 2), (k - N + 5, k - N + 3), \cdots ,$
        $(N - \delta(k)), \left\lceil \dfrac{k}{2} \right\rceil)\}$ DO IN PARALLEL
    COMPUTE $\mathbf{G}(i, j)\mathbf{A}$
  END
END

FIGURE 6.4.2.1
Sameh-Kuck parallel annihilation scheme.

	1	2	3	4	5	6	7	8	9	10	11	12
1	×											
2	11	×										
3	10	12	×									
4	9	11	13	×								
5	8	10	12	14	×							
6	7	9	11	13	15	×						
7	6	8	10	12	14	16	×					
8	5	7	9	11	13	15	17	×				
9	4	6	8	10	12	14	16	18	×			
10	3	5	7	9	11	13	15	17	19	×		
11	2	4	6	8	10	12	14	16	18	20	×	
12	1	3	5	7	9	11	13	15	17	19	21	×

FIGURE 6.4.2.2
An example of the annihilation pattern defined by the Sameh-Kuck algorithm in Fig. 6.4.2.1.

Proof

The time bound is obvious, and the processor bound follows from the fact that a maximum of $\dfrac{N}{2}$ elements are annihilated in any step.

From (6.4.2.8), it follows that each step requires two multiplications, one addition, two divisions, and a square root operation. Since a square root is a complex operation and often takes many steps, it is better, whenever possible, to avoid it. A version of the square-root-free Givens transformation is pursued in Exercise 6.44.

We conclude this section with a description of another related parallel annihilation scheme developed by Cosnard and Robert [1986]. Let m_i and r_i, $1 \le i \le q$, be two sets of integers, where

$$m_i \ge 0 \quad \text{and} \quad m_{i+1} > m_i, \quad \text{for } 1 \le i \le q,$$

and

$$r_i > 0 \quad \text{and} \quad \sum_{i=1}^{q} r_i = N.$$

Let $m_i^{r_i}$ denote a sequence $(m_i, m_i, \cdots, m_i)$, in which m_i is repeated r_i times. Let

$$\mathbf{m} = (m_1^{r_1}, m_2^{r_2}, \cdots, m_q^{r_q})$$

denote a column of N integers. As an example $\mathbf{m} = (1^3, 3, 4^2) = (1, 1, 1, 3, 4, 4)$. Given $\mathbf{m}$, compute a column $\mathbf{n}$ of $N - 1$ integers

$$\mathbf{n} = (n_1^{s_1}, n_2^{s_2}, \cdots, n_p^{s_p}),$$

where $\sum_{i=1}^{p} s_i = N - 1$, as follows:

$$n_1 = \begin{cases} m_2 + 1 \ \text{ and } \ s_1 = \left\lfloor \dfrac{r_1 + r_2}{2} \right\rfloor, & \text{if } r_1 = 1 \\[4ex] m_1 + 1 \ \text{ and } \ s_1 = \left\lfloor \dfrac{r_1}{2} \right\rfloor, & \text{if } r_1 > 1. \end{cases}$$

To obtain n_i, $2 \le i \le p$, assume that

$$s_1 + s_2 + \cdots + s_{i-1} < N - 1.$$

If there exists a k such that

$$m_{k-1} + 1 \le n_{i-1} \le m_k, \tag{6.4.2.9}$$

then define

$$t_{i-1} = (r_1 + r_2 + \cdots + r_{k-1}) - (s_1 + s_2 + \cdots + s_{i-1}) \geq 1.$$

If

$$n_{i-1} < m_k \quad \text{and} \quad t_{i-1} > 1,$$

then

$$n_i = n_{i-1} + 1 \quad \text{and} \quad s_i = \left\lfloor \frac{t_{i-1}}{2} \right\rfloor,$$

else

$$n_i = m_k + 1 \quad \text{and} \quad s_i = \left\lfloor \frac{r_k + t_{i-1}}{2} \right\rfloor.$$

On the other hand, if $n_{i-1} > m_q$ (that is, no k satisfying (6.4.2.9) exists), then

$$n_i = n_{i-1} + 1,$$

and

$$s_i = \left\lfloor \frac{N - (s_1 + s_2 + \cdots + s_{i-1})}{2} \right\rfloor.$$

This process stops when $\sum_{i=1}^{p} s_i = N - 1$.

Let T denote the above operation of obtaining column $\mathbf{n}$ of length $N - 1$ from column $\mathbf{m}$ of length N, that is,

$$\mathbf{n} = T(\mathbf{m}).$$

Thus, given any $\mathbf{m}^{(0)} = \mathbf{m}$, an N-column vector, we can iteratively define the sequence

$$\mathbf{m}^{(i+1)} = T(\mathbf{m}^{(i)}), \qquad (6.4.2.10)$$

where $\mathbf{m}^{(i)}$ is of length $N - i$.

The following example illustrates the process. Let $N = 7$ and $\mathbf{m}^{(0)} = (0^7) = (0, 0, \cdots, 0)$. Then, $m_1 = 0$ and $r_1 = 7$. Clearly,

$$n_1 = 1 \quad \text{and} \quad s_1 = 3.$$

Since n_1 does not satisfy (6.4.2.9), we get

$$n_2 = 2 \quad \text{and} \quad s_2 = 2.$$

To obtain n_3, notice again that n_2 does not satisfy (6.4.2.9), and we get

$$n_3 = 3 \quad \text{and} \quad s_3 = 1.$$

Thus, $\mathbf{m}^{(1)} = (1^3, 2^2, 3^1) = (1, 1, 1, 2, 2, 3)$.

Continuing in this way, we obtain a lower triangular array with $\mathbf{m}^{(i)}$ as the ith column for $i = 1$ to $N - 1$. (Exercise 6.42).

$m^{(1)}$	$m^{(2)}$	$m^{(3)}$	$m^{(4)}$	$m^{(5)}$	$m^{(6)}$	$m^{(7)}$	$m^{(8)}$	$m^{(9)}$	$m^{(10)}$	$m^{(11)}$
×										
4	×									
3	6	×								
2	5	8	×							
2	4	7	10	×						
2	4	6	9	12	×					
1	3	6	8	11	14	×				
1	3	5	7	10	13	15	×			
1	3	5	7	9	12	14	16	×		
1	2	4	6	8	11	13	15	17	×	
1	2	4	6	8	10	12	14	16	18	×
1	2	3	5	7	9	11	13	15	17	19

FIGURE 6.4.2.3
An example of a Cosnard-Robert parallel annihilation scheme.

The interesting feature of the Cosnard-Robert algorithm is that the lower triangular array generated by $m^{(i)}$, for i to $N - 1$, constitutes the parallel annihilation scheme. Figure 6.4.2.3 is an example of such an annihilation scheme.

Referring to Fig. 6.4.2.3, in the *first* step, annihilate $a_{12,1}, a_{11,1}, a_{10,1}, a_{9,1}, a_{8,1}$, and $a_{7,1}$. This can be done, for example, by using $G(6, 12)$, $G(5, 11)$, $G(4, 10)$, $G(3, 9)$, $G(2, 8)$, and $G(1, 7)$, respectively. Similarly, in the *second* step, $a_{12,2}$, $a_{11,2}, a_{10,2}, a_{6,1}, a_{5,1}$, and $a_{4,1}$ are annihilated. Continuing in this way, in the 19th step $a_{12,11}$ is annihilated.

We now state a number of features of this algorithm with proof. For details, refer to Cosnard and Robert [1986].

(P1) The Cosnard-Robert parallel annihilation scheme takes $2N - o(N)$ steps using $O(N^2)$ processors.

(P2) This scheme is *optimal* in the sense that the number of parallel steps used by this algorithm is less than or equal to that of any other parallel annihilation scheme.

(P3) This optimal annihilation scheme is not unique. Another example of a parallel annihilation requiring 19 steps for $N = 12$ is given in Fig. 6.4.2.4.

Another related parallel annihilation scheme independently developed by Modi and Clarke [1984] is given in Exercise 6.43.

$m^{(1)}$	$m^{(2)}$	$m^{(3)}$	$m^{(4)}$	$m^{(5)}$	$m^{(6)}$	$m^{(7)}$	$m^{(8)}$	$m^{(9)}$	$m^{(10)}$	$m^{(11)}$
×										
5	×									
4	7	×								
3	6	9	×							
3	5	8	11	×						
3	5	7	10	13	×					
2	4	6	9	12	14	×				
2	4	6	8	11	13	15	×			
1	3	5	7	10	12	14	16	×		
1	3	5	7	9	11	13	15	17	×	
1	2	4	6	8	10	12	14	16	18	×
1	2	3	5	7	9	11	13	15	17	19

FIGURE 6.4.2.4
Another parallel annihilation scheme for $N = 12$.

6.5 NOTES AND REFERENCES

Section 6.1. For a succinct discussion of the importance and the applications of the parallel methods for solving triangular and banded systems, refer to the book by Kuck [1978]. Chen [1975] and Chen and Kuck [1975] contain analyses of time and processor bounds for many related algorithms for solving triangular and banded systems.

Section 6.2. The column sweep method is described in Kuck [1978]. The wave front method, which is a modified column sweep method, is due to Evans and Dunbar [1983]. Section 6.2.2 follows Heller [1974]. For further properties of Hessenberg matrices, refer to Householder [1964] and Stewart [1973]. Heller attributes Theorem 6.2.2.1 to Schenk, who apparently developed it around 1825. Further historical details can be obtained from Heller [1974].

Sections 6.2.3 and 6.2.4 follow closely Sameh and Brent [1977]. A detailed error analysis of the Sameh-Brent Algorithm-1 is given in Sameh and Brent [1977], where it is shown that the round-off error in the computed solution can be unacceptably high (see Exercise 6.28). This can be somewhat mitigated by accumulating the inner products in double precision (Exercise 6.25). This analysis illustrates the fact that faster algorithms are *not* always stable. For discussion of speed *vs.* stability trade-off, refer to Chapter 7.

Very recently a number of variants of the column sweep method suitable for implementation on distributed memory architecture, such as hypercubes, have been reported in the literature -- see Heath and Romine [1988], Li and Coleman [1988], Eisenstat, Heath, Henkel, and Romine [1988], Romine and Ortega [1988], and Geist and Romine [1988]. Some of the algorithms contained in these papers are pursued in Exercises 6.30 and 6.31. Heath [1986] and [1987] contain a host of papers related all aspects of problem solving using hypercube type multiprocessors.

Section 6.3. The algorithm in Section 6.3.1 is taken from Sameh and Brent [1977], and the algorithm in Section 6.3.2 is taken from Chen, Kuck, and Sameh [1978]. Fast algorithms for solving second-order linear recurrences of the Fibonacci type are covered in Exercises 6.22 and 6.23.

Section 6.4. The **LU** decomposition algorithm is perhaps the most fundamental of all the algorithms for matrix problems. For a treatment of error analysis related to **LU** decomposition, refer to Wilkinson [1965], Forsythe and Moler [1967], Golub and Van Loan [1983], or Stewart [1973]. These references also contain a thorough discussion of the need for pivoting and its effect on the overall error in the solution.

Recently, implementation of the **LU** decomposition algorithm on distributed memory architecture has received considerable attention. Refer to Moler [1986], Geist and Heath [1986], McBryan and Van De Velde [1986], Geist and Romine [1988], and Chamberlain [1987], for details. Geist and Heath [1986] and Chamberlain [1987] describe different strategies for pivoting in implementing **LU** decomposition on distributed memory architecture.

For multivector processors with hierarchical memory, such as the Alliant FX/8, block-oriented algorithms as in Exercise 6.37 are found to be more suitable. Obviously, the size of the block is a function of the properties of the memory hierarchy. For details, refer to Gallivan, Jalby, Meier, and Sameh [1987].

When matrix **A** is symmetric and positive definite, then **A** can be factored as $\mathbf{A} = \mathbf{LL}^t$, where **L** is a lower triangular matrix. This factorization is known as Cholesky factorization. A comprehensive treatment of Cholesky decomposition is contained in George and Liu [1981]. We invite the reader to specialize the parallel implementations of the **LU**-decomposition algorithm given in Exercises 6.33 through 6.38 for the case when **A** is symmetric and positive definite.

Section 6.4.2 is patterned after Sameh and Kuck [1978] and Cosnard and Robert [1986]. Also refer to Modi and Clarke [1984] for another related approach. Sameh and Kuck [1977] and [1978] contain algorithms for **QR** reduction for tridiagonal systems. The square root operation required in finding the matrix $\mathbf{G}(i, j)$ often inhibits speed-up. Square-root-free Givens transformations are described in Gentleman [1973] and Hammarling [1974] (Exercise 6.44). Refer to Golub and Van Loan [1983] for further details of implementation.

6.6 EXERCISES

6.1   (Evans and Dunbar [1983]). Analyze the computations of the wave front method for $N = 31$ using $15 \le p \le 30$ processors.

(a) Compute the number of operations performed in the first and second phases of this method. Compute the time required to complete these phases, when

$$\frac{N-1}{2} \le p < \left\lfloor \frac{2(N-1)}{3} \right\rfloor \quad \text{and} \quad \left\lfloor \frac{2(N-1)}{3} \right\rfloor \le p \le N-1.$$

(b) Compare the performance of the column sweep algorithm in Fig. 6.2.1.1 with that of the wave front method on a multivector processor, such as the Alliant FX/8.

6.2   Prove Theorem 6.2.2.1 using Cramer's rule.

6.3   (Heller [1974]). Let $\mathbf{H} = [h_{ij}]$ be a lower Hessenberg matrix, that is, $h_{ij} = 0$ for $j > i + 1$. Then show that $\mathbf{G} = [g_{ij}]$, where

$$g_{ij} = \begin{cases} h_{ij} \displaystyle\prod_{k=j}^{i-1}(-h_{k,k+1}), & 1 \le j \le i \le N \\ -1, & 1 \le i \le N-1, \quad j = i+1, \\ 0, & 1 \le i \le N-1, \quad i+1 < j \le N, \end{cases}$$

is a normalized Hessenberg matrix.

6.4   (Heller [1974]). A normalized Hessenberg matrix $\mathbf{H}$ is a *banded matrix* if

$$h_{ij} = 0 \quad \text{for} \quad i - j \ge k,$$

that is, $\mathbf{H}$ contains $k + 1$ non-zero diagonals. In this case, show that

$$\mathbf{D}[r:t] = \mathbf{D}[r:s] \ \mathbf{D}[s+1:t]$$

$$+ \sum_{i=1}^{p} \sum_{j=q_i}^{x_i} h_{s+i-j,\,s-j} \ \mathbf{D}[r:s-j-1] \ \mathbf{D}[s+i-j+1:t],$$

where $p = \min\{k-1, t-r\}$, $q_i = \max\{0, i-t+s\}$,   and $x_i = \min\{i-1, s-r\}$.

Hint: Specialize Theorem 6.2.2.3.

6.5   Show that the number of processors required by the algorithm in Fig. 6.2.2.1 to compute $\mathbf{D}[1: i]$ for $1 \leq i \leq N$ in time $T(N) = O((\log N)^2)$ is $O(N^4)$. Hence or otherwise, compute the total number of operations involved.

Hint: The number of processors directly depends on the maximum of the number of multiplications performed in any stage of the algorithm.

6.6   As evident in the example for $N = 8$ in Tables 6.2.2.1 and 6.2.2.2, the algorithm in Fig. 6.2.2.1 generates more information than is subsequently used. Clearly, the type of computations done at any stage depends on the value of s. Discuss the effect of changing s on the overall information generated by the algorithm.

6.7   (Heller [1974]). Consider the following constant coefficient system

$$z_0 = 0,$$

$$z_1 = 1,$$

$$z_i = \sum_{j=0}^{i-1} a_{i-1-j} z_j, \qquad i \geq 2.$$

Express it in the matrix form $\mathbf{Az} = \mathbf{d}$, where $\mathbf{z} = (z_0, z_1, z_2, \cdots)^t$, $\mathbf{d} = (0, 1, 0, 0, \cdots)^t$, and

$$\mathbf{A} = \begin{bmatrix} 1 & 0 & 0 & 0 & 0 & 0 & \cdots \\ 0 & 1 & 0 & 0 & 0 & 0 & \cdots \\ -a_1 & -a_0 & 1 & 0 & 0 & 0 & \cdots \\ -a_2 & -a_1 & -a_0 & 1 & 0 & 0 & \cdots \\ -a_3 & -a_2 & -a_1 & -a_0 & 1 & 0 & \cdots \\ \cdot & \cdot & \cdot & \cdot & \cdot & \cdot & \cdots \\ \cdot & \cdot & \cdot & \cdot & \cdot & \cdot & \cdots \\ \cdot & \cdot & \cdot & \cdot & \cdot & \cdot & \cdots \end{bmatrix}.$$

Let $\mathbf{D}$ be the Hessenberg matrix corresponding to matrix $\mathbf{A}$ given above.

$$D = \begin{bmatrix} 0 & -1 & 0 & 0 & 0 & 0 & 0 & 0 & 0 & \cdots \\ 1 & 0 & -1 & 0 & 0 & 0 & 0 & 0 & 0 & \cdots \\ 0 & a_1 & a_0 & -1 & 0 & 0 & 0 & 0 & 0 & \cdots \\ 0 & a_2 & a_1 & a_0 & -1 & 0 & 0 & 0 & 0 & \cdots \\ 0 & a_3 & a_2 & a_1 & a_0 & -1 & 0 & 0 & 0 & \cdots \\ 0 & a_4 & a_3 & a_2 & a_1 & a_0 & -1 & 0 & 0 & \cdots \\ \cdot & \cdot & \cdot & \cdot & \cdot & \cdot & \cdot & \cdot & \cdot & \cdots \\ \cdot & \cdot & \cdot & \cdot & \cdot & \cdot & \cdot & \cdot & \cdot & \cdots \\ \cdot & \cdot & \cdot & \cdot & \cdot & \cdot & \cdot & \cdot & \cdot & \cdots \end{bmatrix} \cdot$$

(a) Show that $z_i = D[4 : 3 + i]$, $i \geq 1$. (Recall $D[j : j - 1] = 1$.)

(b) Show that for $m \geq 1$ and $n \geq 1$,

$$z_{m+n} = z_{m+1} z_n + \sum_{i=1}^{n-1} \sum_{j=1}^{m} a_{i+m-j} \, z_j z_{n-i}.$$

Hint: Apply Theorem 6.2.2.3.

6.8 (Heller [1974]). Let $y_i = 0$, for $i < 0$,

$$y_i = c_i, \quad \text{for} \quad 0 \leq i \leq k - 1$$

$$y_i = \sum_{j=0}^{i-1} a_{i-1-j} y_j, \quad \text{for} \quad i \geq k.$$

(a) Show that for $n \geq k$,

$$y_n = c_{k-1} z_{n-k+2} + \sum_{j=0}^{k-2} c_j \sum_{i=k}^{n} a_{i-1-j} z_{n+1-i},$$

where z_j's are the solutions of the system defined in Exercise 6.7.

6.9 Consider the banded system

$$x_i = \sum_{j=i-m}^{i-1} - a_{ij} x_j + d_i.$$

(a) Express the solution x_i's in terms of the determinants of the Hessenberg matrices.

(b) Compute the number of processors and parallel time required to solve this system by this method.

6.10 (a) Prove Lemmas 6.2.3.1 through 6.2.3.3.

(b) Show that $\mathbf{A}_i\ (a_i)\ \mathbf{A}_{i+1}\ (a_{i+1}) \neq \mathbf{A}_{i+1}\ (a_{i+1})\ \mathbf{A}_i\ (a_i)$.

6.11 Prove Lemma 6.2.3.4.

Hint: Use (6.2.3.3) and exploit the structure of $\mathbf{A}_i$'s.

6.12 Compute the total number of scalar operations required by the algorithm in Fig. 6.2.3.1. Also compute the redundancy factor, speed-up, and efficiency of this algorithm.

6.13 Describe an implementation of the algorithm in Fig. 6.2.3.1 on a pipelined multivector machine, such as the Alliant FX/8, and hypercube architecture.

6.14 Show that

(a)
$$\left[\mathbf{D}_i^{(0)} \right]^{-1} = \begin{bmatrix} 1 & 0 \\ -a_{2i} & 1 \end{bmatrix}.$$

(b)
$$\left[\mathbf{D}_i^{(j)} \right]^{-1} = \begin{bmatrix} \mathbf{I}^{(j)} & 0 \\ -\mathbf{A}_{2i,\ 2i-1}^{(j)} & \mathbf{I}^{(j)} \end{bmatrix}.$$

6.15 Prove the correctness of the algorithm in Section 6.3.1 by verifying (6.3.1.16).

6.16 Compute the degree of parallelism needed to complete the algorithm in Section 6.3.1. Also compute the total number of scalar operations and the redundancy factor of this algorithm.

6.17 Prove the relation (6.3.2.21).

6.18 Specialize the algorithm in Section 6.3.2 to the case when $m = 1$, and compare the resulting algorithm with those given in Chapter 5.

6.19 Implement the algorithm in Section 6.3.2 on a multivector machine, such as the Alliant FX/8, for different values of m.

6.20 The linear banded lower triangular system (6.3.2.1) with bandwidth $m + 1$ can be solved in $2(N - 1)$ time steps using only m processors by the column sweep method. For a given N and m, find the number of processors p for which the algorithm in Section 6.3.2 performs faster than the column sweep method.

6.21 Compute the total number of operations and the redundancy factor for the algorithm in Section 6.3.2.

6.22 (Lakshmivarahan and Dhall [1985a]). A Parallel Algorithm to Compute the First N Fibonacci Numbers. Let $F_0 = F_1 = 1$, and F_i for $i \geq 2$ be defined as follows:

$$F_i = F_{i-1} + F_{i-2}.$$

(a) Let $N = 2^n$. For $1 \leq j \leq 2^{n-1}$ and $2 \leq s \leq n$, show that

$$F_{2^{s-1}+j} = F_{2^{s-1}} F_j + F_{2^{s-1}-1} F_{j-1}.$$

Hint: Prove by induction.

(b) Based on (a), the following algorithm is immediate:

Step 1 (Initialization).

$$F_0 = F_1 = 1, \quad \text{and} \quad F_2 = 2.$$

Step 2.

    FOR $s = 2$ TO n DO
        FOR $j \in \{1, 2, 3, \cdots, 2^{s-1}\}$ DO IN PARALLEL
            COMPUTE $F_{2^{s-1}+j}$ using (a).
        END
    END

Show that this algorithm generates the first $N = 2^n$ Fibonacci numbers in $2(\log N - 1)$ steps using N processors or in $3(\log N - 1)$ steps using $\dfrac{N}{2}$ processors.

Note: This bound compares very favorably with that given in Section 2.3.5 in Kuck [1978], where it is shown that the first N Fibonacci numbers can be computed in $5 \log N - 3$ steps using $1.25 N$ processors.

6.23 (Lakshmivarahan and Dhall [1985a]). Let $x_0 = 0$ and $x_1 = d_1$ and for $i \geq 2$

$$x_i = x_{i-1} + x_{i-2} + d_i.$$

(a) Show that the solution of this recurrence in closed form is given by

$$x_t = \sum_{i=0}^{t-1} F_i d_{t-i},$$

where F_i's are the Fibonnaci numbers defined in Exercise 6.22.

(b) Define

$$Z(s, t) = \sum_{j=0}^{t-s} F_j d_{t-j}.$$

Show that for $t > s$ and $i \geq 0$,

$$Z(s,\ t+i) = Z(t+1,\ t+i) + F_i\ Z(s,\ t) + F_{i-1}\ Z(s,\ t-1).$$

(c) The following algorithm computes x_i's in parallel. Let $N = 2^n$.

Step 1.

      FOR $i = 1$ TO 2^{n-1} DO

         COMPUTE $Z(2i-1,\ 2i-1)$ and $Z(2i-1,\ 2i)$

      END

Step 2.

      FOR $s = 2$ TO n DO

         FOR $g \in \{0,\ 1,\ 2,\ \cdots,\ 2^{n-s}-1\}$ DO IN PARALLEL

         FOR $i = 1$ TO 2^{s-1} DO

      $Z(2^s\ g + 1,\ 2^{s-1}\ (1+2g) + i)$

         END

        END

      END

Show that the above algorithm computes $Z(1, t)$ for $1 \leq t \leq 2^n$ in at most $3 \log N$ steps using $\frac{3}{2}N$ processors or in at most $4 \log N$ steps using $\frac{3}{4}N$ processors.

6.24 (Heller [1978]). Let A be a unit lower triangular matrix (as in 6.2.1.2). Given $Ax = d$, the following is another algorithm that computes $x = A^{-1}d$. Define $L = I - A$, where L is a strictly lower triangular matrix.

(a) Show that $L^N = 0$, a null matrix.

(b) Show that

$$x = A^{-1}d$$

$$= (I + L + L^2 + \cdots + L^{N-1})\,d$$

$$= (I + L^{2^{n-1}})(I + L^{2^{n-2}}) \cdots (I + L^2)(I + L)\,d,$$

where $n = \lceil \log N \rceil$; that is, successively square L, find the sum $(I + L^{2^j})$, and compute the above product using the associative fan-in algorithm to compute x.

(c) Compute the number of steps and the processors needed to implement this algorithm.

(d) Use the above method of finding the inverse to solve banded systems.

6.25 (Wilkinson [1965]). Let x_1 and x_2 be two real numbers, and let o denote one of the four standard arithmetic operations. The standard model for the floating point operations with round-off error is

$$fl(x_1 \text{ o } x_2) = x_1 \text{ o } x_2(1 + \delta),$$

with $|\delta| \leq \varepsilon$, called unit round-off, $x_1 \text{ o } x_2$ is the actual value, $fl(x_1 \text{ o } x_2)$ is the computed value,

$$\varepsilon = \begin{cases} \dfrac{1}{2} r^{1-t}, & \text{for rounded operation} \\[2ex] r^{1-t}, & \text{for chopped operations,} \end{cases}$$

r is the radix, and t is the number of digits used in the representation.

(a) Let $\mathbf{x} = (x_1, x_2, \cdots, x_N)^t$ and $y = (y_1, y_2, \cdots, y_N)^t$. The inner product $\mathbf{x}^t\mathbf{y}$ can be computed in $1 + \lceil \log N \rceil$ steps by first multiplying $\mathbf{x}$ and $\mathbf{y}$ componentwise in one step and then adding the products using the associative fan-in rule (in a binary tree fashion, refer to Chapter 1) in $\lceil \log N \rceil$ steps. Show that

$$|fl(\mathbf{x}^t\mathbf{y}) - \mathbf{x}^t\mathbf{y}| \leq \varepsilon (1 + \lceil \log N \rceil) \sum_{i=1}^{N} |x_i| |y_i|.$$

(b) If the inner products are accumulated in double precision, then show that

$$|fl(\mathbf{x}^t\mathbf{y}) - \mathbf{x}^t\mathbf{y}| \leq \varepsilon \sum_{i=1}^{N} |x_i| |y_i|.$$

6.26 (Golub and Van Loan [1983]). Let $\mathbf{Ax} = \mathbf{b}$ and $(\mathbf{A} + \delta\mathbf{A}) \tilde{\mathbf{x}} = \mathbf{b}$, where $\delta\mathbf{A}$ is called the perturbation matrix. Show that

$$\frac{\|\tilde{\mathbf{x}} - \mathbf{x}\|}{\|\mathbf{x}\|} \leq \varepsilon \, \kappa(\mathbf{A}) \, \frac{\|\delta\mathbf{A}\|}{\|\mathbf{A}\|},$$

where

$$\kappa(\mathbf{A}) = \|\mathbf{A}\| \, \|\mathbf{A}^{-1}\|$$

is called the *condition number* of the matrix $\mathbf{A}$, and $\|\mathbf{x}\|$ and $\|\mathbf{A}\|$ denote the vector and matrix norms, respectively.

Note: Refer to Chapter 5 (Exercise 5.35) for a discussion of the definition and properties of various norms.

6.27   Compute the condition number for the matrix $\mathbf{A} = \begin{bmatrix} a & b \\ c & d \end{bmatrix}$.

6.28   (Sameh and Brent [1977]). (a) Let $\tilde{\mathbf{x}}$ be the computed solution of system (6.2.3.1) using the Sameh-Brent Algorithm-1, and let $\mathbf{x}$ denote the actual solution. Show that $\tilde{\mathbf{x}}$ satisfies the perturbed system

$$(\mathbf{A} + \delta\mathbf{A})\,\tilde{\mathbf{x}} = \mathbf{d}$$

with

$$\|\delta\mathbf{A}\| = \varepsilon\,\kappa^2(\mathbf{A})\,\|\mathbf{A}\|\ O\,(N^2 \log N),$$

and

$$\frac{\|\tilde{\mathbf{x}} - \mathbf{x}\|}{\|\mathbf{x}\|} = \varepsilon\,\kappa^3(\mathbf{A})\,\|\mathbf{A}\|O\,(N^2 \log N),$$

where $\kappa(\mathbf{A})$ is the condition number of $\mathbf{A}$. (See Exercise 6.26.)

Note: Thus, the relative error in the solution can be quite large even for moderately large values of $\kappa(\mathbf{A})$. This shows that faster algorithms are not always stable.

(b) The above bound was derived assuming all the computations are done in single precision. Derive a new upper bound on the relative error in the solution when the inner products are accumulated in double precision (refer to Exercise 6.25).

6.29   (Chen, Kuck, and Sameh [1978]). Let $\mathbf{A}$ be an $N \times N$ unit lower triangular Toeplitz matrix of bandwidth $m + 1$. (Toeplitz matrices have the same elements along each diagonal. Refer to Section 7.2 for properties of Toeplitz matrices.)

(a) Show that $\mathbf{A}^{-1}$ is also a Toeplitz matrix.

(b) We now present an algorithm which is a specialization of the one given in Section 6.3.2. First partition $\mathbf{A}$ as follows:

$$\mathbf{A} = \begin{bmatrix} \mathbf{L} & 0 & 0 & \cdots & 0 & 0 \\ \mathbf{U} & \mathbf{L} & 0 & \cdots & 0 & 0 \\ 0 & \mathbf{U} & \mathbf{L} & \cdots & 0 & 0 \\ . & . & . & \cdots & . & . \\ . & . & . & \cdots & . & . \\ . & . & . & \cdots & . & . \\ 0 & 0 & 0 & \cdots & \mathbf{L} & 0 \\ 0 & 0 & 0 & \cdots & \mathbf{U} & \mathbf{L} \end{bmatrix},$$

where both $\mathbf{L}$ and $\mathbf{U}$ are Toeplitz matrices of order $s_1 = \left\lceil \dfrac{N}{k-1} \right\rceil$ and $p = km$

is the total number of available processors. Notice that there are only $k - 1$ blocks along the principal diagonal of A as opposed to k blocks in (6.3.2.2). Except for this difference in partition size, this algorithm is the same as in Section 6.3.2.

Step 1: Allot m processors to each of the following $k - 1$ systems, and solve them in parallel using the column sweep method:

$$L \, \overline{d}_i^{(0)} = \overline{d}_i,$$

$d = (\overline{d}_1, \overline{d}_2, \cdots, \overline{d}_{k-1})^t$ is a compatible partition of d, where $Ax = d$. Simultaneously, using the rest of m processors, solve

$$Ly = e_1$$

using the column sweep method, where e_1 is the first unit vector of size s_1.

Note: It is well known that y uniquely defines L^{-1}. See Chapter 7 for details.

(a) Show that step 1 takes a total of $2\left(\left\lceil \dfrac{Nm}{p - m} \right\rceil - 1\right)$ units of time.

(b) Specialize the rest of the algorithm in Section 6.3.2 to this case and show that the system can be solved in

$$2\left\lceil \frac{Nm}{p - m} \right\rceil + O(m^2 \log \frac{p}{m})$$

steps.

(c) Compare this algorithm with the column sweep method, when $N \gg p > 2m$.

6.30 (Heath and Romine [1988]). Let $Ax = b$ be the system to be solved, where A is an $N \times N$ lower triangular matrix. There are two versions of the serial algorithm for solving this system.

Vector Sum Version:

FOR $j = 1$ TO N STEP 1 DO
$\qquad x_j = \dfrac{b_j}{a_{jj}};$
$\qquad$ FOR $i = j + 1$ TO N STEP 1 DO
$\qquad\qquad b_i = b_i - x_i \, a_{ij};$
$\qquad$ END
END

Scalar Product Version:

> FOR $i = 1$ TO N STEP 1 DO
>> FOR $j = 1$ TO $i - 1$ STEP 1 DO
>>> $b_i = b_i - x_j \, a_{ij}$
>>
>> END
>>
>> $x_i = \dfrac{b_i}{a_{ii}};$
>
> END

Based on these two algorithms, parallel implementations suitable for various distributed memory architectures, including the hypercube, can be developed. Let the jth row (column) of $\mathbf{A}$ be assigned to a processor called MAP (j), where the function $j \rightarrow$ MAP(j) is prespecified and is known to all the processors. As an example, it could be the Gray code mapping (see Chapter 2 for details). Let FAN_OUT$[x, root\,]$ denote the operation where the processor *root* broadcasts the data x to all the other processors. This can be effectively done by using the spanning tree based broadcast algorithm (see Chapter 2 for details). Let MYROW (MYCOL) denote the set of rows (columns) of $\mathbf{A}$ assigned to a processor. It is assumed that each processor has a relevant segment of the vector $\mathbf{b}$. With these notations, we describe a collection of algorithms.

For each of the following algorithms, analyze the computation and the communication cost.

(a) **FAN_OUT Vector Sum Algorithm.**

> FOR $j = 1$ TO N STEP 1 DO
>> IF $j \in$ MYROW THEN
>>> $x_j = \dfrac{b_j}{a_{jj}};$
>>
>> FAN_OUT $[x_j,$ MAP$(j)]$;
>> FOR $i \in$ MYROW, AND $i > j$ DO
>>> $b_i = b_i - x_j a_{ij}$
>>
>> END
>
> END

Parallelism is achieved by letting each processor execute the above algorithm. Thus, when $j = 1$, the processor containing the first row of $\mathbf{A}$ computes x_1 and broadcasts it to all the other processors. On receiving x_1, all the processors update their respective b_i's. Then, when $j = 2$, the processor that has the second row of $\mathbf{A}$ computes x_2 and broadcasts it. This cycle continues until all the x_i's are recovered.

(b)

FAN_IN Scalar Product Algorithm:

FOR $i = 1$ TO N STEP 1 DO

   $y = 0$;

   FOR $j \in$ MYCOL, AND $j < i$ DO

     $y = y + x_j a_{ij}$;

     $z =$ FAN_IN[y, MAP(i)];

     IF $i \in$ MYCOL THEN

$$x_i = \frac{b_i - z}{a_{ii}};$$

   END

END

Here FAN_IN $[u, root]$ denotes that the processor *root* receives the sum of the u's from all the other processors by using the broadcast spanning tree in the reverse order.

Remark: These algorithms are quite generic in nature and can be implemented in a variety of distributed memory architecture including hypercube, ring, trees, etc.

6.31 (Heath and Romine [1988]). Following the notations and the conventions of Exercise 6.30, we now describe another algorithm, a column-oriented wave front vector sum algorithm for solving a lower triangular linear system. The processor MAP(1) computes $x_1 = b_1/a_{11}$ and $y_i = x_1 a_{i1}$ for $2 \le i \le k$ for some $1 \le k \le N$. This processor then sends the segment $(y_2, y_3, \cdots, y_k)$ to the processor MAP(2). On receiving this segment, the latter processor first computes $x_2 = (b_2 - y_2)/a_{22}$ and updates y_3 to y_k as follows:

$$y_i = y_i + x_2 a_{i2}, \quad \text{for } 3 \le i \le k.$$

In the meantime, processor MAP(1), soon after sending the above segment to MAP(2), continues to compute $y_i = x_1 a_{i1}$ for $k + 1 \le i \le 2k$ and again sends the new segment $(y_{k+1}, y_{k+2}, \cdots, y_{2k})$ to MAP(2). Processor MAP(2) after updating, sends the segment $(y_3, \cdots, y_k)$ to MAP(3), which in turn computes $x_3 = (b_3 - y_3)/a_{33}$ and updates $(y_4, \cdots, y_k)$ as follows:

$$y_i = y_i + x_3 a_{i3} \quad \text{for } 4 \le i \le k.$$

This process of receiving, updating, and sending continues until all the x_i's are computed.

The number s of segments a processor receives depends on the value k which in turn determines the total communication cost. Also, notice that the first segment shrinks in size by 1 after each component of the solution is recovered. Thus, for processor MAP(k) the second segment becomes the new first segment, and this process of redefining the first segment occurs after passing through a sequence of k processors. The computations in each processor may be represented in the form of an algorithm as follows:

> FOR $i \in$ MYCOL DO
> > FOR $j = 1$ TO s STEP 1 DO
> > > RECEIVE a segment;
> > > IF $j = 1$, THEN
> > > > $$x_i = \frac{(b_i - y_i)}{a_{ii}};$$
> > >
> > > REMOVE y_i from the segment;
> > > FOR $y_r \in$ segment DO
> > > > $$y_r = y_r + x_i a_{ri};$$
> > >
> > > END
> > > IF segment is non-empty THEN
> > > > SEND segment to $MAP(i + 1)$;
> >
> > END
>
> END

(a) Describe the actual sequence of computations for this algorithm for the case when $N = 8$ and k ranging from 1 to 4.

(b) Compute the total computation and communication time as a function of N and k.

(c) In the above algorithm, it was tacitly assumed that the processor MAP(i) had column i and b_i in its memory. Restructure the algorithm for the dual case when the processor MAP(i) contains the ith row and b_i.

6.32 (Li and Coleman [1988]). Let $\mathbf{Ax} = \mathbf{d}$, where $\mathbf{A}$ is an $N \times N$ lower triangular matrix. Consider a distributed memory multiprocessor with k processors where N is a multiple of k. It is assumed that the N columns are distributed in a wraparound fashion, that is, if column i is stored in processor MAP(i), then MAP(i) = MAP(j) if and only if $i \equiv j \pmod{k}$. The basic idea of the Li-Coleman algorithm is described in Fig. E6.1, using an example with $k = 3$ processors. Referring to this figure, processor p_1 computes first x_1 and then the segment $(z_2, z_3, \cdots, z_k)$ of size $k - 1$. This segment is then sent to processor p_2, which, after receiving it, computes x_2, deletes z_2, updates z_3 to z_k, computes z_{k+1}, forms the new segment $(z_3, z_4, \cdots, z_{k+1})$, and sends it to processor p_3. This process continues cyclically until all the variables are recovered. To maximize the overlap in computation, each processor, after sending the segment, accumulates the inner products necessary for recovering the variables. Generalizing this example, calculate the computation time and the communication delay for this algorithm.

Cycle	p_1 $j = 1, 4, 7, \cdots$	p_2 $j = 2, 5, 8, \cdots$	p_3 $j = 3, 6, 9, \cdots$
	$x_1 = b_1/a_{11}$ $z_2 = a_{21}x_1$ $z_3 = a_{31}x_1$ Send (z_2, z_3) to p_2		
1	$t_4 = a_{41}x_1$ $t_5 = a_{51}x_1$ $t_6 = a_{61}x_1$ $t_7 = a_{71}x_1$ $t_8 = a_{81}x_1$ $t_9 = a_{91}x_1$	$x_2 = (b_2 - z_2)/a_{22}$ $z_3 = z_3 + a_{32}x_2$ $z_4 = a_{42}x_2$ Send (z_3, z_4) to p_3	
	$\cdots$	$t_5 = a_{52}x_2$ $t_6 = a_{62}x_2$ $t_7 = a_{72}x_2$ $t_8 = a_{82}x_2$ $t_9 = a_{92}x_2$ $\cdots$	$x_3 = (b_3 - z_3)/a_{33}$ $z_4 = z_4 + a_{43}x_3$ $z_5 = a_{53}x_3$ Send (z_4, z_5) to p_1
2	$x_4 = (b_4 - z_4 - t_4)/a_{44}$ $z_5 = z_5 + t_5 + a_{54}x_4$ $z_6 = t_6 + a_{64}x_4$ Send (z_5, z_6) to p_2	$\cdots$	$t_6 = a_{63}x_3$ $t_7 = a_{73}x_3$ $t_8 = a_{93}x_3$ $t_9 = a_{93}x_3$
	$t_7 = t_7 + a_{74}x_4$ $t_8 = t_8 + a_{84}x_4$ $t_9 = t_9 + a_{94}x_4$	$x_5 = (b_5 - z_5 - t_5)/a_{55}$ $z_6 = z_6 + t_6 + a_{65}x_5$ $z_7 = t_7 + a_{75}x_5$ Send (z_6, z_7) to p_3	
	$\cdots$	$t_8 = t_8 + a_{85}x_5$ $t_9 = t_9 + a_{95}x_5$ $\cdots$	$x_6 = (b_6 - z_6 - t_6)/a_{66}$ $z_7 = z_7 + t_7 + a_{76}x_6$ $z_8 = t_8 + t_8 + a_{86}x_6$ Send (z_7, z_8) to p_1
3	$x_7 = (b_7 - z_7 - t_7)/a_{77}$ $z_8 = z_8 + t_8 + a_{87}x_7$ $t_9 = t_9 + a_{97}x_7$ Send (z_8, t_9) to p_2		
	$\cdots$ $\cdots$	$\cdots$ $\cdots$	

FIGURE E6.1 Li-Coleman cyclic vector sum algorithm.

Note: Refer to Li and Coleman [1988], Heath and Romine [1988], and Eisenstat, Heath, Henkel, and Romine [1988], for details of implementation.

6.33 (Ortega [1988]). In this exercise, we describe an implementation of the **LU** decomposition algorithm given in Fig. 6.4.1.1.

Let there be N processors and let the processor p_i contain the ith row of the original matrix **A**. In the first step, processor p_1 sends a copy of the first row to processors p_2 through p_N using a suitable broadcast algorithm. On receiving this row, processor p_i, $i = 2$ to N, updates its row (namely, the ith row) in parallel as follows:

$$\text{FOR } j = 1 \text{ TO } N \text{ STEP 1 DO}$$

$$a_{ij} = a_{ij} - \left(\frac{a_{i1}}{a_{11}} \right) a_{1j}$$

$$\text{END}$$

In the second step, processor p_2 broadcasts its updated second row to processors p_3 to p_N, who in turn do a similar updating of their rows. Thus, in the ith step, processor p_i broadcasts its updated i^{th} row to processors p_{i+1} to p_N and the algorithm stops after $N - 1$ steps.

(a) Assuming that the N processors are connected in a binary hypercube, compute the total communication cost.

(b) Modify the algorithm if there are only p processors and N is a multiple of p.

(c) Append the vector **d** as the $(N + 1)^{th}$ column of the matrix **A** where **Ax** = **d**. Thus, the ith row is extended by appending d_i on the right. Now perform the above algorithm on this extended row. Show that in the end d_i is transformed into y_i, where $\mathbf{y} = (y_1, y_2, \cdots, y_N)$ and $\mathbf{y} = \mathbf{L}^{-1}\mathbf{d}$, where **L** is given in (6.4.1.7). Notice that in the end we are left with the system **Ux** = **y**, which can be solved by any of the methods in this chapter.

6.34 Modify the algorithm in Exercise 6.33 for the case when the ith column of **A** is stored in p_i instead of the ith row. Compare the computational and communication complexity of these two implementations resulting from the dual storage schemes.

6.35 (Ortega [1988]). The **LU** factorization can be iteratively computed by using the idea of *bordering*. Let $\mathbf{A}_k$ be the leading principal submatrix of **A** of order k, and assume that $\mathbf{A}_k$ has been factorized, that is, $\mathbf{L}_k$ and $\mathbf{U}_k$ are known such that $\mathbf{A}_k = \mathbf{L}_k\mathbf{U}_k$. Consider $\mathbf{A}_{k+1}$, and express it in the partitioned factored form as follows:

$$\mathbf{A}_{k+1} = \begin{bmatrix} \mathbf{A}_k & \mathbf{b}_k \\ \mathbf{c}_k^t & a_{k+1,\,k+1} \end{bmatrix} = \begin{bmatrix} \mathbf{L}_k & \mathbf{0} \\ \mathbf{l}_k^t & 1 \end{bmatrix} \begin{bmatrix} \mathbf{U}_k & \mathbf{u}_k \\ \mathbf{0} & u_{k+1,\,k+1} \end{bmatrix},$$

where $\mathbf{b}_k$ and $\mathbf{c}_k$ are known column vectors of size k, $\mathbf{u}_k$ and $\mathbf{l}_k$ are unknown column vectors of size k, and $u_{k+1,\,k+1}$ is the unknown scalar. The matrix $\mathbf{A}_{k+1}$ partitioned in this way is called a *bordered* matrix. Multiplying the right-hand side of the above relation, it follows that

$$\left. \begin{aligned} \mathbf{L}_k \mathbf{u}_k &= \mathbf{b}_k \\[1em] \mathbf{l}_k^t \mathbf{U}_k &= \mathbf{c}_k^t, \end{aligned} \right\} \tag{*}$$

and

$$u_{k+1,\,k+1} = a_{k+1,\,k+1} - \mathbf{l}_k^t \mathbf{u}_k. \tag{**}$$

Clearly, $\mathbf{u}_k$ and $\mathbf{l}_k^t$ can be obtained by solving the triangular systems in (*) by any of the methods described in this chapter, and $u_{k+1,\,k+1}$ involves an inner product and subtraction.

Describe an implementation of this algorithm on a multivector processor as well as a distributed memory processor such as a Hypercube.

6.36   This exercise describes another partitioned **LU** factorization algorithm. Let $\mathbf{A}[i:j,\ k:l]$ denote the *slice* of the matrix $\mathbf{A}$ contained between the ith and j^{th} rows and k^{th} and l^{th} columns, where $i \le j$ and $k \le l$. If $i = k$ and $j = l$, this slice denotes the principal submatrix bounded by the ith row and column and the jth row and column and is denoted by $\mathbf{A}[i:j]$; if $i = j$, then it is denoted as $\mathbf{A}[i,\ k:l]$, and if $k = l$, as $\mathbf{A}[i:j,l]$. Let

$$\begin{bmatrix} \mathbf{A}[1:k-1] & \mathbf{A}[1:k-1,\,k] & \mathbf{A}[1:k-1,\,k+1:N] \\ \mathbf{A}[k,\,1:k-1] & \mathbf{A}[k,\,k] & \mathbf{A}[k,\,k+1:N] \\ \mathbf{A}[k+1:N,\,1:k-1] & \mathbf{A}[k+1:N,\,k] & \mathbf{A}[k+1:N] \end{bmatrix}$$

$$= \begin{bmatrix} \mathbf{L}[1:k-1] & \mathbf{0} & \mathbf{0} \\ \mathbf{L}[k,\,1:k-1] & \mathbf{I} & \mathbf{0} \\ \mathbf{L}[k+1:N,\,1:k-1] & \mathbf{L}[k+1:N,\,k] & \mathbf{L}[k+1:N] \end{bmatrix} \times$$

$$\begin{bmatrix} \mathbf{U}[1:k-1] & \mathbf{U}[1:k-1,\,k] & \mathbf{U}[1:k-1,\,k+1:N] \\ \mathbf{0} & \mathbf{U}[k,\,k] & \mathbf{U}[k,\,k+1:N] \\ \mathbf{0} & \mathbf{0} & \mathbf{U}[k+1:N] \end{bmatrix}$$

Let $\mathbf{A}[1:k-1] = \mathbf{L}[1:k-1]\mathbf{U}[1:k-1]$ be   known   along   with $\mathbf{L}[k,\,1:k-1]$, $\mathbf{U}[1:k-1,\,k]$, $\mathbf{L}[k+1:N,\,1:k-1]$, and $\mathbf{U}[1,\,k+1:N]$. The problem is to find $\mathbf{L}[k+1:N,\,k]$, $\mathbf{U}[k:k]$, and $\mathbf{U}[k,\,k+1:N]$. Multiplying the right-hand side of the above equation, and equating, we obtain

$$\mathbf{U}[k:k] = \mathbf{A}[k:k] - \mathbf{L}[k, 1:k-1]\mathbf{U}[1:k-1, k]$$

$$\mathbf{L}[k+1:N, k]$$

$$= \frac{1}{\mathbf{U}[k:k]} \times \left[\mathbf{A}[k+1:N, k] - \mathbf{L}[k+1:N, 1:k-1]\mathbf{U}[1:k-1, k] \right]$$

$$\mathbf{U}[k, k+1:N] = \mathbf{A}[k, k+1:N] - \mathbf{L}[k, 1:k-1]\mathbf{U}[1:k-1, k+1:N].$$

(a) Derive an implementation of this algorithm suitable for a multivector processor.

Note: Ortega [1988] attributes this algorithm to Dongarra and Eisenstat.

6.37 Let $\mathbf{A} = \mathbf{LU}$, where $\mathbf{L} = [\, l_{ij} \,]$ is unit lower triangular and $\mathbf{U} = [\, u_{ij} \,]$ is upper triangular. Show that the following algorithm computes $\mathbf{L}$ and $\mathbf{U}$ from $\mathbf{A}$.

> FOR $r = 1$ TO N DO
> > FOR $i = r$ *TO* N DO
> > $$u_{ri} = a_{ri} - \sum_{j=1}^{r-1} l_{rj} u_{ji}$$
> > END
> > FOR $i = r+1$ *TO* N *STEP* 1 DO
> > $$l_{ir} = \frac{(a_{ir} - \sum_{j=1}^{r-1} l_{ij} u_{jr})}{u_{kk}}$$
> > END
> END

(a) Discuss a parallel implementation of this algorithm on a multivector machine and on the hypercube architecture.

(b) Compute the total number of operations and amount of communication needed in each of the above implementations.

Note: This algorithm is known as the *Doolittle reduction*. (Golub and Van Loan [1983]).

6.38 In this exercise, we further extend the **LU** factorization using blocking. Let **A** be expressed as follows:

$$
\begin{bmatrix} A_{11} & A_{12} & A_{13} \\ A_{21} & A_{22} & A_{23} \\ A_{31} & A_{32} & A_{33} \end{bmatrix} = \begin{bmatrix} L_{11} & 0 & 0 \\ L_{21} & L_{22} & 0 \\ L_{31} & L_{32} & L_{33} \end{bmatrix} \begin{bmatrix} U_{11} & U_{12} & U_{13} \\ 0 & U_{22} & U_{23} \\ 0 & 0 & U_{33} \end{bmatrix},
$$

where A_{ii} is a $k_i \times k_i$ matrix and $k_1 + k_2 + k_3 = N$. Recall, by definition, that L_{ii}'s are unit lower triangular and U_{ii}'s are upper triangular, for $i = 1, 2, 3$. Assuming that $A_{11} = L_{11}U_{11}$ is known, along with L_{21}, L_{31}, U_{12}, and U_{13}, the problem is to find L_{22}, U_{22}, L_{32}, and U_{23}. To this end, after multiplying the right-hand side, we obtain

$$ L_{22}U_{22} = A_{22} - L_{21}U_{12}, \tag{1} $$

$$ L_{22}U_{23} = A_{23} - L_{21}U_{13}, \tag{2} $$

$$ L_{32}U_{22} = A_{32} - L_{31}U_{12}. \tag{3} $$

Consider equation (2). Let α_i be the ith column of U_{23} and β_i be the ith column of $A_{23} - L_{21}U_{13}$. If L_{22} is known, then α_i can be recovered in parallel by solving the unit lower triangular system $L_{22}\alpha_i = \beta_i$, for $i = 1$ to k_3. Likewise, if U_{22} is known, the rows of L_{32} can be obtained in parallel by solving a set of upper triangular systems arising from (3).

the unit lower triangular structure of L_{22} as in Exercise 6.36.

Develop an implementation for the block **LU** factorization algorithm described above suitable for multivector and hypercube architectures.

6.39 Compare the suitability of the **LU** factorization algorithms described in Exercise 6.33 through 6.38 for different architectures.

6.40 Show that $G(i, j)$ is orthogonal, that is, $G^{-1}(i, j) = G^t(i, j)$.

6.41 Compare the number of operations involved in computing $M_i A$ and $G(i, j)A$, where A is a matrix, M_i is defined in (6.4.1.1), and $G(i, j)$ in (6.4.2.2).

6.42 For $N = 7$ compute $m^{(i)}$, $i = 2, 3, 4, 5,$ and 6.

6.43 (Modi and Clarke [1984]). In this exercise, we develop a version of a *greedy* strategy for the parallel annihilation scheme. We first illustrate this scheme by an example in Fig. E6.2 below using a 16×4 matrix A, where $\times$ denotes the principal diagonal elements.

In the first step, elements of A at positions $(16, 1), (15, 1), (14, 1), \cdots, (9, 1)$ are annihilated. In the second step, elements at positions $(16, 2), (15, 2), (14, 2), (13, 2), (8, 1), (7, 1), (6, 1),$ and

Rows i	Columns j			
	1	2	3	4
1	×			
2	4	×		
3	3	6	×	
4	3	5	8	×
5	2	5	7	10
6	2	4	7	9
7	2	4	6	9
8	2	4	6	8
9	1	3	5	8
10	1	3	5	7
11	1	3	5	7
12	1	3	4	6
13	1	2	4	6
14	1	2	4	5
15	1	2	3	5
16	1	2	2	4

FIGURE E6.2
A greedy strategy for annihilation.

(5, 1) are annihilated, and so on.

Let $z(t, i)$ be the number of zeros in column i at time t.

(a) Let **A** be an $M \times N$ matrix. Generalizing the above example, show that

$$z(t+1, i) = z(t, i) + \left[\frac{z(t, i-1) - z(t, i)}{2} \right],$$

where $z(0, i) = 0$ for $1 \le i \le N$, $z(t, 0) = M$ for all $t = 0, 1, 2, \cdots$, and $[x]$ denotes the integer part of x.

(b) Using the above recurrence, compute the number of parallel steps needed to annihilate elements below the principal diagonal of an $M \times N$ matrix for $2 \le M \le 100$ and $2 \le N \le 20$.

(c) Show that

$$z(t, 1) \geq z(t, 2) \geq z(t, 3) \geq \cdots \geq z(t, N),$$

for all t.

(d) Since $a + \left[\dfrac{b-a}{2}\right] = \left[\dfrac{b+a}{2}\right]$, for any two integers a and b, the $z(t, i)$ recurrence can be rewritten as

$$z(t+1, i) = \left[\frac{z(t,i-1) + z(t, i)}{2}\right].$$

Define a new recurrence

$$\alpha(t+1, i) = \left[\frac{\alpha(t, i-1) + \alpha(t, i)}{2}\right],$$

where $\alpha(t, 0) = 1$ for all t. Show that

$$z(t, i) \leq M\, \alpha(t, i).$$

(e) Let $Q(x, y) = \sum\limits_{t, i} \alpha(t, i)x^t y^i$. Prove that $\alpha(t, i)$ can be computed by using the generating function

$$Q(x, y) = (1 - \frac{x}{2})\left\{ (1-x)(1 - \frac{x(1+y)}{2}) \right\}^{-1},$$

as

$$\alpha(t, i) = 1 - 2^{-t} \sum_{k=0}^{i-1} \binom{t}{k}.$$

(f) The annihilation process stops when $M - N$ zeros are introduced in the Nth column of $\mathbf{A}$. Let t^* be the number of steps needed to achieve this goal. Then it follows from the definition that t^* must be such that

$$z(t^* - 1, N) \leq M\alpha(t^* - 1, N) < M - N$$

and

$$M\alpha(t^*, N) \geq M - N.$$

Show that $t^* = [t]$, where t is the solution of

$$2^{-t} \sum_{k=0}^{N-1} \binom{t}{k} = \frac{N}{M}. \tag{*}$$

(g) Show that for N fixed, as $M \to \infty$, the solution of (*) can be approximated as

$$t \approx \log M + (N - 1) \log \log M.$$

6.44   (Gentleman [1973], Hammarling [1974]). This exercise develops the concept of a square-root-free Givens transformation. Let

$$\mathbf{A} = \begin{bmatrix} a_1 & a_2 & a_3 & \cdots & a_N \\ b_1 & b_2 & b_3 & \cdots & b_N \end{bmatrix}.$$

First factor **A** in the form $\mathbf{A} = \mathbf{KC}$, where

$$\mathbf{K} = \begin{bmatrix} k_1 & 0 \\ 0 & k_2 \end{bmatrix} \quad \text{and} \quad \mathbf{C} = \begin{bmatrix} 1 & c_2 & c_3 & \cdots & c_N \\ d_1 & d_2 & d_3 & \cdots & d_N \end{bmatrix}.$$

It is assumed that **K** and **C** are given. Let

$$\mathbf{K}' = \begin{bmatrix} k_1' & 0 \\ 0 & k_2' \end{bmatrix} \quad \text{and} \quad \mathbf{C}' = \begin{bmatrix} c_1' & c_2' & c_3' & \cdots & c_N' \\ 0 & d_2' & d_3' & \cdots & d_N' \end{bmatrix}.$$

The problem is to obtain **K**′ and **C**′ from **K** and **C** by applying the standard Givens transformation, that is,

$$\begin{bmatrix} t & s \\ -s & t \end{bmatrix} \mathbf{KC} = \mathbf{K}'\mathbf{C}'.$$

Then, it is well known that

$$c_1' = \frac{r}{k_1'},$$

and, for $i = 2, 3, \cdots, N$,

$$c_i' = \frac{tk_1 c_i + sk_2 d_i}{k_1'}$$

$$d_i' = \frac{-sk_1 c_i + tk_2 d_i}{k_2'},$$

where

$$t = \frac{k_1}{r}, \qquad s = \frac{k_2 d_1}{r},$$

and

$$r = (k_1^2 + k_2^2 d_1^2)^{1/2}.$$

This standard approach requires a square root operation. In the following, the idea of a square-root-free Givens transformation is developed.

Let

$$k_1' = r \quad \text{and} \quad k_2' = tk_2 = \frac{k_1 k_2}{r}. \tag{*}$$

Define

$$h_i = k_i^2 \qquad \text{and} \qquad h_i' = (k_i')^2.$$

Using these, we can rewrite the relations for c_i' and d_i' as follows:

$$\left.\begin{aligned} r^2 = (k_1')^2 = h_1' = (h_1 + h_2 d_1^2) \\[2mm] h_2' = (k_2')^2 = t^2 k_2^2 = \frac{h_1 h_2}{h_1'}, \end{aligned}\right\} \qquad (**)$$

and, for $i = 2, 3, \cdots, N,$

$$\left.\begin{aligned} c_i' = \frac{h_1}{h_1'} c_i + \frac{h_2 d_1}{h_1'} d_i \\[2mm] d_i' = -d_1 c_i + d_i. \end{aligned}\right\} \qquad (***)$$

Thus, given $\mathbf{K}$

(1) Compute h_1' and h_2' using (**), and

(2) Compute c_i' and d_i', using (***), for $i = 2, 3, \cdots, N.$

Evidently, these computations *do not* involve a square root operation and hence are called a square-root-free or fast Givens transformation. Since $\mathbf{K}$ and $\mathbf{C}$ are known, we can assume that h_i' and all the coefficients in (***) involving h_i and h_i' are known. In other words, a (c_i', d_i') pair can be computed in three multiplications. Substituting for d_i in c_i', we can rewrite (***) as follows:

$$\left.\begin{aligned} c_i' = c_i + \frac{h_2 d_1}{h_1'} d_i' \\[2mm] d_i' = d_i - d_1 c_i \end{aligned}\right\}, \quad i = 2, 3, \cdots, N.$$

Clearly, this formulation requires only two multiplications.

(a) Analyze the relative merits of the three- and two-multiplication methods from the point of view of parallel implementation.

(b) There are other ways of choosing k_1' and k_2'. For each of the following choices of k_i', $i = 1, 2$, derive the formula for computing c_i' and d_i', for $i = 2, 3, \cdots, N.$

(1) $k_1' = tk_1', \quad k_2' = tk_2'.$

(2) $k_1' = tk_1, \quad k_2' = -sk_2.$

(3) $k_1' = tk_1, \quad k_2' = \dfrac{t^2 k_1}{s}.$

Note: For a treatment of error analysis for Givens transformations, refer to Gentleman [1973], Hammarling [1974], and Wilkinson [1965].

CHAPTER
7

AN
ASSORTMENT
OF
MATRIX
PROBLEMS

7.1 INTRODUCTION

Parallel algorithms for solving linear bidiagonal, tridiagonal, banded, and triangular systems, along with those for triangular factorization of a matrix, are described in Chapters 5 and 6. In this chapter, we describe parallel algorithms for solving many matrix problems, such as finding the product and powers of matrices, computing the inverse, determinant, characteristic equation, and eigenvalues of a matrix, as well as the solution of triangular Toeplitz systems. To make the exposition self-contained, in Section 7.2 we review a number of relevant properties of matrices. Section 7.3 contains the parallel algorithms for the product of matrices and the powers of a matrix. The algorithms for the inverse of a matrix are contained in Section 7.4.

Section 7.5 deals with the algorithms for computing the determinants and the characteristic polynomials. Parallel methods for solving triangular Toeplitz systems are discussed in Section 7.6. A divide-and-conquer strategy based algorithm for computing the eigenvalues of a real symmetric matrix is covered in Section 7.7

7.2 PROPERTIES OF MATRICES

In this section, we assemble many well-known results from the classical theory of matrices. While these results are widely available in the literature, there are at least two reasons for their inclusion here. First, it makes our treatment independent and less allusive. Second, it helps us to set up the various notations for a unified treatment. An advanced reader may skip this section in the first reading and choose to refer to portions of it when needed.

7.2.1 Basic Concepts

Let

$$\mathbf{A} = [\, a_{ij} \,] \tag{7.2.1.1}$$

be an $N \times N$ matrix and let det[$\mathbf{A}$] denote the *determinant* of $\mathbf{A}$. The *trace* of $\mathbf{A}$, denoted by $tr(\mathbf{A})$, is defined as

$$tr(\mathbf{A}) = \sum_{i=1}^{N} a_{ii}. \tag{7.2.1.2}$$

The *adjoint* of $\mathbf{A}$, denoted by $ADJ(\mathbf{A})$, is an $N \times N$ matrix where (t denotes the *transpose*)

$$[ADJ[\mathbf{A}]]^{t} = [\, A_{ij} \,], \tag{7.2.1.3}$$

and A_{ij} is the *cofactor (signed minor)* of the element a_{ij}. Thus, if m_{ij} is the minor of the element a_{ij}, then

$$A_{ij} = (-1)^{i+j} \, m_{ij}. \tag{7.2.1.4}$$

The following fact is well known:

$$ADJ(\mathbf{A})\,\mathbf{A} = \mathbf{A}\,ADJ(\mathbf{A}) = \det[\mathbf{A}]\,\mathbf{I}, \tag{7.2.1.5}$$

where $\mathbf{I}$ is an identity matrix of the same size as $\mathbf{A}$.

The *characteristic* polynomial $\phi(\lambda)$ of $\mathbf{A}$ is defined by

$$\phi(\lambda) = \det[\mathbf{A} - \lambda\,\mathbf{I}]$$

$$= (-1)^{N}(\lambda^{N} + p_{1}\lambda^{N-1} + p_{2}\lambda^{N-2} + \cdots + p_{N-1}\lambda + p_{N}). \tag{7.2.1.6}$$

The roots $\lambda_{1}, \lambda_{2}, \cdots, \lambda_{N}$ of

$$\phi(\lambda) = 0$$

are known as the *eigenvalues* of the matrix **A**. The characteristic polynomial $\phi(\lambda)$ may also be expressed as

$$\phi(\lambda) = (-1)^N \prod_{i=1}^{N} (\lambda - \lambda_i). \tag{7.2.1.7}$$

The following properties will be needed in the sequel.

Property 7.2.1.1. Referring to (7.2.1.6), it can be shown that

$$\left. \begin{aligned} p_1 &= -\sum_{i=1}^{N} \lambda_i = -tr(\mathbf{A}) \\ p_k &= (-1)^k \times \text{ sum of the principal minors of order } k \\ p_N &= (-1)^N \det[\mathbf{A}], \end{aligned} \right\} \tag{7.2.1.8}$$

where there are $\dfrac{N!}{(N-k)!\,k!}$ principal minors of order k.

Let

$$\mathbf{C}(\lambda) = ADJ(\mathbf{A} - \lambda\,\mathbf{I}). \tag{7.2.1.9}$$

Since the cofactor of each element in the determinant of $\mathbf{A} - \lambda\,\mathbf{I}$ is a polynomial in λ of degree $N - 1$, the matrix **C** can be represented by a polynomial with matrix coefficients as

$$\mathbf{C}(\lambda) = \mathbf{C}_{N-1} + \mathbf{C}_{N-2}\,\lambda + \mathbf{C}_{N-3}\,\lambda^2 + \cdots + \mathbf{C}_0\,\lambda^{N-1}, \tag{7.2.1.10}$$

where $\mathbf{C}_i$, $i = 0, 1, \cdots, N-1$, are $N \times N$ matrices independent of λ.

Comparing the coefficients of the like powers of λ in

$$\mathbf{C}(\lambda)(\mathbf{A} - \lambda\,\mathbf{I}) = \det[\mathbf{A} - \lambda\,\mathbf{I}]\,\mathbf{I}, \tag{7.2.1.11}$$

we obtain the following $N + 1$ equations:

$$\left. \begin{aligned} \mathbf{C}_{N-1}\,\mathbf{A} &= (-1)^N p_N\,\mathbf{I} \\ \mathbf{C}_{N-2}\,\mathbf{A} - \mathbf{C}_{N-1} &= (-1)^N p_{N-1}\,\mathbf{I} \\ \mathbf{C}_{N-3}\,\mathbf{A} - \mathbf{C}_{N-2} &= (-1)^N p_{N-2}\,\mathbf{I} \\ &\vdots \\ \mathbf{C}_2\,\mathbf{A} - \mathbf{C}_3 &= (-1)^N p_3\,\mathbf{I} \\ \mathbf{C}_1\,\mathbf{A} - \mathbf{C}_2 &= (-1)^N p_2\,\mathbf{I} \\ \mathbf{C}_0\,\mathbf{A} - \mathbf{C}_1 &= (-1)^N p_1\,\mathbf{I} \\ -\mathbf{C}_0 &= (-1)^N\,\mathbf{I}. \end{aligned} \right\} \tag{7.2.1.12}$$

Multiplying the ith equation (from the top) by $\mathbf{A}^i$, for $i = 0, 1, \cdots, N$, and adding them, it is readily seen that

$$(-1)^N [\mathbf{A}^N + p_1 \mathbf{A}^{N-1} + p_2 \mathbf{A}^{N-2} + \cdots + p_{N-1} \mathbf{A} + p_N \mathbf{I}]$$

$$= \mathbf{0}, \text{ the null matrix.} \qquad (7.2.1.13)$$

The above discussion is summarized in the following property, called the *Caley-Hamilton* theorem.

Property 7.2.1.2. The matrix $\mathbf{A}$ is a solution of its own characteristic equation, that is,

$$\phi(\mathbf{A}) = 0. \qquad (7.2.1.14)$$

The proof of the next property is left as Exercises 7.1 and 7.2.

Property 7.2.1.3. Let λ_i, $i = 1, \cdots, N$ be the eigenvalues of $\mathbf{A}$ and $f(x) = a_0 + a_1 x + \cdots + a_m x^m$ be the polynomial. Then $f(\lambda_i)$, $i = 1, \cdots, N$ are the eigenvalues of the matrix $f(\mathbf{A})$. In particular, λ_i^k, $i = 1, \cdots, N$, are the eigenvalues of $\mathbf{A}^k$.

7.2.2 Leverrier Method for Computing $\phi(\lambda)$

Define, for $1 \le k \le N$,

$$t_k = \sum_{i=1}^{N} \lambda_i^k = tr(\mathbf{A}^k). \qquad (7.2.2.1)$$

In the following, we derive a set of fundamental identities relating p_k, the coefficients of $\phi(\lambda)$, and t_k for $k = 1, 2, \cdots, N$. By differentiating both sides of (7.2.1.7), we obtain

$$\frac{d\phi(\lambda)}{d\lambda} = \phi(\lambda) \sum_{i=1}^{N} (\lambda - \lambda_i)^{-1}. \qquad (7.2.2.2)$$

Comparing the coefficients of like powers of λ in (7.2.2.2) and using the definition of t_k in (7.2.2.1), we get a recurrence relation defining t_k:

$$t_1 + p_1 = 0,$$

and, for $2 \le k \le N$,

$$t_k + p_1 t_{k-1} + p_2 t_{k-2} + \cdots + p_{k-1} t_1 + k\, p_k = 0. \qquad (7.2.2.3)$$

This is called *Newton's formula*. The following property, which summarizes the above discussion, is called *Leverrier's method* for computing the coefficients of the characteristic polynomial.

Property 7.2.2.1. The coefficients p_i, $i = 1, \cdots, N$, of the characteristic equation are the solution of the linear lower triangular system,

$$\mathbf{T}\,\mathbf{p} = -\mathbf{t}, \tag{7.2.2.4}$$

where

$$\mathbf{p} = (p_1, p_2, \cdots, p_N)^t,$$

$$\mathbf{t} = (t_1, t_2, \cdots, t_N)^t,$$

and

$$\mathbf{T} = \begin{bmatrix} 1 & 0 & 0 & \cdots & 0 & 0 \\ t_1 & 2 & 0 & \cdots & 0 & 0 \\ t_2 & t_1 & 3 & \cdots & 0 & 0 \\ \cdot & \cdot & \cdot & \cdots & \cdot & \cdot \\ \cdot & \cdot & \cdot & \cdots & \cdot & \cdot \\ \cdot & \cdot & \cdot & \cdots & \cdot & \cdot \\ t_{N-1} & t_{N-2} & t_{N-3} & \cdots & t_1 & N \end{bmatrix}.$$

Property 7.2.2.2. Multiplying on the right both sides of $\phi(\mathbf{A}) = 0$ in (7.2.1.14) by $\mathbf{A}^{-1}$ and rearranging, it follows that

$$\mathbf{A}^{-1} = -\frac{\mathbf{A}^{N-1} + p_1\,\mathbf{A}^{N-2} + p_2\,\mathbf{A}^{N-3} + \cdots + p_{N-1}\,\mathbf{I}}{p_N}. \tag{7.2.2.5}$$

Thus, knowing the coefficients of the characteristic polynomial and the powers of $\mathbf{A}$, we can compute $\mathbf{A}^{-1}$ using (7.2.2.5). This constitutes the basis for Csanky's algorithm described in Section 7.4.

7.2.3 Faddeeva-Sominsky Method for Computing $\phi(\lambda)$

The method of Faddeeva and Sominsky for computing $\phi(\lambda)$, and consequently $\mathbf{A}^{-1}$, is closely related to the proof of the Caley-Hamilton theorem and is described below. Define a sequence of matrices as follows:

$$\mathbf{B}_0 = \mathbf{I},$$
$$\mathbf{B}_1 = \mathbf{A}\,\mathbf{B}_0 + r_1\mathbf{I},$$
$$\mathbf{B}_2 = \mathbf{A}\,\mathbf{B}_1 + r_2\mathbf{I},$$
$$\vdots \qquad\qquad\qquad (7.2.3.1)$$
$$\mathbf{B}_i = \mathbf{A}\,\mathbf{B}_{i-1} + r_i\mathbf{I},$$
$$\vdots$$
$$\mathbf{B}_N = \mathbf{A}\,\mathbf{B}_{N-1} + r_N\mathbf{I},$$

where, for $1 \le k \le N$,

$$k\,r_k = -\,tr(\mathbf{AB}_{k-1}). \qquad (7.2.3.2)$$

We now prove by induction that $r_i = p_i$ for $i = 1, \cdots, N$.

It is obvious from the definition that $r_1 = p_1$. Assume that $r_k = p_k$ for all $1 \le k \le i$. From (7.2.3.1), we get

$$\mathbf{B}_i = \mathbf{A}^i + p_1\,\mathbf{A}^{i-1} + p_2\,\mathbf{A}^{i-2} + \cdots + p_i\,\mathbf{I}.$$

Multiplying both sides by $\mathbf{A}$ (on the left), taking traces, and using (7.2.2.1), we obtain

$$tr(\mathbf{A}\,\mathbf{B}_i) = t_{i+1} + p_1\,t_i + p_2\,t_{i-1} + \cdots + p_i\,t_1.$$

Comparing this with Newton's formula in (7.2.2.3), we obtain that $r_{i+1} = p_{i+1}$. Thus, (7.2.3.2) provides an alternative method for computing $\phi(\lambda)$.

From the Caley-Hamilton theorem, it readily follows that $\mathbf{B}_N = \mathbf{0}$, the null matrix. Hence using the last equation in (7.2.3.1), we obtain

$$\mathbf{A}^{-1} = -\,\frac{\mathbf{B}_{N-1}}{p_N}. \qquad (7.2.3.3)$$

A parallel algorithm for computing the inverse of a matrix based on this formula is pursued in Exercise 7.28.

7.2.4 Samuelson Method for Computing $\phi(\lambda)$

Let $\mathbf{A}_N$ be an $N \times N$ matrix partitioned as follows:

$$\mathbf{A}_N = \begin{bmatrix} a_{11} & \mathbf{R} \\ \mathbf{S} & \mathbf{A}_{N-1} \end{bmatrix}, \qquad (7.2.4.1)$$

where

$$\mathbf{R} = (a_{12}, a_{13}, \cdots, a_{1N}),$$

$$\mathbf{S} = (a_{21}, a_{31}, \cdots, a_{N1})^t,$$

and

$$\mathbf{A}_{N-1} = [\, a_{ij}\,], \quad 2 \le i,\, j \le N,$$

that is, $\mathbf{A}_{N-1}$ is obtained by deleting the first row and first column of $\mathbf{A}_N$. $\mathbf{A}_N$ partitioned in this form is called a *bordered* matrix. Let

$$\phi_N(\lambda) = \det[\mathbf{A}_N - \lambda \mathbf{I}_N]$$

and

$$\phi_{N-1}(\lambda) = \det[\mathbf{A}_{N-1} - \lambda \mathbf{I}_{N-1}], \qquad\qquad (7.2.4.2)$$

where $\mathbf{I}_j$ is the identity matrix of order j.

The following property relating $\phi_N(\lambda)$ to $\phi_{N-1}(\lambda)$ provides a framework for iteratively computing $\phi_N(\lambda)$.

Property 7.2.4.1. If $\mathbf{A}_N$ is a bordered matrix of the type given in (7.2.4.1), then

$$\phi_N(\lambda) = (a_{11} - \lambda)\, \phi_{N-1}(\lambda) - \mathbf{R}\, ADJ(\mathbf{A}_{N-1} - \lambda \mathbf{I}_{N-1})\, \mathbf{S}. \qquad (7.2.4.3)$$

To verify this relation, let

$$ADJ'(\mathbf{A}_N - \lambda \mathbf{I}_N) = \begin{bmatrix} \phi_{N-1}(\lambda) & D\,(\lambda) \\ C(\lambda) & B\,(\lambda) \end{bmatrix}. \qquad (7.2.4.4)$$

Since

$$(\mathbf{A}_N - \lambda \mathbf{I}_N)\, ADJ(\mathbf{A}_N - \lambda \mathbf{I}_N) = \mathbf{I}_N\, \phi_N(\lambda), \qquad (7.2.4.5)$$

that is,

$$\begin{bmatrix} a_{11} - \lambda & R \\ \\ S & \mathbf{A}_{N-1} - \lambda \mathbf{I}_{N-1} \end{bmatrix} \begin{bmatrix} \phi_{N-1}(\lambda) & C\,(\lambda) \\ \\ D\,(\lambda) & B\,(\lambda) \end{bmatrix} = \begin{bmatrix} \phi_N(\lambda) & 0 \\ \\ 0 & \phi_N(\lambda)\, \mathbf{I}_{N-1} \end{bmatrix}, (7.2.4.6)$$

we obtain

$$(a_{11} - \lambda)\, \phi_{N-1}(\lambda) + R\, D(\lambda) = \phi_N(\lambda) \qquad (7.2.4.7)$$

and

$$S\, \phi_{N-1}(\lambda) + (\mathbf{A}_{N-1} - \lambda \mathbf{I}_{N-1})\, D(\lambda) = 0. \qquad (7.2.4.8)$$

From (7.2.4.8), it follows that

$$D(\lambda) = -(\mathbf{A}_{N-1} - \lambda \mathbf{I}_{N-1})^{-1}\, S\, \phi_{N-1}(\lambda),$$

which on substitution into (7.2.4.7) and using (7.2.1.5) verifies (7.2.4.3).

Let

$$\det[\mathbf{A}_{N-1} - \lambda \mathbf{I}_{N-1}] = \phi_{N-1}(\lambda)$$

$$= (-1)^N[q_0 \lambda^{N-1} + q_1 \lambda^{N-2} + \cdots + q_{N-2} \lambda + q_{N-1}]. \qquad (7.2.4.9)$$

The following property is useful in the sequel.

Property 7.2.4.2.

$$ADJ(\mathbf{A}_{N-1} - \lambda \mathbf{I}_{N-1})$$

$$= (-1)^{N+1} \sum_{k=2}^{N} [\mathbf{A}_{N-1}^{k-2} q_0 + \mathbf{A}_{N-1}^{k-3} q_1 + \mathbf{A}_{N-1}^{k-4} q_2$$

$$+ \cdots + \mathbf{I}_{N-1} q_{k-2}] \lambda^{N-k}. \qquad (7.2.4.10)$$

To prove this result, first multiply both sides (on the right) by $(\mathbf{A}_{N-1} - \lambda \mathbf{I}_{N-1})$. Since the resulting value of the left-hand side is $\phi_{N-1}(\lambda)$, it is enough to verify that the product of the right-hand side and $(\mathbf{A}_{N-1} - \lambda \mathbf{I}_{N-1})$ is equal to $\phi_{N-1}(\lambda)$. Thus

$$RHS(7.2.4.10) \times (\mathbf{A}_{N-1} - \lambda \mathbf{I}_{N-1})$$

$$= (-1)^{N+1} \sum_{k=2}^{N} (\mathbf{A}_{N-1}^{k-1} q_0 + \mathbf{A}_{N-1}^{k-2} q_1 + \cdots + \mathbf{A}_{N-1} q_{k-2}) \lambda^{N-k}$$

$$+ (-1)^N \sum_{k=1}^{N-1} (\mathbf{A}_{N-1}^{k-1} q_0 + \mathbf{A}_{N-1}^{k-2} q_1 + \cdots + \mathbf{I}_{N-1} q_{k-1}) \lambda^{N-k}$$

$$= \phi_{N-1}(\lambda),$$

which is to be proved.

Now substituting (7.2.4.10) into (7.2.4.3), it follows that

$$\phi_N(\lambda) = (a_{11} - \lambda) \phi_{N-1}(\lambda) + (-1)^N \mathbf{R} \left\{ \sum_{k=2}^{N} [\mathbf{A}_{N-1}^{k-2} q_0 \right.$$

$$\left. + \mathbf{A}_{N-1}^{k-3} q_1 + \cdots + \mathbf{I}_{N-1} q_{k-2}] \lambda^{N-k} \right\} \mathbf{S}. \qquad (7.2.4.11)$$

Combining (7.2.1.6), (7.2.4.9), and (7.2.4.11), we have

$$(-1)^N(p_0 \lambda^N + p_1 \lambda^{N-1} + p_2 \lambda^{N-2} + \cdots + p_{N-1} \lambda + p_N)$$

$$= (-1)^N (a_{11} - \lambda)(q_0 \lambda^{N-1} + q_1 \lambda^{N-2} + \cdots + q_{N-2}\lambda + q_{N-1})$$

$$+ (-1)^N \mathbf{R} \left\{ \sum_{k=2}^{N} (\mathbf{B}^{k-2} q_0 + \mathbf{B}^{k-3} q_1 + \cdots + \mathbf{I} q_{k-2}) \lambda^{N-k} \right\} \mathbf{S},$$

where $\mathbf{B} = \mathbf{A}_{N-1}$ and $\mathbf{I} = \mathbf{I}_{N-1}$ for simplicity in notation. From this, the following linear relation between $\mathbf{P}_{N+1} = (p_0, p_1, p_2, \cdots, p_N)^t$ and $\mathbf{Q}_N = (q_0, q_1, q_2, \cdots, q_{N-1})^t$ readily follows:

$$p_0 = -q_0,$$

$$p_1 = a_{11} q_0 - q_1,$$

$$p_2 = \mathbf{R}\,\mathbf{S} q_0 + a_{11} q_1 - q_2,$$

$$p_3 = \mathbf{R}\,\mathbf{B}\,\mathbf{S} q_0 + \mathbf{R}\,\mathbf{S} q_1 + a_{11} q_2 - q_3,$$

$$p_4 = \mathbf{R}\,\mathbf{B}^2\,\mathbf{S} q_0 + \mathbf{R}\,\mathbf{B}\,\mathbf{S} q_1 + \mathbf{R}\,\mathbf{S} q_2 + a_{11} q_3 - q_4,$$

$$\vdots$$

$$p_{N-1} = \mathbf{R}\,\mathbf{B}^{N-3}\,\mathbf{S} q_0 + \mathbf{R}\,\mathbf{B}^{N-4}\,\mathbf{S} q_1 + \cdots + \mathbf{R}\,\mathbf{S} q_{N-3} + a_{11} q_{N-2} - q_{N-1},$$

$$p_N = \mathbf{R}\,\mathbf{B}^{N-2}\,\mathbf{S} q_0 + \mathbf{R}\,\mathbf{B}^{N-3}\,\mathbf{S} q_1 + \cdots + \mathbf{R}\,\mathbf{S} q_{N-2} + a_{11} q_{N-1}.$$

Let

$$\mathbf{M}_N = \begin{bmatrix} -1 & 0 & 0 & \cdots & & \cdot \\ a_{11} & -1 & 0 & \cdots & & \cdot \\ \mathbf{R}\,\mathbf{S} & a_{11} & -1 & \cdots & & \cdot \\ \mathbf{R}\,\mathbf{B}\,\mathbf{S} & \mathbf{R}\,\mathbf{S} & a_{11} & \cdots & & \cdot \\ \cdot & \cdot & \cdot & \cdots & & \cdot \\ \cdot & \cdot & \cdot & \cdots & & \cdot \\ \cdot & \cdot & \cdot & \cdots & & \cdot \\ \mathbf{R}\,\mathbf{B}^{N-3}\,\mathbf{S} & \mathbf{R}\,\mathbf{B}^{N-4}\,\mathbf{S} & \mathbf{R}\,\mathbf{B}^{N-5}\,\mathbf{S} & \cdots & a_{11} & -1 \\ \mathbf{R}\,\mathbf{B}^{N-2}\,\mathbf{S} & \mathbf{R}\,\mathbf{B}^{N-3}\,\mathbf{S} & \mathbf{R}\,\mathbf{B}^{N-4}\,\mathbf{S} & \cdots & \mathbf{R}\,\mathbf{S} & a_{11} \end{bmatrix} \qquad (7.2.4.12)$$

be an $(N + 1) \times N$ matrix. Then the above linear relation can be succinctly written as

$$\mathbf{P}_{N+1} = \mathbf{M}_N \mathbf{Q}_N. \qquad (7.2.4.13)$$

By iterating the above process (of expressing the characteristic equation of $\mathbf{A}_N$ in terms of that of $\mathbf{B} = \mathbf{A}_{N-1}$), we readily see that

$$\mathbf{P}_{N+1} = \mathbf{M}_N \mathbf{M}_{N-1} \mathbf{M}_{N-2} \cdots \mathbf{M}_2 \mathbf{M}_1. \qquad (7.2.4.14)$$

The matrix $\mathbf{M}_N$ has a special structure, namely, it has the same element along each diagonal. Such a matrix is called a *Toeplitz* matrix. Properties of this class of matrices and efficient methods of finding their product are discussed in Section 7.2.5.

The formula (7.2.4.14) is the basis for Berkowitz's algorithm for computing the characteristic polynomial and determinant, which is described in Section 7.5.

This method of finding the characteristic polynomial, due to Samuelson, is in sharp contrast with Leverrier's method and Faddeeva and Sominsky's method. In particular, the latter methods require division, but Samuelson's method is division-free. The technical implication of this difference is that for the Leverrier and Faddeeva-Sominsky methods to be applicable, the elements of the matrix must be restricted to *fields* that contain the set of all natural numbers, such as the set of all reals. But the method of Samuelson is applicable to matrices with elements from an arbitrary *commutative ring*. (Refer to Appendix C at the end of the book for the definition of rings and fields.)

7.2.5 Toeplitz Matrices

An $N \times N$ matrix $\mathbf{A} = [a_{ij}]$ of the type

$$\mathbf{A} = \begin{bmatrix} a_1 & b_1 & b_2 & b_3 & \cdots & b_{N-2} & b_{N-1} \\ a_2 & a_1 & b_1 & b_2 & \cdots & b_{N-3} & b_{N-2} \\ a_3 & a_2 & a_1 & b_1 & \cdots & b_{N-4} & b_{N-3} \\ \cdot & \cdot & \cdot & \cdot & & \cdot & \cdot \\ \cdot & \cdot & \cdot & \cdot & & \cdot & \cdot \\ \cdot & \cdot & \cdot & \cdot & & \cdot & \cdot \\ a_{N-1} & a_{N-2} & a_{N-3} & a_{N-4} & \cdots & a_1 & b_1 \\ a_N & a_{N-1} & a_{N-2} & a_{N-3} & \cdots & a_2 & a_1 \end{bmatrix}, \qquad (7.2.5.1)$$

where a_{ij} depends only on $i - j$, is called a *Toeplitz* matrix. Clearly, the elements along each *diagonal* of a Toeplitz matrix are the *same* and there are $2N - 1$ distinct elements, one along each diagonal. (See Exercises 7.3 and 7.4.) In (7.2.5.1), if $b_i = 0$ for $i = 1, \cdots , N - 1$, then $\mathbf{A}$ is called *lower triangular Toeplitz* matrix, that is,

$$\mathbf{A} = \begin{bmatrix} a_0 & 0 & 0 & \cdots & 0 & 0 \\ a_1 & a_0 & 0 & \cdots & 0 & 0 \\ a_2 & a_1 & a_0 & \cdots & 0 & 0 \\ \cdot & \cdot & \cdot & & \cdot & \cdot \\ \cdot & \cdot & \cdot & & \cdot & \cdot \\ \cdot & \cdot & \cdot & & \cdot & \cdot \\ a_{N-2} & a_{N-3} & a_{N-4} & \cdots & a_0 & 0 \\ a_{N-1} & a_{N-2} & a_{N-3} & \cdots & a_1 & a_0 \end{bmatrix}. \qquad (7.2.5.2)$$

Notice that the lower triangular Toeplitz matrix is determined by the elements of its first column.

Let $\mathbf{a} = (a_1, a_2, \cdots, a_N)$. An $N \times N$ matrix $\mathbf{A}$ is called a *circulant* matrix if the first row of $\mathbf{A}$ is the row vector $\mathbf{a}$ and the ith row $2 \le i \le N$ of $\mathbf{A}$ is obtained by $(i-1)^{th}$ right circular shift of its first row. Thus, a circulant matrix $\mathbf{A}$ is of the form

$$\mathbf{A} = \begin{bmatrix} a_1 & a_2\ a_3\ a_4 & \cdots & a_{N-1}\ a_N \\ a_N & a_1\ a_2\ a_3 & \cdots & a_{N-2}\ a_{N-1} \\ a_{N-1} & a_N\ a_1\ a_2 & \cdots & a_{N-3}\ a_{N-2} \\ \cdot & \cdot\ \cdot\ \cdot & & \cdot\ \ \cdot \\ \cdot & \cdot\ \cdot\ \cdot & & \cdot\ \ \cdot \\ \cdot & \cdot\ \cdot\ \cdot & & \cdot\ \ \cdot \\ a_3 & a_4\ a_4\ a_6 & \cdots & a_1\ \ a_2 \\ a_2 & a_3\ a_4\ a_5 & \cdots & a_N\ \ a_1 \end{bmatrix} \cdot \tag{7.2.5.3}$$

A circulant matrix is determined by the N elements of its first row. From the definition, it follows that every circulant matrix is a Toeplitz matrix, but not vice versa.

There is a close relationship between convolution and Toeplitz matrices which is often exploited in deriving efficient algorithms relating to operations on Toeplitz matrices, such as the product of lower triangular Toeplitz matrices, or the product of a Toeplitz matrix and a vector, etc.

Let $\mathbf{a} = (a_1, a_2, \cdots, a_N)^t$ and $\mathbf{b} = (b_1, b_2, \cdots, b_N)^t$ be two vectors. The *convolution* of $\mathbf{a}$ and $\mathbf{b}$ denoted by $CON(\mathbf{a}, \mathbf{b})$ is a vector $\mathbf{c} = (c_1, c_2, \cdots, c_{2N})^t$, where

$$\begin{aligned} c_1 &= a_1 b_1, \\ c_2 &= a_2 b_1 + a_1 b_2, \\ c_3 &= a_3 b_1 + a_2 b_2 + a_1 b_3, \\ &\vdots \\ c_N &= a_N b_1 + a_{N-1} b_2 + \cdots + a_2 b_{N-1} + a_1 b_N, \\ c_{N+1} &= a_N b_2 + a_{N-1} b_3 + \cdots + a_2 b_N, \\ c_{N+2} &= a_N b_3 + a_{N-1} b_4 + \cdots + a_3 b_N, \\ &\vdots \\ c_{2N-1} &= a_N b_N, \\ c_{2N} &= 0. \end{aligned} \tag{7.2.5.4}$$

We refer the reader to Chapter 3, where various definitions of convolutions and efficient ways of computing them using FFT techniques are described. The relation (7.2.5.4) can be succinctly represented in the matrix form as

$$\mathbf{c} = \mathbf{A}\,\mathbf{z}, \tag{7.2.5.5}$$

where, for $N = 4$,

$$\mathbf{A} = \begin{bmatrix} a_1 & 0 & 0 & 0 & 0 & 0 & 0 & 0 \\ a_2 & a_1 & 0 & 0 & 0 & 0 & 0 & 0 \\ a_3 & a_2 & a_1 & 0 & 0 & 0 & 0 & 0 \\ a_4 & a_3 & a_2 & a_1 & 0 & 0 & 0 & 0 \\ 0 & a_4 & a_3 & a_2 & a_1 & 0 & 0 & 0 \\ 0 & 0 & a_4 & a_3 & a_2 & a_1 & 0 & 0 \\ 0 & 0 & 0 & a_4 & a_3 & a_2 & a_1 & 0 \\ 0 & 0 & 0 & 0 & a_4 & a_3 & a_2 & a_1 \end{bmatrix}, \tag{7.2.5.6}$$

$$\mathbf{c} = (c_1, c_2, c_3, c_4, c_5, c_6, c_7, 0)^t,$$

and

$$\mathbf{z} = (b_1, b_2, b_3, b_4, 0, 0, 0, 0)^t. \tag{7.2.5.7}$$

Generalizing this, it can be seen that convolution of two vectors $\mathbf{a}$ and $\mathbf{b}$ of size N can be expressed as the product of a lower triangular (banded) Toeplitz matrix (depending only on vector $\mathbf{a}$) of order $2N$ and a vector (depending only on vector $\mathbf{b}$) of size $2N$.

Conversely, consider the problem of computing $\mathbf{d} = \mathbf{A}\mathbf{x}$, where $\mathbf{A}$ is a Toeplitz matrix of order N, $\mathbf{d} = (d_1, d_2, \cdots, d_N)^t$, and $\mathbf{x} = (x_1, x_2, \cdots, x_N)^t$. We illustrate the process of recasting this problem as a convolution problem by an example with $N = 4$. The generalization is rather obvious and is left as an exercise. Let

$$\mathbf{A} = \begin{bmatrix} 2a_1 & b_1 & b_2 & b_3 \\ a_2 & 2a_1 & b_1 & b_2 \\ a_3 & a_2 & 2a_1 & b_1 \\ a_4 & a_3 & a_2 & 2a_1 \end{bmatrix}.$$

Then

$$\begin{aligned} d_1 &= 2a_1 x_1 + b_1 x_2 + b_2 x_3 + b_3 x_4, \\ d_2 &= a_2 x_1 + 2a_1 x_2 + b_1 x_3 + b_2 x_4, \\ d3 &= a_3 x_1 + a_2 x_2 + 2a_1 x_3 + b_1 x_4, \\ d4 &= a_4 x_1 + a_3 x_2 + a_2 x_3 + 2a_1 x_4. \end{aligned} \right\} \tag{7.2.5.8}$$

First express $\mathbf{A}$ as the sum of lower and upper triangular Toeplitz matrices as follows.

$$A = L + U, \tag{7.2.5.9}$$

where

$$L = \begin{bmatrix} a_1 & 0 & 0 & 0 \\ a_2 & a_1 & 0 & 0 \\ a_3 & a_2 & a_1 & 0 \\ a_4 & a_3 & a_2 & a_1 \end{bmatrix}, \tag{7.2.5.10}$$

$$U = \begin{bmatrix} a_1 & b_1 & b_2 & b_3 \\ 0 & a_1 & b_1 & b_2 \\ 0 & 0 & a_1 & b_1 \\ 0 & 0 & 0 & a_1 \end{bmatrix}. \tag{7.2.5.11}$$

Let $\mathbf{g} = (g_1, g_2, g_3, g_4)^t$ and $\mathbf{h} = (h_1, h_2, h_3, h_4)^t$, where $\mathbf{g} = \mathbf{L}\mathbf{x}$ and $\mathbf{h} = \mathbf{U}\mathbf{x}$. Then $\mathbf{d} = \mathbf{g} + \mathbf{h}$. Since the computations of $\mathbf{g}$ and $\mathbf{h}$ are similar, we describe only that of $\mathbf{g}$. Comparing

$$
\left.
\begin{aligned}
g_1 &= a_1 x_1 \\
g_2 &= a_2 x_1 + a_1 x_2 \\
g_3 &= a_3 x_1 + a_2 x_2 + a_1 x_3 \\
g_4 &= a_4 x_1 + a_3 x_2 + a_2 x_3 + a_1 x_4.
\end{aligned}
\right\} \tag{7.2.5.12}
$$

with (7.2.5.4), it follows that $\mathbf{g}$ can be obtained as the first half of $CON(\mathbf{a}, \mathbf{x})$, where $\mathbf{a} = (a_1, a_2, a_3, a_4)^t$ and $\mathbf{x} = (x_1, x_2, x_3, x_4)$. For future reference, the above analysis is summarized in the following property.

Property 7.2.5.1. Computing the product $\mathbf{A}\mathbf{x}$ of an $N \times N$ Toeplitz matrix $\mathbf{A}$ with an N-vector $\mathbf{x}$ is equivalent to computing the convolution of properly chosen vectors. Since the latter can be accomplished in parallel in $O(\log N)$ steps and $O(N \log N)$ operations using FFT techniques (refer to Chapter 3 for details), it follows that the product of a Toeplitz matrix and a vector can be found in $O(\log N)$ steps as well.

In Exercise 7.37, another method based on the simple divide-and-conquer strategy is outlined. We leave it to the reader to compare these two methods.

We now consider the problem of computing the product of two lower triangular Toeplitz matrices. Again, we illustrate the basic idea by an example, which can be readily generalized. Let

$$A = \begin{bmatrix} a_1 & 0 & 0 & 0 \\ a_2 & a_1 & 0 & 0 \\ a_3 & a_2 & a_1 & 0 \\ a_4 & a_3 & a_2 & a_1 \end{bmatrix},$$

and

$$B = \begin{bmatrix} b_1 & 0 & 0 & 0 \\ b_2 & b_1 & 0 & 0 \\ b_3 & b_2 & b_1 & 0 \\ b_4 & b_3 & b_2 & b_1 \end{bmatrix}.$$

If $C = AB$, then

$$C = \begin{bmatrix} c_1 & 0 & 0 & 0 \\ c_2 & c_1 & 0 & 0 \\ c_3 & c_2 & c_1 & 0 \\ c_4 & c_3 & c_2 & c_1 \end{bmatrix},$$

where

$$c_1 = a_1 b_1,$$
$$c_2 = a_2 b_1 + a_1 b_2,$$
$$c_3 = a_3 b_1 + a_2 b_2 + a_1 b_3,$$
$$c_4 = a_4 b_1 + a_3 b_2 + a_2 b_3 + a_1 b_4.$$

Comparing this with (7.2.5.4), it follows that the first column of the product matrix C (which uniquely determines it) corresponds to the first N components of the vector $CON(\mathbf{a}, \mathbf{b})$, where $\mathbf{a}$ and $\mathbf{b}$ correspond to the first column of the matrices A and B, respectively.

Property 7.2.5.2. The product of two $N \times N$ lower triangular Toeplitz matrices can be obtained in parallel in $O(\log N)$ steps and $O(N \log N)$ operations.

The definition of the Toeplitz matrix can be extended to rectangular matrices. In an $N \times M$ matrix, the diagonal corresponding to the elements a_{ii}, $i = 1$ to min $\{N, M\}$, is known as the principal or the main diagonal. An $N \times M$ matrix $A = [a_{ij}]$ is a Toeplitz matrix if

$$a_{ij} = a_{i-l+1, j-l+1}, \tag{7.2.5.13}$$

where $l = \min\{i, j\}$. An example of a 5×4 Toeplitz matrix is

$$A = \begin{bmatrix} a_1 & b_1 & b_2 & b_3 \\ a_2 & a_1 & b_1 & b_2 \\ a_3 & a_2 & a_1 & b_1 \\ a_4 & a_3 & a_2 & a_1 \\ a_5 & a_4 & a_3 & a_2 \end{bmatrix}. \qquad (7.2.5.14)$$

The matrix M_N in (7.2.4.12) is another example of a rectangular Toeplitz matrix. The notion of the lower triangular Toeplitz matrix can likewise be extended as follows. An $N \times M$ matrix A is a lower triangular Toeplitz matrix if in addition to (7.2.5.13)

$$a_{ij} = 0 \text{ for } i < j. \qquad (7.2.5.15)$$

In (7.2.5.14), if $b_i = 0$ for $1 \le i \le 3$, then it becomes a lower triangular Toeplitz matrix.

The product of two lower triangular Toeplitz matrices $A_{N \times M}$ and $B_{M \times K}$ is lower triangular but *not* necessarily Toeplitz.

The following property (whose proof is left as Exercise 7.38) is useful in Section 7.5.

Property 7.2.5.3. The product of two $N \times M$ and $M \times K$ Toeplitz matrices, where $N > M > K$, can be obtained in $O(\log N)$ steps requiring $O(N^2)$ operations.

7.2.6 Householder's Transformation

Two types of orthogonal transformations, known as Householder and Givens transformations, have found extensive use in matrix computations. In this section, we briefly discuss the structure and the use of Householder's transformation. Givens transformations are described in Section 6.4.

Let $a = (a_1, a_2, \cdots, a_N)^t$, and define H to be an $N \times N$ matrix of the form

$$H = I - \frac{2aa^t}{a^t a}. \qquad (7.2.6.1)$$

This matrix H is called Householder's transformation. It is easily verified that H is symmetric and $H^t H = H^2 = I$, that is, H is also orthogonal.

Let $x = (x_1, x_2, \cdots, x_N)^t$ be given, and e_1 be the first unit vector. Choose the vector a to be of the form

$$a = x + \alpha e_1, \qquad (7.2.6.2)$$

for some constant $\alpha \ne 0$. From

$$\mathbf{Hx} = \mathbf{x} - \frac{2\mathbf{aa}^t}{\mathbf{a}^t\mathbf{a}}\mathbf{x}$$

$$= \mathbf{x} - \frac{2\mathbf{a}^t\mathbf{x}}{\mathbf{a}^t\mathbf{a}}\mathbf{a}$$

$$= (\mathbf{x} - \frac{2\mathbf{a}^t\mathbf{x}}{\mathbf{a}^t\mathbf{a}}\mathbf{x}) - \frac{2\mathbf{a}^t\mathbf{x}}{\mathbf{a}^t\mathbf{a}}\alpha\mathbf{e}_1$$

it can be seen that

$$\mathbf{Hx} = -\alpha\mathbf{e}_1 \qquad (7.2.6.3)$$

if

$$\alpha^2 = \mathbf{x}^t\mathbf{x} = \| \mathbf{x} \|_2^2. \qquad (7.2.6.4)$$

That is, if we choose $\mathbf{a}$ as in (7.2.6.2), then the effect of multiplying $\mathbf{x}$ by the matrix $\mathbf{H}$ is to annihilate all the elements from x_2 to x_N.

As an example, let $\mathbf{x} = (1, 1, 3, 5)^t$. Then $\alpha = 6$, $\mathbf{a} = (7, 1, 3, 5)$, $\mathbf{a}^t\mathbf{a} = 84$,

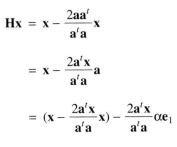

$$\mathbf{H} = \frac{1}{42}\begin{bmatrix} -7 & -7 & -21 & -35 \\ -7 & 41 & -3 & -5 \\ -21 & -3 & 33 & -15 \\ -35 & -5 & -15 & 17 \end{bmatrix},$$

and $\mathbf{Hx} = (-6, 0, 0, 0)^t$.

In practice, if $\mathbf{x}$ is close to a multiple of $\mathbf{e}_1$, then it could happen that $\mathbf{a}^t\mathbf{a}$ is very small and division by $\mathbf{a}^t\mathbf{a}$ could lead to an overflow problem. To avoid such a situation, it is a good practice to choose the vector $\mathbf{a}$,

$$\mathbf{a} = \mathbf{x} + sign(x_1)\,\|\mathbf{x}\|_2\mathbf{e}_1. \qquad (7.2.6.5)$$

By proper choice of $\mathbf{H}$, we can even selectively annihilate any contiguous set of elements of a vector. Let $1 \le r \le s \le N$. Define

$$\mathbf{a} = (0, 0, \cdots, 0, \bar{x}_r, x_{r+1}, \cdots, x_s, 0, 0, \cdots, 0)^t,$$

where

$$\bar{x}_r = x_r + sign(x_r)\,\alpha$$

and

$$\alpha^2 = x_r^2 + x_{r+1}^2 + \cdots + x_s^2.$$

Let

$$\mathbf{H} = \mathbf{I} - \frac{2\mathbf{aa}^t}{\mathbf{a}^t\mathbf{a}}$$

be of the form

$$H = \begin{bmatrix} I_{r-1} & 0 & 0 \\ 0 & \overline{H} & 0 \\ 0 & 0 & I_{N-s} \end{bmatrix},$$

and $\overline{H}$ is the Householder matrix of size $s - r + 1$, where

$$\overline{H} = I_{s-r+1} - \frac{2\mathbf{b}\mathbf{b}^t}{\mathbf{b}^t\mathbf{b}}$$

and

$$\mathbf{b} = (\overline{x}_r, x_{r+1}, \cdots, x_s).$$

It can be easily verified that $\mathbf{Hx}$ has the form

$$(x_1, x_2, \cdots, x_{r-1}, -sign(x_r)\alpha, 0, \cdots, 0, x_{s+1}, \cdots, x_N)^t.$$

Householder's transformations are often used to convert the matrix $\mathbf{A}$ into a prespecified shape, such as a Hessenberg form, triangular form, or tridiagonal form. Given the matrix $\mathbf{A}$, design the matrix $\mathbf{H}_1$ so as to annihilate the elements a_{31} through a_{N1}, that is, in

$$\mathbf{A}_1 = \mathbf{H}_1\mathbf{A}\mathbf{H}_1,$$

all but the first two elements of the first column are zero, where

$$\mathbf{H}_1 = \mathbf{I} - \frac{2\mathbf{b}_1\mathbf{b}_1^t}{\mathbf{b}_1^t\mathbf{b}_1}, \qquad (7.2.6.6)$$

$$\mathbf{b}_1 = (0, \overline{a}_{21}, a_{31}, a_{41}, \cdots, a_{N1})^t,$$

and

$$\overline{a}_{21} = a_{21} + sign(a_{21})\alpha$$

$$\alpha^2 = a_{21}^2 + a_{31}^2 + \cdots + a_{N1}^2.$$

Now, choose $\mathbf{H}_2$ in such a way that it further annihilates all but the first three elements of the second column of $\mathbf{A}_1$ to get

$$\mathbf{A}_2 = \mathbf{H}_2\mathbf{A}_1\mathbf{H}_2.$$

Continuing in this way (Exercise 7.5), we obtain a matrix

$$\mathbf{A}_{N-2} = \mathbf{H}_{N-2} \cdots \mathbf{H}_2\mathbf{H}_1\mathbf{A}\mathbf{H}_1\mathbf{H}_2 \cdots \mathbf{H}_{N-2}, \qquad (7.2.6.7)$$

which has all zero elements below the first subdiagonal, that is, $\mathbf{A}_{N-2}$ is of the form

$$
\mathbf{A}_{N-2} =
\begin{bmatrix}
\times & \times & \times & \cdots & \times & \times & \times \\
\times & \times & \times & \cdots & \times & \times & \times \\
0 & \times & \times & \cdots & \times & \times & \times \\
0 & 0 & \times & \cdots & \times & \times & \times \\
\cdot & \cdot & \cdot & \cdots & \cdot & \cdot & \cdot \\
\cdot & \cdot & \cdot & \cdots & \cdot & \cdot & \cdot \\
\cdot & \cdot & \cdot & \cdots & \cdot & \cdot & \cdot \\
0 & 0 & 0 & \cdots & \times & \times & \times \\
0 & 0 & 0 & \cdots & 0 & \times & \times
\end{bmatrix},
$$

where $\times$ refers to the non-zero elements (Exercise 7.7).

If **A** is symmetric, then it be easily verified (Exercises 7.8, 7.9, and 7.11) that

$$
\mathbf{B} = \mathbf{Q}^t \mathbf{A} \mathbf{Q} \tag{7.2.6.8}
$$

is symmetric and tridiagonal, where

$$
\mathbf{Q} = \mathbf{H}_1 \mathbf{H}_2 \mathbf{H}_3 \cdots \mathbf{H}_{N-2}. \tag{7.2.6.9}
$$

Since **Q** is orthogonal, matrices **A** and **B** have the same set of eigenvalues. Parallel methods for computing the eigenvalues of a symmetric tridiagonal matrix are pursued in Section 7.7.

7.3 PRODUCTS AND POWERS OF MATRICES

7.3.1 A Classical Approach -- Real Matrices

Let $\mathbf{A} = [\, a_{ij}\,]$ and $\mathbf{B} = [\, b_{ij}\,]$ be two $N \times N$ matrices. Let $\mathbf{C} = \mathbf{AB} = [\, c_{ij}\,]$, where

$$
c_{ij} = \sum_{k=1}^{N} a_{ik}\, b_{kj}. \tag{7.3.1.1}
$$

This inner product defining c_{ij} can be computed in $1 + \lceil \log N \rceil$ steps with N processors using the *associative fan-in* algorithm (Chapter 1). Hence, the entire product matrix **C** can be computed in $O(\log N)$ steps using $O(N^3)$ processors. The total number of scalar operations performed in this process is $O(N^3)$. (See Exercise 7.13.)

A method based on Winograd's identity that reduces the number of multiplications needed in multiplying two matrices by 50% is pursued in Exercise 7.12.

The product matrix **C** can still be found in $O(\log N)$ steps (with a slightly larger coefficient) using only $O\!\left[\dfrac{N^3}{\log N}\right]$ processors. This can be accomplished by computing the inner products, namely c_{ij}'s, in $O(\log N)$ steps using only $O(\dfrac{N}{\log N})$ processors. Refer to Chapter 1 for details.

Now to compute $\mathbf{A}^i$, $i = 1, \cdots, N$, where $2^{k-1} < N \leq 2^k$, use the algorithm given in Fig. 7.3.1.1. In this algorithm, in stage i, $\mathbf{A}^{2^{i-1}+1}, \cdots, \mathbf{A}^{\min(2^i, N)}$ are computed in parallel. Clearly, in stage i, for $1 \leq i < k$, 2^{i-1} independent matrix products are computed. Thus, using $2^{i-1} N^3$ processors, all the powers in stage i can be computed in $1 + \lceil \log N \rceil$ steps. Again, stage k takes only $O(\log N)$ steps using $[\min(N, 2^k) - 2^{k-1}] N^3$ processors. Since $N \leq 2^k$, it follows that the entire algorithm takes $O((\log N)^2)$ steps, using at most $N^4/2$ processors. The total number of scalar operations performed in this process is $O(N^4)$. (See Exercise 7.34.) Again the processor count can be reduced to $O\left\lceil \dfrac{N^4}{\log N} \right\rceil$, while maintaining the overall number of steps to be $O((\log N)^2)$ by performing the inner products in $O(\log N)$ steps, using only $O(\dfrac{N}{\log N})$ processors.

/* Given $\mathbf{A}$ and $2^{k-1} < N \leq 2^k$, compute $\mathbf{A}^i$, $i = 1, \cdots, N$. */

FOR $i = 1$ TO k STEP 1 DO
    FOR $j \in \{ 2^{i-1} + 1, 2^{i-1} + 2, \cdots, \min(2^i, N) \}$ DO IN PARALLEL
        COMPUTE $\mathbf{A}^j$
    END
END

FIGURE 7.3.1.1
Computing the powers of $\mathbf{A}$.

7.3.2 A Faster Matrix Multiplication -- Complex Matrices

Let $x = a + ib$ and $y = c + id$, where $i = \sqrt{-1}$, be two complex numbers. The conventional method of computing the product

$$xy = (ac - bd) + i(ad + bc) \tag{7.3.2.1}$$

requires *four* (real) multiplications and *two* (real) additions. However, it is well known (Chapter 3, Exercise 3.14; see also Exercise 7.17) that the product xy can be computed using *three* (real) multiplications and *five* (real) additions, either as

$$xy = [a(c-d)+(a-b)d]+i[b(c+d)+(a-b)d] \qquad \textbf{(7.3.2.2)}$$

or as

$$xy = [(a-b)c+b(c-d)]+i[(a+b)d+b(c-d)]. \qquad (7.3.2.3)$$

Thus, in situations where multiplication is far too expensive compared to addition, these latter forms for computing xy may prove economical. For example, if r is the ratio of the time to multiply two real numbers to that of addition, and if $r > 3$, clearly (7.3.2.2) or (7.3.2.3) provides a faster scheme.

Another important property of (7.3.2.2) and (7.3.2.3) is that it does *not* require *commutativity* of the *product* operation. This immediately suggests that either of these two new forms can be adopted for computing the product of complex matrices. Based on this observation, very recently, Fam [1988] described a faster algorithm to compute complex matrix products.

Let $\mathbf{X} = \mathbf{A}+i\mathbf{B}$ and $\mathbf{Y} = \mathbf{C}+i\mathbf{D}$ be two complex matrices of size $N \times M$ and $M \times K$, respectively. Let $\mathbf{Z} = \mathbf{XY} = \mathbf{E}+i\mathbf{F}$. The conventional method in (7.3.2.1), when applied to computing $\mathbf{Z}$, involves first computing the partial products $\mathbf{AC}, \mathbf{BD}, \mathbf{AD}$, and $\mathbf{BC}$. These computations involve $4NMK$ multiplications and $4NK(M-1)$ additions. Then, computing

$$\mathbf{E} = \mathbf{AC}-\mathbf{BD} \quad \text{and} \quad \mathbf{F} = \mathbf{AD}+\mathbf{BC}$$

requires $2NK$ additions. When expressed in equivalent additions, this method requires

$$T_1 = 4NMK(1+r)-2NK \qquad (7.3.2.4)$$

real additions.

Now, let us analyze the time to compute $\mathbf{Z}$ using (7.3.2.2). In this case, first computing $(\mathbf{C}-\mathbf{D}), (\mathbf{A}-\mathbf{B})$, and $(\mathbf{C}+\mathbf{D})$ requires $2MK+NM$ additions. Computing the products $\mathbf{A}(\mathbf{C}-\mathbf{D}), (\mathbf{A}-\mathbf{B})\mathbf{D}$, and $\mathbf{B}(\mathbf{C}+\mathbf{D})$ requires $3NMK$ multiplications and $3NK(M-1)$ additions. Finally, computing

$$\left. \begin{array}{l} \mathbf{E} = \mathbf{A}(\mathbf{C}-\mathbf{D})+(\mathbf{A}-\mathbf{B})\mathbf{D} \\ \mathbf{F} = \mathbf{B}(\mathbf{C}+\mathbf{D})+(\mathbf{A}-\mathbf{B})\mathbf{D} \end{array} \right\} \qquad (7.3.2.5)$$

requires $2NK$ additions. In all, the total number of equivalent additions turns out to be

$$T_2 = 3NMK(1+r)+2MK+N(M-K). \qquad (7.3.2.6)$$

Likewise, using (7.3.2.3), the product $\mathbf{Z}$ can be computed in

$$T_3 = 3NMK(1+r)+2NM+K(M-N) \qquad (7.3.2.7)$$

equivalent additions. Define $T_4 = \min\{T_2, T_3\}$, then

$$T_4 = 3NMK(1+r)-NK+MK+NM+M\min\{N, K\}. \qquad (7.3.2.8)$$

To quantify the saving in time, let us compute the ratio of T_4 to T_1, when $N = M = K$, that is, $\mathbf{X}$ and $\mathbf{Y}$ are complex matrices of order N. Clearly,

$$\frac{T_4}{T_1} = \frac{3N^3(1+r)+2N^2}{4N^3(1+r)-2N^2}$$

$$= \frac{3N(1+r)+2}{4N(1+r)-2}$$

$$\approx \frac{3}{4} \quad \text{as } N \to \infty, \text{ for any } r.$$

Sample values of this ratio for $1 \leq r \leq 10$ and small values of N are given in Table 7.3.2.1. There is a measurable saving in time for $N \geq 3$ even when $r = 1$, and for large N we can net nearly 25% saving in time.

Combining Fam's method with Winograd's method for multiplying matrices described in Exercise 7.12, we can design a *hybrid* algorithm that further speeds up the process of multiplying complex matrices. More specifically, we can compute the matrix product defining E and F in (7.3.2.5) using Winograd's identity. Assuming that A, B, C, and D are all $N \times N$ matrices, where N is even, the computation of $(C - D)$, $(C + D)$, and $(A + B)$ takes $3N^2$ additions. The products $A(C - D)$, $B(C + D)$, and $(A - B)D$ can be computed (using the method in Exercise 7.12) in $3(\frac{N^3}{2} + N^2)$ multiplications and $3(\frac{3}{2}N^3 + 2N(N-1))$ additions. Finally, computing E and F from these products requires an additional $2N^2$ additions. Thus,

---

TABLE 7.3.2.1

r	N					
	1	4	10	25	50	100
1	1.333	0.8667	0.7949	0.7677	0.7588	0.7544
2	1.100	0.8261	0.7797	0.7617	0.7559	0.7529
3	1.000	0.8065	0.7722	0.7588	0.7544	0.7521
4	0.9444	0.7949	0.7677	0.7570	0.7535	0.7516
5	0.9091	0.7872	0.7647	0.7559	0.7529	0.7515
6	0.8846	0.7818	0.7626	0.7550	0.7535	0.7511
7	0.8667	0.7778	0.7610	0.7544	0.7522	0.7510
8	0.8529	0.7747	0.7598	0.7539	0.7519	0.7509
9	0.8421	0.7722	0.7588	0.7535	0.7518	0.7508
10	0.8333	0.7701	0.7580	0.7531	0.7516	0.7507

in all, this hybrid scheme needs

$$T_5 = N^3(1.5r + 4.5) + N^2(3r + 11) - 6N$$

equivalent additions. The ratio

$$\frac{T_5}{T_1} \approx \frac{N(1.5r + 4.5) + (3r + 11)}{4N(1 + r) - 2}$$

$$\approx \frac{3r + 9}{8r + 8}, \quad \text{as } N \to \infty.$$

Thus, when $r = 2$, the saving can be as large as 37.5% for large N. Typical values of this ratio for various r and N (even) are given in Table 7.3.2.2.

The reader is encouraged to benchmark the performance of the method in (7.3.2.1) and compare it with that in (7.3.2.2) for computing the product of complex matrices on multivector machines such as the Alliant FX/8 as well as on hypercube-based architectures. This method can also be combined with the algorithm in Fig. 7.3.1.1 to compute the powers of a complex matrix.

TABLE 7.3.2.2

r	N				
	4	10	20	50	100
1	1.2667	0.9487	0.8481	0.7889	0.7694
2	1.0217	0.7797	0.7017	0.6555	0.6402
3	0.9032	0.6962	0.6289	0.5889	0.5757
4	0.8333	0.6465	0.5854	0.5491	0.5370
5	0.7872	0.6134	0.5565	0.5225	0.5113
6	0.7545	0.5899	0.5358	0.5036	0.4929
7	0.7301	0.5723	0.5204	0.4894	0.4791
8	0.7113	0.5587	0.5083	0.4783	0.4683
9	0.6962	0.5477	0.4987	0.4695	0.4597
10	0.6839	0.5388	0.4909	0.4622	0.4527

7.3.3 Strassen's Matrix Multiplication Algorithm -- Real Matrices

In 1969, Strassen announced a new method for multiplying matrices which, as a serial algorithm for large N, is considerably faster than the conventional algorithm.

We begin by describing the method for 2×2 matrices. Let

$$\mathbf{A} = \begin{bmatrix} \mathbf{A}_{11} & \mathbf{A}_{12} \\ \mathbf{A}_{21} & \mathbf{A}_{22} \end{bmatrix}, \qquad \mathbf{B} = \begin{bmatrix} \mathbf{B}_{11} & \mathbf{B}_{12} \\ \mathbf{B}_{21} & \mathbf{B}_{22} \end{bmatrix},$$

and

$$\mathbf{C} = \begin{bmatrix} \mathbf{C}_{11} & \mathbf{C}_{12} \\ \mathbf{C}_{21} & \mathbf{C}_{22} \end{bmatrix},$$

where $\mathbf{C} = \mathbf{A}\mathbf{B}$. To compute $\mathbf{C}$, first compute seven intermediate quantities as follows:

$$\left.\begin{aligned} \mathbf{X}_1 &= (\mathbf{A}_{11} + \mathbf{A}_{22})(\mathbf{B}_{11} + \mathbf{B}_{22}) \\ \mathbf{X}_2 &= (\mathbf{A}_{21} + \mathbf{A}_{22})\mathbf{B}_{11} \\ \mathbf{X}_3 &= \mathbf{A}_{11}(\mathbf{B}_{12} - \mathbf{B}_{22}) \\ \mathbf{X}_4 &= \mathbf{A}_{22}(\mathbf{B}_{21} - \mathbf{B}_{11}) \\ \mathbf{X}_5 &= (\mathbf{A}_{11} + \mathbf{A}_{12})\mathbf{B}_{22} \\ \mathbf{X}_6 &= (\mathbf{A}_{21} - \mathbf{A}_{11})(\mathbf{B}_{11} + \mathbf{B}_{12}) \\ \mathbf{X}_7 &= (\mathbf{A}_{12} - \mathbf{A}_{22})(\mathbf{B}_{21} + \mathbf{B}_{22}). \end{aligned}\right\} \qquad (7.3.3.1)$$

Then,

$$\left.\begin{aligned} \mathbf{C}_{11} &= \mathbf{X}_1 + \mathbf{X}_4 - \mathbf{X}_5 + \mathbf{X}_7 \\ \mathbf{C}_{12} &= \mathbf{X}_3 + \mathbf{X}_5 \\ \mathbf{C}_{21} &= \mathbf{X}_2 + \mathbf{X}_4 \\ \mathbf{C}_{22} &= \mathbf{X}_1 + \mathbf{X}_3 - \mathbf{X}_2 + \mathbf{X}_6. \end{aligned}\right\} \qquad (7.3.3.2)$$

Notice that the multiplication operation is confined to computing the intermediate quantities $\mathbf{X}_i$, $i = 1$ to 7. Thus, in all, there are *seven* multiplications and *eighteen* additions/subtractions. The conventional algorithm, however, requires eight multiplications and four additions. Thus, Strassen's algorithm trades *one* multiplication for *fourteen* additions. The real benefit of this approach lies in applying this technique recursively to large matrices. As a first step toward such an extension, observe that the validity of the computations in (7.3.3.1) does *not* require the *commutativity* of the multiplication operation. Consequently, we can use the same algorithm when the $\mathbf{A}_{ij}$ and $\mathbf{B}_{ij}$ elements are themselves matrices.

Consider the case when both $\mathbf{A}$ and $\mathbf{B}$ are $N \times N$ matrices for some $N = 2^n$, $n \geq 2$. Partition $\mathbf{A}$ and $\mathbf{B}$ into 2×2 matrices, where the submatrices $\mathbf{A}_{ij}$ and $\mathbf{B}_{ij}$ for $1 \leq i, j \leq 2$ are of order $\dfrac{N}{2}$. Let $T_m(N)$ and $T_a(N)$ be the total number of multiplications and additions required by this algorithm. From (7.3.3.1), since there are *seven* multiplications of matrices of order $\frac{N}{2}$,

$$T_m(N) = 7T_m(\frac{N}{2}),$$
(7.3.3.3)

where $T_m(2) = 7$. Solving this, we obtain

$$T_m(N) = 7^n = N^{\log_2 7} \leq N^{2.808}.$$
(7.3.3.4)

To quantify the total number of additions, observe that there are 18 *explicit* additions of matrices of order $\frac{N}{2}$ arising from (7.3.3.1) and (7.3.3.2). Further, each of the seven multiplications of matrices involve (implicit) additions. Combining these,

$$T_a(N) = 7T_a(\frac{N}{2}) + 18(\frac{N}{2})^2,$$
(7.3.3.5)

where $T_a(1) = 0$. Solving this, we obtain

$$T_a(N) = 6[7^n - 4^n].$$
(7.3.3.6)

If $T(N)$ is the total count on the number of basic operations, then

$$T(N) = T_m(N) + T_a(N)$$

$$= 7^{n+1} - 6 \times 4^n$$

$$< 7N^{2.808}.$$
(7.3.3.7)

The conventional algorithm requires N^3 multiplications and $N^2(N-1)$ additions, which is a total of $2N^3 - N^2$.

From Table 7.3.3.1, it is clear that for $N \geq 1024$, Strassen's method requires fewer operations than the classical approach. A modified Strassen's method requiring seven multiplications and 15 additions/subtractions is given in Exercise 7.35.

Thus, using a Strassen-like method, we can multiply two $N \times N$ matrices in $O(N^\alpha)$ steps serially, where $\alpha \leq 2.808$. Strassen's method has been improved by a number of authors. Recently, Strassen [1986] improved this by showing that $\alpha < 2.479$, and Coppersmith and Winograd improved it further to $\alpha < 2.376$. These improvements are based on the analysis of the multiplicative complexity of *non-commutative* algorithms for computing bilinear forms. Explicit coverage of this class of algorithm is beyond the scope of this book, and we refer the reader to an excellent monograph by Pan [1984].

We now estimate the parallel time required to evaluate the product of matrices by Strassen's method. Referring to (7.3.3.1), it is clear that in computing X_1, the matrix sums $(A_{11} + A_{22})$ and $(B_{11} + B_{22})$ can be computed in parallel in *one* step using sufficiently many processors. Likewise, all the addition operations involved in the computation of X_i's, $i = 1$ to 7 in (7.3.3.1) can be computed in one step under

TABLE 7.3.3.1

$N = 2^n$	$7^{n+1} - 6 \times 4^n$	$2N^3 - N^2$
2	25	12
4	247	112
8	2,017	960
16	15,271	7,936
32	111,505	64,512
64	798,967	520,192
128	5,666,497	4,177,920
256	3.996×10^7	3.349×10^7
512	2.809×10^8	2.682×10^8
1,024	1.971×10^9	2.146×10^9

unlimited parallelism.

Assuming that the X_i's are available, C_{11} can be computed using (7.3.3.2) in two steps -- computing $(X_1 + X_4)$ and $(X_5 - X_7)$ in parallel in the first step, and in the second step computing the difference $(X_1 + X_4) - (X_5 - X_7)$. It is readily seen that all the other C_{ij}'s can also be computed in at most two steps.

Combining these, it follows that it takes a total of *three* (addition) steps. If $T(N)$ is the parallel time to compute the product using (7.3.3.1) and (7.3.3.2) under unlimited parallelism, then from the above analysis it follows that

$$T(N) = T(\frac{N}{2}) + 3, \tag{7.3.3.8}$$

where $T(1) = 1$. Solving this, we find that

$$T(N) = 1 + 3 \log_2 N = O(\log N). \tag{7.3.3.9}$$

We now summarize the above discussion in the following theorem.

Theorem 7.3.3.1. The product of two $N \times N$ matrices can be computed in

(a) $O(\log N)$ steps requiring $O(N^3)$ operations using the *conventional* method, and

(b) $O(\log N)$ steps requiring $O(N^\alpha)$ operations for $\alpha < 2.376$ using Coppersmith and Winograd's [1987] method.

Computing the minimum number of processors needed to achieve these bounds in either case is left as an exercise. The following corollary provides an asymptotically faster method for computing the first N powers of an $N \times N$ matrix.

Corollary 7.3.3.2. The first N powers of a matrix can be computed in $O((\log N)^2)$ steps requiring only $O(N^{1+\alpha})$ operations.

7.3.4 Strassen's Matrix Multiplication Algorithm -- Boolean Case

Let $\mathbf{A} = [a_{ij}]$ and $\mathbf{B} = [b_{ij}]$ be two $N \times N$ Boolean matrices for some $N = 2^n$, $n \geq 1$. Let $\mathbf{C} = \mathbf{A}\mathbf{B}$, where

$$c_{ij} = \bigvee_{k=1}^{N} (a_{ik} \wedge b_{kj}). \qquad (7.3.4.1)$$

Strassen's algorithm cannot be applied as such to this case since there is no analog of subtraction in the Boolean case. To circumvent this, first compute $\mathbf{C}^* = \mathbf{A}\mathbf{B}$ by considering $\mathbf{A}$ and $\mathbf{B}$ as integer matrices with entries restricted to 0 and 1. That is,

$$c_{ij}^* = \sum_{k=1}^{N} a_{ik} b_{kj} \qquad (7.3.4.2)$$

is an integer in the range

$$0 \leq c_{ij}^* \leq N. \qquad (7.3.4.3)$$

Now combining (7.3.4.1) and (7.3.4.3), it follows that

$$c_{ij} = 0 \text{ if and only if } c_{ij}^* = 0. \qquad (7.3.4.4)$$

To estimate how long it takes to compute c_{ij}'s using (7.3.4.4), we need to analyze the binary representation of c_{ij}^*. To this end, let $m = N + 1$. Since $0 \leq c_{ij}^* \leq N$, we can compute c_{ij}^* exactly if the integer arithmetic in (7.3.4.2) is performed with respect to modulus m. Thus, the integers involved are at most $M = 1 + \log N$ bits long. If $c_{ij}^* = x_M x_{M-1} \cdots x_2 x_1$, then from (7.3.4.4) it follows that

$$c_{ij} = x_M \vee x_{M-1} \vee \cdots \vee x_2 \vee x_1, \qquad (7.3.4.5)$$

which takes $\log M = O(\log \log N)$ steps to compute.

Summarizing this development, we obtain the following theorem.

Theorem 7.3.4.1. The product of two $N \times N$ Boolean matrices can be computed by a Boolean circuit of depth $O(\log N)$ and size $O(N^{\alpha} M \log M \log \log M)$ where $2 < \alpha < 2.376$ and $M = 1 + \log N$.

Proof

The claim on the depth follows by combining (7.3.4.5) with Theorem 7.3.3.1. To quantify the size, recall from Theorem 7.3.3.1 that it takes $O(N^\alpha)$ arithmetic operations to compute $\mathbf{C}^* = [\,c_{ij}^*\,]$, where the arithmetic operations involve multiplication and addition/subtraction of M-bit integers.

It is shown in Chapter 3 that the size of a (near) optimal depth *adder* is at most $M \log M$ and that of the Schonhage and Strassen *multiplier* is at most $O(M \log M \log \log M)$. Thus computing the matrix $\mathbf{C}^*$ requires a size of $O(N^\alpha M \log M \log \log M)$.

Computing c_{ij} from c_{ij}^* using (7.3.4.5) requires $N^2(M-1)$ gates. Since $\alpha > 2$, combining these, the theorem follows.

7.3.5 Speed *vs.* Numerical Stability

In this section we digress to discuss the effect of speed-up on the *quality* of the (numerical) results. The quality of a result is measured in at least two different ways: one is the classical approach, often used in numerical analysis, of bounding a suitable "norm" of the cumulative error, and the other approach is that of computing the sensitivity of the output with respect to the floating point round-off error introduced in each step. Using this second approach, the ensuing analysis shows that the faster algorithms are *not* always numerically stable with respect to certain measures of stability.

We begin by introducing the concept of a polynomial program which is a sequence of instructions of the type

$$V_i = x \circ y,$$

where, for $1 \le i \le m$,

$$x, y \in I \cup \{\bigcup_{j=1}^{i-1} V_j\}.$$

$I = \{d_1, d_2, \cdots, d_N\}$ is the set of *input* or *initial* variables and $\circ \in \{+, -, \times\}$. V_i's are called program variables. Clearly, each program variable is a multivariate polynomial (in the input variables $d_1, d_2, \cdots, d_N$) with integer coefficients and has *no constant terms*.

As an example, let $I = \{x_1, x_2, y_1, y_2\}$. The following polynomial program computes

$$B(I) = x_1 y_1 + x_2 y_2,$$

which is the inner product of the vectors $\mathbf{x} = (x_1, x_2)^t$ and $\mathbf{y} = (y_1, y_2)^t$.

$$
\left.\begin{array}{l}
A = x_1 \times x_2 \\
C = y_1 \times y_2 \\
D = x_1 + y_2 \\
E = x_2 + y_1 \\
F = D \times E \\
G = F - A \\
B = G - C.
\end{array}\right\} \tag{7.3.5.1}
$$

This method of computing the inner products is due to Winograd [1968] (Exercise 7.12).

An instruction that defines a program variable, say $V = V(I)$, can be removed from such a program provided we enlarge the input set I to include V. Thus, if a polynomial program computes $Z = Z(I)$, by removing the instruction that defines V we obtain a new representation for Z, namely (with a slight abuse of notation) $Z = Z(I, V)$. In the above example, if the third instruction defining D is removed, then B becomes

$$
B = D(x_2 + y_1) - x_1 x_2 - y_1 y_2.
$$

Recall that the program variable V is computed by one of the three operations $\{+, -, \times\}$. If these computations are subject to round-off error resulting from finite precision, then it is customary to represent the computed value of V as $V(1 + \varepsilon)$, where ε depends on the machine precision. The induced error in the output polynomial $Z(I, V)$ resulting from the error in the computation of V can be (approximately) expressed as

$$
Z(I, V(1 + \varepsilon)) - Z(I, V) \approx \varepsilon V(I) \frac{\partial Z(I, V)}{\partial V}.
$$

The polynomial

$$
\Delta Z_V \approx V(I) \frac{\partial Z(I, V)}{\partial V} \tag{7.3.5.2}
$$

determines the *sensitivity* of the evaluation of the output Z with respect to the round-off resulting from the computations of $V(I)$. The sensitivity of B with respect to D in the above example is given by

$$
\Delta B_D = (x_2 + y_1)(x_1 + y_2).
$$

In the following, we focus our attention on the analysis of the sensitivity of the (numerical) evaluation of bilinear forms.

Let $\mathbf{x} = (x_1, x_2, \cdots, x_N)^t$ and $\mathbf{y} = (y_1, y_2, \cdots, y_N)^t$, and let $\mathbf{I} = \{x_1, x_2, \cdots, x_N, y_1, y_2, \cdots, y_N\}$. Define a *bilinear* function

$$
B(\mathbf{x}, \mathbf{y}) = \sum_{i=1}^{N} \sum_{j=1}^{M} \alpha_{ij} x_i y_j = \mathbf{x}^t \boldsymbol{\alpha} \, \mathbf{y}, \tag{7.3.5.3}
$$

where $\boldsymbol{\alpha} = [\alpha_{ij}]$ is an $N \times N$ matrix of integer elements. $B(\mathbf{x}, \mathbf{y})$ is called a *permutation* bilinear form, if $\alpha_{ij} \neq 0$ and $\alpha_{kl} \neq 0$ implies either $i = k$ and $j = l$ or $i \neq k$ and $j \neq l$, that is, there is *at most* one non-zero element in each row and each column of the matrix $\boldsymbol{\alpha}$. Clearly, $B = x_1 y_1 + x_2 y_2$ is a permutation bilinear form. Bilinear forms naturally arise in scalar product, matrix - vector product, and matrix - matrix product computations.

Consider a polynomial program that evaluates $B = B(\mathbf{x}, \mathbf{y})$. We now define a useful scheme for *marking* the instructions. If the variable V is defined by an addition/subtraction, then *mark* that instruction. If

$$V = x \circ y,$$

where $\circ \in \{+, -\}$, is marked, and if x is defined by addition/subtraction, then mark x. Do likewise for y. After completing this marking process, *delete* all the *unmarked* instructions. Let I' be the set of all (new) input variables of the resulting polynomial program. Clearly, I' consists of all the original input variables in I and all those program variables defined by multiplication. If B is defined by multiplication, then $I' = \{B\}$.

The *new* representation for B takes the form

$$B = \sum_{V \in I'} a_V V, \tag{7.3.5.4}$$

where a_V is an integer coefficient of V in B.

Applying this marking process to the example in (7.3.5.1), we obtain $I' = I \cup \{F, A, C\}, B = F - A - C, a_F = 1$, and $a_A = a_C = -1$.

The following lemma is crucial.

Lemma 7.3.5.1. If $V \in I'$ in (7.3.5.4) is defined by multiplication and $a_V \neq 0$, then

$$\frac{\partial B}{\partial V} \not\equiv 0.$$

Proof

From (7.3.5.4), we get

$$\frac{\partial B}{\partial V} = a_V + \sum a_U \frac{\partial U}{\partial V}, \tag{7.3.5.5}$$

where the summation is over $U \in I' - \{V\}$. If U is an input variable, then $\frac{\partial U}{\partial V} = 0$. If U is a program variable, then it is defined by multiplication and may depend on V in the sense that $\frac{\partial U}{\partial V} \not\equiv 0$. Let

$$U = P \times Q. \tag{7.3.5.6}$$

Thus,

$$\frac{\partial U}{\partial V} = \frac{\partial P}{\partial V} Q + \frac{\partial Q}{\partial V} P.$$

Clearly, neither of the two terms on the right-hand side has a constant in it. Thus, a_V is the only constant in (7.3.5.5) and the lemma follows.

As an example, for the program in (7.3.5.1), $I' = \{F, A, C\} \cup I$, and $B = F - A - C$. The lemma can be easily verified for this case.

We now define a collection of criteria for judging the stability or robustness of an evaluation process. Let (refer to Exercise 5.35)

$$\|\mathbf{x}\|_\infty = \max_i \{ | x_i | \},$$

and

$$\|(\mathbf{x}, \mathbf{y})\|_B = \max \{ | x_i y_j | : \alpha_{ij} \neq 0 \}.$$

An evaluation of B is said to possess *Brent stability (BS)* if

$$| \Delta B_V(\mathbf{x}, \mathbf{y}) | = O(\|\mathbf{x}\|_\infty \|\mathbf{y}\|_\infty),$$

Brent restricted stability (BRS) if

$$| \Delta B_V(\mathbf{x}, \mathbf{y}) | = O(\|(\mathbf{x}, \mathbf{y})\|_B),$$

Miller strong stability (MSS) if

$$| \Delta B_V(\mathbf{x}, \mathbf{y}) | = O\left(\sum_{i=1}^N | x_i \frac{\partial B}{\partial x_i} | \right) + \sum_{j=1}^M | y_j \frac{\partial B}{\partial y_j} |),$$

or *Miller weak stability (MWS)* if

$$| \Delta B_V(\mathbf{x}, \mathbf{y}) | = O(\|\mathbf{x}\|_\infty \sum_{i=1}^N | \frac{\partial B}{\partial x_i} | + \|\mathbf{y}\|_\infty \sum_{j=1}^M | \frac{\partial B}{\partial y_j} |),$$

for *all* variables V defined by the program evaluating B.

Lemma 7.3.5.2.

(a) MSS => BRS => BS

(b) MSS => MWS => BS

(c) For permutation bilinear forms, BRS = BS.

Proof

From (7.3.5.3)

$$\sum_{i=1}^{N} |\ x_i \frac{\partial B}{\partial x_i}\ | \leq \sum_{i=1}^{N} \sum_{j=1}^{M} |\ x_i\ \alpha_{ij}\ y_j\ |$$

$$\leq \|(\mathbf{x}, \mathbf{y})\|_B \sum_{i=1}^{N} \sum_{j=1}^{M} |\ \alpha_{ij}\ |.$$

A similar inequality holds for $\sum_{j=1}^{M} |\ y_j \frac{\partial B}{\partial y_j}\ |$. Combining these two, we obtain

$$\sum_{i=1}^{N} |\ x_i \frac{\partial B}{\partial x_i}\ | + \sum_{j=1}^{M} |\ y_j \frac{\partial B}{\partial y_j}\ | = O(\|(\mathbf{x}, \mathbf{y})\|_B),$$

that is, MSS => BRS.

From

$$\max\{ |\ x_i y_j\ | : \alpha_{ij} \neq 0 \} \leq \|\mathbf{x}\|_\infty \|\mathbf{y}\|_\infty,$$

we obtain BRS => BS and claim (a) is proved. The proof of (b) is similar and is left as an exercise.

To prove (c), let $\alpha_{ij} \neq 0$. Then

$$|\ x_i y_j\ | = \frac{1}{|\ \alpha_{ij}\ |} |\ x_i \frac{\partial B}{\partial x_i}\ |$$

$$\leq \frac{1}{|\ \alpha_{ij}\ |} \sum_{i=1}^{N} |\ x_i \frac{\partial B}{\partial x_i}\ |.$$

Thus,

$$\|(\mathbf{x}, \mathbf{y})\|_B = \max\{ |\ x_i y_j\ | : \alpha_{ij} \neq 0 \} \leq \frac{1}{|\ \alpha_{ij}\ |} \sum_{i=1}^{N} |\ x_i \frac{\partial B}{\partial x_i}\ |.$$

Similarly,

$$\|(\mathbf{x}, \mathbf{y})\|_B \leq \frac{1}{|\ \alpha_{ij}\ |} \sum_{j=1}^{M} |\ y_j \frac{\partial B}{\partial y_j}\ |.$$

Combining these,

$$\|(\mathbf{x}, \mathbf{y})\|_B = O(\sum_{i=1}^{N} |\ x_i \frac{\partial B}{\partial x_i}\ | + \sum_{j=1}^{M} |\ y_j \frac{\partial B}{\partial y_j}\ |).$$

Thus, BRS => MSS and claim (c) follows from (a).

However, BRS does *not*, in general, imply MSS. The following program evaluates the bilinear form $B(\mathbf{x}, \mathbf{y}) = x_1 y_1 + x_1 y_2 + x_2 y_1 + x_2 y_2$, which is *not* a permutation bilinear form.

$$
\left.\begin{aligned}
A &= x_1 \times y_1 \\
C &= x_1 \times y_2 \\
D &= x_2 \times y_1 \\
E &= x_2 \times y_2 \\
F &= A + C \\
G &= F + D \\
B &= G + E.
\end{aligned}\right\} \tag{7.3.5.7}
$$

For this program $I = \{x_1, x_2, y_1, y_2\}$. The marking process marks the instructions defining B, G, and F. Thus $I' = I \cup \{A, C, D, E\}$, $B = A + C + D + E$, and $\Delta B_A(\mathbf{x}, \mathbf{y}) = x_1 y_1$. If $x_1 = y_1 = 1$, and $x_2 = y_2 = -1$, then $\Delta B_A(\mathbf{x}, \mathbf{y}) = 1$, but

$$
\|\mathbf{x}\|_\infty \sum_{i=1}^{2} \left| \frac{\partial B}{\partial x_i} \right| + \|\mathbf{y}\|_\infty \sum_{j=1}^{2} \left| \frac{\partial B}{\partial y_j} \right| = 0,
$$

that is, this program does *not* possess MWS, and hence (by contrapositive) it does *not* have MSS. Since

$$
\|(\mathbf{x}, \mathbf{y})\|_B = 1,
$$

it does, however, have BRS.

Consider an alternative evaluation for the same $B(\mathbf{x}, \mathbf{y})$:

$$
\left.\begin{aligned}
A &= x_1 + x_2 \\
C &= y_1 + y_2 \\
B &= A \times C.
\end{aligned}\right\} \tag{7.3.5.8}
$$

Clearly,

$$
\Delta B_A = \Delta B_C = AC = (x_1 + x_2)(y_1 + y_2).
$$

It can be verified that this evaluation, while faster, also has MSS.

Let, for $1 \le r \le n$,

$$
B^{(r)}(\mathbf{x}, \mathbf{y}) = \sum_{i=1}^{N} \sum_{j=1}^{M} x_i \, \alpha_{ij}^{(r)} \, y_j
$$

be a set of bilinear forms. This collection is said to possess BS if each bilinear form in the set has BS. Other measures -- BRS, MSS, and MWS -- can be similarly extended to a set of bilinear forms.

In the following, we analyze the effect of requiring a certain type of stability on the structure of the instructions in the polynomial program computing $B(\mathbf{x}, \mathbf{y})$.

Theorem 7.3.5.3. Let $V \in I'$ be defined by multiplication and let $a_V \ne 0$ in (7.3.5.4), where $V(I) \not\equiv 0$ (that is, V does not vanish identically on all input values). If a program that evaluates B has Brent stability, then the instruction defining V must be of the form

$$V = \mathbf{L}_1(\mathbf{x}) \times \mathbf{L}_2(\mathbf{y}),$$

where $\mathbf{L}_i(\mathbf{u})$ is a linear combination of the components of the vector $\mathbf{u}$.

Proof

We will first prove that ΔB_V is bilinear by showing that if it is *not* bilinear then the Brent stability condition, namely

$$\Delta B_V(\mathbf{x}, \mathbf{y}) = O(\|\mathbf{x}\|_\infty \|\mathbf{y}\|_\infty), \tag{7.3.5.9}$$

is *not* satisfied. Assume that ΔB_V does not involve any y_i, $i = 1$ to M, that is,

$$\Delta B_V(\mathbf{x}, \mathbf{y}) = a x_1^{r_1} x_2^{r_2} \cdots x_N^{r_N},$$

where $a \neq 0$. Now, if we fix $y_i = 0$ for all $i = 1$ to M, and allow $\mathbf{x}$ to vary, then $\Delta B_V(\mathbf{x}, \mathbf{0})$ is a non-zero polynomial in $\{x_1, x_2, \cdots, x_N\}$, and $\Delta B_V(\mathbf{x}, \mathbf{0})$ does not vanish identically, but $\|\mathbf{x}\|_\infty \|\mathbf{y}\|_\infty = 0$, which contradicts (7.3.5.9). By changing the role of $\mathbf{x}$ and $\mathbf{y}$, and repeating the above argument, it immediately follows that for Brent stability $\Delta B_V(\mathbf{x}, \mathbf{y})$ must be a function of both $\mathbf{x}$ and $\mathbf{y}$.

Let $J_1 \subseteq \{1, 2, \cdots, N\}, J_2 \subseteq \{1, 2, \cdots, M\}$. Assume

$$\Delta B_V(\mathbf{x}, \mathbf{y}) = a \prod_{i \in J_1} x_i^{r_i} \times \prod_{j \in J_2} y_j^{q_j},$$

where $a \neq 0$ and r_i and q_j are positive integers. Then, for $r = \displaystyle\sum_{i \in J_1} r_i$ and $q = \displaystyle\sum_{j \in J_2} q_j$

$$\Delta B_V(\mathbf{x}, \mathbf{y}) \leq \|\mathbf{x}\|_\infty^r \|\mathbf{y}\|_\infty^q$$

$$= O(\|\mathbf{x}\|_\infty \|\mathbf{y}\|_\infty) \quad \text{for Brent stability}; \tag{7.3.5.10}$$

that is, $r = q = 1$. Since r_i's and q_j's are positive, it follows that $|J_1| = |J_2| = 1$, that is, $\Delta B_V(\mathbf{x}, \mathbf{y})$ is bilinear. Combining this with (7.3.5.2) and Lemma 7.3.5.1, since V is a divisor of ΔB_V, it follows that V is bilinear.

Corollary 7.3.5.4. In order for any evaluation of a set of bilinear forms $B^{(r)}(\mathbf{x}, \mathbf{y})$ using a polynomial program to have simultaneous Brent stability, it must involve multiplications only of the form $\mathbf{L}_1(\mathbf{x}) \times \mathbf{L}_2(\mathbf{y})$.

An immediate consequence of this corollary is that the Strassen method described in Section 7.3.3 has simultaneous Brent stability (Exercises 7.19 and 7.20).

Applying Theorem 7.3.5.3 to the program in (7.3.5.1) that computes the bilinear form $B(\mathbf{x}, \mathbf{y}) = x_1 y_1 + x_2 y_2$, we conclude that this program is *not* Brent-stable, for the defining A, C, and D are *not* bilinear forms. In other words, the Winograd method (Exercise 7.12) of computing the inner product does *not* have Brent stability. Brent [1970b] originally proved this result using the classical approach of bounding the cumulative error. Brent also showed that Winograd's method has Brent stability if the vectors $\mathbf{x}$ and $\mathbf{y}$ are normalized. If $\mathbf{x}$ and $\mathbf{y}$ are normalized (that is, $\|\mathbf{x}\|_\infty = \|\mathbf{y}\|_\infty = 1$), this conclusion also follows from (7.3.5.10).

Hopcroft and Kerr [1971] have shown that it requires $\left\lceil \dfrac{7N}{2} \right\rceil$ multiplications to multiply any 2×2 matrix with a $2 \times N$ matrix using polynomial programs that use multiplications of the form $\mathbf{L}_1(\mathbf{x}) \times \mathbf{L}_2(\mathbf{y})$. Winograd method of Exercise 7.12, on the other hand, requires only $3N + 2$ multiplications. Thus, "preprocessing" in the Winograd method, while it reduces the number of multiplications, also contributes to the *loss* of simultaneous Brent stability.

Theorem 7.3.5.5. Let $V \in I'$ be defined by multiplication and let $a_V \neq 0$ in (7.3.5.4). Further, let

$$V = \sum_{i=1}^{N} \sum_{j=1}^{M} a_{ij}\, x_i\, y_j. \tag{7.3.5.11}$$

Then, if B has Brent restricted stability (BRS), and if a_{ij} in V is non-zero, then the coefficient α_{ij} in $B(\mathbf{x}, \mathbf{y})$ defined in (7.3.5.3) is also non-zero.

Proof

Recall that BRS requires that

$$| \Delta B_V(\mathbf{x}, \mathbf{y}) | = O(\|(\mathbf{x}, \mathbf{y})\|_B).$$

Let $x_i y_j$ be a term in ΔB_V but *not* in B. Then we can choose $\mathbf{x}$ and $\mathbf{y}$ such that $x_k = 0$ for $k \neq i$, $y_l = 0$ for $l \neq j$, $x_i > 0$, and $y_j > 0$. Since $\alpha_{ij} = 0$, we have $\|(\mathbf{x}, \mathbf{y})\|_B = 0$, but $\Delta B_V(\mathbf{x}, \mathbf{y})$ is non-zero. This contradicts the fact that B has BRS. In other words, for BRS to hold, every product $x_i y_j$ that appears in ΔB_V must appear in B as well. Since ΔB_V is a constant multiple of V, if $a_{ij} \neq 0$ in V, it follows from the above argument that α_{ij} in B must also be non-zero.

Theorem 7.3.5.6. Let B be a permutation bilinear form evaluated by a polynomial program, and let B have Miller strong stability (MSS). If a term $x_i y_j$ appears in B with non-zero coefficient, then there is a multiplication in the program of the form $(ax_i) \times (by_j)$.

Proof

Clearly, the term $x_i y_j$ must appear in some V in I' with $a_V \neq 0$ in (7.3.5.4). Let V be such that

$$V = (a_i\, x_i + a_k\, x_k) \times (b_j y_j)$$

where a_i, a_k and b_j are all non-zero. Then, by the above theorem, both $a_i b_j x_i y_j$ and $a_k b_j x_k y_j$ must appear in B. But this contradicts the assumption that B is a permutation bilinear form. Hence the theorem.

Corollary 7.3.5.7. Any polynomial program that evaluates a set $B^{(r)}(\mathbf{x}, \mathbf{y})$ of bilinear forms with simultaneous Miller strong stability must perform q multiplications, one for each of the non-zero coefficients $\alpha_{ij}^{(r)}$ defining $B^{(r)}(\mathbf{x}, \mathbf{y})$.

An immediate consequence of this corollary is that the classical matrix multiplication algorithm requiring n^3 multiplications is *optimal* among the class of algorithms with simultaneous Miller strong stability. Likewise, the classical method of multiplying two complex numbers using four multiplication has simultaneous MSS (Exercise 7.17 and 7.18).

7.4 INVERSE OF A MATRIX

In this section, we describe the best known parallel algorithm for computing the inverse of a matrix.

7.4.1 Csanky's Algorithm

A parallel algorithm due to Csanky for computing the inverse of a matrix is given in Fig. 7.4.1.1. It is based on the Leverrier method described in Section 7.2.2. Let $T_I(N)$ be the time to compute $\mathbf{A}^{-1}$ given $\mathbf{A}$ using this algorithm.

From Section 7.3.1, it is clear that $\mathbf{A}^j$, $j = 1, \cdots, N$, in step 1 can be computed in $O((\log N)^2)$ steps using $O(N^4)$ (or $O(\frac{N^4}{\log N})$) processors. Once $\mathbf{A}^j$, $j = 1, \cdots, N$, are available, t_j, $j = 1, \cdots, N$, can be computed in parallel in $O(\log N)$ steps using only $O(N^2)$ processors.

The coefficients of the characteristic equation $p = (p_1, p_2, \cdots, p_N)$ are obtained by solving the lower triangular system (7.2.2.4) using the methods described in Chapter 6 in $O((\log N)^2)$ steps using only $O(N^3)$ processors.

Finally, step 3 computes $\mathbf{A}^{-1}$ using the p_i, $i = 1, \cdots, N$, computed in step 2, and $\mathbf{A}^j$, $j = 1, \cdots, N$, computed in step 1. Notice $p_i\, \mathbf{A}^{N-j}$ can be computed in *one* step, using N^2 processors. Thus, all the individual terms in the numerator of (7.2.2.5) can be computed in *one* step using $O(N^3)$ processors. Now, the numerator of (7.2.2.5) can be computed (using the associative fan-in algorithm) in $O(\log N)$ time using $O(N^3)$ processors. $\mathbf{A}^{-1}$ is then obtained using *one* more division.

/* Given a non-singular matrix **A**, find its inverse. */

Step 1.

      FOR $j = 1$ TO N STEP 1 DO
          Compute $\mathbf{A}^j$ in PARALLEL
          Compute t_j in (7.2.2.1)
      END

Step 2. Solve the lower triangular system in (7.2.2.4) and find p in parallel.

Step 3. Compute $\mathbf{A}^{-1}$ using the formula (7.2.2.5) in parallel (using the $\mathbf{A}^j$ computed in step 1).

FIGURE 7.4.1.1
Csanky's algorithm.

Thus, the algorithm in all takes

$$T_I(N) = O((\log N)^2) \qquad (7.4.1.1)$$

steps using $O(N^4)$ (or $O(\dfrac{N^4}{\log N})$) processors.

Since the computation det[**A**] depends on all the N^2 elements of **A**, using the standard fan-in arguments it readily follows that

$$T_I(N) \geq 2 \log N. \qquad (7.4.1.2)$$

In other words, the parallel time complexity $T_I(N)$ of the matrix inversion process is such that

$$O(\log N) \leq T_I(N) \leq O((\log N)^2). \qquad (7.4.1.3)$$

Csanky's method, in spite of its attractive property, namely it is the *fastest* known algorithm for inverting matrices, does *not* lend itself for practical implementation. The difficulties arise from two different directions. First, it requires just too many processors to be realistic. Second, even granting that the number of processors is *not* a problem, the method is notoriously unstable. It can be shown (Wilkinson [1965]) that Leverrier's method of computing p_i's, in particular p_N, using (7.2.2.4) is very vulnerable to the rounding errors resulting from the computation of the traces t_i of the matrix $\mathbf{A}^i, i = 1, \cdots, N$.

Two related parallel algorithms for computing $\mathbf{A}^{-1}$ are described in Exercises 7.26 and 7.27.

We conclude this section by deriving a basic relation between the parallel complexities of four related problems. Let $T_I(N)$, $T_D(N)$, $T_S(N)$, and $T_P(N)$ be the parallel time required to compute the inverse of $\mathbf{A}$, to compute the determinant of $\mathbf{A}$, to solve $\mathbf{Ax} = \mathbf{d}$, and to compute the characteristic polynomial of the matrix $\mathbf{A}$, respectively, using a polynomial number of processors.

Let $\mathbf{A}_{i:j}$ be the principal submatrix of $\mathbf{A}$ bounded by the ith row and column and j^{th} row and column. Then, $\mathbf{A} = \mathbf{A}_{1:N}$ and $\mathbf{A}_{N:N} = a_{NN}$. Consider the linear system

$$\mathbf{A}_{k:N}\mathbf{z}(k) = \mathbf{e}_1(N - k + 1), \qquad (7.4.1.4)$$

where $\mathbf{e}_1(j)$ is the first unit vector of size j and $\mathbf{z}(k) = (z_1(k), z_2(k), \cdots, z_{N-k+1}(k))^t$. By Cramer's rule ,

$$z_1(k) = \frac{\det[\mathbf{A}_{k+1:N}]}{\det[\mathbf{A}_{k:N}]}. \qquad (7.4.1.5)$$

Thus, $z_1(k)$ for $k = 1, 2, \cdots, N - 1$ can be obtained in parallel in at most $T_S(N)$ steps.

Now, it takes $\lceil \log N \rceil$ steps to compute

$$\prod_{k=1}^{N-1} z_1(k) = \frac{\det[\mathbf{A}_{N:N}]}{\det[\mathbf{A}_{1:N}]},$$

from which $\det[\mathbf{A}]$ can be extracted in one more division. Thus, we obtain

$$T_D(N) \le T_S(N) + \lceil \log N \rceil + 1. \qquad (7.4.1.6)$$

To compute the solution, first obtain $\mathbf{A}^{-1}$ and compute $\mathbf{x} = \mathbf{A}^{-1}\mathbf{b}$. The former calculation takes $T_I(N)$ steps and, since the latter involves inner product calculations, it can be completed in $\lceil \log N \rceil + 1$ steps, from which we have

$$T_S(N) \le T_I(N) + \lceil \log N \rceil + 1. \qquad (7.4.1.7)$$

Recall that

$$\mathbf{A}^{-1} = \frac{ADJ\,[\mathbf{A}]}{\det[\mathbf{A}]}, \qquad (7.4.1.8)$$

and each element of $ADJ\,[\mathbf{A}]$ is a determinant of order $N - 1$. If $\phi(\lambda)$ is the characteristic polynomial of a matrix $\mathbf{A}$, since $\phi(0) = \det[\mathbf{A}]$, all the determinants needed in computing $\mathbf{A}^{-1}$ can be obtained in parallel in at most $T_P(N)$ steps. The inverse itself can be obtained by performing the division in parallel in one step. Thus,

$$T_I(N) \le T_P(N) + 1. \qquad (7.4.1.9)$$

Finally, the characteristic polynomial $\phi(\lambda)$ of $\mathbf{A}$ can be computed in the following fashion.

Let ω be the $(N + 1)^{th}$ primitive root of unity. Compute

$$\phi(\omega^i) = \det[\mathbf{A} - \omega^i \mathbf{I}] \qquad (7.4.1.10)$$

in parallel for $i = 0, 1, \cdots, N$, using the algorithm for computing determinants in

$T_D(N)$ steps. The coefficients of $\phi(\lambda)$ can be recovered from $\phi(\omega^i)$, $i = 0, 1, \cdots, N$, using the FFT algorithm in $O(\log N)$ steps. Thus,

$$T_P(N) \leq T_D(N) + O(\log N). \tag{7.4.1.11}$$

Combining these, we obtain the following theorem.

Theorem 7.4.1.1. If polynomial (in N) number of processors are available, then $T_I(N)$, $T_S(N)$, $T_D(N)$, and $T_P(N)$ are all of the same order of magnitude.

7.5 DETERMINANT AND CHARACTERISTIC POLYNOMIAL OF A MATRIX

In this section, we describe a parallel algorithm due to Berkowitz [1984] for computing the determinant and the characteristic equation of a general matrix.

7.5.1 Berkowitz's Algorithm

This method is critically dependent on the properties of matrices described in Section 7.2, especially formula (7.2.4.14). Let $\mathbf{A} = [\, a_{ij}\,]$ be an $N \times N$ matrix with

$$\mathbf{P}_{N+1} = (p_0, p_1, p_2, \cdots, p_N) \tag{7.5.1.1}$$

as the vector of coefficients of its characteristic polynomial (refer to (7.2.1.6)). From (7.2.4.14), we obtain that

$$\mathbf{P}_{N+1} = \mathbf{M}_N \mathbf{M}_{N-1} \cdots \mathbf{M}_2 \mathbf{M}_1. \tag{7.5.1.2}$$

The $(N+1) \times N$ matrix $\mathbf{M}_N$ is given in (7.2.4.12). $\mathbf{B} (=\mathbf{A}_{N-1})$ is an $(N-1) \times (N-1)$ matrix obtained by deleting the first row and first column of $\mathbf{A}$. $\mathbf{R}$ is a row vector obtained by deleting the first element of the first row of the matrix $\mathbf{A}$ and $\mathbf{S}$ is a column vector obtained by deleting the first element of the first column. (Refer to 7.2.4.11).

Computation of $\mathbf{P}_{N+1}$ using (7.5.1.2) consists of two parts -- evaluating the elements of $\mathbf{M}_N$ and computing the product on the right-hand side of (7.5.1.2).

Evaluating the elements of the matrix $\mathbf{M}_N$ is equivalent to computing those of the set

$$\mathbf{W} = \{\mathbf{R}\,\mathbf{B}^i\,\mathbf{S} \mid 0 \leq i < N\}. \tag{7.5.1.3}$$

In the following, to simplify the notation, it is assumed that $N = 2^n$ for some *even* $n \geq 2$. Generalization to arbitrary N is left as an exercise (Berkowitz [1984]). Define, for any integer $0 \leq k \leq \dfrac{n}{2}$,

$$\mathbf{U}_k = \{\mathbf{R}\,\mathbf{B}^i \mid 0 \le i < 2^k\} \tag{7.5.1.4}$$

and

$$\mathbf{V}_k = \{\mathbf{B}^{i\,2^k}\mathbf{S} \mid 0 \le i < 2^k\}. \tag{7.5.1.5}$$

Any integer r in the range $0 \le r < N$ can be uniquely expressed as

$$r = a + b\sqrt{N}, \tag{7.5.1.6}$$

where $0 \le a,\ b < \sqrt{N}$. Consequently, any element of $\mathbf{W}$ can be computed as an inner product of vectors (of size $N - 1$) from $\mathbf{U}_{n/2}$ and $\mathbf{V}_{n/2}$ in $O\,(\log N)$ steps requiring $O\,(N^2)$ operations.

The sequence of sets $\mathbf{U}_k,\ 0 \le k \le \dfrac{n}{2}$, can be recursively computed as follows:

$$\mathbf{U}_j = \mathbf{U}_{j-1} \cup \mathbf{Z}_j \tag{7.5.1.7}$$

and

$$\mathbf{Z}_j = \{x\,\mathbf{B}^{2^{j-1}} \mid x \in \mathbf{U}_{j-1}\}, \tag{7.5.1.8}$$

where $\mathbf{U}_0 = \{\mathbf{R}\}$ and $|\,\mathbf{U}_{j-1}\,| = |\,\mathbf{Z}_j\,| = 2^{j-1}$. To compute $\mathbf{Z}_j$, construct a matrix $\mathbf{Y}_j$ (of order $N - 1$) whose first 2^{j-1} rows are the vectors of the set $\mathbf{U}_{j-1}$. The remaining rows of $\mathbf{Y}_j$ are filled with zero entries. Clearly, the elements of $\mathbf{Z}_j$ correspond to the (non-zero) rows of the product matrix

$$\mathbf{Y}_j\,\mathbf{B}^{2^{j-1}}. \tag{7.5.1.9}$$

Thus, $\mathbf{U}_j$ can be obtained from $\mathbf{U}_{j-1}$ in two matrix multiplications (one to compute $\mathbf{B}^{2^{j-1}}$ from $\mathbf{B}^{2^{j-2}}$ and the other in (7.5.1.9)). Let $T\,(j)$ and $s\,(j)$ be the parallel time and the number of operations required to compute $\mathbf{U}_j$. Using Strassen's method for multiplying matrices (refer to Section 7.3), we obtain

$$T\,(j) = T\,(j - 1) + O\,(\log N)$$

and

$$s\,(j) = s\,(j - 1) + O\,(N^{\alpha}),$$

where $T\,(0) = s\,(0) = 0$ and $\alpha < 2.376$.

Hence

$$T\!\left(\frac{n}{2}\right) = O\,((\log N)^2) \tag{7.5.1.10}$$

and

$$s\!\left(\frac{n}{2}\right) = O\,(N^{\alpha}\log N) \quad = \quad O\,(N^{\alpha + \varepsilon}), \tag{7.5.1.11}$$

for any real $\varepsilon > 0$.

To compute the sequence $\mathbf{V}_k$, first compute $\mathbf{B}^{2^k}$ and follow the same recursive procedure as in the computation of $\mathbf{U}_k$, with $\mathbf{B}^{2^k}$ replacing $\mathbf{B}$ and column vectors in place of row vectors.

Summarizing this, we obtain the following lemma.

Lemma 7.5.1.1. Given the vectors $\mathbf{R}$ and $\mathbf{S}$ and the matrix $\mathbf{B}$, the set $\mathbf{W}$ in (7.5.1.3) can be computed in $O((\log N)^2)$ steps requiring $O(N^{\alpha + \varepsilon})$ operations.

Computation of the product of matrices in (7.5.1.2) can be accomplished in a binary tree using the associative fan-in algorithm, where at each internal node a matrix multiplication is performed. Refer to Fig. 7.5.1.1, for an example with $N = 8$. In this figure $\mathbf{M}^{(0)}_{(i+1)\times i} = \mathbf{M}_i$, for $i = 1$ to 8, $\mathbf{M}^{(1)}_{9\times 7} = \mathbf{M}^{(0)}_{9\times 8} \times \mathbf{M}^{(0)}_{8\times 7}$, and so on.

Combining the depth and the number of internal nodes of this binary tree with Property 7.2.5.3, we obtain the following lemma.

Lemma 7.5.1.2. The product in (7.5.1.2) can be found in $O((\log N)^2)$ steps requiring $O(N^3)$ operations.

We now state the principal result of this section.

Theorem 7.5.1.3. For any $\varepsilon > 0$, the coefficients of the characteristic polynomial and the determinant of an $N \times N$ matrix can be computed in $O((\log N)^2)$ steps using only $O(N^{3.376})$ operations.

Proof
By applying the Lemma 7.5.1.1 repeatedly N times, all the component matrices required in (7.5.1.2) can be computed in $O((\log N)^2)$ steps requiring $O(N^{1+\alpha+\varepsilon})$ operations. Since $2 \le \alpha < 2.376$, we can find an $\varepsilon > 0$ such that $1 + \alpha + \varepsilon < 3.376$. Combining this with Lemma 7.5.1.2, the theorem follows.

Computation of characteristic polynomials for tridiagonal matrices is described in Exercises 7.61 and 7.62.

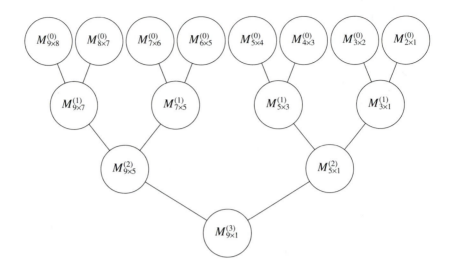

FIGURE 7.5.1.1
An illustration of the computations in (7.5.1.2).

7.6 BINI'S ALGORITHM FOR TRIANGULAR TOEPLITZ SYSTEMS.

In this section, we describe a new class of parallel algorithms for solving triangular Toeplitz systems *approximately* to *any precision* in $O(\log N)$ steps using only $O(N)$ processors. This approximate solution is obtained by solving a special class of Toeplitz systems using standard interpolation techniques. A method for computing the *exact* solution for triangular Toeplitz systems in $O(\log N)$ steps using $O(N^2)$ processors is presented.

7.6.1 Bini's Algorithm -- Approximate Solution

Define, for any $0 \leq \varepsilon \leq 1$, an $N \times N$ matrix $\mathbf{H}(\varepsilon) = [\mathbf{H}_{ij}(\varepsilon)]$, where

$$\mathbf{H}_{ij}(\varepsilon) = \begin{cases} 1, & \text{for } j = i + 1 \\ \varepsilon, & \text{for } i = n, j = 1 \\ 0 & \text{otherwise.} \end{cases} \qquad (7.6.1.1)$$

An example for $N = 4$ is

$$\mathbf{H}(\varepsilon) = \begin{bmatrix} 0 & 1 & 0 & 0 \\ 0 & 0 & 1 & 0 \\ 0 & 0 & 0 & 1 \\ \varepsilon & 0 & 0 & 0 \end{bmatrix}. \tag{7.6.1.2}$$

It can be easily verified that

$$\mathbf{H}^2(\varepsilon) = \begin{bmatrix} 0 & 0 & 1 & 0 \\ 0 & 0 & 0 & 1 \\ \varepsilon & 0 & 0 & 0 \\ 0 & \varepsilon & 0 & 0 \end{bmatrix}, \quad \mathbf{H}^3(\varepsilon) = \begin{bmatrix} 0 & 0 & 0 & 1 \\ \varepsilon & 0 & 0 & 0 \\ 0 & \varepsilon & 0 & 0 \\ 0 & 0 & \varepsilon & 0 \end{bmatrix},$$

$$\mathbf{H}^4(\varepsilon) = \begin{bmatrix} \varepsilon & 0 & 0 & 0 \\ 0 & \varepsilon & 0 & 0 \\ 0 & 0 & \varepsilon & 0 \\ 0 & 0 & 0 & \varepsilon \end{bmatrix},$$

and $\mathbf{H}^0(\varepsilon) = \mathbf{I}$, the identity matrix by definition. Notice, $\mathbf{H}^4(\varepsilon) \neq \mathbf{H}^0(\varepsilon)$ unless $\varepsilon = 1$ (see Exercise 7.39). Define

$$\Phi_N(\varepsilon) = \{ \sum_{i=1}^{N} a_i \mathbf{H}^{i-1}(\varepsilon) \mid a_i \text{ real for } i = 1 \text{ to } N \}, \tag{7.6.1.3}$$

that is, $\Phi_N(\varepsilon)$ is the class of $N \times N$ matrices obtained by linear combinations of powers of $\mathbf{H}(\varepsilon)$. $\Phi(\varepsilon)$ is called the *algebra generated* by the matrix $\mathbf{H}(\varepsilon)$ over the *real* field. As an example, for $N = 4$, if

$$\mathbf{A}(\varepsilon) = a_1 \mathbf{I} + a_2 \mathbf{H}(\varepsilon) + a_3 \mathbf{H}^2(\varepsilon) + a_4 \mathbf{H}^3(\varepsilon),$$

then

$$\mathbf{A}(\varepsilon) = \begin{bmatrix} a_1 & a_2 & a_3 & a_4 \\ \varepsilon a_4 & a_1 & a_2 & a_3 \\ \varepsilon a_3 & \varepsilon a_4 & a_1 & a_2 \\ \varepsilon a_2 & \varepsilon a_3 & \varepsilon a_4 & a_1 \end{bmatrix}, \tag{7.6.1.4}$$

that is, $\mathbf{A}(\varepsilon) \in \Phi_4(\varepsilon)$. Then, $\Phi_N(0)$ denotes the class of $N \times N$ *upper triangular Toeplitz* matrices, and $\Phi_N(1)$ corresponds to the class of *circulant* matrices (refer to (7.2.5.3)). Let

$$\Delta = \begin{bmatrix} 1 & 0 & 0 & \cdot & \cdot & \cdot & 0 \\ 0 & \delta & 0 & \cdot & \cdot & \cdot & 0 \\ 0 & 0 & \delta^2 & \cdot & \cdot & \cdot & 0 \\ \cdot & \cdot & \cdot & \cdot & \cdot & \cdot & \cdot \\ \cdot & \cdot & \cdot & \cdot & \cdot & \cdot & \cdot \\ \cdot & \cdot & \cdot & \cdot & \cdot & \cdot & \cdot \\ 0 & 0 & 0 & \cdot & \cdot & \cdot & \delta^{N-1} \end{bmatrix} \qquad (7.6.1.5)$$

be an $N \times N$ diagonal matrix. The following lemma can be verified by direct multiplication and is left as Exercise 7.40.

Lemma 7.6.1.1. If $\delta^N = \varepsilon > 0$, then

$$\mathbf{H}(\varepsilon) = \delta \Delta \mathbf{H}(1) \Delta^{-1},$$

and, for $0 \le i \le N - 1$,

$$\mathbf{H}^i(\varepsilon) = \delta^i \Delta \mathbf{H}^i(1) \Delta^{-1}.$$

To further understand the relation between the classes $\Phi_N(\varepsilon)$ and $\Phi_N(1)$, let

$$\left. \begin{aligned} \mathbf{a} &= (a_1, a_2, \cdots, a_N)^t \\ \\ \mathbf{b} &= (b_1, b_2, \cdots, b_N)^t, \end{aligned} \right\} \qquad (7.6.1.6)$$

and

where $\mathbf{b} = \Delta \mathbf{a}$, that is, $b_i = a_i \delta^{i-1}$ for $i = 1$ to N.

Let $\mathbf{A}$ and $\mathbf{B}$ be two circulant matrices with $\mathbf{a}$ and $\mathbf{b}$ as their first row, respectively. That is,

$$\left. \begin{aligned} \mathbf{A} &= \sum_{i=1}^{N} a_i \mathbf{H}^{i-1}(1), \\ \mathbf{B} &= \sum_{i=1}^{N} b_i \mathbf{H}^{i-1}(1). \end{aligned} \right\} \qquad (7.6.1.7)$$

Then, from Lemma 7.6.1.1,

$$\mathbf{A}(\varepsilon) = \sum_{i=1}^{N} a_i \mathbf{H}^{i-1}(\varepsilon)$$

$$= \sum_{i=1}^{N} a_i (\delta^{i-1} \Delta \mathbf{H}^{i-1}(1) \Delta^{-1})$$

$$= \Delta (\sum_{i=1}^{N} b_i \, \mathbf{H}^{i-1}(1)) \Delta^{-1}$$

$$= \Delta \mathbf{B} \Delta^{-1}. \tag{7.6.1.8}$$

This relation plays a key role in the development of Bini's algorithm. Using this relation, we can directly *elevate* many of the properties of the class $\Phi_N(1)$ of circulant matrices to $\Phi_N(\varepsilon)$ for $\varepsilon > 0$.

The class $\Phi_N(1)$ enjoys the property of being simultaneously diagonalizable by similarity transformations. To see this, let ω denote the Nth principal root of unity (refer to Chapter 3 for definition). Define an $N \times N$ matrix

$$\mathbf{G} = \frac{1}{\sqrt{N}} [G_{ij}], \tag{7.6.1.9}$$

where, for $1 \leq i, j \leq N$,

$$G_{ij} = \omega^{(i-1)(j-1)}.$$

Thus, $\mathbf{G}$ is a symmetric matrix.

As an example, for $N = 4$,

$$\mathbf{G} = \frac{1}{2} \begin{bmatrix} 1 & 1 & 1 & 1 \\ 1 & i & -1 & -i \\ 1 & -1 & 1 & -1 \\ 1 & -i & -1 & i \end{bmatrix},$$

where $\omega = i = \sqrt{-1}$.

If $\mathbf{G}^*$ denotes the conjugate transpose of $\mathbf{G}$, then it is well known (refer to Chapter 3) that $\mathbf{G}$ is *unitary*, that is,

$$\mathbf{G} \mathbf{G}^* = \mathbf{G}^* \mathbf{G} = \mathbf{I}. \tag{7.6.1.10}$$

The matrix $\mathbf{F} = \sqrt{N} \, \mathbf{G}$ is known as the *Fourier transform matrix*.

Let $\mathbf{B} \in \Phi_N(1)$ with vector $\mathbf{b}$ in (7.6.1.6) as its first row. Define

$$p(x) = \sum_{i=1}^{N} b_i x^{i-1}, \tag{7.6.1.11}$$

and let $\lambda = p(\omega)$. From the properties of ω it follows that

$$\lambda = b_1 + b_2\,\omega + b_3\,\omega^2 + \cdots + b_N\,\omega^{N-1}$$
$$\omega\lambda = b_N + b_1\,\omega + b_2\,\omega^2 + \cdots + b_{N-1}\,\omega^{N-1}$$
$$\omega^2\lambda = b_{N-1} + b_N\,\omega + b_1\,\omega^2 + \cdots + b_{N-2}\,\omega^{N-1}$$
$$\vdots$$
$$\omega^{N-1}\lambda = b_2 + b_3\,\omega + b_4\,\omega^2 + \cdots + b_1\,\omega^{N-1}. \tag{7.6.1.12}$$

If $\mathbf{x} = (1, \omega, \omega^2, \cdots, \omega^{N-1})^t$, then (7.6.1.12) can be represented in matrix notation as

$$\mathbf{B}\mathbf{x} = \lambda\mathbf{x}, \tag{7.6.1.13}$$

from which it follows that $\mathbf{x}$ is an eigenvector and $\lambda = p(\omega)$ is an eigenvalue of $\mathbf{B}$. Starting with

$$\lambda_j = p(\omega^{j-1}), \tag{7.6.1.14}$$

for $j = 1$ to N, and by repeating the above argument, it can be shown that

$$\mathbf{x}_j = (1, \omega^{j-1}, \omega^{2(j-1)}, \cdots, \omega^{(N-1)(j-1)})$$

is the eigenvector of $\mathbf{B}$ corresponding to the eigenvalue λ_j.
Let $\mathbf{D}$ be a diagonal matrix with

$$d_{jj} = \lambda_j. \tag{7.6.1.15}$$

Since $\mathbf{x}_j$ is the jth column of $\mathbf{G}$, combining these, the following result is immediate.

Lemma 7.6.1.2. If $\mathbf{B} \in \Phi_N(1)$, then the matrix $\mathbf{G}$ defined in (7.6.1.9) is such that

$$\mathbf{G}^*\mathbf{B}\mathbf{G} = \mathbf{D}. \tag{7.6.1.16}$$

The following example illustrates these ideas. Let

$$\mathbf{B} = \begin{bmatrix} 1 & 2 & 3 & 4 \\ 4 & 1 & 2 & 3 \\ 3 & 4 & 1 & 2 \\ 2 & 3 & 4 & 1 \end{bmatrix}.$$

Then

$$p(x) = 1 + 2x + 3x^2 + 4x^3.$$

Since $\omega = i$, when $N = 4$ we have

$$\lambda_1 = 10, \qquad \lambda_3 = -2$$

$$\lambda_2 = -2 - 2i, \quad \lambda_4 = -2 + 2i.$$

Let $\mathbf{V} = (\lambda_1, \lambda_2, \cdots, \lambda_N)^t$ be the vector of eigenvalues of the circulant matrix $\mathbf{B}$. It is left as an exercise (Exercise 7.41) to show that the vector $\mathbf{V}$ is, in fact, the discrete Fourier transform of the first row of $\mathbf{B}$, that is,

$$\mathbf{V} = \sqrt{N}\,\mathbf{G}\,\mathbf{b}. \tag{7.6.1.17}$$

We now extend the simultaneous diagonalizability of the class $\Phi_N(1)$ to $\Phi_N(\varepsilon)$, for $\varepsilon > 0$.

Lemma 7.6.1.3. Let $\mathbf{A}(\varepsilon) \in \Phi_N(\varepsilon)$, with $\mathbf{a}$ in (7.6.1.6) as its first row. Then $\mathbf{V} = \sqrt{N}\,\mathbf{G}\,\Delta\,\mathbf{a}$ is the vector of eigenvalues of $\mathbf{A}(\varepsilon)$.

Proof
From (7.6.1.8) and (7.6.1.16), we obtain

$$\mathbf{D} = \mathbf{G}^*\,\mathbf{B}\,\mathbf{G} = (\Delta\mathbf{G})^{-1}\,\mathbf{A}(\varepsilon)\,\Delta\,\mathbf{G}. \tag{7.6.1.18}$$

From this, (7.6.1.17), and $\mathbf{b} = \Delta\mathbf{a}$, the lemma follows.

It should be noted that the class $\Phi_N(0)$ of upper triangular Toeplitz matrices does *not* possess the property of simultaneous diagonalizability. However, since the matrices in this class can be approximated by those in $\Phi_N(\varepsilon)$, we can approximate the solution of a linear system

$$\mathbf{A}(0)\,\mathbf{x} = \mathbf{d}, \tag{7.6.1.19}$$

for $\mathbf{A}(0) \in \Phi_N(0)$ and $\mathbf{d} = (d_1, d_2, \cdots, d_N)^t$ by that of

$$\mathbf{A}(\varepsilon)\,\mathbf{x} = \mathbf{d} \tag{7.6.1.20}$$

to any degree of accuracy, where $\mathbf{A}(\varepsilon) \in \Phi_N(\varepsilon)$. This is the central idea of Bini's approach. Before stating the complete algorithm, we digress to develop some useful matrix - vector products involving the matrix $\mathbf{G}$.

Lemma 7.6.1.4.

(a) If $\mathbf{x}$ is a complex vector, then $\mathbf{G}\mathbf{x}$ and $\mathbf{G}^*\mathbf{x}$ can be computed in $3 \log N$ steps using at most $2N$ processors.

(b) If $\mathbf{y}$ and $\mathbf{z}$ are two real column vectors, then the pairs (i) $(\mathbf{G}\mathbf{y}, \mathbf{G}\mathbf{z})$, (ii) $(\mathbf{G}^*\mathbf{y}, \mathbf{G}^*\mathbf{z})$, and (iii) $(\mathbf{G}\mathbf{y}, \mathbf{G}^*\mathbf{z})$ can be computed in $3 \log N + O(1)$ steps with at most $2N$ processors.

Proof

Since claim (a) involves the computation of the Fourier transform as well as the inverse Fourier transform of $\mathbf{x}$, the time and processor bounds follow from the results in Section 3.4.

To prove (i) in (b), let $\mathbf{x} = \mathbf{y} + i\mathbf{z}$, $\mathbf{u}_x = \mathbf{G}\mathbf{x}$, $\mathbf{u}_y = \mathbf{G}\mathbf{y}$, and $\mathbf{u}_z = \mathbf{G}\mathbf{z}$. Let $\bar{\mathbf{x}} = \mathbf{y} - i\mathbf{z}$ be the complex conjugate of $\mathbf{x}$. Since $\mathbf{G}^2 = \mathbf{P}$, a permutation matrix (Exercise 7.45), using (7.6.1.10) and Exercise 7.46 we obtain, using the symmetry of $\mathbf{G}$,

$$\mathbf{u}_y = \frac{1}{2}\mathbf{G}(\mathbf{x} + \bar{\mathbf{x}})$$

$$= \frac{1}{2}(\mathbf{u}_x + \mathbf{P}\mathbf{G}^*\bar{\mathbf{x}})$$

$$= \frac{1}{2}(\mathbf{u}_x + \mathbf{P}\bar{\mathbf{u}}_x). \qquad (7.6.1.21)$$

Similarly,

$$\mathbf{u}_z = \frac{1}{2i}(\mathbf{u}_x - \mathbf{P}\bar{\mathbf{u}}_x). \qquad (7.6.1.22)$$

Using $2N$ processors, computation of $\mathbf{x}$ takes one step. From part (a) of this lemma, $\mathbf{u}_x$ can be computed in $3 \log N$ steps. Since $\mathbf{P}$ is known *a priori,* the expressions on the right-hand side of (7.6.1.21) and (7.6.1.22) can be computed in a constant number of steps. Combining these, part (i) of (b) follows. Parts (ii) and (iii) can be proved along similar lines.

We now state one of the main results of this section (see Exercise 7.48).

Theorem 7.6.1.5. If $\mathbf{A}(\varepsilon) \in \Phi_N(\varepsilon)$ for $\varepsilon > 0$ is non-singular, then the linear system

$$\mathbf{A}(\varepsilon)\mathbf{x} = \mathbf{d} \qquad (7.6.1.23)$$

can be solved in $6 \log N + O(1)$ steps using $2N$ processors.

Proof

Let $\mathbf{A}(\varepsilon)$ be a matrix with the (row) vector $\mathbf{a}$ in (7.6.1.6) as its first row. From Lemma 7.6.1.3, we have

$$\mathbf{A}^{-1}(\varepsilon) = \Delta\mathbf{G}\mathbf{D}^{-1}\mathbf{G}^*\Delta^{-1}, \qquad (7.6.1.24)$$

where the diagonal elements of the matrix $\mathbf{D}$ are the components of the vector $\mathbf{V}$ in (7.6.1.17). Bini's algorithm for computing $\mathbf{x} = \mathbf{A}^{-1}(\varepsilon)\mathbf{d}$ is given in Fig. 7.6.1.1. Each of the steps 1, 3, and 5 take one unit of time. Steps 2 and 4 (by

/*   Given $\mathbf{A}(\varepsilon)$ and $\mathbf{d}$, compute $\mathbf{A}^{-1}(\varepsilon)\,\mathbf{d}$. It is assumed
         that $2N$ processors are available   */

Step 1. Compute $\mathbf{Z}_1 = \mathbf{A}^{-1}\mathbf{d}$ and $\mathbf{Y}_1 = \sqrt{N}\,\Delta\mathbf{a}$.

Step 2. Compute $\mathbf{Z}_2 = \mathbf{G}^*\mathbf{Z}_1$ and $\mathbf{Y}_2 = \mathbf{G}\,\mathbf{Y}_1$.

Step 3. Compute $\mathbf{Z}_3 = \mathbf{D}^{-1}\mathbf{Z}_2$.

Step 4. Compute $\mathbf{Z}_4 = \mathbf{G}\,\mathbf{Z}_3$.

Step 5. Compute $\mathbf{x} = \Delta\mathbf{Z}_4$.

FIGURE 7.6.1.1
Bini's algorithm -- approximate solution.

Lemma 7.6.1.4) take $3 \log N + O(1)$ units of time. Combining these, the theorem follows.

The following corollaries are immediate.

Corollary 7.6.1.6. In addition to solving (7.6.1.23), we can also compute $\det[\mathbf{A}(0)]$, $\det[\mathbf{A}(\varepsilon)]$, and $\dfrac{\det[\mathbf{A}(\varepsilon)]}{\det[\mathbf{A}(0)]}$ in $6 \log N + O(1)$ steps using only $5N/2$ processors.

Proof
Recall that $\det[\mathbf{A}(0)] = a_1^N$, and $\det[\mathbf{A}(\varepsilon)]$ is the product of the elements of the vector $\mathbf{V} = \sqrt{N}\,\mathbf{G}\Delta\mathbf{a}$. Referring to the algorithm in Fig. 7.6.1.1, modify step 2 by adding the computation of $\det[\mathbf{A}(0)]$.
     Likewise, add the computation of $\det[\mathbf{A}(\varepsilon)]$ to step 4, and computation of the ratio $\dfrac{\det[\mathbf{A}(\varepsilon)]}{\det[\mathbf{A}(0)]}$ to step 5. Since the additional computations in steps 2 and 4 can be done in $\lceil \log N \rceil$ steps using the extra $N/2$ processors, combining with Theorem 7.6.1.5, the corollary follows.

Corollary 7.6.1.7. The solution of a linear system

$$A(0)\, x = d, \tag{7.6.1.25}$$

where the non-singular matrix $A(0) \in \Phi_N(0)$ can be approximated to any degree of accuracy using $6 \log N + O(1)$ steps using $2N$ processors.

Proof

Since $A(0)$ is non-singular, there exists an $\varepsilon_o > 0$, such that if $|\varepsilon| < \varepsilon_o$, then $\det[A(\varepsilon)] \neq 0$, where the first row of $A(\varepsilon)$ is the same as that of A. Since $A^{-1}(\varepsilon) \to A^{-1}(0)$, as $\varepsilon \to 0$, the corollary follows from Theorem 7.6.1.5 and Corollary 7.6.1.6.

It is well known (Exercise 7.54) that $A^{-1}(\varepsilon)$ can be computed by solving

$$A(\varepsilon)\, u = e_1 \quad \text{and} \quad A(\varepsilon)v = e_N \tag{7.6.1.26}$$

where e_i is the ith unit vector,

$$u = (1, u_1, u_2, \cdots, u_{N-1})^t$$

and

$$v = (v_{N-1}, v_{N-2}, \cdots, v_1, 1)^t.$$

In this case, the solution vectors u and v constitute the first column and the first row of $A^{-1}(\varepsilon)$ and uniquely determine the rest of the elements of $A^{-1}(\varepsilon)$.

This discussion leads to the following corollary, whose proof is left to the reader (Exercise 7.55).

Corollary 7.6.1.8. The inverse of a Toeplitz matrix $A(\varepsilon) \in \Phi_N(\varepsilon)$, all of whose principal submatrices are non-singular, can be obtained in $O(\log N)$ steps.

7.6.2 Bini's Algorithm -- Exact Solution

We now describe a method for *refining* the approximate solution of the upper triangular Toeplitz system (7.6.1.25) to get the *exact* solution. The approach is based on the standard interpolation methods. Let $A_m(\varepsilon) \in \Phi_N(\varepsilon)$ be such that

$$A_m(\varepsilon) = \sum_{i=1}^{m} a_i\, H^{i-1}(\varepsilon). \tag{7.6.2.1}$$

As an example, with $N = 4$ and $m = 3$,

$$
A_3(\varepsilon) = \begin{bmatrix} a_1 & a_2 & a_3 & 0 \\ 0 & a_1 & a_2 & a_3 \\ \varepsilon a_3 & 0 & a_1 & a_2 \\ \varepsilon a_2 & \varepsilon a_3 & 0 & a_1 \end{bmatrix}.
$$

(7.6.2.2)

Notice that $A_N(0)$ is an upper triangular Toeplitz matrix.
   Consider the system

$$
A_m(\varepsilon) x(\varepsilon) = d,
$$

(7.6.2.3)

where

$$
x(\varepsilon) = (x_1(\varepsilon), x_2(\varepsilon), \cdots, x_N(\varepsilon))^t
$$

and

$$
d = (d_1, d_2, \cdots, d_N)^t.
$$

(7.6.2.4)

The problem is to solve

$$
A_m(0) x(0) = d
$$

(7.6.2.5)

exactly when $A_m(0)$ is non-singular. Let

$$
A_m^{-1}(\varepsilon) = [\hat{a}_{ij}]
$$

$$
ADJ[A_m(\varepsilon)] = [p_{ij}(\varepsilon)]
$$

(7.6.2.6)

and

$$
\det[A_m(\varepsilon)] = q(\varepsilon).
$$

where $p_{ij}(\cdot)$ and $q(\cdot)$ are polynomials of degree at most m. Since

$$
A_m^{-1}(\varepsilon) = \frac{ADJ[A_m(\varepsilon)]}{\det[A_m(\varepsilon)]},
$$

(7.6.2.7)

it follows that $\hat{a}_{ij}$ is a rational function of ε, that is,

$$
\hat{a}_{ij} = \frac{p_{ij}(\varepsilon)}{q(\varepsilon)}.
$$

(7.6.2.8)

Combining this with (7.6.2.3), it follows that

$$
x_i(\varepsilon) = \frac{\gamma_i(\varepsilon)}{q(\varepsilon)},
$$

(7.6.2.9)

where

$$
\gamma_i(\varepsilon) = \sum_{j=1}^{N} p_{ji}(\varepsilon) d_j
$$

(7.6.2.10)

is a polynomial of degree at most m.

Select a set of $m + 1$ real constants, $\varepsilon_0, \varepsilon_1, \varepsilon_2, \cdots, \varepsilon_m$, such that $\varepsilon_i \neq \varepsilon_j$ for $i \neq j$ and $q(\varepsilon_i) \neq 0$ for $i = 0$ to m. Define the Vandermonde matrix $\mathbf{W} = [\, w_{ij}\,]$ of order $m + 1$, where

$$w_{ij} = [\varepsilon_{i-1}^{j-1}]. \qquad (7.6.2.11)$$

An example of this matrix for $m = 3$ is

$$\mathbf{W} = \begin{bmatrix} 1 & \varepsilon_0 & \varepsilon_0^2 & \varepsilon_0^3 \\ 1 & \varepsilon_1 & \varepsilon_1^2 & \varepsilon_1^3 \\ 1 & \varepsilon_2 & \varepsilon_2^2 & \varepsilon_2^3 \\ 1 & \varepsilon_3 & \varepsilon_3^2 & \varepsilon_3^3 \end{bmatrix}. \qquad (7.6.2.12)$$

Let

$$\mathbf{D}_q = \begin{bmatrix} q(\varepsilon_0) & 0 & 0 & \cdot & \cdot & \cdot & 0 \\ 0 & q(\varepsilon_1) & 0 & \cdot & \cdot & \cdot & 0 \\ 0 & 0 & q(\varepsilon_2) & \cdot & \cdot & \cdot & 0 \\ \cdot & \cdot & \cdot & \cdot & \cdot & \cdot & \cdot \\ \cdot & \cdot & \cdot & \cdot & \cdot & \cdot & \cdot \\ \cdot & \cdot & \cdot & \cdot & \cdot & \cdot & \cdot \\ 0 & 0 & 0 & \cdot & \cdot & \cdot & q(\varepsilon_m) \end{bmatrix}, \qquad (7.6.2.13)$$

and consider the linear system

$$\mathbf{W}^T \mathbf{D}_q^{-1} \mathbf{C} = \mathbf{e}_1 \qquad (7.6.2.14)$$

where $\mathbf{c} = (c_1, c_2, \cdots, c_{m+1})$ and $\mathbf{e}_1 = (1, 0, 0, \cdots, 0)$. From (7.6.2.13), we have

$$\sum_{i=0}^{m} c_{i+1} \frac{\varepsilon_i^{\,j}}{q(\varepsilon_i)} = \begin{cases} 1, & \text{if } j = 0 \\ 0, & \text{otherwise.} \end{cases} \qquad (7.6.2.15)$$

If

$$Q(x) = \alpha_0 + \alpha_1 x + \alpha_2 x^2 + \cdots + \alpha_m x^m, \qquad (7.6.2.16)$$

then, from

$$\sum_{j=0}^{m} \alpha_j \sum_{i=0}^{m} c_{i+1} \frac{\varepsilon_i^{\,j}}{q(\varepsilon_i)} = \alpha_0, \qquad (7.6.2.17)$$

we obtain

$$\sum_{i=0}^{m} c_{i+1} \frac{Q(\varepsilon_i)}{q(\varepsilon_i)} = Q(0). \tag{7.6.2.18}$$

In particular, if $Q(x) = p_{ij}(x)$ defined in (7.6.2.8), then from (7.6.2.17) we obtain a basic relation

$$\sum_{i=0}^{m} c_{i+1} \frac{p_{ij}(\varepsilon_i)}{q(\varepsilon_i)} = p_{ij}(0). \tag{7.6.2.19}$$

When expressed in matrix form, this becomes

$$\sum_{i=0}^{m} c_{i+1} \mathbf{A}_m^{-1}(\varepsilon) = \det[\mathbf{A}_m(0)]\mathbf{A}_m^{-1}(0). \tag{7.6.2.20}$$

Combining this with (7.6.2.5), we have

$$\mathbf{x}(0) = \mathbf{A}_m^{-1}(0)\,\mathbf{d}$$

$$= \frac{1}{\det[\mathbf{A}_m(0)]} \sum_{i=0}^{m} c_{i+1} \mathbf{A}_m^{-1}(\varepsilon)\,\mathbf{d}$$

$$= \frac{1}{a_1^N} \sum_{i=0}^{m} c_{i+1} \mathbf{x}(\varepsilon_i). \tag{7.6.2.21}$$

The above analysis naturally leads to the algorithm in Fig. 7.6.2.1, from which we obtain the following theorem.

Theorem 7.6.2.1. The solution of the linear system (7.6.2.5) can be computed using the algorithm in Fig. 7.6.2.1 exactly in $6 \log N + \log m + O(1)$ steps using $\frac{5}{2} N(m+1)$ processors.

Proof
From Corollary 7.6.1.6, it follows that step 1 of this algorithm can be completed in $6 \log N + O(1)$ steps using $\frac{5}{2} N(m+1)$ processors.

In analyzing step 2, notice that the Vandermonde matrix $\mathbf{W}$ and its inverse can be precomputed and may be considered as input to the algorithm. If

$$\mathbf{W}^{-1} = [\hat{W}_{ij}],$$

we can rewrite (7.6.2.14) using the first row of $\mathbf{W}^{-1}$ as

$$\left[\frac{c_{j+1}}{a_1^N} \right] = \left[\frac{q(\varepsilon_j)}{a_1^N} \right] \hat{w}_{1,j+1}, \tag{7.6.2.22}$$

for $j = 0$ to m. (See Exercise 7.44.) Thus, step 2 can be completed in one step using at most N processors. The sum in step 3 can be computed in $\lceil \log(m + 1) \rceil$ steps. Combining these, the theorem follows.

Since $A_N(0)$ is an upper triangular Toeplitz matrix, the following corollary is immediate.

Corollary 7.6.2.2. The solution of a linear upper triangular Toeplitz system (equation (7.6.2.5) with $m = N$) can be computed in $7 \log N + O(1)$ steps using $2.5N(N + 1)$ processors.

Rewriting (7.6.2.20), we obtain

$$A_m^{-1}(0) = \frac{1}{\det[A_m(0)]} \sum_{i=0}^{m} c_{i+1} A_m^{-1}(\varepsilon). \qquad (7.6.2.23)$$

Combining this with Corollary 7.6.1.8, from Theorem 7.6.2.1, we obtain

Corollary 7.6.2.3. The inverse of an upper triangular Toeplitz matrix can be computed in $O(\log N)$ steps.

/* Given $A_m(0)$ and $\mathbf{d}$, solve $A_m(0)\,\mathbf{x} = \mathbf{d}$. */

Step 1. Compute $\dfrac{q(\varepsilon_i)}{a_1{}^N}$ and solve $A_m(\varepsilon_i)\,\mathbf{x}(\varepsilon_i) = \mathbf{d}$, for $i = 0, 1, 2, \cdots, m$ in parallel.

Step 2. Compute $\dfrac{c_{j+1}}{a_1{}^N}$ for $j = 0$ to m using (7.6.2.14).

Step 3. Compute $\displaystyle\sum_{i=0}^{m} \left[\frac{c_{i+1}}{a_1{}^N} \right] \mathbf{x}(\varepsilon_i)$

FIGURE 7.6.2.1
Bini's Algorithm -- exact solution.

7.6.3 Banded Toeplitz System

Let $\mathbf{A} = [\, a_{ij} \,]$ be an $N \times N$ banded Toeplitz matrix, where

$$a_{ij} = 0 \ \text{for} \ i - j > k \ \text{and} \ j - i > h, \qquad (7.6.3.1)$$

and $k < h$. The bandwidth of $\mathbf{A}$ is $k + h + 1$. When $k = 1$ and $h = n - 1$, $\mathbf{A}$ is called an upper triangular *Hessenberg* Toeplitz matrix. $\mathbf{A}$ is called a *balanced banded* Toeplitz matrix if $k = h$. An example with $N = 5$, $k = 2$, and $h = 3$ is

$$\mathbf{A} = \begin{bmatrix} a_3 & a_4 & a_5 & a_6 & 0 \\ a_2 & a_3 & a_4 & a_5 & a_6 \\ a_1 & a_2 & a_3 & a_4 & a_5 \\ 0 & a_1 & a_2 & a_3 & a_4 \\ 0 & 0 & a_1 & a_2 & a_3 \end{bmatrix}. \qquad (7.6.3.2)$$

Embed the matrix $\mathbf{A}$ as a submatrix of an upper triangular Toeplitz matrix $\mathbf{U}$ of order $N + k$ as

$$\mathbf{U} = \left[\begin{array}{c|c} \mathbf{E}_1 & \mathbf{A} \\ \hline \mathbf{E}_2 & \mathbf{E}_3 \end{array} \right], \qquad (7.6.3.3)$$

where $\mathbf{E}_1$, $\mathbf{E}_2$, and $\mathbf{E}_3$ are Toeplitz matrices of size $N \times k$, $k \times k$, and $k \times N$, respectively. As an example, embedding $\mathbf{A}$ in (7.6.3.2), we obtain

$$\mathbf{U} = \begin{bmatrix} a_1 & a_2 & a_3 & a_4 & a_5 & a_6 & 0 \\ 0 & a_1 & a_2 & a_3 & a_4 & a_5 & a_6 \\ 0 & 0 & a_1 & a_2 & a_3 & a_4 & a_5 \\ 0 & 0 & 0 & a_1 & a_2 & a_3 & a_4 \\ 0 & 0 & 0 & 0 & a_1 & a_2 & a_3 \\ 0 & 0 & 0 & 0 & 0 & a_1 & a_2 \\ 0 & 0 & 0 & 0 & 0 & 0 & a_1 \end{bmatrix}. \qquad (7.6.3.4)$$

Let

$$U^{-1} = \left[\begin{array}{c|c} S_1 & R \\ \hline S_2 & S_3 \end{array} \right], \tag{7.6.3.5}$$

where S_1, S_2, S_3 and R are $k \times N$, $N \times N$, $N \times k$, and $k \times k$ matrices (see Exercise 7.50). It can be shown that the square matrix R of order k is non-singular if A is non-singular (Exercise 7.49). Consider the banded Toeplitz system

$$A x = d, \tag{7.6.3.6}$$

where the bandwidth of A is $k + h + 1$. It is easily seen that x is the solution of (7.6.3.6) if and only if there exists a k-vector y such that

$$U \begin{bmatrix} Z_1 \\ Z_2 \end{bmatrix} = \begin{bmatrix} d \\ y \end{bmatrix} \tag{7.6.3.7}$$

has a solution with $Z_1 = 0$ and $Z_2 = x$. From

$$\begin{bmatrix} Z_1 \\ Z_2 \end{bmatrix} = \left[\begin{array}{c|c} S_1 & R \\ \hline S_2 & S_3 \end{array} \right] \begin{bmatrix} d \\ y \end{bmatrix}, \tag{7.6.3.8}$$

we obtain that $Z_1 = 0$ if and only if

$$R y = - S_1 d. \tag{7.6.3.9}$$

Since R is non-singular, there exists a choice of y that guarantees the solution of (7.6.3.7) with the desired properties.

An algorithm for computing the solution of (7.6.3.7) is given in Fig. 7.6.3.1, from which we obtain the following theorem (see Exercise 7.42 for an alternate scheme).

Theorem 7.6.3.1. The solution of a linear banded Toeplitz system (7.6.3.6) can be computed in $8 \log N + O((\log k)^2) + O(1)$ steps using

$$\max \left\{ \frac{N(N+1)}{2}, \ \frac{5}{2} N(k+h) \right\}$$

processors, where $k < \sqrt{N}$.

/*   Given the matrix **A** and the vector **d**, solve
for **A** **x** = **d** by solving (7.6.3.7).   */

Step 1. Invert the upper triangular Toeplitz matrix **U** using the algorithm in Section 7.6.2, and identify the submatrices S_1 and **R**.

Step 2. Compute $- S_1$ **d**.

Step 3. Solve **R** **y** $= - S_1$ **d** in (7.6.3.9).

Step 4. Compute $\mathbf{U}^{-1} \begin{bmatrix} \mathbf{d} \\ \mathbf{y} \end{bmatrix}$ and identify **x**.

FIGURE 7.6.3.1
Bini's algorithm - banded Toeplitz matrices.

Proof
$\mathbf{U}^{-1}$ in step 1 can be computed in $6 \log (N + k) + \log (k + h) + O(1)$ steps using $\frac{5}{2} N (k + h)$ processors. Step 2 can be completed in $1 + \log N$ steps using $k N$ processors. The $k \times k$ system in step 3 can be solved using Csanky's method (see Section 7.4) in $O((\log k)^2)$ steps using $O(k^4)$ processors. The last step 4 computes a matrix - vector product involving an upper triangular matrix. This can be completed in $1 + \log N$ steps using $\frac{N(N+1)}{2}$ processors. The theorem follows by combining these results.

The special case of $k = 1$ and $h = N - 1$ is worthy of special mention (see Exercise 7.52).

Corollary 7.6.3.2. The upper triangular Hessenberg-Toeplitz system can be solved in $8 \log N + O(1)$ steps using $\frac{5}{2} N^2$ processors.

Another special case of a balanced banded system arises when $k = h$ (see Exercise 7.53).

Corollary 7.6.3.3. The linear system with a balanced banded Toeplitz matrix can be solved in $8 \log N + O((\log k)^2) + O(1)$ steps using $O(N^2)$ processors.

7.7 SYMMETRIC EIGENVALUE PROBLEM

Let A be an $N \times N$ real symmetric matrix. It is well known (Stewart [1973]) that there exists a matrix R such that

$$R'AR = \Delta$$

and

$$R'R = I_N,$$

where $\Delta = \mathbf{diag}(\delta_1, \delta_2, \cdots, \delta_N)$ is a diagonal matrix and I_N is the $N \times N$ identity matrix. The elements of Δ are the *eigenvalues* of A, and the *(orthonormal)* column vectors of R are the *eigenvectors* of A. The problem of computing Δ and R, given A, arises in many application areas, and excellent software packages are available for computing these quantities on serial computers.

In the following, we present a parallel algorithm for this problem when A is a symmetric tridiagonal matrix. Since any real symmetric matrix can be reduced to a symmetric tridiagonal matrix using Householder's transformations (see Section 7.2.6), combining these, one can develop working algorithms for many of the commercially available parallel processors. Alternatively, one could use the Givens transformation for purposes of tridiagonalization. For details on Givens transformation, see Section 6.4.2.

7.7.1 Cuppen's Algorithm

Let A be an $N \times N$ symmetric tridiagonal matrix

$$A = \begin{bmatrix} b_1 & a_2 & 0 & 0 & \cdots & 0 & 0 & 0 \\ a_2 & b_2 & a_3 & 0 & \cdots & 0 & 0 & 0 \\ 0 & a_3 & b_3 & a_4 & \cdots & 0 & 0 & 0 \\ . & . & . & . & & . & . & . \\ . & . & . & . & & . & . & . \\ . & . & . & . & & . & . & . \\ 0 & 0 & 0 & 0 & \cdots & a_{N-1} & b_{N-1} & a_N \\ 0 & 0 & 0 & 0 & \cdots & 0 & a_N & b_N \end{bmatrix} \quad (7.7.1.1)$$

First partition A as follows:

$$
A = \left[
\begin{array}{c|c}
\hat{A}_1 & a_{k+1}e_k(k)e_1^t(N-k) \\
\hline
a_{k+1}e_1(N-k)e_k^t(k) & \hat{A}_2
\end{array}
\right], \qquad (7.7.1.2)
$$

where $\hat{A}_1$ and $\hat{A}_2$ are tridiagonal matrices of order k and $N-k$, respectively, and $e_j(r)$ is the jth unit column vector of size r. Let $b = (e_k(k), e_1(N-k))$ be a column vector obtained by concatenating $e_k(k)$ and $e_1(N-k)$. Then

$$
A = \left[
\begin{array}{c|c}
A_1 & 0 \\
\hline
0 & A_2
\end{array}
\right] + a_{k+1}bb^t, \qquad (7.7.1.3)
$$

where all the elements of A_1 (A_2) are the same as in $\hat{A}_1$ ($\hat{A}_2$) except the last (first) element of the principal diagonal, which is $b_k - a_{k+1}$ ($b_{k+1} - a_{k+1}$).

An example will illustrate this partitioning process. Let $N = 5$ and

$$
A = \begin{bmatrix}
b_1 & a_2 & 0 & 0 & 0 \\
a_2 & b_2 & a_3 & 0 & 0 \\
0 & a_3 & b_3 & a_4 & 0 \\
0 & 0 & a_4 & b_4 & a_5 \\
0 & 0 & 0 & a_5 & b_5
\end{bmatrix}.
$$

Then, for $k = 3$,

$$
A_1 = \begin{bmatrix}
b_1 & a_2 & 0 \\
a_2 & b_2 & a_3 \\
0 & a_3 & b_2 - a_4
\end{bmatrix}, \qquad
A_2 = \begin{bmatrix}
b_4 - a_4 & a_5 \\
a_5 & b_5
\end{bmatrix},
$$

and

$$
a_4 bb^t = \begin{bmatrix}
0 & 0 & 0 & 0 & 0 \\
0 & 0 & 0 & 0 & 0 \\
0 & 0 & a_4 & a_4 & 0 \\
0 & 0 & a_4 & a_4 & 0 \\
0 & 0 & 0 & 0 & 0
\end{bmatrix}.
$$

Let Q_1 and Q_2 be orthogonal matrices such that

$$Q_1^t A_1 Q_1 = D_1, \qquad Q_2^t A_2 Q_2 = D_2,$$
$$Q_1^t Q_1 = I_k, \qquad\qquad Q_2^t Q_2 = I_{N-k}, \qquad\Bigg\} \qquad (7.7.1.4)$$

where

$$D_1 = \mathbf{diag}(d_{11}, d_{12}, \cdots, d_{1k})$$

and

$$D_2 = \mathbf{diag}(d_{21}, d_{22}, \cdots, d_{2,N-k}).$$

Define

$$\mathbf{q}_1 = Q_1^t e_k(k) \qquad \text{and} \qquad \mathbf{q}_2 = Q_2^t e_1(N - k), \qquad (7.7.1.5)$$

that is, $\mathbf{q}_1^t$ is the last row of Q_1 and $\mathbf{q}_2^t$ is the first row of Q_2, and

$$\mathbf{z} = \frac{1}{\sqrt{2}} \begin{bmatrix} \mathbf{q}_1 \\ \mathbf{q}_2 \end{bmatrix}.$$

Clearly, $\|\mathbf{z}\|_2 = 1$, and

$$\mathbf{z} = \frac{1}{\sqrt{2}} \left[\begin{array}{c|c} Q_1^t & 0 \\ \hline & \\ \hline 0 & Q_2^t \end{array} \right] \mathbf{b}. \qquad (7.7.1.6)$$

Combining this with (7.7.1.4), we obtain

$$A = \left[\begin{array}{c|c} Q_1 & 0 \\ \hline & \\ \hline 0 & Q_2 \end{array} \right] [D + \alpha \, \mathbf{z}\mathbf{z}^t] \left[\begin{array}{c|c} Q_1^t & 0 \\ \hline & \\ \hline 0 & Q_2^t \end{array} \right], \qquad (7.7.1.7)$$

where

$$D = \left[\begin{array}{c|c} D_1 & 0 \\ \hline & \\ \hline 0 & D_2 \end{array} \right], \qquad (7.7.1.8)$$

and $\alpha = 2a_{k+1} \neq 0$. From (7.7.1.7), we readily infer that both A and $D + \alpha \, \mathbf{z}\mathbf{z}^t$

have the same set of eigenvalues.

This analysis immediately suggests an algorithm. First partition $\mathbf{A}$ as in (7.7.1.3) and obtain the eigenvalues and eigenvectors of the matrices $\mathbf{A}_1$ and $\mathbf{A}_2$. Then form the new matrix $\mathbf{D} + \alpha \mathbf{z}\mathbf{z}^t$ and compute its eigenvalues. This *divide-and-conquer* approach naturally leads to a recursive procedure.

As an example, let $N = 32$. Partition the given tridiagonal matrix $\mathbf{A}$ as in (7.7.1.3) to obtain tridiagonal matrices $\mathbf{A}_1$ and $\mathbf{A}_2$ each of size 16. Further, partition $\mathbf{A}_1$ and $\mathbf{A}_2$ to obtain four tridiagonal matrices $\mathbf{A}_{11}$, $\mathbf{A}_{12}$, $\mathbf{A}_{21}$, and $\mathbf{A}_{22}$, each of size 8. We thus obtain a collection of problems connected in a binary tree, as shown in Fig. 7.7.1.1. While in principle this recursion can be continued to the lowest level of 2×2 matrices, in practice, from efficiency considerations, one may choose to stop at a certain level, say, $p \times p$ matrices for some integer $p \geq 2$. At this lowest level, the eigenvalues are found by the best known serial algorithms. Once the eigenvalues and vectors at this lowest level are computed, it follows from the above analysis that the rest of the computation is basically that of computing the eigenvalues and vectors of matrices of the form

$$\mathbf{D} + \alpha \mathbf{z}\mathbf{z}^t, \qquad (7.7.1.9)$$

where $\mathbf{D}$ is a diagonal matrix, $\alpha \neq 0$, and $\mathbf{z}$ is a vector with $\|\mathbf{z}\|_2 = 1$. Since $\mathbf{z}\mathbf{z}^t$ is a symmetric *rank* [1] 1 matrix, this is often called a *rank* 1 modification of the symmetric eigenvalue problem.

Thus given $\mathbf{D} = \mathbf{diag}(d_1, d_2, \cdots, d_N)$, the vector $\mathbf{z}$, and the constant $\alpha \neq 0$, the general problem is to find an orthogonal matrix $\mathbf{P}$ such that

$$\mathbf{P}\Lambda\mathbf{P}^t = \mathbf{D} + \alpha \mathbf{z}\mathbf{z}^t, \qquad (7.7.1.10)$$

where

$$\Lambda = \mathbf{diag}(\lambda_1, \lambda_2, \cdots, \lambda_N).$$

Before stating the main result leading to an algorithm for this problem, we shall dispense with a number of easy special cases.

Case 1. If the vector $\mathbf{z}$ is such that one of its components, say z_i, equals 0, then from (7.7.1.10) it follows that

$$\lambda_i = d_i.$$

From

$$(\mathbf{D} + \alpha \mathbf{z}\mathbf{z}^t)\mathbf{e}_i = \mathbf{D}\mathbf{e}_i + \alpha \mathbf{z}z_i = d_i$$

it follows that $\mathbf{e}_i$, the ith unit vector, is the eigenvector for both $\mathbf{D}$ and $\mathbf{D} + \alpha \mathbf{z}\mathbf{z}^t$ corresponding to this eigenvalue.

---

[1] The *rank* of a square matrix is the number of linearly independent columns of it.

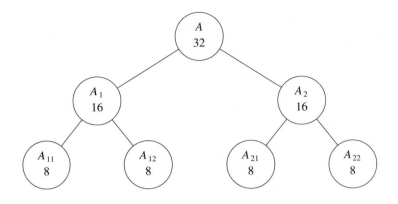

FIGURE 7.7.1.1
A divide-and-conquer approach to the symmetric tridiagonal eigenvalue problem.

Thus, if z_i is zero, we can effectively *reduce* the problem size from N to $N - 1$. This process is called *deflation*.

Case 2. We now investigate the effect of equality among the diagonal elements of **D**. Assume that

$$d_1 = d_2 = \cdots = d_k < d_{k+1} < \cdots < d_N.$$

Let

$$\mathbf{H} = \left[\begin{array}{c|c} \bar{\mathbf{H}} & \\ \hline & \mathbf{I}_{N-k} \end{array}\right] \tag{7.7.1.11}$$

be an orthogonal matrix. It can be verified (Exercise 7.57) that

$$\mathbf{H}\mathbf{D}\mathbf{H}^t = \mathbf{D}. \tag{7.7.1.12}$$

Let $\bar{\mathbf{z}} = (z_1, z_2, \cdots, z_k)^t$, $\mathbf{a} = (a_1, a_2, \cdots, a_N)^t$, where

$$a_1 = z_1 + (sign\,(z_1))\beta$$
$$a_j = z_j, \qquad \text{for } j = 2, 3, \cdots, k,$$

and

$$\beta = (z_1^2 + z_2^2 + \cdots + z_k^2)^{\frac{1}{2}}.$$

If $\bar{\mathbf{H}}$ is a Householder transformation (see Section 7.2.6) of the type

$$\overline{\mathbf{H}} = \mathbf{I}_k - \frac{2\mathbf{a}\mathbf{a}^t}{\mathbf{a}^t\mathbf{a}},$$

then it follows that $\overline{\mathbf{H}}$ annihilates all but the first component of $\overline{\mathbf{z}}$, and $\mathbf{Hz}$ is a vector of the form $\mathbf{y} = (y_1, 0, 0, \cdots, 0, y_{k+1}, y_{k+2}, \cdots, y_N)^t$. From this and (7.7.1.12), we have

$$\mathbf{H}[\mathbf{D} + \alpha \, \mathbf{z}\mathbf{z}^t]\mathbf{H}^t = \mathbf{D} + \alpha \mathbf{y}\mathbf{y}^t.$$

From case 1, we can delete all rows in $\mathbf{D}$ corresponding to the zero components in $\mathbf{y}$. In other words, we can deflate the problem to be of size $N - k + 1$, for some $k \geq 2$.

By repeating this process enough times we can reduce the problem to the case where the diagonal elements of $\mathbf{D}$ are distinct. For further details of the deflation process, refer to Bunch, Nielsen, and Sorensen [1978].

We now state the main result.

Theorem 7.7.1.1. Let $\mathbf{D} = \mathbf{diag}(d_1, d_2, \cdots, d_N)$ with $d_1 < d_2 < \cdots < d_N$. Let $\mathbf{z} = (z_1, z_2, \cdots, z_N)^t$ be such that $z_i \neq 0$, for all $i = 1$ to N, and $\alpha \neq 0$. Then the eigenvalues of $\mathbf{D} + \alpha \, \mathbf{z}\mathbf{z}^t$ are equal to the N roots

$$\lambda_1 < \lambda_2 < \cdots < \lambda_N$$

of the rational function

$$g(\lambda) = 1 + \alpha \mathbf{z}^t(\mathbf{D} - \lambda\mathbf{I})^{-1}\mathbf{z}$$

$$= 1 + \alpha \sum_{i=1}^{N} \frac{z_i^2}{(d_i - \lambda)}. \qquad (7.7.1.13)$$

The corresponding eigenvectors $\mathbf{v}_1, \mathbf{v}_2, \cdots, \mathbf{v}_n$ of $\mathbf{D} + \alpha \, \mathbf{z}\mathbf{z}^t$ are given by

$$\mathbf{v}_i = r(\mathbf{D} - \lambda_i\mathbf{I})^{-1}\mathbf{z} \qquad (7.7.1.14)$$

for some constant r.

Proof

Let $(\lambda, \mathbf{v})$ be an eigenvalue - vector pair. Then from

$$(\mathbf{D} + \alpha \, \mathbf{z}\mathbf{z}^t)\mathbf{v} = \lambda\mathbf{v},$$

we have

$$(\mathbf{D} - \lambda\mathbf{I}) \, \mathbf{v} = -\alpha(\mathbf{z}^t\mathbf{v})\mathbf{z}. \qquad (7.7.1.15)$$

To prove that $(\mathbf{D} - \lambda\mathbf{I})$ is non-singular, assume that it is singular. If $\lambda = d_i$ for some i, then the ith component of the right-hand side of (7.7.1.15), namely,

$$-\alpha(\mathbf{z}^t\mathbf{v})z_i = 0.$$

Since $\alpha > 0$, we have $\mathbf{z}^t\mathbf{v} = 0$, and

$$(\mathbf{D} - d_i\mathbf{I})\mathbf{v} = 0, \tag{7.7.1.16}$$

that is,

$$(d_j - d_i)v_j = 0,$$

from which we obtain $v_j = 0$ for all $j \neq i$ and $v_i \neq 0$, for otherwise $\mathbf{v}$ would be a null vector. Combining this with $\mathbf{z}^t\mathbf{v} = 0$, we obtain $z_i = 0$, a contradiction. Hence $\mathbf{z}^t\mathbf{v} \neq 0$, $(\mathbf{D} - \lambda\mathbf{I})$ is non-singular, and

$$\mathbf{v} = -\alpha(\mathbf{z}^t\mathbf{v})(\mathbf{D} - \lambda\mathbf{I})^{-1}\mathbf{z}, \tag{7.7.1.17}$$

from which (7.7.1.14) follows.

Multiplying both sides of (7.7.1.15) by $\mathbf{z}^t(\mathbf{D} - \lambda\mathbf{I})^{-1}$ and simplifying, we get

$$g(\lambda) = 1 + \alpha\, \mathbf{z}^t(\mathbf{D} - \lambda\mathbf{I})^{-1}\mathbf{z} = 0, \tag{7.7.1.18}$$

from which (7.7.1.13) follows.

Depending on whether α is positive or negative, the eigenvalues of $\mathbf{D}$ and $\mathbf{D} + \alpha\,\mathbf{z}\mathbf{z}^t$ satisfy a very useful separation property (without proof):

If $\alpha > 0$, then

$$\left. \begin{array}{l} d_i < \lambda_i < d_{i+1}, \quad \text{for } i = 1, 2, \cdots, N-1, \\[2ex] d_N < \lambda_N < d_N + \alpha\, \mathbf{z}^t\mathbf{z}, \end{array} \right\} \tag{7.7.1.19}$$

and if $\alpha < 0$,

$$\left. \begin{array}{l} d_1 + \alpha\, \mathbf{z}^t\mathbf{z} < \lambda_1 < d_1 \\[2ex] d_{i-1} < \lambda_i < d_i, \quad \text{for } i = 2, 3, \cdots, N. \end{array} \right\} \tag{7.7.1.20}$$

As may be expected, this separation property plays a crucial role in the development of an algorithm for solving

$$g(\lambda) = 0,$$

known as the *secular equation* (Exercise 7.59).

The graph of the function $g(\lambda)$ for the case $\mathbf{D} = diag(1, 2, 3, 4)$, $\alpha = 2$, and $\mathbf{z} = (0.5, 0.5, 0.5, 0.5)^t$ is given in Fig. 7.7.1.2.

We now move on to solving the secular equation by illustrating the computation of a typical eigenvalue λ_i. In view of the separation property, we can use this procedure in parallel to recover all the eigenvalues. Let

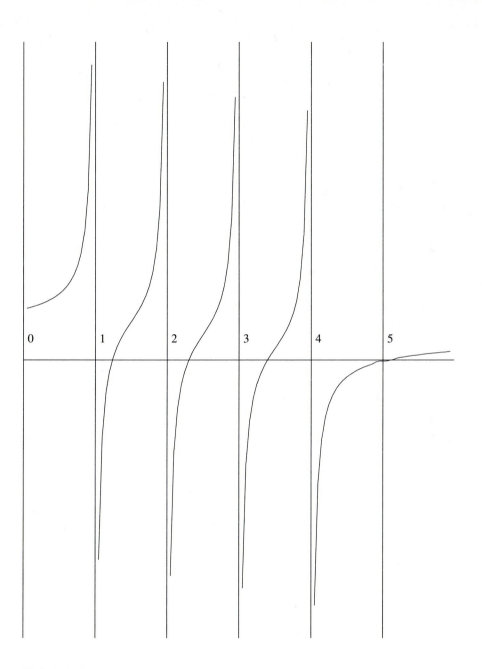

FIGURE 7.7.1.2
An example of the function g(λ).

$$f(\lambda) = \alpha \sum_{j=1}^{i} \frac{z_j^2}{d_j - \lambda}$$

and

$$h(\lambda) = \alpha \sum_{j=i+1}^{N} \frac{z_j^2}{d_j - \lambda}.$$

(7.7.1.21)

Then (7.7.1.13) can be written as

$$g(\lambda) = 1 + h(\lambda) + f(\lambda).$$

(7.7.1.22)

Consider the open interval (d_i, d_{i+1}). In this interval, $f(\lambda) < 0$ and $h(\lambda) > 0$. Further, $1 + h(\lambda)$ is an increasing function and $-f(\lambda)$ is a decreasing function (Exercise 7.58). Hence, the eigenvalue λ_i is obtained by solving

$$-f(\lambda) = 1 + h(\lambda).$$

(7.7.1.23)

A plot of the functions $f(\lambda)$ and $g(\lambda)$ in the open interval $(2, 3)$ is given in Fig. 7.7.1.3.

This equation can be solved in a variety of ways, such as by using Newton's method. However, since $f(\lambda)$ and $h(\lambda)$ are rational functions, they can be approximated locally by simple rational functions.

Let $d_i < \delta_1 < \lambda_i$ be an initial approximation to λ_i. To find the new (better) approximation, δ_2, first define simple interpolating rational functions:

$$\frac{p_1}{p_2 - \lambda}, \quad \text{and} \quad q_1 + \frac{q_2}{d_{i+1} - \lambda},$$

approximating $f(\lambda)$ and $h(\lambda)$, respectively, at point δ_1. The constants p_1, p_2, q_1, and q_2 are defined by the interpolation conditions, namely,

$$\frac{p_1}{p_2 - \delta_1} = f(\delta_1), \qquad \frac{p_1}{(p_2 - \delta_1)^2} = f'(\delta_1)$$

$$q_1 + \frac{q_2}{d_{i+1} - \delta_1} = h(\delta_1), \qquad \frac{q_2}{(d_{i+1} - \delta_1)^2} = h'(\delta_1),$$

(7.7.1.24)

where $f'(\lambda) = \dfrac{df(\lambda)}{d\lambda}$ and $h'(\lambda) = \dfrac{dh(\lambda)}{d\lambda}$.

Solving these equations, we obtain that

$$p_1 = \frac{f^2(\delta_1)}{f'(\delta_1)}, \qquad q_1 = h(\delta_1) - (d_{i+1} - \delta_1)h'(\delta_1)$$

$$p_2 = \delta_1 + \frac{f(\delta_1)}{f'(\delta_1)}, \qquad q_2 = (d_{i+1} - \delta_1)^2 h'(\delta_1).$$

(7.7.1.25)

Using these, the new approximation δ_2 is obtained as the solution (see Exercise 7.63)

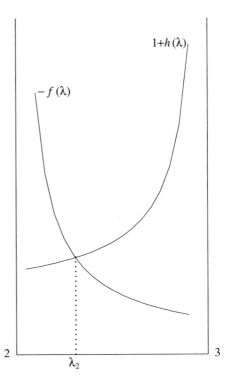

FIGURE 7.7.1.3
An illustration of the computation of the eigenvalue λ_2.

of

$$\frac{-p_1}{p_2 - \delta_2} = 1 + q_1 + \frac{q_2}{d_{i+1} - \delta_2}, \qquad (7.7.1.26)$$

which is a quadratic equation in δ_2. We can now repeat this process by replacing δ_1 by δ_2 to find the third (even better) approximation δ_3 to λ_i. This process is iteratively continued until we find a δ_k which is close to λ_i within a prespecified bound.

We now state a number of facts relating to the properties of the sequence δ_i, $i = 1, 2, 3, \cdots$.

(P1) If $d_i < \delta_1 < \lambda_i$, then $\delta_i < \delta_{i+1}$, for $i = 1, 2, 3, \cdots$, that is, δ_i is a monotonically increasing sequence.

(P2) The sequence δ_i converges quadratically to λ_i, that is,

$$| \delta_{i+1} - \lambda_i | \le \eta \; | \delta_i - \lambda_i |^2,$$

for all $i = 1, 2, \cdots$, where η is a constant independent of i.

The proof of these properties can be obtained from Bunch, Nielsen, and Sorensen [1978], and is left as an exercise. We encourage the reader to develop a program by combining the original reduction of a symmetric matrix to the tridiagonal form and the above divide-and-conquer method.

7.7.2 Krishnakumar-Morf Algorithm

In this section, we present an alternate approach to the symmetric eigenvalue problem for the tridiagonal matrix. This method first computes the characteristic polynomial of a tridiagonal matrix using a divide-and-conquer approach.

Let $\mathbf{A}$ be the tridiagonal matrix in (7.7.1.1), and let

$$p_i(\lambda) = \det[\mathbf{A}_i - \lambda \mathbf{I}_i], \tag{7.7.2.1}$$

where $\mathbf{A}_i$ is the *leading* principal submatrix of order i. By expanding along the last row of $\mathbf{A}_i$, it can be shown that (Exercise 7.61)

$$p_i(\lambda) = (b_i - \lambda) p_{i-1}(\lambda) - a_i^2 p_{i-2}(\lambda), \tag{7.7.2.2}$$

where $p_0(\lambda) = 1$ and $p_1(\lambda) = (b_1 - \lambda)$. For $i \ge j$, let $p_{i:j}(\lambda)$ denote the characteristic polynomial of the principal submatrix (of order $j - i + 1$) $\mathbf{A}_{i:j}$ contained within the ith row and column and j^{th} row and column. Clearly, $\mathbf{A}_k = \mathbf{A}_{1:k}$ and $p_k(\lambda) = p_{1:k}(\lambda)$, for $k = 1, 2, \cdots, N$. As an example,

$$\mathbf{A}_{3:5} = \begin{bmatrix} b_3 & a_4 & 0 \\ a_4 & b_4 & a_5 \\ 0 & a_5 & b_5 \end{bmatrix}$$

and

$$p_{3:5}(\lambda) = \det[\mathbf{A}_{3:5} - \lambda \mathbf{I}_3 \,].$$

We now derive a new type of recurrence for computing $p_N(\lambda)$. First partition $\mathbf{B} = (\mathbf{A} - \lambda \mathbf{I})$, as follows:

$$\mathbf{B} = \left[\begin{array}{c|c} \mathbf{B}_{1:k} & a_{k+1} e_k(k) e_1'(N-k) \\ \hline a_{k+1} e_k(k) e_1'(N-k) & \mathbf{B}_{k+1:N} \end{array} \right], \tag{7.7.2.3}$$

where $e_j(r)$ is the jth unit (column) vector of size r. Expanding $\mathbf{B}$ along the $(k+1)^{th}$ row, we obtain

$$p_N(\lambda) = -a_{k+1} \det[\mathbf{E}_1]$$

$$+ (b_{k+1} - \lambda)p_{1:k}(\lambda)p_{k+2:N}(\lambda) - a_{k+2} \det[\mathbf{E}_2], \qquad (7.2.2.4)$$

where

$$\mathbf{E}_1 = \left[\begin{array}{c|c} \mathbf{B}^{(1)}_{1:k} & a_{k+1}e_k(k)e_1^t(N-k) \\ \hline \mathbf{0} & \mathbf{B}^{(2)}_{k+1:N} \end{array} \right], \qquad (7.7.2.5)$$

$$\mathbf{E}_2 = \left[\begin{array}{c|c} \mathbf{B}_{1:k} & a_{k+1}e_k(k)e_1^t(N-k-1) \\ \hline \mathbf{0} & \mathbf{B}^{(3)}_{k+1:N} \end{array} \right], \qquad (7.7.2.6)$$

$\mathbf{B}^{(1)}_{1:k}$ is obtained from $\mathbf{B}_{1:k}$ by deleting its *last column*,

$\mathbf{B}^{(2)}_{k+1:N}$ is formed by deleting the *first row* of $\mathbf{B}_{k+1:N}$, and

$\mathbf{B}^{(3)}_{k+1:N}$ is obtained from $\mathbf{B}_{k+1:N}$ by deleting its *first row* and *second column*.

The following example illustrates this computation. Let $N = 8$ and $k = 4$. Then

$$\mathbf{E}_1 = \begin{bmatrix} b_1 - \lambda & a_2 & 0 & 0 & 0 & 0 & 0 \\ a_2 & b_2 - \lambda & a_3 & 0 & 0 & 0 & 0 \\ 0 & a_3 & b_3 - \lambda & 0 & 0 & 0 & 0 \\ 0 & 0 & a_4 & a_5 & 0 & 0 & 0 \\ 0 & 0 & 0 & a_6 & b_6 - \lambda & a_7 & 0 \\ 0 & 0 & 0 & 0 & a_7 & b_7 - \lambda & a_8 \\ 0 & 0 & 0 & 0 & 0 & a_8 & b_8 - \lambda \end{bmatrix}.$$

The fourth row of $\mathbf{E}_1$ has only two non-zero elements. Expanding along this row, we obtain that the cofactor of a_5 is $p_{1:3}(\lambda)p_{6:8}(\lambda)$. The cofactor of a_4 is related to the following:

$$\det \begin{bmatrix} b_1 - \lambda & a_2 & 0 & 0 & 0 & 0 \\ a_2 & b_2 - \lambda & 0 & 0 & 0 & 0 \\ 0 & a_3 & 0 & 0 & 0 & 0 \\ 0 & 0 & a_6 & b_6 - \lambda & a_7 & 0 \\ 0 & 0 & 0 & a_7 & b_7 - \lambda & a_8 \\ 0 & 0 & 0 & 0 & a_8 & b_8 - \lambda \end{bmatrix}.$$

The third column has only one element, and expanding along this column, it can be seen that the above determinant is related to the following

$$\det \begin{bmatrix} b_1 - \lambda & a_2 & 0 & 0 & 0 \\ a_2 & b_2 - \lambda & 0 & 0 & 0 \\ 0 & a_3 & 0 & 0 & 0 \\ 0 & 0 & a_7 & b_7 - \lambda & a_8 \\ 0 & 0 & 0 & a_8 & b_8 - \lambda \end{bmatrix}.$$

Now expanding along the third column containing a_7 and subsequently along the column containing a_8, it follows that the cofactor of a_4 is zero, and hence, in this example,

$$\det[\mathbf{E}_1] = a_5 p_{1:3}(\lambda) p_{6:8}(\lambda).$$

Generalizing this (Exercise 7.64), we obtain

$$\det[\mathbf{E}_1] = a_{k+1} \, p_{1:k-1}(\lambda) \, p_{k+2:N}(\lambda). \tag{7.7.2.7}$$

Proceeding along similar lines, it can be shown that

$$\det[\mathbf{E}_2] = a_{k+2} \, p_{1:k}(\lambda) \, p_{k+3:N}(\lambda). \tag{7.7.2.8}$$

Combining these with (7.7.2.4), and simplifying, we have

$$p_N(\lambda) = -a_{k+1}^2 \, p_{1:k-1}(\lambda) \, p_{k+2:N}(\lambda) + (b_{k+1} - \lambda) \, p_{1:k}(\lambda) \, p_{k+2:N}(\lambda)$$

$$- a_{k+2}^2 \, p_{1:k}(\lambda) \, p_{k+3:N}(\lambda). \tag{7.7.2.9}$$

Considering the matrix $\mathbf{A}_{k+1:N}$ and expanding along its first row, it can be seen that

$$p_{k+1:N}(\lambda) = (b_{k+1} - \lambda) \, p_{k+2:N}(\lambda) - a_{k+2}^2 \, p_{k+3:N}(\lambda). \tag{7.7.2.10}$$

Substituting (7.7.2.10) in (7.7.2.9) results in the following basic relation:

$$p_N(\lambda) = p_{1:k}(\lambda) \, p_{k+1:N}(\lambda) - a_{k+1}^2 \, p_{1:k-1}(\lambda) \, p_{k+2:N}(\lambda). \tag{7.7.2.11}$$

With this development as a background, we now turn to the symmetric eigenvalue problem. Let

$$\mathbf{A} = \mathbf{A}^* + a_{k+1} \mathbf{b} \mathbf{b}^t, \tag{7.7.2.12}$$

where

$$\mathbf{A}^* = \left[\begin{array}{c|c} \mathbf{A}_{1:k}^* & \mathbf{0} \\ \hline \mathbf{0} & \mathbf{A}_{k+1:N}^* \end{array} \right], \tag{7.7.2.13}$$

and the vector $\mathbf{b}$ is defined in (7.7.1.3). This method of splitting $\mathbf{A}$ is called the *rank 1 update*. From the above definition, it follows that $\mathbf{A}_{1:k}^*$ ($\mathbf{A}_{k+1:N}^*$) is the same as $\mathbf{A}_{1:k}$ ($\mathbf{A}_{k+1:N}$) except that the last (first) element of its principal diagonal is $b_k - a_{k+1}$ ($b_{k+1} - a_{k+1}$). Let $q_{i:j}(\lambda)$ be the characteristic polynomial of $\mathbf{A}_{i:j}^*$. Again from the definition, it follows that (Exercise 7.65)

$$
\left.\begin{aligned}
q_{1:k}(\lambda) &= p_{1:k}(\lambda) - a_{k+1}\, p_{1:\,k-1}(\lambda) \\
q_{k+1:\,N}(\lambda) &= p_{k+1:\,N}(\lambda) - a_{k+1}\, p_{k+2:\,N}(\lambda) \\
q_{1:\,k-1}(\lambda) &= p_{1:\,k-1}(\lambda) \\
q_{k+2:\,N}(\lambda) &= p_{k+2:\,N}(\lambda).
\end{aligned}\right\}
\tag{7.7.2.14}
$$

The new algorithm depends on two key ideas. The first of them consists in expressing the characteristic polynomial of $\mathbf{A}$ in terms of those of $\mathbf{A}^*$, where $\mathbf{A}$ and $\mathbf{A}^*$ are related through the rank 1 update in (7.7.2.12). This is done by exploiting the relation between the $p(.)$ polynomials and $q(.)$ polynomials given in (7.7.2.14). Indeed, combining the right-hand side of (7.7.2.11) with (7.7.2.14), we get

$$
p_{1:N}(\lambda) = [q_{1:k}(\lambda) + a_{k+1}\, p_{1:\,k-1}(\lambda)]\, [q_{k+1:\,N}(\lambda) + a_{k+1}\, p_{k+2:\,N}(\lambda)]
$$

$$
- a_{k+1}^2\, p_{1:\,k-1}(\lambda)\, p_{k+2:\,N}(\lambda).
$$

Using the last two relations in (7.7.2.14), it follows that

$$
p_{1:N}(\lambda) = q_{1:k}(\lambda)\, q_{k+1:\,N}(\lambda)
$$

$$
+ a_{k+1}\, [q_{1:k}(\lambda)\, q_{k+2:\,N} + q_{1:\,k-1}(\lambda)\, q_{k+1:\,N}(\lambda)].
\tag{7.7.2.15}
$$

Notice that the quantities on the right-hand side of this relation depend only on $\mathbf{A}^*$. Since $\mathbf{A}^*_{1:k}$ and $\mathbf{A}^*_{k+1:\,N}$ are themselves tridiagonal matrices, we can, in fact , apply this relation recursively to $\mathbf{A}^*_{1:k}$ and $\mathbf{A}^*_{k+1:\,N}$ by splitting them again using proper rank 1 updates. For purposes of later reference, we record the following three recurrences obtained from (7.7.2.15) by changing the subscript[2]:

$$
p_{1:N-1} = q_{1:k}\; q_{k+1:\,N-1} + a_{k+1}[q_{1:k}\; q_{k+2:N-1} + q_{1:\,k-1}\; q_{k+1:N-1}],
$$

$$
p_{2:N} = q_{2:k}\, q_{k+1:\,N} + a_{k+1}[q_{2:k}\, q_{k+2:N} + q_{2:\,k-1}\; q_{k+1:N}],
$$

$$
p_{2:N-1} = q_{2:k}\, q_{k+1:\,N-1} + a_{k+1}[q_{2:k}\, q_{k+2:N-1} + q_{2:\,k-1}\; q_{k+1:N-1}].
$$

Define

$$
e_1 = \frac{q_{1:\,k-1}}{q_{1:k}}, \qquad e_2 = \frac{q_{k+1:\,N-1}}{q_{k+1:\,N}},
$$

$$
f_1 = \frac{q_{2:k}}{q_{1:k}}, \qquad f_2 = \frac{q_{k+2:\,N}}{q_{k+1:\,N}},
$$

---

[2] For simplicity in notation, the argument λ is suppressed.

$$g_1 = \frac{q_{2:\,k-1}}{q_{1:\,k-1}}, \qquad g_2 = \frac{q_{k+2:\,N-1}}{q_{k+1:\,N-1}},$$

$$h_1 = \frac{q_{2:\,k-1}}{q_{2:\,k}}, \qquad h_2 = \frac{q_{k+2:\,N-1}}{q_{k+2:\,N}}.$$

Similarly, let

$$e = \frac{p_{1:\,N-1}}{p_{1:\,N}}, \qquad f = \frac{p_{2:\,N}}{p_{1:\,N}},$$

$$g = \frac{p_{2:\,N-1}}{p_{1:\,N-1}}, \qquad h = \frac{p_{2:\,N-1}}{p_{2:\,N}}.$$

The second idea is to relate the number of eigenvalues of **A** that are less than λ to the value of the ratio

$$w(\lambda) = \frac{p_{1:\,N}}{q_{1:\,k}q_{k+1:\,N}}.$$

From (7.7.2.15), using the above ratios, we readily see that

$$w(\lambda) = 1 + a_{k+1}[e_1 + f_2]. \qquad (7.7.2.16)$$

Likewise, from the three recurrences following (7.7.2.15), we obtain

$$\frac{p_{1:\,N-1}}{q_{1:\,k}\,q_{k+1:\,N-1}} = 1 + a_{k+1}[e_1 + g_2].$$

$$\frac{p_{2:\,N}}{q_{2:\,k}\,q_{k+1:\,N}} = 1 + a_{k+1}[h_1 + f_2].$$

$$\frac{p_{2:\,N-1}}{q_{2:\,k}\,q_{k+1:\,N-1}} = 1 + a_{k+1}[h_1 + g_2].$$

Using these, it can be shown (Exercise 7.66) that

$$\left.\begin{aligned}
e &= e_2 \left[\frac{1 + a_{k+1}(e_1 + g_2)}{1 + a_{k+1}(e_1 + f_2)}\right] \\[6pt]
f &= f_1 \left[\frac{1 + a_{k+1}(h_1 + f_2)}{1 + a_{k+1}(e_1 + f_2)}\right] \\[6pt]
g &= f_1 \left[\frac{1 + a_{k+1}(h_1 + g_2)}{1 + a_{k+1}(e_1 + g_2)}\right] \\[6pt]
h &= e_2 \left[\frac{1 + a_{k+1}(h_1 + g_2)}{1 + a_{k+1}(h_1 + f_2)}\right].
\end{aligned}\right\} \qquad (7.7.2.17)$$

Clearly (7.7.2.17) provides a recursive framework for computing the ratios e, f, g, and h for the matrix $\mathbf{A}$ in terms of those for matrices $\mathbf{A}^*_{1:k}$ and $\mathbf{A}^*_{k+1:N}$. Since $w(\lambda)$ depends on these ratios, we can indeed compute $w(\lambda)$ recursively.

Let $\#\mathbf{A}(\lambda)$ denote the number of eigenvalues of $\mathbf{A}$ that are strictly less than λ. In relating $w(\lambda)$ to $\#\mathbf{A}(\lambda)$ and $\#\mathbf{A}^*(\lambda)$, the following two lemmas are crucial.

Lemma 7.7.2.1. If $\mathbf{A}$ and $\mathbf{A}^*$ are two matrices that are related through the rank 1 update as in (7.7.2.12), then

$$(\#\mathbf{A}(\lambda) - \#\mathbf{A}^*(\lambda)) \in \{-1, 0, 1\}.$$

Proof

Let

$$\lambda_1 < \lambda_2 < \lambda_3 < \cdots < \lambda_N$$

be the eigenvalues of $\mathbf{A}$ and

$$d_1 < d_2 < d_3 < \cdots < d_N$$

be those of $\mathbf{A}^*$. From (7.7.1.19) and (7.7.1.20), we obtain (since $\mathbf{z}^t\mathbf{z} = \mathbf{b}^t\mathbf{b} = 2$, where $\mathbf{b}$ is given by (7.7.1.3))

$$d_1 < \lambda_1 < d_2 < \lambda_2 < d_3 < \cdots < d_N < \lambda_N < d_N + 2a_{k+1}, \qquad (7.7.2.18)$$

if $a_{k+1} > 0$, and

$$d_1 + 2a_{k+1} < \lambda_1 < d_1 < \lambda_2 < d_2 < \lambda_3 < \cdots < d_{N-1} < \lambda_N < d_N, \quad (7.7.2.19)$$

if $a_{k+1} < 0$.

Let $\#\mathbf{A}^*(\lambda) = m$. If $a_{k+1} > 0$, then $d_m < \lambda$, $\lambda_{m-1} < \lambda$, and λ_m lies in either the interval (d_m, λ) or $[\lambda, d_{m+1}]$. If it lies in (d_m, λ), then $\#\mathbf{A}(\lambda) = m$, and $\#\mathbf{A}(\lambda) - \#\mathbf{A}^*(\lambda) = 0$. On the other hand, if λ_m lies in $[\lambda, d_{m+1}]$, then $\#\mathbf{A}(\lambda) = m - 1$ and $\#\mathbf{A}(\lambda) - \#\mathbf{A}^*(\lambda) = -1$.

If $a_{k+1} < 0$, then by a similar argument, it follows that $\#\mathbf{A}(\lambda) - \#\mathbf{A}^*(\lambda) = 0$ or 1, and hence the lemma.

Let

$$u(x) = \begin{cases} 1 & \text{for } x \geq 0 \\ 0 & \text{for } x < 0, \end{cases}$$

that is, $u(x)$ is a unit step function.

Lemma 7.7.2.2. Let $\mathbf{A}$ and $\mathbf{A}^*$ be two matrices that are related through the rank 1 update as in (7.7.2.12). If $w(\lambda)$ is the ratio defined in (7.7.2.16), then

$$(\#\mathbf{A}^*(\lambda) - \#\mathbf{A}(\lambda)) = u(-w(\lambda)) \, sign(a_{k+1})$$

$$= \begin{cases} 0 & \text{if } w(\lambda) > 0 \\ 1(sign(a_{k+1})) & \text{if } w(\lambda) \le 0. \end{cases}$$

Proof

Let

$$\det[\mathbf{A} - \lambda\mathbf{I}] = p_{1:N}(\lambda) = (-1)^N \prod_{i=1}^{N} (\lambda - \lambda_i)$$

and

$$\det[\mathbf{A}^* - \lambda\mathbf{I}] = q_{1:k}(\lambda)q_{k+1:N}(\lambda) = (-1)^N \prod_{i=1}^{N} (\lambda - d_i).$$

Then

$$w(\lambda) = \frac{\displaystyle\prod_{i=1}^{N}(\lambda - \lambda_i)}{\displaystyle\prod_{i=1}^{N}(\lambda - d_i)}.$$

If $\#\mathbf{A}^*(\lambda) = \#\mathbf{A}(\lambda)$, then the corresponding terms in the numerator and the denominator of $w(\lambda)$ have the same sign. Thus, $w(\lambda)$ is positive and the theorem is true in this case.

If $\#\mathbf{A}^*(\lambda) - \#\mathbf{A}(\lambda) = \pm 1$, then there is one pair of corresponding terms in the numerator and denominator of $w(\lambda)$ that are of opposite sign, and $w(\lambda)$ is negative. From Lemma 7.7.2.1, it follows that $\#\mathbf{A}^*(\lambda) - \#\mathbf{A}(\lambda)$ is equal to $+1$ if $a_{k+1} > 0$, and -1 if $a_{k+1} < 0$. Hence the lemma.

In other words, the above lemma states that if we know the distribution of the eigenvalues of $\mathbf{A}^*$ and the value of the ratio $w(\lambda)$, then we can ascertain the distribution of the eigenvalues of $\mathbf{A}$. Comparing this lemma with Exercise 7.61, it is clear that this ratio $w(\lambda)$ plays a role similar to the *Strum* sequence. We now seek to compute this ratio in parallel.

Let $N = 2^n$, and recursively define a sequence of rank 1 updates in the form of a complete binary tree with the root at level n and leaves at level 0. Let

$$\mathbf{A}_1^{(n)} = \mathbf{A} \tag{7.7.2.20}$$

be a given tridiagonal matrix of order 2^n at level n. Express $\mathbf{A}_1^{(n)}$ as

$$\mathbf{A}_1^{(n)} = \left[\begin{array}{c|c} \mathbf{A}_1^{(n-1)} & 0 \\ \hline 0 & \mathbf{A}_2^{(n-1)} \end{array} \right] + \mathbf{B}_1^{(n)}, \qquad (7.7.2.21)$$

where $\mathbf{A}_1^{(n-1)}$ and $\mathbf{A}_2^{(n-1)}$ are tridiagonal matrices of order 2^{n-1} at level $n-1$, and $\mathbf{B}_1^{(n)} = a_{N/2+1}\mathbf{bb}'$ (refer to (7.7.1.3)) is a rank 1 matrix of order 2^n. Generalizing this, we can express

$$\mathbf{A}_j^{(l)} = \left[\begin{array}{c|c} \mathbf{A}_{2j-1}^{(l-1)} & 0 \\ \hline 0 & \mathbf{A}_{2j}^{(l-1)} \end{array} \right] + \mathbf{B}_j^{(l)}, \qquad (7.7.2.22)$$

where $\mathbf{A}_j^{(l)}$ is a tridiagonal matrix of order 2^l at level l, $\mathbf{B}_j^{(l)}$ is a rank 1 matrix of order 2^l for $j = 1$ to 2^{n-l}. Clearly, $\mathbf{B}_j^{(0)} = 0$ for $j = 1$ to 2^n. Refer to Fig. 7.7.2.1 for an illustration of this splitting process.

Define

$$\mathbf{A}^{(l)} = \mathbf{diag}(\mathbf{A}_1^{(l)}, \mathbf{A}_2^{(l)}, \cdots, \mathbf{A}_{2^{n-l}}^{(l)}), \qquad (7.7.2.23)$$

that is, $\mathbf{A}^{(l)}$ is a block diagonal matrix with 2^{n-l} blocks, where each block corresponds to a node at level l of the tree of matrices and is a tridiagonal matrix of order 2^l. Clearly, $\mathbf{A}^{(n)} = \mathbf{A}_1^{(n)} = \mathbf{A}$. Let $\psi_k^{(l)}(\lambda)$ be the characteristic polynomial of the matrix $\mathbf{A}_k^{(l)}$. Define

$$w_j^{(l)}(\lambda) = \frac{\psi_j^{(l)}(\lambda)}{\psi_{2j-1}^{(l-1)}(\lambda)\psi_{2j}^{(l-1)}(\lambda)}, \qquad (7.7.2.24)$$

where, for $l = 0$, the terms in the denominator are taken to be unity. Thus, for $j = 1$ to 2^n,

$$w_j^{(0)}(\lambda) = \psi_j^{(0)}(\lambda). \qquad (7.7.2.25)$$

Let

$$\mathbf{A}^{(0)} = \mathbf{diag}(c_1, c_2, \cdots, c_N),$$

where c_i's are real. Then

$$w_j^{(0)}(\lambda) = (c_j - \lambda)$$

and

$$\#\mathbf{A}^{(0)}(\lambda) = |\{j \mid w_j^{(0)}(\lambda) < 0\}|. \qquad (7.7.2.26)$$

Since $\mathbf{A}^{(l)}$ is a block diagonal matrix, it follows from the definition that for $l > 0$,

$$\#\mathbf{A}^{(l)}(\lambda) = \sum_{j=1}^{2^{n-l}} \#\mathbf{A}_j^{(l)}(\lambda). \qquad (7.7.2.27)$$

Applying Lemma 7.7.2.2, we obtain

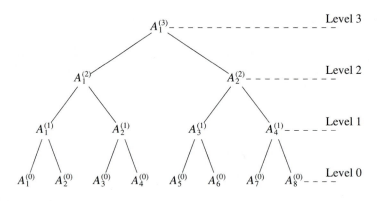

FIGURE 7.7.2.1
An example of a recursive splitting used in the Krishnakumar-Morf algorithm.

$$\# A_j^{(l)}(\lambda) = \# A_{2j-1}^{(l-1)}(\lambda) + \# A_{2j}^{(l-1)}(\lambda) - u(-w_j^{(l)}(\lambda))\, sign(\alpha_j^{(l)}), \quad \textbf{(7.7.2.28)}$$

where $\alpha_j^{(l)}$ is the off-diagonal element used in combining $A_{2j-1}^{(l-1)}$ and $A_{2j}^{(l-1)}$ using a rank 1 update[3]. Stated in other words, as we move up the tree from level $l-1$ to l, the number of eigenvalues less than λ decreases by

$$\sum_{j=1}^{2^{n-l}} u(-w_j^{(l)}(\lambda))\, sign(\alpha_j^{(l)}).$$

Adding up this difference over the levels 1 through n, and combining it with (7.7.2.26), we obtain

$$\# A^{(n)}(\lambda) = \# A^{(0)}(\lambda) - \sum_{l=1}^{n} \sum_{j=1}^{2^{n-l}} u(-w_j^{(l)}(\lambda))\, sign(\alpha_j^{(l)}). \quad (7.7.2.29)$$

Summarizing this development, we get the following theorem.

Theorem 7.7.2.3. If **A** is a symmetric tridiagonal matrix, then the number of eigenvalues less than λ is given by (7.7.2.29).

In concluding this section, we present a method for computing $w_j^{(l)}$ recursively.[4] Let

---

[3] That is, $\alpha_j^{(l)}$ plays a role similar to a_{k+1} in (7.7.1.3).

[4] The argument λ in $w_j^{(l)}$ is suppressed for simplicity in notation.

$\overline{\mathbf{A}}_j^{(l)}$ be the matrix obtained from $\mathbf{A}_j^{(l)}$ by deleting its *last row* and *column*.

$\underline{\mathbf{A}}_j^{(l)}$ be the matrix obtained from $\mathbf{A}_j^{(l)}$ by deleting its *first row* and *column*, and

$\hat{\mathbf{A}}_j^{(l)}$ be the matrix obtained from $\mathbf{A}_j^{(l)}$ by deleting the *first row* and *column* and *last row* and *column*.

Let $\overline{\psi}_j^{(l)}$, $\psi_j^{(l)}$, and $\hat{\psi}_j^{(l)}$, be the characteristic polynomials[3] of the matrices $\overline{\mathbf{A}}_j^{(l)}$, $\underline{\mathbf{A}}_j^{(l)}$, and $\underline{\mathbf{A}}_j^{(l)}$, respectively. Define

$$e_j^{(l)} = \overline{\psi}_j^{(l)} / \psi_j^{(l)}, \qquad f_j^{(l)} = \psi_j^{(l)} / \psi_j^{(l)}, $$
$$g_j^{(l)} = \hat{\psi}_j^{(l)} / \overline{\psi}_j^{(l)}, \qquad h_j^{(l)} = \hat{\psi}_j^{(l)} / \underline{\psi}_j^{(l)}. \qquad (7.7.2.30)$$

At the leaf level, define

$$e_j^{(0)} = (c_j - \lambda)^{-1}, \qquad f_j^{(0)} = (c_j - \lambda)^{-1}, \qquad g_j^{(0)} = h_j^{(0)} = 0. \quad (7.7.2.31)$$

Now applying (7.7.2.16) and (7.7.2.17) to $\mathbf{A}_j^{(l)}$, we obtain

$$w_j^{(l)} = 1 + \alpha_j^{(l)} [e_{2j-1}^{(l-1)} + f_{2j}^{(l-1)}] \qquad (7.7.2.32)$$

and

$$e_j^{(l)} = e_{2j}^{(l-1)} [\frac{1 + \alpha_j^{(l)}(e_{2j-1}^{(l-1)} + g_{2j}^{(l-1)})}{1 + \alpha_j^{(l)}(e_{2j-1}^{(l-1)} + f_{2j}^{(l-1)})}]$$

$$f_j^{(l)} = f_{2j-1}^{(l-1)} [\frac{1 + \alpha_j^{(l)}(h_{2j-1}^{(l-1)} + f_{2j}^{(l-1)})}{1 + \alpha_j^{(l)}(e_{2j-1}^{(l-1)} + f_{2j}^{(l-1)})}]$$

$$\qquad\qquad\qquad\qquad\qquad (7.7.2.33)$$

$$g_j^{(l)} = f_{2j-1}^{(l-1)} [\frac{1 + \alpha_j^{(l)}(h_{2j-1}^{(l-1)} + g_{2j}^{(l-1)})}{1 + \alpha_j^{(l)}(e_{2j-1}^{(l-1)} + g_{2j}^{(l-1)})}]$$

and

$$h_j^{(l)} = e_{2j}^{(l-1)} [\frac{1 + \alpha_j^{(l)}(h_{2j-1}^{(l-1)} + g_{2j}^{(l-1)})}{1 + \alpha_j^{(l)}(h_{2j-1}^{(l-1)} + f_{2j}^{(l-1)})}].$$

Notice in passing that $w_j^{(l)}$ is the same as the denominator of $e_j^{(l)}$ or $f_j^{(l)}$. Thus, by carefully organizing the computations of $e_j^{(l)}$, $f_j^{(l)}$, $g_j^{(l)}$, and $h_j^{(l)}$, it can be seen that *no additional computations are necessary to obtain* $w_j^{(l)}$.

Let λ_1 and λ_2 be such that $\lambda_1 < \lambda_2$ and

$$\#\mathbf{A}(\lambda_2) - \#\mathbf{A}(\lambda_1) = 1. \tag{7.7.2.34}$$

Define $\bar{\lambda} = \dfrac{\lambda_1 + \lambda_2}{2}$. Then,

either
$$\#\mathbf{A}(\lambda_2) - \#\mathbf{A}(\bar{\lambda}) = 1$$

or
$$\#\mathbf{A}(\bar{\lambda}) - \#\mathbf{A}(\lambda_1) = 1. \tag{7.7.2.35}$$

Applying this *bisection* method repeatedly, we can indeed locate the eigenvalues to any desired degree of accuracy. The algorithm is given in Fig. 7.7.2.2.

We invite the reader to investigate efficient implementations of this algorithm on hypercubes and on multivector processors.

/* Given a symmetric tridiagonal matrix $\mathbf{A}$ of order $N = 2^n$.
Find its eigenvalues. */

Step 1. Compute the tree of matrices $\mathbf{A}_j^{(l)}$ using the rank 1 update (7.7.1.3), for $l = 0, 1, \cdots, n$, and $j = 1, 2, \cdots, 2^{n-l}$. (Refer to Fig. 7.7.2.1 for an example.)

Step 2. Combining the bisection method and the recursive procedure for computing $w_j^{(l)}$ determine the eigenvalues to any desired accuracy.

FIGURE 7.7.2.2
The Krishnakumar-Morf algorithm.

7.8 NOTES AND REFERENCES

Section 7.2. The material in this section is adopted from the classic works of Faddeeva [1959] and Householder [1964]. Leverrier developed the method in Property 7.2.2.1 around 1840. Faddeeva and Sominsky's method is taken from Faddeeva [1959]. The method of computing the characteristic polynomial of the matrix $\mathbf{A}_N$ in terms of that of $\mathbf{A}_{N-1}$ described in Property 7.2.4.1 is due to Samuelson [1942]. The proof of Property 7.2.4.2 is taken from Berkowitz [1984]. Further properties of Toeplitz matrices and Householder and Givens transformations can be obtained from Golub and Van Loan [1983].

Section 7.3. Development of faster algorithms to multiply matrices has dominated the literature over the past two decades. Strassen in 1969 (Strassen [1969]) broke new ground in finding faster serial algorithms for multiplying matrices. He showed that the product of 2×2 matrices with elements from a *non-commutative ring* can be computed using only 7 multiplications and 18 additions. Winograd describes a similar algorithm for multiplying 2×2 matrices requiring only 15 additions (Exercise 7.35), the effect of which is to reduce the value of the constant without changing the order of magnitude of the time. Fast algorithms known for multiplying two $N \times N$ matrices at the time of this writing are due to Coppersmith and Winograd [1980] with complexity $O(N^{2.496})$, Strassen [1986] with complexity $O(N^{2.479})$, and Coppersmith and Winograd [1987] with complexity $O(N^{2.376})$. For a fascinating and authoritative account of the development of faster algorithms to multiply matrices and their varied applications, refer to the monograph by Pan [1984].

Array-oriented hardware implementable matrix multiplication algorithms have been extensively developed -- refer to Ramakrishnan and Varman [1984], Varman and Ramakrishnan [1986], and Jagadish and Kailath [1989].

Subsection 7.3.2 is patterned after Fam [1988].

Section 7.3.5 follows very closely the developments in Miller [1975]. Stability analysis of fast matrix multiplication algorithms are covered in Brent [1970b], Bini and Lotti [1980], and Pan [1984]. The monograph by Miller and Wrathall [1980] develops the tools and software needed for automating the round-off analysis of matrix algorithms.

Madsen, Rodrigue, and Karush [1976] developed very efficient methods for multiplication of banded matrices by diagonals. Their algorithm is pursued in Exercise 7.56.

Very recently Bailey [1988b] demonstrated (see Exercise 7.20) the practical effectiveness of the Strassen method. He showed that on Cray-2 for matrices of sizes up to 2048, Strassen method requires only half the number of cycles compared to the best known routines.

Section 7.4. Csanky, in 1976, for the first time showed that the inverse, the determinant, and the characteristic polynomial of a matrix can be computed in $O((\log N)^2)$ steps using $O(N^4)$ processors. Csanky's method exploits the method due to Leverrier [1840] for computing the characteristic polynomial as well as Faddeeva's method announced in 1937. Technically, Csanky's method is applicable only for matrices with elements over fields of *characteristic zero*. Borodin, Van zur Gathen, and Hopcroft [1982] extended Csanky's method for computing determinants and characteristic polynomials over arbitrary commutative rings with unity, including finite fields. Their proof is existential in nature and is based on two key results. The first one is due to Valiant, Skyum, Berkowitz, and Rackoff [1983], according to which a serial algorithm for computing a polynomial of degree $m \leq N$ in t steps can be converted into a parallel algorithm that takes $O(\log N \log t)$ steps using $O(t^3)$ operations. The second idea is due to Strassen [1973] for eliminating the division. Using these ideas, Borodin, Van zur Gathen, and Hopcroft [1982] showed that the determinant of a matrix can be computed in $O((\log N)^2)$ steps using

$O(N^{15})$ operations. Berkowitz in 1984 gave an algorithm for computing the characteristic polynomial, adjoint, and determinant over an arbitrary commutative ring in $O((\log N)^2)$ steps using $O(N^{3.496})$ operations. His approach is based on the well-known Samuelson method for computing the characteristic polynomial of matrices of order N in terms of the characteristic polynomial of matrices of order $N - 1$, and is given in Section 7.5. A short description of the properties of rings and fields is contained in Appendix C.

Parallel methods for the inversion of matrices based on the bordering and partitioning methods were earlier discussed by Pease [1967, 1969]. These algorithms are suitable for implementation on multivector machines. See Exercise 7.14.

Section 7.5. This section is adopted from Berkowitz [1984]. The method of this section is applicable to matrices with elements from an arbitrary commutative ring with unity. The possibility of computing the determinant, characteristic polynomial, and adjoint of a matrix with elements from an arbitrary commutative ring with unity was first established by Borodin, Van zur Gathen, and Hopcroft [1982]. Since their method is not explicit and is based on existential arguments, it requires $O(N^{15})$ operations. Berkowitz [1984] attributes the idea of the proof of Lemma 7.5.1.1 to S. Winograd.

Section 7.6. Bini's paper [1984] constitutes the core of this section. The concept of approximate solution and its relation to the exact solution is very useful. Approximation can be used to reduce the overall complexity. Bini has successfully used similar approximations to evaluate Toeplitz bilinear forms (Bini [1980]).

The best known previous result for solving triangular Toeplitz systems is due to Chen [1975], who solves it in $(\log N)^2 + 2 \log N + O(1)$ steps using $N^2/4$ processors. Grcar and Sameh [1981] describe three different parallel algorithms for solving a balanced ($k = h$) banded Toeplitz system. Their algorithm requires a restrictive condition of *positive definiteness* of the underlying matrix, but Bini's algorithm requires no such additional condition.

All the known algorithms (Chapter 6) for inverting a general triangular matrix still continue to require $O((\log N)^2)$ parallel steps. Until recently, the special structures, such as Toeplitz, have been exploited only to reduce the number of processors. Bini's approach, using the concept of approximate solution, *reduces* the complexity of the inverse of the special class of triangular Toeplitz matrices to $O(\log N)$ steps using $O(N^2)$ processors.

There are a number of excellent references on the properties and applications of Toeplitz matrices -- Roebuck and Barnett [1978], Kailath, Viera, and Morf [1978], Ammar and Gragg [1988], Chun, Kailath, and Lev-Ari [1987], Zohar [1969], Trench [1964], and Gustavson and Yun [1979]. Grenander and Szego [1958] is a classic reference on this topic. More recently, iterative methods for solving Toeplitz systems are gaining attention. For details, refer to Chan [1988].

Section 7.7. The idea of computing the eigenvalues of a real symmetric tridiagonal matrix in parallel using the divide-and-conquer strategy is due to Cuppen [1981]. The algorithm used to solve the secular equation using rational approximation was earlier developed by Bunch, Nielsen, and Sorensen [1978]. Our treatment in Section 7.7.1 is patterned after these two important papers in this area. For a proof of the separation property of eigenvalues of matrices under perturbations, refer to Wilkinson [1965] and Stewart [1973]. The review paper by Golub [1973] provides a unified treatment of the eigenvalue problem in many application areas. Dongarra and Sorensen [1987] provides a performance comparison of the "complete" algorithm, including the initial reduction to tridiagonal form and the computation of the eigenvalues by solving the secular equation.

Recently, Lo, Philippe, and Sameh [1987] described another parallel algorithm for computing eigenvalues and vectors. Isolating the eigenvalues by using the properties of the Strum sequence (Exercise 7.61), they use parallel versions of the *bisection* algorithm to extract the actual eigenvalues. This paper contains a wealth of information regarding implementation and performance of this class of algorithms on multivector machines.

The parallel algorithm for finding the eigenvalues of a real symmetric matrix based on the rank 1 update is directly applicable to updating the singular value decomposition. This latter problem often arises in least squares problems. Refer to Bunch, Nielsen, and Sorensen [1978] for details.

Section 7.7.2 is patterned after Krishnakumar [1984] and Krishnakumar and Morf [1986]. It should be interesting to compare the methods of Cuppen [1981], Krishnakumar and Morf [1986], and Lo, Philippe, and Sameh [1987].

7.9 EXERCISES

7.1 A matrix A is said to be *similar* to a matrix B if and only if there exists a non-singular matrix C such that $A = C^{-1}BC$, and this method of computing A from B is called *similarity transformation.* Show that the similarity transformation satisfies the following:

(a) $C^{-1}(B_1 + B_2 + \cdots + B_k)C = C^{-1}B_1C + C^{-1}B_2C + \cdots + C^{-1}B_kC.$

(b) $(C^{-1}BC)^k = C^{-1}B^kC$ for any integer $k \geq 1$.

(c) $f(C^{-1}BC) = C^{-1}f(B)C$, where $f(x)$ is a polynomial.

Remark: Since $C^{-1} = C^t$, if C is orthogonal, it is computationally advantageous to restrict to the special class of orthogonal similarity transformations.

7.2   Prove Property 7.2.1.3.

       Hint: Use similarity transformation.

7.3   An $N \times N$ matrix $\mathbf{A} = [\, a_{ij} \,]$ is called a *persymmetric* matrix if

$$a_{ij} = a_{n-j+1,\, n-i+1}.$$

       Show that every Toeplitz matrix is persymmetric.

7.4   Let $\mathbf{e}_i = (0, 0, \cdots, 0, 1, 0, \cdots, 0)^t$ be the ith unit vector, that is, a vector with the ith element unity and all the other elements zero. Define an $N \times N$ matrix

$$\mathbf{E}_N = [\, \mathbf{e}_N, \mathbf{e}_{N-1}, \cdots, \mathbf{e}_2, \mathbf{e}_1 \,]$$

       called an *exchange* matrix. As an example,

$$\mathbf{E}_3 = \begin{bmatrix} 0 & 0 & 1 \\ 0 & 1 & 0 \\ 1 & 0 & 0 \end{bmatrix}.$$

       Show that

       (a) $\mathbf{E}_N^t = \mathbf{E}_N$ and $\mathbf{E}_N^2 = \mathbf{I}_N$, the unit matrix.

       (b) If $\mathbf{A}$ is persymmetric then $\mathbf{E}_N \mathbf{A}' \mathbf{E}_N = \mathbf{A}$.

       (c) If $\mathbf{A}$ is persymmetric, then so is $\mathbf{A}^{-1}$.

7.5   Analogous to the expression in (7.2.6.6) for $\mathbf{H}_1$, compute explicitly the elements of $\mathbf{H}_i$ using the appropriate column of the matrix $\mathbf{A}_{i-1}$ for $i = 2, 3, \cdots, N-2$.

7.6   Let $\mathbf{H} = \mathbf{I} - \beta \mathbf{aa}'$,   where $\beta = \dfrac{2}{\mathbf{a}'\mathbf{a}}$.   Then $\mathbf{HA} = \mathbf{A} - \beta \mathbf{aa}'\mathbf{A} = \mathbf{A} - \beta \mathbf{a}(\mathbf{A}'\mathbf{a})'$.   Compute the number of operations required by this transformation.

7.7   Compute the total number of operations required in obtaining $\mathbf{A}_{N-2}$ in (7.2.6.7).

7.8   (a) Show that if $\mathbf{A}$ is symmetric and $\mathbf{H}_1$ is as defined in (7.2.6.6), then in

$$\mathbf{B}_1 = \mathbf{H}_1 \mathbf{A} \mathbf{H}_1$$

       all but the first two elements of the first row and first column are zero.

       (b) Continuing this argument, show that $\mathbf{B} = \mathbf{Q}'\mathbf{A}\mathbf{Q}$ is a symmetric tridiagonal matrix, where $\mathbf{Q} = \mathbf{H}_1 \mathbf{H}_2 \cdots \mathbf{H}_{N-2}$.

7.9   (Dongarra and Sorensen [1987]). Let $\mathbf{H} = \mathbf{I} - \beta\mathbf{aa}'$, where β is a properly chosen constant. Let

$$\mathbf{B} = (\mathbf{I} - \beta\mathbf{aa}')\mathbf{A}(\mathbf{I} - \beta\mathbf{aa}'),$$

where $\mathbf{A}$ is symmetric.

(a) Show that $\mathbf{B}$ can be computed as follows:

(1) $\mathbf{b} = \mathbf{Aa}$.
(2) $\mathbf{c}' = \mathbf{b}' - \beta(\mathbf{a}'\mathbf{b})\mathbf{a}'$.
(3) $\mathbf{B} = \mathbf{A} - \beta\mathbf{ba}' - \beta\mathbf{ac}'$.

(b) Discuss how you would implement this computation in parallel.

(c) Compute the total number of operations required.

7.10 (a) Compute the number of operations needed to perform the Givens update $\mathbf{G}(i, j)\mathbf{A}$, and compare it with that for computing $\mathbf{HA}$ in Exercise 7.6.

(b) Find a proper schedule of Givens transformations for transforming a real symmetric matrix into a tridiagonal form. Compute the total number of operations needed by this procedure, and compare it with that of Householder method in Exercise 7.8.

7.11 Describe a parallel algorithm to compute the product $\mathbf{Q} = \mathbf{H}_1 \mathbf{H}_2 \cdots \mathbf{H}_{N-2}$ described in Exercise 7.8. Compute the parallel time and number of processors.

7.12 (Winograd [1968]). Let $\mathbf{x} = (x_1, x_2, \cdots, x_N)'$ and $\mathbf{y} = (y_1, y_2, \cdots, y_N)'$ be two vectors where N is even. The Winograd identity for the inner product is given by

$$\sum_{i=1}^{N} x_i y_i = \sum_{i=1}^{m} (x_{2i-1} + y_{2i})(x_{2i} + y_{2i-1}) - (\alpha + \beta),$$

where

$$\alpha = \sum_{i=1}^{m} x_{2i-1} x_{2i}$$

$$\beta = \sum_{i=1}^{m} y_{2i-1} y_{2i}$$

and $N = 2m$.

(a) Using this identity for computing the inner product, show that the product of two $N \times N$ matrices can be computed using $\dfrac{1}{2}N^3 + N^2$ multiplications and

$\frac{3}{2}N^3 + 2N(N-1)$ additions.

(b) Extend this to the case when N is odd.

(c) How would you parallelize the matrix multiplication algorithm obtained in part (a)? Compute the time and processor bounds, and compare them with those for the classical method.

7.13 Let $\mathbf{A} = [\, a_{ij}\,]$, $\mathbf{B} = [\, b_{ij}\,]$, and $\mathbf{C} = [\, c_{ij}\,]$ be three $N \times N$ matrices such that

$$c_{ij} = \sum_{k=1}^{N} a_{ik}\, b_{kj}.$$

The standard algorithm for computing $\mathbf{C}$, called the *ijk* algorithm, may be stated as follows:

FOR i = 1 TO N
   FOR j = 1 TO N
   c_{ij} = 0.
   FOR k = 1 TO N
     c_{ij} = $c_{ij} + a_{ik} \times b_{kj}$
   END
  END
END

In this scheme, the loop with index k is contained in the loop with index j, which in turn is contained in the loop with index i. By permuting the i, j, and k loops, and making appropriate changes, we can, in principle, obtain six different schemes -- *ijk, ikj, jik, jki, kij,* and *kji* algorithms for computing $\mathbf{C}$. Discuss the merits of implementing these six different schemes on multivector machines, such as the Alliant FX/8.

7.14 Let $\mathbf{A}$ be an $N \times N$ matrix partitioned as

$$\mathbf{A} = \begin{bmatrix} \mathbf{A}_{11} & \mathbf{A}_{12} \\ \mathbf{A}_{21} & \mathbf{A}_{22} \end{bmatrix}.$$

Assume that $\mathbf{A}_{11}$ and Δ are non-singular, where $\Delta = \mathbf{A}_{22} - \mathbf{A}_{21}\, \mathbf{A}_{11}^{-1}\, \mathbf{A}_{12}$.

(a) Show that

$$\mathbf{A}^{-1} = \begin{bmatrix} \mathbf{A}_{11}^{-1} + \mathbf{A}_{11}^{-1}\,\mathbf{A}_{12}\,\Delta^{-1}\,\mathbf{A}_{21}\,\mathbf{A}_{11}^{-1} & -\mathbf{A}_{11}^{-1}\,\mathbf{A}_{12}\,\Delta^{-1} \\ & \\ -\Delta^{-1}\,\mathbf{A}_{21}\,\mathbf{A}_{11}^{-1} & \Delta^{-1} \end{bmatrix}.$$

Hint: $\mathbf{A} = \begin{bmatrix} \mathbf{I} & 0 \\ \mathbf{A}_{21}\,\mathbf{A}_{11}^{-1} & \mathbf{I} \end{bmatrix} \begin{bmatrix} \mathbf{A}_{11} & 0 \\ 0 & \Delta \end{bmatrix} \begin{bmatrix} \mathbf{I} & \mathbf{A}_{11}^{-1}\mathbf{A}_{12} \\ 0 & \mathbf{I} \end{bmatrix}.$

(b) Show that the above result does not apply to all non-singular matrices.

Hint: $\mathbf{A} = [\,a_{ij}\,]$ and $a_{ij} = 1$ for $i + j = N + 1$ and 0 otherwise.

(c) If $\mathbf{A}$ is an upper (lower) triangular matrix, then show that $\mathbf{A}_{11}$ and Δ are also upper (lower) triangular matrices. Compute the inverse of $\mathbf{A}$ in either case.

(d) (Pease [1967]). Consider the special case when $\mathbf{A}_{11}$ is the leading principal submatrix of size $N - 1$. In this case, $\mathbf{A}_{12}$ and $\mathbf{A}_{21}$ are column and row vectors of size $N - 1$, and $\mathbf{A}_{22}$ is a scalar. Show that

$$\mathbf{A}^{-1} = \begin{bmatrix} \mathbf{A}_{11}^{-1} & 0 \\ 0 & 0 \end{bmatrix} + \Delta^{-1} \begin{bmatrix} \mathbf{A}_{11}^{-1}\mathbf{A}_{12} \\ -1 \end{bmatrix} (\mathbf{A}_{21}\mathbf{A}_{11}^{-1},\ -1\,),$$

where Δ is a scalar. Develop a parallel iterative algorithm for computing $\mathbf{A}^{-1}$. Compute the complexity of your algorithm.

Remark: This method of iteratively finding the inverse of a matrix of size $k + 1$ based on the inverse of a matrix of size k is called the *bordering* technique. For a related method of inversion by partitioning, refer to Pease [1969].

7.15 (Aho, Hopcroft, and Ullman [1974]). Let $T_m(N)$, the serial time required to multiply two $N \times N$ matrices, be such that $T_m(1) \ge 1$ and

$$8\,T_m(N) \ge T_m(2N) \ge 2^{2 + \varepsilon}\,T_m(N)$$

for some $\varepsilon > 0$. Let

$$\mathbf{A} = \begin{bmatrix} \mathbf{A}_{11} & 0 \\ \mathbf{A}_{21} & \mathbf{A}_{22} \end{bmatrix}$$

be a non-singular lower triangular matrix of order $N = 2^k$, $k \ge 1$. Then, clearly,

$$A^{-1} = \begin{bmatrix} A_{11}^{-1} & 0 \\ -A_{22}^{-1} A_{21} A_{11}^{-1} & A_{22}^{-1} \end{bmatrix}.$$

(a) If $T_I(N)$ is the time required to invert $\mathbf{A}$, then show that

$$T_I(N) = 2 T_I(\frac{N}{2}) + 2 T_m(\frac{N}{2}) + \frac{N^2}{4}.$$

(b) Since $T_m(\frac{N}{2}) \geq \frac{N^2}{4}$, the above relation becomes

$$T_I(N) \leq 2 T_I(\frac{N}{2}) + 3 T_m(\frac{N}{2}).$$

Show that

$$T_I(N) \leq 1.5 \, T_m(N).$$

(c) Extend this argument to the case where N is not a power of 2.

7.16 (Miller [1975]). Show that any polynomial program using only multiplications of the form $\mathbf{L}_1(\mathbf{x}) \times \mathbf{L}_2(\mathbf{y})$ must exhibit simultaneous Brent stability.

7.17 (Miller [1975]). Let $x = x_1 + ix_2$, $y = y_1 + iy_2$. Define

$$\begin{aligned}
A &= x_1 + x_2 \\
C &= A \times y_1 \\
D &= y_1 + y_2 \\
E &= x_2 \times D \\
F &= y_1 - y_2 \\
G &= x_1 \times F \\
B_1 &= C - E \\
B_2 &= C - G
\end{aligned}$$

Since this method requires only three multiplications, it is called the "faster" method.

(a) Show that for x and y, if $\|(\mathbf{x}, \mathbf{y})\|_{B_1}$ is very small compared to the product $\|\mathbf{x}\|_{\infty} \|\mathbf{y}\|_{\infty}$, then the effect of round-off error on B_1 is quite large.

(b) For $x = 0.0015 + 1.01i$ and $y = 1.01 + 0.001i$, compute B_1 (i) correctly, (ii) using three-digit floating point arithmetic, that is, round to three significant digits after each operation, and (iii) using the above "fast" method requiring only three multiplications.

7.18   Analyze the stability properties of polynomial programs described in Section 7.3.2 for multiplying complex matrices.

7.19   Prove that Strassen's method for matrix multiplication satisfies the conditions for simultaneous Brent stability.

7.20   (Bailey [1988b]). Consider the process of multiplying the following two matrices by Strassen's method.

$$
\begin{bmatrix} \delta^2 & 1 \\ 1 & \delta \end{bmatrix} \begin{bmatrix} 1 & \delta \\ \delta^2 & 1 \end{bmatrix} = \begin{bmatrix} 2\delta^2 & 1 + \delta^3 \\ 1 + \delta^3 & 2\delta \end{bmatrix}.
$$

where $\delta = O(2^{-t})$, where t is the number of mantissa digits in the representation of floating point numbers. Clearly $c_{11} = 2\delta^2$, but when calculated by this method, we get

$$
c_{11} = 2\delta(1 + \delta) - \delta(1 - \delta^2) - (1 + \delta^2) + (1 - \delta)(1 + \delta^2).
$$

Show that the computation of c_{11} does not satisfy the conditions for Miller strong stability.

7.21   (Faddeeva [1959]). If $A = [a_{ij}]$ is an $N \times N$ matrix such that all the *leading* or *principal* submatrices are non-singular, that is,

$$
a_{11} \neq 0; \quad \det \begin{bmatrix} a_{11} & a_{12} \\ a_{21} & a_{22} \end{bmatrix} \neq 0, \quad \cdots , \mid A \mid \neq 0,
$$

then there exists a unit lower triangular matrix (with unity along the principal diagonal) L and an upper triangular matrix U such that $A = LU$.

Hint: Prove it by induction on the order of A.

7.22   (Aho, Hopcroft, and Ullman [1974]). If the matrix $A = [a_{ij}]$ is such that it is non-singular but not all of its leading or principal submatrices are non-singular, then there exists a permutation matrix P, a unit triangular matrix L, and an upper triangular matrix U such that $AP^{-1} = LU$.

7.23   (Aho, Hopcroft, and Ullman [1974]). Let $T_m(N)$, the serial time required to multiply two $N \times N$ matrices, be such that

$$
T_m(2N) \geq 2^{2+\varepsilon} \, T_m(N)
$$

for some $\varepsilon > 0$, and $T_m(1) \geq 1$.

Let $\mathbf{A}$ be a non-singular matrix. From the **LUP** decomposition of $\mathbf{A}$ (from Exercise 7.22), it follows that

$$\mathbf{A}^{-1} = \mathbf{P}^{-1}\mathbf{U}^{-1}\mathbf{L}^{-1}.$$

(a) Show that $\mathbf{P}^{-1}$ can be computed in $O(N)$ steps.

(b) Combining (a) and Exercise 7.22, show that $\mathbf{A}^{-1}$ can be computed in $O(T_m(N))$ steps. (See also Exercise 7.15.)

(c) Since $\det[\mathbf{A}] = \det[\mathbf{L}]\det[\mathbf{U}]\det[\mathbf{P}]$, show that $\det[\mathbf{A}]$ can be computed in $O(T_m(N))$ steps.

(d) Show that the linear system $\mathbf{A}\mathbf{x} = \mathbf{b}$ can be solved in $O(T_m(N))$ steps.

7.24 Let $T_m(N)$ and $T_I(N)$ be the serial times required to multiply two $N \times N$ matrices and invert an $N \times N$ matrix, where

$$8\,T_m(N) \geq T_m(2N) \geq 2^{2+\varepsilon}\,T_m(N)$$

and

$$8\,T_I(N) \geq T_I(2N) \geq 2^{2+\varepsilon}\,T_I(N)$$

for some $\varepsilon > 0$.

(a) Show that $T_m(N) = O(T_I(N))$.

Hint:
$$\begin{bmatrix} \mathbf{I} & \mathbf{A} & \mathbf{0} \\ \mathbf{0} & \mathbf{I} & \mathbf{B} \\ \mathbf{0} & \mathbf{0} & \mathbf{I} \end{bmatrix}^{-1} = \begin{bmatrix} \mathbf{I} & -\mathbf{A} & \mathbf{A}\mathbf{B} \\ \mathbf{0} & \mathbf{I} & -\mathbf{B} \\ \mathbf{0} & \mathbf{0} & \mathbf{I} \end{bmatrix},$$

where $\mathbf{A}$ and $\mathbf{B}$ are $N \times N$ matrices, since $T_m(N) \leq T_I(3N) \leq T_I(4N) \leq 64\,T_I(N)$.

Remark: Combining this with Exercise 7.15, it follows that the matrix inversion problem and matrix multiplication problem are equivalent.

7.25 (Csanky [1976]). Let $\mathbf{B}$ be an $N \times N$ matrix. If $T\mathbf{B} = tr(\mathbf{B})$, then show that for any matrix $\mathbf{A}$ considered as an operator,

$$(TA)T = T(AT).$$

7.26 (Csanky [1976]). Let $g(\lambda) = (-1)^N[\lambda^N + d_1\,\lambda^{N-1} + d_2\,\lambda^{N-2} + \cdots + d_{N-1}\,\lambda + d_N]$ be the characteristic polynomial for the matrix $\mathbf{T}$ given in (7.2.2.4). Since $\lambda_i = i$, for $i = 1, \cdots, N$, are characteristic roots of $g(\lambda) = 0$, it follows that

$$g(\lambda) = \prod_{i=1}^{N} (\lambda - i).$$

Construct a parallel algorithm for computing the coefficients of $g(\lambda)$ in $2 \log N + O(1)$ steps.

Hint: $d_k = (-1)^k$(sum of the product of integers in every subset of k integers from the set $\{1, 2, \cdots, N\}$). There are $\begin{pmatrix} N \\ k \end{pmatrix}$ such subsets. Use the associative fan-in algorithm to compute d_k.

7.27 (Csanky [1976]). Here is another way of computing $\mathbf{A}^{-1}$.

(1) Given $\mathbf{A}$, compute the powers $\mathbf{A}^i$, $i = 1, \cdots, N$.

(2) Using the powers computed in step 1, construct the matrix $\mathbf{T}$ in (7.2.2.4), where $t_k = tr(\mathbf{A}^k)$.

(3) From $\mathbf{T}$, now compute the powers $\mathbf{T}^i$, $i = 1, \cdots, N$.

(4) Using the coefficients of $g(\lambda)$ found in Exercise 7.26, compute $\mathbf{T}^{-1}$ using

$$\mathbf{T}^{-1} = \frac{\mathbf{T}^{N-1} - d_1 \mathbf{T}^{N-2} - d_2 \mathbf{T}^{N-3} - \cdots - d_{N-1} \mathbf{I}}{d_N}.$$

(5) Compute the solution p of (7.2.2.4) as $p = \mathbf{T}^{-1}t$.

(6) Compute (using the powers of $\mathbf{A}$ from step 1),

$$\mathbf{A}^{-1} = \frac{\mathbf{A}^{N-1} - p_1 \mathbf{A}^{N-2} - p_2 \mathbf{A}^{N-3} - \cdots - p_{N-1} \mathbf{I}}{p_N}.$$

(a) Compute the overall parallel complexity of this scheme. Compute the number of processors needed to achieve this time.

(b) $T_{PR}(N)$ is the parallel complexity of computing the first N powers of a matrix $\mathbf{A}$. Show that

$$T_{PR}(N) \geq \log N$$

$$T_I(N) \leq 2 T_{PR}(N) + O(\log N)$$

and

$$T_I(N) = O(T_{PR}(N)) \leq O((\log N)^2).$$

7.28 (Csanky [1976]). Consider a typical relation from (7.2.3.1),

$$\mathbf{B}_i = \mathbf{A}\mathbf{B}_{i-1} - \frac{tr(\mathbf{A}\mathbf{B}_{i-1})}{i}\mathbf{I}.$$

Using the operator T defined in Exercise 7.25, this relation can be rewritten as

$$\mathbf{B}_i = (\mathbf{I} - \frac{\mathbf{I}T}{i})\mathbf{A}\,\mathbf{B}_{i-1}.$$

Thus,

$$\mathbf{B}_1 = (\mathbf{I} - \mathbf{I}T)\,\mathbf{A}\,\mathbf{I}.$$

$$\mathbf{B}_2 = (\mathbf{I} - \frac{\mathbf{I}T}{2})\,\mathbf{A}\,(\mathbf{I} - \mathbf{I}T)\,\mathbf{A}\,\mathbf{I}$$

$$= (\mathbf{A} - \frac{T\,\mathbf{A}}{2})\,(\mathbf{A} - T\,\mathbf{A})\,\mathbf{I}.$$

Hence

$$\mathbf{B}_{N-1} = (\mathbf{A} - \frac{\mathbf{I}}{N-1}T\,\mathbf{A})\,(\mathbf{A} - \frac{\mathbf{I}}{N-2}T\,\mathbf{A}) \cdots (\mathbf{A} - \frac{\mathbf{I}}{2}T\,\mathbf{A})\,(\mathbf{A} - \mathbf{I}T\,\mathbf{A}).$$

(a) Since $(T\,\mathbf{A})T = T(\mathbf{A}\,T)$, that is, T and $\mathbf{A}$ associate, show that the above expression for $\mathbf{B}_{N-1}$ can be computed using the associative fan-in algorithm in $O\,((\log N)^2)$ steps.

(b) Compute the number of processors required to achieve this time bound.

7.29 (Csanky [1976]). If $\mathbf{A}^{-1}$ can be computed in $O\,((\log N)^2)$ time, then show that

(a) The system $\mathbf{A}\mathbf{x} = \mathbf{b}$ can be solved in $O\,((\log N)^2)$ steps.

(b) $\phi(\lambda)$, the characteristic polynomial of $\mathbf{A}$ and hence $det[\mathbf{A}] = \phi(0)$ can be computed in $O\,((\log N)^2)$ time.

Hint: Computation of $\mathbf{B}_i$ in (7.2.3.1) yields $p_i(\ = r_i)$, $i = 1, \cdots, N$, the coefficients of $\phi(\lambda)$.

7.30 Let $\mathbf{A}$ be a $k \times N$ complex matrix and $\mathbf{b}$ an $N \times 1$ complex vector. Compute the elements of the vector $\mathbf{A}\mathbf{b}$ using the classical method in (7.3.2.1) and the alternative method in (7.3.2.2).

(a) Compare the performance of these two modes of computation by computing the number of equivalent additions.

(b) Apply this method to computing the FFT described in Chapter 3.

7.31 Let $\mathbf{X} = \mathbf{A} + i\mathbf{B}$ and $\mathbf{Y} = \mathbf{C} + i\mathbf{D}$ be two $N \times N$ complex matrices. Let $\mathbf{Z} = \mathbf{X}\mathbf{Y} = [\, z_{ij}\,]$, where $z_{ij} = \sum\limits_{k=1}^{N} x_{ik}\, y_{kj}$. First compute the product $x_{ik}\, y_{kj}$ using (7.3.2.2) using three multiplications and five additions. Then find z_{ij} by performing the complex addition. Compute the number of equivalent additions for this method and compare it with (7.3.2.7).

7.32 (Moharir [1985]). Given a complex number $\mathbf{x} = a + ib$, define a 2×2 matrix induced by $\mathbf{x}$ as

$$\mathbf{M}_x = \begin{bmatrix} a & b \\ -b & a \end{bmatrix}.$$

Let $\mathbf{M}_y$ be a 2×2 matrix corresponding to $\mathbf{y} = c + id$.

(a) Verify that $\mathbf{M}_x + \mathbf{M}_y = \mathbf{M}_{x+y}$ and $\mathbf{M}_x\, \mathbf{M}_y = \mathbf{M}_{xy}$.

In view of this similarity between complex numbers and 2×2 real matrices, we can, in fact, extend the idea of (7.3.2.2) to matrix - vector computations as follows. To compute

$$\begin{bmatrix} \alpha \\ \beta \end{bmatrix} = \begin{bmatrix} a & b \\ -b & a \end{bmatrix} \begin{bmatrix} x \\ y \end{bmatrix} = \begin{bmatrix} ax + by \\ ay - bx \end{bmatrix}, \qquad (*)$$

first compute ay and bx. Then $\beta = ay - bx$ and $\alpha = (ax + by) = (a+b)(x+y) - (ay - bx)$. That is, instead of the conventional four multiplications and two additions, we can compute α and β in *three* multiplications and *five* additions. Note that a, b, x, and y can be complex, or even matrices.

(b) Show that

$$\begin{bmatrix} a & b \\ b & a \end{bmatrix} \begin{bmatrix} x \\ y \end{bmatrix}$$

can be computed in *three* multiplications and *four* additions.

(c) If $\sin A$, $\sin B$, $\cos A$, $\cos B$ are known, then express the computation of $\sin(A + B)$ and $\cos(A + B)$ in the form of matrix - vector computation as in (*) above.

7.33 (Moharir [1985]). Let ω be the cube root of unity. Let $\mathbf{x} = (x_0, x_1, x_2)^t$ be a complex vector. Define $f = (f_0, f_1, f_2)^t$ as

$$\begin{bmatrix} f_0 \\ f_1 \\ f_2 \end{bmatrix} = \begin{bmatrix} 1 & 1 & 1 \\ 1 & \omega & \omega^2 \\ 1 & \omega^2 & \omega \end{bmatrix} \begin{bmatrix} x_0 \\ x_1 \\ x_2 \end{bmatrix}.$$

Clearly, $f_0 = x_0 + (x_1 + x_2)$ and

$$\begin{bmatrix} f_1 \\ f_2 \end{bmatrix} = \begin{bmatrix} x_0 \\ x_0 \end{bmatrix} + \begin{bmatrix} g_1 \\ g_2 \end{bmatrix},$$

where

$$\begin{bmatrix} g_1 \\ g_2 \end{bmatrix} = \begin{bmatrix} \omega & \omega^2 \\ \omega^2 & \omega \end{bmatrix} \begin{bmatrix} x_1 \\ x_2 \end{bmatrix}.$$

(a) Show that $g_1 = \omega x_1 + \omega^2 x_2$ can be computed using *four* real multiplications and *six* real additions.

Hint: ω and ω^2 are complex conjugates.

(b) Show that $g_2 = -(x_1 + x_2) - g_1$.

(c) Compute the total number of real multiplications and additions needed to compute f by the above method.

(d) The above computation is called a three-point discrete Fourier transform of complex samples. Generalize this to five-point and $(2k + 1)$-point for $k \geq 1$.

7.34 Let N be an integer such that $\sqrt{N}$ is an integer. The following algorithm computes A^i, $i = 1$ to N.

Step 1. Given A, compute A^i, for $i = 1, 2, \cdots , \sqrt{N}$, using the parallel prefix algorithm.

Step 2. Compute $A^{j\sqrt{N}}$, for $j = 1, 2, \cdots , \sqrt{N}$, using the parallel prefix algorithm.

Step 3. Multiply $\{ A^0, A^1, A^2, \cdots , A^{\sqrt{N}} \}$ and $\{ A^{\sqrt{N}}, A^{2\sqrt{N}}, A^{3\sqrt{N}}, \cdots , A^{(\sqrt{N} - 1)\sqrt{N}} \}$.

(a) Analyze the algorithm and quantify the parallel time, the number of operations and the number of processors needed.

(b) Compare this algorithm with that given in Fig. 7.3.1.1.

7.35 Let $A = [A_{ij}]$ and $B = [B_{ij}]$ be two 2×2 matrices. Let $C = A B = [C_{ij}]$. Define

$$
\begin{array}{lll}
x_1 = A_{21} + A_{22} & y_1 = x_2 x_6 & z_1 = y_1 + y_2 \\
x_2 = x_1 - A_{11} & y_2 = A_{11} B_{11} & z_2 = z_1 + y_4 \\
x_3 = A_{11} - A_{21} & y_3 = A_{12} B_{21} & \\
x_4 = A_{12} - x_2 & y_4 = x_3 x_7 & \\
x_5 = B_{12} - B_{11} & y_5 = x_1 x_5 & \\
x_6 = B_{22} - x_5 & y_6 = x_4 B_{22} & \\
x_7 = B_{22} - B_{12} & y_7 = A_{22} x_8 & \\
x_8 = x_6 - B_{21} & &
\end{array}
$$

(a) Show that

$$
\begin{aligned}
C_{11} &= y_2 + y_3 \\
C_{12} &= z_1 + y_5 + y_6 \\
C_{21} &= z_2 - y_7 \\
C_{22} &= z_2 + y_5.
\end{aligned}
$$

(b) Does this method require commutativity of the product operation involved in computing y_i's?

(c) This method, due to Winograd, requires 7 multiplications and 15 additions/subtractions. Derive the total number of additions required in multiplying two $N \times N$ matrices by this method for $N = 2^n$. Compare this method with that given in Section 7.3.3.

7.36 Show that the sum/difference of two Toeplitz matrices can be obtained in linear time.

7.37 Let $\mathbf{A}$ be an $N \times N$ Toeplitz matrix for some $N = 2^n$. Partition $\mathbf{A}$ as follows.

$$
\mathbf{A} = \begin{bmatrix} A_1 & A_2 \\ A_3 & A_1 \end{bmatrix} = \begin{bmatrix} 0 & A_2 - A_1 \\ A_3 - A_1 & 0 \end{bmatrix} + \begin{bmatrix} A_1 & A_1 \\ A_1 & A_1 \end{bmatrix},
$$

where A_1, A_2, and A_3 are $\dfrac{N}{2} \times \dfrac{N}{2}$ matrices. Let $\mathbf{x} = (x_1, x_2, \cdots, x_N)$ be partitioned into two $\dfrac{N}{2}$ vectors as $\mathbf{x} = (\mathbf{y}, \mathbf{z})$, where $\mathbf{y} = (x_1, \cdots, x_{N/2})$, and $\mathbf{z} = (x_{N/2+1}, x_{N/2+2}, \cdots, x_N)$. Then

$$
\mathbf{A}\mathbf{x} = \begin{bmatrix} A_1(\mathbf{y} + \mathbf{z}) + (A_2 - A_1)\mathbf{z} \\ (A_3 - A_1)\mathbf{y} + A_1(\mathbf{y} + \mathbf{z}) \end{bmatrix}.
$$

(a) If $T(N)$ is the time to compute $\mathbf{A}\mathbf{x}$, show that

$$T(N) \le 3\, T(\frac{N}{2}) + (\frac{7}{2}N - 2).$$

(b) Show that $T(N) \le 7[3^n - 2^n] = O(N^{1.59})$.

(c) What is the parallel complexity of this approach?

Compare this approach with that outlined in Property 7.2.5.1.

7.38   Prove Property 7.2.5.3.

7.39   Let $\mathbf{H}(\varepsilon)$ be the 4×4 matrix given in (7.6.1.2).

(a) Compute $\mathbf{H}^i(\varepsilon)$ for $i = 5, 6, 7, 8$.

(b) Compute $\mathbf{H}^i(1)$ for $i = 0$ to 8, and compare it with the powers of $\mathbf{H}^i(\varepsilon)$.

(c) Find $\lim_{k \to \infty} \mathbf{H}^k(\varepsilon)$ and $\lim_{k \to \infty} \mathbf{H}^k(1)$.

7.40   Verify Lemma 7.6.1.1.

7.41   Prove relation (7.6.1.17).

7.42   (Bini [1984]).
Let $\mathbf{A}$ be a 3×3 Toeplitz matrix

$$\mathbf{A} = \begin{bmatrix} a_1 & a_2 & a_3 \\ 0 & a_1 & a_2 \\ 0 & 0 & a_1 \end{bmatrix}.$$

$\mathbf{A}$ can be embedded in a 5×5 *circulant* matrix obtained by *bordering* $\mathbf{A}$ on the left and the bottom as follows:

$$\mathbf{B} = \begin{bmatrix} 0 & 0 & | & a_1 & a_2 & a_3 \\ a_3 & 0 & | & 0 & a_1 & a_2 \\ a_2 & a_3 & | & 0 & 0 & a_1 \\ \text{----} & & | & \text{--------} & & \\ a_1 & a_2 & | & a_3 & 0 & 0 \\ 0 & a_1 & | & a_2 & 0 & 0 \end{bmatrix}.$$

By extending this approach, any $N \times N$ upper triangular Toeplitz matrix can be embedded in a $(2N - 1) \times (2N - 1)$ circulant matrix. Using this technique, we describe an alternative method for performing the computations in step 4 of the algorithm in Fig. 7.6.3.1. Recall from Section 7.6.3 that $\mathbf{U}$ and hence $\mathbf{U}^{-1}$ (see Exercise 7.50) are upper triangular Toeplitz matrices. Thus, to compute $\mathbf{U}^{-1}(\mathbf{d}, \mathbf{y})^t$, first embed $\mathbf{U}^{-1}$ in a $(2N-1) \times (2N-1)$ circulant matrix, say, $\mathbf{C}$. Extend the $(N+k)$-vector $(\mathbf{d}, \mathbf{y})^t$ to a $(2N-1)$-vector, say, $\mathbf{f}$, by adding zeros.

(a) Show that the matrix - vector product $\mathbf{Cf}$ can be obtained in $6 \log(2N-1) + O(1)$ steps using $4N-2$ processors.

(b) Using this result, derive new time and processor bounds in Theorem 7.6.3.1 and Corollaries 7.6.3.2 and 7.6.3.3.

7.43 Show that the determinant of the 3×3 Vandermonde matrix

$$\begin{bmatrix} 1 & x_0 & x_0^2 \\ 1 & x_1 & x_1^2 \\ 1 & x_2 & x_2^2 \end{bmatrix}$$

is $(x_1 - x_0)(x_2 - x_0)(x_2 - x_1)$.

(b) Show that the determinant of the $N \times N$ Vandermonde matrix

$$\begin{bmatrix} 1 & x_0 & x_0^2 & \cdots & x_0^{N-1} \\ 1 & x_1 & x_1^2 & \cdots & x_1^{N-1} \\ 1 & x_2 & x_2^2 & \cdots & x_2^{N-1} \\ . & . & . & \cdots & . \\ . & . & . & \cdots & . \\ . & . & . & \cdots & . \\ 1 & x_{N-1} & x_{N-1}^2 & \cdots & x_{N-1}^{N-1} \end{bmatrix}$$

is $(x_1 - x_0)(x_2 - x_0)(x_2 - x_1)(x_3 - x0)(x_3 - x_1)(x_3 - x_2) \cdots (x_{N-1} - x_{N-2})$.

(c) Derive a parallel method for computing this determinant.

7.44 Prove relation (7.6.2.22).

7.45 Show that $\mathbf{G}^2 = \mathbf{P}$, a permutation matrix, where $\mathbf{P} = [p_{ij}]$ is such that for $1 \le i, j \le N$,

$$p_{ij} = \begin{cases} 1 & \text{if } (i+j) \equiv 2 \pmod{N} \\ 0 & \text{otherwise.} \end{cases}$$

7.46 Let $\mathbf{x}$ be a complex vector and $\bar{\mathbf{x}}$ its conjugate. If $\mathbf{u}_x = \mathbf{G}\mathbf{x}$, then show that $\bar{\mathbf{u}}_x = \mathbf{G}^* \bar{\mathbf{x}}$, where $\mathbf{G}^*$ is the conjugate transpose of $\mathbf{G}$.

Hint: Recall that $\mathbf{G}$ is symmetric.

7.47 (Bini [1984]). Find the solution of (7.6.2.14) when $\mathbf{W} = [\, w_{ij}\,]$ in (7.6.2.11) is such that $w_{ij} = \omega^{(i-1)(j-1)}$, where ω is the $(m+1)^{th}$ primitive root of unity.

7.48 (Bini [1984]). Extend the definition of $\Phi_N(\varepsilon)$ in (7.6.1.3) to the *complex* field as follows:

$$\Phi_N^c(\varepsilon) = \{\, \sum_{i=1}^{N} a_i \, \mathbf{H}^{i-1}(\varepsilon) \mid a_i \text{ is a complex number for } i = 1 \text{ to } N\}.$$

Prove the analogs of Theorem 7.6.1.5 and Corollary 7.6.2.3, when $\mathbf{A}(\varepsilon) \in \Phi_N^c(\varepsilon)$.

7.49 Show that if $\mathbf{A}$ is non-singular, then the submatrix $\mathbf{R}$ in (7.6.3.5) is also non-singular.

7.50 (Traub [1966]). (a) Show that the inverse of a lower triangular Toeplitz matrix

$$\mathbf{A} = \begin{bmatrix} 1 & 0 & 0 & \cdots & 0 & 0 \\ a_1 & 1 & 0 & \cdots & 0 & 0 \\ a_2 & a_1 & 1 & \cdots & 0 & 0 \\ \cdot & \cdot & \cdot & \cdots & \cdot & \cdot \\ \cdot & \cdot & \cdot & \cdots & \cdot & \cdot \\ \cdot & \cdot & \cdot & \cdots & \cdot & \cdot \\ a_{N-1} & a_{N-2} & a_{N-3} & \cdots & a_1 & 1 \end{bmatrix}$$

is a lower triangular Toeplitz matrix

$$\mathbf{B} = \begin{bmatrix} 1 & 0 & 0 & \cdots & 0 & 0 \\ b_1 & 1 & 0 & \cdots & 0 & 0 \\ b_2 & b_1 & 1 & \cdots & 0 & 0 \\ \cdot & \cdot & \cdot & \cdots & \cdot & \cdot \\ \cdot & \cdot & \cdot & \cdots & \cdot & \cdot \\ \cdot & \cdot & \cdot & \cdots & \cdot & \cdot \\ b_{N-1} & b_{N-2} & b_{N-3} & \cdots & b_1 & 1 \end{bmatrix},$$

where $b_0 = 1$ and

$$b_m = \sum_{k=1}^{m} - a_k \, b_{m-k}.$$

Note: This latter expression is called a *generalized Lucas polynomial*.

(b) Develop an algorithm to compute **B** based on this formulation.

(c) Extend this to block lower triangular Toeplitz matrices.

7.51 (Roebuck and Barnett [1978]). (a) Show that a 3×3 unit lower triangular Toeplitz matrix can be expressed as a product of two unit bidiagonal Toeplitz matrices, that is,

$$
\begin{bmatrix}
1 & 0 & 0 \\
a_1 & 1 & 0 \\
a_2 & a_1 & 1
\end{bmatrix}
=
\begin{bmatrix}
1 & 0 & 0 \\
-x_1 & 1 & 0 \\
0 & -x_1 & 1
\end{bmatrix}
\begin{bmatrix}
1 & 0 & 0 \\
-x_2 & 1 & 0 \\
0 & -x_2 & 1
\end{bmatrix},
$$

where x_1 and x_2 are the roots of the quadratic equation

$$x^2 + a_1 x + a_2 = 0.$$

(b) Generalize this to $N \times N$ matrices as follows. Let

$$
\mathbf{A} =
\begin{bmatrix}
1 & 0 & 0 & \cdots & 0 & 0 \\
a_1 & 1 & 0 & \cdots & 0 & 0 \\
a_2 & a_1 & 1 & \cdots & 0 & 0 \\
\cdot & \cdot & \cdot & \cdots & \cdot & \cdot \\
\cdot & \cdot & \cdot & \cdots & \cdot & \cdot \\
\cdot & \cdot & \cdot & \cdots & \cdot & \cdot \\
a_{N-1} & a_{N-2} & a_{N-3} & \cdots & a_1 & 1
\end{bmatrix}
$$

and

$$
\mathbf{X}_i =
\begin{bmatrix}
1 & 0 & 0 & \cdots & 0 & 0 \\
-x_i & 1 & 0 & \cdots & 0 & 0 \\
0 & -x_i & 1 & \cdots & 0 & 0 \\
\cdot & \cdot & \cdot & \cdots & \cdot & \cdot \\
\cdot & \cdot & \cdot & \cdots & \cdot & \cdot \\
\cdot & \cdot & \cdot & \cdots & \cdot & \cdot \\
0 & 0 & 0 & \cdots & -x_i & 1
\end{bmatrix}.
$$

Show that

$$A = X_1 X_2 \cdots X_{N-1},$$

where $x_1, x_2, \cdots, x_{N-1}$ are the roots of the polynomial

$$x^{N-1} + a_1 x^{N-2} + a_2 x^{N-3} + \cdots + a_{N-2} x + a_{N-1}.$$

(c) Let $A = [a_{ij}]$ be a bidiagonal matrix, where

$$\begin{aligned}
a_{ii} &= 1 \quad \text{for } i = 1 \text{ to } N \\
a_{i, i-1} &= x \quad \text{for } i = 2 \text{ to } N \\
a_{ij} &= 0 \quad \text{otherwise.}
\end{aligned}$$

Show that $A^{-1} = [\hat{a}_{ij}]$ is a lower triangular Toeplitz matrix, where

$$\hat{a}_{ij} = \begin{cases}
1 & \text{for } i = j, \\
(-x)^{i-j} & \text{for } i > j, \\
0 & \text{for } i < j.
\end{cases}$$

(d) Using this approach, develop an algorithm to invert a lower triangular Toeplitz matrix.

7.52   Prove Corollary 7.6.3.2.

7.53   Prove Corollary 7.6.3.3.

7.54   (Gohberg and Feldman [1974]). Let A be an $N \times N$ Toeplitz matrix with all its leading principal submatrices being non-singular. Let

$$\mathbf{u} = (1, u_1, u_2, \cdots, u_{N-1})^t \text{ and } \mathbf{v} = (v_{N-1}, v_{N-2}, \cdots, v_1, 1)^t,$$

where

$$A\mathbf{u} = \mathbf{e}_1, \qquad A\mathbf{v} = \mathbf{e}_N, \qquad (*)$$

and $\mathbf{e}_i$ is the ith unit vector. Define

$$L(\mathbf{u}) = \begin{bmatrix}
1 & 0 & 0 & \cdots & 0 & 0 \\
u_1 & 1 & 0 & \cdots & 0 & 0 \\
\cdot & \cdot & \cdot & \cdots & \cdot & \cdot \\
\cdot & \cdot & \cdot & \cdots & \cdot & \cdot \\
\cdot & \cdot & \cdot & \cdots & \cdot & \cdot \\
u_{N-2} & u_{N-3} & u_{N-4} & \cdots & 1 & 0 \\
u_{N-1} & u_{N-2} & u_{N-3} & \cdots & u_1 & 1
\end{bmatrix},$$

$$\mathbf{U(v)} = \begin{bmatrix} 1 & v_1 & v_2 & \cdots & & v_{N-2} & v_{N-1} \\ 0 & 1 & v_1 & \cdots & & v_{N-3} & v_{N-2} \\ \cdot & \cdot & \cdot & \cdots & & \cdot & \cdot \\ \cdot & \cdot & \cdot & \cdots & & \cdot & \cdot \\ \cdot & \cdot & \cdot & \cdots & & \cdot & \cdot \\ 0 & 0 & 0 & \cdots & & 1 & v_1 \\ 0 & 0 & 0 & \cdots & & 0 & 1 \end{bmatrix},$$

$$\mathbf{L_1(v)} = \begin{bmatrix} 0 & 0 & 0 & \cdots & & 0 & 0 \\ v_{N-1} & 0 & 0 & \cdots & & 0 & 0 \\ \cdot & \cdot & \cdot & \cdots & & \cdot & \cdot \\ \cdot & \cdot & \cdot & \cdots & & \cdot & \cdot \\ \cdot & \cdot & \cdot & \cdots & & \cdot & \cdot \\ v_2 & v_3 & v_4 & \cdots & & 0 & 0 \\ v_1 & v_2 & v_3 & \cdots & & v_{N-1} & 0 \end{bmatrix},$$

$$\mathbf{U_1(u)} = \begin{bmatrix} 0 & u_{N-1} & u_{N-2} & \cdots & & u_2 & u_1 \\ 0 & 0 & u_{N-1} & \cdots & & u_3 & u_2 \\ \cdot & \cdot & \cdot & \cdots & & \cdot & \cdot \\ \cdot & \cdot & \cdot & \cdots & & \cdot & \cdot \\ \cdot & \cdot & \cdot & \cdots & & \cdot & \cdot \\ 0 & 0 & 0 & \cdots & & 0 & u_1 \\ 0 & 0 & 0 & \cdots & & 0 & 0 \end{bmatrix}.$$

(a) Show that

$$\mathbf{A}^{-1} = \mathbf{L(u)U(v)} - \mathbf{L_1(v)U_1(u)}. \qquad (**)$$

Note: Stated in other words, $\mathbf{A}^{-1}$ is obtained by solving the two special systems of equations in (*).

(b) In addition, if the matrix $\mathbf{A}$ in (*) is *symmetric,* show that

$$\mathbf{u} = \mathbf{E}_N \mathbf{v} \quad \text{and} \quad \mathbf{A}^{-1} = \mathbf{L(u)} \, \mathbf{L}^t(\mathbf{u}) - \mathbf{U}_1^t(\mathbf{u}) \, \mathbf{U}_1(\mathbf{u}),$$

where $\mathbf{E}_N$ is the exchange matrix defined in Exercise 7.4.

(c) If $\mathbf{A}$ is a lower triangular Toeplitz matrix, then show that

$$\mathbf{A}^{-1} = \mathbf{L(u)}.$$

7.55 Prove Corollary 7.6.1.8. Compute the number of processors needed to achieve this time bound.

Hint: Since e_1 and e_N are constants, in the case when $d = e_1$ or e_N, the computation of the vector Z_2 in step 2 of Bini's algorithm in Fig. 7.6.1.1 can be avoided by precomputing it, that is, Z_2 may be considered as input. Also exploit the Toeplitz structure of the matrices $L(u)$, $U(v)$, $L_1(v)$, and $U_1(u)$ defined in Exercise 7.54.

7.56 (Madsen, Rodrigue, and Karush [1976]). This exercise develops a fast algorithm for matrix multiplication by diagonals. This is very useful for banded matrices. Let $A = [a_{ij}]$ be an $N \times N$ matrix. Define vectors $A_{\pm k}$ as follows. For $k = 0, 1, 2, \cdots, N - 1$, let

$$\left. \begin{array}{l} A_k(m) = a_{m, k+m}, \\ A_{-k}(m) = a_{k+m, m}, \end{array} \right\} \quad \text{for } m = 1 \text{ to } N - k.$$

It can be verified that A_0 is the principal diagonal of A, and A_k and A_{-k} are the kth super (upper) and sub (lower) diagonals of A, respectively. Notice that if a matrix is stored by diagonals, then the transpose operation is trivial.

Let $x = (x_1, x_2, \cdots, x_N)$. Define for $q \geq p$, $x(p:q) = (x_p, x_{p+1}, \cdots, x_q)$. Let $a = (a_1, a_2, \cdots, a_N)$ and $b = (b_1, b_2, \cdots, b_M)$, with $N > M$. Let $c = (c_1, c_2, \cdots, c_N)$. Define two types of componentwise additions of a and b as follows:

$$c = a +_u b = b +_u a,$$

where

$$c_i = a_i + b_i, \quad \text{for } i = 1 \text{ to } M,$$
$$c_i = a_i, \quad\quad \text{for } i = M + 1 \text{ to } N.$$

Similarly,

$$c = a +_l b = b +_l a,$$

where

$$c_i = a_i, \quad\quad\quad\quad\quad \text{for } i = 1 \text{ to } N - M,$$
$$c_{N-M+i} = a_{N-M+i} + b_i, \quad \text{for } i = 1 \text{ to } M.$$

Let $x\, y$ denote componentwise multiplication of two vectors x and y of equal length.

(a) Show that the matrix - vector product Ax can be computed by multiplying along the diagonals as follows:

$$Ax = A_0 x(1:N) +_u A_1 x(2:N) +_u \cdots +_u A_{N-1} x(N:N)$$

$$+_l A_{-1} x(1:N-1) +_l A_{-2} x(1:N-2) +_l \cdots +_l A_{-(N-1)} x(1:1).$$

(b) Let $\mathbf{A}$ and $\mathbf{B}$ be two tridiagonal matrices with diagonals $\mathbf{A}_{-1}$, $\mathbf{A}_0$, and $\mathbf{A}_1$ and $\mathbf{B}_{-1}$, $\mathbf{B}_0$, and $\mathbf{B}_1$, respectively. $\mathbf{A}_0$ and $\mathbf{B}_0$ are N-vectors, but $\mathbf{A}_1$, $\mathbf{A}_{-1}$, $\mathbf{B}_1$, and $\mathbf{B}_{-1}$ are $(N-1)$-vectors. Let $\mathbf{C}=\mathbf{AB}$ be the product matrix with diagonals $\mathbf{C}_0$, $\mathbf{C}_{\pm 1}$, and $\mathbf{C}_{\pm 2}$, which are vectors of size N, $N-1$, and $N-2$, respectively. Show that

$$\mathbf{C}_0 = \mathbf{A}_0\mathbf{B}_0 +_l \mathbf{A}_{-1}\mathbf{B}_1 +_u \mathbf{A}_1\mathbf{B}_{-1},$$

$$\mathbf{C}_1 = \mathbf{A}_0(1\!:\!N-1)\mathbf{B}_1 + \mathbf{A}_1\mathbf{B}_0(2\!:\!N-1),$$

$$\mathbf{C}_{-1} = \mathbf{A}_0(2\!:\!N)\mathbf{B}_{-1} + \mathbf{A}_{-1}\mathbf{B}_0(1\!:\!N-1),$$

$$\mathbf{C}_2 = \mathbf{A}_1(1\!:\!N-2)\mathbf{B}_1(2\!:\!N-1),$$

$$\mathbf{C}_{-2} = \mathbf{A}_{-1}(2\!:\!N-1)\mathbf{B}_{-1}(1\!:\!N-2).$$

(c) Compute the complexity of multiplying two tridiagonal matrices using this method.

(d) Extend this to compute the product of two pentadiagonal matrices.

7.57　Using the matrix $\mathbf{H}$ defined in (7.7.1.11), prove the relation (7.7.1.12).

7.58　(Bunch, Nielsen, and Sorensen [1978]). From the definitions in (7.7.1.21), show that $1 + h(\lambda)$ is an increasing convex function and $-f(\lambda)$ is a decreasing convex function.

7.59　(Golub [1973]). Under the conditions of Theorem 7.7.1.1, since
$$(\mathbf{D} + \alpha\,\mathbf{zz}' - \lambda\mathbf{I}) = (\mathbf{D} - \lambda\mathbf{I})\,[\mathbf{I} + \alpha(\mathbf{D} - \lambda\mathbf{I})^{-1}\mathbf{zz}'],$$
we obtain
$$\det[\mathbf{D} + \alpha\,\mathbf{zz}' - \lambda\mathbf{I}\,] = \det[\mathbf{D} - \lambda\mathbf{I}\,]\,\det[\mathbf{I} + \alpha(\mathbf{D} - \lambda\mathbf{I})^{-1}\mathbf{zz}'].$$
From the separation property in (7.7.1.19), we have
$$\det[\mathbf{D} - \lambda\mathbf{I}\,] = \prod_{i=1}^{N}(d_i - \lambda) \neq 0.$$
Show that $\det[\mathbf{I} + \alpha(\mathbf{D} - \lambda\mathbf{I})^{-1}\mathbf{zz}'] = g(\lambda)$.

Hint: Show that $\det[\mathbf{I} + \mathbf{uv}'] = 1 + \mathbf{u}'\mathbf{v}$, where $\mathbf{u}$ and $\mathbf{v}$ are two column vectors.

7.60　(Golub [1973]). Let $\phi_N(\lambda)$ be the characteristic equation for the matrix $\mathbf{D} + \alpha\,\mathbf{zz}'$. Show that $\phi_N(\lambda)$ can be computed using the following recurrence relation:

$$\phi_{k+1}(\lambda) = (d_{k+1} - \lambda)\phi_k(\lambda) + \alpha z_{k+1}^2 \, \psi_k(\lambda), \text{ for } k = 0, 1, 2, \cdots, N-1,$$

where

$$\psi_k(\lambda) = (d_k - \lambda)\psi_{k-1}(\lambda), \quad \text{for } k = 1, 2, \cdots, N-1,$$

and

$$\phi_0(\lambda) = \psi_0(\lambda) = 1.$$

Hence or otherwise show that

$$\phi(\lambda) = \prod_{i=1}^{N}(d_i - \lambda) + \alpha \sum_{i=1}^{N} z_i^2 \prod_{j \neq i} (d_j - \lambda).$$

7.61 (Golub and Van Loan [1983]). Consider the symmetric tridiagonal matrix **A** in (7.7.1.1). Let $p_k(\lambda) = \det[\mathbf{A}_k - \lambda\mathbf{I}_k]$, where $\mathbf{A}_k$ is the leading principal submatrix of **A** or order k.

(a) Show that

$$p_i(\lambda) = (b_i - \lambda)\, p_{i-1}(\lambda) - a_i^2\, p_{i-2}(\lambda),$$

where $p_0(\lambda) = 1$ and $p_1(\lambda) = b_1 - \lambda$.

Remark: This sequence of polynomials defined by the above linear second-order recurrence is known as the *Strum sequence*. The sequence $p_0(\lambda), p_1(\lambda), p_2(\lambda), \cdots p_N(\lambda)$ has a remarkable property, namely, the number of sign changes in the sequence is equal to the number of eigenvalues of **A** that are less than λ.

(b) Show that the numerical values of this sequence $\{ p_i(\lambda) \}$, $i = 0$ to N, at a point λ can be computed in linear time.

(c) Compute the Strum sequence when $N = 4$, $b_i = 2$ for $i = 1$ to N, and $a_i = -1$ for $i = 2$ to 4. Test the above property of the Strum sequence for two values of λ.

7.62 (Lo, Philippe, and Sameh [1987]). The second-order linear recurrence defining polynomials $p_k(\lambda)$ in Exercise 7.61 can be written in matrix form as

$$\mathbf{Lx} = \mathbf{d},$$

where $\quad \mathbf{x} = (p_0, p_1, p_2, \cdots, p_N)^t; \quad p_i = p_i(\lambda), \quad i = 0, 1, \cdots, N,$
$\mathbf{d} = (1, 0, 0, \cdots, 0)^t,$

$$L = \begin{bmatrix} 1 & 0 & 0 & \cdots & 0 & 0 & 0 \\ \beta_1 & 1 & 0 & \cdots & 0 & 0 & 0 \\ \alpha_2 & \beta_2 & 1 & \cdots & 0 & 0 & 0 \\ \cdot & \cdot & \cdot & \cdots & \cdot & \cdot & \cdot \\ \cdot & \cdot & \cdot & \cdots & \cdot & \cdot & \cdot \\ \cdot & \cdot & \cdot & \cdots & \cdot & 1 & \cdot \\ 0 & 0 & 0 & \cdots & \alpha_N & \beta_N & 1 \end{bmatrix},$$

$$\alpha_i = a_i^2, \quad \text{and} \quad \beta_i = -(b_i - \lambda).$$

(a) Using the methods of Chapter 6, derive parallel algorithms for computing the Strum sequence.

(b) Compute the number of operations for your parallel method and compare it with that of the serial algorithm.

7.63 (Bunch, Nielsen, and Sorensen [1978]). Rewriting (7.7.1.26) as

$$\delta_2^2 - (a + 2\delta_1)\delta_2 + (b + a\delta_1 + \delta_1^2) = 0,$$

where

$$a + 2\delta_1 = \frac{p_1 + q_2}{1 + q_1} + (p_2 + d_{i+1})$$

and

$$b + a\delta_1 + \delta_1^2 = d_{i+1} p_2 + \frac{p_1 d_{i+1} + q_2 p_2}{1 + q_1},$$

show that $\delta_2 = \delta_1 + \dfrac{2b}{a + \sqrt{a^2 - 4b}}$.

7.64 Prove relations (7.7.2.7) and (7.7.2.8).

7.65 Derive relations (7.7.2.14).

7.66 Derive recursive relations (7.7.2.17).

7.67 Compute the number of scalar operations needed by the algorithm in Fig. 7.7.2.2.

APPENDIX A

SOME BASIC CONCEPTS

Let f and g be positive real-valued functions of positive integer-valued variables.

Definition A.1. $O(g)$ defines the set of functions f such that f/g is bounded above, that is, there exist $c > 0$ and $n^* > 0$ such that for all $n \geq n^*$

$$f(n) < cg(n).$$

Definition A.2. $o(g)$ defines the set of functions f such that f/g tends to zero, that is, for every $\varepsilon > 0$, there exists an n^* such that for all $n \geq n^*$,

$$f(n) < \varepsilon g(n).$$

Definition A.3. $\Omega(g)$ is the set of functions f such that f/g is bounded away from zero, that is, there exist $c > 0$ and $n^* > 0$ such that for all $n \geq n^*$

$$f(n) > cg(n) > 0.$$

Definition A.4. $\Theta(g)$ is the set of functions f such that f/g is bounded above and below, that is, there exist $c_1 > 0$, $c_2 > 0$, and $n^* > 0$ such that for all $n \geq n^*$,

$$0 < c_1 g(n) < f(n) < c_2 g(n).$$

For further details, refer to Knuth [1976], Gottlieb and Kruskal [1984], and Brassard and Bratley [1988].

APPENDIX B

HALL'S THEOREM

This appendix contains a version of a fundamental theorem of Hall [1935] which plays a key role in the development of an algorithm for controlling Benes networks described in Section 2.3.

Let S be a finite set and $C = \{ A_i \mid 1 \leq i \leq n\}$ be a family of (not necessarily distinct) subsets of S. A set of elements a_i, $1 \leq i \leq n$, such that $a_i \in A_i$ and $a_i \neq a_j$ is called a *system of distinct representatives* (SDR) for C. Obviously, for SDR to exist, it is necessary that every subfamily of k sets from C must contain at least k distinct elements, that is, for $1 \leq k \leq n$,

$$\left| \bigcup_{j=1}^{k} A_{i_j} \right| \geq k, \tag{B1}$$

where $1 \leq i_j \leq n$. A family $\{A_i \mid 1 \leq i \leq k\}$ is said to be *critical* if

$$\left| \bigcup_{i=1}^{k} A_i \right| = k. \tag{B2}$$

Example 1. Let $S = \{a, b, c, d, e\}$, $n = 4$. Let $A_1 = \{a, b\}$, $A_2 = \{b, c\}$, $A_3 = \{c, a\}$, and $A_4 = \{d, e\}$. Then $a_1 = a$, $a_2 = b$, $a_3 = c$, and $a_4 = d$ constitute a system of distinct representatives. This is *not* unique, for $a_1 = b$, $a_2 = c$, $a_3 = a$, and $a_4 = d$ is also a system of distinct representatives.

Also notice that the subcollection consisting of $\{A_1, A_2, A_3\}$ is critical.

Example 2. Let $A_1 = \{a, b\}$, $A_2 = \{b, c\}$, $A_3 = \{a, c\}$, and $A_4 = \{a, b\}$. This collection has no SDR, since their union contains only three elements.

P. Hall, in 1935, proved that the above obvious necessary condition is indeed sufficient for the existence of an SDR. It is this sufficiency part that is often useful in applications.

Hall's Theorem. Let S be a finite set and $C = \{A_i \mid 1 \leq i \leq n\}$ be a family of (not necessarily distinct) subsets of S. The family C possesses an SDR if and only if condition (B1) is satisfied.

Proof

The proof is by induction. Clearly, for $n = 1$, the theorem is obvious. Let the theorem be true for families with less than m sets in them. Consider a family with m sets. It is convenient to distinguish two cases.

Case 1. There is no subfamily that is critical. Then for $1 \leq r < m$,

$$|\bigcup_{j=1}^{r} A_{i_j}| \geq r+1,$$

where $1 \leq i_j \leq m$ and $1 \leq j \leq r$. From (B1) it follows that $A_1 \neq \emptyset$. Pick $a_1 \in A_1$, and consider the collection $A_i - \{a_1\}$ of $m - 1$ sets for $2 \leq i \leq m$. By the induction hypothesis, there exist distinct $a_i \in A_i - \{a_1\}$, for $2 \leq i \leq m$. Combining these with a_1, we obtain a system of distinct representatives for the family of m sets.

Case 2. There is a critical subfamily. Let $A_1, A_2, \cdots, A_r$ be a critical subfamily. Then

$$|\bigcup_{i=1}^{r} A_i| = r, \tag{B3}$$

where $1 \leq r < m$. By the induction hypothesis, there exists a system of distinct elements $a_i \in A_i$, $1 \leq i \leq r$. Let

$$B_i = A_i - \{a_1, a_2, \cdots, a_r\},$$

for $r + 1 \leq i \leq m$. Define

$$B = \bigcup_{j=1}^{t} B_{i_j},$$

for some $1 \leq t \leq n - r$, where $k + 1 \leq i_j \leq m$ and $1 \leq j \leq t$. Then

$$|B| = |\bigcup_{j=1}^{t} B_{i_j}| + |\bigcup_{l=1}^{r} A_l| - r \qquad \text{(using } (B\,3))$$

$$= |(\bigcup_{j=1}^{t} B_{i_j}) \cup (\bigcup_{l=1}^{r} A_l)| - r$$

$$= |(\bigcup_{j=1}^{t} A_{i_j}) \cup (\bigcup_{l=1}^{r} A_l)| - r$$

$$\geq (t+r) - r = t \qquad \text{(from } (B\,1)).$$

Thus, the family $\{B_i \mid r+1 \leq i \leq m\}$ also satisfies (B1). By the induction hypothesis, there exist distinct $b_i \in B_i$ for $r+1 \leq i \leq m$. Clearly,

$$(\bigcup_{i=1}^{r} \{a_i\}) \cup (\bigcup_{i=r+1}^{m} \{b_i\})$$

constitutes a system of distinct representatives for the family of m sets. Hence the theorem.

The above proof is due to Halmos and Vaughan [1950]. Mirsky and Perfect [1966], Ryser [1963], and Roberts [1984] contain various forms of Hall's theorem and their applications.

CONCEPTS FROM ABSTRACT ALGEBRA

This appendix assembles many definitions and facts about *groups, rings,* and *fields* that are useful in understanding portions of Chapters 3 and 7. We use the following notations:

N : the set of all *non-negative* integers.
E : the set of all *even* integers.
P : the set of all *positive* integers.
Z : the set of all integers.
Q : the set of all *rational* numbers.
R : the set of all *real* numbers.
C : the set of all *complex* numbers.
Z_m : $\{ 0, 1, 2, \cdots , m - 1 \}$.
R^+ : the set of all *positive* real numbers.
R^* : the set of all *non-negative* real numbers.

The sets Q^+, Q^*, and C^* are similarly defined.

An *ordered pair $G = (B, \text{o})$ is called a group* if B is a (non-empty) set that is closed under the *binary* operation o, such that

(g1) If a, b, $c \in B$, then the *associative* law holds, that is

$$a \circ (b \circ c) = (a \circ b) \circ c,$$

(g2) There exists a unique element e_0, called the *identity*, such that

$$a \circ e_0 = e_0 \circ a = a,$$

for all $a \in B$, and

(g3) For every element $a \in B$, there exists a unique element $a^{-1} \in B$, called the *inverse* of a, such that

$$a \circ a^{-1} = e_0.$$

G is a *finite* group if the underlying set B is finite; otherwise it is an infinite group. G is called a *commutative* (or *Abelian*) group if

$$a \circ b = b \circ a,$$

for all a, $b \in B$.

Example 1. $(Z, +)$ is a commutative group, with $+$ denoting the usual addition of integers. In this case $e_+ = 0$ (zero), and the inverse of any integer is obtained by changing its sign. Likewise, $(R, +)$, $(Q, +)$, and $(C, +)$ are all examples of commutative groups, when $+$ denotes the addition of real, rational, and complex numbers, respectively. Clearly, $(P, +)$ is *not* a group (why?). $(Z_m, +_m)$ is a commutative group if $+_m$ denotes the addition of integers modulo m.

Example 2. Let R^+ denote the set of all *non-negative* real numbers. If $\times$ denotes the multiplication of real numbers, then $(R^+, \times)$ is a commutative group with 1 (unity) as the identity and the reciprocal as the inverse.

Example 3. Let M_n denote the set of all $n \times n$ *non-singular* matrices $(n \geq 2)$ and $\times$ denote the *matrix product*. Clearly, $(M_n, \times)$ is a non-commutative group, since the matrix product is, in general, *not* commutative. $(R, \times)$, $(Q, \times)$, and $(C, \times)$ are *not* groups, but $(R^*, \times)$, $(Q^*, \times)$, and $(C^*, \times)$ are groups.

Let $G = (B, +)$ be a group. Let $G' = (S, +)$, where $S \subseteq B$ is called a *subgroup* denoted by $G' \leq G$, if the elements of S satisfy conditions (g1) to (g3). If S is a proper subset of B, then G' is called a proper subgroup and is denoted as $G' < G$.

From this definition and Example 1, it readily follows that

$$(Z, +) < (Q, +) < (R, +) < (C, +)$$

and

$$(Q^*, \times) < (R^*, \times) < (C^*, \times).$$

Notice that $(Z^*, \times)$ is *not* a group.

An ordered triplet $R = (B, +, \times)$ is called a *ring* if B is a set and $+$ (called addition) and $\times$ (called multiplication) are two *binary operations* such that

(r1) $(B, +)$ is a *commutative* (Abelian) group.

(r2) If $a, b, c \in B$, then the *associative* law for multiplication holds, that is,

$$(a \times b) \times c = a \times (b \times c),$$

and

(r3) If $a, b, c \in B$, then the left and right *distributive* laws hold, that is,

$$a \times (b + c) = a \times b + a \times c$$

and

$$(a + b) \times c = a \times c + b \times c.$$

Depending on the properties of the $\times$ (multiplication) operation, a number of special cases arise.

The ring R is called a *commutative* ring if

$$a \times b = b \times a$$

for all $a, b \in B$. R is said to be a ring with *identity* if there exists an element $e_\times \in B$ such that

$$a \times e_\times = e_\times \times a = a,$$

for all $a \in B$. This identity $e_\times$ is *not* the identity under the (addition) operation $+$. The (additive) identity e_+ is often called zero.

Example 4. $(Z, +, \times)$ is a commutative ring with identity, where $+$ and $\times$ denote the usual integer addition and multiplication, respectively. Clearly, $e_+ = 0$ (zero) and $e_\times = 1$ (unity). Similarly, $(R, +, \times)$, $(Q, +, \times)$, and $(C, +, \times)$ are all examples of commutative rings with identity when $+$ and $\times$ denote the addition and multiplication of real, rational, and complex numbers, respectively. $(Z_m, +_m, \times_m)$, with $+_m$ and $\times_m$ denoting the addition and multiplication of integers modulo m, is also a commutative ring with identity.

Example 5. The set M_n of all $n \times n$ non-singular matrices $(n \geq 2)$ with the matrix addition and multiplication operations is an example of a *non-commutative* ring with identity.

We can define a subring of a ring quite like the subgroup of a group. The following relation holds among rings:

$$(Z, +, \times) < (Q, +, \times) < (R, +, \times) < (C, +, \times).$$

Consider the ring $R = (B, +, \times)$. Let $e_+ = 0$, be the additive identity. It can be shown that for any $a \in B$, $a \times 0 = 0$. Let a, b be such that $a \neq 0$ and $b \neq 0$. Then, if $a \times b = 0$, a and b are known as *divisors of zero*. a is called the *left* and b the *right* divisor of zero. In a commutative ring, the left and the right divisors are the same and are simply called the *divisor*.

Example 6. $\{Z_6, +_6, \times_6\}$ is an example of a commutative ring with zero divisors. In this case, 2, 3, and 4 are all divisors of zero.

If a ring has *no* divisors of zero, and if $a \times b = 0$, then either $a = 0$ or $b = 0$. In such a ring (with no divisors of zero), the *cancellation* law for multiplication ($\times$) holds, that is, if $a \times x = b \times x$, then $a = b$.

A commutative ring with no zero divisors is called an *integral domain*.

Example 7. Let E be the set of all even integers. Then $(E, +, \times)$ is an integral domain *without identity*, where $+$ and $\times$ denote the usual integer addition and multiplication.

Example 8. Let $Z[x]$ denote the set of all univariate polynomials with integer coefficients. $(Z[x], +, \times)$, where $+$ and $\times$ denote the usual polynomial addition and multiplication, is an *integral domain with identity*. Clearly, $Z[x]$ is an infinite set.

If the ring $R = (B, +, \times)$ is such that $(B - \{0\}, \times)$ is a group, where 0 is the additive identity, e_+, then it is called a *division* ring. If a division ring is commutative, then it is called a *field*.

Example 9. $(R, +, \times)$, $(Q, +, \times)$, and $(C, +, \times)$ are all examples of fields. But $(Z, +, \times)$ is not a field. Similarly, $(Z_m, +_m, \times_m)$ is a field when m is prime. The set M_n of all $n \times n$ non-singular matrices under the usual matrix addition and multiplication is an example of a division ring which is *not* a field.

The notion of a subfield can be defined quite similarly to that of subgroups and subrings.

We now state a number of facts without proof.

(f1) A division ring must contain at least two elements.

(f2) Every finite division ring must be a field.

(f3) Since any *subfield* $(S, +, \times)$ of the field of reals $(R, +, \times)$ must contain 1 (the multiplicative identity) and all integral multiples and reciprocals of integers, S must contain the set of all rational numbers.

Let $R = (B, +, \times)$ be a ring. If there exists a *least positive integer* $n \in B$, such that

$$a + a + \cdots + a = n \times a = 0$$

for all $a \in B$, then the *characteristic* of R is said to be n and is denoted as $CH(R) = n$. If no such integer exists, then $CH(R) = 0$ by definition.

Example 10. If $R = (Z, +, \times)$, then $CH(R) = 0$. But, if $R = (Z_6, +_6, \times_6)$, then $CH(R) = 6$.

We now state a number of facts relating to the characteristic of a ring.

(f4) Let $R = (B, +, \times)$ be an integral domain (which is a commutative ring with no zero divisors) with $CH(R) = m$. Then $m = 0$ or m is a prime.

For, let $m \neq 0$ and $m = m_1 m_2$, where $1 < m_1, m_2 < m$. If $e_\times$ is the multiplicative identity, then $m \times e_\times = (m_1 \times e_\times) \times (m_2 \times e_\times) = 0$. Since R is an integral domain, there are no zero divisors. Thus, either $m_1 \times e_\times = 0$ or $m_2 \times e_\times = 0$. In either case, $CH(R) = m_1$ or m_2, which is less than m, a contradiction. Thus, if $m \neq 0$, then m must be a prime.

(f5) Let $R = (B, +, \times)$ be a field. Since every field is also an integral domain, then $CH(R) = 0$ or m, a prime.

Let $F = (B, +, \times)$ be a field. If F is the only subfield of F, then F is called the *prime field*. If F' is a prime field that is *also* a subfield of a field F, then F' is called the *prime subfield of F*. Clearly, the prime subfield is the smallest subfield.

(f6) Every field contains a unique prime subfield.

(f7) If F is a field such that $CH(F) = 0$, then the prime subfield of F is *isomorphic* to $(Q, +, \times)$, the field of rational numbers.

(f8) Fields of characteristic zero are indeed *infinite* fields.

(f9) If F is a field with $CH(R) = p$, a prime, then the prime subfield of F is isomorphic to Z_p.

(f10) If F is a field with subfield F_1, then

$$CH(F) = CH(F_1).$$

(f11) If p is a prime integer, then there exists an *infinite field* of characteristic p.

For further reading, consult Birkhoff and Bartee [1970], Lipson [1981], and Stone [1973a].

REFERENCES

Abramson, N. [1963]. *Information Theory and Coding.* McGraw-Hill, New York.

Agerwala, T., and Arvind (eds) [1982]. Data Flow Systems -- Special Issue. *IEEE Computer,* February 1982.

Aggarwal, V.B., S.K. Dhall, J.C. Diaz, and S. Lakshmivarahan [1985]. A Parallel Algorithm for Solving Large Scale Sparse Linear Systems Using Block Preconditioned Conjugate Gradient Method on MIMD Machine. *Proceedings of the Workshop on Parallel Processing Using the HEP,* University of Oklahoma, Norman, Oklahoma, pp 97-114.

Agrawal, D. P. [1983]. Graph Theoretical Analysis and Design of Multistage Interconnection Networks. *IEEE Transactions on Computers,* Vol 32, pp 637-648.

Aho, A. V., J. E. Hopcroft, and J. D. Ullman [1974]. *The Design and Analysis of Computer Algorithms.* Addison-Wesley, Reading, MA.

Ajtai, M., J. Komlos, and E. Szemeredi [1984]. An $O(n \log n)$ Sorting Network. *Combinatorica,* Vol 3, pp 1-19.

Akl, S. G. [1985]. *Parallel Sorting Algorithms.* Academic Press, New York.

Akl, S. G. [1989]. *The Design and Analysis of Parallel Algorithms.* Prentice-Hall, Engelwood Cliffs, NJ.

Al-Hallaq, A. Y., and S. Lakshmivarahan [1987]. Self Routing Control Algorithms and the Passability of Random Inputs by the Base-line Networks. *Information Sciences,* Vol 43, pp 139-154.

Allen, J. R. [1983]. Dependence Analysis for Subscripted Variables and its Application to Program Transformations. Ph.D. Thesis, Rice University, Houston, TX.

Allen, J. R., and K. Kennedy [1983]. PFC: A Program to Convert Fortran to Parallel Form. Technical Report, MASC TR82-6, Rice University, Houston, TX.

Allen, J.R., and K. Kennedy [1985]. A Parallel Programming Environment. *IEEE Software,* Vol 2, No 4, pp 21-29.

Alliant [1985]. *Alliant Product Summary.* Alliant Computer Systems Corporation, Acton, MA.

Almasi, G. S., and A. Gottlieb [1989]. *Highly Parallel Computing.* Benjamin/Cummings, Redwood City, CA.

Alt, H. [1984]. Comparison of Arithmetic Functions with Respect to Boolean Circuit Depth. *Proceedings of the ACM Symposium on Theory of Computing,* pp 466-470.

Amdahl, G. M. [1967]. Validity of the Single Processor Approach to Achieving Large Scale Computing Capabilities. *Proceedings of the AFIPS Spring Joint Computer Conference,* Vol 30, pp 40-54.

Ammar, G. S., and W. B. Gragg [1988]. Superfast Solution of Real Positive Definite Toeplitz Systems. *SIAM Journal on Matrix Analysis and Applications.* Vol 9, pp 61-76.

Anderson, S. F., J. G. Earle, R. E. Goldschmidt, and D. M. Powers [1967]. The IBM System/360 Model 91: Floating Execution Unit. *IBM Journal of Research and Development,* Vol 11, pp 34-53.

Andre, F., D. Herman, and J. P. Verjus [1985]. *Synchronization of Parallel Programs.* MIT Press, Cambridge, MA.

Baase, S. [1978]. *Computer Algorithms: Introduction to Design and Analysis.* Addison-Wesley, Reading, MA.

Baba, T. [1987]. *Microprogrammable Parallel Computer.* MIT Press, Cambridge, MA.

Babb, R.G., II, (ed) [1988]. *Programming Parallel Processors.* Addison-Wesley, Reading, MA.

Baer, J. L. [1974]. A Survey of Some Theoretical Aspects of Multiprocessing. *Computing Surveys,* Vol 5, pp 31-80.

Baer, J. L., and D. P. Bovet [1969]. Compilation of Arithmetic Expressions for Parallel Computation. *Proceedings of the IFIP Congress,* North-Holland, Amsterdam, pp 340–346.

Bailey, D. H. [1988a]. The Computation of Pi to 29,360,000 Decimal Digits Using Borwein's Quartically Convergent Algorithm. *Mathematics of Computation,* Vol 50, pp 283-296.

Bailey, D. H. [1988b]. Extra High Speed Matrix Multiplication on the Cray-2. *SIAM Journal on Scientific and Statistical Computing,* Vol 9, pp 603-607.

Banerjee, U. [1979]. Speedup of Ordinary Programs. Technical Report UIUCDCS-R-79-989, Department of Computer Science, University of Illinois, Urbana, IL.

Barasch, L., S. Lakshmivarahan, and S. K. Dhall [1988]. Generalized Gray Codes and Their Applications. *Proceedings of the Second International Super Computing Conference,* Boston, MA, pp 331-337.

Barasch, L., S. Lakshmivarahan, and S. K. Dhall [1989a]. Embedding Arbitary Meshes and Complete Binary Trees in Generalized Hypercubes. *Proceedings of the First Annual IEEE Symposium on Parallel and Distributed Processing,* Dallas, TX, pp 202-209.

Barasch, L., S. Lakshmivarahan, and S. K. Dhall [1989b]. Generalized Gray Codes and Their Properties. *Mathematics for Large Scale Computing, Lecture Notes in Pure and Applied Mathematics,* Vol 120, J.C. Diaz (ed). Marcel Dekker, New York, pp 203-216.

Barnes, G. H., R. M. Brown, M. Kato, D. J. Kuck, D. L. Slotnick, and R. A. Stokes [1968]. The ILLIAC IV Computer. *IEEE Transactions on Computers,* Vol 17, pp 746-757.

Batcher, K. [1968]. Sorting Networks and Applications. *Proceedings of the AFIPS Spring Joint Computer Conference,* Vol 32, pp 307-314.

Batcher, K. [1980]. Design of a Massively Parallel Processor. *IEEE Transactions on Computers,* Vol 29, pp 836-840.

Beame, P. W. [1986]. Limits on the Power of Concurrent-Write Parallel Machines. *Proceedings of the ACM Symposium on Theory of Computing,* pp 169-176.

Beame, P. W., S. A. Cook, and H. J. Hoover [1986]. Log Depth Circuits for Division and Related Problems. *SIAM Journal on Computing,* Vol 15, pp 994-1003.

Beatty, J. C. [1972]. An Axiomatic Approach to Code Optimization for Expressions. *Journal of ACM,* Vol 19, pp 613-640.

Beetem, J., M. Denneau, and D. Weingarten [1985]. The GF 11 Supercomputer. *Proceedings of the Symposium on Computer Architecture,* pp 108-115.

Bell, C. G. [1985]. Multis: A New Class of Multiprocessor Computers. *Science,* Vol 228, pp 462-467.

Bellman, R. [1960]. *Introduction to Matrix Analysis.* McGraw-Hill, New York.

Bellman, R. K., L. Cooke, and J. A. Lockett [1977]. *Algorithms, Graphs, and Computers.* Academic Press, New York.

Benes, V. E. [1962]. On Rearrangeable Three-Stage Connecting Networks. *The Bell System Technical Journal,* Vol 41, pp 1481-1492.

Benes, V. E. [1965]. *Mathematical Theory of Connecting Networks and Telephone Traffic.* Academic Press, New York.

Benes, V. E. [1975a]. Proving the Rearrangeability of Connecting Networks by Group Calculations. *The Bell System Technical Journal,* Vol 54, pp 421-434.

Benes, V. E. [1975b]. Towards a Group Theoretic Proof of the Rearrangeability Theorem for Clos' Network. *The Bell System Technical Journal,* Vol 55, pp 797-805.

Benes, V. E. [1975c]. Applications of Group Theory to Connecting Networks. *The Bell System Technical Journal,* Vol 54, pp 407-420.

Berkowitz, S. J. [1984]. On Computing the Determinant in Small Parallel Time Using a Small Number of Processors. *Information Processing Letters,* Vol 18, pp 147-150.

Berry, M., and A. H. Sameh [1988]. Multiprocessor Schemes for Solving Block Tridiagonal Linear Systems. CSRD Report 739, University of Illinois, Urbana, IL.

Bertsekas, D. P., and J. N. Tsitsiklis [1989]. *Parallel and Distributed Computation: Numerical Methods.* Prentice-Hall, Engelwood Cliffs, NJ.

Bhatt, S. N., and I.C.F. Ipsen [1985]. How to Embed Trees. Research Report/DCS/RR-443, Department of Computer Science, Yale University, New Haven, CT.

Bhatt, S. N., F. Chung, T. Leighton, and A. Rosenberg [1986]. Optimal Simulation of Tree Machines. Research Report-DCS-TR-495, Department of Computer Science, Yale University, New Haven, CT.

Bhuyan, L. N., and D. P. Agrawal [1984]. Generalized Hypercube and Hyperbus Structures for a Computer Network. *IEEE Transactions on Computers,* Vol 33, pp 323-333.

Bilardi, G., and F. P. Preparata [1987]. Size-Time Complexity of Boolean Networks for Prefix Computations. Technical Report UICU-ENG-87-2202, Coordinated Science Laboratory, University of Illinois, Urbana, IL.

Bilgory, A., and D. Gajski [1986]. A Heuristic for Suffix Solutions. *IEEE Transactions on Computers,* Vol 35, pp 34-42.

Bini, D. [1980]. Border Rank of a $p*q*2$ Tensor and the Optimal Approximation of Bilinear Forms. *Lecture Notes in Computer Science,* Vol 85. Springer-Verlag, New York, pp 98–108.

Bini, D. [1984]. Parallel Solution of Certain Toeplitz Linear System. *SIAM Journal on Computing,* Vol 13, pp 268-276.

Bini, D., and G. Lotti [1980]. Stability of Fast Algorithms for Matrix Multiplication.

Numerische Mathematik, Vol 36, pp 63-72.

Birkhoff, G., and T. C. Bartee [1970]. *Modern Applied Algebra.* McGraw-Hill, New York.

Blum, N. [1983]. A Note on Parallel Computation Thesis. *Information Processing Letters,* Vol 17, pp 203-205.

Borodin, A. [1977]. On Relating Time and Space to Size and Depth. *SIAM Journal of Computing,* Vol 6, pp 733-744.

Borodin, A., and J. E. Hopcroft [1982]. Routing, Merging and Sorting on Parallel Models of Computation. *Proceedings of the ACM Symposium on Theory of Computing,* pp 338-344.

Borodin, A., and I. Munro [1975]. *The Computational Complexity of Algebraic and Numeric Problems.* American Elsevier, New York.

Borodin, A., Van zur Gathen, and J. E. Hopcroft [1982]. Fast Parallel Matrix and GCD Computations. *Proceedings of the Annual Symposium on the Foundations of Computing,* pp 65-71.

Brandenberg, J. E., and D. E. Scott [1985]. Embeddings of Communication Trees and Grids into Hypercubes. Technical Report, Intel Scientific Computers, Beaverton, OR.

Brassard, G., and P. Bratley [1988]. *Algorithmics: Theory and Practice.* Prentice-Hall, Englewood Cliffs, NJ.

Brent, R. P. [1970a] On the Addition of Binary Numbers. *IEEE Transactions on Computers,* Vol 19, pp 758-759.

Brent, R. P. [1970b]. Error Analysis of Algorithms for Matrix Multiplication and Triangular Decomposition Using Winograd's Identity. *Numerische Mathematik,* Vol 16, pp 145–156.

Brent, R. P. [1973]. The Parallel Evaluation of Arithmetic Expression in Logarithmic Time. *Complexity of Sequential and Parallel Numerical Algorithms,* J.F. Traub (ed). Academic Press, New York, pp 83-102.

Brent, R. P. [1974]. The Parallel Evaluation of General Arithmetic Expression. *Journal of ACM,* Vol 21, pp 201-206.

Brent, R. P. [1976]. Fast Multiprecision Evaluation of Elementary Functions. *Journal of ACM,* Vol 23, pp 242-251.

Brent, R.P., D. J. Kuck, and K. Maruyama [1973]. The Parallel Evaluation of Arithmetic Expressions Without Division. *IEEE Transactions on Computers,* Vol 22, pp 532-534.

Brent, R.P., and H. T. Kung [1982]. A Regular Layout for Parallel Adders. *IEEE Transactions on Computers,* Vol 31, pp 260-264.

Budnik, P., and D. J. Kuck [1971]. The Organization and Use of Parallel Memories. *IEEE Transactions on Computers,* Vol 20, pp 1566-1569.

Bunch, J. R., C. P. Nielsen, and D. C. Sorensen [1978]. Rank One Modification of the Symmetric Eigenproblem. *Numerishe Mathematik,* Vol 31, pp 31-48.

Buneman, O. [1969]. A Compact Non-Iterative Solver. Report 294, Institute for Plasma Physics, Stanford University, Stanford, CA.

Buzbee, B. L. [1973]. A Fast Poisson Solver Amenable to Parallel Computation. *IEEE Transactions on Computers,* Vol 22, pp 793-796.

Buzbee, B. L., and F. W. Dorr [1974]. The Direct Solution of the Biharmonic Equation on Rectangular Regions and the Poisson Equation on Irregular Regions. *SIAM Journal on Numerical Analysis,* Vol 11, pp 753-763.

Buzbee, B. L., G. H. Golub, and C. W. Nielson [1970]. On Direct Methods for Solving Poisson's Equations. *SIAM Journal on Numerical Analysis,* Vol 7, pp 627-655.

Calahan, D. A., and W. G. Ames [1979]. Vector Processors: Models and Applications. *IEEE Transactions on Circuits and Systems,* Vol 26, pp 715-726.

Carlson, D. A., and B. Sugla [1985]. On the Area Requirements of Very Fast VLSI Adders. Technical Report, Department of Electrical and Computer Engineering, University of Massachusetts, Amherst, MA.

Chamberlain, R. M. [1987]. An Alternative View of LU Factorization with Partial Pivoting on a Hypercube. *Hypercube Multiprocessor,* M. T. Heath (ed). SIAM Publications, Philadelphia, PA.

Chambers, F. B., D. A. Duce, and G. P. Jones (eds) [1984]. *Distributed Computing.* Academic Press, New York.

Chan, T. [1988]. An Optimal Circulant Preconditioner for Toeplitz Systems. *SIAM Journal on Scientific and Statistical Computing,* Vol 9, pp 766-771.

Chan, T., and D. C. Resasco [1987]. Hypercube Implementation of Domain-Decomposed Fast Poisson Solvers. *SIAM Second Hypercube Conference,* M. T. Heath (ed). SIAM Publications, Philadelphia, PA, pp 738-746.

Chandra, A. K., S. Fortune, and R. Lipton [1983]. Unbounded Fan in Circuits and Associative Functions. *Proceedings of the ACM Symposium on Theory of Computing,* pp 52-60.

Chandra, A. K., L. Stockmeyer, and U. Vishkin [1984]. Constant Depth Reducibility. *SIAM Journal on Computing,* Vol 13, pp 423-439.

Chandy, K. M., and J. Misra [1988]. *Parallel Program Design: A Foundation.* Addison-Wesley, Reading, MA.

Chen, S. C. [1975]. Speedups of Iterative Programs in Multiprocessing Systems. Ph. D. Thesis, Department of Computer Science, University of Illinois, Urbana, IL.

Chen, S. C., and D. J. Kuck [1975]. Time and Parallel Processor Bounds for Linear Recurrences. *IEEE Transactions on Computers,* Vol 24, pp 701-717.

Chen, S. C., D. J. Kuck, and A. H. Sameh [1978]. Practical Parallel Band Triangular Systems Solvers. *ACM Transactions on Mathematical Software,* Vol 4, pp 270-277.

Chun, J., T. Kailath, and H. Lev-Ari [1987]. Fast Parallel Algorithms for QR and Triangular Factorization. *SIAM Journal on Scientific and Statistical Computing,* Vol 8, pp 899-913.

Clos, C. [1952]. A Study of Non-Blocking Switching Networks. *The Bell System Technical Journal,* Vol 32, pp 406-424.

Cohen, J. [1979]. Non-Deterministic Algorithms. *Computing Surveys,* Vol 11, pp 79-94.

Cook, S. A. [1985]. A Taxonomy of Problems with Fast Parallel Algorithms. *Information and Control,* Vol 64, pp 2-22.

Cook, S., and C. Dwork [1982]. Bounds on the Time for Parallel RAMS to Compute Simple Functions. *Proceedings of the ACM Symposium on Theory of Computing,* pp 231-233.

Cook, S. A., C. Dwork, and R. Reischuk [1986]. Upper and Lower Time Bounds for Parallel Random Access Machines Without Simultaneous Writes. *SIAM Journal on Computing,* Vol 15, pp 87-97.

Cooley, J. M., and J. W. Tukey [1965]. An Algorithm for Machine Calculation of Complex Fourier Series. *Mathematics of Computation,* Vol 19, pp 297-301.

Coppersmith, D., and S. Winograd [1980]. On the Asymptotic Complexity of Matrix Multiplication. *SIAM Journal on Computing,* Vol 11, pp 472-492.

Coppersmith, D., and S. Winograd [1987]. Matrix Multiplication via Arithmetic Progressions. *Proceedings of the Nineteenth Annual ACM Symposium on Theory of Computing,* pp 1-6.

Cosnard, M., and Y. Robert [1986]. Complexity of Parallel QR Factorization. *Journal of the ACM,* Vol 33, pp 712-723.

Crowther, W., J. Goodhue, E. Starr, R. Thomas, W. Milliken, and D. Blackadar [1985]. Performance Measurements on a 128-Node Butterfly Parallel Processor. *Proceedings of the International Conference on Parallel Processing,* pp 531-540.

Csanky, L. [1976]. Fast Parallel Matrix Inversion Algorithms. *SIAM Journal on Computing,* Vol 5, pp 618-623.

Cuppen, J. J. M. [1981]. A Divide and Conquer Method for the Symmetric Eigenproblem. *Numerische Mathematik,* Vol 36, pp 177-195.

Cyberplus [1984]. *Multiparallel Processing System.* Control Data Corporation, Hardware Reference Manual, St. Paul, MN.

Davis, P. J. [1979]. *Circulant Matrices.* Wiley, New York.

DeGroot, D. [1983]. Expanding and Contracting SW-Banyan Networks. *Proceedings of the International Conference on Parallel Processing,* pp 19-24.

Dennis, J. B. [1980]. Data Flow Supercomputers. *IEEE Computer,* Vol 18, November, pp 42-56.

Deo, N. [1974]. *Graph Theory with Applications to Engineering and Computer Science.* Prentice-Hall, Englewood Cliffs, NJ.

Dhall, S. K., S. Lakshmivarahan, and M. V. R. Seshacharyulu [1985]. Solving for Cascade Sums and First-Order Linear Recurrences on the HEP. *Proceedings of the Workshop on Parallel Processing Using the HEP,* The University of Oklakoma, Norman, OK, pp 303–326.

Diaz, J.C. (ed) [1989]. *Mathematics for Large Scale Computing, Lecture Notes in Pure and Applied Mathematics,* Vol 120. Marcel Dekker, New York.

Dongarra, J. J. [1986]. How Do the Minisupers Stack Up? *IEEE Computer,* March, pp 99–100.

Dongarra, J. J. (ed) [1988]. *Experimental Parallel Computing Architectures.* North-Holland, Elsevier, New York.

Dongarra, J. J., F. Gustavson, and A. Karp [1985]. Implementing Linear Algebra Algorithms for Dense Matrices on a Vector Pipeline Machine. *SIAM Review* Vol 26, pp.91-112.

Dongarra, J. J., C. B. Moler, J. R. Bunch, and G.W. Stewart [1979]. *LINPACK, User's Guide.* SIAM, Philadelphia, PA.

Dongarra, J. J., and D. C. Sorensen [1987]. A Fully Parallel Algorithm for the Symmetric Eigenvalue Problem. *SIAM Journal on Scientific and Statistical Computing,* Vol 8, pp s139-s154.

Dorn, W. S. [1962]. Generalization of Horner's Rule for Polynomial Evaluation. *IBM Journal of Research and Development,* pp 239-245.

Dowers, K., S. Lakshmivarahan, and S. K. Dhall [1987]. On the Comparison of the Performance of ALLIANT FX/8, IBM 3081, and VAX 11/780 in Solving Linear Tridiagonal Systems. *Proceedings of the IEEE Region 5 Conference,* Tulsa, OK, pp 117–122.

Dowers, K., S. Lakshmivarahan, and S. K. Dhall [1989]. Block Tridiagonal System on the Alliant FX/8. *Parallel Processing for Scientific Computing,* G. Rodrigue (ed), pp 56-60.

Eckstein, D. M. [1979]. Simultaneous Memory Access. Technical Report-79-6, Iowa State University, Ames, IA.

Eisenstat, S. C., M. T. Heath, C. S. Henkel, and C. H. Romine [1988]. Modified Cyclic Algorithms for Solving Triangular Systems on Distributed-Memory Multiprocessors. *SIAM Journal on Scientific and Statistical Computing,* Vol 9, pp 589-600.

Estrin, G. [1960]. Organization of Computer Systems -- The Fixed Plus Variable Structure Computer. *Proceedings of the Western Joint Computer Conference,* No. 5, pp 33-40.

Evans, D. J. (ed) [1980a]. *Parallel Processing Systems.* Cambridge University Press, London.

Evans, D. J. [1980b]. On the Solution of Certain Toeplitz Tridiagonal Linear Systems. *SIAM Journal on Numerical Analysis,* Vol 17, pp 675-680.

Evans, D. J., and R. C. Dunbar [1983]. The Parallel Solution of Triangular Systems of Equations. *IEEE Transactions on Computers,* Vol 32, pp 201-204.

Even, S. [1980]. *Graph Algorithms.* Computer Science Press, Rockville, MD.

Faddeeva, V. N. [1959]. *Computational Methods of Linear Algebra.* Dover Publications, New York.

Fagin, R., M. M. Klawe, N. J. Pippenger, and L. Stockmeyer [1983]. Bounded Depth, Polynomial Circuits for Symmetric Functions. IBM Report RJ-4440, Yorktown Heights, NY.

Fam, A. T. [1988]. Efficient Complex Matrix Multiplication. *IEEE Transactions on Computers,* Vol 37, pp 877-879.

Fich, F. E. [1983]. New Bounds for Parallel Prefix Circuits. *Proceedings of the ACM Symposium on Theory of Computing,* pp 100-109.

Flynn, M. J. [1972]. Some Computer Organizations and Their Effectiveness. *IEEE Transactions on Computers,* Vol 21, pp 948-960.

Forsythe, G., and C. B. Moler [1967]. *Computer Solution of Linear Algebraic Systems,* Prentice-Hall, Englewood Cliffs, NJ.

Fortune, S., and J. Wyllie [1978]. Parallelism in Random Access Machines. *Proceedings of the ACM Symposium on Theory of Computing,* pp 114-118.

Fox, G. C., and W. Furmanski [1987]. Communication Algorithms for Regular Convolutions and Matrix Problems on the Hypercube. *Hypercube Multiprocessors,* M. T. Heath (ed). SIAM Publication, Philadelphia, PA, pp 223-238.

Fox, G. C., M. Johnson, G. Lyzenga, S. W. Otto, J. Salmon, and D. Walker [1988]. *Solving Problems on Concurrent Processors.* Vol 1. Prentice-Hall, Englewood Cliffs, NJ.

Fox, G. C., and S. W. Otto [1984]. Algorithms for Concurrent Processors. *Physics Today,* Vol 37, pp 50-59.

Fujishiro, I., Y. Ikebe, A. Harashima, and M. Watanabe [1989]. A Note on Cyclic Reduction Poisson Solvers with Application to Bioconvective Phenomena Problems. *Computers and Fluids,* Vol 17, pp. 419-435.

Furst, M., J. B. Saxe, and M. Sipser [1981]. Parity, Circuits, and Polynomial Time Hierarchy. *Proceedings of the Symposium on Foundations of Computer Science,* pp 260-270.

Gajski, D. [1980]. Recurrence Semigroups and Their Relation to Data Storage in Fast Recurrence Solvers. Technical Report UIUCDCS-R-80-1037, University of Illinois, Urbana, IL.

Gajski, D. [1981]. An Algorithm for Solving Linear Recurrence Systems on Parallel and

Pipelined Machines. *IEEE Transactions on Computers,* Vol 30, pp 190-206.

Galil, Z. [1985]. Optimal Parallel Algorithms in VLSI: Algorithms and Architectures. *Proceedings of the International Workshop on Parallel Computing and VLSI.* North-Holland, Amsterdam, pp 3-11.

Galil, Z., and W. J. Paul [1983]. An Efficient General Purpose Parallel Computer. *Journal of ACM,* Vol 30, pp 360-387.

Gallivan, K., W. Jalby, U. Meier, and A. H. Sameh [1987]. The Impact of Hierarchical Memory Systems on Linear Algebra Algorithm Design. Technical Report CSRD 625, Center for Supercomputing Research and Development, University of Illinois, Urbana, IL.

Gannon, D. B., and J. V. Rosendale [1984]. On the Impact of Communication Complexity of Parallel Numerical Algorithms. *IEEE Transactions on Computers,* Vol 33, pp 1180–1194.

Garey, M. R., and D. S. Johnson [1979]. *Computers and Intractability: A Guide to the Theory of NP-Completeness.* W. H. Freeman, San Francisco, CA.

Garner, H. L. [1959]. The Residue Number System. *IRE Transactions on Electronic Computers,* Vol 8, pp 140-147.

Geist, G. A., and M. T. Heath [1986]. Matrix Factorization on a Hypercube Multiprocessor. *Hypercube Multiprocessor,* M. T. Heath (ed). SIAM Publications, Philadelphia, PA, pp 161-180.

Geist, G. A., and C. H. Romine [1988]. LU Factorization Algorithms on Distributed-Memory Multiprocessor Architectures. *SIAM Journal on Scientific and Statistical Computing,* Vol 9, pp 639-649.

Gentleman, W. M. [1973]. Least Square Computations by Givens Transformations Without Square Roots. *Journal of the Institute of Mathematics and Applications,* Vol 12, pp 329–336.

Gentleman, W. M. [1978]. Some Complexity Results for Matrix Computation on Parallel Processors. *Journal of ACM,* Vol 25, pp 112-115.

Gentleman, W. M., and G. Sande [1966]. Fast Fourier Transforms -- For Fun and Profit. *Proceedings of the Fall Joint Computer Conference,* pp 563-578.

Gentzsch, W. [1983]. *Vectorization of Computer Programs With Applications to Computational Fluid Dynamics.* Vol 8, *Notes on Numerical Fluid Mechanics.* Friedr. Vieweg & Sohn, Braunschweig, West Germany.

George, A., and J. W. Liu [1981]. *Computer Solution of Large Sparse Positive Definite Systems.* Prentice-Hall, Englewood Cliffs, NJ.

Gohberg, I.G., and I. A. Feldman [1974]. *Convolution Equations and Projection Methods for Their Solutions.* Translation of Mathematical Monographs, Vol 41, American Mathematical Society.

Goke, L. R., and G. J. Lipovski [1973]. Banyan Networks for Partitioning Multiprocessor Systems. *Proceedings of the First Annual Computer Architecture Conference,* pp 21-28.

Goldschlager, L. M. [1977]. The Monotone and Planar Circuit Value Problems Are Log Space Complete for *P. SIGACT News,* Vol 9, No. 2, pp 25-29.

Goldschlager, L. M. [1978]. A Unified Approach to Models of Synchronous Parallel Machines. *Proceedings of the ACM Symposium on Theory of Computing,* pp 89-94.

Goldschlager, L. M. [1982]. A Universal Interconnection Pattern for Parallel Computers.

Journal of ACM, Vol 29, pp 1073-1086.

Golub, G. H. [1973]. Some Modified Matrix Eigenvalue Problems. *SIAM Review,* Vol 15, pp 318-334.

Golub, G. H., and C. F. Van Loan [1983]. *Matrix Computations.* Johns Hopkins University Press, Baltimore, MD.

Gottlieb, A., R. Grishman, C. P. Kruskal, K.P. McAuliffe, L.Rudolph, and M.Snir [1983]. The NYU Ultracomputer -- Designing an MIMD Shared Memory Parallel Computer. *IEEE Transactions on Computers,* Vol 32 pp 175-189.

Gottlieb, A., and C. P. Kruskal [1984]. Complexity Results for Permuting Data and Other Computations on Parallel Processors. *Journal of ACM,* Vol 31, pp 193-209.

Grcar, J., and A. H. Sameh [1981]. On Certain Parallel Linear System Solvers. *SIAM Journal on Scientific and Statistical Computing,* Vol 2, pp 238-256.

Grenander, U., and G. Szego [1958]. *Toeplitz Forms and Their Applications.* University of California Press, Berkeley, CA.

Gupta, A. [1987]. *Parallelism in Production Systems,* Pitman, London.

Gustafson, J. L. [1988]. Reevaluating Amdahl's Law. *Communications of ACM,* Vol 31, pp 532-533.

Gustafson, J. L. [1989]. Author's Response. *Communications of ACM,* Vol 32, pp 263-264.

Gustafson, J. L., R. Montry, and R. E. Benner [1988]. Development of Parallel Methods for a 1024-Processor Hypercube. *SIAM Journal on Scientific and Statistical Computing,* Vol 9, pp 609-638.

Gustavson, F. G., and D. Y. Y. Yun [1979]. Fast Algorithms for Rational Hermite Approximation and Solution of Toeplitz System. *IEEE Transactions on Circuits and Systems,* Vol 26, pp 750-755.

Hall, P. [1935]. On Representatives of Subsets. *Journal of London Mathematical Society,* Vol 10, pp 26-30.

Halmos, P. R., and H. E. Vaughan [1950]. The Marriage Problem. *American Journal of Mathematics,* Vol 72, pp 214-215.

Hammarling, S. [1974]. A Note on Modifications to the Givens Plane Rotation. *Journal of the Institute of Mathematics and Applications,* Vol 13, pp 215-218.

Han, T., D. A. Carlson, and S. P. Levitan [1987]. VLSI Design of High Speed, Low-Area Addition Circuitry. Technical Report, Department of Electrical and Computer Engineering, University of Massachusetts, Amherst, MA.

Hardy, G. H., and E. M. Wright [1960]. *Introduction to the Theory of Numbers.* Clarendon Press, Oxford, England.

Harel, D. [1987]. *Algorithmics: The Spirit of Computing.* Addison-Wesley, Reading, MA.

Haynes, L. S., R. L. Lau, D. P. Siewiorek, and D.W.Mizzell [1982]. A Survey of Highly Parallel Computing. *IEEE Computer,* January 1982, pp 9-24.

Heath, M. T. (ed) [1986]. *Hypercube Multiprocessors.* SIAM Publications, Philadelphia, PA.

Heath, M. T. (ed) [1987]. *Hypercube Multiprocessors.* SIAM Publications, Philadelphia, PA.

Heath, M. T., and C. H. Romine [1988]. Parallel Solution of Triangular Systems on Distributed-Memory Multiprocessors. *SIAM Journal on Scientific and Statistical Computing,* Vol 9, pp 558-588.

Heath, M. T., and P. Worley [1989]. Once Again, Amhahl's Law. *Communications of ACM,* Vol 32, pp 262-263.

Heideman, M. T. [1988]. *Multiplicative Complexity, Convolution, and the DFT.* Springer-Verlag, New York.

Heller, D. [1974]. A Determinant Theorem with Applications to Parallel Algorithms. *SIAM Journal on Numerical Computing,* Vol 11, pp 559-568.

Heller, D. [1976]. Some Aspects of the Cyclic Reduction Algorithm for Block Tridiagonal Linear Systems. *SIAM Journal on Numerical Analysis,* Vol 13, pp 484-496.

Heller, D. [1978]. A Survey of Parallel Algorithms in Numerical Algebra. *SIAM Review,* Vol 20, pp 740-777.

Hillis, W.D. [1985]. *The Connection Machines.* MIT Press, Cambridge, MA.

Hirschberg, D. S. [1982]. Parallel Graph Algorithms Without Memory Conflicts. *Proceedings of the 20th Allerton Conference,* pp 257-263.

Ho, C. T., and S. L. Johnsson [1987]. On Embedding of Arbitrary Meshes in Boolean Cubes with Expansion Two and Dilation Two. *Proceedings of the International Conference on Parallel Processing,* pp 188-191.

Hockney, R. W. [1965]. A Fast Direct Solution of Poisson's Equation Using Fourier Analysis. *Journal of ACM,* Vol 12, pp 95-113.

Hockney, R. W., and C. R. Jesshope [1981]. *Parallel Computers.* Adam and Hilger Ltd, Bristol.

Hofri, M. [1987]. *Probabilistic Analysis of Algorithms.* Springer-Verlag, New York.

Hoover, H. J., M. M. Klawe, and N. J. Pippenger [1984]. Bounding Fan-out in Logical Networks. *Journal of ACM,* Vol 31, pp 13-18.

Hopcroft, J. E., and L. R. Kerr [1971]. On Minimizing the Number of Multiplications Necessary for Matrix Multiplication. *SIAM Journal on Computing,* Vol 20, pp 30-36.

Horowitz, E., and S. Sahni [1978]. *Fundamentals of Computer Algorithms.* Computer Science Press, Rockville, MD.

Householder, A. S. [1964]. *The Theory of Matrices in Numerical Analysis.* Ginn (Blaisdell), Boston, MA.

Hu, T. C. [1982]. *Combinatorial Algorithms.* Addison-Wesley, Reading, MA.

Hwang, K. [1979]. *Computer Arithmetic: Principles, Architecture, and Design.* Wiley, New York.

Hwang, K. [1984]. *Supercomputers: Design and Applications -- Tutorial.* IEEE Computer Society Press, Silver Spring, MD.

Hwang, K. [1987]. Advanced Parallel Processing with Supercomputer Architectures. *Proceedings of the IEEE,* Vol 75, pp 1348-1379.

Hwang, K., and F. A. Briggs [1984]. *Computer Architecture and Parallel Processing.* McGraw-Hill, New York.

Hwang, K., and D. DeGroot (Ed) [1989]. *Parallel Processing for Supercomputers and Artificial Intelligence.* McGraw-Hill, New York.

Hyafil, L., and H. T. Kung [1977]. The Complexity of Parallel Evaluation of Linear Recurrences. *Journal of ACM,* Vol 24, pp 513-521.

Ja' Ja', J., and V. K. Prasanna Kumar [1984]. Information Transfer in Distributed Computing with Applications to VLSI. *Journal of ACM,* Vol 31, pp 150-162.

Jagadish, H. V., and T. Kailath [1989]. A Family of New Efficient Arrays for Matrix Multiplication. *IEEE Transactions on Computers,* Vol 38, pp 149-155.

Johnson, D. B., and S. M. Venkatesan [1982]. Parallel Algorithms for Minimum Cuts and

Maximum Flows in Planar Networks. *Proceedings of the IEEE Symposium on Foundations of Computer Science,* pp 244-254.

Johnsson, S. L. [1984]. Odd-Even Cyclic Reduction on Ensemble Architecture and the Solution of Tridiagonal Systems of Equations. Technical Report DCS-RR339, Department of Computer Science, Yale University, New Haven, CT.

Johnsson, S. L. [1985]. Communication Efficient Basic Linear Algebra Computations on Hypercube Architectures. Technical Report DCS-RR361, Department of Computer Science, Yale University, New Haven, CT.

Johnsson, S. L., and C. T. Ho [1986]. Spanning Graphs for Optimum Broadcasting and Personalized Communication in Hypercubes. Technical Report DCR-RR500, Department of Computer Science, Yale University, New Haven, CT.

Jones, N. D., and W. T. Lasser [1977]. Complete Problems for Deterministic Polynomial Time. *Theoretical Computer Science,* Vol 3, pp 105-117.

Jordan, H. F. [1984]. Experiences with Pipelined Multiple Instruction Streams. *Proceedings of IEEE,* Vol 72, pp 113-123.

Kailath, T., A. Viera, and M. Morf [1978]. Inverses of Toeplitz Operators, Innovations and Orthogonal Polynomials. *SIAM Review,* Vol 20, pp 106-119.

Kallman, R. [1983]. A Faster Carry 8-bit Circuit. *IEEE Transactions on Computers,* Vol 32, pp 1209-1211.

Karatsuba, A., and Yu. Ofman [1963]. Multiplication of Multidigit Numbers on Automata. *Soviet Physics Doklady,* Vol 7, pp 595-596.

Karp, R. M., R. E. Miller, and S. Winograd [1967]. The Organization of Computations for Uniform Recurrence Relations. *Journal of ACM,* Vol 14, pp 563-590.

Karp, R. M., and V. L. Ramachandran [1988]. A Survey of Parallel Algorithms for Shared-Memory Machines. Report No. UCB/CSD 88/408, March, University of California, Berkeley, CA.

Katseff, H. P. [1988]. Incomplete Cubes. *IEEE Transactions on Computers,* Vol 37, pp 604–608.

Kennedy, K. [1980]. Automatic Translation of Fortran Programs to Vector Form. Technical Report 476-029-4, Rice University, Houston, TX.

Kim, K., and V. K. Prasanna Kumar [1987]. A Simple Proof of Rearrangeability of Five Stage Shuffle/Exchange Network for $N = 8$. Technical Report CRI-87-42, University of Southern California, Los Angeles, CA.

Knuth, D. E. [1968]. *The Art of Computer Programming: Fundamental Algorithms,* Vol 1. Addison-Wesley, Reading, MA.

Knuth, D. E. [1969]. *The Art of Computer Programming: Semi Numerical Algorithms,* Vol 2. Addison-Wesley, Reading, MA.

Knuth, D. E. [1973]. *The Art of Computer Programming: Sorting and Searching,* Vol 3. Addison-Wesley, Reading, MA.

Knuth, D. E. [1976]. Big Omicron, Big Omega and Big Theta. *SIGACT News,* April-June, pp 18-24.

Kogge, P. M. [1973]. Maximal Rate Pipelined Solutions to Recurrence Problems. *Proceedings of the Symposium on Computer Architecture,* pp 71-76.

Kogge, P. M. [1974]. Parallel Solution of Recurrence Problems. *IBM Journal of Research and Development,* pp 138-148.

Kogge, P. M. [1981]. *The Architecture of Pipelined Computers.* McGraw-Hill, New York.

Kogge, P. M., and H. S. Stone [1973]. A Parallel Algorithm for the Efficient Solution of a General Class of Recurrence Equations. *IEEE Transactions on Computers,* Vol 22, pp 786-792.

Kosaraju, S. R. [1986]. Parallel Evaluation of Division-Free Arithmetic Expressions. *Proceedings of the Symposium on Theory of Computing,* pp 231-239.

Kosaraju, S. R., and M. J. Atallah [1988]. Optimal Simulations Between Mesh-Connected Arrays. *Journal of the ACM,* Vol 35, pp 635-650.

Kothari, S. C., S. Lakshmivarahan, and H. Peyravi [1985]. On the Problem of Computing the Number of Permutations Realized by a Class of SW-Banyan Networks. Technical Report, School of EECS, University of Oklahoma, Norman, OK.

Kowalik, J. S. (ed) [1985]. *Parallel MIMD Computation: The HEP Supercomputer and Its Applications.* MIT Press, Cambridge, MA.

Kowalik, J. S., and S. P. Kumar [1985]. Parallel Algorithms for Recurrence and Tridiagonal Equations. In *Parallel Computation: HEP Supercomputer and Its Applications,* J.S. Kowalik (ed). M.I.T. Press, Cambridge, MA. pp. 295-308.

Kozen, D. [1976]. On Parallelism in Turing Machines. *Proceedings of the IEEE Symposium on Foundations of Computer Science,* pp 89-97.

Krapchenko, V. M. [1970]. Asymptotic Estimation of Addition Time of a Parallel Adder. *Systems Theory Research,* Vol 19, pp 105-122.

Krishnakumar, A. S. [1984]. Divide and Conquer Algorithms and Architectures for the Symmetric Tridiagonal Eigenproblem. Ph. D. Dissertation, Department of Electrical Engineering, Stanford University, Stanford, CA.

Krishnakumar, A. S., and M. Morf [1986]. Eigenvalues of a Symmetric Tridiagonal Matrix: A Divide and Conquer Approach. *Numerische Mathematik,* Vol 48, pp 349-368.

Krizanc, D., D. Peleg, and E. Upfal [1988]. A Time Randomness Tradeoff for Oblivious Routing. *Proceedings of the Symposium on the Theory of Computing,* pp 93-102.

Kronsjo, L. [1987]. *Algorithms: Their Complexity and Efficiency.* Wiley, New York.

Krumme, D. W., K. N. Venkataraman, and G. Cybenko [1986]. Hypercube Embedding is NP-Complete. *Hypercube Multiprocessor,* M. T. Heath (ed). SIAM Publications, Philadelphia, PA, pp 148-157.

Kruskal, C. P., L. Rudolph, and M. Snir [1985]. The Power of Parallel Prefix. *IEEE Transactions on Computers,* Vol 34, pp 965-968.

Kruskal, C. P., and M. Snir [1982]. Some Results on Packet Switching for Multiprocessors. *Princeton Conference on Information Sciences and Systems,* pp 305-310.

Kuck, D. J. [1976]. Parallel Processing of Ordinary Programs. *Advances in Computers,* Vol 15, M. Yovits (ed). Academic Press, New York, pp 119-179.

Kuck, D. J. [1978]. *The Structure of Computers and Computations,* Vol 1. Wiley, New York.

Kuck, D. J., D. Lawrie, R. Cytron, A. H. Sameh, and D. Gajski [1983]. The Architecture and Programming of the CEDAR System. Technical Report, Department of Computer Science, University of Illinois, Urbana, IL.

Kuck, D. J., and K. M. Maruyama [1975]. Time Bounds on Parallel Evaluation of Arithmetic Expressions. *SIAM Journal on Computing,* Vol 4, pp 147-162.

Kuck, D. J., and Y. Muraoka [1974]. Bounds on the Parallel Evaluation of Arithmetic Expressions Using Associativity and Commutativity. *Acta Informatica,* Vol 3, pp 203–216.

Kuck, D. J., and R. A. Stokes [1982]. The Burroughs Scientific Processor (BSP). *IEEE Transactions on Computers,* Vol 31, pp 363-376.

Kuhn, R. H., and D. A. Padua [1981]. *Parallel Processing: Tutorial.* IEEE Computer Society Press, Silver Spring, MD.

Kumar, M., D.M. Dias, and J.R. Jump [1985]. Switching Strategies in Shuffle-Exchange Networks. *IEEE Transactions on Computers,* Vol 34, pp 180-186.

Kung, H. T. [1980]. The Structure of Parallel Algorithms. *Advances in Computers,* Vol 19, M. Yovits (ed). Academic Press, New York, pp 65-112.

Kung, H.T., and C.E. Leiserson [1980]. Systalic Arrays. *Introduction to VLSI Systems,* C. A. Mead and L. A. Conway (eds). Addison-Wesley, Reading, MA.

Kung, H. T., B. Sproull, and G. Steele (eds) [1981]. *VLSI Systems and Computations.* Computer Science Press, Rockville, Maryland.

Ladner, R. E., and M. J. Fischer [1980]. Parallel Prefix Computation. *Journal of ACM,* Vol 27, pp 831-838.

Lakshmivarahan, S. (ed) [1985]. *Proceedings of the Workshop on Parallel Processing Using the Heterogeneous Element Processor.* Parallel Processing Institute, School of Electrical Engineering and Computer Science, University of Oklahoma, Norman, OK.

Lakshmivarahan, S., and S. K. Dhall [1985a]. New Class of Parallel Algorithms for Solving First-Order and Certain Classes of Second-Order Linear Recurrences. *Proceedings of the International Conference on Parallel Processing,* August 20-23, pp 843-845.

Lakshmivarahan, S., and S. K. Dhall [1985b]. Parallel Algorithms for Solving Certain Classes of Linear Recurrences. *Lecture Notes in Computer Science,* Vol 26, S. N. Maheshwari (ed). Springer-Verlag, New York, pp 457-476.

Lakshmivarahan, S., and S. K. Dhall [1986a]. A New Class of Parallel Algorithms for Solving Linear Tridiagonal Systems. *Proceedings of the Fall Joint Computer Conference,* pp 315-324.

Lakshmivarahan, S., and S. K. Dhall [1986b]. A Lower Bound on the Communication Complexity in Solving Linear-Tridiagonal Systems on a Cube Architecture. *Proceedings of the Second SIAM Conference on Hypercube Multiprocessors,* pp 560-568.

Lakshmivarahan, S., and S. K. Dhall [1988]. A New Hierarchy of Hypercube Interconnection Schemes for Parallel Computers. *Journal of Supercomputing,* Vol 2, pp 81-108.

Lakshmivarahan, S., and S. K. Dhall [1989]. *Parallel Prefix Computation.* Monograph in preparation.

Lakshmivarahan, S., C. M. Yang, and S. K. Dhall [1987]. Optimal Parallel Prefix Circuits with (size + depth) $= 2n - 2$ and $\lceil \log n \rceil \leq depth \leq \lceil 2\log n \rceil - 3$. *Proceedings of the International Conference on Parallel Processing,* pp 58-65.

Lakshmivarahan, S., S. K. Dhall, and L. L. Miller [1984]. Parallel Sorting Algorithms. *Advances in Computers,* Vol 23, M. Yovits (ed). Academic Press, New York, pp 295–354.

Lambiotte, J. J., and R. Voigt [1975]. The Solution of Tridiagonal Linear Systems on CDC STAR-100 Computer. *ACM Transactions on Mathematical Software,* Vol 1, pp 308-329.

Lawrie, D. H. [1975]. Access and Alignment of Data in an Array Processor. *IEEE Transactions on Computers,* Vol 24, pp 1145-1155.

Lawrie, D. H., and A. H. Sameh [1984]. The Computational Complexity and Communication Complexity of a Parallel Banded System Solver. *ACM Transactions on Mathematical*

Software, Vol 10, pp 185-195.

Le Veque, W. J. [1961]. *Elementary Theory of Numbers.* Addison-Wesley, Reading, MA.

Lee, K. Y. [1985]. On the Rearrangeability of $2(\log N) - 1$-Stage Permutation Networks. *IEEE Transactions on Computers,* Vol 34, pp 412-425.

Lenfant, J. [1978]. Parallel Permutation of Data: A Benes Network Control Algorithm for Frequently Used Permutations. *IEEE Transactions on Computers,* Vol 27, pp 637-647.

Lev, G., N. J. Pippenger, and L. G. Valiant [1981]. A Fast Parallel Algorithm for Routing in Permutation Networks. *IEEE Transactions on Computers,* Vol 30, pp 93-100.

Li, G., and T. F. Coleman [1988]. A Parallel Triangular Solver for a Distributed-Memory Multiprocessor. *SIAM Journal on Scientific and Statistical Computing,* Vol 9, pp 485–502.

Lint, B., and T. Agerwala [1981]. Communication Issues in the Design and Analysis of Parallel Algorithms. *IEEE Transactions on Software Engineering,* Vol 7, pp 174-188.

Lipovski, G. J., and M. Malek [1987]. *Parallel Computing: Theory and Comparisons.* Wiley, New York.

Lipson, J. D. [1981]. *Elements of Algebra and Algebraic Computing.* Addison-Wesley, Reading, MA.

Lo, S. S., B. Philippe, and A. H. Sameh [1987]. A Multiprocessor Algorithm for the Symmetric Tridiagonal Eigenvalue Problem. *SIAM Journal on Scientific and Statistical Computing,* Vol 8, pp s155-s165.

Lord, R. E., J. S. Kowalik, and S. P. Kumar [1983]. Solving Linear Algebraic Equations on an MIMD Computer. *Journal of ACM,* Vol 30, pp 103-117.

Lorin, H. [1972]. *Parallelism in Hardware and Software.* Prentice-Hall, Englewood Cliffs, NJ.

Lorin, H. [1975]. *Sorting and Sort Systems.* Addison-Wesley, Reading, MA.

Lubeck, O., J. Moore, and R. Mendez [1986]. A Benchmark Comparison of Three Supercomputers: Fujitsu VP-200, Hitachi S810/20, and Cray X-MP/2. *IEEE Computer,* December, pp 10-24.

McBryan, O. A., and E. Van De Velde [1986]. Hypercube Programs for Computational Fluid Dynamics. *Hypercube Multiprocessors,* M .T. Heath (ed). SIAM Publications, Philadelphia, PA, pp 221-243.

McKenzie, P. [1984]. Parallel Complexity and Permutation Groups. Ph.D. Thesis, Department of Computer Science, University of Toronto, Toronto, Canada.

McKeown, J. J. [1980]. Aspects of Parallel Computation in Numerical Optimization. *Numerical Techniques for Stochastic Systems,* F. Archetti and M. Cugiani (eds). North-Holland, Amsterdam, pp 297-327.

Madsen, N. K., G. H. Rodrigue, and J. I. Karush [1976]. Matrix Multiplication by Diagonals on a Vector/Parallel Processor. *Information Processing Letters,* Vol 5, pp 41-45.

Maples, C. [1985]. Pyramids, Cross-bars and Thousands of Processors. *Proceedings of the International Conference on Parallel Processing,* pp 681-688.

Maruyama, K. [1973]. On The Parallel Evaluation of Polynomials. *IEEE Transactions on Computers,* Vol 22, pp 2-5.

Matelan, N. [1985]. The FLEX/32 Multiprocessor. *Proceedings of the Symposium on Computer Architecture,* pp 209-213.

Mead, C. and L. Conway [1980]. *Introduction to VLSI Systems*. Addison-Wesley, Reading, MA.

Mehlhorn, K. [1984a]. *Data Structures and Algorithms*, Vol 1. *Sorting and Searching*. Springer-Verlag, New York.

Mehlhorn, K. [1984b]. *Data Structures and Algorithms*, Vol 2. *Graph Algorithms and NP-Completeness*. Springer-Verlag, New York.

Mehlhorn, K. [1984c]. *Data Structures and Algorithms*, Vol 3. *Multidimensional Searching and Computational Geometry*. Springer-Verlag, New York.

Mehlhorn, K., and F. P. Preparata [1983]. Area-Time Optimal VLSI Integer Multiplier with Minimum Computation Time. *Information and Control*, Vol 58, pp 137-156.

Miller, W. [1975]. Computational Complexity and Numerical Stability. *SIAM Journal on Computing*, Vol 4, pp 97-107.

Miller, W., and C. Wrathall [1980]. *Software for Roundoff Analysis of Matrix Algorithms*. Academic Press, New York.

Miranker, W. [1971]. A Survey Parallelism in Numerical Analysis. *SIAM Review*, Vol 13, pp 524-547.

Mirsky, L., and H. Perfect [1966]. Systems of Representatives. *Journal of Mathematical Analysis and Applications*, Vol 15, pp 520-568.

Modi, J. J., and M. R. B. Clarke [1984]. An Alternative Givens Ordering. *Numerische Mathematik*, Vol 43, pp 83-90.

Moharir, P. S. [1985]. Extending the Scope of Golub's Method Beyond Complex Multiplication. *IEEE Transactions on Computers*, Vol 34, pp 484-487.

Moitra, A., and S. Sitharama Iyengar [1987]. Parallel Algorithms for Some Computational Problems. *Advances in Computers*, Vol 26, M. Yovits (ed). Academic Press, New York, pp 94-154.

Moler, C. B. [1986]. Matrix Computations on Distributed Memory Multiprocessors. *Hypercube Multiprocessors*, M. T. Heath (ed). SIAM Publications, Philadelpha, PA, pp 181-195.

Morgenstern, J. [1973]. Note on a Lower Bound of the Linear Complexity of the Fast Fourier Transform. *Journal of ACM*, Vol 20, pp 305-306.

Motzkin, T. S. [1955]. Evaluation of Polynomials and Evaluation of Rational Functions. *Bulletin of American Mathematical Society*, Vol 61, pp 163.

Muller, D. E., and F. P. Preparata [1976]. Restructuring of Arithmetic Expressions for Parallel Evaluation. *Journal of ACM*, Vol 23, pp 534-543.

Munro, I., and M. Patterson [1973]. Optimal Algorithms for Parallel Polynomial Evaluation. *Journal of Computers and System Sciences*, Vol 7, pp 189-198.

Muraoka, Y. [1971]. Parallelism Exposure and Exploitation in Programs. Ph.D. Dissertation, Department of Computer Science, University of Illinois, Urbana, IL.

Nassimi, D., and S. Sahni [1981a]. A Self Routing Benes Network and Parallel Permutation Algorithms. *IEEE Transactions on Computers*, Vol 30, pp 332-339.

Nassimi, D., and S. Sahni [1981b]. Data Broadcasting in SIMD Computers. *IEEE Transactions on Computers*, Vol 30, pp 101-107.

Nassimi, D., and S. Sahni [1982]. Parallel Algorithms to Set Up the Benes Permutation Network. *IEEE Transactions on Computers*, Vol 31, pp 148-154.

Ofman, Yu. [1963]. On the Algorithmic Complexity of Discrete Functions. *Soviet Physics*

Doklady, Vol 7, pp 589-591.

Opferman, D. C., and N. T. Tsao-Wu [1971]. On a Class of Rearrangeable Switching Networks. Part 1: Control Algorithms. *The Bell System Technical Journal,* Vol 50, pp 1579-1600.

Ortega, J. M. [1988]. *Introduction to Parallel and Vector Solution of Linear Systems.* Plenum Press, New York.

Ortega, J. M., and R. G. Voigt [1985]. Solution of Partial Differential Equations on Vector and Parallel Computers. *SIAM Review,* Vol 27, pp 149-240.

Oruc, A. Y., and M. Y. Oruc [1986]. Equivalence Relations Among Interconnection Networks. *Journal of Parallel and Distributed Computing,* Vol 2, pp 30-49.

Ostrowski, A. M. [1954]. On Two Problems in Abstract Algebra Connected with Horner's Rule. *Studies Presented to R. von Mises.* Academic Press, New York, pp 40-48.

Ouchark, W. J., J. A. Davis, S. Lakshmivarahan, and S. K. Dhall [1987]. An Experimental Comparison of Four Different Communication Schemes on INTEL Hypercube. Technical Report OU-PPI-TR-87-05, School of Electrical Engineering and Computer Science, University of Oklahoma, Norman, OK.

Pan, V. Y. [1966]. Methods of Computing Values of Polynomials. *Russian Mathematical Surveys,* Vol 21, No. 1, pp 105-136.

Pan, V. Y. [1984]. *How to Multiply Matrices Faster.* Lecture Notes in Computer Science, Vol 179. Springer-Verlag, New York.

Papadimitriou, C. H., and K. Steiglitz [1982]. *Combinatorial Optimization.* Prentice-Hall, Englewood Cliffs, NJ.

Parberry, I. [1987]. *Parallel Complexity Theory.* Pitman, London.

Parker, D. S. [1980]. Notes on Shuffle/Exchange-Type Switching Networks. *IEEE Transactions on Computers,* Vol 29, pp 213-222.

Patel, J. [1981]. Performance of Processor Memory Interconnections for Multiprocessors, *IEEE Transactions on Computers,* Vol 30, pp 771-780.

Pease, M. C. [1967]. Matrix Inversion Using Parallel Processing. *Journal of ACM,* Vol 14, pp 757-764.

Pease, M. C. [1969]. Inversion of Matrices by Partitioning. *Journal of ACM,* Vol 16, pp 302–314.

Pease, M. C. [1977]. The Indirect Binary n-Cube Microprocessor Array. *IEEE Transactions on Computers,* Vol 26, pp 458-473.

Peters, G., and J. H. Wilkinson [1970]. $Ax = \lambda Bx$ and the Generalized Eigenproblem. *SIAM Journal on Numerical Analysis,* Vol 7, pp 479-492.

Pfister, G. F., and V. A. Norton [1985]. "Hot Spot" Contention and Combining in Multistage Interconnection Networks. *Proceedings of the International Conference on Parallel Processing,* pp 790-795.

Pfister, G. F., W. C. Brantley, D. A. George, S. L. Harvey, W. J. Kleinffelder, K. P. McAuliffe, E. A. Melton, V. A. Norton, and J. Weiss [1985]. The IBM Research Parallel Processor Prototype (RP3): Introduction and Architecture. *Proceedings of the International Conference on Parallel Processing,* pp 764-771.

Pippenger, N. J. [1979]. On Simultaneous Resource Bounds. *Proceedings of the IEEE Symposium on Foundations of Computer Science,* pp 307-311.

Pippenger, N. J., and M. J. Fischer [1979]. Relations Among Complexity Measures. *Journal of ACM,* Vol 26, pp 361-381.

Pradhan, D. J., and K. L. Kodandapani [1980]. A Uniform Representation of Single and Multistage Interconnection Networks Used in SIMD Machines. *IEEE Transactions on Computers,* Vol 29, pp 777-790.

Prasanna Kumar, V. K., and C. S. Raghavendra [1987]. Array Processor with Multiple Broadcasting. *Journal of Parallel and Distributed Computing,* Vol 1, pp 173-190.

Prasanna Kumar, V. K., and Yu-Chen Tsai [1989]. On Mapping Algorithms to Linear and Fault Tolerant Systolic Arrays. *IEEE Transactions on Computers,* Vol 38, pp 470-478.

Pratt, V. R., and L. Stockmeyer [1976]. A characterization of the Power of Vector Machines. *Journal of Computers and Systems Science,* Vol 12, pp 198-221.

Preparata, F . P., and D. E. Muller [1975]. The Time Required to Evaluate Division-Free Arithmetic Expressions. *Information Processing Letters,* Vol 3, pp 144-146.

Preparata, F. P., and D. E. Muller [1976]. Efficient Parallel Evaluation of Boolean Expressions. *IEEE Transactions on Computers,* Vol 27, pp 548-549.

Purdom. P. W., Jr., and C. A. Brown [1985]. *The Analysis of Algorithms.* Holt, Rinehart, and Winston, New York.

Purdy, C. N., and G. B. Purdy [1987]. Integer Division in Linear Time with Bounded Fan-In. *IEEE Transactions on Computers,* Vol 36, pp 640-644.

Quinn, M. J. [1987]. *Designing Efficient Algorithms for Parallel Computers.* McGraw-Hill, New York.

Quinn, M. J., and N. Deo [1984]. Parallel Graph Algorithms. *Computing Surveys,* Vol 16, pp 319-348.

Raghavendra, C. S., and A. Varma [1986]. Rearrangeability of the 5-Stage Shuffle/Exchange Network for $N = 8$. Technical Report CRI-86-05, University of Southern California, Los Angeles, CA.

Raghavendra, C. S., and A. Varma [1987]. Rearrangeability of Multistage Shuffle/Exchange Networks. *Proceedings of the 14th Symposium on Computer Architecture,* pp 154-162.

Ramakrishnan, I. V., and P. J. Varman [1984]. Modular Matrix Multiplication on a Linear Array. *IEEE Transactions on Computers,* Vol 33, pp 952-958.

Ramamoorthy, C. V., and H. F. Li [1977]. Pipeline Architecture. *Computing Surveys,* Vol 9, pp 61-102.

Randell, B., and P.C. Treleaven (ed) [1983]. *VLSI Architecture.* Prentice-Hall, Engelwood Cliffs, NJ.

Reed, D. A., and R. M. Fujimoto [1988]. *Multicomputer Network: Message Based Parallel Processing.* MIT Press, Cambridge, MA.

Reghbati, E., and D. G. Corneil [1978]. Parallel Computations in Graph Theory. *SIAM Journal on Computing,* Vol 7, pp 230-237.

Reif, J. [1986]. Logarithmic Depth Circuits for Algebraic Functions. *SIAM Journal on Computing,* Vol 15, pp 231-242.

Reingold, E. M. [1972]. Establishing Lower Bounds on Algorithms: A Survey. *AFIPS Spring Joint Computer Conference,* Vol 40, pp 471-481.

Reingold, E. M., J. Nievergelt, and N. Deo [1977]. *Combinatorial Algorithms: Theory and Practice.* Prentice-Hall, Englewood Cliffs, NJ.

Rettberg, R., and R. Thomas [1986]. Contention is No Obstacle to Shared Memory Multiprocessor. *Communications of ACM,* Vol 29, pp 1202-1212.

Riganati, J. P., and P. B. Schneck [1984]. Supercomputing. *IEEE Computer*, October, pp 97-113.

Roberts, F. S. [1984]. *Applied Combinatorics*. Prentice-Hall, Englewood Cliffs, NJ.

Roebuck, P. A., and S. Barnett [1978]. A Survey of Toeplitz Matrices. *International Journal of Systems Science*, Vol 9, pp 921-934.

Romine, C., and J. Ortega [1988]. Parallel Solution of Triangular Systems of Equations. *Parallel Computing*, Vol 6, pp 109-114.

Ruzzo, W. L. [1981]. On Uniform Circuit Complexity. *Journal of Computers and System Science*, Vol 22, pp 365-383.

Ryser, H. J. [1963]. *Combinatorial Mathematics*. The Carus Mathematical Monograph, The Mathematical Association of America.

Saad, Y., and M. H. Schultz [1985a]. Topological Properties of Hypercubes. Technical Report DCS-RR-389, Department of Computer Science, Yale University, New Haven, CT.

Saad, Y., and M. H. Schultz [1985b]. Data Communications in Hypercubes. Technical Report DCS-RR-428, Department of Computer Science, Yale University, New Haven, CT.

Salamin, E. [1976]. Computation of Pi Using Arithmetic-Geometric Mean. *Mathematics of Computation*, Vol 30, pp 565-570.

Salas, S. A., and E. Hille [1982]. *Calculus*. 4th Ed. Wiley, New York.

Sameh, A. H. [1977]. Numerical Parallel Algorithms-A survey. *High Speed Computer and Algorithm Organization*, Academic Press, New York, pp 207-228.

Sameh, A. H., and R. P. Brent [1977]. Solving Triangular Systems on a Parallel Computer. *SIAM Journal on Numerical Analysis*, Vol 14, pp 1101-1113.

Sameh, A. H., and D. J. Kuck [1977]. A Parallel QR-Algorithm for Symmetric Tridiagonal Matrices. *IEEE Transactions on Computers*, Vol 26, pp 147-153.

Sameh, A. H., and D. J. Kuck [1978]. On Stable Parallel Linear System Solvers. *Journal of ACM*, Vol 25, pp 81-91.

Samuelson, P. [1942]. A Method for Determining Explicitly the Coefficients of the Characteristic Equation. *Annals of Mathematical Statistics*, Vol 13, pp 424-429.

Satyanarayanan, M. [1980]. *Multiprocessors: A Comparative Study*. Prentice-Hall, Englewood Cliffs, NJ.

Savage, J. E. [1987]. *The Complexity of Computing*. Krieger, Malabar, FL.

Schendel, U. [1984]. *Introduction to Numerical Methods for Parallel Computers*. Ellis Horwood Limited, Chichester.

Schonhage, A., and V. Strassen [1971]. Schnelle Multiplikation Grosser Zahlen. *Computing*, Vol 7, pp 281-292.

Schwartz, J. T. [1980]. Ultracomputers. *ACM Transactions on Programming Languages and Systems*, Vol 2, pp 484-521.

Sedgewick, R. [1983]. *Algorithms*. Addison-Wesley, Reading, MA.

Seitz, C. L. [1985]. The Cosmic Cube. *Communications of ACM*, Vol 28, pp 22-33.

Sequent Computer Systems [1985]. *Balance 8000 Guide to Parallel Programming*. Reference Manual.

Shiloach, Y., and U. Vishkin [1981]. Finding the Maximum, Merging, and Sorting in a Parallel Computation Model. *Journal of Algorithms*, Vol 2, pp 88-102.

Shiloach, Y., and U. Vishkin [1982]. An $O(n^2 \log n)$ Parallel Max-Flow Algorithm. *Journal of Algorithms*, Vol 3, pp 128-146.

Siegel, H. J. [1985]. *Interconnection Networks for Large-Scale Parallel Processing.* Lexington Books, D. C. Heath and Company, Lexington, MA.

Sklansky, J. E. [1960a]. An Evaluation of Several Two-Sum and Binary Adders. *IRE Transactions on Electronic Computers,* Vol 9, pp 213-226.

Sklansky, J. E. [1960b]. Conditional-Sum Addition Logic. *IRE Transactions on Electronic Computers,* Vol 9, pp 226-231.

Snir, M. [1985]. On Parallel Searching. *SIAM Journal on Computing,* Vol 14, pp 688-708.

Snir, M. [1986]. Depth-Size Tradeoffs for Parallel Prefix Computation. *Journal of Algorithms,* Vol 7, pp 185-201.

Snyder, L. [1982]. Introduction to the Configurable, Highly Parallel Computer. *IEEE Computer,* January, pp 47-56.

Snyder, L. [1984]. Supercomputers and VLSI. In *Advances in Computers,* Vol 23, M. Yovits (ed). Academic Press, New York, pp 1-33.

Spira, P. M. [1969]. The Time Required for Group Multiplication. *Journal of ACM,* Vol 16, pp 235-245.

Stewart, G. W. [1973]. *Introduction to Matrix Computations.* Academic Press, New York.

Stockmeyer, L., and U. Vishkin [1984]. Simulation of Parallel Random Access Machines by Circuits. *SIAM Journal on Computing,* Vol 13, pp 409-422.

Stone, H. S. [1971]. Parallel Processing With Perfect Shuffle. *IEEE Transactions on Computers,* Vol 20, pp 153-161.

Stone, H. S. [1973a]. *Discrete Mathematical Structures and Their Applications.* Science Research Associate, Inc., Chicago.

Stone, H. S. [1973b]. An Efficient Parallel Algorithm for the Solution of Tridiagonal System of Equations. *Journal of ACM,* Vol 20, pp 27-38.

Stone, H. S. [1975]. Parallel Tri-diagonal Equation Solvers. *ACM Transactions on Mathematical Software,* Vol 1, pp 289-307.

Stout, Q. F., and B. Wager [1987]. Intense Hypercube Communication 1. Computing Research Lab-TR-9-87, University of Michigan, Ann Arbor, MI.

Strassen, V. [1969]. Gaussian Elimination Is Not Optimal. *Numerische Mathematik,* Vol 13, pp 354-356.

Strassen, V. [1973]. Vermeidung von Divisionen. *Journal of Reine Angewante Mathematics,* Vol 264, pp 182-202.

Strassen, V. [1986]. The Asymptotic Spectrum of Tensors and the Exponent of Matrix Multiplication. *Proceedings of the Conference on the Foundations of Computer Science,* pp 49-54.

Swamy, M. N. S., and K. Thulasiraman [1983]. *Graphs, Networks and Algorithms.* Wiley, New York.

Swan, R. J., S. H. Fuller, and D. P. Siewiorek [1977]. Cm* -- A Modular Multi-Microprocessor. *Proceedings of the AFIPS Conference,* Vol 46, pp 637-643.

Swarztrauber, P. N. [1974]. A Direct Method for the Discrete Solution of Separable Elliptic Equations. *SIAM Journal on Numerical Analysis,* Vol 11, pp 1136-1150.

Swarztrauber, P. N. [1977]. The Methods of Cyclic Reduction, Fourier Analysis and the FACR Algorithm for the Discrete Solution of Poisson's Equation on a Rectangle. *SIAM Review,* Vol 19, pp 490-501.

Swarztrauber, P. N. [1979]. A Parallel Algorithm for Solving General Tridiagonal Equations.

Mathematics of Computation, Vol 33, pp 185-199.

Swarztrauber, P. N. [1982]. Vectorizing the FFTs. *Parallel Computations,* G. Rodriguez (ed). Academic Press, New York, pp 51-83.

Swarztrauber, P. N. [1987]. Approximate Cyclic Reduction for Solving Poisson's Equation. *SIAM Journal on Scientific and Statistical Computing,* Vol 8, pp 199-209.

Sweet, R. A. [1974]. A Generalized Cyclic Reduction Algorithm. *SIAM Journal on Numerical Analysis,* Vol 11, pp 506-520.

Sweet, R. A. [1977]. A Cyclic Reduction Algorithm for Solving Block Tridiagonal Systems of Arbitary Dimension. *SIAM Journal on Numerical Analysis,* Vol 14, pp 706-720.

Sweet, R. A. [1988]. A Parallel and Vector Variant of the Cyclic Reduction Algorithm. *SIAM Journal on Scientific and Statistical Computing,* Vol 9, pp 761-765.

Syslo, M. M., N. Deo, and J. S. Kowalik [1983]. *Discrete Optimization: Algorithms.* Prentice-Hall, Englewood Cliffs, NJ.

Theis, D. J. (ed) [1981]. Array Processors -- Special Issue. *IEEE Computer,* September.

Thompson, C. D. [1978]. Generalized Connection Networks for Parallel Processor Interconnection. *IEEE Transactions on Computers,* Vol 27, pp 1119-1125.

Thompson, C. D. [1979]. Area Time Complexity for VLSI. *Proceedings of the ACM Symposium on Theory of Computing,* pp 81-88.

Thurber, K. J., and G. M. Masson [1979]. *Distributed Processor Communication Architecture.* Lexington Books, Lexington, MA.

Toffoli, T., and N. Morgolus [1987]. *Cellular Automata Machines.* MIT Press, Cambridge, MA.

Traub, J. F. [1966]. Associated Polynomials and Uniform Methods for the Solution of Linear Problems. *SIAM Review,* Vol 8, pp 277-301.

Traub, J. F. [1973]. Iterative Solution of Tridiagonal Systems on Parallel or Vector Computers. *Complexity of Sequential and Parallel Algorithms,* J. F. Traub (ed). Academic Press, New York, pp 49-82.

Traub, J. F., G. W. Wasilkowski, and H. Wozniakowski [1983]. *Information, Uncertainty, Complexity.* Addison-Wesley, Reading, MA.

Traub, J. F., and H. Wozniakowski [1980]. *A General Theory of Optimal Algorithms.* Academic Press, New York.

Trench, W. F. [1964]. An Algorithm for the Inversion of Finite Toeplitz Matrices. *SIAM Journal on Applied Mathematics,* Vol 12, pp 515-522.

Uhr, L. [1984]. *Algorithms -- Structured Computer Arrays and Networks.* Academic Press, New York.

Uhr, L. [1987]. *Parallel Multicomputer Architectures for Artificial Intelligence.* Wiley Interscience, New York, NY.

Upfal, E. [1984]. Efficient Schemes for Parallel Communication. *Journal of ACM,* Vol 31, pp 507-517.

Uspensky, J . V. [1948]. *Theory of Equations.* McGraw-Hill, New York.

Valiant, L. G. [1975]. Parallelism in Comparison Problems. *SIAM Journal on Computing,* Vol 4, pp 348-355.

Valiant, L. G. [1982]. A Scheme for Fast Parallel Communication. *SIAM Journal on Computing,* Vol 11, pp 350-361.

Valiant, L. G., and G. J. Brebner [1981]. Universal Schemes for Parallel Computation.

Proceedings of the ACM Symposium on Theory of Computing, pp 263-277.

Valiant, L. G., S. Skyum, S. Berkowitz, and C. Rackoff [1983]. Fast Parallel Computation of Polynomials Using Few Processors. *SIAM Journal on Computing,* Vol 12, pp 641-644.

Varah, J. M. [1972]. On the Solution of Block-Tridiagonal Systems Arising from Certain Finite-Difference Equations. *Mathematics of Computations,* Vol 26, pp 859-868.

Varga, R. S. [1962]. *Matrix Iterative Analysis.* Prentice-Hall, Englewood Cliffs, NJ.

Varman, P. J., and I. V. Ramakrishnan [1986]. Synthesis of an Optimal Family of Matrix Multiplication Algorithms on Linear Arrays. *IEEE Transactions on Computers,* Vol 35, pp 989-996.

Vinogradov, I. M. [1961]. *An Introduction to the Theory of Numbers.* Dover, New York.

Vitter, J.S., and R. A. Simons [1986]. New Classes for Parallel Complexity: A Study of Unification and Other Complete Problems for *P. IEEE Transactions on Computers,* Vol 35, pp 403-418.

Wagner, A., and D. G. Corneil [1987]. Embedding Trees in a Hypercube is NP-Complete. Technical Report 197/87. Department of Computer Science, University of Toronto, Toronto, Canada.

Waksman, A. [1968]. A Permutation Network. *Journal of ACM,* Vol 15, pp 159-163.

Wallace, C. S. [1964]. A Suggestion for Fast Multiplier. *IEEE Transactions on Computers,* Vol 13, pp 14-17.

Waser, S., and M. J. Flynn [1982]. *Introduction to Arithmetic for Digital Systems Designers.* Holt, Rinehart and Winston, New York.

Wegener, I. [1987]. *The Complexity of Boolean Functions.* Wiley-Teubner Series in Computer Science, Wiley, New York.

Weide, B. [1977]. A Survey of Analysis Techniques for Discrete Algorithms. *Computing Surveys,* Vol 9, pp 292-313.

Wijshoff, H. A. G., and J. Van Leeuwen [1987]. On Linear Skewing Schemes and *d*-Ordered Vectors. *IEEE Transactions on Computers,* Vol 36, pp 233-239.

Wilkinson, J. H. [1960]. Error Analysis of Floating-Point Computations. *Numerische Mathematik,* Vol 2, pp 317-340.

Wilkinson, J. H. [1965]. *The Algebraic Eigenvalue Problem,* Clarendon Press, Oxford, England.

Wimp, J. [1984]. *Computation with Recurrence Relations.* Pitman Advanced Publishing Program, Boston, MA.

Winograd, S. [1965]. On the Time Required to Perform Addition. *Journal of ACM,* Vol 12, pp 277-285.

Winograd, S. [1967]. On the Time Required to Perform Multiplication. *Journal of ACM,* Vol 14, pp 793-802.

Winograd, S. [1968]. A New Algorithm for Inner Product. *IEEE Transactions on Computers,* Vol 17, pp 693-694.

Winograd, S. [1975]. On The Parallel Evaluation of Certain Arithmetic Expressions. *Journal of ACM,* Vol 22, pp 477-492.

Winograd, S. [1980]. *Arithmetic Complexity of Computations.* SIAM, Philadelphia, PA.

Wolfe, M. [1982]. Optimizing Supercompilers for Supercomputers. Ph.D. Thesis, Report No. UIUCDCS-R-82-1105, Department of Computer Science, University of Illinois, Urbana, IL.

Wu, A. Y. [1985]. Embedding of Tree Networks into Hypercubes. *Journal of Parallel and Distributed Processing,* Vol 2, pp 238-249.

Wu, C. L., and T. Y. Feng [1980a]. On a Class of Multistage Interconnection Networks. *IEEE Transactions on Computers,* Vol 29, pp 694-702.

Wu, C. L., and T. Y. Feng [1980b]. The Reverse-Exchange Interconnection Network. *IEEE Transactions on Computers,* Vol 29, pp 801-811.

Wulf, W., and C. G. Bell [1972]. C.mmp -- A Multi-miniprocessor. *Proceedings of AFIPS Fall Joint Computer Conference,* Vol 41, pp 765-778.

Yao, A. C. [1976]. On the Evaluation of Powers. *SIAM Journal on Computing,* Vol 5, pp 100-103.

Yao, A. C. [1979]. Some Complexity Questions Related to Distributive Computing. *Proceedings of the Annual Symposium on Theory of Computing,* pp 209-213.

Zakharov, V. [1984]. Parallelism and Array Processing. *IEEE Transactions on Computers,* Vol 33, pp 45-78.

Zohar, S. [1969]. Toeplitz Matrix Inversion: An Algorithm of Trench. *Journal of ACM,* Vol 16, pp 592-601.

AUTHOR INDEX

SUBJECT INDEX